B. W. Sprinkle

B. W. Sprinkle

Complete Guide
To Residential
Remodeling

Complete Guide To Residential Remodeling

MORTIMER P. REED

Prentice-Hall, Inc., Englewood Cliffs, NJ, 07632

Library of Congress Cataloging in Publication Data

Reed, Mortimer P.
  Complete guide to residential remodeling.

  Includes index.
  1. Dwellings—Remodeling. I. Title.
TH4816.R426   643'.7   82-7627
ISBN 0-13-160671-9   AACR2
ISBN 0-13-160663-8 (pbk.)

Editorial production/supervision and interior design by *Barbara Bernstein*.
Manufacturing buyer: *Joyce Levatino*.

Cover photos courtesy of American Plywood Association.

Printed in the United States of America

10 9 8 7 6 5 4 3 2 1

ISBN 0-13-160671-9
ISBN 0-13-160663-8 {PBK}

PRENTICE-HALL INTERNATIONAL, INC., *London*
PRENTICE-HALL OF AUSTRALIA PTY. LIMITED, *Sydney*
PRENTICE-HALL CANADA LTD., *Toronto*
PRENTICE-HALL OF INDIA PRIVATE LIMITED, *New Delhi*
PRENTICE-HALL OF JAPAN, INC., *Tokyo*
PRENTICE-HALL OF SOUTHEAST ASIA PTE. LTD., *Singapore*
WHITEHALL BOOKS LIMITED, *Wellington, New Zealand*

To my wife, Helen, who either participated in or stoically endured the remodeling of every house we have lived in but one—and we designed that one from scratch.

Contents

Preface

Every successful residential remodeling has four phases: making the decision to remodel, planning the work to be done, preparing for the adjustments in living while the remodeling is in progress, and finishing the actual work of destruction and construction.

Only you can make the decision to remodel. This book helps you decide whether it is practical for you.

You can hire someone to plan the work, but with a little help and a lot of patience you can do the planning yourself. This book shows and tells you how.

Only you can prepare for remodeling. This book tells you what to expect, and how to cope with the unexpected.

You can hire someone to do all the work. This book tells you how to select and work with a remodeling contractor. You can do all the work yourself if you have the tools and experience in all aspects of building. This book helps you organize and schedule the work to be done.

But this book is aimed more directly at the homeowner who hires contractors to do part of the work and does the rest himself or herself. It suggests which parts each should handle. It gives step-by-step procedures for adding rooms and for making changes from basement floor to roof ridge. It tells what tools you need for various tasks. And it shows how to make better use of the space you have in your present home.

To get a start on the first phase, simply start with Chapter 1.

ACKNOWLEDGEMENTS

Concepts and procedures can seldom be presented clearly in words alone. It takes photographs and drawings to flesh out those words and give them meaning.

The photographs in this book were furnished by the firms and individuals named in the captions with those photographs. Their cooperation and diligence in matching the author's requests with prints in their files were a joy and a solace.

More than half the drawings were developed specifically for this book. The other illustrations were selected from:

Architectural Graphic Standards by Ramsey & Sleeper (copyright John Wiley & Sons, Inc., 1970; editor Harold D. Hauf, FAIA)

Building Construction by Reed (copyright McGraw-Hill, Inc., 1976)

Handbook of Vacation House Planning and Building by Reed (copyright Prentice-Hall, Inc., 1979)

Residential Carpentry by Reed (copyright John Wiley & Sons, Inc., 1980)

Permission by these publishers to reprint is most gratefully appreciated.

Mortimer P. Reed

1

A Reason To Remodel

(a)

(b)

Minor changes can bring big dividends. Built 60 years ago, this house had a porch close to the street (a) where its owners could sit and enjoy talking with people walking by. Now too close to today's traffic, the porch is enclosed (b) and the entrance is on the side closer to the middle of the house. Top-hinged louvered panels shield windows from summer sun and provide privacy, yet still allow air to circulate. (Designer: Jim Clamp, ASID. Photographer: Wes Walker.)

Nearly everyone who has ever owned a house has thought at least once about remodeling. No house is perfect. Any house that you have lived in awhile, or that someone has lived in before you, is bound to have some things that you would like to change.

Unfortunately, few people ever make those changes. Their desire to remodel seldom passes from the thinking stage to action. Instead, they continue to put up with the flaws and annoyances of a house that doesn't suit their family, or else they move to another house with a different list of things they'd like to change. Thus they miss out on one of life's greatest satisfactions.

The main reason so few people remodel is that they don't know how to go about it. They harbor a fear

of the unknown. If you want to build a new house, you find a site you like, a set of plans you like, a builder you like, and start digging. If you want to buy a house, either new or used, you find a realtor you like, who finds a house you like, and you buy it. In both cases your primary participation is selection.

Remodeling the house you live in is more complex, but at the same time more satisfying. Part of your input into the project is selection, yes. But you must become deeply involved in planning what you'd like to do, in getting your ideas down on paper, in scheduling the work to be done (even when you don't do it yourself), and in finding people to do the work for you. None of these steps is beyond your capacity. The period while a remodeling is in progress is a time of excitement, frustration, upset, reward, mess, and gratification all at the same time. But when your project is completed, and you've done the job right, your first feeling is pride of accomplishment, and the second is regret that you didn't take action sooner.

The idea of remodeling your house has undoubtedly crossed your mind. But is it a *good* idea? For you and your family it may be the most practical and economical solution to your housing problems. For your neighbor it may be the wrong thing to do. Or vice versa. The decision depends largely on the honest answers you give to the following questions:

- What is your purpose in wanting to remodel?
- What problems do you expect to solve?
- Has your family reached a remodeling stage?
- Are you satisfied with your neighborhood and community?
- What is the structural condition of your house?
- Can you afford the cost of remodeling? Can you afford the alternatives?

These questions and the answers you give to them are valid whether you now own a home, or are thinking about buying an older home with the intention of remodeling it. In the latter case you have an advantage: you have more leeway in choosing the problems that need to be corrected. Many older homes give you more space for your money than a new house. But the costs of remodeling, maintenance, and repair will probably be more, too.

Before going any further, let's define some commonly used and misused terms.

In the simplest possible concept, a house consists of its structure (the skeleton), exterior and interior surfaces (the skin), and utility systems (the lifelines). Each of these elements may be repaired, modified, or replaced when necessary. The process followed may be maintenance, restoration, renovation, or remodeling.

Maintenance is the continuing process of keeping all parts of the house in good working order. **Restoration** is the process of refurbishing an old house as close as possible to its original condition. The term usually applies to houses more than a century old and of historical importance. **Renovation** is the process of updating parts of a house that are outmoded, usually as the result of technological change. **Remodeling** is the process of altering a house structurally to meet the changing needs of its owners and contemporary standards of living. **Repair** is a vital part of all four processes.

The subject of this book is remodeling. But few projects are pure remodeling. To make maximum use of the money you spend to improve your living conditions, you probably should do a little renovating, some maintenance, and some repair at the same time.

To get back to your reason for remodeling, there should be only one: to make your house more pleasant, suitable, comfortable, and/or economical for you and your family to live in.

Seems obvious, doesn't it? Yet many, many people, who should and can afford to remodel, put it off until they decide to sell the house. Then, to put the house in salable condition, they spend a lot of money to make it more pleasant, comfortable, or economical for the *next* family! By remodeling when you have the need, you can remodel for less money and enjoy the benefits of your efforts yourselves. And you will still get your money back when you finally do sell.

The point is this: if you decide to remodel, do it now!

Exploring The Possibilities

Old houses that are still structurally sound (a) make excellent remodeling prospects. Spend little money to update the exterior, however. Instead, replace and repair, and use paint of a neutral color to soften and subdue awkward lines (b). Then modernize the interior to your heart's content (see attic photos, page 126). (Courtesy American Plywood Association.)

The problems that make most people like yourself consider the possibility of remodeling fall into two categories: major and minor. A major problem can usually be corrected only by remodeling or moving out. Typical examples are out-of-date bathrooms, kitchens with inefficient work space, not enough bedrooms, too little living space, inadequate storage space, and structural flaws. Problems of this type develop over a period of time. A house is seldom designed to accommodate the constantly changing needs of the family members living in it. Human beings are highly adaptable creatures who adjust to their surroundings. Yet there is a limit to that adaptability.

Minor problems are less obvious. They become apparent after you have lived in a house for awhile; often they are simply the differences between the house you used to live in and this one. Typical of these annoyances are doors that bump when both are open, hot and cold faucets that are reversed or turn in the opposite direction, a cabinet door that opens to the right instead of the left, no electrical outlet where you need it, a light switch where you wouldn't have put it, and heat outlets where you want to place furniture or hang draperies.

Although it would be nice to correct these peculiarities, they alone aren't a good enough reason for remodeling. You can adjust to them. But there may come a day when you tire of adjusting.

The first step in exploring the possibilities of remodeling is to make a complete list of major problems and minor annoyances. Keep the lists separate. Your purpose is to get a good grip on the scope of the work to be done. Whether and how it is done come later.

YOUR FAMILY STATUS

Most remodelings take place at one of three stages in the life of a family unit:

1. When family size has grown to the point where the house doesn't provide adequate space for normal family activities.

2. When family size has stabilized, but the needs of its members and their use of space have changed considerably.

3. When family size has shrunk as children have grown and gone, and remaining family members have more space to heat, cool, clean, and maintain than they use on a regular basis.

The Expanding Family

A young couple just beginning family life seldom needs more space than an apartment or manufactured housing provides, and often can't afford much more. They may have only enough furniture to keep rooms from looking bare. Except for a place to put clothes, sports equipment, food, and the utensils for preparing, serving, and eating it, they need little storage space. Children up to school age don't need or take up much space, and can share bedrooms.

But Americans are accumulators, and their need for space increases rapidly. A cozy eating nook that was romantic for two becomes cramped for four. Beds take up more floor space than cribs. Toys need a resting place. Food preparation takes more counter space and more utensils. More shelves are needed for food storage. And suddenly there is no place where each member of the family can be alone.

When this point is reached, it's time for action.

The Maturing Family

The living values that a house should provide don't change much from the time the first child starts elementary school until he or she enters high school. Then the requirements of older children become more adult and less juvenile. Teenagers tend to socialize less with their parents and more with their peers. They want to spend more time by themselves, and need more privacy. They need a quiet place for study and self-contemplation. At the same time they need a place where they can meet, not with just one close friend, but with a gang of friends. If they had their own way, they would have their own all-purpose room, their own bathroom, their own telephone, and their own refrigerator.

When this point is reached, it is time to consider action.

The Contracting Family

During the life of a house trying its best to be a home, the phase of family shrinkage is the most difficult. Children away at college or living out of town no longer need rooms of their own most of the year. Yet when they do return home, and until they establish homes of their own, many of them want and need to reestablish their roots in the place where they grew up. The familiarity of their own room reinforces those ties to home. Later, when they return as a family unit of their own with your grandchildren, space is often at a premium during their visit.

When this point is reached, it may be time to take action.

THE QUALITY OF YOUR NEIGHBORHOOD OR COMMUNITY

For remodeling to be a serious possibility for you, you should be able to answer "yes" to most, if not all, of the following questions concerning the area where you now live:

- Do you like and get along well with your immediate neighbors?
- Are the distances you must travel to work or public transportation, schools, church, shops, and recreation within the bounds that you are willing to drive?
- Are the services satisfactory that you pay for with your tax dollars?
- Is the quality of local schools sufficiently high to meet your family's needs?
- Have property values risen more than inflation over the past five years?
- Is the community of which your neighborhood is a part still a good place to live?
- Is the neighborhood as desirable or more desirable than when you moved into it?

If more than half your answers to these questions are negative, your best action probably is to sell and relocate. But before you buy another house somewhere else, ask these same basic questions about the new location.

If most of your answers are "yes," look thoroughly into the trend of zoning within a mile of your home.

Zoning

Most communities large enough to have local government have zoning laws. Their primary purpose is to protect the landowner's investment by controlling the use of land in an area, or **zone**. The most common zones are residential, multifamily, commercial, light industrial, heavy industrial, and farm. Residential zones in suburban areas may be further divided according to minimum lot size, such as less than 1 acre or more than 1 acre.

You may find houses in any zone. Zoning laws simply restrict what can be built in any zone to the types of buildings shown in Table 2-1, plus all those in the zone or zones above it. Farms, of course, are in a zone classification by themselves.

Of concern to you is not only the zone you are in, but also the trend of zoning nearby. Even in subdivisions where most of the land is zoned residential, there are frequently strips along main streets that are zoned commercial, or pockets zoned for apartments and other multifamily buildings. Yet at one time the entire area was probably zoned residential. Land is often rezoned when its value for one zoning purpose surpasses its value for the more restrictive zoning purpose above it in Table 2-1. And rezoning is almost always for more permissive than more restrictive use.

Thus the protection provided by zoning laws is only as good as the ability of local officials to withstand the pressure of commercial enterprise. If you have lived in your house for many years, you are probably aware of how changes in zoning have gradually affected the character of some streets and neighborhoods that you see regularly. If you are a newer resident, by all means study the pattern of zoning changes before you consider investing in the cost of remodeling a house in a slowly changing neighborhood.

To find out how your land is zoned, look in your telephone book under your local government listings. At the very end you may find "Zoning" or something similar. Call the number listed. Ask also whether maps are maintained showing current and past zoning. It could be well worth your time to visit the zoning office to look over those maps. If you're planning a room addition, you will need additional information available at the zoning office (see page 31).

If the zoning picture still looks favorable, take a good long look at your house to be sure that it is worth the expense of remodeling.

THE CONDITION OF YOUR HOUSE

After you have lived in a house for a couple of years, you should have a good idea of how well it is built and how well it has been maintained. The most important test is how well it withstands extremes. Does it creak and leak air in high winds? Does water leak, seep, or run in at any point during heavy rains or sudden thaws? Is there enough insulation to keep you comfortable and fuel bills within reason during periods of extreme heat or cold?

In half a day you can complete a thorough inspection of your house. It has two purposes: to search for major structural problems that could make remodeling a questionable investment, and to look for minor defects that should be corrected at the time of remodeling. During the inspection wear old clothes that completely cover arms and legs, shoes with nonskid soles, work gloves to protect your hands, safety glasses to protect your eyes, and possibly a gauze mask to protect your nose, throat, and lungs. An inspection is a messy job, but well worth the trouble.

For writing down the results of your inspection you need a pad of paper and a pen or mechanical pencil. Avoid an ordinary lead pencil; you'll probably break the point when you're farthest from a sharpener. Divide the paper into two columns, one for major problems and one for minor flaws. At the left of the paper list the structural parts or members you inspected.

Check the structure first, then exterior surfaces, and finally interior surfaces. For equipment take along a flashlight or a trouble light with a long cord, a screwdriver and putty knife, a carpenter's level at least 24 " long, and a piece or two of chalk.

The Structure

To determine the structural soundness of a house, look carefully in three places—the basement or crawl space, the attic, and around window and door openings. If your house is built on a concrete slab, or has a flat or shed roof and therefore no attic, concentrate your inspection at openings and on all surfaces, including the roof.

Table 2-1. Zoning classifications and the types of buildings that can be legally built in each zone.

Zone	Types of building permitted
Residential	Family houses, schools, churches, hospitals
Multifamily	Apartments, duplexes, townhouses, condominiums
Commercial	Retail stores, service stations, eating places, small office buildings
Light industrial	Small plants that produce very little noise and pollution; e.g. a bottling plant
Heavy industrial	Large factories such as steel mills, oil refineries, and chemical plants
Farm	Large tracts (usually 10 acres)

The Foundation. Pick a day during or right after a heavy rain or spring thaw to look at the foundation. Work inside the house, either in the basement or crawl space. Look first for cracks in the foundation walls. Fine hairline cracks in mortar joints are neither uncommon nor cause for alarm. A clearly visible zigzag crack through mortar joints (Fig. 2-1a) indicates either structural stresses or poor mortar joints. A vertical crack that runs half the height of the wall and goes through concrete blocks as well as joints (Fig. 2-1b) is a sign of settling. The cause may be an inadequate soil base under footings, or stresses caused by wet soil. It may be footings under the wall that are too small or improperly reinforced. Or it may be a poorly poured or poorly laid foundation wall. A crack of either type will only get wider, and is a sign of structural weakness that is expensive to correct.

Look next at the surface of foundation walls. If walls are built of concrete block, brick, stone, or clay

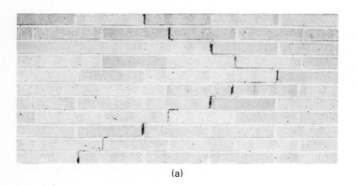

(a)

(b)

Fig. 2-1. Clearly visible cracks along mortar joints (a) or cracks that split masonry units (b) are signs of severe structural stress and an almost certain source of leaks. (Courtesy Brick Institute of America.)

tile, joints between masonry units should be full of mortar. If walls are concrete, surfaces should be solid and not chipped. There should be no signs of stains from water leaks. Rub your hand over the surface; it should come away slightly dusty. If your hand has a powdery white film on it, the powder is probably **efflorescence**—a deposit on the surface that points to excess moisture in the wall. Obviously, moisture is present if the wall is damp, and moisture in any wall can cause damage.

While you are checking out the foundation, look for any mud tunnels running up the walls. Tunnels are a sure sign of termites. Termites are soft-bodied antlike insects that feed on the cellulose in wood. They must have access to moisture, and cannot stand exposure to light and air. They live in damp ground and, to reach their favorite meal, build mud tunnels as protection against light and air if they can't travel unseen through cracks in the foundation walls.

Most houses built in the last 30 years were protected against termites at the time of construction. This protection used to be a metal shield laid across the top of the foundation wall and bent downward (see Fig. 2-2b). The shield prevents termites from reaching wood sill members. For protection today the soil around the foundation and in any crawl space is usually treated with chemicals that poison termites. To be effective, however, soil poisoning must be repeated once a year.

You aren't likely to find termite tunnels. If you do, however, cut away 6 to 12″ of tunnel, and watch for any activity along the corridor within 15 or 20 minutes. Use as little light as possible. If termites are active, they will begin to run down the broken tunnel line seeking the safety of the soil. If you see no activity, look next at the top of the foundation wall.

Atop the wall is the **sill plate,** a wood member (usually a 2 × 6) laid flat and inset from the inside wall surface (Fig. 2-2). It should run continuously along the wall without any gaps, although there will be joints between lengths of sill plate. About every 4′ around the perimeter of the wall, probe the plate with your screwdriver. The blade should sink only slightly beneath the surface of the wood. If the blade goes into the wood easily and meets little resistance inside, the sill plate has been weakened by rot, termites, or other wood-boring insects. A weak sill plate means a weak structure. The wall isn't about to fall down, but you do have a problem that must be corrected.

Check along the top of the sill plate between joists. Near the corners of the foundation and at intervals of 6 to 8 ft along the wall you should find the tops of sill bolts or wall anchors. These devices are embedded in the wall and hold the sill plate to it; they prevent hurricane-force winds from listing the house off its foundation.

Next, feel along the top of the wall and see what ends up on your gloves. There is sure to be some debris—an accumulation of dust, powdered concrete,

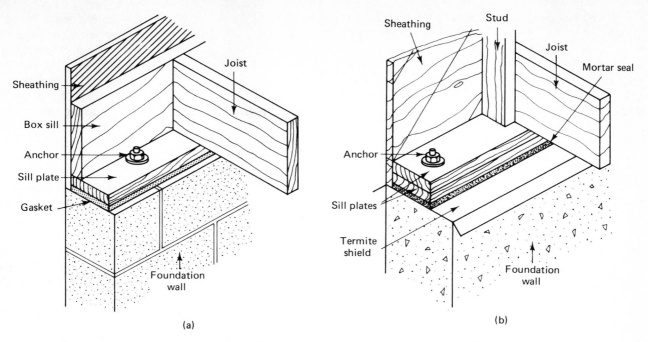

Fig. 2-2. In most houses the sill plate is a single member (a), but in older houses it may be doubled and rest on a termite shield (b). This lowest wood member should be at least 8″ above ground and not easily pierced with a screwdriver. Sill plates should be anchored to the foundation wall.

even some sawdust and wood chips. These are normal. Wings of insects, little piles of fresh sawdust, and puddled moisture are not. They indicate a potential problem with wood-eating insects or water leakage.

Now sight along the top of the wall looking outward. You shouldn't be able to see daylight, especially if you have a basement. In good construction the joint between the foundation wall and sill plate is closed tight with a seal of cement, a manufactured gasket, or mineral insulation (see Fig. 2-2). Outside the house the exterior surface material should extend over the bottom edge of sheathing and below the top of the foundation wall to keep out air and moisture. The absence of some sort of seal is not necessarily a structural defect, but close the joint when you remodel.

Floor Support System. To complete your investigation in the basement or crawl space, turn your attention to the floor structure. It consists of floor joists and girders. **Girders** may be steel I-beams, timbers, or built-up wood beams made of two or three thicknesses of joists. Ends of girders rest either in pockets in foundation walls or on sill plates, and are often supported in between on posts, piers, columns, or an interior partition. **Joists,** which carry the floor, are shorter and lighter members that butt or overlap at girders. Except under wings of a house, joists rarely extend in one piece from foundation wall to foundation wall.

Look first for splices. Wood girders may be spliced along their length, but the splices should be staggered for maximum strength. Joists should never be spliced unless the splice falls directly above a point of support.

Now look for long diagonal splits. Wood is an imperfect building material, and every piece has some defects. Often these defects affect only the appearance of the lumber but not its strength. Some two dozen defects, their size, and their location in the piece are taken into consideration when lumber is graded at the sawmill according to national standards. The standards for structural or stress-graded lumber permit knots up to a certain size in certain locations in the piece. They also permit lengthwise separations of limited length—called checks, splits, or shakes depending on where they occur (Fig. 2-3). **Checks** are a lengthwise separation along the grain on one surface. **Splits** are like checks, but extend from one surface through to the opposite surface, and are more serious. **Shakes** are lengthwise separations along annular rings—the growth rings of a tree. What you need to look for and hope you don't find are splits that have lengthened and widened since the house was built. They are signs of future structural problems, and should be corrected during remodeling.

Every house settles a little, and settling isn't likely to be uniform. If you suspect that your house has settled more than it should, or that joists are sagging more than you'd like, lay your carpenter's level on the underside of joists, beginning at the foundation wall and moving toward the center of the house in increments of about 3′. In the typical house the level will show a slight slope downward from points of support to the centers of joists. The bubble in the level, however, shouldn't be

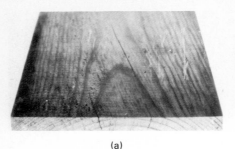  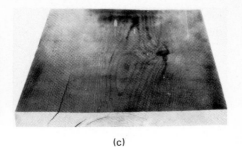

(a)   (b)   (c)

Fig. 2-3. Signs of potential structural problems in floor framing members are checks (a), splits (b), and shakes (c). (Courtesy U.S. Forest Products Laboratories.)

more than ⅛″ off dead center at any point along the joist. Sag can be corrected, but the job is often expensive and can create as many problems in interior surface materials as it solves. Unless the sag is extreme and floors are far out of level, you are usually better off to leave the structure alone and live with the condition.

When joists slope steadily downward from outside walls to center supports, look at conditions at the bottoms of posts or columns. They should have their own footings, which won't be visible if the area is floored. Bottoms of wood posts should not touch the ground, and should be raised above the level of any concrete floor (see Fig. 18-2). If sinking posts are the cause of first-floor sag, the floor structure should be raised on jacks, and adequate footings installed under the posts.

Roof Support System. The best time to investigate structural conditions in an attic is a cool cloudy

Fig. 2-4. In good roof construction a collar beam connects pairs of roof rafters. Spaced no more than 48″ apart, collar beams resist the outward thrust by rafters at side walls. (Photo: Drew: Leviton-Atlanta.)

day—ideally a few hours after a heavy rain or toward the end of a spring thaw. As with your inspection of the foundation, you look for signs of leakage and structural weakness. Leaks are most likely to originate where chimneys and vents go through the roof, but they may show up anywhere.

Begin at the point where you enter attic space. Work your way along one side of the ridge to the end of the attic, then down the other side, and back to your starting point. In an attic that isn't floored, work clockwise if you are right-handed and counterclockwise if you are left-handed. Carry the flashlight in one hand, and use your other hand to steady yourself on the rafters or chords of trusses as you step from joist to joist.

Look and feel for moisture along all roof supports and on the underside of roof sheathing. The source of a leak is sometimes very hard to pinpoint. A leak may actually begin near the ridge, yet show up at some lower point. When you do find signs of a leak, you know that its source is somewhere above the point where it appeared, and probably within a foot in either direction from the rafter. Mark with chalk the highest point on the rafter or truss chord where you find moisture. By measuring from the mark to the ridge and to an end wall, you can orient yourself when you climb onto the roof later to seek the point of leakage.

Be sure to check for leaks as far as you can see toward the lower ends of rafters. When the roof pitch is low and head room is limited, the help of a small but sure-footed child is invaluable for checking in corners.

After you complete your inspection of individual rafters, stand at one end of the attic and sight down the series of rafters at about their midpoints. There should be a collar beam (Fig. 2-4) across every second or third pair of rafters. Look specifically for any rafters that sag below your line of sight more than, say, about ½″. If you find any, look them over carefully for splits, rot, or other signs of structural weakness. The rafter may only be warped or a little wider than the others. But if it is actually lower than its neighbors, the roof above it will also be lower, giving rainwater and melting snow a chance of lingering and increasing the damage. Such rafters should be raised to the level of other rafters during remodeling.

Door and Window Openings. It isn't possible to check out the condition of wall structure without removing surface materials. You can learn a lot, however, from the condition of those materials, and from the operation of exterior doors and windows.

Unless your house is more than 30 years old, chances are good that there is some insulation between studs in exterior walls. It may not be enough by today's standards, but nevertheless it does act as a barrier between indoor and outdoor temperatures in very hot or cold weather. The air space between storm windows or storm doors and the openings they protect also acts as an insulator. Even so, the difference in temperature on opposite sides of a door or window is great, especially in winter, and warpage, shrinkage, and condensation are common problems.

Start your investigation of openings with either a putty knife or a piece of paper about the thickness of stationery. Working from the outside, insert it all the way around the opening, and also at any point where two window sashes meet. When windows and doors fit tightly in their frames, you won't be able to slide the putty knife along the opening without some effort. If the knife moves freely, try to shake the window. If you can make it rattle, the problem can sometimes be corrected by resetting the window stop. More often, however, a rattle indicates that a door or window has shrunk over the years, and may need to be replaced.

A loose window or door is seldom a structural problem—just a source of air leaks and a cause of high fuel costs. A sticky window or door—one that binds at some point as you open it—is likely to result from a slight structural shift. Doors and windows are installed to fit tight, with just enough clearance around the edges for easy operation. When a house settles unevenly, the movement may cause a door or window to stick. Similarly, if the structural frame around an opening is not strong enough to carry the loads above it, or if the frame was not absolutely square to begin with, windows and doors may stick. When all doors and windows operate easily, and are tight in their openings even on windy days, wall structure is sound. If not, the problems should probably be corrected when you remodel.

Exterior Surfaces

If you found structural cracks in foundation walls, start your inspection of exterior surfaces by locating these cracks outside. Measure how far up they extend, and mark this down on your inspection sheet. Then move to any corner of the house and work all the way around in one direction. Pick a sunny day this time, and time your inspection so that you can study one wall with the sun hitting it at a sharp angle. Under such light conditions the texture of materials shows up strongly, and so do flaws.

Masonry Walls. You can expect to find some hairline cracks in mortar joints; they are harmless. Make note, however, of any joints where mortar is loose or missing. Look closely at brickwork above and below windows and exterior doors where stresses are greatest. Occasionally, run your screwdriver along mortar joints to see how firm the mortar is. Nothing should happen. If much mortar comes loose in fine granules, it is usually a sign that the mortar mix had too much sand in it, or that water is puddling at joints instead of running off. Poor joints can be corrected by remortaring (called **pointing**), but the job is expensive to have done and tedious for the amateur.

Make a note, too, of any holes or gaps in mortar. These can be filled by **tuckpointing** (pressing mortar into the opening) at the time other mortar is mixed during remodeling. Look especially closely where entrance stoops and porches join the house. Sometimes steps are built without adequate support and tend to split away from the house's foundation. These cracks should be filled to prevent moisture from being trapped along the foundation wall.

Nonmasonry Walls. Because wood is a flexible building material, it adjusts to some settling. The main signs of structural problems are horizontal splits in siding, and courses of shingles that have dropped out of line. Note any places where these faults occur, and look for further signs of problems on interior walls at these points. Other problems with wood exteriors—warped lengths, knots that are loose or have fallen out, and cracks at ends of siding—are easily corrected when remodeling takes place.

Trim. While exterior trim serves as decoration around openings and where two surfaces meet at an angle, its main purpose is to protect joints from weather. Trim is milled from high grades of lumber. If properly primed before it is nailed in place, it will last a long time with no care except for painting. As you inspect the exterior of your house, look for joints that have opened up over the years, and make a note to seal them with caulking compound applied with a caulking gun. The openings should be cleaned first so that caulking will penetrate into them and stick to exterior surfaces. Any trim that shows signs of rot or other water damage should be replaced.

Flashing. Wherever two exterior surfaces meet at an angle, the joint should be flashed. **Flashing** is one of several materials—metal or treated paper—applied in strips at the angles to prevent moisture from getting into structural members. At many joints flashing is applied to wall and roof sheathing behind exterior finish materials, and you can't see it. But you should see flashing above window and door openings; at outside corners of wood siding in the form of metal corner caps; at horizontal joints between different materials when the lower material is thicker than the upper material; and at several places on roofs (Fig. 2-5). If the flashing is metal, simply make sure it fully overlaps the material below it. If flashing is building paper, look for tears or holes, which should be sealed with roofing compound.

Roofing. Inspect your roof on a cloudy day for comfort's sake. If you found signs of leaks in your attic, transfer the measurements you took there, and mark an × on the roof with chalk. In a 90° arc above that point, 45° on either side of a line running straight up the roof, inspect the roofing carefully for loose nails, or cracked, split, or missing shingles, any one of which could be the source of your leak.

Check the condition of flashing—in valleys where two roof slopes meet, around pipes and vents that protrude through the roof, around chimneys, and where roofs butt against any walls. The upper edges of horizontal flashing strips should not be visible, but be tucked behind siding or into mortar joints. The lower edges should overlap the roofing. Both edges of flashing that follows the slope of the roof should be concealed.

Finally, look at the condition of the chimney's brickwork and of the roofing itself. Chimneys should have a concrete or metal cap that prevents rain from getting into interior mortar joints and bricks around flues. Chimney tops are fully exposed to weather extremes, and the most common sign of incipient problems is chunks and flakes of clay on the roof around and below the chimney. If you find such signs,

replace the cap and upper courses of bricks whether or not you remodel.

Asphalt shingles have a life of 15 to 20 years, and should be replaced when their surfaces begin to blister, when edges curl upward, and when the mineral grains that provide color begin to wash away. To see how much shingles have deteriorated, carefully raise an occasional shingle and compare the protected surface with the exposed surface.

Wood shingles have long life if they have the chance to dry out thoroughly after rains. Three or four days after a rain carefully lift a few wood shingles at various points in the roof, particularly at eaves where shingles are most subject to soaking. The concealed surfaces should be dry. If not, squeeze the shingles to see whether they are only damp but firm, or soft and spongy. Wet or rotting shingles should be replaced as soon as possible. Unfortunately, the chances are good that sheathing underneath is also damp and rotting, and should also be replaced.

Gutters and Downspouts. An inch of rain falling on a house with 1000 sq ft of floor space translates into more than 750 gallons of water running off the roof. Water is the probable cause of more structural damage than any other element. Each section of roof must direct rain and melting snow toward the eaves. At the eaves this water must be gathered in gutters or it will fall to the ground near the foundation. Unless the ground on all sides of the house slopes away from it, water is likely to seep into the ground and eventually work its way into your basement or crawl space.

The slope and placement of gutters are critical.

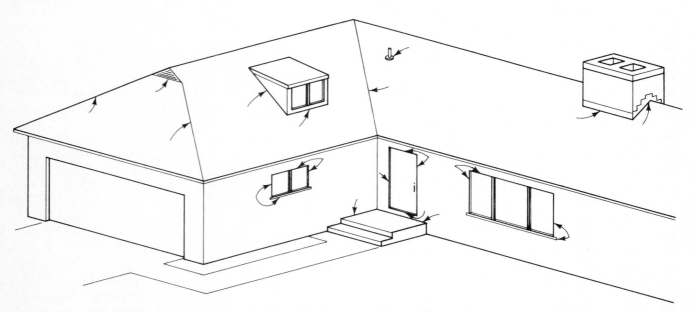

Fig. 2-5. You should find flashing at all points indicated by arrows: wherever any two roof surfaces meet, and wherever a wall, chimney, or vent comes through a roof. Flashing is also required around all window and exterior door openings.

Gutters must be located to catch water as it comes down the roof, whether it runs off or drips off. In climates where daytime thaws and nighttime freezes are common, gutters must lie far enough below eaves so that water won't back up under the roof. Gutters must also be sloped toward downspouts so that water runs off before it can turn to ice or gather in sufficient depth to cause gutters to sag. Downspouts in turn must channel the water away from the foundation of your house, but not toward your neighbor's.

Unpleasant as the task is, the only time to check how well your water removal system works is under adverse conditions—during a heavy rain (without lightning, of course) or during a spring thaw. Make sure that the water moves freely in the directions intended, that gutters are without holes, and that joints between sections are tight. Then watch how water flows from downspouts, looking particularly for low spots where the water forms into puddles or runs toward the house rather than away from it. Any problems you spot should be corrected promptly, even if you decide not to remodel.

Interior Surfaces

Signs of structural stress in walls show up inside a house in two places—in corners and at openings. Uneven settling causes small cracks to open up in corners where two walls or a wall and a partition come together. If their cause is settling, cracks tend to show up in the first year after a house is built, can be filled, and may never show up again. If the cause is structural weakness, the cracks will reopen within six months.

Cracks that begin at upper corners of windows and doors and run upward at about a 45° angle away from the opening also indicate framing that is not fully adequate for the loads imposed upon it. Your house isn't going to collapse, but if you intend to remodel a wall with recurrent cracks, plan to add studs or bracing. A crack below a window is more likely the result of settling.

Even though your inspection of the area below floor joists doesn't indicate any sagging, there are two signs visible in rooms supported by those joists. One is tall furniture, such as a bookcase or hutch, that leans into the room because the floor isn't level. When joists run at right angles to a wall, the chances are that the floor isn't level because all joists have deflected somewhat. When joists run parallel to the wall, it may be that only the first joist sags, or that the edge joist under the wall wasn't doubled to support the extra weight. Sagging joists can be corrected without great difficulty or cost, but the improvement probably won't justify the expense unless the sag is severe.

The other sign of invisible sag is liquids that run rather than puddle when spilled on the floor. You can test the level of the uncarpeted floor of a room by setting a marble (any small, round, hard ball will do) on the floor at various points to see which way it rolls. In a carpeted room set the ball in a track, such as a C-shaped curtain rod, and turn the track in various directions. This test shows you where the low point is in each room, and gives you a good gauge of where you may need to add supports to offset the tilt.

Occasionally, you will find small cracks where walls and ceilings meet without trim. These are normal. Most ceiling materials are flexible enough to deflect slightly as ceiling joists deflect. Large cracks toward the middle of the ceiling beneath attic space often result from the weight of items stored there that are too heavy for ceiling joists to carry. The heaviest boxes and furniture should be stored above walls and partitions.

REMODELING COSTS

A thorough inspection will give you a good picture of how sound your house is structurally, and any areas where correction is needed. If you do uncover major structural problems, which isn't likely, call in a builder or remodeling contractor promptly. Show him the evidence you have found, ask him to verify your judgment, and get from him an estimate to correct the problem. Get a second estimate if the first one seems too high or too low. See Chapter 3 for suggestions on selecting a contractor.

If the builder confirms that your house is structurally deficient, you have a rather unpleasant choice. You can repair the house and continue to live in it, even though the cost of repairs cuts into the amount you could spend on remodeling. You can repair the house and sell it, perhaps finding something closer to your needs than your present home unremodeled. Or you can try to sell the house without repairing it. If you decide on this get-out-from-under course, investigate current local laws on selling real estate. In more and more communities every year the responsibility for the acceptable condition of a house for sale lies on the shoulders of the seller, not the buyer.

So much for the dark side of the picture. Much more likely your inspection will uncover nothing wrong that would prevent or seriously limit funds for remodeling. Then what is the next step forward? Actually, there are two that go hand in hand—planning the job and estimating the cost. With a rough idea of what remodeling you'd like to do, you can make a rough estimate of its cost. The more specific your plans become, the more accurate your estimate can be.

Types of Remodeling

There are three basic types of remodeling: adding new space, converting existing space to another purpose, and improving the usefulness, appearance, and/or comfort of available rooms. Once you decide which type of remodeling best suits your needs, and approximately how many square feet of area are involved, you can make a preliminary estimate of cost, based on the current cost per square foot or per cubic foot of new houses. More in a moment about finding out what these costs are in your community.

The cost of building an addition will range from 10 to 25% more than the cost per square foot or per cubic foot of the same space in a new house. The percentage depends on the size of the addition and how difficult it is to connect the new space to the original house. The larger the addition, the greater the total cost, of course, but the smaller the cost per foot.

To convert existing space costs about one-half to two-thirds of the cost of new space. A carport, porch, or unfinished attic or basement already has the necessary structure in place. If this structure is adequate for the new purpose to which you want to put it, the major cost elements are for closing openings, installing new finish materials, and extending heating, lighting, and possibly plumbing systems into the space. The less tearing out and the shorter the extension of utilities, the closer the cost will be to half the cost of new construction.

The cost of improving existing space is very difficult to estimate in advance because you have so many variables. Each remodeling project is different. The final cost depends on how much work must be done on the structure (removing a bearing wall, for example, or shoring up a sagging floor); how much tearing out is required; how much of existing plumbing, wiring, or heating systems need to be replaced to meet current building codes; and how extensive the remodeling job is.

Here are two examples. Suppose that you need another bedroom in a small house, and that you decide the best way to remodel is to convert a cramped living room into a master bedroom, and add a larger living room. Estimate the cost of the new living room at the going rate for new construction plus about 15%. To convert the old living room to a large bedroom you will undoubtedly need new closets, perhaps a new partition to form a hall, and some repair work on surfaces. You can safely estimate this conversion at half the cost of new construction. If, however, your plans also include an extra bathroom off the master bedroom, but still within the walls of the old living room, estimate the conversion at the same cost as new construction.

Now suppose that you want to remodel your 25-year-old kitchen, which is short on counter and storage space, has poor traffic flow, and looks its age. To do the job right, you will probably need to gut the space, which costs little for materials but a lot for labor. To improve traffic flow or brighten the room, you may need to replace a bearing wall with a supporting beam or to enlarge window areas. By the time the kitchen is stripped of cabinets and counters, the ceiling and walls will probably need resurfacing. You'll need new cabinets and countertops. You may be able to reuse your appliances, but if they are more than 10 years old, they will look shabby beside new cabinets. Then, seen against new appliances, the floor covering will look old, and cry for replacement. Furthermore, most good kitchen remodeling requires some changes in plumbing, electrical, and gas lines. So by the time you have your kitchen the way you want it, the cost could be almost twice the cost of new construction. And worth every cent.

Cost per Square Foot

Many builders experienced in new construction calculate costs on a per-square-foot basis. On each job they keep close track of their expenses for materials, labor, and overhead. Then they divide this total by the number of square feet of floor space in the house. They figure main living areas at full square footage and other areas, such as basements, garages, and porches, at half square footage. The resultant figure is their cost per square foot. Then they add their profit. When they estimate the next job, they adjust these costs for any increases or decreases in the costs of materials, labor, or overhead, and for differences between houses—a brick exterior instead of siding, an extra bathroom, interior paneling instead of wallboard, and so on.

Builders may not be willing to tell you their costs per square foot, but you can find out the going rate in your community in two other ways. One is to ask at a real estate office that sells new homes. The second is to talk to the loan officer at your regular bank. It's a good idea to ask both places, because the figures aren't likely to be exactly the same, and the two answers will give you a range to work with.

Armed with this information, you can then measure the width times the length of the space you plan to remodel. Then multiply by the cost per square foot, and adjust as just discussed. You will come up with a reasonably close estimate of what you would have to pay a reputable contractor to do the work for you. Measure as shown in Fig. 2-6a. When measuring square footage, include the thickness of exterior walls (dimensions A, B, C, D, and F), including the wall against which you build an addition. Include only half the thickness of interior partitions (dimensions C, D, E, and F).

Cost per Cubic Foot

For remodeling work, a cost per cubic foot is a little more accurate than a cost per square foot. The cost of a cubic foot is roughly one-eighth to one-tenth of the cost of a square foot. To arrive at cubic footage, you multiply the square footage of each area to be remodeled by the height of that area, measuring as shown in Fig. 2-6b. A current cost per cubic foot in your community may also be hard to obtain, but try the same sources mentioned earlier.

Chapter 2 / Exploring The Possibilities

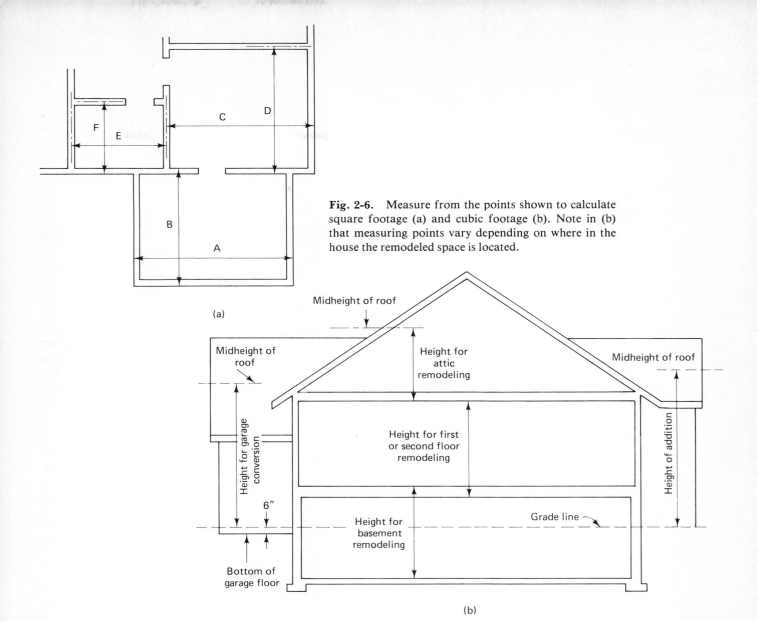

Fig. 2-6. Measure from the points shown to calculate square footage (a) and cubic footage (b). Note in (b) that measuring points vary depending on where in the house the remodeled space is located.

At this stage in your progress toward remodeling, avoid talking with a builder or remodeling contractor unless you happen to have one as a personal friend. Usually, contractors are unwilling to give you an estimate or per foot cost until they know exactly what you have in mind and have a reasonable assurance of landing the job. Even then you may not get a firm price. Remodeling contractors can't always be certain what they will find when they break into walls, particularly in a house built before 1940. They much prefer to work on a cost-plus basis so that they have an opportunity to make a reasonable profit. More about contracts and quotations in chapter 3.

Now, where's the money coming from?

Sources of Financing

If you must borrow money to finance a remodeling, there are many possible sources, and it pays to shop around for the best rate and terms. In these days of economic unrest, conditions change almost daily, and any information given here today may be outdated tomorrow.

One source of financing is the Department of Urban Development (HUD), which was once known as the Federal Housing Administration (FHA). Through the Housing Division of HUD you can arrange a loan of up to $15,000 for a maximum term of 15 years at a fixed annual percentage rate (APR). The rate is about 19%, but call to learn the current figure. Any loan of more than $7500 must be secured by a first, second, or third mortgage, depending on how many mortgages you already have on your home. For loans of less than $7500 no such security is required.

To be eligible for such an FHA loan you must already own the property and have occupied the house for at least 90 days. This restriction is to prevent loans to people who have bought a shell house and intend to finish it themselves. You may apply for a loan whether you intend to hire a remodeling contractor or plan to do the work yourself.

The Veterans Administration has similar arrangements and restrictions on a VA loan. Few veterans use a VA loan for remodeling, however, because they have already used it for the purchase of the house.

The banks where you have savings accounts and checking accounts, and are therefore a known customer, are a good source of loans. But shop around among their competitors, too. Half a percentage point over a dozen years can make quite a difference in the total cost of a remodeling.

If you work for a firm that has a credit union, it may be another source of financing. Credit unions have a top limit on the amount you can borrow, so it pays to have a reasonably good estimate in hand when you investigate.

Even if you have enough money in an interest-bearing account to cover the cost of remodeling, consider the possibility of a loan. Say that the interest rate you would have to pay will be about 5% higher than the interest you receive on your savings. In effect, then, you would be paying only 5% for the loan. This may seem like an avoidable expense, but sometimes there are tax advantages to taking out a loan and leaving your sources of ready cash untouched.

Remodeling versus Moving

The main alternative to remodeling is moving. Moving in itself entails some expenses that might be better spent on remodeling. These include the costs of selling your present home—real estate fees, advertising, and the like. There are the expenses of buying another house—automobile expenses during the search, closing costs, and new arrangements for mortgaging, probably at a much higher interest rate. There are the actual costs of moving, which aren't tax deductible. It costs almost as much to move one block as to move 100 miles. And you are likely to need or want to put money into new draperies or carpeting or redecorating in another house. Of course, you can reduce these costs by advertising and selling the house yourself, and handling the moving with strong-backed friends, but many of the expenses of moving are unavoidable.

Doing the Work Yourself

The rough estimates of remodeling costs discussed earlier in this chapter are based on hiring a professional remodeler to do the work. How much can you save by doing it all yourself? Or part of it?

If you have more time than money, you can cut costs roughly in half. You eliminate the builder's profit and his overhead on all the work you do. In some remodelings you can also eliminate labor costs, such as finishing off or enclosing existing space. In others that involve changes in the structure or utility lines, you will probably need specialists that you can hire yourself as owner-contractor. Your costs for materials, which are approximately 40% of total cost in remodeling, will be higher than a professional contractor's costs. You will have more waste than he will, and you have no place to use up leftover materials.

If you are blessed with the talents to build, and have the time and patience to do the job, you'll find in this book the information necessary to do the job right. If you have done any building before, your experience will stand you in good stead. But if you have never done any remodeling before, be aware of what you are getting into. Don't let the lack stop you from going ahead; just be prepared.

For remodeling is a slow, messy, frustrating experience that is at the same time exciting and thoroughly satisfying. The tearing-out stage is fun and an adventure. What will you find when you remove the plaster or wallboard? Yet during this stage you must live in and run a household amid layers of gypsum dust, the debris of discarded materials, and the clutter of tools. Dust infiltrates cabinets, and even soup tastes a little gritty. You have to find new routes between rooms because the familiar ones are temporarily blocked. And the floors and carpets clearly show the new routes in a trail of footprints.

If your remodeling requires cutting through exterior walls or the roof, you must time your work to coincide with good weather, and plan your actions to be completed with the greatest practical haste. Even if the weather is perfect, you will have moments of anxiety whenever the sun ducks behind a cloud or the temperature drops two degrees.

When you begin to apply finish materials to the ceiling, walls, and floor, it looks as if the end is in sight. Yet at this point you are little more than halfway through the job, and from then on the work seems to go agonizingly slowly. By now you and your family wish the remodeling were done, but it doesn't pay to hurry. It's better to take the time to do everything right.

The big advantage of remodeling is that, a week or two after the job is done and routines are back to normal, you can be proud of your "new" house and gratified with the improvements. And you have provided yourself with a year's worth of tales to tell and laugh about that weren't funny at all at the time.

Preliminary Planning

(a)

(b)

Nothing is seriously wrong with the lines of the original house (a). When the owners reorganized and expanded existing space, however, they corrected a foundation problem at the same time, and put more emphasis on the main entrance (b). Windows grouped in a recess are the focal point of the streetside elevation, and a low railing leads the eye to the front door. Broad boards at the base of walls echo the fascia boards, but with siding they would make the house look very low. The vertical lines of plywood panels and battened joints correct the proportions. (Courtesy American Plywood Association.)

The purpose of all the steps to this point is to determine if you should *not* remodel. As long as remodeling is still a reasonable prospect, the next step is to plan in detail what work should be done.

To plan properly takes time and some study. To a great extent you must rely on your own resources to plan any remodeling, particularly in the early stages. Later, after your ideas have jelled, you can go to several sources for help.

Many people who plan their own remodeling start out by putting a floor plan down on paper. Actually, the floor plan should be the final step—after you know what to put down. The best way to attack the problem is to begin with a concept of what you want to accomplish

by remodeling. To do this, you must look at your entire house, not just one area.

Suppose that your primary need is another bedroom. The obvious solution is to build a small addition with the extra bedroom in it. But to do so you would probably have to cut down the size of some existing room to form a hallway to your new space. This approach may work or it may not.

So before you make any final decision, look at alternatives, and also at other problems you have listed that might be corrected at the same time. Another possible solution, for example, is to build a shed dormer and put the bedroom in unused attic space. Another is to create a bedroom in basement space that is dry, warm, and has good light and ventilation. Still another is to convert an existing room, such as a living room, into the needed bedroom, and put a larger, brighter living room in an addition.

So begin your long-range planning by listing your primary purposes, then write down all the problems that, ideally, you would like to correct at the same time. You won't be able to solve them all, but the more you solve the happier you will be with your remodeling, and the more you get for the money you spend.

Once you know exactly what you want to achieve, you can start putting plans on paper.

WHERE TO GET HELP

Two good sources of ideas are the so-called "shelter" magazines, such as *Better Homes & Gardens*, and the remodeling books put out by shelter magazine publishers. These are available at many bookstores, drugstores, and other retail outlets across the country. You aren't likely to see the solution to a remodeling problem exactly like yours; no two are alike. But seeing what someone else has done may trigger an idea that will work for you.

From two other sources you can hire limited help in design and construction: an architect and a remodeling contractor.

An Architect

Few architectural firms are interested in designing your remodeling for you. It just isn't profitable. If a firm sets its fee high enough to cover the time spent, that fee would probably be more than you are willing to pay.

Many firms, however, permit their younger members to gain experience by moonlighting on design work that doesn't conflict in any way with their regular work. You may find such a person willing and able to develop a floor plan and the necessary elevations, sections, and details for you, although he or she probably won't have time to supervise construction.

In addition, you can hire most architects, from principals of firms on down, as consultants. To take full advantage of this arrangement, however, consult only after you have developed your ideas as far as you can yourself.

Any search for the best architect for you requires two steps. First, find out which ones may be interested in working with you, and second, select the right one from among the prospects. In large metropolitan areas look in the telephone book first for a listing under American Institute of Architects. The local chapter offices often have records that indicate which firms and which members of firms might help you. The AIA won't recommend any one firm, but will send you a list of architects that design residential remodelings, in-

cluding retired members who like to design occasionally on short-term projects.

If consultations will take place in the architect's office during the day, look for addresses convenient for you to reach. Then call. Tell the switchboard operator why you called. She is likely to know which members of the firm are interested in and available for remodeling design work, and can put you in touch directly.

After you make telephone contact, perhaps you and the architect can arrange to meet for lunch just to make sure you are compatible in thinking and temperament, and can agree on a fee. Fees and time of payment vary. You may hire a starting architect for as little as $15 to $20 per hour. Older and more experienced architects will charge several times as much. If you feel that you can afford only so much for design consultation, say so immediately. And before you actually begin to work together, establish the amount of the fee, what it will and will not cover, and a specific time for consultation.

If you hire an architect to design your entire remodeling, you meet first at your home. Have ready your list of problems to correct, and any clippings of magazines that show the type of result you like. A floor plan of your house as it exists, if available, will save the architect the time and you the expense of measuring. A few weeks later the architect will show you some sketches describing his or her ideas for your review and approval. After you approve the sketches, the architect will prepare final drawings from which you and your builder can work.

If you hire an architect as a consultant, you meet in the architect's office. Bring along a "before" floor plan drawn to scale, and a floor plan at the same scale showing how you visualize the layout of the remodeled house. Also bring along your list of problems to correct, and a list of the finish materials you want to use inside and out. If your remodeling includes changes in the exterior, particularly involving roof lines, take photos of the house from all sides. Then show the architect either elevations you have drawn, or sketches laid over the photographs that show how the new roof will look.

The architect won't criticize or snicker at your drawings, but will be pleased that you have taken so much time to present clearly what you have in mind.

The architect will first make sure that your plans are structurally sound. He or she may then recommend some minor changes that will save you construction costs. The architect may suggest a change or two that will improve the appearance of the house with little or no additional cost, and may even make a couple of rough sketches to guide you. Most architects will give you more than your money's worth. In essence they can take what may be your practical but rather pedestrian solution to your remodeling needs, and give it a little flair and individuality. But don't let anyone talk you into any changes you don't want. It's your money, and you have the right to full veto.

A Contractor

For help in designing a remodeling, a building contractor is rarely the best person to talk to. Unlike architects, contractors are not trained in spatial relationships, scale, and residential design, although they may offer design service to customers.

On the other hand, if you have any questions as to the structural condition of your house, or the practicality of remodeling it, talk to a contractor experienced in residential remodeling. A remodeling contractor may charge a fee for a firsthand inspection and recommendations, but will almost always apply this fee toward any resulting remodeling work. He or she can verify which walls in your house are bearing walls if you aren't sure. And if there is more than one direction your remodeling can take, he or she can tell you which is the most economical approach. An architect can do this, too, but would have to make an on-site inspection, which may not be part of your agreement.

Wherever you go for help, the job of preliminary planning is yours. But before you can successfully develop a floor plan of remodeled space, you need a floor plan of existing space.

THE "BEFORE" PLAN

If a set of drawings was among the papers that you acquired when you bought your house, work from the floor plan as your "before" plan. Just make sure that the plan in the drawings agrees with the plan of the house as built. Sometimes changes made during construction aren't recorded on drawings. Verify especially the locations of windows and doors.

Dimensioning

Note on the drawings the points to and from which measurements are taken. The overall dimensions of a house are measured from exposed outside corner to exposed outside corner, whatever the exterior material. Framing dimensions on floor plans above foundation or basement level, however, are measured from the outside corners of structure—that is, from corner stud to corner stud in frame construction, regardless of the exterior material, and in solid masonry from outside corner to outside corner like overall dimensions (see Fig. 3-1).

If your plans were drawn by a professional, doors and windows are dimensioned to their centerlines.

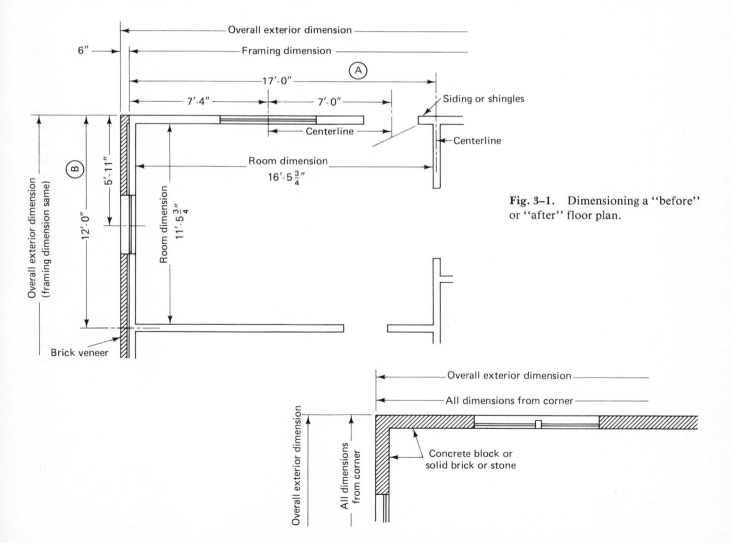

Fig. 3–1. Dimensioning a "before" or "after" floor plan.

Similarly, interior partitions are dimensioned to their centerlines, not their surfaces. Therefore, when you take interior measurements from wall surface to wall surface, they won't agree with dimensions on drawings. You must compensate.

Suppose that you have a room dimensioned like the one in Fig. 3-1. The exterior dimension of 17'-0" (A) doesn't include the brick veneer wall or air space, but does include the thickness of the stud wall and half the thickness of an interior partition. To find the actual room dimension corresponding to dimension A, you subtract the thickness of an exterior wall stud (3½"), half the width of a partition stud (1¾"), and the thickness of interior surface materials. Here are typical thicknesses:

- Plywood paneling: ¼" or ⁵⁄₁₆".
- Solid wood panels: ¾".

- Gypsum wallboard: ⅜", ½", or ¾". Generally, the more expensive the house, the thicker the wallboard.
- Plaster: ¾" to 1". As a rule, the older the house, the greater the total thickness of plaster and supporting lath.

Therefore, if walls are ½" wallboard, the total thickness you subtract from the framing dimension is 6¼", and the long dimension of the room should be 16'-5¾".

Even though the side wall of the house in Fig. 3-1 is wood siding, you still subtract 6¼" from dimension B to find the short dimension of the room: 11'-5¾".

How to Measure

For the most accurate possible dimensioning, measure cumulatively. In other words, take all measurements

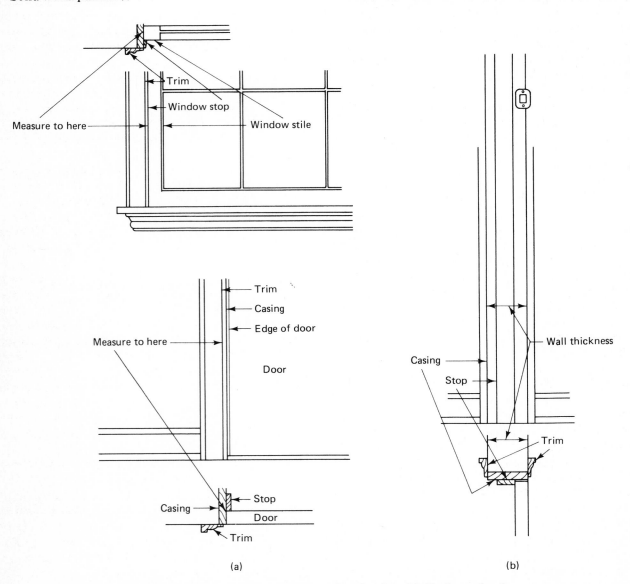

(a) (b)

Fig. 3-2. At openings measure to the insides of casings (a). To determine the thickness of a partition, measure the width of a door casing (b).

Chapter 3 / Preliminary Planning

along one wall from the same starting point, usually a corner of the room. While someone else holds the end of a 50′ steel tape steady, unreel it along the wall. As you come to a door or window jamb or a corner, read off the dimension and write it down. You'll save a lot of time later if you list in reverse order the points to which you measure, beginning with the far corner of the room. Then you write in your measurements from the bottom up, something like this:

From northwest corner of living room to:

northeast corner	16′-5¾″
east door jamb	15′-10″
west door jamb	12′-10″
east window jamb	10′-0⅛″
west window jamb	4′-7⅞″

Cumulative measuring is not only faster than any other method but is more accurate. Suppose that you are off only ⅛″ in every measurement you make. If you measure from corner to jamb, then across the window, then along the wall in this way, moving the tape each time, you make five measurements and are off ⅝″ at the other corner. By holding one end of the tape fixed, you are off at most ⅛″.

To locate the position of a window or door, measure to the inside edge of the casing (Fig. 3-2a). To find the dimension from the corner of the room in Fig. 3-1 to the centerline of the window, add the dimensions to the jambs and divide by 2:

$$\frac{10′-0\frac{1}{8}″ \; + \; 4′-7\frac{7}{8}″}{2}$$

The centerline is 7′-4″ from the corner.

To determine the thickness of an interior partition with a door in it, measure the width of the casing (Fig. 3-2b). Interior partitions of most houses less than 40 years old are 4½″ thick. Almost all interior partitions will be identical in thickness. There may be two exceptions. Walls behind toilets are often 2″ thicker to hide the plumbing stack, and partitions around closets may be 2″ thinner.

Making Your Own "Before" Plan

If you don't already have a floor plan to work from, it isn't too difficult to make your own. First measure the overall dimensions of the outside of your house; accuracy within 6″ is good enough for the moment. Floor plans are almost always drawn at a scale of ¼″ = 1′-0″. If your outside dimensions are 40′ × 24′, for example, you know that the plan drawn to scale will be 10″ × 6″. Therefore, you need a sheet of paper at least 12″ × 8″ to show the plan of the basic house and its outside dimensions.

You can work on a plain sheet of paper, but it is easier to use graph paper divided with very light lines into ⅛″ or ¼″ squares. A straight-edged ruler is ade-

quate for measuring. Let each 1/16″ on the ruler equal 3″ of actual dimension. Use a sharp pencil; a No. 2 or 3 is best because you can erase easily. Draw lightly until you have the entire plan on paper, then go back and strengthen lines when you are sure they are right.

Start your drawing an inch in from the top and left-hand edges of the paper, and let this point be the corner of the room at a corner of the house. You can add the exterior wall thickness later. Measure as outlined in Figs. 3-1 and 3-2. You'll save time and effort if you locate all windows and doors while you are in one room before you go on to the next room. Remember to allow for thickness of partitions in your drawing. Don't worry about showing the shape of trim at doors and windows; draw openings as square-sided.

If remodeling calls for any changes in walls or partitions, locate on your drawing the positions of heat registers, return air grilles, and radiators. Be accurate, and use the symbols shown in Fig. 3-3. Also mark the locations of electrical outlets, switches, and ceiling or wall lights, this time with reasonable accuracy. It doesn't cost as much to relocate wiring as it does to relocate heat ducts or plumbing pipes.

As shown in Fig. 3-4, a "before" plan during development should include dimensions of the house, of rooms, and to openings—all indicated outside the plan itself. Inside, show heat and electrical outlets, door swings, and the direction of stairways from the floor level depicted.

With the interior of the house lightly laid out, add the thickness of exterior walls. Then measure to see how close the overall dimensions on your drawing come to the actual overall dimensions of the house. A difference of an inch or two isn't important. If you are off by more than 3″, however, recheck your measurements along that side, and the thicknesses of partitions.

Incidentally, if you draw on unlined paper, be sure that all corners are square. To make a square corner you need a compass. Mark the corner of the room on your paper (point A in Fig. 3-5) and from it draw a long horizontal line. Measure off 4″ along this line and make a light mark (point B). Next, set the point of your compass in the corner (point A), and draw an arc 3″ away from it at approximately a right angle to your line. Then move the compass to the 4″ mark (point B), and draw another arc 5″ away. From the point where the two arcs cross (point C), draw a line to point A, and you will have a wall at right angles.

You have just used the old Pythagorean theorem to form a square corner. Remember it? "The square on the hypotenuse of a right triangle is equal to the sum of the squares on the other two sides." On your drawing the square on the hypotenuse is 5 × 5 or 25, and the sum of the squares of the other two sides, 3 × 3 plus 4 × 4, is also 25. Keep this theorem in mind. You will use it many times during construction.

After you have checked the accuracy of your lightly drawn plan of the house as it exists, strengthen

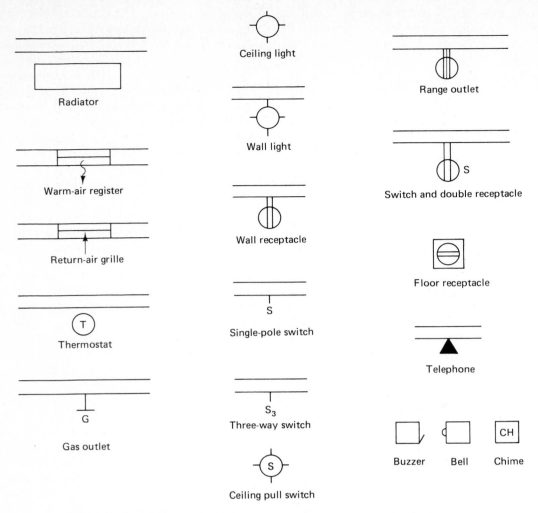

Fig. 3-3. Typical architectural symbols for elements of heating and electrical systems. These are for use on plans; symbols for use on elevations are often different.

the lines and add dimensions. Show only the dimensions pertinent to the areas you plan to remodel, and, if possible, dimension outside these areas to avoid confusion (see Fig. 3-4). Do not use cumulative dimensions; list only the actual dimensions from point to point by subtracting one cumulative dimension from another.

Finally, add a compass point somewhere on the drawing so that you can keep orientation straight (see Fig. 3-4). **Orientation** is the relationship to the points of a compass, and is important in planning any changes in rooms or in locating a room addition. Orientation and how to develop ''after'' drawings are discussed in later chapters on specific remodeling projects.

SELECTING CONTRACTORS

Unless you are an experienced do-it-yourselfer, versed in all phases of residential construction, you will probably have at least one contractor working for you at some time during your remodeling. He may be a remodeling contractor to whom you entrust the entire project. Or he may be a specialist, such as a plumber or electrician, whom you hire to do only part of the work. Whatever he does, you must pick with care.

The remodeling specialist you select to do all your work for you must be experienced, reputable, financially sound, and someone you like personally. During any remodeling this contractor and his crew will be almost as close as members of your family, and making a bigger mess. It is extremely important that everyone who is at home during remodeling like the contractor. There will be days when they are in each other's way, and they must be compatible.

Qualifications

For this reason alone look for a contractor who specializes in remodeling, rather than a builder whose work is mostly new houses. Builders are used to working solely with their own crews, and they are the only ones that must put up with the mess they make until they get around to cleaning it up. Their goal is to build quickly,

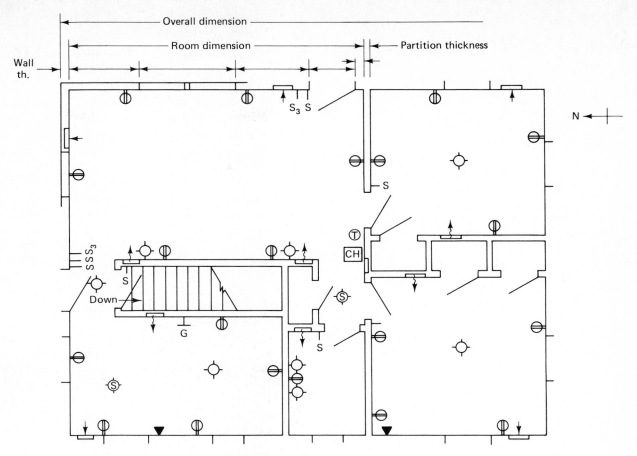

Fig. 3-4. A typical "before" plan during development. Lines marking the outsides of exterior walls are added after all else is drawn.

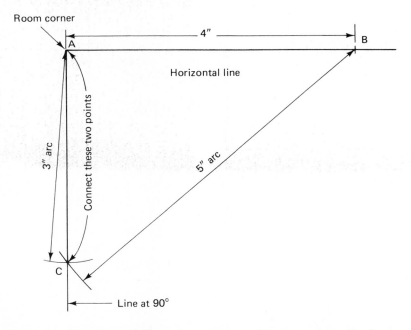

Fig. 3-5. Drawing a right angle on paper without a square. To form a similar right angle when laying out an addition or during construction, follow the same procedure but use 4′, 3′, and 5′, or any convenient multiple of these dimensions.

and as well as possible at that speed. They establish the pace and routine, and have no one else to consider.

A good remodeling contractor, on the other hand, knows that his work interrupts household routines, and that he has your entire family to consider. He will mesh his schedule with the family's schedule, timing the various aspects of the job so they cause a minimum of disruption. During the tearing-out stage he will work quickly and clean up his mess frequently. When water, gas, or electricity must be shut off temporarily, he will let you know well in advance so that you can adjust your schedule to the interruption. The remodeling contractor and the owner's family must work closely together as a team and, to keep schedules, costs, and tempers under control, they must be teammates.

Where to Look

The best way to find your contractor is to talk with owners for whom he has worked. Ask friends or business associates who have remodeled for their recommendations. If you draw a blank here, keep your eyes open as you drive by remodeling projects that are under way. Knock on the door and explain why you stopped. Although homeowners may be suspicious initially, most people are proud to show you what remodeling they are doing. Be prepared to identify yourself with a calling card or something similar, make the visit brief and businesslike, and ask permission to call later when the contractor isn't there to discuss the owners' opinion of him.

If you still have no good leads, try the classified pages of your telephone book. Tell the contractor what you are planning, and ask him for the names, addresses, and telephone numbers of owners for whom he has completed jobs. He may not give them to you over the telephone, but will ask to meet you at your home to see what you have in mind. This is a good sign of reputability; he is protecting his former clients until he has checked *you* out.

Checking Him Out

By visiting the homes of a contractor's clients, you can see for yourself the quality of work he does. By talking with his clients you can learn the answers to these important questions:

- How prompt is he? When he sets a time for starting the day, ending the day, or shutting off water, can you count on it?
- Does he work out a schedule with you and stick to it?
- How neat is he? Remodeling is messy, but good contractors move debris out of the house as quickly as possible and dispose of it themselves. And they sweep up before they leave for the day.

- Does he store incoming materials for your convenience rather than his?
- Are the contractor and his crew good workers, but at the same time good-natured and pleasant to have around?
- Is he businesslike in his dealings with you? Are his estimates of cost and time accurate? Are his billings complete and easy to understand?
- Would you invite him back if you remodeled again?

From the answers given by both the husband and wife and any other adults home during remodeling, you can get a good idea of the experience and congeniality of the contractor and his crew. To verify his reputation and financial stability, ask him for a bank reference. His banker can and will tell you how long he has been a customer, whether his bank account is sound and has adequate reserves for emergencies, and what his reputation is in the community.

Finally, ask your contractor who his primary suppliers are. Talk to the managers of these building supply houses, and ask how promptly he pays his bills. The fact that he *does* pay his bills promptly is a plus. The fact that he *can* pay his bills promptly is a bigger plus. It means that his customers are also paying him promptly, and are not withholding payment because of poor workmanship or other failure to do the job as contracted.

Preliminary Discussion

After you are satisfied that you have found the right contractor for you, set up an evening meeting to go over your plans. Have a set of prints ready for him to take with him. (If you talk with more than one contractor, have a set of prints for each.) He will walk around the house, inside and out, with the prints in hand. He will probably check out some measurements and make notes. His main purpose at this time is to size up the job, but at the same time to size up you and your family as potential clients.

If he knows that he is competing against other remodeling contractors—and you should tell him so—he will do little else at the first meeting. If he knows that he can have the job if his quotation is within your budget, he may make a suggestion or two that can save him some time and therefore reduce your cost. Such suggestions are more likely to come from him, however, after he has studied the plans in his office.

Consider very carefully any suggestions he makes in light of his knowledge. The right contractor knows construction, good building procedures, and building materials. Rarely is he trained in planning and design, although he may do both when required. He may spot a structural problem that you missed, and suggest an alternative solution. Unless the suggestion defeats one of your goals in remodeling, go along with it. He may see a place where construction will be difficult and expensive, and suggest a way to simplify and reduce the cost of his work. Again, as long as the suggestion doesn't alter your purposes and use of the space, go along with it. But if he thinks you are on the wrong track with your ideas, and wants to make wholesale changes, he's not the right contractor for you.

Undoubtedly, there will be times when you have to compromise. If your contractor *can't* carry out your wishes—they don't comply with codes, for instance—you must be the one to accede. If he *can* carry out your wishes, but prefers to do something else, you have to decide whether his reasons are better than your reasons—a reduction in cost, for example. Here is one place where an architectural consultant can be invaluable. But if he thinks his solution is better than yours, and it is only one opinion against another, stick to your guns. He should compromise.

THE QUOTATION

A week or so after he talks with you, your contractor will give you a quotation, or bid. The quotation will state the scope of the work to be done—what work he will do, what work he won't do (to be done by others, including you), and the documents on which his quotation is based. It will set forth the basis for billing; it probably will not contain a fixed cost figure, but may include an approximation.

Most remodeling contractors are unwilling to state a fixed price. It's not because they are out to overcharge you, but because they can't always foresee all their costs until they have removed surface materials and can see what is between studs, joists, and rafters. You can demand a final price, but there are two good reasons for not doing so. First, you are in essence telling your contractor, with whom you must work in harmony, that you don't trust him to charge you fairly. Second, any price you force him to name will be high enough to cover any eventuality and assure that he makes a profit. This cost will undoubtedly be higher than if the work were done on a cost-plus basis.

Cost-Plus Basis

Under a cost-plus arrangement the contractor charges you for all the materials he buys, and for the labor of his crew to install all materials used on the job, whether he buys them or you do. To this total he then adds a fixed percentage to cover his overhead costs and give him a profit. This percentage is usually 15 to 20%, but may be higher in suburban areas of large cities. The advantage of a cost-plus contract is its fairness to both sides. The contractor is assured of a fair profit, regardless of the problems he encounters on the job, and you pay no more and no less than a fair price.

The disadvantage to you is that you don't have a firm price on which to base any loan you may need to negotiate. To get around that difficulty, you and your contractor can usually work out a cost-plus arrangement with a fixed maximum. The fixed maximum is high enough to assure the contractor a profit under the most adverse circumstances. The fixed maximum is also the most he can charge you. If the contractor's actual costs are below the fixed maximum—and they almost always are—you get the saving. Under a fixed-price arrangement, the contractor pockets the saving. Cost-plus with a fixed maximum is fair to both parties.

THE CONTRACT

Some small contractors aren't used to working under a written contract. An honest person is content with a verbal agreement and a handshake to confirm your acceptance of his bid. But a contract is a good idea nevertheless, and protects you both. A quotation isn't a legal document; a contract is. If your contractor doesn't have a standard contract form that he uses, pick one yourself. You can buy standard contract forms at most office supply and stationery stores with blanks that you fill in with the variables.

A word of caution. For a small fee a lawyer will review a contract to make sure it is in good order and legally acceptable. That's fine. But don't ask the lawyer to write the contract. Use a standard form. A specially written contract isn't necessary, will cost you money, and opens up suspicions you want to avoid. Your contractor will want his lawyer to look over a strange contract, too, and that adds to his costs. A contract should be a simply stated, friendly agreement that forms a legal basis for working together.

The contract should include a copy of each of your drawings, with any changes you have agreed on clearly shown and listed on a separate sheet of paper. It should include a copy of any specifications, or a list of the surface materials you have agreed to. It should include the maximum price figure, and the percentage the contractor will add to his costs of materials and labor. And it should show the terms of payment.

Terms of Payment

Contractors bill in a number of ways, depending on the extent of their work. Yours may bill you at fixed times, such as every other Monday. He may bill you after he orders the materials, and again at the end of the job. He may bill at fixed points in construction, such as after completion of various phases—tearing out, structural work, finishing, and acceptance. Whatever method he prefers should be stated in the contract so that you know when to expect bills and how to compare them with the work accomplished to that point.

More about paying bills a little later in this chapter.

THE IDEAL HOMEOWNER

In the last few pages you have read how you should look for and look at a remodeling contractor. Now let's reverse the roles and see how the remodeling contractor looks at a homeowner, and what he expects of you and from you.

From the contractor's viewpoint, you the homeowner should be financially sound and with a credit rating indicating prompt payment. You should be aware of the extent and the limits of your own knowledge of construction. You should be able to show clearly what you want done, then leave it to the contractor to accomplish that result. You must be both trustworthy and trusting. You should be open in your questions and just in your criticisms. And if you are quick with praise for a job well done, you are a winner!

The contractor looks over the homeowner's family with equal care. As the ideal wife and homemaker, you should go about your regular routine with as few adjustments as possible. When you have to leave for a meeting or to run errands, you let the crew know of your departure, and have full faith that your household will be intact when you return. You are interested in progress of the job, but don't look over anyone's shoulder except in passing. You maintain your equanimity in spite of dust, noise, and confusion. When the mess gets to you, you walk away from it, knowing that the work of the contractor of necessity creates dust, noise, and confusion. You are friendly but not forward, conversational but not chatty. And if you bake cookies for your family, you bake a few extra for its temporary members.

Of equal importance, you instruct your children on their behavior. "No complaints if something is moved or misplaced. Watch if you want, but stay out of the way and skip the questions. Your father is paying while your questions are being answered. If the crew is working in your room, keep yourself elsewhere except to get something to take somewhere else out of the way. Treat the remodelers as if they are your friends, and they will be your friends."

If you have a pet trained to protect, confine him well away from areas of work and materials storage. And if you have a pet that treats everyone who comes to the house as a friend, let him greet the crew when they arrive and wag goodbye when they leave, but keep him confined out of the way the rest of the day.

You get the picture. In brief, you are the ideal homeowner-client if you pride yourself on selecting the best contractor you can find, then leave him alone to vindicate your judgment.

BEING YOUR OWN CONTRACTOR

For his fee a contractor secures a building permit, hires specialists such as a plumber or electrician to do the work he can't do with his regular crew (they are usually carpenters), schedules the work, and supervises it. When you do most of the work yourself, and hire tradespeople to do only what you can't or don't want to do, you must take on all these responsibilities.

Select your subcontractors—the specialists—as soon as possible, following the procedures for selecting a remodeling contractor. While you are narrowing the field to your ultimate choice, develop a schedule for the work you intend to do. Then, when you talk with each prospect, show him your schedule, and have him tell you at what point in your work he wants to begin his. Go over the drawings with each person, and on your set of prints note the places where you have to leave room for him to work, or make provision for the work he installs.

Ask each subcontractor, too, to give you a sketch showing where he intends to run ducts, pipes, or wiring. A rough sketch is adequate as long as it shows exactly where you have special work to do. Include the sketch as part of your agreement with him. Finally, about a week before he is scheduled to start work, ask him to stop by and inspect your work to make sure that nothing further needs to be done.

Remember that one of the attributes of a good contractor is promptness. A good contractor or subcontractor schedules his crews to keep them busy at all possible times. To do this, he fits small jobs in among the big ones. If you as a contractor aren't ready for your subcontractor when he has your job scheduled, you may have to wait until he has another opening. This throws your entire schedule out of kilter, and delays completion.

So schedule your work with as much flexibility and accuracy as possible. In Tables 3-1 to 3-4 you'll find estimates of the times required to complete various tasks in new construction. The man-hours given are based on the pace of experienced professionals, adjusted upward for the capable amateur. Your own pace may be slower; it isn't likely to be faster.

The time required to remove old construction is much more difficult to assess. It will go more slowly than you might expect. For every hour spent on putting up a new wall surface, for example, you will probably take two to remove the old surface. One reason is that you must dispose of the debris frequently, and this takes many extra steps.

Incidentally, all members of your family can be very helpful during tearing out, given proper direction.

Table 3-1. Approximate manhours required to complete various framing jobs. Estimates are based on your having the proper tools in good condition, basic knowledge of the work to be done, and a pace geared to the muscles of an amateur.

Task	Estimate	Manhours	Includes:
Install sill plates	40 lin ft	1	Laying gasket or mortar seal
Set header and edge joists	35 lin ft	1	Any ledger
Build a girder	4 lin ft[a]	1	Positioning and attachment
Set posts	1½ posts	1	
Set columns	1 column	1	
Set floor joists	30 lin ft[a]	1	Cutting
Lay subflooring	50–60 sq ft[a]	1	Cutting and fitting
Install bridging	8 sets	1	
Build window frames	1 frame	1	Bracing
Build door frames	1 frame	¾	Bracing
Frame exterior walls	4 lin ft[a]	1	Raising and attachment
Install ceiling joists	25 lin ft[a]	1	Trimming
Cut common rafters	4 rafters	1	Marking, cutting, and testing the sample
Set common rafters	2 pairs[a]	1	
Install ridgeboard	18–20 lin ft[a]	1	Splicing
Install hip and valley rafters	1 rafter	1½	Cutting and fitting
Install jack rafters	1 pair	1	Cutting and fitting
Install collar beams	4 beams	1	Cutting
Build gable ends	4 lin ft of wall	1	Cutting
Install plywood roof sheathing	45 sq ft[a]	1	
Install sheathing boards	40 sq ft	1	
Install wall sheathing	50 sq ft[a]	1	
Apply building paper	75 sq ft[a]	1	
Install flashing	15 lin ft	1	
Install windows[a]	1 window[a]	1	
Install exterior doors	1 door[a]	1½	Hanging the door
Install louvers	1 louver	¾	
Build dormer walls	3 lin ft	1	Cutting and assembling all posts, studs, and plates
Build knee walls	6 lin ft	1	
Build partitions	5 lin ft	1	
Install blocking	15 pieces	1	
Insulate ceilings	40 lin ft	1	
Insulate walls	50 lin ft	1	
Insulate floors in crawl space	35 lin ft	1	
Box in pipes and ducts	4 lin ft	1	
Install furring over cabinets	6 lin ft	1	Does not include cutting through an existing ceiling for attachment

[a]With a helper, increase this estimate by 25%. The helper needs no experience, but can be useful to help you carry, hold, and set materials.

Table 3-2. Approximate manhours needed to complete various tasks below ground after excavating.

Task	Estimate	Manhours	Includes:
Form for wall footings	12–15 lin ft	1	Cutting stakes and form boards
Pour footings, premixed concrete	25 lin ft	1	Reinforcement
Pour footings, you mix concrete	10–12 lin ft[a]	1	Reinforcement
Lay drain tiles	16–18 lin ft	1	Base preparation and sloping
Lay concrete blocks	10 sq ft	1	Mixing mortar
Set anchor bolts	6 bolts	1	Positioning and embedding
Pour basement floor	40 sq ft	1	Reinforcement and finishing with help from two friends whose time is not figured in manhours
Pour caps and pedestals	1 cap or pedestal	1	Forming and reinforcement

[a]With a helper, increase this estimate by 25%.

Table 3-3. Approximate manhours required to install surface materials and their bases.

Task	Estimate	Manhours	Includes:
Apply asphalt strip shingles on roof	25–28 sq ft	1	
Apply wood shingles on roof	20 sq ft	1	
Apply wood siding	25–30 sq ft[a]	1	Caulking
Apply wood shingles on walls	20–25 sq ft	1	Caulking
Lay bricks	7–8 sq ft	1	Mixing mortar
Install gutters and downspouts	10–12 lin ft	1	Assembly and attachment
Install furring strips	80 sq ft of wall or ceiling	1	
Install underlayment	50 sq ft	1	
Install a grid ceiling	25 sq ft of ceiling area	1	All work except fitting lay-in panels
Apply ceiling tiles with mastic	12–15 sq ft[a]	1	
Apply ceiling tiles with staples	25–28 sq ft	1	
Apply wallboard to ceilings	25–30 sq ft[a]	1	Cutting and attachment only
Apply wallboard to walls	40 sq ft[a]	1	Cutting and attachment only
Finish wallboard joints, each of three steps	25 lin ft	1	
Apply wall paneling	40–50 sq ft	1	
Lay ceramic wall tiles	2 sq ft	1	Spreading mastic and grouting
Apply tileboard	20 sq ft	1	Installing moldings
Lay ceramic floor tiles	3 sq ft	1	Spreading mastic and grouting
Lay resilient tiles	12–15 sq ft	1	Spreading mastic
Lay sheet flooring	15–20 sq ft[a]	1	Spreading adhesive and seaming
Install wood block flooring	12–15 sq ft	1	
Install wood strip flooring	12–15 sq ft	1	
Lay carpeting	25–30 sq ft[a]	1	

[a]With a helper, increase this estimate by 25%.

Table 3-4. Approximate manhours required to complete finish carpentry jobs and trimming.

Task	Estimate	Manhours	Includes
Install soffits	12 lin ft[a]	1	Cutting and fitting
Install fascias	20 lin ft[a]	1	
Hang shutters	1 pair	1½	
Build a stairway	Each step	3–4	Framing, and cutting and installing all parts
Frame cabinets	Per cabinet	1½–2	
Assemble drawers	Per drawer	1½	Hardware installation
Hang cabinet doors	Per door	1	Cutting, shaping, and hardware application
Hang or set cabinets	2[a]	1	
Build countertops	16 sq ft	1	Backsplash and edge
Apply laminate	10–12 sq ft	1	Applying contact cement
Install countertops	Per piece	¾[b]	
Install a sink or lavatory in a countertop	Each	2	Cutting the hole, but does not allow time for plumbing
Install ceiling cove	10 lin ft	1	Cutting and fitting
Install interior door trim	Per door	2–2½	Door stops
Install window trim	Per window	4–5	Casings, stool, and apron
Install baseboard	12 lin ft	1	Cutting and fitting
Install base shoe	12 lin ft	1	Cutting and fitting
Install corner trim	8 lin ft	½	
Hang interior doors	Per door	3	Installation of hardware
Paint doors	Per coat per side	2	
Paint windows	Per coat, per side	3–3½	
Paint exterior trim	10 lin ft per coat	1	
Paint ceilings	25 sq ft per coat	1	
Paint walls	30 sq ft per coat	1	
Paint interior trim	15 lin ft per coat	1	
Hang wallpaper	25–28 sq ft[a]	1	

[a]With a helper, increase this estimate 25%.
[b]With a helper, decrease this estimate 20%.

Older children thrive on destruction, and toddlers as young as three can help pile up materials removed from walls and ceilings and carry them out. Just be sure that their hands and feet are protected from nails and sharp edges, and that their lungs are protected against dust.

Allow yourself some leeway in your schedule. Don't plan a fast pace and drive yourself to meet it. Your remodeling will become drudgery instead of a satisfying project. There will be weekends and evenings when you want to do something else, or perhaps nothing at all. Allow for it. But don't set such a slow schedule that the project drags on, and you all grow irritable from living under upset conditions.

Most important, stay on the schedule you set. If you get ahead, call your subcontractors and tell them. This gives them a little flexibility in their scheduling. They may not be able to come sooner, but if they can, you gain time to devote to later phases of construction. If you get behind schedule, call them immediately to allow them the maximum time for rescheduling. Don't expect them to make up the time *you* lost, however.

Paying Your Bills

A contractor or subcontractor working for you under a cost-plus contract should include with each billing a copy of every bill for materials, marked paid, and a copy of the time record of each member of his crew. Check all bills for accuracy. If you have any questions, inquire. But be friendly about it. Your contractors hope that you will become a good reference for them on future work, and they are as interested in a correct billing as you are.

Because you are living with the work being done, you quite naturally will keep an eye on contractors' progress day to day. When you spot something that doesn't seem right or may cause you an unexpected problem, question it. If there is a good reason for it, the contractor will tell you what it is. If he can't, tell him to correct the mistake. When you pay a bill for work done, that work should be done the way you want it.

But avoid nitpicking. And, except for the final payment, pay your bills promptly when the work is satisfactory. Your contractor has spent his money in your behalf, and is entitled to prompt reimbursement.

The Final Bill. Before you pay the final bill, which should be for no less than 10% of the total cost of remodeling, go over the contractor's work with meticulous care. Make a checklist of the items that you think should be corrected, then go over each one with the contractor on hand. As each item is corrected or explained to your satisfaction, cross it off. Then, with final payment, send a brief letter indicating your satisfaction with his work. When you pay that last bill, your contractor is no longer legally obligated to make any corrections. If, in the first month after completion, something goes wrong, a good contractor will make a

callback to correct it, but he does so to maintain his reputation.

DOING ALL THE WORK YOURSELF

Beginning with the next chapter, the information in this book is organized by the type of remodeling, and is put together on the assumption that you intend to do all the work yourself that doesn't require a license. Even if you have no such intention, the procedures will serve as a checklist for work done by others.

As soon as you have your drawings in order, you are almost ready to go to work. But not quite. You have a few preliminaries to take care of.

The Building Permit

In most communities you need to obtain a building permit before you can start any kind of remodeling that affects the structure of the house. You will certainly need a permit to add a room, enclose a carport, raise a roof, remove a bearing wall, or make any change in your plumbing, heating, or electrical system. You probably won't need a permit to refinish existing surfaces, add storage space, or make repairs. If you have any doubt, ask the person who issues the permits.

In cities the person to see is usually the building inspector, whose office is in the city hall. In smaller communities it may be the county engineer in the courthouse. In outlying areas it may be the tax assessor.

Bring with you your "before" and "after" plans, a plot plan if you are adding a room, any specifications, and your estimate of the cost. Unless he or she is out of the office, the person responsible for permits will usually review your documents while you wait, and issue the permit right then and there. The cost of a permit is nominal; for remodelings it is usually based either on the cost estimate or on the square footage of space added, with a minimum fee regardless of cost or size.

Nail the permit to a tree, post, corner of the house, or some other spot where it is clearly visible from the street. The permit is your authorization to get on with the work.

Other Preparation

Before you pick up the first tool, you have five important decisions to make: how to clear the area where you will be working, what to do with building debris and scrap materials, when to order materials, where to store them, and what tools you will have to buy or rent.

Clearing Land. The part of your lot that an addition will occupy obviously must be cleared of trees, overhanging branches, shrubs, and perennials. Trees within the building area or close enough to interfere should be cut down and the stumps removed. Small trees and shrubbery must be dug up. Those to be saved should have a ball of soil protecting the roots, and burlap wrapped around the ball and tied at the trunk. Set the shrubbery somewhere else on your property where it is not only out of the way but also has approximately the same light conditions as it had before removal. Keep the burlap damp until you replant. Replant perennials. If you want to use them around the new foundation, plant them later in the soil you remove when you trench for the foundation.

Clearing Rooms. When your remodeling plans require work in more than one room, it is usually more convenient to complete work in one room before going on to the next. The main reason is that most people don't have enough space to store the furniture from more than one room.

Clear out all furniture. One possible exception is a grand piano that can't be moved without taking it apart. Cover such pieces with a sheet of polyethylene, and tape the seams to keep out as much dust as possible. Since you will probably have to move large furniture within the room, make sure that the casters are free to roll.

Remove and store draperies and curtains. Cover carpeting you expect to keep with a sheet of polyethylene at least 4 mm thick, and tack it around the edges. Again seal all seams.

Debris. Most garbage pickup services will not accept building materials on their regular rounds. Often, however, they will remove such debris for a fee. Call your local sanitation department to find out how to arrange for a pickup, and in what form the debris should be containerized.

Your best bet is to start saving corrugated boxes long before you start work, and have several in the room as you begin demolition. Put scrap plaster, wallboard, and gypsum lath in boxes no larger than 18″ in any dimension. Gypsum is very heavy, and you won't be able to carry a full box much larger than that. Toss scrap lumber and plywood into a larger box, such as half a refrigerator carton. Separate noncombustible materials—glass, insulation, metal—in their own box.

To collect scrap materials outdoors, use containers not affected by moisture. Plastic garbage cans are best for leftover mortar, which tends to react with metal. Metal containers are adequate for broken masonry, shingles, flashing, and roofing. Make a habit of tossing scrap into containers as it develops; cleanup then takes little time.

As alternatives to public trash disposal services, you have two choices. One is a private hauler, listed in the telephone classified pages under "Rubbish Removal." Private collection services supply containers of various sizes, and charge you by the container for the trash they haul away. You tell them the size and quantity of containers you need; they deliver empties and pick up full ones.

The other alternative is to dispose of debris at a local dump, now often called a landfill. You provide the containers and transportation. You may be able to use the landfill free, or there may be a small charge. Investigate first; landfills sometimes accept anything except garbage, but others limit what you may dump.

Ordering Materials. You will order few, if any, materials in large enough quantities to benefit from a volume discount. So place your orders only far enough ahead to have materials on hand when you need them. Most materials will be stock items at your building supply dealer's store or yard, and can be delivered within 24 hours after you place an order. For any item that the dealer himself must order, find out well in advance how much lead time he requires, and then allow for it.

In each chapter is information on estimating your basic materials requirements. To make ordering a regular routine, make out your list once a week, say on Sunday, and place the order on Monday for materials you will need during the week beginning on the next weekend. On the 10th of the month, for example, you decide what you will need for the 16th through the 22nd, and order on the 11th for delivery on the 15th. Keep in mind what you already have on hand. You can usually return unused materials that are still packaged as they arrived, but there is no advantage to overstocking.

Storing Materials. All materials should be kept under cover at all times. Sand for mortar may be dumped on the ground near the point where you will mix, but should be covered with a tarpaulin or sheet of polyethylene. Concrete blocks and bricks should be stored on pallets and similarly covered. Lumber should be raised off the ground on **stickers** (lengths of scrap 2 × 4) and covered to prevent it from absorbing moisture from either the ground or air. Under roof in a carport or garage is best if you have the room. Leave any metal bands on lumber until you are ready to use it. Store siding like lumber. Keep boxed materials, such as asphalt and wood shingles, under cover and raised above ground level.

Store materials used indoors in the rooms where you will use them. Some materials take up a lot of floor space; that's one reason for clearing rooms completely. The truck driver who delivers your materials will store them where you want them, but he has to know where that is. So plan well ahead.

Tools. As a final step in preparation, check over all your tools. Make sure they are clean, that cutting edges are sharp and well oiled, and that you have the tools you will need. You probably won't own a few tools that are either too expensive or too seldom used even for a well-outfitted workshop. But you can almost always rent them from building materials dealers or firms listed in the classified telephone directory under "Rental Service Stores and Yards." The charge is nominal.

Now let's get that project under way.

Planning New Living Space

(a)

(b)

Only a limited view outward relieved the cell-like atmosphere in this master bedroom (a). High sills offered some privacy, but draping was difficult. Now (b) sliding glass doors let in more and better light, are more easily draped for privacy, provide access to a secluded deck, and give the entire room a much cozier air. The closets extend into a small addition. (Courtesy American Plywood Association.)

You can increase living space in an existing house in four ways. One is to build outward in an addition. Another is to enclose open space already outlined within the overall dimensions of the house. A third is to build upward to create another living level. The fourth is to finish off existing but unfinished space.

Although the goal of more space is the same in each of these remodelings, the approaches to planning them are quite different. An addition is similar in many ways to new construction; as long as you have enough land, you have few other restrictions on your planning. The conversion of a garage, porch, or carport has few structural aspects, but you are more limited in what you can do with design and space arrangement. An upward addition involves extensive structural change, and a lot of careful planning in three dimensions. Finishing off existing space scarcely involves new structure, but you must plan within the straitjacket of structure that is already there.

The planning and structural considerations of each of these options are discussed fully within the next eight chapters. Let's begin with the room addition, certainly the most popular solution to the need for more space.

Plan where to build an addition before you decide how to use it. The two major problems you must solve are access to the new space and its orientation. When room additions don't turn out as well as expected, the main reason is that their effect on other rooms wasn't fully considered.

LEGAL LIMITATIONS

But before you get at these problems, find out where you can add legally. In incorporated communities the amount of building space on most lots is limited by local zoning laws. These laws state that you can build only so close to your property lines. This closest building point is called a **setback line.** On the street side of your house the property line is not the same as the curb line, so the front setback line is usually well back from the street. Most houses are built right on the front setback line; therefore, the opportunity to add onto the front is rare.

Setbacks

Front setbacks are usually stated in feet, such as "30 feet from the front property line." Zoning laws may refer to side setbacks as a specific distance, such as 10', or as a percentage of the width of your lot. A 10% setback on a lot 75' wide, for example, means that you can build no closer than 7.5 or 7½' to either side property line. These dimensions, by the way, are measured to the foundation of the house, and do not include roof overhangs. On small city lots houses often extend from side setback line to side setback line, or stop just short enough to allow for a driveway on one side. On larger lots houses are sometimes placed off center so that there is room to expand on one side.

Local zoning may also require a rear setback. It may be a fixed distance or a limiting percentage, such as "20% of the depth of the property but not less than 20 feet."

Floor Area

Zoning laws sometimes contain a limitation on the area of the first floor of the house. Setbacks are the usual governing limitation as long as the entire house is under one roof. Only if you plan to build a separate building, such as a combination garage and workshop or a cottage for an elderly relative, does the limitation on total floor area of all buildings come into effect. This allowable floor area is commonly stated as a maximum percentage of the total land area inside property lines.

Sources of Information

To learn what zoning restrictions apply to your lot, look in the telephone book under the listings for city government. There you should find an entry for "Zoning," "Zoning Desk," or something similar. Give your address, and someone in that office can tell you in what classification your property is zoned, and what the setbacks are.

If you live in a medium-size city, the listing under city government may be "Zoning," "Planning Department," "Building Inspector," or "City Engineer." In a town the listing is usually "City Clerk."

If you live in a suburb, the place to find setback information depends on the size and type of local government. Look first under your community's name and its government listing, if any. When you don't see any listing similar to those in other categories above, look under your county government listings. Many suburbs that are primarily bedroom communities look to the county for specialized services they themselves can't afford to provide.

If you live in an unincorporated area—whether rural, village, or outside a big city—the listing will usually be under county government. There may be a listing under "Zoning," "County Clerk," or "County Engineer." In some counties with only one city of any size, the City Building Inspector handles both city and county zoning.

Deed Restrictions

In some residential communities, particularly those with homes of the best quality and design, the deed to property contains certain restrictions. These restrictions exceed local codes, and apply not only to the original house but also to modifications of any kind that are visible outside the house. For the sake of continuity of appearance in the subdivision, for example, you may be forced by the deed to use certain materials, such as brick for walls and clay tiles on the roof. Or you may be required to use a specified style of architecture or type of roof. Or there may be a limitation on the height and size of any addition you can build.

So before you get very far along in your thinking, look at your deed.

Zoning Variance

Later, should you find that what you want to add and what you can legally add are in conflict, you still have some options available. The best solution, although not the easiest, is to rework your plans until they conform. When deed restrictions are your downfall, this is your only solution. To secure a variance in a deed restriction almost always requires unanimous approval of all property owners living under the same deed restrictions you are, and the chances of that happening are mighty slim.

But if you feel that a zoning ordinance unfairly limits what you can do and creates a hardship, you can appeal to local zoning officials. Communities with zoning laws usually have a zoning board made up of civic-minded citizens. They meet either on a regularly scheduled night of the month, or whenever the backlog of zoning work requires it. You must appear before the board to present your case. You ask the board for a hearing, the board schedules your case, and through local newspapers advises anyone interested to appear at the hearing.

To present your case you must come armed with

"before" and "after" plot plans, floor plans, and elevations showing the appearance of the new exteriors, and a statement giving your reasons for requesting the variance. Be prepared to answer questions on the effect the variation would have on the property of immediate neighbors. When possible, bring photographs to back up your statements.

What are your chances of being granted a zoning variance? That depends on the board, and boards are human. You are likely to receive approval when you have a legitimate request, present your case well, can prove that similar variances have already been granted to others, and/or have no one at the hearing speak in opposition. You are likely to be turned down if your plans are vague, you either antagonize or bore the board, you don't have a legitimate argument, and/or there is vociferous opposition. Securing a zoning variance involves a good bit of public relations, not only with the board but with your neighbors. Show your neighbors in advance what you want to do and, if they see no harm, they may even give you a letter saying so to present to the board.

On the other hand, always think in terms of staying within the restrictions imposed on you. Request a zoning variance only as a last resort. There are few clear justifications for one when you do a good job of planning in the first place.

LOT AREA AVAILABLE FOR EXPANSION

With setback information in hand, the next step is to relate it to the position of your home on its lot. This isn't necessary when you have a large lot with ample room for expansion, or when you know the house was built right on the setback lines of a small lot. But if you have any doubt about the lot space available, you have three choices:

1. Among the papers you received when you bought your house may be a plot plan or copy of a survey that shows the shape and dimensions of your lot, and how far the house lies from all property lines. Mark the setback lines on this drawing and add dimensions to them.

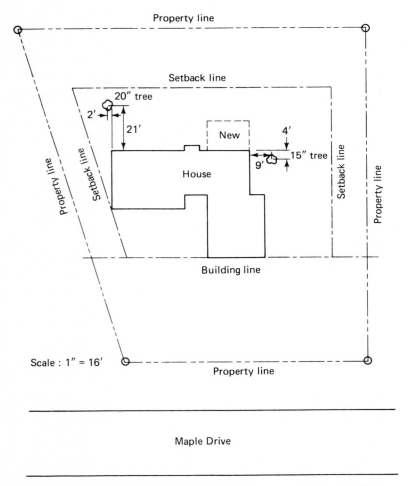

Fig. 4-1. A good plot plan shows the shape of your property, setback lines, an outline of your house and any addition, and is drawn to a scale indicated on the plan. Locating major obstructions such as trees is not required, but is useful in visualizing the limitations on planning.

Chapter 4 / Planning New Living Space

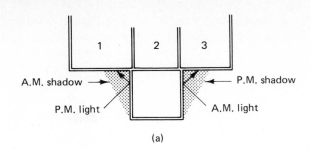

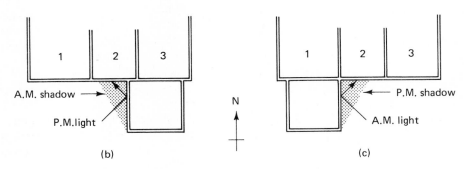

Fig. 4-2. Placement of an addition greatly affects light conditions in existing rooms.

2. If you can't find a plot plan, draw your own (Fig. 4-1). Use a scale of 1″ = 20′ if you have an engineer's scale, or 1″ = 16′ if you have an ordinary ruler. If you have an architect's scale, use the ¾″ scale; let ¾″ = 12′, which is the same as 1″ = 16′. Show the shape of your house as drawn on your "before" plan, but at the new scale.

3. Stake out the available area on the site.

Locate Property Lines

For either of the last two choices, you must locate your property lines. This isn't always easy. In recent years the corners of residential property have been marked with pieces of metal rod or iron pipe. Many years ago the markers were more likely stone cylinders. The longer ago the survey was made, the farther below the surface of the ground you are likely to find the markers. In your front yard they are buried so you don't hit them with a lawn mower. At the back corners they are more likely to be at or even above ground level, so look there first.

When you can't find the markers, estimate as best you can where the property lines are, and pace off the distance from them to your house. You don't need to know the exact location unless you expect to add right to the setback line. And you aren't that far along yet.

From your work with setback lines, you determine the maximum amount of floor space you can *add*. From your preliminary cost estimate you have a general idea of how much floor space you can *afford*. If you can reconcile these two square footages with how much

space you *need*, you are ready to find the best place to add it.

As you develop your plans, keep the size of your addition in mind. Build as large as necessary to meet your family's needs, but don't overdo it. As a rule of thumb, don't spend more than 25% of the present value of your house on an addition, nor increase the appraised value of your remodeled house significantly above other homes in the neighborhood. Even though you have no intention of selling at the present time, and aren't remodeling as an investment except in your own family, there's no sense in making your house difficult to sell.

ORIENTATION

When you add a wing, it will change the light conditions in the rooms near it. It may affect the flow of air around and through the house. In cold climates it may sometimes act as a snow fence, either causing or preventing drifts that block doors and driveways.

Light Conditions

To understand how a room addition can darken or brighten existing rooms, study Fig. 4-2. Suppose that your house faces north, and any addition must go on the south side. Yet it can go in the middle or on either corner.

Added in the middle of the wall, as in Fig. 4-2a, the addition effectively blocks all direct daylight out of existing room 2. Even if the new space and old space are completely open to each other, the interior area will be dim. In a one-story house you can correct this light problem with a skylight cut into the roof or with artificial light.

At the same time, room 3 will be brighter in the morning and room 1 brighter in the afternoon because of sunlight bouncing off the exterior walls of the addition. The lighter in color these walls are, the more light is reflected. Conversely, when the addition shades room 3 in the afternoon and room 1 in the morning, they will be darker than they were.

An addition as shown in Fig. 4-2b, will reduce the amount of light in room 3 even if there is a window in its east wall. It will reduce the light in room 2 in the morning and increase it in the afternoon. It won't affect the light in room 1.

Conversely, an addition as shown in Fig. 4-2c, will reduce the amount of light in room 1, increase the light in room 2 in the morning but reduce it in the afternoon, and have no effect on room 3.

If your house faces south and the room addition

goes on the north side, light conditions in the three rooms will vary as on the south, except that there will be less light in all rooms. They won't get direct sunlight except for a few weeks in late spring and early summer.

When you place an addition on either a west wall or an east wall, rooms to the north of it will be darker than they have been, and rooms to the south will be lighter.

Don't underestimate the effect of reflected or "bounce" light, because it penetrates farther into rooms than direct sunlight. Even a little reflected sunlight brightens a house in a wooded area that doesn't get much sun to begin with. On the other hand, too much bounce light, particularly in warm climates, increases the temperature several degrees in rooms receiving the light.

Trees

No matter where you place an addition, some growing things will be in the way. Bushes and small trees can be

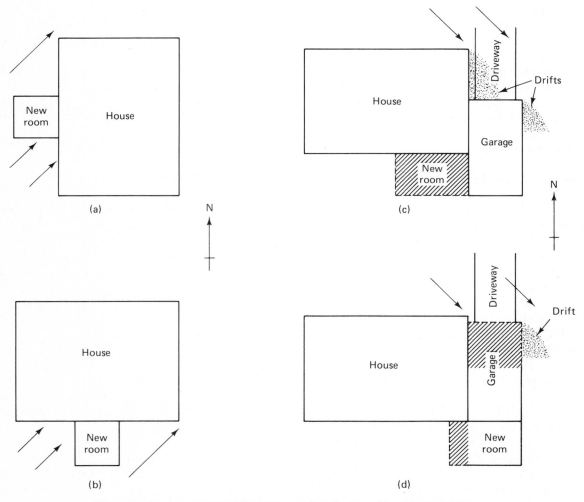

Fig. 4-3. In summer an addition exposed to the prevailing breeze is likely to increase airflow into rooms on one side and decrease airflow on the other side (a, b). In winter in snowy climates, you can sometimes place an addition (d) to correct a problem with drifts (c).

Chapter 4 / Planning New Living Space

dug up and set aside for replanting. When bushes have grown too large, remodeling offers an excellent excuse for removing and replacing them with others more appropriate to the size of the house.

Large trees are expensive to move and, for the shade, shelter, and beauty they provide, are usually too valuable to destroy. On your plot plan mark the locations of all trees you want to save (see Fig. 4-1), measuring as accurately as possible to the center of the trunk. Then look up the characteristics of each species of tree to be saved. You need to know the shape of the root system and the maximum dimensions of the tree when fully grown. Some encyclopedias list this information and show a picture of a leaf for positive identification. If your home library fails you, try the public library. Your county agent and local nurseryman can also give you the necessary information.

Try to plan an addition where it completely misses all existing roots and isn't in the way of expansion of a tree's root system. It's possible to cut roots up to 4″ in diameter without killing a tree, as long as you don't cut too many of them. The trouble is, with tall old trees, you don't know where the roots are until you start construction. So it's better to avoid them entirely.

Keep in mind, too, that as trees grow, their branches spread as well as their roots. As you narrow down the possible locations for your addition, stake them out roughly, then measure upward to the height where future eaves will be. Branches should clear a roof slope by at least 3′ to allow for movement in winds, and for deflection under snow, sleet, and freezing rain when they don't shed their leaves in winter.

Summer Air Movement

Throughout most of the United States and southern Canada the prevailing summer breeze comes from the southwest. An addition on the north or east side of an existing house, therefore, has little effect on air movement. Placed on the west, however, the addition increases airflow into rooms to the south of it and decreases flow into rooms north of it, as in Fig. 4-3a. Similarly, an addition on the south forces more air into rooms to the west of it, and tends to block air into rooms to the east (Fig. 4-3b).

Summer air movement isn't often a critical consideration. But if you rely on breezes and cross-ventilation to keep you cool in summer, the effect of an addition on airflow is worth keeping in mind when you have a choice of places to put it.

Winter Air Movement

Just before a heavy snowfall the wind usually comes out of the east. But by the time the snow begins to fall, the wind shifts around to the northwest. Drifting is caused by strong winds picking up light snow and depositing it in pockets of calm. With lightweight snow and strong winds the ground on the north and west sides of a building may be bare, while snow piles up on the other two sides.

If drifting is a winter problem on your lot, be sure you don't make the problem worse with placement of an addition. And perhaps you can correct the problem.

Take the house in Fig. 4-3c. To make the street side more attractive, the garage is offset a dozen feet from the setback line on which the front of the house is built. Suppose that you plan an addition on the back flush with the rear wall of the garage. Suppose also that one of the problems you listed for possible correction is snow that piles up in drifts right in front of the garage door.

As an alternative solution, consider adding to the front of the house, retaining only a little offset for the sake of appearance (Fig. 4-3d). Then move the garage space forward. The new room is in approximately the same location but blocks less south light, you add the same amount of space, but now snow will drift beside the driveway instead of on it.

As another example, look back at Fig. 4-2. A door into the backyard located just to the right of an addition will be in a pocket sheltered from wind, rain, and snow. A door placed on the left side is much more exposed and less practical.

Keep the effects of sun, wind, and precipitation in mind when you think about where to place an addition. But be prepared to compromise, because the most important problem you must solve is access to the new space.

ACCESS TO NEW SPACE

Access is seldom a problem to an addition that is simply the expansion of an existing room. But when you add another room with three new walls, you will probably have to create a hallway to it.

In a good floor plan you can reach every room in the house without going through another room. If this isn't possible in your present house, make it one of your remodeling goals. Whenever a room must also serve as a passageway, good arrangements of furniture are difficult, floor covering wears excessively in the pathway, and uninterrupted privacy just isn't possible.

Because hall space costs the same per square foot as living space, many people think of halls as wasted space that could be put to better use. This isn't true. Can you imagine a school without corridors? The sole purpose of a passageway is to permit people to move from one room to another in a building without disturbing the occupants of any rooms. The need is not as great in a house as in a school because the amount of movement is less, but the need is there nevertheless.

So concentrate on how to provide hall space. An existing hallway that ends in a closet can be economically extended (Fig. 4-4a). This ideal op-

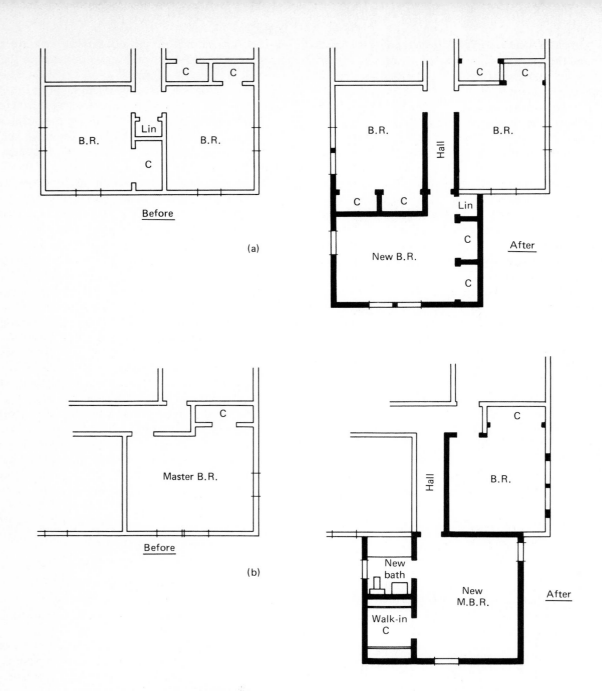

Fig. 4-4. A hallway leading to an addition may be created out of closet space (a) which you then include in the addition, out of an existing room large enough to be made smaller (b), or out of an outdated bathroom (c, on the next page) which you replace with a master bath.

portunity isn't often available, however, on the wall of the house where you have enough land to add on.

Sometimes you can carve a hallway out of an existing room. Suppose that you want to add a child's bedroom which, with closet space, contains about 120 sq ft. The best place is behind the master bedroom, which is 11' × 14', but the only access would be by taking hallway space from that room. Instead of reducing the size of the master bedroom too much, convert it into the child's bedroom and add a new master bedroom, perhaps with its own bath (Fig. 4-4b).

You add a little more space at greater cost, true, but you solve your need for an extra bedroom without creating new problems with a cramped master bedroom.

The point made here is very important. Never limit your thinking solely to the room you need. A much better answer may be to convert existing space to the room you need, and build a different room in the addition.

Here's another equally important point. You add to your remodeling cost if you relocate plumbing fixtures in a bathroom or kitchen. But don't let this extra cost blind you to what is often the best overall solution. Sometimes the present bathroom is the only logical place for a hallway to new space, as in Fig. 4-4c, left. It is typical of bathrooms in small tract houses 20 years ago, but cramped for a family of four. For a family of five it is inadequate.

Look what happens when you move it (Fig. 4-4c, right). Small bedroom 3 becomes 2' wider, and its door can be moved to a more practical location. The new hallway doesn't reduce the size of any bedroom. The new bathroom is larger, has entrances from both the hallway and the new bedroom, and is arranged for use by more than one person at a time. Furthermore, a new rear door offers direct access from the outdoors. Certainly, you increase your cost over the cost of a bedroom alone. But you have improved two existing rooms as well, and gotten your money's worth.

LAYING OUT THE ADDITION

Before you finally settle on an acceptable floor plan, you will make many false starts and go through periods of frustration when nothing seems to work. Be prepared for this and allow plenty of time for planning. Never rush it.

At the beginning, work from the floor plan of your existing house that you found or drew. Tape it to a flat, hard surface. Use masking tape rather than the more common transparent tape; it won't tear or damage the drawing or working surface when you remove it, and holds just as well. The ideal surface is a drawing board, but the top of a card table, a piece of smooth plywood, or other stiff sheet material will suffice. Less convenient to use are such surfaces as countertops, dining table tops, the sides of appliances, and even walls.

Do your planning on transparent tracing paper. You can always buy it at artist's supply stores, and many office supply and stationery stores carry it. It comes in pads ranging in size from $9'' \times 12''$ to $18'' \times 24''$, and in long rolls 18 to 24'' wide. Architects and designers prefer rolls because they are easier to handle and you don't need to tape them down while you are testing your ideas.

Working where light is good for close work, lay the paper over the existing floor plan. Begin by marking the four corners of the house; as you draw, the paper is bound to slip occasionally, and marking the corners helps you quickly realign your sketch with the floor plan. For sketching the changes you want to make, you need only a soft pencil, an eraser, and probably a 12'' ruler for measuring. Don't worry about drawing straight lines or measuring to exact scale. Your main goal at this time is to rough out your ideas to see how well they solve your remodeling problems. A more accurate and detailed drawing comes later when you have settled on an approach.

Points to Keep in Mind

While you plan, keep in the back of your mind the need for access to new space, and the effects of sun, wind,

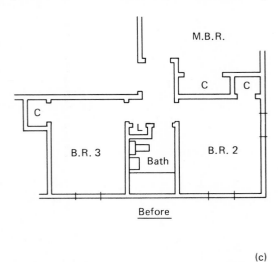

Before

(c)

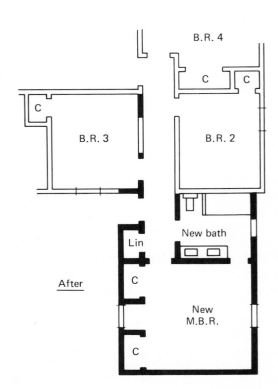

After

and weather. Then, as you rearrange and reorganize existing space, keep these points in mind, too:

Bearing Walls. To open up two rooms that are separated by a bearing wall, it is possible to remove that wall. But something must replace it to support the weight of structure above it. The least expensive way—and it usually works well—is to build a beam to carry the load, then support the beam on posts made of 2 × 4s. On your plan you must show these posts as stub walls; allow a minimum of 6″ on each side of the opening.

New Openings. Whenever you add a new door or window, or widen an existing door or window

bathroom, and possibly the living room. With so much movement, make sure that you plan enough floor space to serve the room's main purposes, and enough wall space for furniture.

Until the preliminary floor plan is almost worked out, you need to think in only two dimensions—length and width. Then you have to begin to think in the third dimension—height—which affects exterior appearance and the materials you choose.

EXTERIOR APPEARANCE

The shape of a room addition involves more design considerations than any other type of remodeling. The

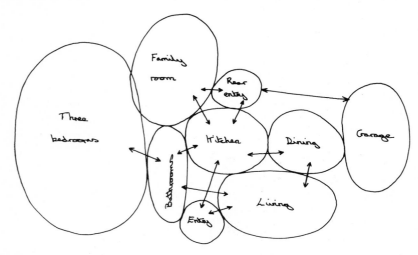

Fig. 4-5. To free your thinking in planning room relationships, try working with ovals instead of rectangles. After you have relationships right, you can work with straight lines.

opening, you must cut a bigger hole than you fill. Without enough working room, installation of a new door or window is difficult or even impossible economically. Therefore, make sure that you have at least 6″ of working space on each side of the finished opening.

Traffic Patterns. As you develop a preliminary floor plan, your main concern should be with spatial relationships—how each area of the house relates to the new space. Some designers of new houses use a series of circles or ovals to denote areas of specific usages (Fig. 4-5), and never draw a straight line until the circles are in a satisfactory relationship to each other. In this approach to planning, traffic patterns between areas show up clearly.

After you have roughed out a floor plan that appears feasible, draw in lightly with a colored pencil the probable traffic patterns. In many rooms, such as new bedrooms, the only traffic is into the room and out of it through the same door. But if the room is a new family room, for example, there will be traffic between the new room and the outdoors, the kitchen, a

style and slope of the new roof, its intersection with the old one, the relationship of windows and doors to solid walls, and the selection of exterior materials all must be carefully planned.

The New Roof

Sometimes you see houses with a roof of one style on the main house and of a different style on a wing or addition. But combining roof styles is tricky, not only from the standpoint of design but also in construction where the two styles meet. So if your house has a gable roof on it, plan on a gable roof of the same pitch and the same overhang on your addition. Similarly, use a hip roof with a hip roof, a gambrel with a gambrel, and a mansard with a mansard. If your lot is fairly level and eaves are at the same height around the house, maintain that same eave height on the addition.

Unless deed restrictions say otherwise, you do have alternatives, and under certain conditions another roof style may be a better answer. A flat or almost flat roof can look attractive on an addition, regardless of the shape of the main roof. A flat roof is frequently the best solution if the addition will be a step or two below floor level of the rest of the house. Then the new roof doesn't intersect the old roof at all, but butts against a side wall (Fig. 4-6).

Occasionally, a shed roof works well on an addition. Here the slope of the roof becomes critical. Asphalt shingles should never be used on a slope of less than 2 in 12—that is, the vertical height of the roof drops no less than 2″ for every 12″ of horizontal run (see Fig. 7-6). A low slope can be covered with roll roofing or metal, however. Applying a roof of asphalt shingles, wood shingles, or metal is well within the scope of most talented amateurs. Roll roofing must be mopped with hot asphalt, which requires special equipment.

One more point on the best roof shape: if possible, do not design the roof of the addition as a direct continuation of one side of the existing roof. The addition will look better if it is inset slightly, even as little as 18″.

Windows

The size of windows you select and where you locate them are very important to maximum use of the new

(a)

(b)

Fig. 4-6. You can cover most additions with a flat roof. Here any roof shape but flat would cover windows that afford cross-ventilation in an upstairs bedroom (a). Note that the new roof (b) butts against the original slope, not against the two-story rear wall of the house. (Courtesy American Plywood Association.)

space and to exterior appearance. Decide first whether you want to use the same type of windows installed in the main house. Your addition will look less like an addition and more like part of the original house if you use the same building components. But there is no reason not to change if you like something else better. Just be consistent in the addition; use the same style of window throughout the new space. You may vary sizes according to your needs, however.

From your building materials dealer you can get literature that gives the available sizes, rough opening dimensions, and installation details of the windows he stocks or will order for you. Before you establish these sizes and their exact centerlines, lay another sheet of tracing paper over your plan and make a furniture layout. This will help you to figure out where you need unbroken wall space for furniture, and where you need light during the daytime. It will also help you decide where to place windows to take maximum advantage of breeze, sunlight, and any view.

On the subject of view, many people think of a worthwhile view only as distant—of mountains or a lake or a valley. A long view may be beautiful, but it becomes like a calendar picture; after awhile you forget to look at it. Many times a short view is much more satisfying—a view of nature in action. Birds at a feeder, flowers nodding in the sun, leaves bobbing in the breeze, rain pelting onto a deck—all are views worth watching. Make sure that you place windows so that you can see these things going on without having to get up to look at them.

Knowing where you need windows comes first. Their sizes and their arrangement come next. An arrangement of windows is known as **fenestration,** and is critical to good exterior appearance. A series of small windows marching along a wall make a house look like a fortress. Group windows when you can (Fig. 4-7). A group provides better light and a broader view. Where you need wall space for furniture but also need daylight, consider a band of high windows. Since they won't offer much view, plan other windows with sills that reach almost to the floor. Small children and family pets love them; they like to see out, too, at their eye level. Rooms with windows with low sills are brighter, also. The light reflects off the floor and other horizontal surfaces, and helps to lighten otherwise dark corners.

Exterior Doors

Do you want a door to your yard out of the addition? Possibly not from a bedroom. On the other hand, what could be nicer than a small deck right off the new

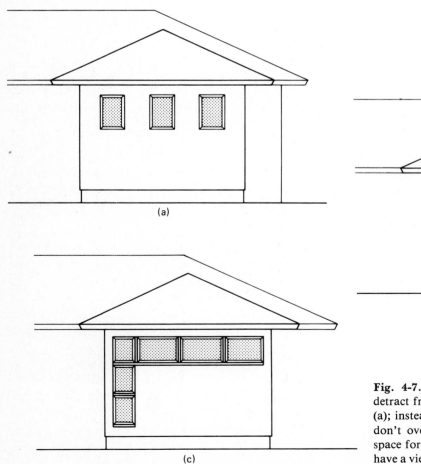

(a)

(c)

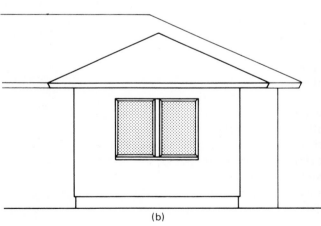

(b)

Fig. 4-7. Arrangement of windows can add to or detract from exterior appearance. Avoid regimentation (a); instead, group windows wherever possible (b). But don't overlook fenestration that not only leaves wall space for furniture but also lets small children and pets have a view outside, too (c).

Chapter 4 / Planning New Living Space

bedroom where you can sit on warm summer and spring evenings and relax in privacy before you retire? A deck isn't expensive, is easy to build along with the addition, and just could be the most gratifying part of your home's expansion.

Where wall space is limited, plan for a single 3'-0"-wide door that swings in against a wall. Even then, consider a pair of sliding glass patio doors. They are made 5', 6', and 8' wide with two doors, and in widths up to 12' with three doors. Because the doors slide, you don't have to find a place to swing them. Because their glass area is large and extends to the floor, they provide excellent light and view. They provide good ventilation if you are willing to leave them open at night. Otherwise, make sure that some of your windows open to give you good cross-ventilation without draft.

Exterior Materials

Few materials are exactly the same size, shape, and color that they were a generation ago. So before you decide to use the same material on the exterior wall of an addition that was used on the existing house, make sure that you can buy it. This problem of matching materials is greatest when your remodeling includes closing up or enlarging existing openings.

If you can't match existing materials, aim for color contrast. You can usually buy new shingles that match old shingles, and new siding that will closely match old siding. The most common difficulty is matching the colors of new bricks or new manufactured materials with old ones. Therefore, if your old bricks are a dark red, for example, and you can't match them, go to a tan or burnt orange. Stay in the same color scheme—warm colors such as reds, oranges, yellows, and browns, or cool colors such as blues, greens, and grays. Too great a contrast is often glaring. Too little contrast looks like you missed when you tried to match colors. A noticeable contrast looks planned.

You can also achieve pleasant contrast by using a different material on the addition. An addition finished with wood shingles or siding can look very nice on a brick or stone house, particularly if the wood is painted or stained no darker than the masonry. A small addition looks its best under most circumstances when its color is either the same color as the main house, or slightly lighter.

Roofing

When the roof of an addition butts against the main roof, you must use the same type of roofing material. Wood shingles can be stained to match the color of the existing roof, no matter to what color it has weathered. Matching the color of asphalt shingles exactly isn't always possible; just come as close as you can. If your old roof is nearing the end of its natural life (15 to 20 years), during remodeling is a fine time to reshingle it.

PREPARING "AFTER" DRAWINGS

From your many sketches you and your family decide which offers the best solution. Then draw that floor plan to scale. This time tape the floor plan of the existing house to a working surface, and tape a piece of tracing paper over it. On the new floor plan you need to show only the areas of the house you intend to remodel, including any additions. So place the paper to allow for this, and leave 1½" on all sides for dimensioning.

The final floor plan should be as accurate as you can make it—not to make it pretty, but to make sure that everything works, particularly in spots where you don't have much leeway in dimension or working space. If you are careful, you can do the job with a straight-edged ruler, a No. 3 pencil kept sharp, a pencil compass, and an eraser. You'll do a much better job more quickly, easily, and accurately with a T-square for drawing horizontal lines and for use as a base for triangles, a 45° or 30°–60° triangle for drawing vertical and diagonal lines, an architect's scale for accurate measuring, a 2H drafting pencil (mechanical pencils are the easiest to keep sharp), a compass, and an eraser.

Drawing Tips

Here are a few simple tips to help you with your drawing:

- Draw lines lightly until you are certain they are correct. A light line is easy to erase; a heavy line isn't.
- Keep your pencil sharp. You can keep a point sharper for a longer time if you rotate the pencil slightly as you draw a line—clockwise if you are right-handed and counterclockwise if you are left-handed.
- If you don't have a mechanical pencil, use a knife to cut back the wood around the lead so that about ½" is exposed. There are three reasons for this. First, wood should never come in contact with the T-square or triangle; your lines won't be straight. Second, you can sharpen the lead on a piece of fine sandpaper to get a sharp point. Third, if you press too hard you'll break the lead; this forces you to draw lightly.
- To sharpen the lead, draw the pencil lightly across the sandpaper while slowly twisting the pencil in the opposite direction. This gives you a sharp point and keeps the lead itself round.
- Hold the pencil at about a 60° angle to the drawing, with the point against the T-square or triangle. This assures a straight line and reduces the chance of breaking the lead.
- Blow away lead particles that fall on the drawing. Don't try to wipe or brush them away; they will smear.

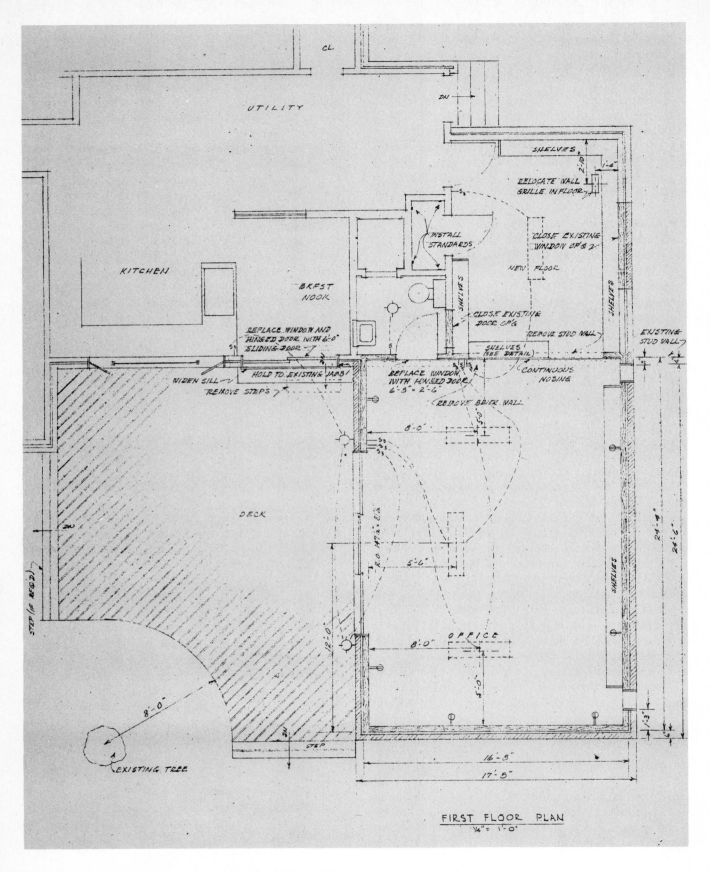

Fig. 4-8. The completed floor plan of an addition, and the adjacent areas that were remodeled. Your finished drawing does not need to look this professional, but should include the type of information shown here.

- Wash your tools occasionally with soap and warm water, and dry them thoroughly before reuse. Dirty tools make dirty drawings.

- Keep your eraser clean and the edge sharp. If you make a lot of mistakes, buy an **eraser shield**—a thin piece of metal with various shapes cut into it. With the shield you can cover areas you won't want to erase, and save having to redraw them.

- Draw reference lines first, such as two outside walls that meet at a corner. Then, if the paper slips for any reason, you can quickly realign your drawing over the "before" plan.

- Next draw in the walls and partitions that won't be changed, then work on the areas to be remodeled. As much as possible, work from the upper left of the drawing toward the lower right. By doing so, you move drawing tools over finished areas no more than necessary, and the drawing stays cleaner.

- When all lines showing structure are drawn lightly, and the plan still works to your satisfaction, strengthen the lines.

- Next, mark where ducts and pipes will come through walls and partitions, simply as a reminder to provide for them. Use the typical symbols shown in Fig. 3-3.

- Similarly, mark the locations of light fixtures, electrical outlets, and switches. Use the electrical symbols shown in Fig. 3-3. Add dash lines between lights and/or outlets and the switches that operate them. Draw the dash lines freehand or with a French curve; they should not be straight lines.

- Finally, add dimension lines and dimensions themselves. To save time and space, show only critical dimensions—that is, those that must be followed exactly. For example, if a door in a partition is close to one corner of a room, dimension from that corner to the centerline of the opening. You don't need to dimension from the opposite corner.

Elevations

When you finish your floor plan (Fig. 4-8), draw on a fresh sheet of paper the elevations of the exterior walls of the addition. Maintain the same ¼″ scale that you use for the floor plan. You need elevations for several purposes. First, any official who must approve your plans before you get a permit will want to see them. From your own standpoint elevations will help you visualize how the addition will look by itself and in relation to the existing house. Equally important, elevations are the only place to show heights that can't be shown on a floor plan. Heights you need to know are the finished floor level, heads of windows and exterior doors, eaves, and roof ridges. To determine these heights, the easiest way is to work from a section.

A Section

You can save time in construction if you take time now to develop a section through the house where the addition will fit onto it. A floor plan is a horizontal slice through a building taken at about eye level. **A section** is a vertical slice—through structure, or a cabinet, or any part of the house that you need to study to understand the relationship of heights.

Figure 4-9 shows typical sections. The first floor of most houses is carried on wood joists that rest on a sill plate, which in turn rests on a foundation wall (a or b). The foundation wall rests on a concrete footing. A house built on a concrete slab floor usually rests on a foundation wall also (c). The exception is a floating or thickened-edge slab (d), which rests directly on the ground.

To draw a section through a house with floor joists, start with a straight line representing the top of the foundation wall (A in Fig. 4-10). Then draw two vertical lines downward (B) to indicate the thickness of that wall, using a scale of ½″ or ¾″ = 1′-0″. You can determine the thickness of your foundation wall by measuring at an opening in it, or by taking an overall outside dimension, subtracting the matching inside dimension, and dividing by 2. Most foundation walls, whether built of poured concrete or of concrete blocks, are 8″ thick when exterior walls of the house are finished with wood, and 10″ thick when the house has a brick or stone veneer exterior. Houses built around the turn of the century often have stone or brick foundation walls of greater thickness.

At the bottom ends of the foundation wall lines (about 2 to 2½ actual inches down from the top of the wall), draw a footing (C, Fig. 4-10) centered under the wall. Make the footing the same height as the wall's thickness (8″ or 10″) and twice as wide as the wall (16″ or 20″).

Now "break" the wall with a pair of diagonal lines (D). Such lines indicate that the part of the wall between the lines is just like the wall above and below them. You use this breaking device when the wall is too high to draw in its entirety at scale, or when you don't know the exact height. If you have a basement, measure the height of the wall from floor to top, and add this measurement to your drawing. If you have crawl space, the dimension is unknown at the moment, so leave it blank.

Next work upward from the foundation. First draw in the sill plate (E, Fig. 4-10). Take measurements if you can; sill plates are usually 2 × 6s or sometimes 2 × 4s (1½″ × 5½″ or 1½″ × 3½″, respectively). Then measure the height of any floor joist, and draw in the edge joist (F). Across the top of the edge joist, which is 1½″ thick, draw a horizontal line (G) representing the underside of the subfloor.

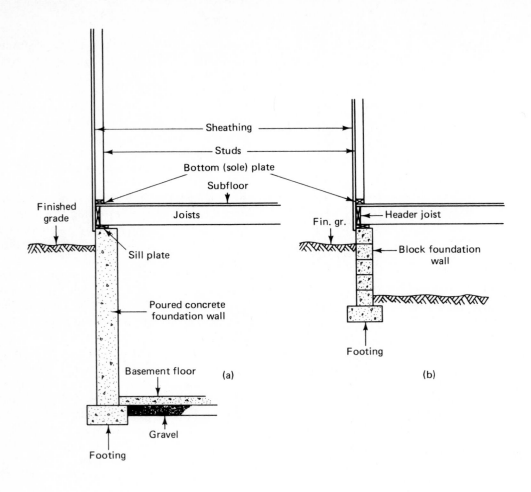

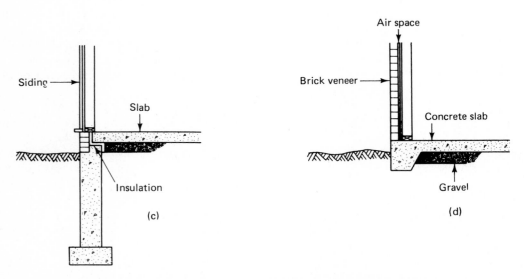

Fig. 4-9. Typical sections through foundations and first-floor construction. Poured concrete and concrete block walls are interchangeable.

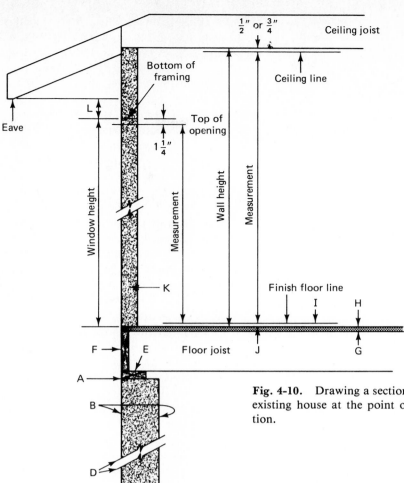

Fig. 4-10. Drawing a section through the wall of your existing house at the point of attachment of an addition.

From this point upward to the finished floor you can't always be sure of thicknesses without tearing out, but you can work from clues. Look upward between floor joists at the underside of the subfloor. If you see boards, your subfloor is ¾″ thick. If you see plywood, it is probably ½″ thick. Add another horizontal line (H, Fig. 4-10) showing the top of the subfloor.

Finally, show the level of the finish floor (I). Table 4-1 shows typical thicknesses of flooring (J) to allow. Note that materials such as resilient tiles and linoleum require both subflooring and **underlayment**—a smooth base in sheet form. Carpeting and wood blocks are applied directly over subflooring. Wood strip flooring requires neither underlayment nor subflooring.

Now locate the first floor wall at the edge of the subfloor (K, Fig. 4-10), and draw its structural thickness at scale (3½″). Add two more lines for any masonry veneer. Carry the lines upward about 4″ in actual dimension, and break them.

For planning purposes you need to mark three more points on the wall: the heights of the heads of typical windows and doors, the height of the exterior wall, and the height of the eave of the roof. Measurements should be calculated from the top of the subfloor (H). To find wall height, measure from the finish floor to the ceiling, add the thickness of flooring (J, Fig. 4-10) and either ¾″ for a plaster ceiling or ½″ for a ceiling of gypsum wallboard. To tell the difference, knock on the surface. Plaster sounds the same—solid—wherever you knock. Wallboard sounds solid at joists and hollow between.

To find the height to the top of framing for windows and exterior doors, measure from finish floor to the top of the opening, not the trim (refer to Fig. 3-2). Then add finish floor thickness and 1¼″ for the window frame.

For the time being you can approximate eave height. Outside the house hold a board level against the

Table 4-1. Typical thicknesses of finish flooring materials and the base materials beneath them.

Flooring Material	Base Required	Total Thickness (in.)
Asphalt tiles	Underlayment	³⁄₁₆
Carpeting (with pad)	None	⅜ to ¾
Ceramic tiles, glazed	Mastic	⅜ to ¹³⁄₁₆ (¾ standard)
Ceramic tiles, unglazed	Mastic	⁵⁄₁₆
Linoleum	Underlayment	⅛ to ³⁄₁₆ (⅛ standard)
Rubber tiles	Underlayment	³⁄₁₆
Vinyl tiles	Underlayment	⅛
Wood blocks, thick	None	¾ to ⅞ (¾ standard)
Wood blocks, thin	Mastic	⅜ to ½ (⅜ standard)
Wood planks	None	¾
Wood strips, prefinished	None	⅜ to 1⅛ (¾ standard)
Wood strips, unfinished hardwood	None	⅜ to 1⅛ (¾ standard)
Wood strips, unfinished softwood	None	¾ to 1⅜ (¾ standard)

underside of the existing eave, and mark that height on the wall. Then measure down to the top of the window opening and subtract 1¼". That gives you dimension L.

The reason for all these measurements is that your addition will look best if eave and window heights are the same there as in the main house. That assumes that floor levels will be the same. If your addition will have a different floor level, drawing an accurate section is even more important, as you will see in Chapter 5.

What to Do with Drawings

Even though you aren't experienced in draftsmanship, don't let the need for drawings scare you off. You aren't making them to win a prize. Their sole purpose is to help you visualize what problems you may run into, and to reach solutions *on paper*. Once you start work on a remodeling, solving unexpected problems can be expensive. So do everything you can to avoid surprises. The time you spend on accurate drawings can save hours of remodeling time, and prevent errors in construction that are sometimes costly to correct.

After you finish your drawings, take them to a blueprint shop and get two prints of each. Always work with prints. Store the originals either flat in a drawer and protected by a sheet of cardboard, or rolled in a mailing tube. Use one set of prints for discussion, and use the other set for marking any changes to be made in the originals.

If you intend to do all or much of the work yourself, now is the time to take your drawings to an architect for consultation. His main responsibility as a consultant is to give you sound professional advice. How much of that advice you take is up to you.

If you intend to hire a remodeling contractor to do all the work, go over your plans with him first. As long as he sees no structural problems that will run up his costs and yours, you may be tempted to bypass architectural advice. Don't; if the architect's suggestions improve your results, you have spent money wisely. And if he says you have done a fine job on your own, you can proceed with full confidence.

When you and the contractor disagree, by all means use the architectural consultant for a third opinion. Even if you're wrong, you can't lose.

As you make changes or corrections to your plans, note them on one set of prints. Then change the originals all at one time to save working on them any more times than is necessary. When the originals are at last correct, get one copy for submission with the permit, one for each contractor or subcontractor, and a couple of prints for yourself. You will wear out several sets of prints during a remodeling.

Mechanical Systems

During an overall remodeling is the ideal time to replace an aging furnace with a more energy-efficient heating and cooling unit. In this basement flat ceiling panels of plywood cover ducts, while spaces between are vaulted with curved sheets of plywood. Light troughs (left) provide soft indirect light. After the new heating plant is installed, it will be screened from view. (Courtesy American Plywood Association.)

Unless you are experienced in assembling residential utility systems, hire subcontractors to install the necessary electrical, plumbing, heating, and cooling lines and extra equipment. These systems are carefully inspected by local officials for conformance to building codes, and without a thorough knowledge of those codes you could easily make a costly mistake. Leave the work to professionals.

You should, however, provide all possible input into the design of those systems. To do so, take time to study the systems in your existing house. It will pay you to know where ducts, pipes, and conduits run, and where you can tie new lines into the existing systems. While you are still in the planning stage you should

determine whether existing equipment, such as your furnace or boiler, air conditioner, and water heater, has sufficient capacity to take care of new living space. And if the equipment isn't adequate, you should know what alternatives are available and allow for them.

Let's look at heating first.

YOUR HEATING SYSTEM

When you drew your "before" plan, you showed the locations of heating outlets in a warm-air system or radiators in a hot-water or steam system. That step is easy, because grilles and radiators are visible. More difficult but just as necessary is tracing the lines from furnace or boiler to those visible outlets.

Heat Ducts

With rare exception heat ducts run horizontally away from the furnace, then vertically between studs in walls. In a one-story house you can tell where ducts are by the locations in walls of registers and return air grilles. Ducts run up or down behind them. In a multistory house there will also be a duct in the wall behind every grille. To determine where ducts to upper floors pass through walls of lower floors, measure from the corner of an outside wall to the center of each grille. Then measure off this same distance on the wall below. If the upper floor overhangs the lower floor, allow for the offset. You can verify the duct location by looking in the basement, crawl space, or attic (wherever the furnace is) to see where ducts turn upward into walls.

If you have any choice, avoid cutting into stud cavities occupied by heat ducts. New ducts are difficult to install in existing walls.

Heat Pipes

Piping to and from radiators in a hot water or steam heating system usually enters a room through the floor rather than a wall. To reach upper floors, however, piping rises through interior partitions from the boiler to the floor structure. At that point it may jog between joists before turning upward through the floor. Measure to the locations of vertical pipes in the basement, then measure again in rooms. In most cases the measurements will be the same when you allow for differences in thickness of exterior walls. Feeder and return piping usually runs side by side vertically between the same two studs, and any horizontal adjustments occur in the floor structure.

Heating Capacity

To determine whether your present furnace or boiler has enough excess capacity to heat the added space, call the company that regularly services your equipment, and ask them to send over an engineer. Be prepared to tell him the cubic footage of your house, and the cubic footage of additional space you want to heat. He will relate your needs to the rated Btu output of your heating plant. **Btu** stands for British thermal unit, and is a standard for measuring heat. If furnace capacity is great enough, the engineer can suggest where to tie in new ducts or piping, and how to lay out the heating system most efficiently in the new space.

Of course, he'll try to sell you on the idea of his company doing the work. By all means get a quotation in writing. Then get additional quotations, and compare the cost of alternative methods.

A Separate Heating System

Your existing heating system will seldom be adequate to heat your existing house plus an addition, converted garage, or entire attic. One alternative—and often the best solution of all—is to heat the new space separately with its own heating system. There are several advantages. First, you have no guess work about the adequacy of the equipment, and no worry about the effect that heating the new space will have on the quality of the system in heating existing space. Second, a separate system is easier to install. Third, and perhaps the biggest plus: if something goes wrong with your main heating system, you still have some warm rooms to live in.

If the new space to be heated is one large room, an individual space heater is one good solution. Space heaters are tall and narrow, and designed to fit between studs. They operate on gas, oil, or electricity. Electrical units do not need to be vented; oil- and gas-fired units must be. Therefore, they must be placed in an exterior wall where they can be vented directly outdoors or, if placed in a partition, must be vented through the roof. Some models are designed for installation in a partition between two rooms, and heat them both.

To warm converted space that you have partitioned into several rooms, you have a choice between resistance heaters and radiant panels. An electrically operated resistance heater may be installed in the ceiling, in a wall or partition, or along the baseboards of exterior walls. These units provide clean, dry heat, and require no venting. They are more expensive than oil- or gas-fired wall heaters, however, and take a little longer to meet the thermostat's call for heat.

Radiant panels may be installed in the ceiling or under the floor. Heat may be distributed through tubing carrying water heated by a small boiler, or through ducts carrying air heated in a furnace. With radiant panels you have complete freedom to arrange furniture as you want, and you avoid the variation in air temperature common with on-and-off space heaters and resistance heaters. On the other hand, radiant systems are slow to heat and slow to cool. Carpeting reduces the efficiency of a floor system, although the floor is always warm—a decided advantage in a garage conversion. The heat from a ceiling system does not penetrate tables, and people sometimes complain about cold feet while sitting at them.

If the heating system you decide on requires either heat ducts or hot water piping under the floor, you must establish the floor level of the finished space to allow for installation and maintenance of the system. Your heating subcontractor can tell you how much space he needs. But unless you are trained in heating systems, hire a professional to design and install the system, even if it is no more complex than individual baseboard units.

AIR CONDITIONING

Cooling converted space requires the same considerations as heating it. Your existing central air conditioning system is not likely to have enough capacity to cool added space to your satisfaction unless it was oversized to begin with. Thus your choices are a combination heating-air conditioning unit, or individual space coolers.

Combination heating and air conditioning units have gradually shrunk in size over the years as efficiency has increased. Today you need a floor space no larger than 24″ × 24″ to house most units. You must provide access to the space with a removable panel that permits repairs and maintenance, and a grille that allows air to circulate through the furnace compartment. Since some noise will emanate from the unit when it is operating, locate the equipment as far as possible from quiet rooms. The ideal location is off a hallway as close as practicable to the center of the converted space.

YOUR PLUMBING SYSTEM

A residential plumbing system has three parts: water lines, both hot and cold; drain lines that carry waste out of the house; and vent lines that carry off gases in the waste system.

Water Lines

The smallest of all plumbing lines, water supply pipes run both vertically and horizontally. Hot and cold water lines usually run close together—side by side horizontally at the same level between floor joists, then side by side vertically to their point of use (Fig. 5-1). Occasionally, they run horizontally one above the other in walls, but only near plumbing fixtures at the very end of the line. If you locate the point in your basement or crawl space where pipes disappear upward, they almost always emerge again at the same point above.

Drain Lines

The drainage system in a house includes the pipes that carry waste to the sewer or septic system (Fig. 5-2). As previously discussed, the soil stack or soil pipe is the largest pipe in the drainage system, and is almost always located in a thicker wall directly behind the toilet, technically called a **water closet**. The pipe between the water closet and the soil stack, called a **closet bend,** is located between floor joists. Waste piping from other plumbing fixtures must eventually reach the soil stack, sloping slightly over its entire length. When the fixtures are close to the stack, the sloping drain lines usually run between floor joists when joists run the same direction, as from lavatory A. They hang from joists running at

right angles (B). Waste piping from isolated fixtures (C in Fig. 5-2) may run horizontally in the wall for a short distance.

Vent Lines

All fixtures must be vented to permit trapped gases to escape into the air. Plumbing codes permit a fixture within 5′ of the main stack to be vented into that stack. More distant fixtures must be vented separately. Vent piping rises at the point where waste piping turns downward—either directly behind the fixture as at A in Fig. 5-2, or at the end of a short horizontal run as at C. If the location of walls permits, as at D, vent piping runs straight upward into attic space. Then it continues either up through the roof, or jogs slightly to clear the roof structure at the eaves. Or, as at E, it runs horizontally above or between floor joists in the attic until it connects with the main stack.

But note what happens at A. The horizontal section of vent piping from the lavatory does not go into the soil stack directly. Instead it rises in the wall, then turns again before reaching the soil stack. The reason for this is that plumbing codes do not permit any vent piping to enter a soil stack below the waste line from another fixture.

Where Is the Piping?

Without digging into walls, how can you tell where the plumber ran his pipes? You can't always be sure where pipes *are,* but you can almost always figure out where pipes *aren't.*

Follow the main stack through first. It must be vertical. It will be the same distance from exterior walls in the basement or crawl space, on each floor, in the attic, and where it goes through the roof. Normally, it will be in the stud space directly behind the centerline of the water closet.

Bathrooms that are back to back or one above the other share a single stack. Otherwise, there must be a soil stack for each water closet. Any group of fixtures with a water closet requires a stack. You can tell how many stacks there are in your house by standing far enough away from it so that you can see the entire back half of the roof. Because vents on a roof are rather ugly, they are usually on the back of the house where they aren't visible from the street.

You can safely assume that as many fixtures as possible will be vented into the main stack. Maximum horizontal distances between the point where waste lines enter a wall and their soil stack, by today's codes, are:

- 2½′ for lavatories and small sinks
- 3½′ for bathtubs, kitchen sinks, and laundry trays
- 5′ for shower stalls and urinals
- 6′ for water closets

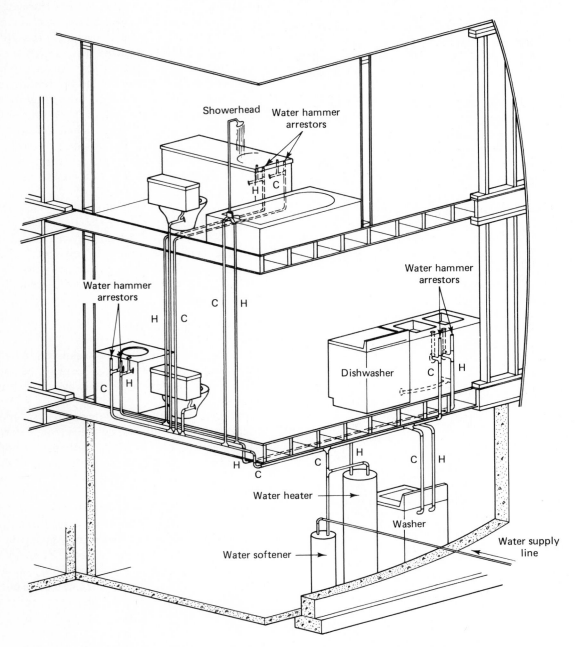

Figure 5-1. This section through a two-story house with basement shows a typical water system. Note that horizontal runs lie between first-floor joists as much as possible, then turn upward directly to the fixtures they serve.

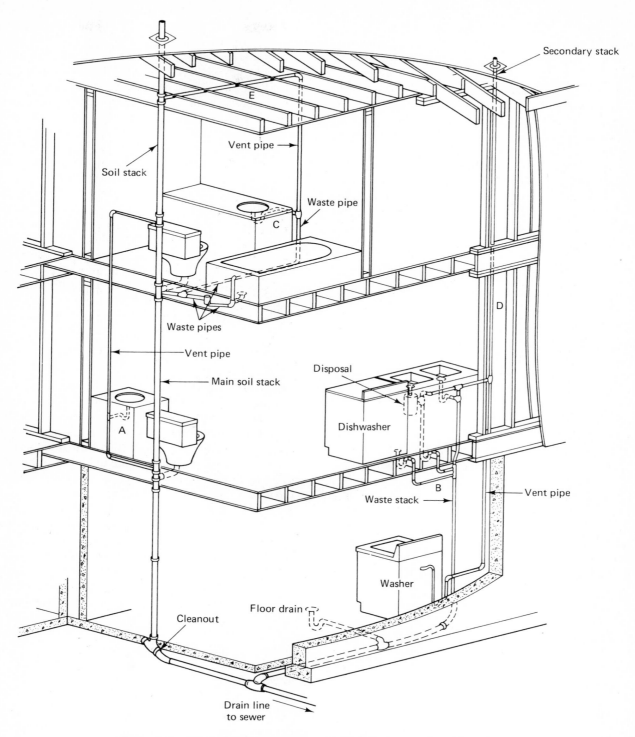

Figure 5–2. Typical drainage system, showing the house connection pipe to a sewer or septic tank. Drainage piping must slope downward to meet plumbing codes.

These distances may be greater in houses built prior to present-day codes or in isolated areas beyond the reach of codes. Code restrictions will apply to almost all houses built in the past 50 years, however.

Fixtures farther from the main stack than the distances noted above must be vented through a secondary stack. As you can see in Fig. 5-2, secondary stacks rise vertically between floors, but they aren't necessarily directly behind the fixture they vent. The stack for a sink beneath a window, for example, runs to one side of the window. Similarly, the stack for a lavatory beneath an inset medicine cabinet runs beside the cabinet. But which side?

Look outdoors first, and line up the stack where it breaks through the roof with the kitchen window. Now you know which side. Although the vent pipe may jog in the attic, the jog will be up the slope rather than across it. The only exception is to avoid a rafter, and then the jog is only a few inches. If you want to check, look in the attic.

Extending Existing Lines

The size of water inlet piping from your source of fresh water is established by code. Requirements vary with available water pressure, the distance to your house from the water main, and the number and type of plumbing fixtures connected to the water lines. If your present water supply isn't always satisfactory, now is the best time to investigate the cause. If the problem is either undersized water pipes or mineral deposits from hard water that have narrowed their usable inside diameter, the cost of new and larger water piping could be well worth the expense.

Houses less than 50 years old built in cities with a sound water supply system usually have water inlet piping large enough to accept the demands of another bathroom. To be certain, measure the outside diameter of the water inlet pipe where it enters the house. It will come through a foundation wall of a house with a basement or deep crawl space. If crawl space is shallow, piping may come up from the ground near the foundation wall. In a house on a concrete slab it will come up either through the slab or in a recess in it in the garage or kitchen. Call your local water department and give the diameter to an engineer. Tell him what fixtures you now have and what you plan to add. He can tell you whether your existing supply pipe is large enough, or else what size it should be.

If at all possible, locate new rooms that require plumbing against the existing wall of the house for several reasons. First, the shorter new water and drain lines are, the lower their cost. Second, although water lines can run horizontally, drain lines must slope at least ¼" per foot of horizontal run. Furthermore, they can't begin to run horizontally until they are below floor structure. You can't notch joists for drain piping.

Suppose that you want to add a toilet and lavatory in the new space, and that the nearest drain line is 5' from the wall between the house and your addition. Directly beneath the toilet you need a closet bend, an ell-shaped pipe with a long tail that carries waste from the floor of the bathroom to horizontal below floor structure. The open end of the bend will already be about 4" below the subfloor. To this vertical dimension add the fall of ¼" per foot. If your toilet is centered 2' from the house wall, you add only ½". But if your toilet is 20' from the wall, you must add 5". If the drain line runs between joists, the drop won't cause any problems. But if the line must run underneath crossing joists, it will cut into basement headroom, or in a crawl space may drop too far to fit into your existing system.

So before you go ahead with any remodeling that requires plumbing, get the help of a plumbing contractor to rough out the water and drain lines. They must meet local codes, and the building inspector must approve the system before you can complete construction. By getting professional advice, even if you install the plumbing yourself, you avoid the danger of having to tear out what you installed, or having to change your design after you have begun construction.

YOUR ELECTRICAL SYSTEM

Electric power comes into your house through a line called a **service entrance,** and is distributed through a **service panel**—either a fuse box or a circuit breaker box. When you bring power to new living space, you will need at least one new electrical circuit and probably two. Power to any existing light or outlet in an attic, garage, carport, or porch travels over a circuit unlikely to be able to carry the extra load you'll put on it.

The solution is to run new wiring from the service panel. Circuit breaker boxes in most homes have extra capacity for just such purposes, and adding a circuit or two creates no problem. In older homes equipped with fuse boxes, however, that capacity may not be available. The boxes were large enough when the house was built, but with appliances added and use of electricity increased geometrically, all extra circuits are often filled. Sometimes you will find two fuse boxes for that very reason. The best answer is to replace all fuse boxes with a circuit breaker panel of adequate capacity, and rewire the entire house at the same time. Many codes won't permit you to add or modify existing wiring unless all wiring throughout the house is updated to meet current electrical codes.

Locating Receptacles

The National Electrical Code is quite specific on locations of electrical receptacles. It says that all areas used for living—and that includes all rooms except bathrooms, laundry rooms, and rooms with special

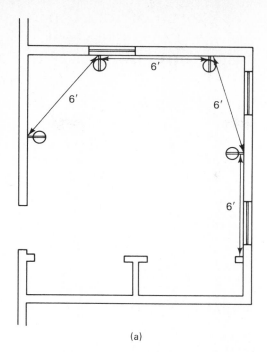

(a)

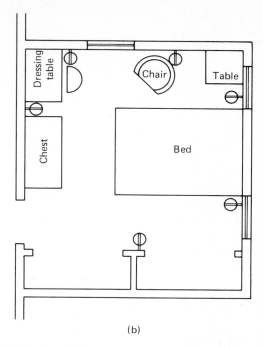

(b)

Figure 5–3. Both these layouts for electrical outlets in a bedroom meet code requirements. Once the room in (a) is furnished, however, two of the four outlets will be difficult to reach. Addition of another outlet and more judicious spacing puts all outlets within reach (b). The outlet between closets is a convenience for vacuuming.

equipment such as workshops—must have electrical receptacles or outlets spaced so that no point along the floor line below any wall space is more than 6′ from an outlet, measured horizontally. This rule applies to any wall area 2′ wide or wider.

Study the layout of outlets in Fig. 5-3a. It meets the code. But before you finalize a similar layout, superimpose your furniture layout on it. You may find that you have put a receptacle behind a sofa or desk where it is very inconvenient to reach. So relocate these outlets (Fig. 5-3b) for the sake of convenience, and add another outlet or two where necessary to meet the 6′ rule.

The standard location for wall receptacles is 12″ to 14″ above a floor and 6″ above a counter. Switches are normally centered about 48″ above the floor, but you may want to raise them to 54″ to keep them beyond the reach of small children, or lower them to 42″ to put them within reach. Indicate on your floor plan where you want switches, the type required, and what outlet or fixture they will turn on (see Fig. 4-8).

A single-pole switch (symbol is S) is the only control point for an outlet or light, although it may turn on more than one light, such as a pair flanking a bathroom mirror. A single-pole switch is adequate for rooms with one entrance. A room with two entrances should have three-way switches (symbol S₃). Mentally walk through each space to determine the best locations for switches. Within 6″ of doorways on the knob side of the door is the common location.

LIGHTING

As you plan your lighting in new space, answer these three questions:

1. How much light do I need?
2. What type of lighting do I want?
3. Where is each type of lighting needed?

How Much Light

The intensity of light—the amount you need—is measured in footcandles. A **footcandle** is the amount of light that a candle casts on a square foot of curved wall 1′ away. On a clear day your yard is drenched with about 10,000 footcandles of sunlight. Just inside a window, however, intensity is about 200 footcandles, and in the center of a medium-size room it is about 10 footcandles. A 75-watt bulb provides 30 footcandles at a distance of 3′ and 20 footcandles at a distance of 6′.

For casual activities, such as talking, watching television, playing cards, or setting a table, 10 footcandles is adequate. For cleaning house, distinguishing colors of socks in a drawer, or knitting, you need 20 to 30 footcandles. For shaving, washing dishes, preparing food, or reading this book, you need 30 to 50 footcandles. For intermittent fine work, such as sewing, writing, or making repairs, you need 50 to 70 footcandles. For prolonged fine work you need 70 to 100 footcandles.

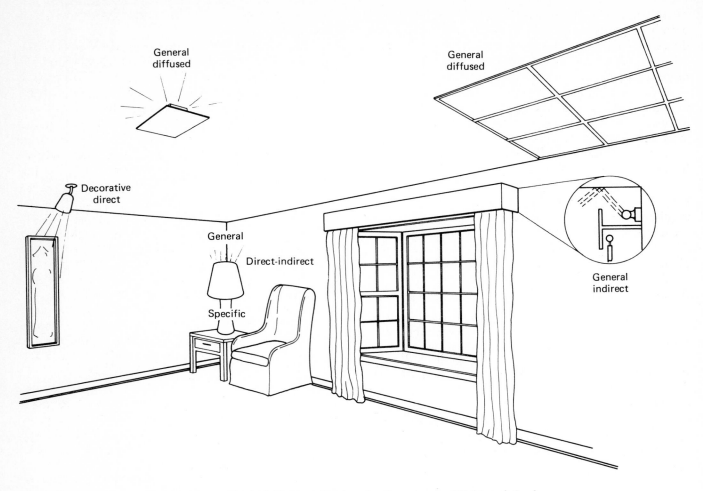

Figure 5-4. Typical fixtures showing the three types of light and the four ways of distributing that light.

Table 5-1. Basic lighting requirements for various rooms and for common activities in those rooms.

	Living Room	Family Room	Dining Room	Kitchen and Utility	Bedrooms	Bathrooms	Hallways and Stairways	Storage
General lighting								
Intensity (footcandles)	10	25–30	10–15	30–50	10	10–15	20	10
Type	Diffused or indirect	Direct or direct-indirect	Direct, indirect	Direct or diffused	Indirect	Direct	Direct	Direct
Specific lighting for:	Reading Card playing	Games	Dining	Food preparation Cooking Dishwashing	Dressing Reading Personal care	Shaving Washing Applying cosmetics	Safety	
Decorative lighting on:	Paintings Statuary Objets d'art Bookshelves		Silverware China Glassware				Planting in an entry hall	

Types of Light

There are three types of lighting: general, specific, and decorative. And there are four ways of dispersing light: directly, indirectly, combined direct-indirect, and diffused. The type of lighting and its method of dispersal depend on how you plan to use a room.

General lighting provides a low intensity of illumination at a relatively uniform level. It should be diffused light without glare. The best general light—ideal for casual activities—is indirect, and comes from lights that are not themselves visible (Fig. 5-4). Direct light is the least desirable general lighting.

For specific lighting, however, direct light is the best. You need specific lighting for any activity that requires more intensity than casual activities. It adds to the level of general light.

Decorative lighting is usually low in intensity and planned either to create a pleasant atmosphere or to highlight a prized possession. It may be direct and focused on a painting or statue, or it may be indirect to achieve the effect of candlelight.

Room Requirements

As you plan lighting requirements room by room, use Table 5-1 as a general guide. The thinking behind these recommendations follows.

Living Room. General lighting may come from overhead fixtures, or indirectly from tube lights behind valances above window draperies. A dimmer switch permits you to keep lighting at a soothingly low level for conversation, or to increase the level for card games. If your room is large enough, consider a hanging fixture over a permanently located game table. Plan receptacles for lamps that provide specific lighting for reading and at the desk or table where you work on home records and pay bills.

Family Room. If you have a special table for pool, billiards, or table tennis, provide strong specific lighting directly above it. Light in the remainder of the room can come from lamps. If the family room is the scene of less vigorous activities, such as watching television or playing recordings, provide a middle level of direct general lighting, and specific lighting from lamps or ceiling spotlights where you need it.

Dining Room. Although a dining room or dining area serves primarily a single purpose, you can light it in many ways. For young families who have small children but seldom entertain at dinner, a hanging fixture that provides about 15 footcandles works well. For middle-aged couples a lower level of lighting is more comfortable and more relaxing. For older couples who want to see what they're eating but whose eyes aren't as

strong as they used to be, 15 footcandles is again a good level. Provide the maximum level you need, then reduce the intensity with a dimmer switch as the occasion demands.

For families that entertain frequently or who like the subdued atmosphere of fine restaurants, a spotlight recessed in the ceiling provides an ideal setting for dining. The strong light focused on the center of the table adds luster to good glassware, china, and silver, but lights the faces of diners with a soft glow reflected off the tablecloth. With the main light concentrated on the table, you can balance light levels with indirect valance lighting or with decorative lighting in a china cabinet.

Kitchen. To serve the work triangle (see Chapter 14) a kitchen needs a high level of general lighting that you can provide with a large ceiling fixture or a series of lighting panels recessed into the ceiling (see Chapter 13). But you also need good specific lighting. Ideal above the sink is a light placed close enough to the wall so that the washer of dishes doesn't cast a shadow on the sink. Above counters tube lights tucked under cabinets illuminate work surfaces without glare in your eyes. A light in a range hood offers good specific light for cooking.

Utility Areas. As in the kitchen, you need good general lighting in the laundry area, with sources so placed that they shine into the interiors of washers and dryers. Provide direct specific light and a receptacle at the spot where you set up an ironing board.

A workshop, whether in a basement, garage, or room of its own, needs the same type of lighting as a kitchen—a high level of general light plus specific lighting over the workbench and above tools in a fixed location.

Halls and Stairways. Lighting in entrance halls should be general and of medium intensity. The fixture should be overhead, placed high enough to be out of the way of people and furniture moving through the area, and aimed to highlight differences in floor level at the entrance door. The level of light should not be so bright that people coming in out of the dark are blinded by it.

Lighting in bedroom halls should be either recessed in or set close to the ceiling. Low intensity is adequate and best. For family members and guests likely to be up in the middle of the night, small night lights about 12″ above floor level are ideal. They may be recessed into walls or be plugged into wall outlets on both sides near the ends, midpoint, and turns in the hall.

For maximum safety place lights at stairways so that they highlight the edges of steps. One ceiling light just forward of the bottom step and another just behind the top step (Fig. 5-5) provide safe lighting. The lights should be operated together by a three-way switch.

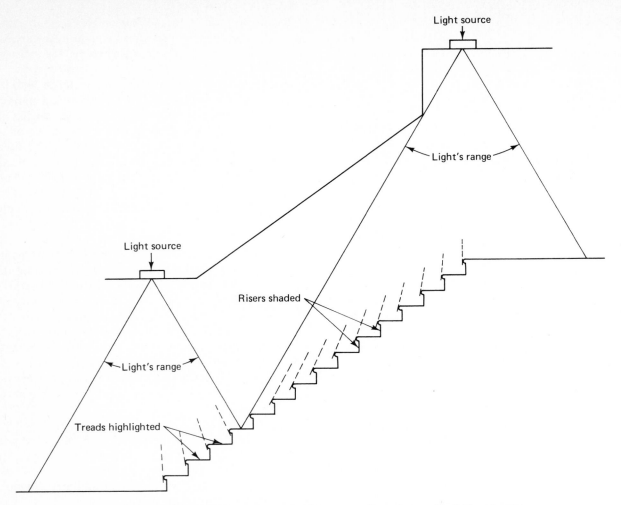

Figure 5–5. Lights at the top and bottom of a stairway should be placed to throw light on the edges of steps, with the treads receiving more light than the vertical risers between them.

Bedrooms. Bedrooms used primarily for sleeping, dressing, and undressing need only a low level of general lighting. Avoid direct light from overhead fixtures, which may wake sleeping people and offers little privacy from outside the house. Instead use indirect light; valance lighting is excellent and assures privacy. Supplement it with specific lighting at mirrors, dressing tables, and for reading in bed.

Bathrooms. Here you need a medium level of general lighting for most bathroom purposes, provided either by a single fixture or a ceiling panel. General lighting is poor, however, when you are looking in a mirror, because it throws shadows on your face and neck. Instead, plan on a pair of tube lights, warm in tone, flanking the mirror. Put them on a different switch than the ceiling light, or get the type with a switch at the end of the tubes. For those middle-of-the-night calls when your eyes don't need or want to see much light, use a night light in an outlet.

Storage Areas. Every closet should be lighted. If it is large enough to walk into, locate a small fixture either in the closet ceiling or on the wall above the closet door. If the closet is shallow, place a small spotlight in the ceiling outside the closet high enough to clear the doors, but low enough to light the floor of the closet, the entire hanging area, and shelves.

A single light with a low-wattage bulb is adequate for bulk storage areas in a basement, crawl space, garage, or under attic eaves. You can even use a bare bulb as long as the socket is out of the way where you won't hit it and shatter it.

Building An Addition— Foundation

The All-Weather Wood Foundation has neither concrete nor masonry. Its design is based on the same principles as a stud wall. A 2x8 footing plate rests on a bed of gravel. Vertical members are specially treated 2x6s spaced 12" on centers, and covered on the outside with special ½" plywood sheathing. This foundation system can be built in any weather, and built upon immediately. It meets all major building codes. (Courtesy American Plywood Association.)

An addition must have a foundation strong enough to support its own weight and the weight of its contents. The soil beneath it must be solid enough to support the same weights. Floor, wall, ceiling, and roof construction must meet the same code requirements as a new house. And utility systems—plumbing, heating, and electrical—must meet current codes, even if your house was built before those codes went into effect.

PREPARATION

Before you begin any actual construction, you need to take four important steps: establish the relationship between the floor level of the addition and the existing house, determine the type of foundation to build and the size of flooring members, work out the depth of the foundation, and test the soil.

Floor Levels

The starting point for all planning of heights is the finished floor level of the present house. If you build the floor of the addition at the same level, you must decide early what finish flooring material to use. You can compensate for a small variation in level with a threshold, but your remodeling will be more successful if you match the level exactly.

For the typical thicknesses to allow, refer back to Table 4-1. Remember that such flooring materials as resilient tiles and linoleum require underlayment. Other flooring materials do not.

If you plan to step either up or down into an addition, make the height of that step no less than 6″ nor more than 7″. Any lesser or greater dimension for a single step is generally considered a safety hazard.

Joist Size

The size of joists you need depends on their spacing and their length. Standard spacing is 16″ on centers (**o.c.**). Maximum length is determined by code.

Building codes state load requirements in one of two ways. Some specify the load joists must be capable of carrying. **Dead load**—the weight of the joists themselves and the structure resting on them—is taken into consideration in joist tables. The **live load** includes furnishings and people (on rafters it also includes wind and snow). Typical live load is 40 psf (pounds per square foot).

Other codes limit the amount any structural member may deflect. **Deflection** is the amount of sag, and relates to stiffness. The measure of stiffness—a member's ability to return to its original straightness—is **modulus of elasticity**, also known as the **E factor**. A typical maximum deflection is $\frac{1}{360}$ of the span between supports, measured in inches.

Tables 6-1 and 6-2 show the proper size of joist to select. Suppose that your addition is 14′-0″ wide, and joist spacing will be 16″ o.c. With 2 × 6 sill plates the clear span is 13′-1″, subtracting the 5½″ width of two plates. Assuming that your local code calls for a 40-lb live load, you can meet requirements as shown in Table 6-1 with:

- 2 × 8s with a fiber stress (f) of 1300 psi (pounds per square inch)
- 2 × 10s or 3 × 8s with a fiber stress of 900 psi
- 3 × 6s with a fiber stress of 1500 psi

Now suppose that your code is based on deflec-

tion. Referring to Table 6-2, you see that you can meet requirements with:

- 2 × 8s with an E greater than 1,600,000
- 2 × 10s with an E of 1,000,000
- 3 × 8s with an E of 1,200,000

Various species of lumber have widely varying f and E ratings, and are graded accordingly at lumber mills. Most lumber dealers stock joists with an f rating of 1200 or more, and an E rating of 1,400,000 or more. So the simplest way to buy what you need is to tell your dealer the distance you need to span and the joist spacing you prefer, and let him tell you what to buy. If he is honest and knows you are likely to buy your supplies from him, he will recommend the most economical size of joist to buy to meet code.

But before you talk to your dealer, consider two other points. First, it is frequently to your advantage to use the same size joists as in your existing house, even though you could safely use smaller ones. Then all your heights match. This is of particular value when you are matching floor levels. When you have a difference in floor levels, heights won't match anyway.

Finally, lay out the floor structure in both directions. Suppose that your addition is 14′ × 10′, and you don't need to match joist heights. You can frame the floor in two ways—by running the joists of the addition parallel to the common wall or at right angles to it (Fig. 6-1). With either framing plan you have the same amount of foundation wall and sill plate. Perimeter joists are the same length—34 linear feet.

In Fig. 6-1a you need eight joists 13′-9″ long. These must be cut from 14′ lengths, so you need 112 linear feet of joist. In Fig. 6-1b you have 10 joists about 9′-10½″ long, plus a ledger. These must be cut from 10′ lengths, so you need 114 linear feet of joist and ledger. Is the saving of 2 linear feet worth it? Well, you have three more pieces to cut in b, but each piece is shorter, lighter, and easier to handle.

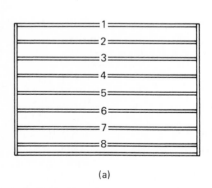

(a)

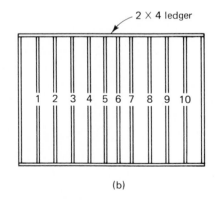

2 × 4 ledger

(b)

Figure 6–1. Always lay out floor joists on paper in both directions to see which is the more economical and practical layout. In this example layout (a) has fewer pieces but greater lumber usage.

Table 6-1. Joist sizes limited by the loads they carry[a]

Size (Nominal) (in.)	Spacing (C to C) (in.)	f=	900 Ft	In.	1000 Ft	In.	1100 Ft	In.	1200 Ft	In.	1300 Ft	In.	1400 Ft	In.	1500 Ft	In.	1600 Ft	In.	1700 Ft	In.	1800 Ft	In.
2 × 6	12	L=	9	6	10	0	10	5	10	11	11	4	11	9	12	3	12	7	13	0	13	4
	16	L=	8	3	8	8	9	1	9	6	9	11	10	3	10	8	11	0	11	4	11	8
2 × 8	12	L=	12	6	13	2	13	10	14	5	15	0	15	7	16	2	16	8	17	2	17	8
	16	L=	10	11	11	6	12	1	12	7	13	1	13	7	14	1	14	7	15	0	15	5
2 × 10	12	L=	15	9	16	7	17	5	18	2	18	11	19	7	20	4	21	0	21	7	22	3
	16	L=	13	9	14	6	15	2	15	10	16	6	17	2	17	9	18	4	18	11	19	5
2 × 12	12	L=	18	11	19	11	20	11	21	10	22	9	23	7	24	5	25	2	26	0	26	9
	16	L=	16	7	17	5	18	3	19	1	19	11	20	8	21	4	22	1	22	9	23	5
2 × 14	12	L=	22	0	23	3	24	4	25	5	26	6	27	6	28	5	29	4	30	3		
	16	L=	19	4	20	4	21	4	22	4	23	3	24	1	24	11	25	9	26	6	27	4
3 × 6	12	L=	11	10	12	6	13	1	13	8	14	3	14	9	15	4	15	10	16	3	16	9
	16	L=	10	4	10	11	11	5	12	0	12	5	12	11	13	4	13	10	14	3	14	8
3 × 8	12	L=	15	7	16	6	17	3	18	0	18	9	19	6	20	2	20	10	21	6	22	1
	16	L=	13	8	14	5	15	2	15	10	16	5	17	1	17	8	18	3	18	10	19	4
3 × 10	12	L=	19	7	20	7	21	8	22	7	23	6	24	5	25	3	26	1	26	11	27	8
	16	L=	17	2	18	1	19	0	19	10	20	8	21	5	22	2	22	11	23	7	24	4
3 × 12	12	L=	23	5	24	8	25	10	27	0	28	1	29	2	30	2						
	16	L=	20	7	21	9	22	9	23	10	24	9	25	9	26	7	27	6	28	4	29	2
3 × 14	12	L=	27	2	28	8	30	0														
	16	L=	24	0	25	3	26	6	27	8	28	10	29	11	31	0						

[a]To use this table, first find L values (lengths) that are closest to but longer than your joist span. Then look to the left of the table on that line to find the size of joist needed and its spacing, and look at the top of the column for the minimum fiber stress value of the wood. Use 16″ spacing unless low basement headroom is a problem. You need more lumber with 12″ spacing, but you can gain a couple of inches in headroom.

Table 6-2. Joist sizes limited by amount of deflection[a]

Size (Nominal) (in.)	Spacing (C to C) (in.)	E=	1,000,000 Ft	In.	1,200,000 Ft	In.	1,400,000 Ft	In.	1,600,000 Ft	In.
2 × 6	12	L=	9	1	9	8	10	2	10	8
	16	L=	8	4	8	10	9	3	9	8
2 × 8	12	L=	12	1	12	10	13	6	14	1
	16	L=	11	0	11	8	12	4	12	11
2 × 10	12	L=	15	2	16	1	17	0	17	9
	16	L=	13	11	14	9	15	6	16	3
2 × 12	12	L=	18	4	19	5	20	5	21	4
	16	L=	16	9	17	9	18	9	19	7
2 × 14	12	L=	21	4	22	7	23	10	24	11
	16	L=	19	7	20	9	21	10	22	10
3 × 6	12	L=	10	7	11	3	11	10	12	4
	16	L=	9	8	10	3	10	10	11	3
3 × 8	12	L=	13	11	14	10	15	7	16	4
	16	L=	12	9	13	7	14	4	14	11
3 × 10	12	L=	17	5	18	7	19	7	20	6
	16	L=	16	1	17	1	18	0	18	10
3 × 12	12	L=	21	0	22	3	23	6	24	6
	16	L=	19	4	20	6	21	7	22	7
3 × 14	12	L=	24	5	25	11	27	4	28	7
	16	L=	22	6	23	11	25	2	26	4

[a]To use this table, go down the column showing the code's E value until you find the L value (length) that is closest to but longer than your joist span. Then look to the left of the table on that line to find the size of joists you need and their spacing.

But there is another important factor. Because the span in layout (b) is less, you can use joists one size smaller. If you buy 2 × 8s that meet live-load requirements in layout (a), you need 194.67 board feet of lumber. But if you buy 2 × 6s for layout (b), you need only 143.33 board feet of lumber.

How do you arrive at these figures? Lumber is sold by the board foot, and a **board foot** is 1″ × 12″ × 12″, or 144 cu in. Therefore, every linear foot of 2 × 8 contains 1.33 board feet (b.f.); that's $\frac{2 \times 8}{1 \times 12}$. Multiply 1.33 times the 112 l.f. of 2 × 8 required, and you get 149.33; add 45.33 b.f. for edge joists. Every linear foot (l.f.) of 2 × 6 contains exactly 1 b.f. Multiply 1 times 134 l.f. of 2 × 6, and 0.67 times 14 l.f. of ledger, and you get 143.33. The cost per board foot of 2 × 8s and 2 × 6s is not necessarily the same, but by framing the floor as in layout (b) you can cut the cost of joists about 30%. Now that *is* worth the saving.

Keep in mind also that joists should probably run toward the house if you will be installing drain lines that tie in with existing drain lines, regardless of the saving in the cost of joists. If joist size matches existing joist size, you can run joists in either direction; the cost saving is a minor consideration.

Foundation Walls

Whether you build your addition over a basement or over crawl space, the components are the same. Only the height of the foundation wall differs.

The typical foundation wall supporting wood floor joists consists of a continuous concrete footing and a foundation wall of concrete blocks (see Fig. 4-9). The wall may be built of poured concrete, bricks, or stone, but if you do the work yourself, concrete blocks are the best material.

Concrete blocks are made in a number of shapes and sizes (Fig. 6-2). For most of the wall you need two-core or three-core stretcher blocks (a or b). At each corner of the foundation you need corner blocks (c). The top course on which the sill plate rests should be cap blocks (d or e). The other blocks shown are for special purposes. In a foundation with a basement you may need jamb blocks beside an entrance door (g), sash blocks at steel basement windows (h), and partition blocks to divide interior space (i). Double corner blocks (f) are used to build piers, and 10″ stretchers replace 8″ stretchers when exterior walls are brick or stone veneer, or the wall supports a concrete slab.

The standard footing is 8″ thick and twice as wide as the thickness of the foundation wall. Under 8″

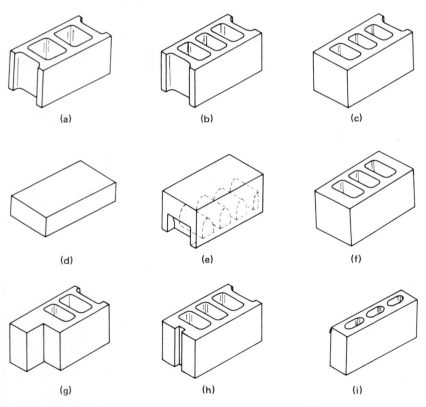

(a)   (b)   (c)

(d)   (e)   (f)

(g)   (h)   (i)

Figure 6-2. Typical concrete blocks: (a) two-core stretcher; (b) three-core stretcher; (c) corner block; (d) 4″ cap block; (e) 8″ cap block; (f) double-corner block; (g) jamb block; (h) sash block; (i) 4″ partition block. You build straight, unbroken expanses of wall with stretcher blocks. All other types are for special purposes.

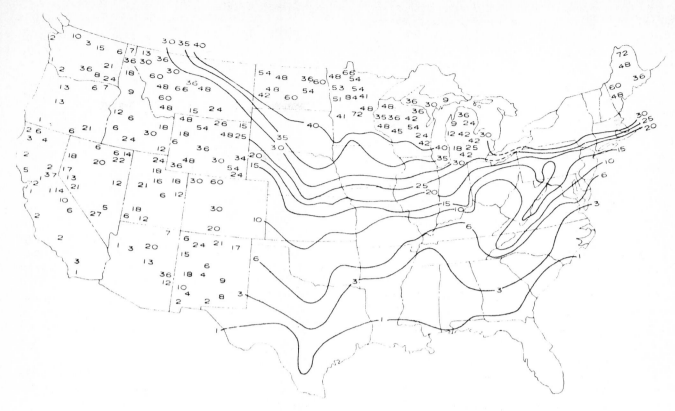

Figure 6-3. This map shows the depth in inches to which the ground normally freezes in winter. It is a general guide only. To find where the frost line is in your community, call local building officials.

blocks, then, you need a footing 8″ × 16″. Under 10″ blocks you need a footing 10″ × 20″. Blocks are centered on the footing.

A new type of foundation wall, pioneered by the American Plywood Association, uses neither concrete nor concrete blocks. It is called the All-Weather Wood Foundation (AWWF). Footings and the top and bottom plates are pressure treated lumber. Studs, also pressure treated, are faced on the outside with plywood bonded with exterior glue, which in turn is protected by a polyethylene film. All fasteners must withstand corrosion. A carefully leveled bed of gravel supports the footings and continues part way up foundation walls. Inside the basement, walls may be insulated and finished like any stud wall above ground level. The AWWF system meets all code requirements. Because of the care in leveling and the special materials needed, a wood foundation should be built only by a builder experienced with the system.

Basement Wall Height. Plan the floor of any basement under an addition at the same level as the existing basement floor. Then the bottom of the footing is at the same level as the bottom of footings under the existing house. Usually, this is 12″ below basement floor level.

Build the new foundation wall at the same height as the old wall. This is easy if the old wall is 8″ blocks; then all courses line up. The inside height of a poured concrete wall may not be divisible by 4″, however. When you face this condition, reduce the height of the new wall until it is divisible by 4″, and slope the concrete where the new and old floors meet. Do not have the floor of the addition lower than the old floor unless you install a floor drain and a drain pipe.

Foundation Wall around Crawl Space. Footings must always rest on soil that won't freeze. The point to which ground freezes is called the **frost line**. When frozen ground thaws in the spring, it heaves with enough force to crack concrete. You must place footings below the frost line to avoid damage. Your local building inspector or engineer can tell you what the depth is in your community. In the United States the frost line varies from a few inches to as much as 7′ (Fig. 6-3).

In standard building practice the bottom of the footing lies 12″ below the frost line, and the top of the foundation wall is at least 8″ about finished **grade** (ground) level. Line up the top of the wall with the top of the existing foundation wall, whether it surrounds a basement or crawl space. Then make the total wall height divisible by 4″, and place footings accordingly.

Concrete Slabs. Most concrete slab floors are supported around their edges on regular foundation walls, and in their centers on a bed of gravel (see Fig. 4-9). Note that the edge of the slab must be insulated to prevent cold floors. Rigid foam insulation is commonly used here. A standard slab floor may be used under an addition, whatever the floor construction is in the main house.

Some houses and additions are built on concrete slabs that are thicker and deeper around their perimeter than they are in their center. Called a **floating slab, turned-down slab,** or **thickened-edge slab,** this type of construction should be used under an addition only when the main house rests on the same type of slab (see Fig. 4-9).

Testing the Soil

An optimist assumes that the soil where he or she wants to add has enough bearing strength to support the weight of an addition, and starts digging. A pessimist, aware that soil conditions may vary greatly within a few yards, checks out soil samples to make sure that building can proceed safely and economically.

Even an amateur can learn a lot by digging test holes. The most commonly used tool is a posthole auger, which you can rent from many equipment rental stores. Mark the approximate locations of the corners of your addition. Then twist the auger into the ground at these corners like a screwdriver. You get a soil sample about 6″ in diameter.

Dig as deep as you expect to excavate for the foundation—7′ to 8′ for a basement, 2′ to 6′ for crawl space, and 1½′ to 5′ for a concrete slab. Then study the last sample from the bottom of the hole. Break it apart with your hands. The best bearing soils are firm and dry, and won't crumble easily. Feel the sample for moisture. A little dampness is normal, especially in the spring. But if the soil is wet, or the hole slowly fills with water, you will probably need to install a foundation drainage system.

If you hit a rock ledge, dig other holes along the proposed foundation line to see where the ledge runs. As long as a ledge is deep enough below ground level, you can pour footings on it. But don't count on building a basement.

If you have any doubt about the soil you find, take your samples to the county engineer for an opinion. Some companies specialize in testing soil samples, and you can go to them to be absolutely sure. But a soil analysis is not cheap, and as long as your present house shows no signs of settling unevenly because of poor soil, you can probably proceed safely.

OUTLINING THE EXCAVATION

Using your dimensioned floor plan as a guide, locate the two points where the foundation walls of the addition will meet the existing foundation. Measure with a steel tape from the nearest corner of the house. Work from the foundation itself if it is exposed. When the wall is brick veneer, measure from the corner of the bricks. Use a grease pencil or chalk to make the marks, one about 6″ above the ground and the other at the approximate level of the top of the foundation.

Drive a small stake into the ground as close as possible to the foundation at the two lower marks. Then drive a nail partway into the top of each stake exactly on the mark.

Now use the Pythagorean theorem, as shown in Fig. 3-5 on page 21, to locate the two outer corners of the addition. From each nail measure 8′ away from the wall, and swing an arc in the dirt. Then measure from each nail 6′ toward the other nail and make marks.

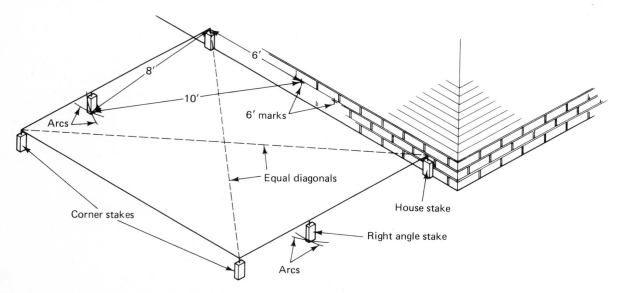

Figure 6–4. To lay out an addition, mark the two points where it meets the existing house, use the Pythagorean theorem to establish square corners, stake the outer corners, and measure the diagonals to assure that all corners are square.

Make sure that the nails and marks are at the same level. Then from each of the two marks measure off 10', and swing arcs that cross the two 8' arcs. Drive a stake at each of these intersections, and drive a nail into the top of the stakes directly above the intersection. You have now formed right angles at the wall.

Next, measure off the other dimension of the addition, beginning at each nail at the wall and stretching your tape directly over the corresponding nail in the right-angle stake. Mark these two corners with stakes and nails as before (Fig. 6-4). Then stretch a length of nylon cord from one stake at the house to the corresponding corner, over to the next corner, then back to the other stake at the house. Wrap the cord several times around each nail, but don't pull the stakes out of line.

The cord outlines the shape of the addition, and the shape should be rectangular. To make sure, measure diagonally from each corner stake to the opposite house stake. The two readings should be identical. A difference up to ¼" is acceptable. If the difference is greater, start over. The four corners of your foundation *must* be square if your addition is to be square.

Establishing Foundation Height

With the shape of the foundation wall established, you next establish its height. First mark the height of the existing foundation wall on the side of the house. The top of the wall won't be visible from outside, so go into the basement or crawl space. There measure the distance (if any) between the top of the wall and the head or sill of an opening for a window or ventilator.

Now, back outdoors, transfer this dimension to the outside of the wall at the same opening. Carry this height horizontally to your other two marks on the wall; the best way is to use a straight board with a carpenter's level set on it. Where the horizontal and vertical marks cross, nail boards horizontally to the wall with their tops at foundation level. Drive a nail part way into the top of each board on the vertical mark. You have now established the top of the foundation wall of the addition, and its outside edges where it butts against the house.

Batter Boards

The stakes that mark the corners of your addition will be in the way once you start excavating the foundation. To replace them, and to establish foundation height at these outside corners, build **batter boards**. The simplest batter board consists of two 2 × 4 stakes about 4' long and one piece of 1 × 6 about 6' long (Fig. 6-5).

At least 4' outside the foundation line at corners,

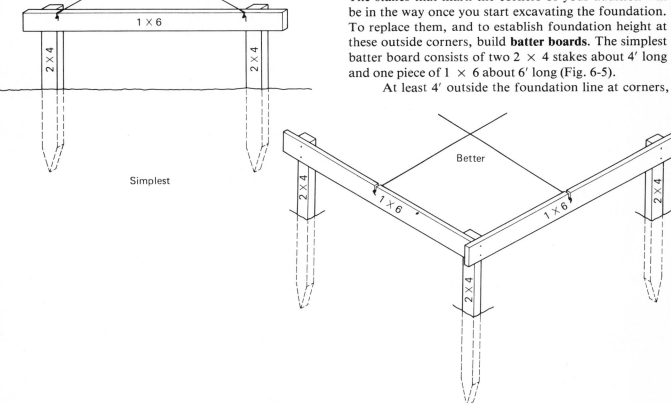

Figure 6–5. Typical batter boards for marking corners. Those shown are the most common and are equally useful when the site is reasonably level. A different type is needed on sloping ground. Note that the horizontal members are nailed on the back sides of stakes to withstand the pull of the cords.

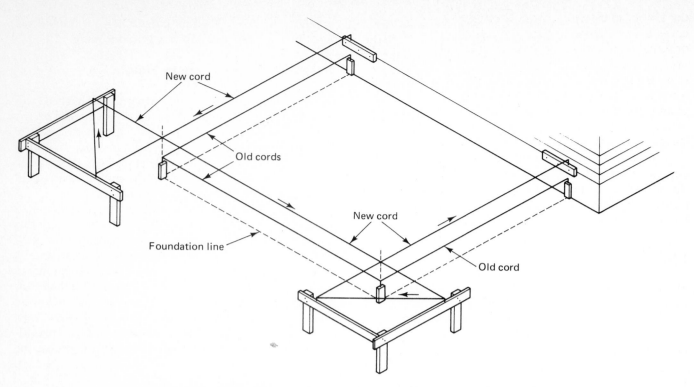

Figure 6–6. After you string cords between batter boards to outline the foundation for your addition, your work should look like this.

and 5 to 6' apart, drive batter board stakes partway into the ground. At this time their tops should be above foundation level. Next, nail the 1 × 6s to the back sides of the stakes, with the top edges flush with the tops of the stakes as in Fig. 6-5. Use only one nail at each stake.

Level Batter Boards. The next step is to get batter boards level with foundation height. There are two ways. One is to rent or borrow an optical level and a leveling rod. Either a transit level or dumpy level will do. Set up the optical level at any point in the yard from which you can clearly see all four corners of the addition. Adjust the instrument on the tripod so that it is absolutely level.

Then have someone set the leveling rod on one of the boards you nailed to the house. Focus on the rod, and read the figure you see there. Write the figure down; it will be in feet and tenths of feet. Repeat this process at the other board to make sure that the reading is identical. If it isn't, at least one of your boards is not level with the top of the existing foundation. So recheck their location now, and correct any error.

When the readings are identical, swing the optical level toward one batter board, and focus on the rod set atop one of the stakes. Let's say that your readings at the house are 3.2', and the reading at the stake is 2.9'. This means that your helper must drive the stake 0.3' deeper into the ground until the reading there is also 3.2'. If the reading at the stake is greater than the reading at the house, cut a longer stake, and drive it into the hole until its top is at the 3.2' mark.

Repeat this process at the other two stakes, and at all three stakes of the other batter board. The tops of all stakes should now be level and at foundation height. To check, place your carpenter's level diagonally across the horizontal batter boards. Once you are sure that batter boards are level, add a second nail through the boards at each stake.

Making Your Own Level. As an alternative to renting an optical level, you can make a simple level yourself from a length of clear plastic garden hose, a funnel, and a pair of clamps. Leveling with a hose is slow but just as accurate.

Clamp one end of the hose to the corner stake of a batter board, and secure the other end to the board at the house. Both ends must be higher than the top of the existing foundation. Then, using the funnel, fill the hose until the water level at the house is exactly even with the foundation height. Wait until the water in the hose stops surging, and mark the water level at the stake. No matter how many turns the hose makes or how uneven the ground, the water level in the two ends will be identical.

Nail batter boards to the corner stake on the mark, then use your carpenter's level to set the other ends level. Use two nails at each end. The stakes will extend above foundation level with this method, but that doesn't matter. The horizontal boards will be at the proper height. Repeat this process at the other corner.

Once batter boards are set, string cords as shown in Fig. 6-6. Attach one end of two cords to the nails at the house, and stretch them directly over the nails in corner stakes. Where the cords touch the batter boards, drive nails and tie the cords to the nails. Then repeat the process to mark the third wall of the addition. Do not remove the old cords until you verify the accuracy of location of the new cords. Where lines cross, hang a plumb bob to make sure that the lines cross directly above the nails in the corner stakes. Leave foundation stakes in place as a guide to excavating.

Before going any further, run a tape between corners of the addition to make certain that your overall dimensions are those shown on your drawing. Then check the diagonals once more. When everything checks, prepare to excavate.

EXCAVATING

No matter how much work you plan to do yourself, hire someone to excavate. Look in the classified telephone directory under "Excavating Contractors" or "Grading Contractors." With a backhoe an experienced operator can dig a trench of required depth and width in a couple of hours. With a small power shovel or a front-end loader an operator can dig a basement or crawl space in less than a day when the soil is dry. If you value your time at more than $2 per hour, get help. It will pay for itself.

When the contractor arrives, be prepared to tell him how deep to dig, how wide a trench you need, where to deposit dirt from the excavation, and where to set shrubbery that you want to save and replant.

How Deep to Dig

You have already established the depth of your footings, measured either from the top of the foundation or to a point below the frost line. The dimension appears on the section you drew (Fig. 4-10). The operator should dig to that depth.

Grade level beneath a concrete slab should be about 10″ below the finished slab level. Ask the backhoe operator to pile enough dirt inside the foundation to build up grade to this level when necessary, and place the rest outside the foundation for backfilling. Let any fill settle for a couple of weeks before placing any slab.

How Wide to Dig

The width of an excavation varies with the height of the foundation wall, the type of floor construction in your addition, and soil conditions. Figure 6-7 shows typical sections through excavations at the foundation wall. A trench needs to be no wider than your footings if (1) its depth is no more than 3′, (2) the floor of the addition will be a concrete slab, and (3) you have no problems with ground water. The sides of the trench can serve as forms for footings.

If you build over crawl space, allow at least 3′ between the undersides of floor joists and the surface of

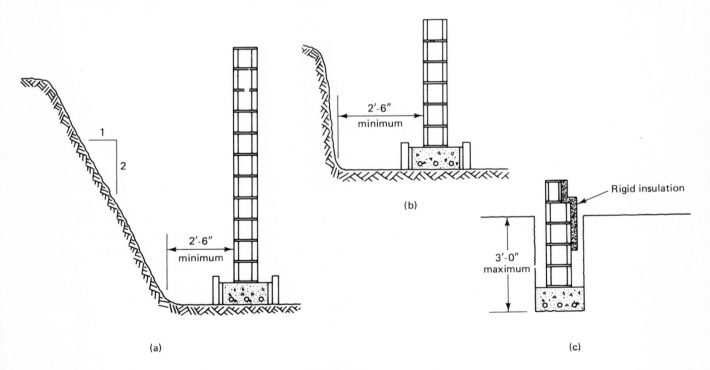

Figure 6–7. An excavation must be wide enough so that you can place footings, and high banks must be cut back to protect against cave-ins. Here are typical sections through an excavation for a basement (a), crawl space (b), and foundation wall under a concrete slab (c).

the crawl space. Allow at least 2½' outside the foundation wall to give you room for forming for footings and/or to install drain tiles.

If you build a basement, the excavation should also be 2½' wider than the foundation, and the bank should be no steeper than 2 to 1—in other words, it should slope outward one foot for every 2' of height. This prevents a cave-in from soft soil or a heavy rain.

Where to Pile Dirt

With any type of excavation some dirt is needed for backfilling between the finished wall and the sides of the cut. This dirt should be placed a few feet back from the edge of the cut where you don't have to carry it far but where it won't spill into the excavation.

Make arrangements to have excess dirt hauled away, but not until you have completed grading around the finished foundation. If your topsoil is good and you have much of it, ask the excavator to place it in a separate pile for finished grading.

Where to Set Shrubbery

With the bucket of a backhoe or power shovel, a good excavator can gently dig under shrubs and move them with a large ball of soil still around the roots. For bushes and small trees that you want to replant, find a place out of the way of construction where sun and shade conditions are similar to what they experienced before you moved them. While they are out of the ground, water frequently to counteract evaporation. Cover the balls with burlap soaked with water to reduce loss of soil moisture.

Cleaning Up

Before the excavator removes his equipment, check his work. Make sure that the hole or trench is of the required size and depth, and reasonably level at the bottom. Be sure that the excess dirt and shrubbery are stored where you want them.

You will have some handwork to do. Clean all dirt away from the existing foundation wall where the new walls will meet it. With a spade, shape the sides of trenches at footing level until they are vertical. Lay your carpenter's level both along and across the excavation under footings, then cut away high spots and fill low spots. Finally, clean away all loose soil where you will form for footings.

FOOTINGS

During excavation the contractor probably removed the cords in your batter boards, and worked from corner stakes. Now that he is gone, put the cords back in place to use as a guide for marking the locations of footings

on batter boards. This procedure isn't necessary when the trench acts as a form.

Locating Forms

From each nail holding a cord, measure 4" *away* from the foundation wall (Fig. 6-8). Measure half the width of the wall if it is not 8" thick. At these points cut saw kerfs (inset) in batter boards, and drive new nails at the house. They mark the outside of your footings.

Now move your cords to these outer kerfs and nails. Where cords cross, tie a plumb bob on a string so that it clears the excavation by a few inches. When the plumb bob stops swinging, it will mark the exact corner of your footing. Temporarily mark the spot with a piece of steel reinforcing rod. Repeat process at all corners.

Building Forms

To build forms use 2 × 2s for stakes and 2 × 8s, a pair of 2 × 4s, or ¾" exterior-grade plywood for sides. Drive a pair of stakes at each outside corner as shown in Fig. 6-8, and a single stake at the corners against the house. Measure up 8" from the bottom of the excavation on each stake, and make a mark. Then stretch a cord between all stakes on the marks.

Begin forming at a corner, nailing form boards to the insides of stakes, with their tops against the cord. Add stakes about every 8' and near the end of each side piece. When you finish forming the outside edge of the footing, the top inside edge of all form boards should be touching the cords at all points.

Now cut a piece of 2 × 2 or 1 × 4 to the width of your footing, and use it as a spacer to locate the inside faces of the other set of form boards. Drive stakes for support as before. With both sets of forms in place, lay your carpenter's level across them to make sure that their tops are exactly level. This level is critical to building a vertical foundation wall.

When a Trench Is the Form

With no forms to guide you to the proper depth of a footing poured in a trench, you must use other means. The simplest solution is to drive 1 × 2 stakes into the bottom of the trench. Place the stakes in the center of the trench near the house, at each corner, and about every 8' between. To determine how far in to drive stakes, measure down from the cord above them the height you established for the block foundation wall, excluding its footing. You fill the trench with concrete to the tops of the stakes, then remove them before the concrete begins to set.

Reinforcement

Footings must be reinforced with steel. The common reinforcement is a pair of No. 3 steel rods, often called **rebars**, placed about 2½" from the sides of forms.

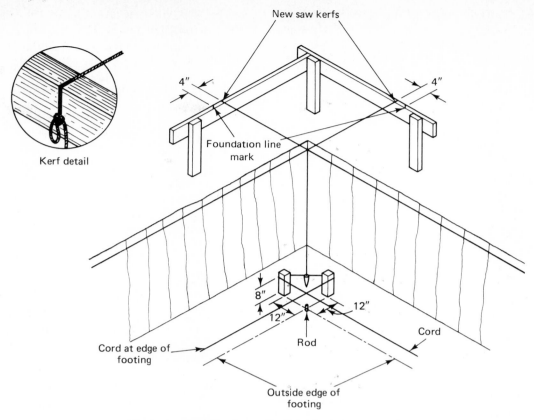

New saw kerfs

4"

4"

Foundation line mark

Kerf detail

8"

12"

12"

Rod

Cord

Cord at edge of footing

Outside edge of footing

Figure 6-8. Locating forms for footings in an excavation.

Rebars may be cut with a hacksaw and bent in a vise. Where two lengths meet, they should overlap 12 to 18″ and be wired together so that they stay in position. The bars are usually laid in position in forms, then raised about an inch by hand after the concrete is poured.

Concrete Mix

You can buy ready-mixed concrete in small quantities, but if you are a long way from a supplier, you may want to mix your own. The best mix is 1 part portland cement to 2¾ parts sand to 4 parts aggregate no larger than 1½″. With dry or damp sand add about 6 gallons of clean water for every sack of cement. With wet sand, add only 5 gallons. These proportions will give you about 8½ cu ft of concrete per 94-lb sack of cement, or enough for about 9½ linear feet of 8″ × 16″ footing.

For a 10′ × 14′ addition with 34 linear feet of footing, then, you would need four sacks of cement (each sack contains 1 cu ft), 11 cu ft of sand, 16 cu ft of aggregate, and 20 to 24 gallons of water. You'll have a little concrete left over.

If you rent a cement mixer, build a wood box with *inside* dimensions 1 ft square and 1 ft deep. Draw lines on the inside at depths of 3″, 6″, and 9″ so that you can measure as little as ¼ cu ft accurately. Place the mixer as close as possible to the point of use. That way you'll spill and waste less. Make a chute if you have to pour from a height of more than 4′.

As you pour, force the mix against the sides of forms with a spade, working it up and down to release trapped air. Position rebars after you spade. Be sure that the forms are filled right to the top but not over the top. Use a straight board to level the concrete, working the board back and forth across the mix while resting it on the tops of forms. Use a small metal float to bring excess water to the surface.

While fresh concrete is curing, keep it covered with straw, burlap, or any other material that retains moisture. Keep the covering damp for four to five days. This prevents water from evaporating too quickly and weakening the footing.

You can remove the forms after 48 hours in warm weather or 96 hours in cold weather. Remove the stakes first, then gently pry off the forms, being careful not to damage the concrete. If you intend to put form boards to other use—and there's no reason not to—clean them as you remove them. You can save cleanup time by coating the sides of forms with clean oil before installing them.

FOUNDATION WALLS

Brush off the tops of footings after they have cured, and snap chalk lines on them to mark the outside and inside edges of your foundation wall. Then set the first course of concrete blocks in place without mortar to see how the spacing works out. Begin at the four corners; any partial blocks should fall in midwall. The standard mortar joint to allow is ⅜″, but you can reduce it to as little as ¼″ if necessary to avoid cutting blocks to fit. Do not increase the spacing; you only invite leaks.

Mortar Mix

For mortar, mix one part masonry cement with three parts fine, clean sand. These proportions are by volume, so use your measuring box. Mix cement and sand together on a mortar board, then gradually add water until the mortar is wet enough to spread easily but sticky enough to hang on your trowel. If the mix is too stiff, add water and remix thoroughly. If the mix is too runny, add a little sand and mix it in completely. Do not add cement.

Mix only enough mortar to last for 2½ hours. Until you learn from experience how much this is, start with the minimum porportions above. Once mortar stiffens or hardens, throw it out.

Where New and Existing Walls Meet

New foundation walls under a concrete slab or around crawl space don't need to interlock with existing foundation walls, as long as you have good load-bearing soil and a sturdy footing. Just butt the two walls together with a good mortar joint, and seal the joint with parging. More about parging later in this chapter.

If you are expanding your basement, however, you'll have a stronger foundation if you tie the two walls together. A tie-in is practical for the amateur, however, only when both new and old walls are concrete blocks. You must break out part of the old wall where the new wall meets it.

Begin by snapping vertical chalk lines that run between the outer chalk lines on your footings and the nails in the boards that you attached to the house early in construction. If you built properly, these chalk lines will be plumb. If you planned wisely, the chalk lines will fall at mortar joints in every other course of blocks, making the job of breaking out much easier.

You probably won't be able to save the blocks you knock out. Take care, however, to avoid disturbing the mortar joints or the blocks that remain in the wall. Remove only the blocks shown in Fig. 6-9.

The best method is to make two vertical cuts along lines A and B with a power saw equipped with a masonry-cutting wheel. Cut so that you remove not only the block but the masonry mortar joint on both ends. Then chip around the remaining half-blocks on each side of the opening, and knock them outward with a sledge or masonry hammer. Remove all mortar from the exposed blocks. Have a piece of polyethylene available to cover the opening in case of a sudden rain.

As a final step before beginning to lay blocks,

remove all exterior wall material that hides the top of the old foundation between the vertical chalk lines. If any material, such as a length of siding, extends beyond the chalk lines, carefully pry off the entire piece and set it aside for reuse. Do not remove any sheathing yet; leave it to protect the interior of the house from weather as long as possible.

A Course Pole

To keep courses of concrete block level, make a course pole. A **course pole** is simply a board at least as long as your foundation wall is tall, with marks on it every 8″. The marks indicate the level of the top of each course. A course pole is a valuable tool when you are interlocking with an existing wall or matching an existing wall height.

The First Course

Beginning at the house, spread a full bed of mortar about 1″ deep and 6′ long on the footing between the chalk marks. Then, with your trowel, cut a furrow down the middle of the bed to make sure you have ample mortar along the entire edge of each block. Basic procedures for laying blocks are illustrated in Figs. 13-15, 13-16, and 13-17.

Set your supply of blocks within easy reach and with the greater core surface *face up*. Most blocks have one core surface slightly greater than the other. By placing this surface up, you provide the maximum mortar bed for the next course.

Lay the first block at the existing foundation wall. Choose a stretcher block if its end butts against the existing foundation. Butter with mortar the end that will touch the old wall. Then press the block into the bed of mortar until its top is 8″ (or whatever the mark on your course pole) above the footing. Use the handle of your trowel to tamp the block level, and check that level with a carpenter's or mason's level. At the same time make sure that you are aligned between chalk lines.

If you have cut into your existing foundation wall, and the end of the first block lies flush with the inside surface of the old foundation, use a corner block. Before setting it in the mortar bed, however, butter the end of the exposed block in the existing wall and half the top core surface of the corner block. Set the block carefully so that you don't wipe off the mortar. Use plenty of mortar to assure a solid joint. Removing excess mortar is easy; correcting a poorly filled joint is not.

With the first block laid, now lay three or four more stretcher blocks on the footing. Butter the end face of each block fully with mortar, and set it in place against the previously laid block. After you set each block, check the thickness of mortar joint, block alignment, plumb, and level. Make any adjustments *now* before the mortar begins to set. Adjusting after

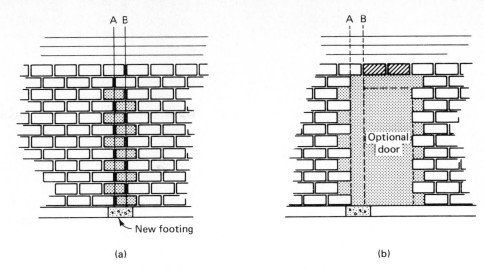

Figure 6-9. The foundation wall of an addition should meet an existing foundation wall at mortar joints if possible. Then, to tie walls together, you need to remove only the blocks shown shaded in (a). To cut a door through the wall, remove blocks in the shaded area in (b), and set the door jamb flush with blocks on the side away from the new wall. Crosshatched blocks (b) may either be removed or supported on jacks if there is more than one course above the opening.

mortar begins to stiffen breaks the bond and leads to leaks. Then scrape off excess mortar with the edge of the trowel, and drop some in each core hole to form a better bond with the footing. Throw the remainder back onto your mortar board.

Corner Pyramids

Experienced masons build corners four or five courses high in a pyramid. Thus they can stretch a cord between corners as a guide for laying each course level.

Before laying successive courses of blocks, spread mortar generously on the exposed surface of the finished course below. Then apply mortar to both ends of blocks (Fig. 6-10). This method, known as **face-shell bedding**, provides a double thickness of mortar at each vertical joint and assures tight, well-filled joints. As you set each block, tip it slightly toward you so that you can see the edge of the course below. Swing the block into place; never drag it through the mortar.

Spread mortar in advance only for as many blocks as you can lay in 30 to 45 minutes. You won't set many blocks in the first hour, but will gradually gain speed as you get the hang of the job. Don't rush, however. It pays to build a foundation wall right.

At outside corners lay three or four more blocks along the adjacent footing. When you have four blocks at corners against the house and four in each direction at outside corners, start the second course.

After you have built your pyramids, fill in the courses between them. Always lay blocks so that vertical joints are half a block apart in adjacent courses. This pattern is known as **running bond** or **regular bond**.

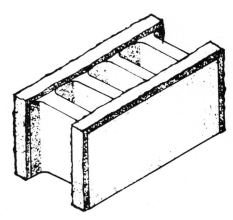

Figure 6-10. Apply mortar to shells at the top and both ends of each concrete block.

By alternating the direction of corner blocks in courses, you automatically lay a running bond pattern.

When you must break or cut a block to fit in the middle of a wall, use a power saw with a masonry blade for a clean vertical cut. You can break blocks by scoring them and hitting them sharply with a hammer, but they won't always break where you want them to. Remember to allow for mortar joints at both ends when you determine the lengths of cut blocks.

Ventilators

In the foundation for an addition you shouldn't have to provide openings for plumbing or electrical connections. You will need to ventilate crawl space, however, and also to provide access either to crawl space or a basement from the existing house.

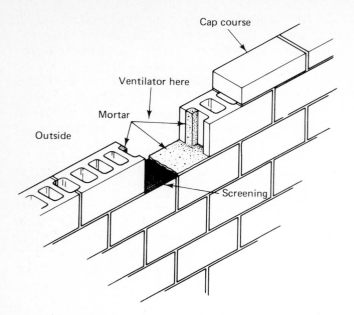

Figure 6–11. The floor of the opening for a ventilator must be covered with screening as a base for mortar. You install ventilators at the same time as you lay the course of blocks directly above them—usually the cap course.

Ventilators are exactly the size of a concrete block—8″ high and 16″ wide. Two are adequate under small additions open to other crawl space, placed opposite each other near outside corners. Otherwise use three, two opposite each other near the house and one near the middle of the third wall. Ventilators allow air to circulate, and prevent moisture problems in crawl space. They should be left open all year long.

Ventilators go in the course just below the cap course, so omit a block when you lay that course. Then set the ventilators when you lay the cap course. Cover the two half-blocks in the course below the opening with a piece of screening (Fig. 6-11). Then spread mortar on the screening to form a sill, and on the sides of the opening toward the outside of the wall. Set the ventilator in place, add mortar in the top channel, and proceed with the cap course.

Windows and Doors

You install steel basement windows like ventilators, except that you use sash blocks instead of stretcher blocks at the sides. You can set them on a precast concrete sill or form one out of mortar.

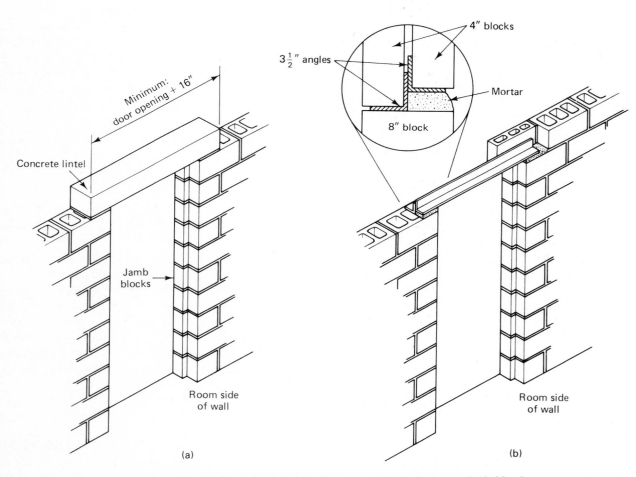

Figure 6–12. Walls above openings for doors and windows may be bridged by concrete lintels (a) or pairs of angles supporting blocks only 4″ thick (b). Both lintels and angles must extend at least 8″ on both sides of an opening.

The weight of any masonry above an opening more than 16″ wide must be supported. There are two ways (Fig. 6-12). One is to use a precast concrete lintel 16″ longer than the width of the opening. The other is to install two 4″ blocks instead of 8″ blocks across the opening, and support each on 3½″ × 3½″ × ⁵⁄₁₆″ angles set back to back and offset for the door or window frame. The depth of the offset is the same as the offset in a jamb block.

The best location for a door through an existing basement wall into new basement space is at one corner of the addition. You have already broken through the wall here anyway, and filled the outside wall with full blocks and half blocks as you built your pyramid. Inside the basement enlarge the opening one block in height and two more blocks in width (Fig. 6-9b). Support the masonry above the opening temporarily with a pair of jacks. Then square off the opening to a 32″ width by using full-size corner blocks in every other course, and half-size double corner blocks in the alternate courses. Over the door opening, install a lintel.

The Top Course

Cap blocks are made in two sizes (see Fig. 6-2). Blocks 4″ thick are solid; 8″ blocks have partial cores on the bottom. Both types are laid like stretcher blocks, and form a smooth, solid surface on which to lay the wood sill plate.

The sill plate must be anchored to the foundation wall. One way is with ½″ anchor bolts 18″ long, made in the shape of a J (Fig. 6-13a). The bent end fits into the

core of the block below the cap block, which you fill with mortar. Set bolts every 8′ between cap blocks, 3″ from the outside edge of the wall. Let the threaded ends stick up 2½″ above the cap blocks.

For the top course you can use stretcher blocks instead of cap blocks, but you must lay strips of ¼″ hardware cloth two courses below (Fig. 6-13b), and fill all cores of the top two courses with mortar, troweled smooth at the top of the wall.

The other type of anchor, ideal when stretcher blocks form the cap course, is the V anchor. It consists of two lengths of flat metal which you fit together into a V, and a spacing tab that establishes the correct width to fit over the sill plate (Fig. 6-13b). Set the anchors into wet mortar in cores until the spacer is flush with the top of the wall. Make sure that all anchors are the same distance from the edge of the wall—at the outside edge of the core.

Tooling Joints

After mortar in the joints is hard enough so that you can't push your thumb into it, but still soft enough to show your thumbprint, tool the joints. Use a **sled-runner**, a masonry tool with a handle and a rounded blade, or a **jointer**, which has the same blade but no handle. Pull the tool along the joint with just enough pressure to compact the mortar. Tool horizontal joints first, then vertical joints. Scrape off loose mortar with your trowel. Where horizontal and vertical joints meet, you will probably have to tool twice in each direction for a smooth joint.

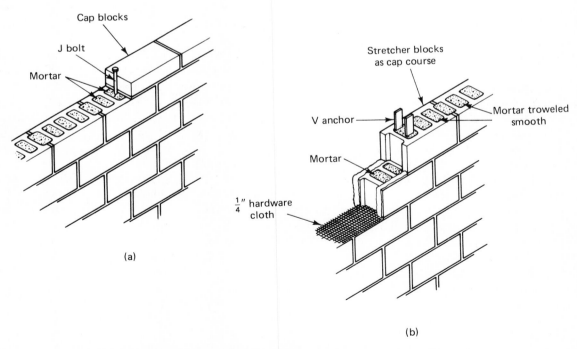

(a)

(b)

Figure 6–13. J-bolts (a) and V-anchors (b) connect sill plates to the foundation. Note that hardware cloth (screening) must be laid in the mortar joint two courses below stretcher blocks that are used in place of cap blocks.

PARGING

A foundation wall around crawl space or under a slab does not need to be waterproofed. A basement wall does. The process is called **parging**, and it has seven steps.

First, with a nozzle spray, dampen the wall but don't soak it. Second, using a mortar mix, trowel a first or **scratch** coat ¼″ thick on the outside of walls from the top of the footing to a point about 6″ above finished grade. Because soil must slope away from the wall, finished grade is about 2″ higher than the original ground level.

Third, before the scratch coat fully hardens, roughen the surface with the point of a trowel, a hand cultivator, or a garden rake. Roughening assures a good bond with the next coat. Let the coat dry for 24 hours. Then, as the fourth step, dampen it with a nozzle spray.

Fifth, apply a second ¼″ coat of mortar mix. Feather the coat at the top of the wall, and curve it over the top of the footing to help water drain away from the house. Sixth, keep this coat damp for at least 48 hours by spraying. Then let it dry thoroughly.

Finally, apply two coats of a mixture of asphalt or hot tar—a waterproofing compound—over a prime coat recommended by the manufacturer of the compound. You can either brush or spray these three thin coats. For best results with a brush, apply the first finish coat horizontally and the second finish coat vertically.

DRAIN LINES

You should install drain tiles around your new footings under two conditions: (1) if you cut through a similar drain line when you excavated, or (2) if you have problems with moisture coming through your existing foundation wall.

Drain tiles are usually 4″ in diameter, and come in lengths from 1 to 8′. Some types have small perforations so that groundwater can enter on all sides. Lay the tiles with a ¼″ gap between their ends, and cover the top half of the joint with a strip of building paper that keeps dirt out of the drain line.

Drain lines must slope at least 1″ for every 8′ of length, and drain into a dry well, sewer, or other disposal point. The layout of your drainage system depends on more factors than can be covered here. Obviously, you can't simply extend an existing drain line around an addition and achieve the required fall. For help in laying out the system and learning code restrictions on disposal, contact your building inspector or county engineer.

Lay tiles in a bed of coarse gravel. To assure proper slope, nail a block cut from 1″ lumber (and therefore ¾″ thick) to one end of a 2 × 4 exactly 6′ long. Set this device on the tile line with the block down,

and use a level to check the 1-in-8 slope required. Add more gravel until drain lines are covered about 18″, then add fine gravel to about 6″ below finished grade.

BACKFILLING

There are three advantages to backfilling as soon as possible after parging the foundation and installing drain tiles. First, you eliminate the danger of falling into the trench. Second, it is easier to move framing members because you can stack them closer to their point of use. But most important, you prevent a sudden heavy rain from filling the trench and making it too muddy to work for several days.

Before you backfill, remove all debris from around the foundation, including roots and building materials. Then shovel dirt into the trench by hand. Backfill in layers about 8″ deep, and tamp each layer before adding the next. By compacting the soil as you fill, you reduce the amount the soil will settle. Place the final couple of inches of backfill when you finish grading at the end of the job, and rake the soil so that it slopes away from the foundation.

SILL PLATES

The first wood members to go into place are sill plates. Cut plates from 2 × 6 lumber that has been chemically treated at the mill to protect against insects and moisture. Sill plates should be a single length of lumber if possible. If not, plan the joint between pieces so that it does not fall directly under a joist.

Edges of sill plates should lie ¾″ back from foundation walls (Fig. 6-14). If you hold them in position with anchor bolts, lay out the plates on the top of the wall, mark the locations of bolts, and drill ¾″-diameter holes. With V anchors this step isn't necessary.

Sill plates don't touch the foundation, but rest on a seal. For a seal you can buy asphalted gaskets that are ½″ thick but compress to about ¼″ under structural weight. Simply cut gasket strips to length, punch holes to fit tightly around anchor bolts, and set them on the foundation.

As an alternative you can use mortar as a seal. Dampen the top of the wall, then brush or trowel on a thin bonding coat. You can buy a manufactured bonding coat that comes in quarts and gallons, or you can make your own from a mixture of cement and water. Before the bonding coat dries, trowel on a layer of mortar to a depth of about ½″. Set sill plates in the mortar, place a 1½″ washer over each bolt, and thread on the nuts. Tighten the nuts with a wrench, using your carpenter's level constantly to make sure that you set the plates exactly level. This process will squeeze out excess mortar. Wipe off the excess with your trowel, and tool the joint on both sides.

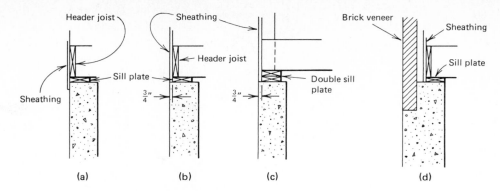

Figure 6–14. Sill plates may be positioned in three ways: flush with the outside of foundation walls (a), with sheathing extending down the wall 1″; inset ¾″ from the outside edge in platform (b) or balloon framing (c), with sheathing resting atop the wall; or flush with the inside edge of foundation walls (d) when exterior material is brick or stone veneer.

With either type of seal, toenail lengths of sill together at corners and where lengths butt together.

TERMITE PROTECTION

Termites are soft-bodied antlike insects that feast on the cellulose in wood. They have been found in all 48 states of the continental United States, but are found most commonly in areas where trees are abundant and rainfall is heavy. You should protect any addition, as well as your entire house, against them.

A sill of treated lumber won't stop termites; they will bypass it with an earth tunnel. One solution is to bend a shield made of galvanized metal over the foundation wall beneath the gasket. A still better and more common solution today is chemical soil poisoning. Companies that offer this type of termite protection are listed in classified telephone directories under "Pest Control." For an annual fee they will respray and assure that your house is free of termites. Have this done after you have backfilled and before you lay subflooring on floor joists. But compare prices and quality of service; they vary, and you want to choose a company that stands behind its guarantee.

A LEDGER

As long as floor joists run parallel to the existing wall of the house, sill plates are the only support those joists need. If joists run at right angles to the wall, however, you must add a ledger at the wall for support. A ledger is a 2 × 4 or 2 × 6 securely nailed to the edge joist at the house (Fig. 6-15).

Sheathing on the existing wall will be in the way of setting a ledger. Remove only enough to expose the edge joist and bottom plate of the exterior wall. Leave the rest of the sheathing in place to protect the wall against weather until you have the addition enclosed. Cut the ledger to the length of the sill plate opposite it. Then set it so that its bottom edge is about flush with the top of the foundation wall and its top edge is absolutely level. Attach it with a pair of 12-penny (12d) nails near the ends and about every 16″ between.

Although your foundation is now complete, this is not a good stopping point. Get the floor framed and covered to protect your new basement or crawl space from weather. Put off pouring a basement floor (see Chapter 11) until you have the roof on your addition, but remember to allow some access from outside for chuting concrete.

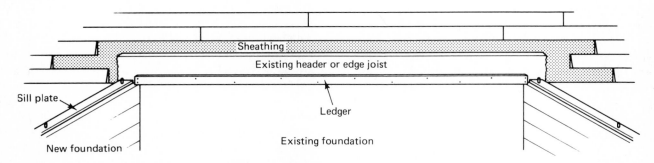

Figure 6–15. Ends of joists perpendicular to an existing house wall are supported on a ledger, and notched to fit over it. The top of the ledger must be level, and the bottom at the same height as the top of the foundation wall.

Building An Addition— Framing

(a)

(b)

When you add on, remove only as much exterior material as is in the way of attaching new walls and roof. During construction (a) vertical siding and the sheathing behind it are gone, but insulation and windows are still in place. After the walls are framed but before they are raised, the eave must be cut and windows removed. Note in the finished addition (b) that exterior materials, window style, and roof pitch match those of the existing house, even though the new roof is a shed with clerestory windows that throw light deep into new rooms. (Courtesy American Plywood Association.)

The platform framing system is now by far the most common method of framing a house. The floor structure consists of a sill plate, header joists, edge joists, regular joists, and bridging (Fig. 7-1). Complete houses usually have a girder or beam to support joists too short to extend from wall to wall, but few additions are that large. The inset in Fig. 7-1 shows typical girder construction when required.

THE FLOOR FRAME

With foundation work done and sill plates in place, assemble a box sill consisting of header joists and edge joists the same size as regular joists. When your joists

run parallel to the existing wall, cut two header joists the same length as the sill plate; the single edge joist is the same length as regular joists (Fib. 7-1a). When joists run at a right angle to the existing wall, cut one header joist the same length as the parallel sill plate, and two edge joists the length of regular joists (Fig. 7-1b).

With parallel joists, set one header in place so that its side is flush with the sill plate, and its ends are flush with the end of the sill plate and the edge joist of the existing house. Use a framing square to mark the cuts so that both ends are square. With 8d nails toenail the header joist to the sill every 16″. Keep the joist as vertical as possible, but don't worry if it leans slightly. Set the opposite header joist in the same way.

Now measure the distance between header joists at

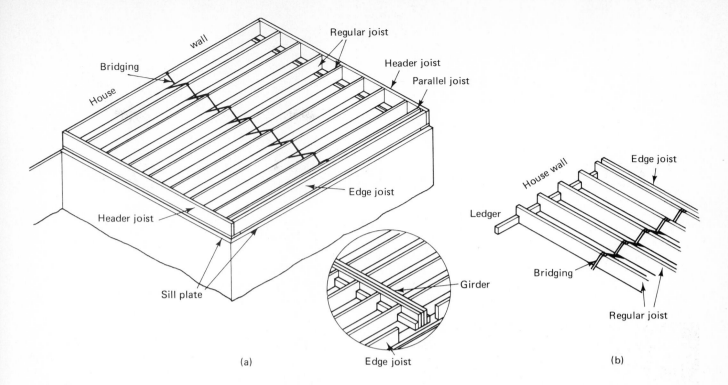

Fig. 7-1. Platform framing consists of regular joists surrounded by header and edge joists of the same size, all resting on a sill plate and stiffened by bridging. Shown is framing with joists parallel to the house wall (a), and with joists perpendicular to the house wall (b). Shown in the inset is construction at a girder when the distance between opposite walls is too great to span with a single length of joist.

the sill plate, and cut all joists to this length. Set the edge joist first to complete the box sill and to straighten header joists. Check corners for square. Toenail the edge joist to the sill, then drive three 16d nails through header joists into each end of the edge joist.

With right-angle joists, set the single header joist flush with sill plates at the side and both ends. Then measure the distance between the header joist and the existing edge joist at the house to determine the length of edge and regular joists. All regular joists must be notched to fit over the ledger (Fig. 7-1b).

After you complete the box sill, snap a chalk line between the tops of edge joists along the wall above the ledger. Then measure the distance from the line to the ledger at various points. If the foundation, ledger, and edge joists are all level, the dimension should be constant. This dimension is the end height of regular joists after they are notched. The depth of the notch is 1½″. Cut all joists before you notch or set any.

Next, measure off 47¼″ from the corner of the addition along the top of each header joist (or header joist and ledger), and make a mark. Then measure every 16″ in each direction and make additional marks, all measured from the 47¼″ mark. With a framing square carry the marks down both faces of the joists (Fig. 7-2). Place an × next to each line on the side *away* from the

corner. You use these lines to locate joists, and the ×s tell you on which side of the line to set regular joists.

Do you see the reason for the 47¼″ dimension? The sheets of plywood you use for subflooring are 48″ wide. The edges of each piece must meet on the centerline of a joist. Because joists are 1½″ wide, the edge of the first supporting joist is ¾″ from the centerline and 47¼″ from the corner, where subflooring is flush at the edge.

Standard joist spacing is 16″, which is a maximum. Under most additions you won't need to vary this spacing. The dimension of your addition across joists should be divisible by 16″. Here are the possible exceptions:

- Always add a joist parallel to the edge joist and flush with the opposite edge of the sill plate (see Fig. 7-1a). This joist helps to support the exterior wall.

- When joists run parallel with the existing house wall, add a joist at the house, nailing it not only to the sill plate but also to the existing floor frame.

- Under any partitions in the addition that run parallel with floor joists, double the joists. No extra support is needed when partitions are at right angles to joists. The centerline of the par-

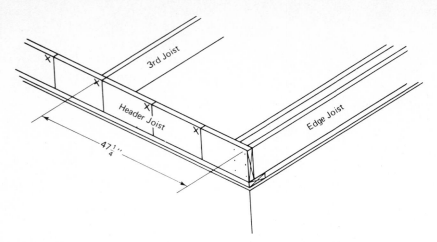

Fig. 7–2. For joists parallel to the house wall, measure off 47¼″ from each outside corner along header joists, then every 16″ from that mark in both directions. The Xs tell you on which side of the mark to set joists. For joists perpendicular to the house wall, measure off 47¼″ from all four corners along the header joist and ledger, then every 16″ until the distance between the two middle marks is 16″ or less.

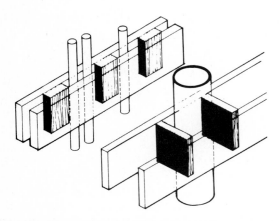

Fig. 7–3. When pipes rise into a partition parallel to joists, separate the supporting joists with spreaders— 2 x 4s nailed flat when pipes are 1″ or less in outside diameter, or joist stock nailed at right angles beside larger pipes.

tition should fall directly above the centerline of the pair of joists.

• When a partition contains pipes, ducts, or electrical conduit, separate the doubled joists with **spreaders** (Fig.7-3). The centerline of the partition should lie above the centerline of the spreaders.

• If spacing doesn't come out evenly when joists rest on a ledger, space joists evenly from outside walls toward the center, and let the smallest spacing occur in the middle of the floor framing.

All extra joists and spreaders must be the same depth and thickness as regular joists, and should be cut from the same lumber stock.

Setting Joists

Lumber today is quite consistent in depth, but it pays to measure the heights of joists at their ends just to make sure. The tops of regular joists must be flush with the tops of header joists. If necessary, notch the underside of a too-deep joist to fit over the sill plate. Add a shim under a too-shallow joist to raise it to flush.

Before you set any joist on its marks, recheck all joist locations to make sure they are correct. Also look at each joist that you've cut to length, to make sure that the piece is straight, and that any **crown** (high point) is up. Almost all lumber has some crown in it; when placed up, the weight of the floor helps to straighten it.

Setting joists is easiest with two people, one to hold one end of a joist on its mark while you nail the other end on its mark. If you must work alone, drive a nail part way into one end of the joist about ½″ from the top, and set the joist in rough position. Then go to the other end and nail it. Now go back to the first end, remove the helping nail, drop the joist into correct position, and nail it.

At each end of each joist nail through the header joist with three 16d nails. Drive the top nail first, then recheck the end of the joist for position, plumb, and level. Drive the bottom nail next and the middle nail last. Then toenail through the joist into the header near its top and bottom.

Before you go any further, check your floor structure one more time. Header and edge joists must be straight and corners square if walls are to be straight and corners square. Sight down all regular joists to be sure that all crowns are up, the sides are plumb, and all tops are flush. Unless they are, you'll never get the subfloor smooth. Make certain also that joists under joints in subflooring are straight.

Bridging

Bridging serves several purposes. It stiffens joists and therefore assures a firmer floor. It holds joists in line at the correct spacing. And it spreads heavy loads over more than one joist, thus preventing sag, uneven deflection, and future cracks in the floor, walls, and ceiling.

Of the three types of bridging, two are easy for the amateur to install. Use solid bridging if you had to trim at least 14½″ off joists when you cut them to length. **Solid bridging** consists of lengths of joist material fitted between joists at their midpoints and staggered slightly for easier nailing (Fig. 7-4a). Under any other circum-

sheets slightly less than 48″ wide and 96″ long, the difference allowing for expansion. Edges may be square, shiplapped, or tongue-and-groove. All are satisfactory; the cost and quality of subfloor increase with the complexity of the edge.

Check the corners of the first sheet for square, then position it at an outside corner of your addition, with its long dimension across joists. With tongue-and-groove plywood, set the grooved edges outward. With shiplapped plywood, trim the outer edges square, and lay the first piece with the longer shiplapped edges down. With 8d nails, first secure the three corners over header and edge joists, then the fourth corner. Space other nails 6″ apart into the box sill, and 10 to 12″ apart into regular joists.

Sheet 2 (see Fig. 7-5) will probably complete the

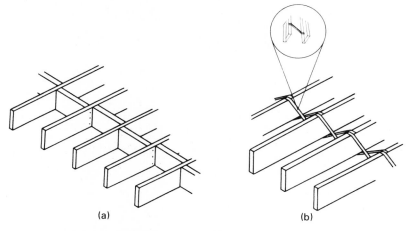

Fig. 7-4. Use solid bridging (a) when you have the scrap lumber available. Otherwise, use manufactured steel bridging (b). The inset shows method of nailing.

stance, use manufactured bridging. **Manufactured bridging** is made of steel bent to fit over the top of one joist and against the bottom of the adjacent joist (Fig. 7-4b). You install this bridging in pairs, and nail through the holes provided.

Cross-bridging, the third type, consist of pairs of 1 × 3 struts. It is the least expensive type, but the ends must be cut at an angle to assure a good fit. This takes time that you can better spend on other construction.

Bridging should be installed as soon as joists are in place, and before you lay subflooring. Nail the bottom ends of steel bridging after the subflooring is in place. Delaying this step lets you adjust joist spacing.

Subflooring

The best and most common material for subflooring is ½″ CDX plywood. It is made with exterior glue, and will withstand a rain until you get the roof on. It comes in

first row. Cut it to length, allowing for a gap about the thickness of a dime at sheet 1 and an equal gap at the house.

Sheet 3 is usually a half sheet, but it can also be one-third or two-thirds of a sheet, depending on the dimensions of your addition. Plan your subflooring layout for minimum waste, but install no piece less than 32″ long. Stagger joints between panels so that they are at least two joists apart for a stronger floor. If sheet 2 is no more than 60″ long, use the offall as sheet 3. Set the factory edge on the centerline of the joist, nail, then trim the edge with a power saw. When you come to the final row, again cut to length, nail, then trim to width along the header joist.

A COMMON RAFTER

The next step in construction is to cut a common roof rafter. You'll see why shortly. To cut a rafter you have to know the pitch of the roof on your addition.

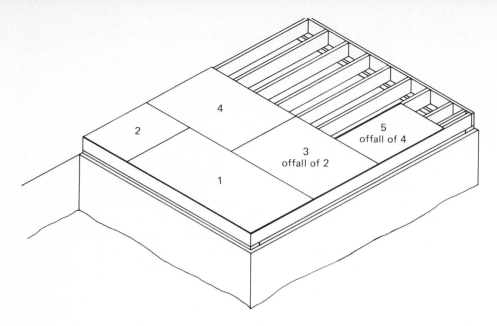

Fig. 7-5. Typical layout for subflooring in a small addition.

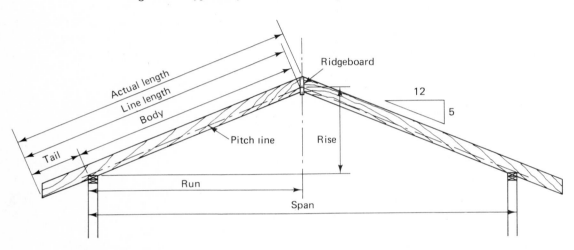

Fig. 7-6. Common terminology used in framing roofs, and the triangular symbol for roof pitch.

Roof Pitch

As long as your addition is not as wide as the house, use the same roof pitch. If the addition is wider, maintain the same ridge and eave heights, and lower the pitch. This is an acceptable solution when the pitch on the addition is no less than 3 in 12.

To understand how to frame a roof, learn the meanings of four terms: span, run, rise, and pitch (Fig. 7-6). The **span** of any roof is the distance between the outer edges of the plates atop exterior stud walls. The **run** is half the span, or the distance from the edge of one wall plate to the centerline of the ridgeboard.

If you draw an imaginary line parallel to a roof beginning at the edge of the plate, that line, called the **pitch line**, intersects the ridgeboard somewhere below its midpoint. The vertical height of the roof between the top of the plate and this point of intersection is called the **rise**. The **pitch** of a roof is the ratio of rise to run, with the run always stated as 12. Thus a roof with a 5 in 12 pitch rises 5' for every 12' of run.

Existing Pitch. How do you find the pitch of your existing roof? If you have a set of plans, look there first. The pitch is usually shown as an inverted triangle just above a roof slope in one or more of the elevation drawings (see Fig. 7-6). If you have no drawings to go by, you'll have to measure, but this isn't too difficult.

Climb a ladder until your eyes are just slightly above the **rake** (side edge) of a gable, shed, or gambrel roof. Carry with you a carpenter's level, a folding rule, and a pencil. Against a smooth section of the **fascia** board—the broad piece of trim along the rake—set your level. Adjust it until the bubble is centered, then draw a horizontal line along the top (Fig. 7-7a) to the trim board. Next, measure off 12" from the trim along this line, and make a mark. Place your level upright on this mark and draw a vertical line to the trim board. Lay your level against the trim between the two marks to make sure that it is reasonably straight. Then measure the length of the vertical line. If the dimension is 5", for example, the roof pitch is 5 in 12.

To find the pitch of a roof with constant eave height, such as a hip or mansard, you may have to get on the roof. Take the same tools as above, plus a sheet of plywood at least 18" square. Set the plywood upright on the roof slope; the job is easier if someone else holds it in place. With your level, draw a horizontal line to the edge of the board (Fig. 7-7b). About 15" from the edge, make a mark. Through the mark draw a vertical line, and carry it downward to the edge of the plywood. Then from the intersection of the two lines, measure off 12" on the horizontal line. Through that point draw a line parallel to the bottom edge of the plywood until it intersects the vertical line. The length of the vertical line is the rise.

Incidentally, save that piece of plywood, and carefully saw along the lines. The triangle is called a **pitch board,** and you use it many times while framing a roof.

Laying Out a Rafter

A common rafter lies at right angles to the plate supporting it, and extends from the eave to the ridgeboard. Most of the rafters in the roof of an addition are common rafters, so it pays to lay out a sample rafter accurately, then cut all others like it.

The shortest side of a pitch board represents **unit rise,** and the side that meets it at right angles represents **unit run,** which is always 12". The hypotenuse represents **unit length.** To determine the length of the **body** of the rafter—the part between the ridgeboard and plate—you simply multiply the unit length times the run of your roof stated in feet.

Let's suppose that your addition is 12'-0" wide, and the roof overhangs 18" on each side. Then the run of the roof is 7½':

$$\frac{12 + 1\frac{1}{2} + 1\frac{1}{2}}{2}$$

If the pitch is 5 in 12, the unit length is 13", as calculated by the Pythagorean theorem. Therefore, the line length of a common rafter here is 7½ × 13" or 97½"—a little over 8'. Table 7-1 gives unit lengths for common rafter pitches.

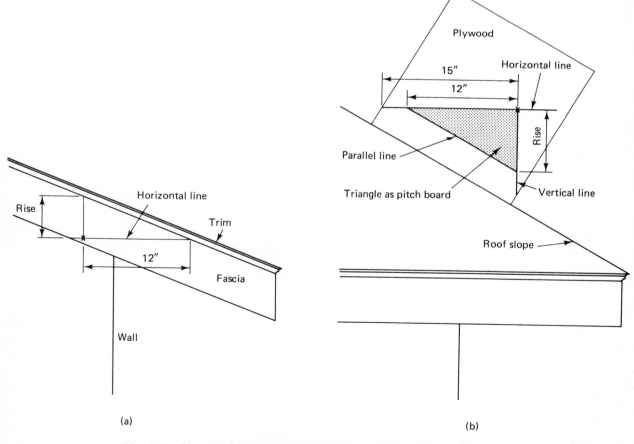

(a)

(b)

Fig. 7-7. How to determine the pitch of an existing gable roof (a) or hip roof (b). The shaded area of plywood in (b) is a pitch board.

Table 7-1. Determining the unit length of a common rafter.

When unit rise (in.) is:	Pitch is:	Unit length (in.) is:
2	2 in 12	12.17
3	3 in 12	12.37
3½	3½ in 12	12.50
4	4 in 12	12.65
5	5 in 12	13.00
6	6 in 12	13.42
8	8 in 12	14.42
12	12 in 12	16.97

The **line length** of a rafter is the body length plus the tail length (see Fig. 7-6), but it is not actual cut length. Because rafters run at an angle, you have some cutting waste at both ends. But line length does guide you to what length of rafter stock to order. In this case you need 10' lengths, or you can cut two rafters out of one 18' length.

For additions less than 16' wide (8' span), 2 × 6s spaced 16" o.c. are adequate to support loads in most of the country. But live loads range from 20 to 50 lb. The usual wind load is 15 lb, but may be 25 lb in hurricane areas. Snow loads range from none in Florida to 90 lb in parts of Maine and some areas of the Rockies. So check with your building inspector or county engineer, or rely on your building supply dealer for selecting the right size rafter stock.

Mark the Sample Rafter. From the rafter stock you receive, select the straightest piece you can find for your sample. Then use a carpenter's square and a sharp pencil to lay out the cuts. Check the rafter for any crown, and lay it flat with the crown toward you. You mark on the bottom edge—the edge away from you.

Start near the end to your right. Lay your framing square on the lumber with the **blade**—the longer side—to your left. Set it so that the 12" mark on the blade is at the top edge of the rafter (the edge nearest you), and the unit rise mark (5" in our example) on the **tongue**—the short side of the square—is also at the same edge (Fig. 7-8a). It doesn't matter whether you use the marks on the outer or inner edges of the square, as long as you are consistent. When you have the square properly placed, draw a line along the outside edge of the tongue. This marks the **plumb cut**—the line at the centerline of the ridgeboard.

You can lay out the length of the rafter either by measuring it on the side nearest you, or by stepping it off. In the **step-off-method,** lay your square against the plumb cut line and slide it up or down the line until the unit rise mark on the tongue and the 12" mark on the blade lie at the edge of the rafter *nearest* you. Make a mark on the edge of the rafter at the 12" point, then move the square down the rafter as shown in Fig. 7-8b. If the run of your roof is 7' and the run of its overhang

is 2', for example, you move and mark nine times, then draw a line through the final mark parallel to the plumb cut line. This marks the **tail cut.** If your run is not in even feet, say 9'-6", set the square against the plumb cut line with the 6" mark on the blade (instead of the 12" mark) at the edge of the rafter. Mark that point, then step off full-length units.

To mark the **bird's mouth**—the notch that fits over the plate at the wall—step off the body length of the rafter from the plumb cut line, just as you stepped off the total length. Draw the plumb cut line for the bird's mouth parallel to the plumb line at the ridge (see Fig. 7-8c). Then measure 3½" at a right angle to this line toward the top of the rafter and draw a parallel line (Fig. 7-8d). Finally, where this line touches the edge of the rafter, draw another line at right angles. This line marks the **seat cut** (Fig. 7-8e).

You now have only one more line to draw. The plumb line at the ridge marks the centerline of the ridge, and you must allow for half the thickness of the ridgeboard. A ridgeboard may be either a board, which is ¾" thick, or a plank, which is 1½" thick. Mark off half its thickness at right angles to the plumb cut line and draw a parallel line (Fig. 7-8f). This is the **shortening line.**

With your sample rafter marked, lay out another just like it so that you have a pair to test for fit. Do not make any cuts until you complete the test.

Testing the Fit. To test the accuracy of your work, snap a chalk line down the center of your sub-floor under the future ridge. Then lay the rafters flat on the floor so that the bird's mouths fit at the corners of the floor, and the plumb cuts overlap the thickness of the ridgeboard. If the cut lines are just slightly off, adjust them. Otherwise, lay out a new pair of rafters. Don't try to force a fit.

When you are satisfied, cut along both shortening lines. Then set a short piece of ridgeboard material upright along the chalk centerline and retest the fit. Then and *only* then can you safely make the cuts at the tails and bird's mouths.

Determine how many pairs of common rafters you need, and cut them to match your samples. Include the samples in your count. You need a pair at the end of the rafter plate where it meets the existing wall. In a gable roof without an overhang at the rake you need another pair over the gable, and a pair every 16" between the two pairs. In a gable roof with a side overhang you need the same number, but omit the bird's mouth in one pair. In a hip roof the final pair falls at the end of the ridgeboard, and you may need one more single common rafter (see "Framing A Hip Roof" later in the chapter).

THE ROOF INTERSECTION

To help you visualize what happens where the old and new roofs meet, draw a plan of the roof. Lay a sheet of

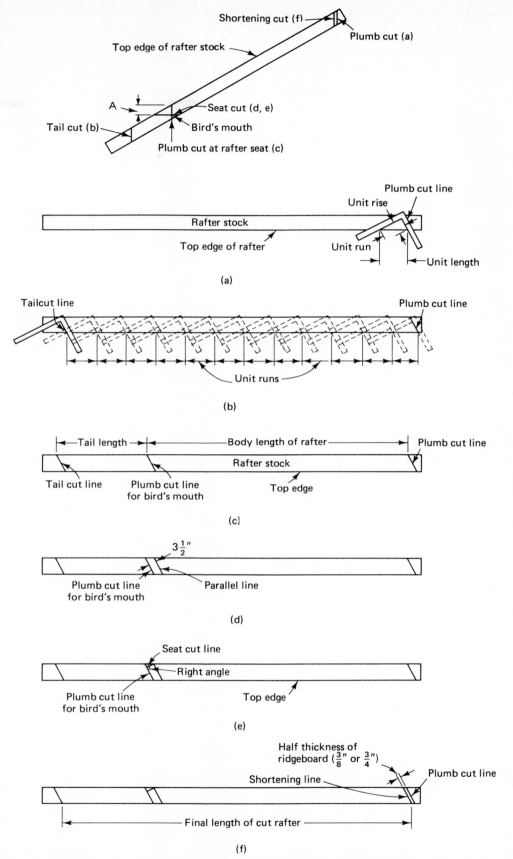

Fig. 7–8. Marking the various cuts in a common rafter: (a) plumb cut; (b) tail cut; (c) plumb cut at bird's mouth; (d) plumb line for seat cut; (e) seat cut at bird's mouth; (f) shortening cut.

tracing paper over your floor plan and tape it down at the corners. Show the intersections of exterior walls in dotted lines. Where these lines intersect, draw a pair of lines at 45° representing the roof valleys. Then draw the ridge line of the addition midway between the wall lines. It should meet the two valley lines where they intersect. Finally, draw in the eave lines of the existing house and its addition. They, too, should meet on the 45° valley lines.

Now transfer this information to the actual roof. Earlier you marked on the existing wall with a chalk line where the new walls would intersect. Carry these lines (A in Fig. 7-9) onto the fascia and edge of the roof by dropping a plumb bob from the fascia until it lines up with the new walls. Then measure over the horizontal width of overhangs on the addition, and mark these points (B). Next, mark the centerline of the addition (C).

Up on the roof, snap three chalk lines (D, E, F) at 90° to the eave; they represent a continuation of wall and ridge lines. Follow the Pythagorean theorem to assure that the lines are at right angles to the eave and parallel to each other. Then measure on your sample rafter the distance from the tail cut to the plumb cut at the bird's mouth. (This distance is the unit length of the rafter times the amount of overhang expressed in feet.) Lay off this distance (G) on the roof along both extended wall lines, measuring from the eave. Make sure to allow for overhanging roofing materials when you lay off these distances. Now connect the two marks with one more chalk line (H). This line should lie directly above the stud wall below. If you are working with brick veneer, you have to adjust all measurements by 6″ taken horizontally. You need the stud line, not the veneer line.

Finally, stretch a cord from the intersection of the eaves (B) over the intersection of the walls (where D and H meet) and to the centerline. Mark this point (I) with chalk. Then repeat this step on the other side of the addition. The second cord should meet the centerline at point I. If not, go through the process again. When lines are correct, drive a nail into the roof at point I, and snap a pair of chalk lines (J and K) from there to the eaves. These lines mark the location of the valleys between roofs.

Cutting Away

The eave of the house is in the way of wall erection and roof construction. To give you working room, cut with a power saw along chalk lines. If the undersides of rafters are covered by soffits, cut them first from underneath to expose roof construction. Then you can see whether anything is in the way of cutting that might cause a problem.

Cut through gutters with metal shears, and remove the section between cuts. Then either raise the open ends or dam them with cement or putty so that rain will flow away from new construction. With your power saw set for a shallow cut, slice through the roofing material and sheathing and ¼ to ½″ into rafters. You may hit some nails, so use a metal-cutting blade. Be careful to hold the saw plumb, not at right angles to the roof slope. Cut upward along lines J and K in Fig. 7-9 from the eaves to the wall line. Then work from the midpoint of the wall line (H) toward the other cuts. Finish the cuts with a saber saw.

WALL FRAMING

The easiest way to build walls is flat on the subfloor, then raise them into position. Build them in order of length, with the longest wall first. Your walls will pro-

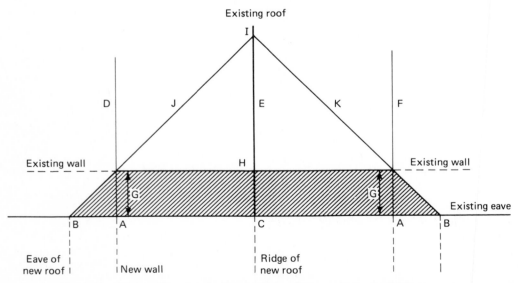

Fig. 7–9. How to lay out the intersection of the roof of an addition on an existing roof.

bably be short enough so that you can build them with window and any door openings already framed, and still be light enough to raise with a little help from your friends.

Stud Length

As long as your addition is not an enlargement and completely open to an existing room, exact ceiling height isn't important. The standard ceiling height today is a nominal 8'. Add ½" for the thickness of ceiling material, and a ½" gap at the floor to allow for installing 8'-high wall materials, and you have 97" between the top of the subfloor and the undersides of ceiling joists. This is also the height of your walls. Since you have a **bottom plate** (also called a **sole plate**), a **top plate**, and a **cap plate** each 1½" thick, the total length of studs is 92½". If your dealer can provide you with studs cut to length (they are called **P.E.T.** for precision end trimmed), order them this length.

But if you intend to cut your own, calculate *all* your lumber needs before ordering. As you know, 2 × 4s of stud grade come in lengths of 8', 10', 12', 14', 16', and sometimes 18'. Suppose that you order all 8' lengths. You can cut your studs all right, but you will have a pile of useless 3¼" blocks left over. Remember that you have window sills, **cripples** (short studs) below windows, and perhaps some blocking in walls and partitions. So make a list of all the lengths you need, and the quantities of each length. Allow ¼" for each saw cut. Then work out the most economical mix. You may find that a mixture of 8', 12', and 16' lengths works out most economically.

Corner Posts

Build posts for outside corners first. They consist simply of two studs and four or five spacers 8 to 12" long. Nail the spacers to one stud as shown in Fig. 7-10, then nail the other stud over the spacers. The corner posts fit at the ends of the longest wall or walls.

Window Frames

Next assemble window frames. In his literature the window manufacturer tells what size opening (called the rough opening) to provide. The **rough opening** is the horizontal dimension between **trimmers** (Fig. 7-11a) and the vertical dimension between **sill** and **header**. For best appearance the header should be at the same level as headers for other windows in the house when floor levels are the same. Keep the header level constant, and let sill heights vary as necessary.

The length of a window header equals the width of the rough opening plus 3". The height of a header depends on this same width. Use the following data as a guide:

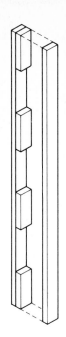

Fig. 7-10. Corner posts of walls consist of a pair of studs with 2 x 4 spacers between them, each 8 to 12" long.

Rough opening	Use a pair of:
Up to 4'	2 × 4s
4 to 6'	2 × 6s
6 to 8'	2 × 8s

Between the pairs of header pieces fit a piece of ½" plywood cut to the same dimensions. Then the header is the same 3½" thickness as a 2 × 4 stud. Assemble the header by nailing through the plywood from both sides with 8d nails.

To assemble the window frames, lay a pair of studs together edge up, and mark on both the location of the underside of the header. Then separate the studs, set the header on its marks and square and flush, and fasten it in place with 16d nails driven through the studs. Cut a pair of trimmers the length of the rough-opening height, and nail them in place from the window side. Cut the sill member the same length as the header, and install it square and flush at the end of the trimmers. Finally, cut cripples to fit above the header and below the sill. Nail one to each length of stud; don't install the remaining cripples until you erect the wall and know the correct locations.

Door Frames

Assemble the frame for any exterior door in the same general way, using two studs, a header, two trimmers, and two cripples (Fig. 7-11b). To keep the frame square, tack a 1 × 6 across the face of the opening near the bottom, then add a diagonal brace from corner to corner.

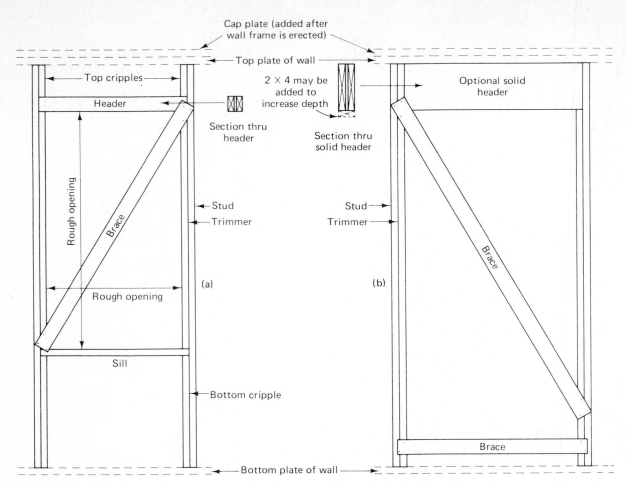

Fig. 7-11. Window frames (a) consist of a header, sill, and a pair of trimmers around the rough opening specified by the window manufacturer. A door frame (b) is similiar without a sill. Frames should be attached to studs and braced before you set them in position.

Plates

The top and bottom plates of any stud wall are the same length, and should be cut from single lengths of 2 × 4 when possible. If the wall is longer than available lengths of plate stock, you must splice. Plan splices so that they fall between studs.

Put the two plates together edge up, and mark stud locations on both at the same time. How do you know where they fall? Well, you know that you will have corner posts at the end of the longest wall or walls (1 in Fig. 7-12), and a single stud where a wall butts against either a corner post or an existing wall (1A). Mark them with lines and ×s to show on which side of the line to set the stud or assembly. Then measure in 18¾″ from the end of a plate with a corner post to mark the location of the first stud.

Next, mark the locations of studs that will support joints between sheets of interior surface materials (2 in Fig. 7-12). Measure in 50¾″ from the end of a plate with a corner post to the location of the first supporting stud, and every 48″ thereafter. Measure 47¼″ from the end of

a plate that butts against a corner post, then every 48″. Let irregular measurements fall at the opposite corner from where you start.

Now, from drawings, find the centerlines of windows and doors, and their rough-opening widths. Mark the centerlines on the plates, then measure off half the rough-opening dimension in each direction to locate inside edges of trimmers (3 in Fig. 7-12). Next, mark the locations of the other studs spaced at 16″ o.c. (4 in Fig. 7-12).

Where Partitions Intersect

Finally, mark on the subfloor with chalk the centerlines of intersecting partitions. Then measure 1¾″ on either side to locate the sides of studs in the partitions. To provide a nailing base for a strong corner and also a surface for attachment of interior wall materials, you must have a stud in exterior walls (5) with ¾ to 1″ of its edge exposed on each side of the partition. If the partition falls against one stud, simply add another (Fig. 7-13). If the partition falls between studs, add two. Sometimes you

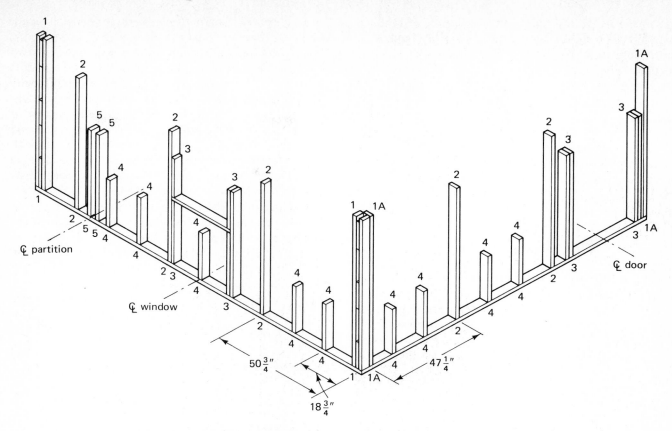

Fig. 7–12. Where to place studs in exterior walls. In a wall with a corner post (1) the first stud lies 18¾" from the end of the plate, and the first stud to support interior materials (2) is 50¾" from the corner. These dimensions are 3½" less in a wall with no corner post but only a stud (lA). Other members shown are door and window frames (3), regular studs (4), and studs to support interior partitions (5).

can adjust a marked stud location to accommodate a partition, but you are wise not to tamper with standard spacing when you can avoid it.

WALL ASSEMBLY

Within a foot or two of the edge of the subfloor where it belongs, lay the bottom plate on edge with stud marks up. Next set corner posts and end studs in position, then the top plate. Next, position window and door frames, then all full-length studs. At this point you should have all wall components laid out ready for assembly except for cripples above and below openings.

Before you assemble the parts, check all studs for straightness. Replace any with twist or crook; a bow of not more than ½" can be corrected. **Crook** is warp from plumb in the width of a member; **bow** is warp from plumb in the thickness of a member. **Twist** is warp in both directions.

When all parts meet your approval, nail posts and studs on their marks with a pair of 16d nails driven through the plates. Drive nails part way into the bottom plate, then check alignment with your square before you

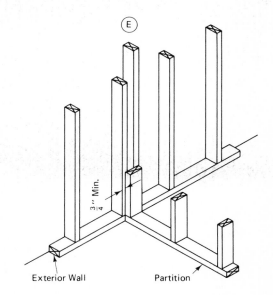

Fig. 7–13. Where a partition butts against a wall or other partition, you need two studs to support edges of wall materials. If one stud already exists with at least ¾" of its face exposed, simply add another (E). Under all other circumstances add two studs.

drive nails home. Complete all nailing to the bottom plate first. Then tack 4′ lengths of 1 × 6 diagonally across corners to hold them square while you nail the top plate. The braces will assure a square wall.

After you nail the top plate, add the cripples at openings. Then give the assembly one final look. Make sure that no studs are cocked, that all studs are flush with both edges of both plates, and that studs are perpendicular to both plates. Finally, measure the diagonals to make sure that the wall is square. If not, remove the braces and rack the wall until diagonals are equal. Then renail the braces. Braces should not extend beyond the edges of the assembly.

RAISING A WALL

As you raise a wall, it tends to slide on the floor until you get it upright. To keep the wall from sliding off the subfloor, tack a pair of 2 × 4 stops to the edge joist about a foot from each end of the floor. Stops should extend about 6″ above the subfloor so that you can easily knock them off when they have served their purpose.

Where a wall meets the house, snap a vertical chalk line on each side of the addition as a setting guide. At this time remove any exterior wall materials that are still in the way, and sheathing at the points of intersection. You can remove all sheathing between the new walls at this time if the weather looks good, but the more you leave in place the better your old wall is protected until you have the addition under cover.

Where the new walls will intersect the existing wall, there must be a stud into which to nail the corner stud. If there isn't, add it now. Finally, at outside corners lay a 12′ length of 1 × 6 where you can reach it in a hurry. You use it to brace the wall once it is raised.

With preparation out of the way, call on two people to help raise each wall. With you in the middle and a helper at each end, lift the wall at a uniformly slow speed and let it slide against the stops. Avoid racking the wall as you move it. When the wall is close to final position—flush with the subfloor at the side and ends—you can move it the final fraction of an inch with a couple of hammer blows. Then with 16d nails, nail the bottom plate through the subflooring into edge joists between the corners and first studs *only*. Finally, while your helpers hold the wall plumb and you use a level to make sure, attach a brace running from the side of the corner post to the edge joist. Repeat this procedure at the other end if that end is an outside corner, or nail the end stud into the stud in the existing wall.

Build other exterior walls as just described, and set them in position. Again nail only at ends. At corners nail walls securely together with 16d nails, driving them through end studs into corner posts every 8″.

Tieing Walls Together

Atop the top plate you need to add a cap plate to tie walls together. Cap plates are not the same length as top plates because they overlap them at corners (Fig. 7-14). They will be either 3½″ or 7″ shorter or longer, depending on which walls contain corner posts. Cut cap plates from the straightest lumber you have available. Avoid splices, but leave 3½″ gaps where cap plates of partitions will intersect the exterior wall.

Before you nail cap plates in place, tack a pair of small 1 × 2 blocks at the corners of the wall so that

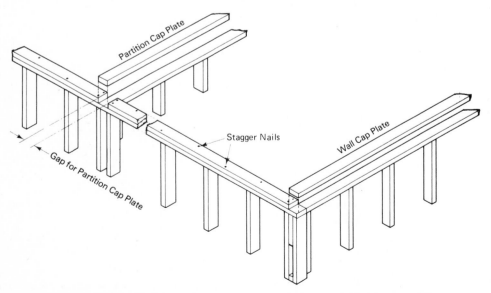

Fig. 7–14. Cap plates of shorter exterior walls and interior partitions overlap the top plate of long walls to tie corners together. Note that nails are staggered from side to side except at the ends of cap plates.

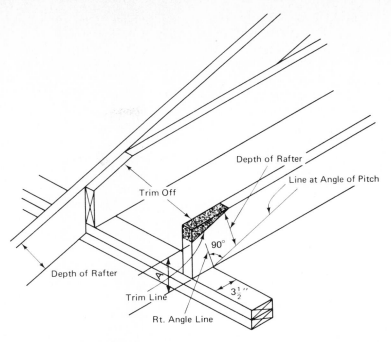

Fig. 7–15. Ends of ceiling joists under sloping roofs must be trimmed flush with the tops of rafters. Dimension A is the vertical distance from the seat cut to the top edge of a common rafter.

they stick up 2″ above the top plate. Then stretch a cord between the blocks and tie it. Cut a third block of the same size and stick it in your pocket.

Set the cap plate in position, flush with the top plate and the end of the partition. Nail with a pair of 16d nails at one end. Then work your way toward the other end of the wall, placing nails ¾″ from an edge about every 24″ and staggering locations from side to side. Drive nails part way in, then slip the block in your pocket, called a **gauge block**, between the plates and the cord. Move the plates until the block lightly touches the cord, then nail. The gauge block helps you straighten the wall, and the cap plate maintains straightness.

If you are working on a long wall with splices in both the cap plate and top plate, set the cap plate so that there is at least 24″ between splices. A 48″ gap is better. Then strengthen the splice in the top plate with a 14½″ block beneath it nailed to both plate and adjoining studs.

Final Nailing

Only after your walls are straight should you go back to the bottom plate and finish nailing it to the floor structure. Nail straight down between studs into header and edge joists, and either at an angle beside joists into regular joists or through studs into an edge joist.

To check the quality of your attachment job, look underneath the subfloor. If you see the ends of many nails that have missed joists completely, your nailing job isn't satisfactory.

CEILING FRAMING

Ceiling joists should always run the same direction as common rafters in the roof, and almost always the same direction as floor joists. They are usually 3″ longer and 2″ narrower than floor joists. Code requirements for live loads on ceiling joists are less—most often 20 lb instead of 40 lb. Where 2 × 10s may be required for a floor, 2 × 8s are adequate for a ceiling. Because ceiling joists not only support roof load but prevent walls from bowing out under that load, they must be strong in tension as well as resistant to bending. And they must be securely nailed.

Cut joists to length, which is equal to the span of the addition's roof. But before you install them, you must trim their ends. (If your roof is flat, no trimming is needed.) Lay joists down with their crowns *away* from you, and the end to be trimmed to your left.

Pick up one of your sample rafters, and measure the distance between the seat cut and the top of the rafter along the plumb cut line for the seat (A in Fig. 7-8, top). Transfer this dimension to the ends of all ceiling joists. Then, using your pitch board, draw a diagonal line parallel to the roof pitch (Fig. 7-15). The little triangle of wood above this line must be trimmed off so that ceiling joists don't stick up above rafters.

On the cap plate mark the locations of ceiling joists, just as you marked the top plate for studs. In most cases studs and joists will line up.

For the moment don't install the joists nearest to and farthest from the house. With 12d nails toenail the other joists to the cap plate (which is known as a **rafter plate** to roof craftsmen) on the side away from the × s. Rafters go on the other side. Set joists as upright as possible. They may get a little out of plumb as you toenail, but you can correct that when you install rafters. Staying on the marks is more important.

THE RIDGEBOARD

As stated earlier, a ridgeboard may be either ¾ or 1½″ thick. Straightness is more important than thickness. Boards are less likely to be straight than planks, but they are easier to cut and lighter to handle.

The ridgeboard should be at least as wide as your plumb cut on the ends of rafters is long. As a rule of thumb, use a ridgeboard 2″ deeper than rafters—a 1 × 8 ridgeboard with 2 × 6 rafters, for example.

As long as the pitches of the roof of the house and your addition are the same, you can easily calculate the ridgeboard's length. With a gable roof its length is equal to the length of the addition parallel to the ridgeboard, plus half the span of the addition. With a hip roof its length is the same as the length of the addition, plus any overhang at the rake. Order a ridgeboard at least 2′ longer than this calculated length. It's better to waste a little material than to cut the ridgeboard too short and waste all of it.

Along the top of the ridgeboard, working from the sloping cut, measure off the distance equal to the run of a common rafter plus 1½″, make a mark, and put an × beyond it. The × indicates the location of the pair of common rafters nearest to the house. To mark the locations of all other rafters, follow the spacing of the ceiling joists below.

If your ridgeboard is longer than you can cut from one piece of lumber, you must splice. Let the splice fall between rafters. Cut the two ends square, then nail a piece of ridgeboard stock no less than 12″ nor more than 14″ long across the joint. The ridgeboard should be raised in one piece, so splice before you assemble.

One end of the ridgeboard must be cut to the shape of the roof. Mark the cut with your pitch board. The outer end of the ridgeboard gets a plumb cut, which you make after the roof is assembled.

ROOF ASSEMBLY

To assemble the roof, you need a working platform about 4′ wide centered under the ridgeboard. Use sheets of plywood for this purpose. Place them so ends meet over ceiling joists, and nail them at the outside corners with double-headed nails that are easy to remove later. You can reuse the plywood for sheathing.

Where the ridgeboard butts against the house roof, remove only enough shingles to permit nailing. Do not remove or cut into the roofing paper beneath. Then call upon three agile people to help you assemble the roof frame in midair. Lean cut rafters against the rafter plate where they will be installed, with tails down and plumb cuts up.

Select two common rafters. With three 8d nails driven through the ridgeboard into rafter ends, attach one rafter on the second mark from the outside end of the ridgeboard, and the other on the second mark from the inside end. Nail both rafters on the same side of the ridgeboard.

Now raise the ridgeboard slowly until the bird's mouths of the two rafters rest on the rafter plate. Have your three helpers support the ridgeboard—one at each end of the working platform and the third at the end against the house roof at the chalk line. You shove the rafters tight against the rafter plate and tight against the ceiling joists. Then with at least eight 16d nails attach the rafter, toenailing into the rafter plate (3 nails) and directly into the joist (5 nails).

Next, set the two opposite common rafters in place. Nail at the rafter plate as before. At the ridgeboard toenail through the plumb cut into the ridgeboard with three 8d nails.

Check both sets of rafters for plumb, and make sure that the ridgeboard is level. Then toenail the cut end of the ridgeboard to the sheathing of the existing roof. Your roof frame should now be stable and self-supporting.

Install two more pairs of rafters next to each pair of rafters already installed, working toward the center of the addition. After each pair, sight down the ridgeboard to make sure that it is straight, recheck its level, and check the rafters for plumb. Continue to install pairs until the middle of the roof is completely framed.

If your roof has no overhang at the end, install the pair of end rafters flush with the outside edge of the plate. They must be absolutely plumb. Cut the end of the ridgeboard flush with the rafters.

More likely, however, your roof will overhang. In that case you have no end rafters. Instead, you have a pair of **fly rafters**, which are common rafters without a bird's mouth (Fig. 7-16). Fly rafters are supported at their ends by the ridgeboard and a fascia board, and in the middle by ladders. The ladders rest on the gable wall, which you build shortly.

First, however, set the outside ceiling joist with its outside edge flush with the *inside* edge of the end rafter plate. At the other end of the addition nail the final ceiling joist across the ends of cut rafters in the existing roof. It is because of the location of this joist that cuts through the roof must be plumb.

To stiffen the roof structure add 1 × 6 collar beams across every third pair of rafters as in Fig. 2-4. You don't really need them, however, with roof spans of 16′ or less.

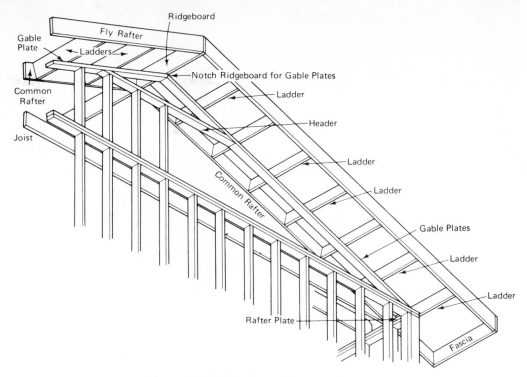

Fig. 7–16. Detail of a roof overhang at a gable.

The Gable Wall

A gable may be framed in several ways. The simplest way is to mark the centerline of the roof on the cap plate, measure off ¾" in each direction, then mark every 16" in both directions from that first set of marks. Gable studs vary in length, but with this method you have two of each length.

Studs in a gable wall without overhang run from the cap plate to the underside of the end rafter. In a wall with an overhang they butt against the underside of a gable plate (see Fig. 7-16). The line length of a gable plate is the same as the length of the underside of a rafter from the *plumb line* (not the shortening line) to the seat cut for the bird's mouth. Each plate gets a plumb cut at one end and a horizontal heel cut at the other. The plates meet at a notch cut into the ridgeboard. Use your pitch board to mark the cuts at the proper angle.

The space under the roof of your addition must be ventilated. You can install ventilators at the eaves or the ridge (see Figs. 8-12 and 8-13, respectively), or you can install louvers in the gable. You need 1 sq in. of free ventilating area for every 2 sq ft. of floor space. **Free ventilating area** is the size of openings for vents less the areas of louvers or screening that block the free flow of air. You can buy metal louvers for gables that adjust to your roof pitch. Frame the bottom of the louver opening with a header. All studs beneath it are the same length.

To mark and cut remaining studs, measure from any mark on the cap plate vertically to the underside of the gable plate or end rafter. The difference between the lengths of adjacent studs is the same. It is called the **common difference**, and is equal to $1\frac{1}{3}$ times the unit rise. (The $1\frac{1}{3}$ is the ratio of standard stud spacing of 16" to the unit run of 12.) So if your roof pitch is 5 in 12, the common difference is $1\frac{1}{3} \times 5$ or $6\frac{2}{3}"$, or about $6\frac{11}{16}"$. Cut all gable studs to length. Then, with a pair of 10d nails, toenail studs into the cap plate, and with two more toenail into the gable plate or end rafter.

To assemble the overhanging roof at the rake (Fig. 7-16), first cut ladders out of rafter stock. Their length is the distance from the face of the last pair of common rafters to the edge of the cap plate, plus the amount of overhang, less $1\frac{1}{2}"$ for the thickness of the fly rafter. Space ladders 24" apart, beginning at the ridge. Avoid hitting ceiling joists by placing one ladder just above them, and adding another just below them after you install the fly rafter. Nail through the fly rafters into the ridgeboard and ladders with three 8d nails at each point. Then trim the end of the ridgeboard flush with the fly rafter. Fit and trim the fascia as a final step.

Where the new roof meets the old, you can complete construction in two ways. If you don't intend to open attic spaces to each other, remove the roofing material between your diagonal chalk lines (J and K in Fig. 7-9), and cut jack rafters to fit between the ridge and the old roof's sheathing.

To open the spaces to each other—and you'll have

a cooler addition if you do—you must cut through the entire roof structure along the diagonal chalk lines. Be sure to keep the cuts plumb. Connect the unsupported ends of the cut rafters with valley rafters. Then cut jack rafters to fit between the valley rafters and the new ridge.

FRAMING A HIP ROOF

The center part of a hip roof is built of common rafters like a gable roof. At the hip end, however, you place the first pair of common rafters at a distance from the end wall equal to the span of a common rafter (Fig. 7-17).

Cut the ridgeboard flush at that point, and brace it with a common rafter set at the midpoint of the end wall. Then determine the length of the two hip rafters and the shorter jack rafters in the hip.

To find these lengths, look on the blade of your framing square. On one side you will find a column of six numbers. If your unit rise is 5, say, look in the column under the number 5. The first number down is 13.00", which is the unit length of a common rafter in a roof with a 5-in-12 pitch. The next number is the unit length of a hip rafter. You multiply this number times the same number of units you have in a common rafter to find the length of the two hip rafters. At their upper ends these rafters get a double cheek cut (Fig. 7-18c). At their lower ends give them a plumb cut if the ends will be exposed, or a double cheek cut if you cover them with a fascia board. Cut the bird's mouth as shown in Fig. 7-18d.

Jack rafters get the same cut at the eave as a common rafter, and a single cheek cut (see Fig. 7-18b) at the other. The difference in lengths of adjacent jack rafters is a common difference, as in gable studs. This common difference is the third number in the column on your framing square; with a 5-in-12 pitch the common difference is 17⅝". Cut the first jack rafter this much shorter than a common rafter, and each successive jack rafter the same amount shorter again. You need four jack rafters of each length to complete the hip.

To start either a single or double cheek cut, mark the centerline on the top of a piece of rafter stock. Mark the plumb cut (AB, in Fig. 7-18a) as shown in Fig. 7-8, and square this line across the top of the rafter (BC, Fig. 7-18a). At 90° to line AB measure off half the 45° thickness of the roof member it butts against (¹⁷⁄₃₂" if the member is a board and 1¹⁄₁₆" if the member is a plank). At this point draw line DE parallel to AB. This is the shortening line. Square this line across the top of the rafter (EF). Then at 90° to line DE measure off half the thickness of the rafter stock (usually ¾"), and draw line GH parallel to DE. Square this line across the top of the rafter (HI). Point J marks the intersection of line EF with the centerline.

To make a single cheek cut, Fig. 7-18b, draw a line

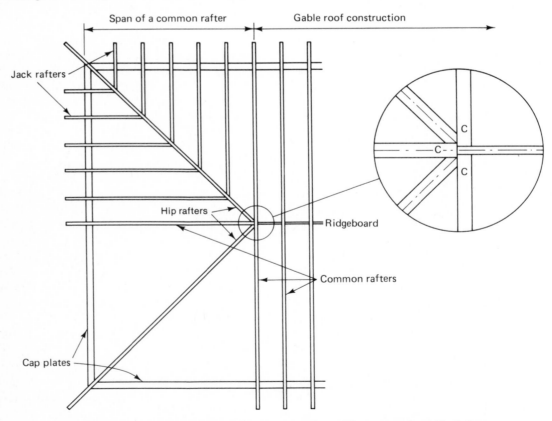

Fig. 7–17. In a hip roof three common rafters (C) meet at the end of the ridgeboard (inset). The centerlines of hip rafters extend outward from the intersections of these common rafters.

Chapter 7 / Building An Addition—Framing

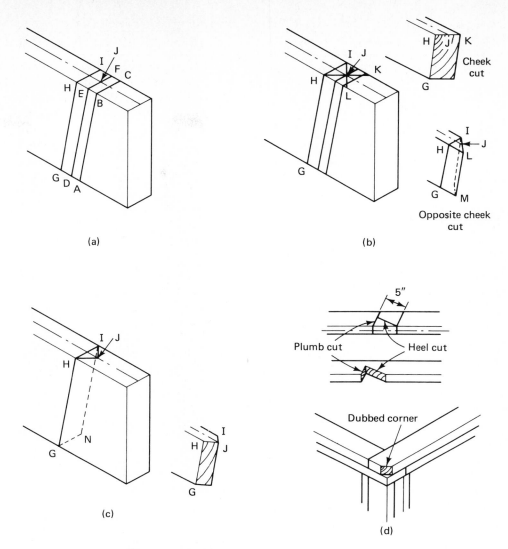

Fig. 7-18. The first step (a) is identical for laying out any cheek cut. Jack rafters need a single cheek cut (b) at the end abutting hip or valley rafters. Hip rafters need a double cheek cut (c) at one end, and a specially cut bird's mouth (d) at the other.

from H through J to K, and cut along lines GH and HK. To make an opposite cheek cut, draw a line from I through J to L, draw line LM parallel to AB, then cut along lines IL and LM. To make a double cheek cut, Fig. 7-18c, square line GH across the bottom of the rafter (GN), and draw line IN. Then cut along lines GH and HJ to the centerline, and along IN and IJ to complete the cut.

To fit a hip rafter plate, mark the heel cut as in Fig. 7-8, but measuring 5″ instead of 3½″. Then dub (trim) the rafter plate to fit (Fig. 7-18d).

ROOF SHEATHING

Before you complete the roof structure where it overlies the existing roof, apply sheathing to the roof and walls. To protect your construction, sheathe the roof first. Use ½″ exterior-grade plywood if your roofing material will

be shingles made of asphalt or asbestos. Under wood shingles or shakes use 1 × 4 boards.

Plywood

Start with a square sheet at one outside edge of the roof at the eave, with the long dimension running across rafters. Set the lower edge in one of two ways. If you leave the ends of rafters exposed, protect them by carrying the lower edge of the sheathing ½″ beyond their ends. Otherwise, set sheathing flush with the ends. Set the inner edge on the centerline of a rafter, and let the outer edge hang over. Trim the excess after you have the entire roof sheathed.

Stagger joints between sheets as you did in laying the subfloor. At the ridge let the top course overlap, and trim it flush with the tops of rafters in the other slope. When you trim the top course on the other side of the ridge, cut flush with the sheathing on the first side.

Table 7-2. Spacing of fasteners in sheathing

Type of sheathing	Plywood	Gypsum	Insulating
Recommended fastener	6d common nails	1¾″ roofing nails	1¾″ roofing nails
Spacing at edges	Every 6″	Every 4″	Every 3″
Spacing into other framing	Every 12″	Every 8″	Every 4½″

Boards

To determine the spacing between boards used for sheathing, measure the exposure of the wood shingles on the main roof. The spacing from centerline of board to centerline of board must be the same as shingle exposure. Normal exposure is 5 to 7½″.

Pick a straight board for attachment at the eave, and set it in one of the two ways described for plywood sheathing. Cut each board so that it ends on the center of a rafter, and stagger the ends so that no two adjacent boards end on the same rafter. Use a pair of 8d nails in each board at each rafter.

WALL SHEATHING

For sheathing walls you can use plywood for bracing strength, gypsum sheathing to protect against fire, or composition sheathing to reduce costs. All three materials are available in sheets 4′ wide and of varying lengths for vertical application. For horizontal application gypsum and insulating sheathing are manufactured in sheets 2′ × 8′, and plywood 4′ × 8′.

Set the first piece of sheathing on the ¾″-wide exposed top of the foundation wall, and line up one edge on the centerline of a stud. Let the other edge hang over the corner. Nail as shown in Table 7-2. If you apply sheathing vertically, order pieces long enough to extend from foundation to rafters to avoid horizontal joints. Apply sheathing horizontally with joints staggered.

When you come to an opening for a door or window, the easiest method is to sheathe into the opening, then cut out the excess, rather than to measure and precut before you apply.

With the roof and wall sheathed, your addition is now fully shaped, structurally sound, and partially protected from weather. But sheathing should be protected from rain as soon as possible. Applications of roofing materials is discussed in Chapter 10, and exterior wall materials in Chapter 13. Interior finishing is covered in Chapters 19, 20, and 21.

Converting Nonliving Space

(a)

(b)

(c)

Garage space next to the living room, even only one car wide, is ideal for conversion. The garage door opening of this small house (a) was fitted with large glass panels and a glass door, all screened by a lattice network (b) on the street side of a narrow deck. A broad 2'-deep bay added on the side (c) increases the visual width of the narrow room, and built-in seating carries through the bay and across the rear wall. Walls and ceiling are surfaced with plywood paneling. (Courtesy American Plywood Association.)

One of the simplest and most economical ways to increase your living space is by converting nonliving space that is already under roof and at least partially enclosed. This solution presents fewer structural problems than an addition, requires less time, and scarcely interferes with household routine. Most likely prospects at first-floor level are, in order of practicality, an attached garage, carport, covered porch, and detached garage. The other possibilities—attic or basement space—are discussed separately in Chapters 9, 10, and 11.

AN ATTACHED GARAGE

A garage connected to the house must meet the same structural code requirements as the house itself. It has

an adequate foundation and a concrete slab floor that may need only finish flooring to be acceptable. It has structurally sound exterior walls, finished on the outside with exterior materials. Studs may be surfaced inside the garage, but chances are slim that there is any insulation between them. The roof is in place and surfaced against weather. Rafters and ceiling joists are likely to be in the same condition as studs.

So you have structurally sound, weather-protected space to work in. You undoubtedly have direct access from the house. Your major costs are for closing the garage door opening, partitioning the space, finishing interior surfaces, and providing insulation, heat, and light. As you develop your floor plan, you have four design problems to work out.

DESIGN PROBLEMS

The most important and first problem to solve is: What are you going to do with the contents of the garage? Where will you store bicycles and tricycles, sports gear, yard and garden tools and equipment, and the miscellaneous things you now keep there? What will you do with your cars?

There are several possible solutions. One is to store the miscellaneous items from the garage in the basement, and provide an outdoor access stairway from the basement directly to your yard. Details of planning and installing a basement access stairway are covered in Chapter 11.

If you don't have a basement, you can build or buy a separate storage shed to place elsewhere on your property, or add storage space outside the garage but attached to it, or partition some storage space inside the old garage. Much depends on what you need to store and where you use it. If the majority of items to be stored are used outdoors, then access to their storage area should be from outdoors. Under other circumstances you may want all storage space accessible from inside the remodeled space, or have part of it open in and part open out. The decision on storage must be made first, because it usually affects the floor level.

Floor Level

When your land slopes away from the garage doors, and good drainage is assured, the garage floor is sometimes at the same level as the concrete slab under part or all of the rest of the house. More often, however, the garage floor is one or two steps down from the level of the main living area. This gives you the opportunity to raise the floor level of the converted space.

When conditions are ideal, it is possible to apply a finish floor of resilient tiles or sheets directly over the concrete slab floor of a garage. But conditions are seldom ideal.

For one thing a good garage floor slopes, either toward a drain or toward the garage doors. This very provision for drainage that is an advantage in a garage is a drawback for most uses to which you are likely to put the converted space. Second, good floor construction calls for a vapor barrier under a concrete floor slab. Its purpose is to prevent ground moisture from entering the slab and causing deterioration of finish flooring. A properly built floor slab will be warm and dry. The question is: Does the garage floor slab have a vapor barrier? Codes don't require it, builders often omit it, and you can't be sure without digging under the slab.

To assure a warm, dry, level floor, then, you will be wise to raise the level of the floor in the new space. In storage space reached only from outdoors, use the old floor. Support the new floor on sleepers (see Fig. 8-3) or a joist system (Fig. 7-1). Often you can do this without affecting the heights of existing doors. Furthermore, if you plan in the new space a bathroom, lavatory, washing machine, or anything that requires a drain, you can make full use of the difference in floor levels to install the plumbing system.

Car Storage

When you convert a garage, there aren't many other places to store a car. In most parts of the country, particularly in snowy climates, garages are as close as possible to the street, to reduce shoveling. So there isn't room to add a garage or carport in front of the one you plan to convert. Seldom is there room on the side of the house, either. There may not even be enough room on the side to put a driveway.

Your only option may be to park cars in the driveway all year long. This has its disadvantages in cold, wet, and very hot climates. Furthermore, some community officials, prodded by real estate sales people, are beginning to pass ordinances that prevent people from parking their cars permanently exposed. At the present time many communities have ordinances that require owners to store boats, campers, and trailers behind the building line. In order to keep communities as attractive as possible, and from looking like used-car lots, officials are extending these restrictions to cars.

So investigate local ordinances and talk to your local political representative to find out if anything might prevent you from converting a garage into livable space. If not, you'll probably need most of your driveway for parking. Consider adding a curb across it, however, to keep cars from bumping into the new room.

The Garage Door Opening

With a driveway still leading up to converted garage space, you won't be able to disguise the old garage completely. But you can minimize the driveway's effect and improve the appearance of your house with good design and planting.

Leave the headers over the garage door or doors alone, and use that height as your starting point. Most garage doors today are 7'-0" high, and the underside of the header is about 7'-1½" above the level of the garage floor. That height is just about ideal when you raise floor level. If your garage doors are 8' high, you may want to add a new header 10 to 12" below the existing one.

But before you decide, make some sketches. First, develop the floor plan of the space by the methods described in Chapter 4. With the space laid out to your satisfaction, draw an overlay showing placement of furniture. Then you can see better where you need daylight, and where you must have artificial light.

A couple of thumbnail sketches may help you visualize what will work best for you. Look at Fig. 8-1. When the garage door opening is close to the main entrance to the house, plan the window arrangement so

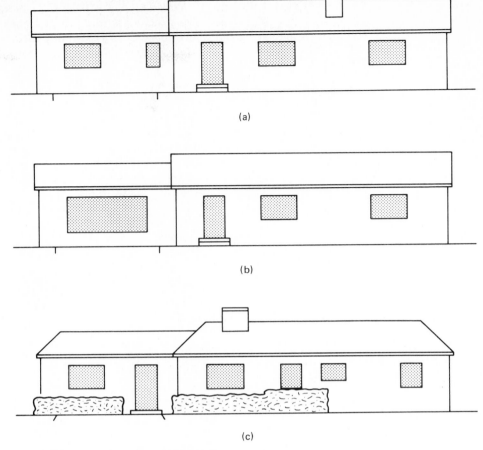

Fig. 8–1. Three possible solutions to closing the opening for a wide garage door. In (a), two windows, one matching existing windows, disguise the old opening. In (b), the entire width is glassed for maximum light, but you do not fool anybody. In (c), planting not only emphasizes a new main entrance, but helps to conceal the old door, which is now a window.

that it visually directs visitors toward the front door and away from the garage. On the other hand, when the garage will be converted to a new living room, screen off the old door and emphasize the new one.

The Driveway

There is nothing appealing about an old driveway that leads to a former garage. But there aren't many practical things you can do about it. Digging it up seems like a needless expense; even if you converted the space into a garden you would need a truckload of topsoil. You could camouflage it by painting it green, but that only helps a little in summer and none in winter.

Perhaps the best solution is to keep the old driveway in use. Build a series of portable planters, large enough to serve as screens but small enough to be easily moved. When you need the entire driveway for parking, set the planters close to the house where they serve as base planting. When you don't need the entire driveway, move the planters out to form a patio. There they offer some privacy to outdoor living space, even though it is on the street side of the house.

STRUCTURAL PROBLEMS

In a garage conversion, structural problems are few. To bring existing space to the point of readiness for interior finishing, the main work includes raising the floor level, installing insulation in walls and ceilings, and closing up openings.

Making a converted garage comfortable for year-round use may be the most difficult part of the remodeling. In much of the country garages are not heated. In cold climates where heated garages are more common, the design temperature in the garage is frequently about 40°F (4½°C)—just warm enough to prevent anything stored there from freezing. Furthermore, few garages are insulated, and many are placed on the most exposed corner of the house.

Before you begin work, then, you must decide how you intend to heat the space, where any water and drain lines will run, and what allowance, if any, must be made for a separate electrical service panel within the converted space. These considerations are discussed in detail in Chapter 5.

The Floor Structure

Ideally, the floor of your converted space should be at the same level as the floor of the room off which it opens. The next best solution is one full step down of 6 to 7″. The most dangerous solution is a difference in level of less than a full step.

So determine first the present difference in height between the finished floor of the house and the finished floor of the garage at the doorway between them. If there is no door, drive a long nail horizontally through the wall at the point where you plan a future door, and measure the distance to the nail on both sides of the wall.

Sleepers. Sleepers are short lengths of straight, flat lumber spaced no more than 16″ apart (see Fig. 8-3). Over a concrete floor you lay them in a bed of adhesive.

You can lay a new floor over sleepers when you have these conditions:

- The garage floor is reasonably level over most of its surface. You can compensate for variations up to ½″ and for slope at a floor drain.

- You don't need the space under the floor for an extension of plumbing or heating systems.

- The floor level in the garage needs to be raised between 2 and 4″. For a minimum raise, use boards a nominal 1″ thick as sleepers, a subfloor of ½″ plywood, and resilient flooring. For a maximum raise, use 2 × 4 sleepers, a subfloor of ¾″ plywood, and wood block flooring. For intermediate raises, use the combination that comes closest to your requirements.

For any other set of conditions, use regular floor joists.

Preparation

If the walls of your garage have finished surfaces, remove a small piece of the finish material in an inconspicuous spot to learn whether walls are insulated. If they are not, start work by clearing walls and ceiling down to the bare structure. Carefully remove trim around windows and doors and elsewhere, and set it aside for reuse. Pry it loose gently with a wood chisel driven behind the trim with the flat surface outward to minimize damage. Let the nails pull through, and remove them later with a cat's paw or the claw of a hammer.

To remove wood or plywood paneling, start at a window or door opening, and pry carefully along the edge. The finish material may be nailed, glued, or attached with contact cement. By working with extreme care you can probably save most panels that were nailed or glued. Panels attached with contact adhesive can't be saved. Your best bet is to cut the panels with a power saw along the edges of studs and plates, and leave the structure covered with strips of paneling.

If walls are finished with either plaster or gypsum wallboard, you can't save any of it. Be sure that you have a means of disposing of the debris before you begin work. Most garbage pickup services won't accept building materials unless you make a special request to the private or municipal service and pay a fee for the pickup.

If you find that the ceiling and exterior walls are adequately insulated, patch the exploratory hole with pieces of the same material cut for a tight fit (see Chapter 18). If you must insulate, or want to be sure that what insulation you have is adequate, follow the instructions in Chapter 10.

Next, dismantle the garage door. Open the door fully, then release the tension on the two cables running between the door and the counterbalancing mechanism. The method of releasing tension and detaching the cable varies with the manufacturer of the door. To avoid injury from a flying cable, call your local distributor for the safest procedure. After you detach the cables, close the door carefully; it is no longer counterbalanced, and will drop quickly.

Now remove the horizontal sections of track and their supports, then the curved sections if they are separate. The door panels will remain stacked in the door opening after the upper track is removed.

Then, from the top panel, remove the roller hardware and the hinges connecting it to the panel below. Lift this panel off the stack. Repeat this step with the remaining panels, working from top to bottom. Finally, remove the remainder of the track, all supporting brackets, the stop molding at the sides of the opening, and any trim. The door opening should now be clean down to structural framing.

CLOSING THE GARAGE DOOR OPENING

You can build the entire frame that closes the opening on the floor of the garage, then raise it into position. It is generally easier, however, to install the frame piece by piece to assure a tight fit.

First, fill the door opening up to the height of the surrounding foundation. Use concrete blocks as described in Chapter 6 if and when the floor is level at this point and you can work out the heights evenly. If not, build a form to the required height, and pour a low wall of concrete as you would a footing. You don't need sill bolts, however.

To avoid problems with condensation and rot in the space between the old and new floors, set a ventilator at some inconspicuous point in the low wall. To do the job right you should cut another ventilator

Chapter 8 / Converting Nonliving Space

through the opposite wall to allow cross-ventilation. But one vent is far better than none.

Next, measure the width of the opening at the top of the foundation, and cut a 2 × 4 plate to fit. Atop the low foundation set either an asphalted gasket or a bed of mortar ½″ thick (see Chapter 6). This seal assures an airtight fit between the foundation and plate. If you use mortar, press the plate into the seal while it is still wet, then trowel off the excess. Toenail the plate into jamb studs immediately, and let the mortar set while you cut other structural members. Make sure that the plate is absolutely level in both directions, and flush with adjacent framing inside the garage.

Then determine where you need studs. You need a stud at each end (A in Fig. 8-2), a stud flanking each side of any opening for a window or entrance door (B), a pair of studs to support any interior partition (C), and studs to support joints between panels of interior wall materials (D). There must be no more than 16″ between the centerlines of adjacent studs.

As you can see, you may be able to save some studs by carefully laying out the wall in advance. If you apply wood paneling, you'll need a stud every 48″ measured from one corner. If you apply wallboard vertically, which is the easier way, you also need a stud every 48″. If you apply wallboard horizontally, you need a stud every 8 to 12′, depending on the length of board you can handle.

Before you mark stud locations on the plate, lay out the spacing on paper, then adjust the dimensions to fit your needs. If you do move a window, door, or partition a few inches, make absolutely sure that the change doesn't adversely affect anything else in your plan. Then mark the plate.

Next, before you cut studs to length, measure at several points the distance between the new bottom plate and the header across the old door. The header probably deflects. Ideally, you should apply a jack at the center to raise the header to level, then cut all studs the same length. An easier way is to cut jamb studs to full dimension. Then, where sag is greatest, cut studs about ⅛″ too long and wedge them in position. The sag in the header won't ever increase with the studs in place, and by attempting to force the header upward with full-length studs, you may put a bend in them that makes attachment of wall materials difficult. Cut remaining studs for an exact fit.

Toenail all studs to the plate. Be sure to stay on your marks; hammering tends to knock studs out of position. Then use a level or plumb bob to set each stud vertical before toenailing into the header. With all full-height studs in place, recheck your work for plumb and flush fits, and all measurements. If anything is wrong, you can adjust a little with well-placed hammer blows. But don't try to correct an error of more than ¼″. Instead, cut the misplaced stud as close as possible to one end (you can use it later for shorter cripples), and remove it in two pieces.

Exterior Materials

The distance from door jambs to exterior corners of most garages is less than 4′. Rather than piece materials in the opening, you will have a better looking job if you remove wood siding all the way to the corner, and replace the short pieces with longer pieces. Note how corners are finished. If they are metal-covered, remove the metal corners before removing the siding. If corners

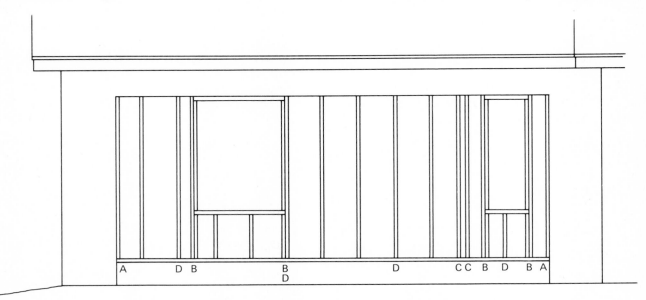

Fig. 8-2. Typical elevation of a former garage door opening shows how to determine where to place studs. Note the absence of a top plate, which can be omitted unless you assemble the framing on the floor of the garage and raise it into place.

are mitered, save the old siding as a cutting guide, numbering the pieces from bottom to top before you remove them, even though you remove them from top to bottom.

When the door opening is near one end of a long wall, remove the alternate pieces of short siding, leaving the long ones in place. Loosen all pieces at the jamb enough so that you can remove the pieces to be replaced and the nails holding them.

If walls are wood shingles, remove only edge shingles in about two-thirds of the courses, and replace them later with wider shingles. In this way you break up the lines of demarcation of the old door opening.

When exterior walls are masonry, remove only units at jambs that are less than full size. With a power saw fitted with a masonry-cutting blade, cut horizontally as close as possible to the edges of masonry units you won't remove. Then use a cold chisel and hammer to break the mortar bond at vertical joints. With the chisel, clean away all loose mortar so that you have three clean surfaces against which to lay new masonry. Removing masonry is a slow job that takes great care; crack a mortar joint and you invite leaks.

Sheathing

Next sheathe the opening, applying the sheathing horizontally. Depending on your house's construction, the bottom piece will overlap the low foundation ½ to 1″ if the outside faces of studs are flush with the edge. If studs are inset, fit the sheathing to the top of the wall. Cut lengths to meet at the centerline of a stud, and locate joints in the upper course on different studs. You will probably have to rip upper pieces of sheathing to width; be sure to allow for any variation in the size of the opening. At window and door openings let the sheathing extend into the opening, then trim it to fit after it is in place.

Unless you are remodeling in cold weather, leave openings for new windows and doors in their rough state. The openings provide light, air circulation, and a means of moving construction materials into the old garage. Complete floor construction and install insulation before you enclose the remaining openings.

FLOOR CONSTRUCTION

During the preparation stage you marked with a nail the height of the finished floor in the house. Using this point as a guide, mark on a nearby stud or wall surface the height of the finished floor in converted space, whether it is at this same level or down a step. Then calculate the thickness of the subfloor plus the finish flooring you plan to install. (Table 4-1 shows the most common thicknesses.) Mark on the stud or wall the underside of this thickness; it indicates the point to which you must build the floor frame.

To mark this point all the way around the garage, look for the longest straight board you can find. Set the board on your mark, lay a carpenter's level on the board, and move the board until it is absolutely level. Then mark all studs, or every 16″ on the wall. Move the board to the last mark and repeat the process. After you have marked all the way around the room, stretch a taut nylon cord between marks on opposite sides of the area, set your level on it, and recheck. This operation takes three people. Once you are assured of the level to which you are working, you can lay out the floor structure.

If your garage floor is very uneven and you want to lay the new floor over sleepers, clean the surface thoroughly, then pour over it a lightweight concrete mix to level it (see Chapter 18). The mix should not be more than 1″ thick at any point. Unless you have the necessary tools and are experienced in concrete flatwork, hire this work done.

If your garage floor has a drain, either install a plug to cap the opening, or remove the drain cover and fill the pipe with mortar. The chances of water ever backing up in the drain are slight, but the problems a backup causes are worth taking this extra step to avoid.

With Sleepers

When you install sleepers (Fig. 8-3), you need two layers, one against the concrete floor and one atop a vapor barrier. If the two layers are different in thickness, install the thinner layer first. To support the edges of subflooring or wood strip flooring, you need sleepers around the perimeter of the area set 1″ away from wall structure. In the center of the area set sleepers every 16″ o.c.—staggered if you apply wood strip flooring, and in straight lines if you apply wood subflooring.

Which way do sleepers run? That depends on the direction you run strip flooring or subflooring. Strip flooring should run the same direction as any strip flooring in the adjoining room, and sleepers must run at right angles to the flooring. Lay out subflooring for the most economical use of material, and run sleepers at right angles to the long sides (see Fig. 7-5). You must have a sleeper under every edge joint between sheets of plywood.

After you have determined the best layout, sweep the floor as clean as possible. Then pick up the last bit of sawdust and dirt with the tube attachment on a vacuum cleaner. Next apply an asphalt waterproofing compound over the concrete surface, following the manufacturer's directions. Let the primer dry overnight.

The next day, snap chalk lines on the floor as a guide to placement of sleepers. Cut sleepers to length out of 1 × 4s or 2 × 4s of treated material—that is, wood that has been impregnated under pressure at the mill with chemicals that prevent rot and keep out wood-

(a)

Moisture barrier ——→   ——— Plain, untreated strips

Adhesive ——→   Treated strip ——→   ——— 25/32" strip flooring

(b)

Fig. 8–3. Sleepers may be 2″ planks laid in mastic (a), which forms a vapor barrier, or treated 1″ boards set in strips of mastic, covered with a polyethylene vapor barrier, then capped with another set of boards not treated (b). (Photo courtesy National Oak Flooring Manufacturers Association.)

loving insects. The ideal length is 18 to 30″ so that the sleepers lie flat on an uneven floor. Then lay beads of adhesive across your concrete, following chalk lines, and press the sleepers into the adhesive. The adhesive must be formulated to provide a strong bond between wood and concrete. If you plan to run wiring under the floor, leave small gaps between sleepers where necessary. Check their level constantly.

As soon as the first layer of a two-layer application of sleepers is in place and you have rechecked their spacing, lay sheets of polyethylene film from wall to wall, overlapping 4 to 6″ at seams. Then, before the adhesive has time to set, nail the second layer of sleepers directly over the first layer. Use 4d nails if you are applying 1″ boards, and 7d nails if you are nailing through 2 × 4s.

With Joists

You can frame with floor joists in two ways. In both cases joists should run the short dimension of the area. When the space is narrow enough, and you have enough height between old and new floor levels, buy joists long enough to span the entire width. Otherwise, you must buy shorter joists and support them at or near their midpoints.

Let's say that you are converting a double garage, and the width to be spanned is just under 20′. To span that width with single joists you would need 2 × 12s spaced either 16″ or 12″ o.c., depending on the grade of lumber available. If your lumber dealer carries 20′ lengths of 2 × 12s—and not all of them do—your cost is likely to be high. On the other hand, you have a minimum of cutting and fitting, and eliminate the need for intermediate support. You will need help to set the joists, however, because they are heavy and awkward to handle alone.

To span the same width with pairs of joists that meet over center support, you would need only 10′ lengths of 2 × 6s spaced 16″ o.c. An alternative is one set of 12′ lengths and a set of 8′ lengths, perhaps cut from 16-footers. You will also need enough length of 2 × 6 to build a girder running the other direction (Fig. 8-4), plus scrap for supporting this beam above the floor. In addition you will need a pair of joist hangers every 16″.

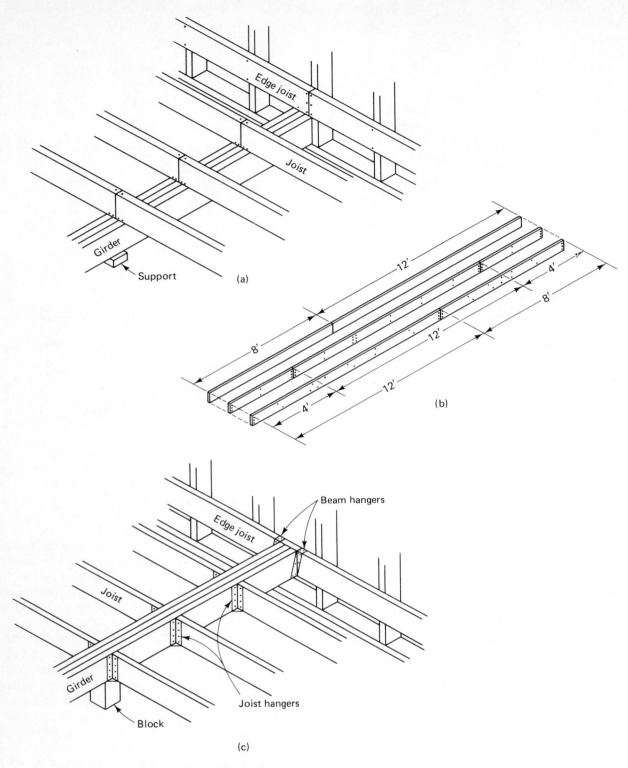

Fig. 8–4. When you cannot span between walls with single lengths of joists, you can support shorter lengths on a girder (a) provided that the new floor level is two or more steps above the existing floor level. When vertical height is more limited (c), you can butt joists against a girder and attach them with joist hangers. Typical girder construction is shown in (b).

As another alternative, you can sometimes buy 20′ lengths of 2 × 6. By supporting them at their midpoints on short pieces of 2 × 4 or 4 × 4, you can build a strong floor structure with minimum cutting and no center beam.

So as you lay out your joist system, check the availability and compare the cost of joist stock in various lengths and depths. Then go with the system that costs the least for materials, as long as you can afford the extra time required for cutting and fitting.

Begin floor construction by nailing header joists below your marks along the two longest walls. Individual lengths must be cut to meet on the centerlines of studs. Next, cut and nail edge joists (see Fig. 7-1) along the shorter walls at the same level. Be sure that the tops of these perimeter joists are level around the entire space.

On the two header joists mark the locations of regular joists. Use a line to mark the edge and an × to indicate on which side of the line to place the joists. Remember that 16″ is the maximum spacing. For general instructions on joist layout, see Chapter 7.

If you need a center beam or girder, build it from three widths of joist stock (Fig. 8-4), with joints between lengths staggered at least 4′. Attach widths to each other with 10d nails, three near the end of each piece and a pair about ¾″ from the top and bottom every 24″ between. The length of the girder is the distance between the two edge joists.

Attach the girder to edge joists with beam hangers. Then cut posts from treated 2 × 4s or 4 × 4s to provide support approximately every 8′. To determine the length of the posts, stretch a taut cord between header joists at each point of support. Measure the distance from cord to floor, and subtract the depth of the girder. Cut each post to its particular length, set the bottom end in adhesive, raise the girder, and wedge the post in place. Check each post for plumb, then toenail the girder to it.

Mark joist locations on the top of the girder. Then install joist hangers at each joist mark on header joists and on both sides of the girder. Cut regular joists to length, drop them into the hangers, and nail through the holes provided.

Your floor framing is now complete. To assure a warm floor in extremely cold climates, install insulating batts between joists with the vapor barrier side *up*. Do not do so, however, unless you have provided ventilation in the enclosed space beneath the new floor.

As a final procedure before framing the ceiling, lay subflooring as described in Chapter 7 and shown in Fig. 7-5.

CEILING JOISTS

If the garage you are converting has nothing overhead but rafters and a roof, and you have no plans for partitioning the space, you can insulate between rafters, and add ceiling material to the undersides of those rafters. This gives your room a cathedral ceiling which follows the shape of the roof. It can be very attractive, but does make the room harder to heat.

To have a flat ceiling you must install ceiling joists. There are two ways. Normally, joists spanning a wide area are supported on a bearing partition. A bearing partition should be placed as close as possible to the center of the space being divided. Thus your planning for use of garage space is restricted, but you can use the space above joists for storage. An alternative solution is to support the ceiling joists from the rafters. This gives you full use of living space, but eliminates all possible use of space above the joists.

Joists Supported by a Bearing Partition

Design, build, and install the bearing partition as described in the following section of this chapter. Brace it temporarily to hold it absolutely plumb. Then measure the span from face to face of rafter plates, and divide by two. If rafters butt at the ridgeboard above, add 5¼″ to this dimension. If rafters are offset at the ridge, add 7″. You'll see why in a moment.

Beginning at the end of the area to be framed, measure to the side of each rafter adn write down the series of measurements. Then transfer these measurements to the cap plate of the bearing partition. Indicate on which side of the marks to place the joists. When rafters line up, joists will also line up on the same side of the mark, but the opposite side from rafters. When rafters are offset, joists will lie on opposite sides of teh marks and overlap the width of the plate. That's why joists are a little longer when rafters are offset.

Cut a pair of 2 × 6 joists each to the dimension you worked out above, and give both ends a square cut. Then trim one end as shown in Fig. 7-15 to match the slope of the rafter. Test the fit; the pair of joists should either meet at the centerline of the bearing partition or overlap the width of that partition. When the fit is good, use one joist as a template for cutting the others.

If ceiling joists run at 90° to rafters, the ends do not require trimming. For strong construction, however, rafters should be secured to outer joists. There are two methods, shown in Fig. 8-5; the choice is yours. For perpendicular joists, work out a 16″ spacing on the cap plate of the partition, then mark the plates on end walls identically.

Now raise each joist into position on its marks. Nail it horizontally to any rafter with three 8d nails, and toenail to the plate with two more nails. Complete this step for all joists, including joists against end walls needed for attachment of ceiling materials. Then move to the partition. Where joists overlap, toenail them to the plate on one side, then nail through one joist into the other with three more nails. Where joists butt, line up the ends and toenail them to the plate on the marks.

(a)

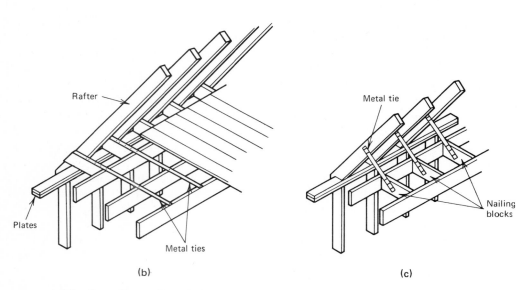

(b)   (c)

Fig. 8–5. To counteract the outward thrust of rafters that run at right angles to ceiling joists, these members should be tied together. The ties may be short lengths of rafter stock, trimmed at one end like ceiling joists (a); short lengths of rafter stock and horizontal metal ties (b); or metal ties running diagonally and secured to nailing blocks between the first and second rafters (c). (Photo: Jay: Leviton-Atlanta.)

Then connect joists with splice plates applied to both sides.

For **splice plates** you can use (1) 5″ × 8″ plates of perforated metal manufactured for this purpose, (2) 5″ × 12″ pieces of plywood ⅜″ or ½″ thick, or (3) 1″ boards trimmed to 5″ × 24″. Metal splice plates need no fasteners; you hammer on their sides to attach them. Attach plywood plates with two rows of 4d nails spaced 3″ apart. Attach boards with 6d nails also spaced 3″ apart.

Joists Hung from Rafters

If you omit a bearing partition, you need 2 × 4 joists that either span from cap plate to cap plate, or are spliced at the center as just described but with entirely different splice plates. Total joist length is equal to the span of the roof: the distance from face to face of cap plates plus 7″. Any splice falls at the midpoint of the span.

Cut two end joists to length, and fit them against end walls with their bottoms level. Toenail them to plates at their ends, and nail into studs along their length. Connect ends at the midpoint with a 3″ × 6″ metal splice plate or a 3″ × 12″ plywood plate on the exposed side. Make sure that the plate doesn't protrude below the bottom edge of the joist.

Next, find the approximate midpoint of the nearest rafter, and mark this point directly above the end joist. Then take a 2 × 4 long enough to reach between the mark and the midpoint of the joist (Fig. 8-6). Hold the 2 × 4 across studs and mark the ends for cutting. This web member should just touch the top of the joist at one side of the splice, and miss the underside of sheathing at the chalk mark by about ½″.

Cut your sample web member and test the fit. When the fit is proper, cut all other web members. You need two for each joist except the end ones.

While you are on the ladder checking the fit, measure from the underside of the joist to the subfloor. Cut a brace of this length from a 2 × 4. You need this brace to support joists during attachment.

When you lay out the remaining rafters for splicing, lay the two pieces of joist end to end, flat on the subfloor, and against a third length of straight 2 × 4 to assure good alignment. Then lay the two web members in position, and install gusset plates to hold all four pieces together. For **gussets** use either 8″ × 16″ metal splice plates or ½″ plywood plates 12″ high and 24″ wide, with the grain of the face layer of plywood running horizontally. Apply a splice plate on one side, turn the assembly over, and splice on the other side. With plywood gussets use 18 4d nails per gusset, as shown in Fig. 8-6.

Raise each assembly into place with help, set it on its marks on rafter plates, and toenail at each end. Then brace the center of the joist to level it, and nail through each web member into a rafter with four 10d nails.

Ceiling Openings

When headroom is great enough and the ceiling structure strong enough, the space above ceiling joists is excellent for storage, provided that the space is ventilated. To reach this space from below, you may install a folding stairway or an access door. When you plan the location of a folding stairway, leave enough room at the lower end so that you can carry up boxes and other bulky items in safety. An access door can fit above a space as small as 3′ square.

There are two types of folding stairways. Where headroom is limited, the best type has steps in sections, hinged together to fold against the access door. When closed, the stairway extends only a few inches into attic space. The other type is a one-piece stairway that slides into the attic and takes up some floor space when closed.

Both types come ready to install in a framed opening, and with instructions for installation. Framing is similar to that shown in Fig. 8-7 for an access door.

No access door should be smaller than 24″ × 24″, and 30″ × 30″ is the most practical size. Above the

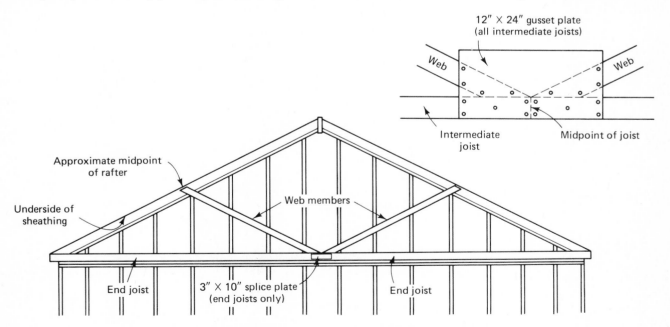

Fig. 8–6. Ceiling joists hung from rafters must be supported by web members. Determine lengths of joists and web members by working first at a gable, then splice the four pieces together with a gusset plate (inset) when joists are not fastened to end walls.

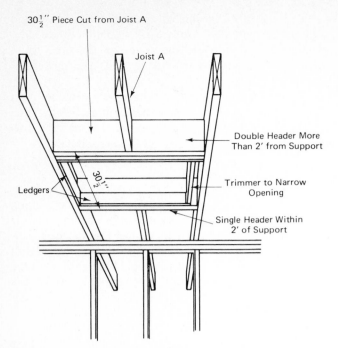

30½'' Piece Cut from Joist A

Joist A

Double Header More Than 2' from Support

Ledgers

30½''

Trimmer to Narrow Opening

Single Header Within 2' of Support

Fig. 8–7. A typical access opening in a ceiling is 30″ square, and fits between two rafters on 16″ centers. The opening may be narrowed with a trimmer. The access door rests on ledgers.

center of the door opening omit a ceiling joist temporarily. This leaves a space between joists of 30½″ (see Fig. 8-7). Cut headers to this length. You need one at each end of the opening when it is within 2′ of a wall or bearing partition, and two at each end under any other conditions. Install two headers 30½″ apart and add the second pair, if required, outside the first pair. Around the inside of the opening add 1 × 2 ledgers—two cut to 30½″ and two cut to 29″. Then from a sheet of plywood cut a door 30″ square. You can use plywood as thin as ¼″, but it will warp from attic heat in summer, and leak air. A door of ½″ plywood is much better.

PARTITIONS

Professional builders usually build interior partitions just like exterior walls, with built-up headers over door openings. They start with a continuous bottom plate, add studs, top plate, and cap plate, and raise the partition. Then they cut away the part of the plate across door openings with a power hand saw.

But a few things about a partition are different. Where two partitions meet at a corner, you double the end stud of the longer partition (Fig. 8-8). On drawings, partitions are dimensioned from the outsides of wall

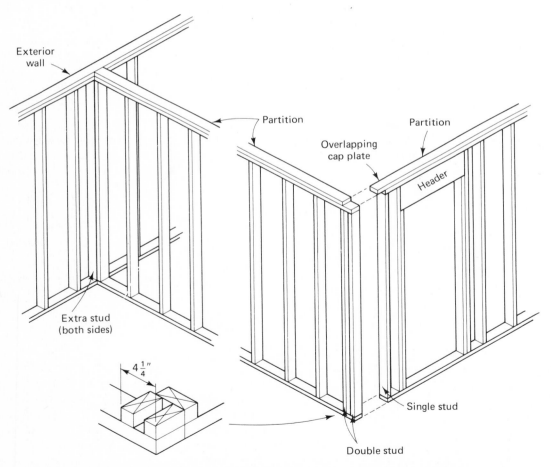

Exterior wall

Partition

Overlapping cap plate

Partition

Header

Extra stud (both sides)

4¼″

Single stud

Double stud

Fig. 8–8. Details of partition construction at intersections with walls and other partitions.

studs in exterior walls and to the centerlines of other partitions (see Fig. 3-1). Therefore, the actual length of a partition that abuts an exterior wall is its dimension on the drawing less the width of an exterior stud (3½″) and less half the width of an interior stud (1¾″). Similarly, the actual length of a partition between other partitions is its length on the drawing less twice the width of half a stud (1¾″ + 1¾″).

To locate a partition on the subfloor, mark its centerline at both ends. Then measure 1¾″ to one side of the marks and snap a chalk line. It is easier to set a partition on a line marking its edge than its center.

Build all partitions flat on the subfloor, starting with the longest first. In this way you always have enough floor space to lay out the next-shorter partition.

In new construction, such as an addition, you build and erect partitions, then install ceiling joists. When ceiling joists are already in place, as in a garage conversion and in the method for additions in Chapter 7, you build partitions with the cap plate already in place before you erect them. Where partitions meet exterior walls, you let the cap plate overlap in new construction (see Fig. 7-14), but cut it flush with the end of the top plate in remodeling. Where two partitions meet at a corner, the cap plate on the shorter partition must overlap the top plate of the longer partition (see Fig. 8-8).

Existing ceiling joists probably sag a little at the center of a long span. This makes erection of full-height partitions difficult. You can rent a jack and raise joists temporarily, or you can avoid the problem by building your partitions with a bottom plate cut from a 1 × 4 instead of a 2 × 4. Set these slightly short partitions on chalk lines, then raise them into position by driving shims under the bottom plate at studs, working from alternate sides. Wood shingles make excellent shims.

Attachment

With no overlapping cap plate to secure the tops of partitions at exterior walls, you must add studs (see Fig. 7-13) to assure solid attachment the full height of the partition.

Set each partition on its chalk line, and nail every 8″ through the end stud into a stud or corner post of an existing wall or previously installed partition. Then at the opposite end nail downward in the last stud spacing into the subfloor and, if possible, on into a floor joist or sleeper. Do not drive this nail all the way in until you have set adjoining partitions. After all partitions are set, drive the nails home and nail between all other studs into the floor structure.

To secure partitions at their tops, they must be nailed to ceiling framing. When ceiling joists cross a partition, toenail through each joist on both sides downward into the cap plate (Fig. 8-9a). When a partition runs the same direction as joists, build a **ladder**

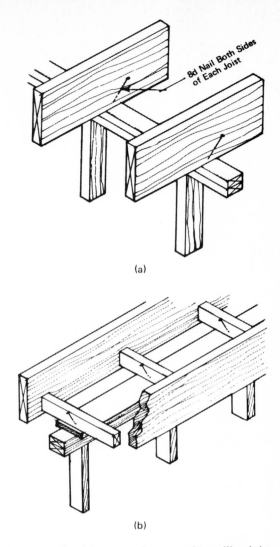

(a)

(b)

Fig. 8-9. Partitions must be secured to ceiling joists—by toenailing when joists run at right angles (a), and with a ladder when they run parallel (b). The ladder consists of a 1 x 6 and a series of 2 x 4 rungs.

(Fig. 8-9b) consisting of a 1 × 6 centered over and nailed to the cap plate, and 2 × 4 ladder rungs placed upright between the joists. The 1 × 6 provides for attachment of ceiling material. After you check each partition for plumb, toenail ladder rungs into the 1 × 6, then nail through joists into the ends of the 2 × 4s.

A STACK WALL

If your plans call for a full or half bathroom in new space, one partition must be built differently from all others. It is the **stack wall**, so-called because the pipe or stack that ventilates the system lies behind it. The vent stack almost always lies directly behind a toilet fixture and is centered on it.

Before you build a stack wall, make sure that you and your plumbing subcontractor are in agreement on

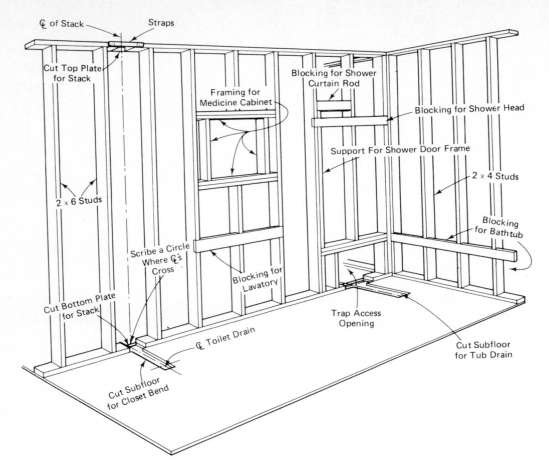

Fig. 8–10. Partitions around bathrooms should be built with blocking for any bathtub, showerhead, lavatory, and shower door or curtain rod, and framing for an access door to bathtub plumbing and any medicine cabinet.

the exact location of the stack and its size. Usually, a stack wall is a nominal 6″ thick, but some codes permit smaller vent piping that will fit in a wall built of 2 × 4s. You can make the entire wall thicker, or use 2 × 6s only in the area behind the toilet. It's easier to finish walls when the stack wall is uniform in thickness.

Except for the thickness of plates and studs, a stack wall is built much like any other partition. The soil stack should be approximately centered between studs, however, and you need to add blocking to support any lavatory, showerhead, curtain rod, or shower door (Fig. 8-10). You also need special framing at the end and side of the tub, and around a medicine cabinet.

Work out in advance with subcontractors of any mechanical systems at what points in construction they want to do their work. They will probably want to install any duct and plumbing lines that run below the floor after you have finished framing but before you add the subfloor. If floor joists run at right angles to the centerline of the toilet, you may have to frame the floor to allow for piping. Under no circumstances can you notch a joist without reinforcing it.

Figure 8-11a shows how to reinforce a notch in the top, middle, and bottom of a joist, provided (1) that the notch is no more than one-sixth of the depth of the joist, (2) that it does not occur in the middle of ⅓ of the joist's length, and (3) that the notch occurs within 2′ of the ends of the joist. Most codes do not permit notching under any other conditions.

You can cut or drill a hole in the bottom plate of a partition because you don't affect its structural integrity. A cut in top and cap plates, however, must be reinforced as shown in Fig. 8-11b.

Most codes permit you to notch studs up to half their width in a nonbearing partition, but only up to one-third their width in a bearing partition. No notch can be in the middle third of the length of the stud, however. Nor can you notch more than two adjacent studs without reinforcing all you cut. Figures 8-11c and d show acceptable methods of reinforcing 2 × 6 and 2 × 4 studs respectively.

Locating the Hole for the Vent Stack

Where a vent goes upward, it should rise between ceiling joists and rafters. To find the point where a vent goes through the roof, wait until the plumbing subcontractor has carried his lines to the point where they will rise

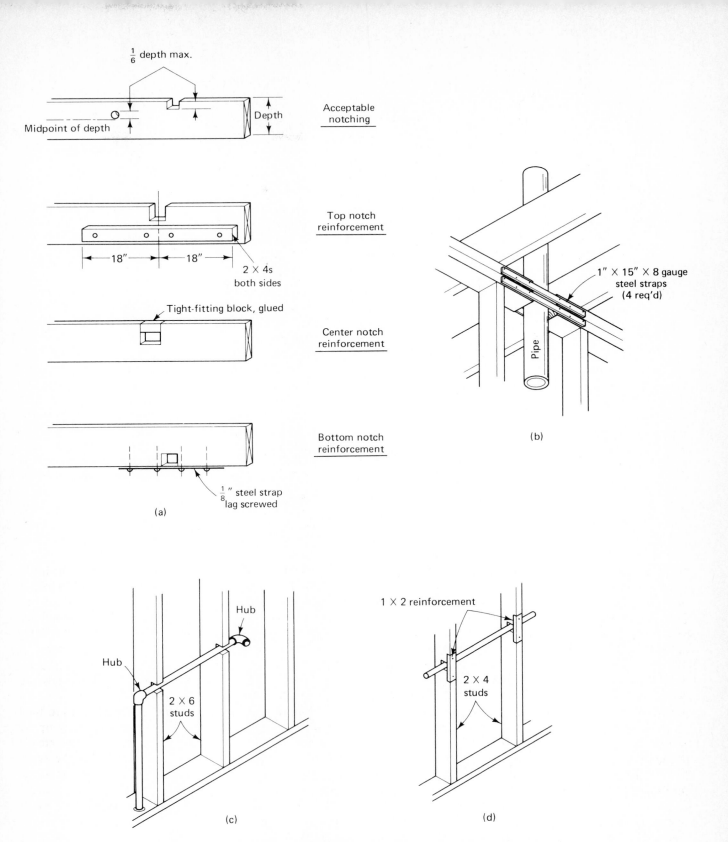

Fig. 8-11. Notching framing members within code requirements: (a) reinforcing a notch in the top, middle, and bottom of a joist; (b) reinforcement for cut top plates; (c) acceptable notching in a stack wall; (d) reinforcement for cut studs in a standard partition. Codes place strict limitations on what structural members you can notch, where and how much you can notch them, and the type of reinforcement needed.

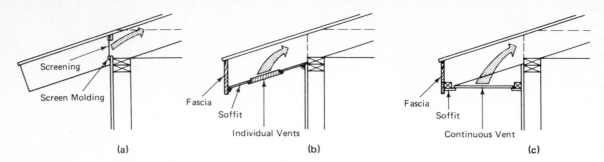

(a)   (b)   (c)

Fig. 8-12. Three ways to ventilate roofs by providing air intakes and exhausts at eaves. Vents set in exterior walls may be individual units or a continuous screened opening (a). Vents in soffits may also be individual (b) or continuous (c). Make sure that insulation between ceiling joists above exterior walls does not restrict airflow.

vertically. Then hold a plumb bob against the underside of roof sheathing, and move it around until it hangs directly over the center of the pipe. Mark this point with an ×, then drive a long nail vertically through the ×.

The hole you cut in the roof will be oval, not circular, and should be about ¼″ bigger than the pipe. For a 4″ pipe, then, the dimension *across* the roof will be 4¼″. To determine the dimension *along the slope*, the simplest way is to draw the conditions on the fascia board at the rake of the roof. Draw two vertical lines 4¼″ apart, then measure the distance between these lines at the sloping edge of the fascia. If your roof has a 5-in-12 pitch, for example, the dimension will be 4⅝″.

To cut the hole, carefully remove finish roofing around the protruding nail until you bare an area of sheathing about 1′ square. On the sheathing draw a rectangle with the two dimensions you established, mark the midpoints of all four sides, then draw an oval through the four marks. Drill a hole *vertically* just inside the oval large enough to accept the blade of a saber saw. Then cut the hole on the lines, again cutting vertically, not at right angles to the roof.

After the vent pipe is installed, it must be flashed—that is, the hole sealed with **flashing**. The most practical flashing for this purpose is a small sheet of plastic manufactured and shaped for the purpose that fits tightly around the stack. Install the flashing, then replace the roofing material, cutting for a close fit. Apply a liberal coat of roofing cement under all cut edges, over all holes left by old nails, and over any exposed nails. Cut asphalt shingles with a utility knife; shears also do the job but are harder to clean. Spread roofing cement with a putty knife.

VENTILATION

With all structural work done, the only steps remaining before application of wall materials are to insulate and ventilate. These steps for the area under the floor are discussed earlier in this chapter. Apply insulation between studs as described in Chapter 10.

Attic space that you have sealed off with a ceiling must be ventilated. One method, discussed in Chapter 7, is with louvers set in a gable just below the roof line. This method requires the most cutting and fitting and is the least effective. Another is to add roof ventilators; they are manufactured in a variety of sizes and shapes. None are objects of beauty, however, and therefore should be installed in the roof least visible from the street.

A third method, ventilating under the eaves of the roof, is adequate if you have eaves on opposite sides, but inadequate when you have only one eave to work with. Figure 8-12 shows three places to set ventilators in eaves. They may be individual units or continuous from rake to rake.

The most effective method of exhausting air from an existing roof is eave ventilation coupled with a ridge ventilator (Fig. 8-13). It is made of thin metal shaped to fit along a roof ridge—the point at which heat gathers. Ventilators come in 10′ sections that fit together with watertight gaskets. You need 8′ of ventilator for every 300 sq ft of attic area.

To install a ridge ventilator on an existing roof, first determine the length you need. Ends should come

Fig. 8-13. A ridge ventilator exhausts hot air at the ridge where it accumulates, but is scarcely visible from the street. It can be installed easily in an existing roof. (Courtesy H.C. Products Co.)

no closer than 6″ to gable walls or hips. Mark the location with chalk, and remove the ridge course of shingles between the marks. Then snap chalk lines along the roof about 1½″ from the ridge on each side. With a roofer's knife or a similar sharp cutting tool, slice through the courses of shingles along the chalk lines until sheathing is exposed. Then set your power saw to cut only to the thickness of the sheathing, and cut along the same two lines.

You will now see the ridgeboard and upper ends of rafters. Assemble the ridge ventilator and center it over the opening, bending the flanges to fit the slope of your roof. Nail through the flanges. Then reuse the ridge shingles, cut in half, to form a watertight seal over the flanges. Cover exposed nails and any cracks with roofing cement.

A CARPORT

Converting a carport is similar to converting a garage, with a few extra steps required.

First, determine whether the roof and its supporting structure are worth saving, or should be removed. When the roof is an integral part of the main roof of the house, or alike in construction, and supports are wood posts or brick pillars, keep what you have. Then frame between the supports as described for framing around a garage door opening. You will probably need to remove any carport ceiling and replace it, since there is little likelihood of insulation above it.

When the carport has its own roof supported by metal posts, your best bet is to remove the existing structure carefully, and treat the conversion as a room addition, working upward from the carport floor instead of a new foundation. But read the limitations that follow.

A SCREENED PORCH

The wisest method of converting a porch to enclosed living space depends on both the roof and floor structure. A porch with a wood plank floor raised above ground level rarely has a foundation strong enough to support the weight of a new room, nor a roof that does much more than shed weather. Unless it has a standard foundation, dismantle the porch, carefully saving as many structural members as possible for reuse. Then dig out the foundation. Usually, it will consist only of some individual footings and piers. You may have to hire someone with the equipment to lift these supports out of the ground and dispose of them. You could leave them in place and pour a foundation against them, but the result will be much weaker and more subject to uneven settling than if you start from scratch.

A porch with a concrete or masonry floor probably rests on a foundation, or has a thickened-edge slab strong enough to support walls and roof. Dig down at some point along the side of the porch until you can see what the support is and how deep it bottoms out below the ground. If it meets either of the specifications in Fig. 4-9, it should be strong enough to support a completed and enclosed room. There is no simple way to determine whether the slab is reinforced, but the chances are good that if the edges are properly supported, the slab is adequately reinforced.

If there is even the slightest doubt in your mind as to the strength of a foundation and/or slab, have them torn out and start over. You could have future structural problems that cost a lot more than the expense of breaking up and removing old concrete.

Could you pour a thinner, reinforced slab over the existing slab? Yes, under certain conditions. The new slab should be a minimum of 4″ thick, and the added height will alter the relationship with the floor level of the existing house. If this doesn't cause a problem, dig outside the existing slab, form as described in Chapter 6 for a thickened-edge slab as shown in Fig. 4-9, and pour a new floor with its own support. Be sure to add a vapor barrier between the two slabs to prevent moisture from coming through and ruining new flooring. To do this, of course, you must tear down the existing porch, but you will have a slightly larger room, and in the long run will probably have it ready to use more quickly.

Reaching Attic Space

Of all stairways a spiral staircase manufactured of metal takes up the least floor space. But be sure you have another way to move furniture. A center pipe is first bolted to the lower floor. Then triangular steps are threaded over it and welded in place. the floor opening is framed with joist stock, and trimmed with thin plywood bent to follow the circular cutout in upper floor and lower ceiling materials. (Courtesy American Plywood Association.)

Of all types of remodelings that increase living space, finishing an attic is the most economical. In most houses attic floor joists are strong enough to carry the weight of finished rooms without further strengthening. There is often a subfloor over at least part of the floor area. The roof is finished, and lets you work at your convenience regardless of weather conditions.

Furthermore, because of an attic's location above existing living space, it is comparatively easy to extend heat ducts, electric wiring, and even plumbing into finished attic space.

DESIGN PROBLEMS

Yet not all attic space is convertible. Much of it, particularly in houses built since World War II, is under roofs too low to provide adequate headroom. You may be able to lift the existing roof and build a second story under it. But get professional help with the design from an architect, and help on construction from a contractor. Furthermore, if you would be the only homeowner in your neighborhood with a two-story house, don't think twice. Think three times.

Even in a house where attic space isn't completely ideal, most of the problems can be solved with careful planning, even to floor joists too light for the load. But there are at least two conditions that must be present in order for conversion to be feasible: (1) the house must have a roof ridge that is at least 8' above the floor of the attic, and (2) there must be some practical place to build an attic stairway if the house doesn't already have one.

Headroom

Before low-pitched roofs became popular a generation ago, most houses were built with gable or hip roofs steep enough to leave some usable space in an attic. How usable such space was—and is—depends on the pitch of the roof and the depth of the house.

Suppose that a house is 24' wide and has a gable roof with a 12-in-12 pitch (that's a 45° slope) and 2 × 6 rafters. Attic height just below the ridge is about 11½'. At a point 8' above the attic floor—standard ceiling height—the space between rafters is about 7' wide. At 6' above the floor—the lowest point with minimum headroom—space between rafters is about 11'.

The wider the house, the wider the usable space. In a house 28' wide with the same roof pitch, the ceiling at the 8' mark would be about 11' wide. Conversely, the lower the roof pitch, the narrower is the usable attic space. A house 28' wide with a 5-in-12 pitch, which is common today, has maximum headroom under the ridge of less than 6', and the space isn't usable for living.

To determine the usable space in your attic, drop a plumb bob from the underside of the ridgeboard to the subfloor or tops of floor joists (Fig. 9-1a). Mark this spot (X) with chalk. Measure the height with a steel tape. Then move the tape down the underside of a rafter until the vertical height is 7' (adequate headroom), and mark the spot (Y) with chalk. Now measure between the chalk marks; the measurement will be half the usable width of an attic room, as long as the slopes of both roofs are the same.

Unless the vertical measurement from the ridge is at least 8', use of the attic isn't practical. Ceiling height in attic rooms used for sleeping can be as low as 7', but 7½' is preferable. By raising the roof on one side of the ridge and building a shed dormer, you can add rooms that are half the width of the house or close to it (Fig. 9-1b). But to be able to give enough slope to the dormer roof for drainage, you must have that 8' at the ridge.

Sidewalls of attic space, called **knee walls**, can be as short as 4'. In areas with insufficient headroom for standing upright you can put bunk beds, a desk, and built-in storage. Because attic space is almost always

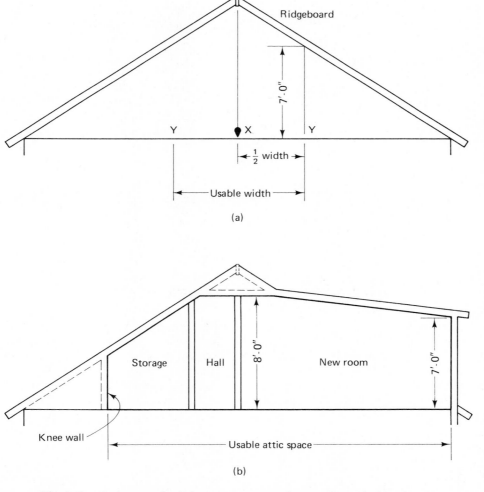

(a)

(b)

Fig. 9–1. Attic space for living purposes must have at least 7' of headroom. The width of usable space is twice the distance from X to Y in (a). Limited space can be economically increased with a shed dormer (b).

long and narrow, attic rooms are also long and narrow. So put knee walls as far apart as possible. If the measurement between chalk marks X and Y in fig. 9-1a is at least 4′, any room will be at least 8′ wide. Thus you can skip the structural discussion in this chapter after you read the following discussion of attic access. You won't need to raise the roof, although you should consider adding dormers.

Access

Unless you are lucky enough to have a permanent attic stairway already in the house, you must provide one. You won't be able to secure a building permit to convert an attic to living space without it. Trap doors and pull-down stairways don't meet code requirements for quick egress.

The biggest problem is where to find room for a stairway. It must be at least 30″ wide between flanking walls. It must be about 10′ long measured from the bottom of the first step to the edge of the finished attic floor. It must have floor space at least 30″ × 30″ at both ends for landings.

You have a choice of eight possible solutions (Fig. 9-2). One is a straight stairway that runs parallel to the roof ridge, and reaches attic level at a point with full headroom (Fig. 9-2a). This point is usually either under the ridge or just to one side of it. Building such a stairway is difficult for the amateur because it runs at right angles to attic floor joists. They must all be cut and reinforced for a stairwell.

A second solution (Fig. 9-2b) is a straight stairway that starts up near an outside wall of the existing house and follows the roof slope upward, again ending under or almost under the ridge. Of the first two possible stairway placements, the second is usually the better answer because it runs parallel to joists. In either case you must steal some living space from the floor below for stairs, and it's usually easier and more attractive to take the space from the end of a room rather than the side. Furthermore, if the stairway can rise near the center of the house, it provides access to all new attic rooms with a minimum of upstairs hallway.

When there is no place in your house for 10′ of straight stairway plus landing space at both ends, perhaps you can use winders (Fig. 9-2c, d, e, or f). **Winders** are steps with a triangular tread that radiate from the same center point. The overall length of a winding stairway is about the same as a straight stairway, but the landing area is at one side of it instead of at the end.

If space for stairs is at a premium, you may be able to fit in a circular stairway (Fig. 9-2g), which you can either build or buy. Manufactured stairways consist of a center steel pole to which are attached metal steps that wind around it. Circular stairways take up the least space: they fit within a circle 48″ in diameter. But they are quite steep, and will defy efforts to move box

springs and dressers up or down. You should consider a circular stairway only when attic space will be used infrequently and you have no other alternative.

As a very last resort consider one other possibility: a stairway addition (Fig. 9-2h). Here you add a stairway outside the house and simply enclose it. Usually, such a stairway must wind and rise at one end of the house, which brings it upstairs at an inopportune place. But at least it gets you upstairs, and can be designed as a feature of the house.

ATTIC STRUCTURE

Assuming that you have adequate headroom for finishing your attic, begin by studying its structure. Determine the size of floor joists and how they are supported. In most houses pairs of joists meet over a bearing wall directly or almost directly beneath the roof ridge. Calculate the span of these joists—that is, their length between points of support. As mentioned before, attic joists are usually sized to carry the loads likely to be placed on them if the space were finished. Even when joist size is marginal, a subfloor of ¾″ plywood, engineered grade, adds sufficient strength to carry and distribute these loads safely on the structure.

If there is any doubt in your mind, check with your local building inspector, building materials dealer, or a remodeling contractor before proceeding.

Sometimes older houses, primarily in small towns and rural areas, have roofs built like barn roofs. Rafters are heavier than normal, joists are lighter than normal, and they are connected by diagonal web members. In effect, the dead loads on the joists are carried by the rafters. With such construction the joists are not strong enough to carry live loads. Rather than give up your remodeling project or replace the joists, you can often lay a deck of ¾ (1¼″) plywood over them, applied with nails and glue. The plywood acts as a membrane that stiffens the structure, spreads loads, and provides an excellent subfloor.

STAIRWAY LAYOUT

Once you have made a decision about the thickness of the subfloor and agree on the material you want to use for a finish floor, you can get at stairway design.

Riser Height

To establish the height of each **riser** in a stairway—the vertical part of a step—find the vertical height *in inches* from the top of attic floor joists to the finished floor of a room below (Fig. 9-3). Measure at a ceiling opening when possible. Use a plumb bob to establish true vertical, mark the point of the plumb bob, and measure to that point. If you have no ceiling opening, measure the height of attic joists, then measure the height from

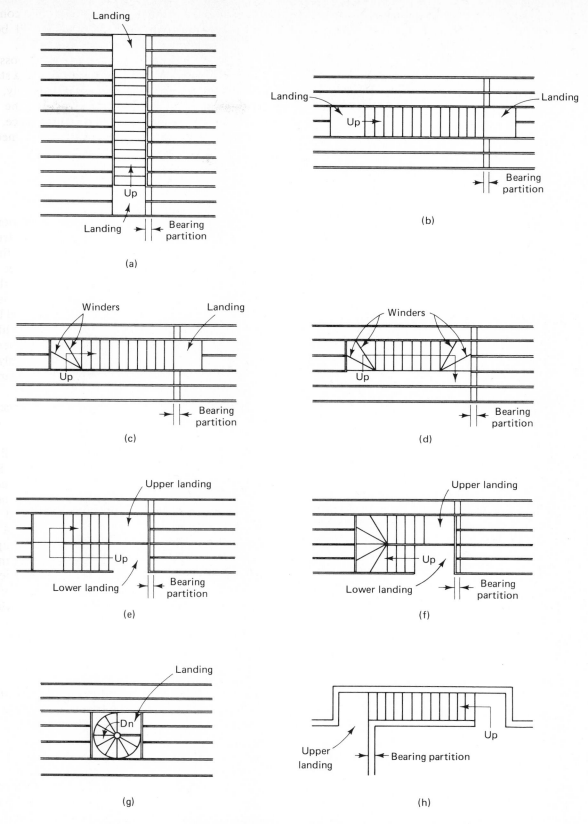

Fig. 9-2. Eight possible placements for a new stairway to attic space: (a) straight stairway across joists; (b) straight stairway with joists; (c, d, e, f) stairways with winders; (g) circular stairway; (h) outside stairway. Straight stairways (a, b) are by far the best and safest.

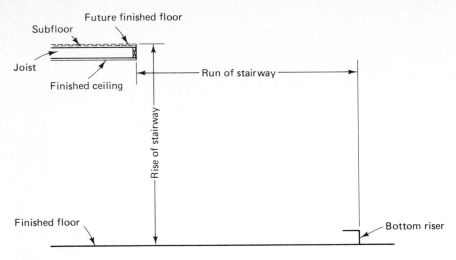

Fig. 9–3. To lay out a stairway, first find its rise—the distance in inches from floor level to floor level. The run of a stairway is the horizontal distance between the top and bottom risers. The rise is the basis for determining the number of steps, and the run for the depth of stair treads.

floor to ceiling of the room below. Add these two dimensions, and add in the thickness of ceiling material. If you don't know that thickness, use ¾" to be on the safe side.

To this height from joist tops to finished floor add either ¾" or 1¼" for the thickness of a subfloor. Then add the thickness of finish flooring material in the attic (see Table 4-1). The total is the **rise** of your stairway.

To avoid having to work with fractions, convert all numbers to decimals. Suppose that your overall height is 105⅞". Convert is to 105.875. Maximum riser height is 7¾" or 7.75. To avoid problems with decimal points, move the decimal over two places to the right, and divide 10587.5 by 775. The answer is 13.6 + . That is the number of risers you need. Because all risers should be the same height, you increase your answer to the next whole number, in this case 14.

Now divide the number of risers into the total height to establish the height of each riser in your stairway. In the example, divide 14 into 105.875, and you get 7.5625", or 7⁹⁄₁₆".

Tread Depth

A stairway always has one more riser than it does treads; the top tread is the upper floor itself. Therefore, in the stairway used as an example, you need 13 treads. A **tread** is the horizontal part of a step. The minimum depth of a tread is 9". Multiply the number of treads times the depth of each tread. Here the answer is 117", or 9'-9". This dimension is the *minimum* **run** of the stairway—its length measured horizontally (Fig. 9-3)

The 7¾" and 9" dimensions used in this example are code limitations. No riser should be *more* than 7¾", and no tread should be *less* than 9". The ideal ratio is 7½ to 10, but you will seldom have the space for an ideal attic stairway.

When you have established the minimum run of your stairway, look for a place on the floor plan where you can block out a space as long as your minimum run and 30" wide, with room for landings at both ends—a total space in the example of 30" × 177" (see Fig. 9-2a and b).

If you can't find one, you can fit a stairway with winders at one end into a space 30" × 150" (Fig. 9-2c). If you still can't find enough space, you can fit a stairway with winders at both ends into a space 30" × 120" (Fig. 9-2d).

Still no luck? If the problem is length rather than width, you may be able to work in a stairway 64" wide that turns back on itself. In 90" of length you can fit a stairway with two landings and a step between (Fig. 9-2e). In 60" of length you can fit a stairway with winders (Fig. 9-2f). In both (e) and (f), however, you need landing space at each end, and probably some other means of getting furniture into the attic space. Circular and turnback designs make moving not only hazardous but sometimes impossible.

Headroom for a Stairway

When you have found a tentative location for a stairway, make sure that you have enough headroom, particularly at the point where the stairs pass under the framing for the stairwell. To check, draw a section through the stairway (Fig. 9-4). You have determined its height and its minimum run. Draw a line to scale equal in length to the run. Then at one end draw the vertical height to scale. At the opposite end draw a vertical line equal to the height of a single riser. Now draw a diagonal line between these two points. This is the **nosing line**, the line through the front edge of each tread, which is called a **nose**.

From each end of the nosing line measure off 6'-8"

vertically, to scale, and draw another line at this point parallel to the nosing line. Any structure, including finished ceiling, must lie above this headroom line. By marking off the thickness of attic floor framing, including the finished floor above and finished ceiling below, you can determine how long the stairwell must be.

In this design process you determined the minimum run. If you have more room available, calculate the maximum run of the stairway—that is, the maximum space you have available. Divide this new dimension by the number of treads to establish tread depth. As long as the new tread depth is not more than 10″, draw a new section using the new tread dimension but keeping the same riser height. With deeper treads you will have a longer stairway and a longer stairwell, but the steps will be much safer and more comfortable to climb up and down.

All this drawing effort is solely to determine the practicality of the location and shape of your attic stairs. When you are ready to remodel, you must retake every measurement with great accuracy. In a stairway an error of as little as an inch can make a difference in safety.

DORMERS

Even when fully insulated, attic space is warmer in summer than rooms below. At some time of the day the sun shines perpendicularly on one side of the roof, and heat builds up quickly. In your planning, then, you should provide as much cross-ventilation as conditions permit.

Most older homes have windows in the gables at ends of attics. Newer homes are more likely to have ventilating louvers. When you partition attic space into more than one long room, the single window in end rooms won't provide satisfactory ventilation. You need to provide more air circulation—and extra light—through windows in the sides of rooms, and that means a dormer or two.

"Dormer" is a French word (pronounced door-may) meaning to sleep. Originally, a dormer was a sleeping room, then the name for a window in a projection through a sloping roof. Today a dormer is the projection itself, usually with a window in it. A dormer may be not much wider than the window itself, or it may extend from side wall to side wall of the house.

Building a single dormer is not as difficult as it might look. A typical dormer has a front wall taller than it is wide, with a window in it, and two triangular walls on the sides. The dormer roof should match the main roof in style and pitch. The simplest dormer is just wide enough to fit between two rafters 32″ apart. Headers support the cut rafter between them. The ridgeboard of a single dormer must be no higher than the main ridgeboard of the house from which it projects. It can be lower, however, and usually is.

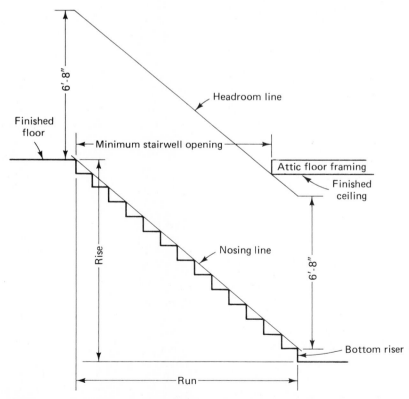

Fig. 9–4. Draw a section through your proposed attic stairway to see whether you can provide minimum headroom, and what size to make the stairwell.

For best appearance single dormers should be placed symmetrically. One broad dormer can look well on a roof not more than 12' wide. On a wider roof, plan on two or even three dormers, depending on attic room arrangement. Space two equidistant from the rakes of the roof, and any others equally between.

A shed dormer is a little more difficult to build only because it is larger and heavier. Its front wall is always a rectangle, but the rectangle is wider than it is tall—the opposite of a single dormer. It also contains more than one window, and may provide light and ventilation to more than one room. Side walls are triangular, but the roof is a shed type sloping away from the ridge. The upper edge of the shed roof may slope from the ridge itself, or from some point farther down the slope, depending on the headroom available. Rafters of a single dormer are 2 × 4s; rafters in a shed dormer are 2 × 6s or 2 × 8s, based on their length and the probable snow load.

The side walls of a long shed dormer may be built directly above the side walls of the main house if the roof overhangs at least 12" at the rake. But a shed dormer looks best when its sides lie inside the planes of walls below. Then the existing roof forms a visual frame around the dormer, and greatly improves its appearance.

YOUR ATTIC FLOOR PLAN

Up to this point you have established only the feasibility of remodeling your attic. Now you must get your ideas down on paper accurately. You have already done part of this work; you made a stairway layout and drew a section through the attic. The remaining drawing is a floor plan of attic space, complete with locations of heat sources, electrical outlets and lights, and any plumbing extensions.

When you plan a room addition, you are only slightly limited in planning its size and shape. When you plan a garage or carport conversion, you are working within fixed walls, but everything you need to see for planning is on one level. With an attic remodeling, however, you have two floor levels to contend with, nonrectangular space, and an existing structure that must be strengthened temporarily while you work.

As you develop your floor plan, work back and forth between the existing structure and your drawing. First draw an elevation of the wall up which your stairway will climb, and draw in the stairway. Then lightly mark on the wall itself the location of the first riser, the nosing line, and a horizontal line 6'-8" down from the ceiling.

From the ceiling drop a plumb bob so that the cord lies exactly over the intersection of the nosing and 6'-8" lines. Mark this point on the ceiling. Then from this point measure at 90° to the wall the width of your stairway, and make another mark on the ceiling.

Connect the two marks with a lightly drawn line. This line marks the approximate end of the stairwell above its lower end. You still have to allow for the thickness of material used to finish the stairwell.

Now from the first riser mark, measure off the run of the stairway along the wall and mark that point. From the mark draw a light vertical line to the ceiling, again using your plumb bob to establish the upper end of the line. From the upper end of the line measure at 90° to the wall the width of your stairway, and mark it. Then connect the two marks, thus locating the upper end of the stairwell. Finally, connect the ends of the two 90° lines with a line drawn parallel to the wall. Now the shape of your stairwell is drawn on the ceiling.

By placing boards, furniture, or something similar on the floor directly below the lines on the ceiling, you can see just how much space the stairway will occupy, and how it will affect the size, shape, and usefulness of the room from which the stairs rise. If you plan to enclose the stairway completely, hang a sheet from the two corners to get the proper effect. If the stairway will be open on one side, fold the sheet diagonally and drape it between the upper corner and the first riser to see how the stairway will look.

If the result isn't what you had hoped, you may have to look for another place to run stairs. But if you are satisfied with the results so far, then transfer the corner points into the attic by driving a nail at least 3" long upward at each corner. If you hit wood, pull out the nail and drive another 2" from the corner. Whether you move 2" along the end line or side line depends on which way the ceiling joists run.

Then climb into the attic and dig through the insulation between joists until you find the nails. If you are lucky, the nails will just miss a joist, and you will need to cut only one to install a stairway. Otherwise, you must cut two. Using the nails as a guide, mark the ends of the stairwell on the side of the nearest joist, then carry the lines across the top of the joist. Next draw the outline of the stairwell across the tops of other joists so that it matches the outline on the ceiling below.

Now study the outline. If you need to cut more than one joist, can you move the stairway slightly to avoid this? Chances are that you can't, but it's worth a long look to save you materials and labor. Next, measure from the head of the stairwell to rafters. Do you have at least 6'-8" of height here and at all other points above the stairway? If not, you must relocate it. Finally, see if there are any pipes, wiring, or ducts within the outline. They will have to be moved, and you must figure out where they can be relocated before you proceed.

If the stairway location still appears good, recheck all dimensions, particularly the location of the nosing line, headroom at all points, and the size of the stairwell opening. Then remove all insulation within the stairwell's outline, and assemble the tools for cutting away the ceiling.

STAIRWAY CONSTRUCTION

The best time to remodel an attic is in late spring or early fall, when you need neither heat from the furnace nor cooling from an air conditioning system, and the chances of fair weather are reasonably good. While you build a stairway, the floor below the attic is completely open. The opening can provide good ventilation in warm weather, but will lose a lot of heat in cool weather. Yet the stairway is the logical place to start, so that you have a way of moving building materials into the attic.

There are five basic steps in a complete attic remodeling: building a stairway, modifying the roof, insulating, installing subflooring, and erecting partitions. The order in which you attack these steps depends partly on the time of year, and how many steps you must complete. Under most circumstances it's best to build the rough stairway first, then install subflooring, next build supporting partitions, then open the roof, insulate, and finally complete partitioning and finish the stairway.

If the ceiling is gypsum wallboard, you will need a sharp utility knife, a utility saw, and goggles. Don't use a good saw for cutting; the gypsum will dull it quickly. If you don't have an old saw you're willing to part with, buy an inexpensive utility saw just for this purpose. Using a metal straightedge to cut against, first cut along your ceiling lines with a knife to score the surface and make a clean break line. Then drill a hole near one corner large enough to accept the saw. Cut in both directions away from the corner, then go back and cut the corners. Where you cross a joist, cut into it as little as possible to save effort. You don't shorten the joist at this point anyway.

For cutting away plaster you can use a utility saw, but the job will go much more quickly with a power saw and a carbide-tipped blade. If your ceiling has acoustical tiles, cut all the way through the border tiles with your knife, and remove the tiles before cutting the backing material.

Work carefully, and take your time. Cutting any gypsum-based material is dusty and messy, and some loose insulation is bound to fall through. A drop cloth over good carpeting or wood flooring offers the best protection against damage, and makes it easier to remove the debris.

If you expect that the ceiling will be open for some time, have a sheet or two of plywood available to cover the opening. A tarpaulin or layer of polyethylene will provide cover, but neither of them will support you if you accidentally step into the opening.

Framing the Stairwell

All framing members around a stairwell must be double—that is, two joists on each side and two headers at each end (see Fig. 9-5). Pairs of joists are exactly alike. Therefore, you may have to remove any attic subflooring to determine the length of the added joists and how their ends are shaped. The inner end is cut square and overlaps the bearing wall that supports it. The outer end must be trimmed to the slope of the roof.

You will need to cut one new joist if one of the existing joists lies atop a partition and is supported by it. You will need to cut two if your stairway fits between existing joists. You will need three if you can use an existing joist on one side, but can't fit the stairway against an existing joist on the other side. You must cut four if no existing joists are useful. However many you need, mark and cut one first and test its fit. When the fit is right, use that joist as a template for cutting the rest.

The sides of joists should be covered to give the stairwell a finished appearance. When you work between existing joists, the space will be 30½", and the best finishing material is ¼" plywood so that you hold to the 30" width of stairway. If you have a little more room, you can finish the sides with ½" gypsum wallboard, but must leave 31" between joists. Adjust your chalk marks as necessary to allow for finish materials.

First install any new joists on their marks (step 1 in Fig. 9-5), but don't install the doubling joists yet. Toenail these joists into the top plates of supporting walls or partitions, driving one 8d nail on each side of the joist at each end.

The marks you made at the end of the stairwell show the length of the finished opening. To allow for headers, measure off 3" away from your marks at the upper end of the stairway, and draw new marks across the framing joists and those to be cut. Carry these marks down the sides of the joists; use a framing square to make sure that the lines are plumb. At the other end of the stairwell measure off 3" plus the thickness of finish material, and again mark.

Cut all joists to be removed along these new sets of marks (step 2, Fig. 9-5). Make all cuts at one end first, then have someone support the cut ends while you cut the other ends. Cut carefully; the cuts must be plumb or headers won't fit properly. Save the offall for use as headers.

Now cut one header to length and test the fit. Use it as a template for cutting the other headers. Set the two outer headers on the vertical marks on uncut joists, and nail through the headers into all cut joists with three 8d nails (step 3, Fig. 9-5). Complete attachment with three 8d nails driven through the sides of joists into the ends of headers. Drive the first nail partway in, then check plumb before driving the nail home.

Next, fit the inner headers in place (step 4, Fig. 9-5), and nail them into the outer headers at each end and at some point between where you won't hit other nails. Finish the job with three nails through joists into the ends of the inner headers.

Finally, add the doubling joists outside the stairwell opening. Toenail them into the top plates at each end (one side only), then nail them to regular joists

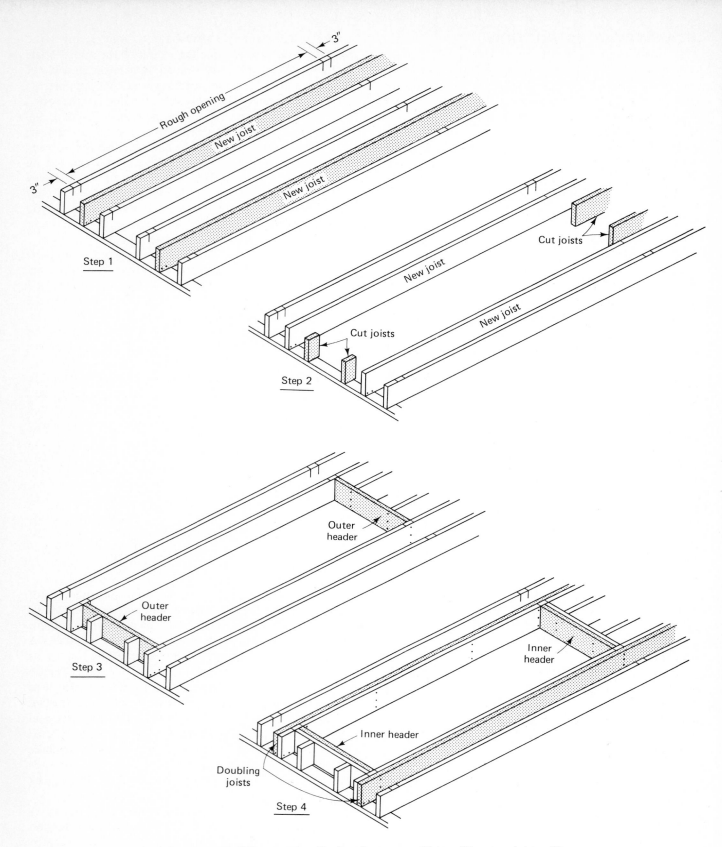

Fig. 9–5. Building a stairwell takes four steps: (1) installing new joists, (2) cutting existing joists that are in the way, (3) installing outer headers, and (4) doubling headers and framing joists.

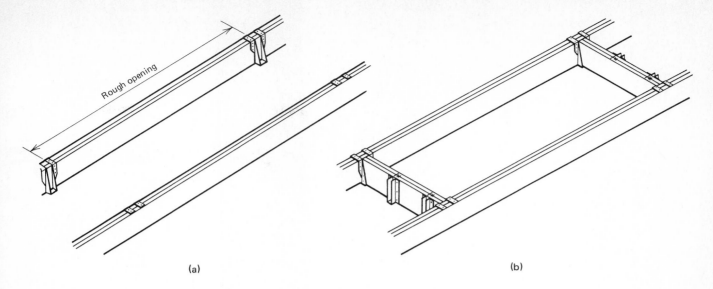

(a)   (b)

Fig. 9–6. When headers are supported by joist hangers, the doubled joists are installed first (a), then the pairs of headers (b). The work leading up to this stage—steps (1) and (2) in Fig. 9–5—is the same.

at the ends and every 4′ between. Nail about ¾″ from the top and bottom and at a midpoint.

Builders often use joist hangers to assure that headers fit properly. If you use hangers, you install the side joists first, then the doubling joists. Place hangers on your marks as shown in Fig. 9-6a; they must be wide enough to take two headers. Drop outer headers in first, and nail them to the cut joists. Then insert inner headers (Fig. 9-6b), and nail them to the outer headers. End nailing is not required.

Cover the stairwell opening with plywood until it is in your way when you build the stairway.

Building the Stairway

Unless you have the tools and are experienced in finish carpentry, have the stairway built for you. You can hire a carpenter to do the complete job, including rails and trim. Or you can have the stairway built to order in a local millwork shop; shops are listed in classified telephone directories under "Stairways."

To build the stairway yourself, first measure diagonally from the top of the stairwell opening to the mark for the bottom riser (refer to Fig. 9-4). Tack pieces of material on the header to represent the thickness of the subfloor and finish flooring. You will need two 2 × 12s at least this long for **stringers** to support the steps.

Stringers are supported at their lower ends on a 2 × 4 kick plate laid flat and nailed into the floor (Fig. 9-7). At their tops they may be notched to fit over a 2 × 4 ledger, or attached with metal joist hangers.

Marking and Cutting Stringers. To mark the locations of treads and risers on stringers you can use either a framing square or a pitch board. On the

framing square carry the riser height on the tongue and the tread depth on the blade. Set the square on the stringer so that the two dimensions fall exactly at the edge of the stringer. Then mark the shape. You can work from either the outside or inside edges of the square, whichever is more comfortable for you. This method is similar to that shown in Fig. 7-8b for laying out a rafter.

A **pitch board** for marking stringers is simply a triangle of scrap plywood or 1 × 8 nailed to a short length of 2 × 4. One side of the triangle is equal to riser height, and the other side is equal to tread depth (Fig. 9-8). Cut the triangle with maximum accuracy, and attach it down the center to the 2 × 4.

With either your framing square or pitch board, first mark the floor line across one end of the stringer. Then work upward, marking the locations of all treads and risers. At the top, mark the plumb cut where the stringer will butt against the stairwell header.

Cut along the floor line and plumb cut line, notch for the ledger if necessary, raise the stringer into position, and test the fit. The stringer should fit flush at both ends; if not, adjust the cuts until it does. Measure headroom to make sure that it is adequate beneath the other stairwell header. The top of the stringer should lie 2¾″ to 3″ below the nosing line, measured vertically.

When the fit is good, make the cuts you've marked for risers and treads, and use this stringer as a template for marking and cutting the other stringers. If you are good with a power saw, you can save time by laying the two stringers flat across sawhorses, tacking them together to prevent movement, and cutting them both simultaneously.

If you find that you have miscalculated somewhere, and either you have too little headroom or clearance is tight, you can save vertical space in three

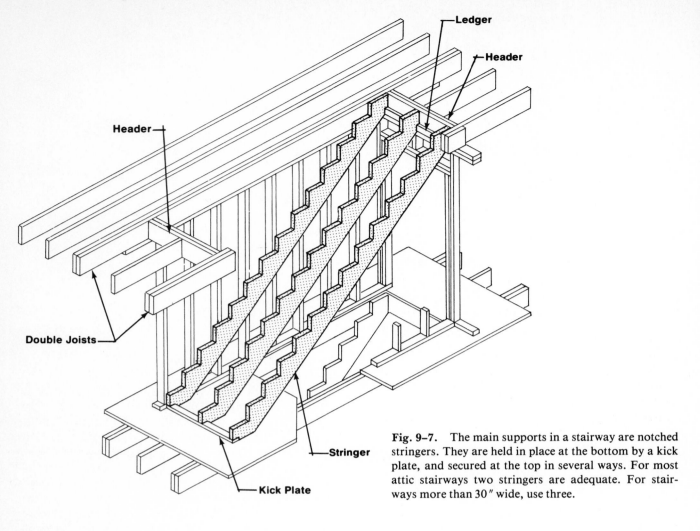

Fig. 9–7. The main supports in a stairway are notched stringers. They are held in place at the bottom by a kick plate, and secured at the top in several ways. For most attic stairways two stringers are adequate. For stairways more than 30″ wide, use three.

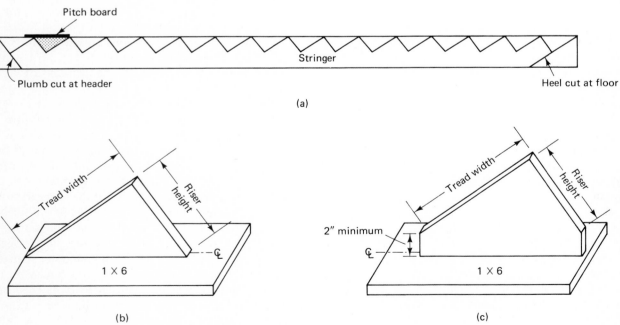

Fig. 9–8. The simplest way to mark stringers (a) is with a pitch board made from scrap boards. Make a triangular pitch board (b) for marking open stringers, where treads and risers fit onto stringers. Make a pitch board with an extension (c) for marking closed stringers, where treads and risers fit into grooves in stringers.

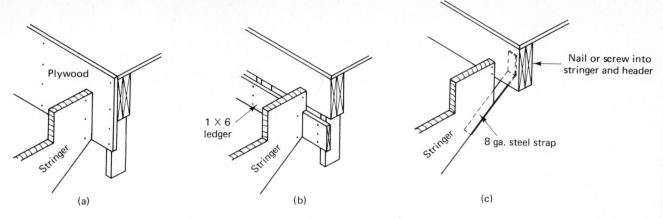

Nail or screw into
stringer and header

Stringer

1 × 6
ledger

Stringer

Stringer

8 ga. steel strap

(a)   (b)   (c)

Fig. 9–9. At the top of a stairway stringers are usually notched to fit over a ledger (see Fig. 9–7) or attached with joist hangers. When conditions do not permit these common methods, the three shown here are acceptable alternatives.

ways. You can attach the ends of stringers to a wide piece of plywood, locating the first tread a full riser height below the upper floor level (Fig. 9-9a). Or you can set a ledger into notches in studs below the header, and in turn notch the stringers to fit over the ledger (Fig. 9-9b). Both of these methods require a stud wall below the header. If you don't have a wall, you can butt the stringers against the header, and secure them with metal straps (Fig. 9-9c).

Strings. You will almost always have a wall the full length of a stairway on one side. On the other side you may have one of three conditions: another full-length wall, forming a closed stairway; a stub wall along part of its length; or no wall at all, forming an open stairway.

In a closed stairway stringers fit against a length of 1 × 12, called a **string**, which is capped with a small molding (Fig. 9-10a). In a partially open stairway with a full-height stub wall, the lower wall is triangular, with a sloping top plate that lies flush with the top of the string. In an open stairway the triangular wall fits under the stringer, and the string is notched to the same shape as the stringer (Fig. 9-10b).

To lay out a string that fits against a wall, mark a plumb cut at its lower end. Along this line measure down the height of the baseboard at the floor, and draw the cut for the floor line at 90° at this point. On the wall measure vertically about 1½″ above the nosing line, and draw a line at this point parallel to the nosing line. Tack the string in position along this line. Then mark the cut at the upper end, and at the same time mark the cut for shortening the baseboard.

Usually, you will have a partition in the attic above the wall beside the stairway. In this case give the upper end of the string a plumb cut to fit against a future baseboard upstairs. If you have a railing instead of a wall around the stairwell, give the string a horizontal cut that is flush with the future finish floor.

Mark the second string for cutting, using the first one as a template, but don't cut it yet.

Installing Strings and Stringers. Strings and stringers must be nailed into studs. One device for locating studs hidden behind wall materials is a **stud finder**, available at hardware stores. Mark the centers of studs along the base of the wall, check the spacing for accuracy (assuming that the spacing was uniform to begin with), then carry the marks lightly up the wall. Set the string in place, and nail it with three 8d casing nails at each stud, being careful to keep the string on a diagonal parallel to the nosing line.

Next, cut and nail the kick plate to the floor (see Fig. 9-7), and add the support at the top of the stairwell. Cut both these pieces to exact length—the clear width of your stairway—and set the stringers flush with the ends. Before nailing, check the cuts for treads to be sure that they are level, and set your level across both stringers to make sure that they are at the same level. If not, shim the lower one on top of the kick plate. Nail any stringer that fits against a string with a pair of 16d nails, driven all the way into studs between the three nails holding the strings.

As long as you use the stairway for moving building materials upward and scrap downward, defer finishing the stairway to avoid damaging the treads. Cut temporary treads out of 1″ boards or ½″ plywood, lay them across the stringers, and nail once at each end near the middle of the tread. Don't drive the nails all the way home; let the heads stick up just enough so that you can remove them later. Or use double-headed (duplex) nails.

Finishing the Stairway

When the day arrives to complete your stairway, order the treads, risers, railings, balusters, and all other parts from your lumber dealer or a local millwork company. Treads and risers are stock items, and you order by the

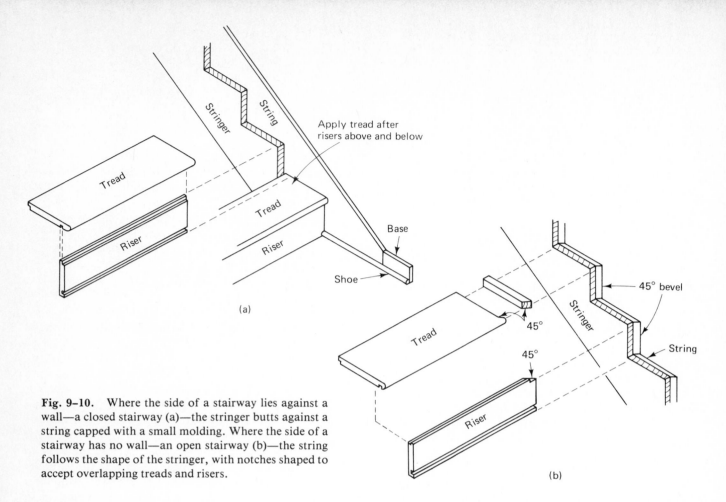

Fig. 9-10. Where the side of a stairway lies against a wall—a closed stairway (a)—the stringer butts against a string capped with a small molding. Where the side of a stairway has no wall—an open stairway (b)—the string follows the shape of the stringer, with notches shaped to accept overlapping treads and risers.

tread depth and riser height, which won't vary, and by length, which may. Parts that fit between two strings are all the same length. But where the stairway has no string on one side, lengths will be greater.

To determine exactly how much greater, cut and install the second string. It fits flush with the stringer at each tread, but extends the thickness of a riser beyond each riser, with the extra thickness beveled at a 45° angle (see Fig. 9-10). Riser length is equal to the width of the stairway plus the thickness of the string, with one end cut at 45°. Tread length is equal to the width of the stairway, plus the thickness of the string, plus the width of the nosing. Sometimes the return nosing is included as part of the tread, but more often it is a separate piece that you glue on later.

To install treads and risers, begin at the bottom of the stairway. Nail the first riser about 2″ from its bottom edge; use 6d nails if treads will be exposed, or 5d nails if you plan to carpet the stairway. Install addition risers as far up as you can comfortably reach.

Then spread glue liberally into the grooves in both risers and treads. Fit the tread into the groove in the back riser, and press it firmly onto the shiplapped edge of the front riser. To hold the treads in place until the glue dries, drive a single 12d finishing nail at the center of the tread into each stringer. A good job of gluing is the secret to a stairway without squeaks.

Repeat this process on up the stairway, completing three or four steps at a time. Let the glue set thoroughly on one set of treads before you step on them. If you don't have time to wait, work quickly so that all treads are in place before the glue dries. Otherwise, you may break the glue bond and the stairs may squeak.

Handrails

In a closed stairway the handrail is usually attached to the right-hand wall as you descend, at a point between 30 and 34″ above the nosing line. Wood handrails are a stock item at most lumberyards, and you simply decide which shape you like and order them cut to length. They are supported on metal brackets attached with screws to the underside of the railing and through finish wall material into studs. Three brackets are enough—one about a foot from each end and the third midway between.

On a Cap Plate. In a partially open stairway the handrail should be on the open side. Where the stairway is open and between strings, cover the string and top plate of the triangular wall under the stairway with a cap cut from ¾ stock. The cap must be wide enough to cover the combined thickness of the string, 2 × 4 top plate, and wall material, and overhang about ¾″ on each side—roughly 6¼" total from edge to edge.

At many metalworking shops you can buy handrails fabricated from standard parts and assembled to meet your stairway's specific conditions. They are attached with screws into the cap and the finished end of the stub wall. Or you can buy the necessary wood parts and fit your own. The parts are shown in Fig. 9-11a. Locate the lowest baluster flush with the first riser, then space other balusters equally from that point to the stub wall—between 6 and 10″ apart measured horizontally.

On the cap mark the centerline of the handrail; it should line up with the centerline of the end of the stub wall. From the centerline measure off on one side half the width of the grooved subrail, and draw a line at that point parallel to the centerline. Cut the subrail to length; let it extend about 2″ beyond the lower baluster. Give both ends a plumb cut.

With glue and 6d finishing nails attach the subrail. Then mark the locations of balusters, and trim both ends of all of them to the slope of the subrail. Glue the balusters in place on the marks. Then fill the gaps between balusters with fillets, including a short fillet below the lowest baluster. Fillets must be cut to fit tightly into the groove in the subrail and against balusters. They should project slightly above the subrail, but can be flat, rounded, or molded to any shape you like. Test the fit of all parts before gluing any in place.

Handrails designed for attachment over balusters are often grooved on the underside. Cut fillets to fit in the groove of the same lengths as fillets in the subrail below. Wedge the fillets in place, gapping for the balusters, fit the handrail over the balusters, and test the fit. When all pieces mesh smoothly, fill the gaps with glue and reset the handrail on the balusters. Let the glue dry thoroughly before you use the handrail.

If the bottom of the handrail is flat, attach a subrail to it and space the balusters with fillets. Glue the ends of balusters, then drive screws into predrilled holes through all fillets and into the handrail.

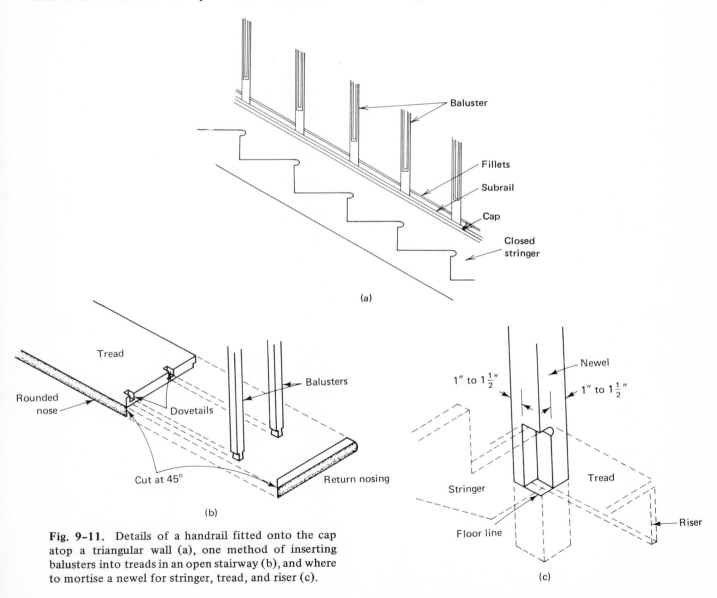

Fig. 9-11. Details of a handrail fitted onto the cap atop a triangular wall (a), one method of inserting balusters into treads in an open stairway (b), and where to mortise a newel for stringer, tread, and riser (c).

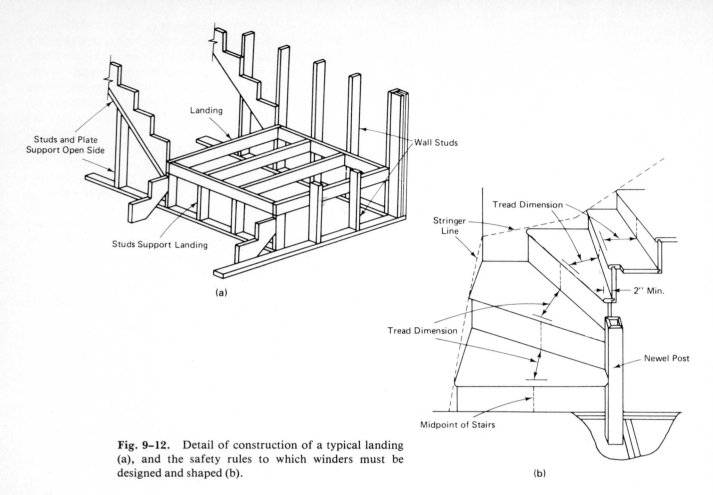

Fig. 9–12. Detail of construction of a typical landing (a), and the safety rules to which winders must be designed and shaped (b).

Trim

To trim a closed stairway, add a small cove molding along the tops of exposed strings. If you don't add carpeting, add another small cove molding under the nosing of each tread. Attach both moldings with glue and brads.

In an open stairway the lower ends of balusters are either doweled or dovetailed to fit into treads (see Fig. 9-11b). Balusters are spaced closer together than when they fit into subrails. They are usually set flush with the face of each riser and at the midpoint between. Therefore, you have two lengths of balusters, one longer than the other by half a riser height. Cut the upper ends to the slope of the handrail, and attach them between fillets as just described.

Cut the lower ends square, and fit them against the side edge of treads. If the ends are doweled, drill holes about ¾″ deep into treads at the proper spacing, and of a diameter just great enough for a tight fit. If the ends are dovetailed, cut matching dovetails of the same dimensions in the edges of treads.

Fill the holes or dovetails with glue, and insert the balusters. Then cut nosing returns for the edges of treads. Attach them with glue and just enough finishing nails to hold them firmly until the glue dries. Add a small cove molding under the return nosings.

Newels

When a handrail is long and the stairway will receive a lot of use, the lowest point of the balustrade should be a **newel**. The newel should rise about 2″ beyond the face of the first riser, and center on the handrail. In good-quality construction the stringer, bottom riser, and bottom tread are all mortised into the newel for maximum strength (Fig. 9-11c). If you don't have mortising equipment, cut the bottom riser a little short for a butt fit, and notch the bottom tread to fit around the newel.

Landings

A landing is simply a lightweight floor frame (Fig. 9-12a). You support it on studs when it butts against a wall. You support it on a post and short studs nailed to a bottom plate when there is no wall. The post consists of two 2 × 4s, one cut square on top and the other beveled to support the diagonal plate atop a triangular wall.

Landings are usually square, with both dimensions equal to the stairway's width. The platform is simply an oversized tread, made of the same wood and with a similar nosing.

Winders

Two rules govern the shape of winders. First, at the midpoint in the length of the tread, the depth of a winder should be the same as the depth of a rectangular tread in that stairway. For example, if your stairway is 30″ wide and treads are 9″ deep, then at a point 15″ from the bend in the stairway the winders must be 9″ deep (Fig. 9-12b). Second, winders must not come to a point at the newel, but taper to a smaller tread. A newel is required with open winders.

The only sure way to lay out winders is full size on the floor. Each will be a different size and shape. Usually, there are three together. The upper one is a triangle with its hypotenuse at the nosing. The lower one is a similar triangle, but with the hypotenuse at the upper riser. The middle one is a trapezium, with no sides parallel but two meeting at right angles. Strings on the straight portion of stairway above and below the winders are standard. Where the stairway turns, however, they must be shaped to meet stair conditions.

In other words, if you must have winders, you would be wise to have them built and assembled for you, even if you build the stairway yourself from the winders upward.

With your stairway built or at least usable, your next steps are to shape and protect attic rooms.

10

Shaping Attic Space

(a)

(b)

(c)

The attic of this Victorian house (a) was finished generations ago, but it was uninsulated, plaster was falling off old wood lath, and the space had limited light. Headroom was excellent, however. First the rafters were completely exposed (b), and old wall materials torn off. Then the roof was resurfaced and the entire exterior insulated. Today (c) skylights and a new floor-to-ceiling window make the roof bright and cheerful, and comfortable under all weather conditions. End walls are gypsum wallboard, and other surfaces are cedar siding. Note the center ceiling board, which permits a change of direction of the lap siding. (Courtesy American Plywood Association.)

Attic space between rafters and joists is seldom completely open. Roofs built with standard rafters usually have **collar beams**—horizontal members between pairs of rafters every 32 or 48″. Collar beams may lie anywhere from 2 to 6′ above floor level. They will be in your way, but leave them in place until you build a supporting structure to replace them.

A roof supported by trusses is a more difficult problem, and may defy solution. For one thing web members of trusses will be in your way. Yet they not only brace the roof but also support the chords that act as ceiling joists, which are not strong enough alone to support an attic floor. It is sometimes possible to build a membrane of heavy plywood, attached to chords with screws and glue, sufficient to support attic rooms, and

to carry the weight of the roof on knee walls built near the midpoints of rafters. But such a design requires professional knowledge of construction and the interrelationship of members. If you have roof trusses, consult with an architect or with a builder who employs a professional engineer. They can tell you whether attic remodeling is practical for you. Otherwise, you can begin work on the subfloor.

SUBFLOOR

If your attic already has a subfloor, study its condition. A subfloor adequate for attic storage may not be good enough as a base for finish flooring. Your choice of

126

finish flooring has an important bearing on the subfloor beneath it.

A floor of hardwood strips may be laid over any subfloor that is reasonably solid and level. The strips are a structural material, and can actually be fastened to joists with no subfloor at all. Any other material—wood blocks, linoleum, tiles of all kinds, and carpeting—require a subfloor, and all but carpeting also require underlayment. **Underlayment** is a thin material, usually hardboard, that bridges the joints between sheets of subflooring and provides a smooth base for finish flooring.

But you can't lay a smooth underlayment when the joints beneath it are uneven. Seams will eventually telegraph through any thin finish flooring material, such as vinyl tile or linoleum. A subfloor of plywood that has been laid with care should have few uneven joints to correct. A subfloor of boards has probably been in place for many years, and cupping at edges is likely. You can use a power floor sander to knock down the high spots, but in the long run you will have a smoother and stronger subfloor if you replace the boards with plywood.

Inspection

To determine how much work you must do, walk the entire subfloor slowly, with good light on it, and preferably with someone in the rooms below who can tell you how much sound of people walking you transmit through the floor. Look and listen for these problems, and mark their locations:

- *Squeaks.* A squeak occurs when two pieces of wood rub together, and can usually be corrected with added fasteners. Mark with chalk the spot where you caused the squeak.
- *Springy spots.* Their cause may be a weak board or a weak spot in the floor framing below. Determine whether just the subfloor is moving or its support by removing the board and stepping on the joist. Either replace the board, or strengthen the structure with **cleats** on both sides of the weak joist. For cleats use 1″ boards the same depth as the joist and as long as you can install. Attach cleats with pairs of 6d nails every 18 to 20″.
- *Broken or split boards.* Such boards must be replaced.
- *Large gaps between sheets or boards.* Plywood is laid with a gap of about 1/16″ between edges, and boards with a gap of about 1/8″. A gap of more than 1/2″ must be corrected.
- *Uneven edges.* With a power floor sander you can smooth off differences in height up to 1/16″. When the difference is greater, try to determine why. Sometimes you can level the edges with additional

fasteners. But if the problem is warping, replace the faulty pieces.

- *Uneven surface.* Set a carpenter's level across seams and at various points in the middle of sheets or boards. Sometimes boards are tight at edges but bow upward in the center. This condition prevents a level underlayment, and the bowed pieces must be replaced.

A New Subfloor

To prepare for laying subflooring, first remove any insulation that extends above the tops of joists. Otherwise, it acts as a cushion, and squeaks will develop. Then lay your carpenter's level across every three adjacent joists and at right angles to them. When properly installed, floor joists are set with their crowns up—that is, with any high spot in the middle upward instead of downward. Occasionally, a joist is set with its crown down, and your floor will have a low spot at that point. To correct any difference in height of more than 1/4″, add a shim of an equal height when you lay your subfloor. But mark the spot for the shim now. Usually, a variation of less than 1/4″ will correct itself when you attach the subfloor.

Next look for cocked joists—those that aren't plumb. A ridge in the ceiling below is one sign of a cocked joist. To straighten the offending member, cut several 2 × 4 blocks just long enough to fit between the cocked joist and flanking joists and to force the member upright. Wedge the blocks in place like solid bridging (see Fig. 7-4), with their tops flush with the tops of the joists. Nail through the sides of joists into the ends of blocks. Then add a set of blocks on the other side, offset just far enough so you can nail them.

Finally, check the ends of joists where they meet over a bearing partition below. They must be level, but sometimes deflection over the years causes ends to rise slightly. Knock down any high spots with a hand sander, wood file, or rasp.

When you have the floor structure ready to accept subflooring, begin at the stairwell opening and work outward in all directions. Use a subflooring grade of plywood designed for the spacing of your joists. A type manufactured with interior glue is adequate. It comes in 4′ × 8′ sheets with either square or tongue-and-groove edges. If your floor framing is level, order square-edged material. But if the framing is still a little uneven, order tongue-and-groove material for a better result. As long as joists are spaced no more than 16″ on centers, you can use 1/2″ material, but you'll have a stronger, quieter floor with a 3/4″ subfloor.

Planning Seams. By taking the time to plan a layout for sheets of subflooring, you can save material and the number of cuts. First snap a chalk line from one end of the attic to the other—along the header at the top

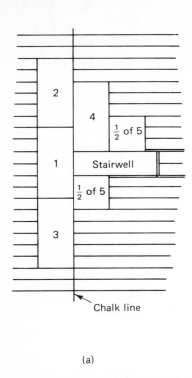

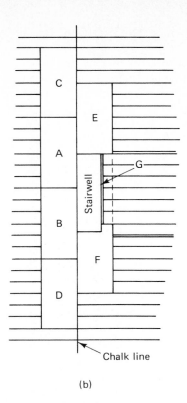

(a)   (b)

Fig. 10–1. Follow the subflooring layout in (a) when your stairwell runs the same direction as joists, and the layout in (b) when the stairwell crosses floor joists.

of the stairway if the stairway runs parallel to joists, or along the header nearest the center of the attic if the stairway runs across joists. Except at an opening, the end of each sheet must fall on the centerline of a joist. At the stairwell the first sheet fits flush with the inner edge of the header. Plan your layout so that you end up with one-third, one-half, or two-thirds of a sheet at end walls.

When your stairway runs parallel to joists, set sheet 1 with one end on the centerline of a joist and one side overlapping the header at the top of the stairs (Fig. 10-1a). Set pieces 2 and 3 on the chalk line, making sure that their edges form a straight line. Lay sheet 4 with its outer end centered on a joist and the other end at or overlapping the stairwell framing. Then cut sheet 5 into two pieces and lay them as shown. Lay the next sheet at the end of 2, and continue laying sheets in a diagonal pattern until you have completely floored one side of the attic to a point beneath the future knee wall. Trim subflooring flush with stairwell framing members where necessary. Then lay the other side of the subfloor in the same general pattern.

When your stairway runs at right angles to joists, set sheets A and B with their ends meeting over a joist at about the midpoint of the stairwell (Fig. 10-1b). Then lay sheets C and D along the chalkline. Next, at whichever end of the stairwell is framed by joists, lay full sheet E. Fit sheet F so that its edge is 96″ from the edge of sheet E. Complete the other side of the subfloor

to the knee wall and end walls, then come back to the open side. You can cut piece G at any time, but it's better to wait until you know what size pieces of scrap you have available.

Cutting. By laying at least four full sheets of plywood before you need to cut any, you have enough for a working platform. Check corners of all pieces for square and trim them if necessary before you haul them upstairs. Mark all cuts with a square to assure a right-angle cut, and be sure that the blade is plumb when you cut. Even a slight angle from square or plumb can cause attachment problems.

With square-edged plywood, it doesn't matter which side or edge you set flush with the stairwell opening. With tongue-and-groove subflooring, however, it does. Set the grooved edges of pieces 1 and 4 flush at the opening. Similarly, set the grooved edges of pieces A, B, and E at the opening. You can slide piece G into place from the stairwell side.

When a piece must be notched to fit around any opening, such as piece F, lay the piece first, attach it, then cut along framing members with a power saw.

Attachment. When you have the first sheet of square-edged subflooring in exact position, nail at the four corners with 8d threaded nails, setting them about ⅜″ in from the two edges. Complete attachment with nails spaced about 6″ apart across the ends and into joists under the edges of the sheet, and about every 9 to 10″ between—six nails per joist. Nail all other sheets in the same manner.

With tongue-and-groove subflooring nail 6″ apart into the framing around the stairwell *only*. Fit adjoining pieces tight before nailing at the seam. A single row of nails driven through both panels at about the midpoint of the tongue provides ample holding power.

To make sure that joints are tight, but to avoid damaging the edges of tongue-and-groove panels, pound on a piece of scrap held against the edge. Never pound on the edge itself. Use a piece of 2 × 4 against grooved edges, and a piece of grooved material fitted over tongued edges.

At Obstructions. Rising through your attic space somewhere you are bound to find such obstructions as a vent stack and chimney. Framing around a chimney should already be completed with doubled joists and headers by the original builder (Fig. 10-2a). At a smaller opening, perhaps for a flue or duct that fits between joists, frame with headers to support the edge of the subfloor (Fig. 10-2b). Building codes require a gap of 2″ between a chimney or flue and the nearest wood framing, so allow this space when you install the headers.

At small openings for such things as heat ducts and piping that do not yet extend above subfloor level but will eventually, mark their locations on the sheet of subflooring that covers them, then lay the sheet uncut. You can cut or drill later when you are ready to extend the system.

Where a stack interferes, cut subflooring so that the distance from the end of one sheet is at least 16″ from the centerline of the pipe. Then cut the next sheet to end at least 16″ from the centerline on the other side of the pipe (see Fig. 10-2b). With a saber saw, cut out of each piece a half circle with a diameter ¼″ greater than the diameter of the pipe. Then install short pieces of 2 × 4 blocking between joists and on each side of the pipe to support the notched edges.

KNEE WALLS

A knee wall is much like any other wall, with a bottom plate and a doubled top plate. The only difference is that studs are shorter. Knee walls vary in height, but should not be less than 4′-0″ high. A common height is 5′-4⅜″, measured from the surface of the subfloor to the underside of rafters. Why that odd dimension? Because each stud is then 4′-11⅞″ long, and you can cut two of them from a 10′ length of 2 × 4 without waste.

To establish the location of a knee wall after you decide on its height, measure that height upward from the subfloor at both ends of the attic, and mark it with chalk. Then drop a plumb bob from each mark, and mark the subfloor with chalk at these points. Next, snap chalk lines across the attic between both pairs of marks. Your subflooring must extend at least 3½″ beyond the bottom chalk line; it needs to go no farther unless you plan to use under-the-eaves space for bulk storage.

To accept a knee wall rafters must be notched. On the side of each rafter, starting at the upper chalk line, draw a horizontal line 3½″ long. From the end of this line draw a vertical line to the bottom edge of the rafter. The two lines shape the notch—the equivalent of a

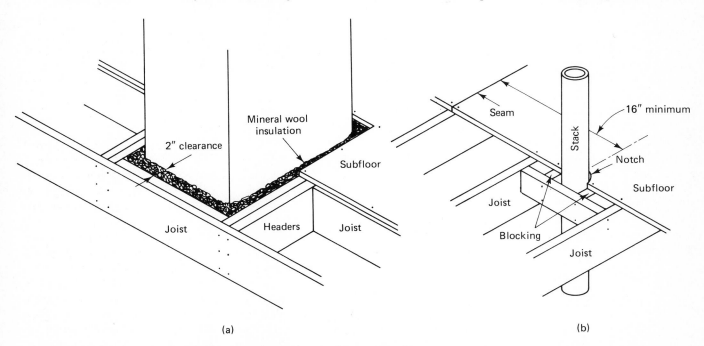

(a)   (b)

Fig. 10–2.   Framing a floor around a chimney (a) or vent stack (b).

bird's mouth. Use a level and square for accurate marking, and recheck the vertical height between the horizontal chalk line and the subfloor at each rafter. Delay cutting until you assemble the wall.

Assembly

Because many knee walls are long, build them in sections short enough for you to handle alone. Plan top and bottom plates of the same length so that one section meets the next between studs. Plan the cap plate so that it overlaps the top plate on an adjoining section by at least 24″. If the rafters are spaced 24″ o.c., a 32″ overlap makes nailing easier.

Cut top and bottom plates together, and lay the bottom plates along their chalk lines to confirm a proper fit. Then set the top plates on them, and on both sets mark stud locations; each stud should lie directly under a rafter. If you need an access door to under-the-eaves space, mark its location on both plates and omit the stud marks there.

Cut studs to length, and assemble knee wall sections flat on the subfloor. Nail through the bottom plate into the ends of studs with a pair of 8d nails, then through the top plate into the other end with another pair of 8d nails. Be sure that studs are plumb and flush with plates before you drive nails home. Then set the cap plate in place, and test its fit against chalk lines on the rafters. When the fit is good, attach the cap plate onto the top plate with a single 10d nail every 16″, nailing first about ¼″ from one edge, then ¼″ from the other (refer to Fig. 7-14). Use a pair of nails where lengths of cap plate butt.

If you have miscalculated slightly in your measurements, you can increase the height of the knee wall by driving shims under the bottom plate next to studs, and nailing through them into the subfloor. To reduce the height you can rip the top plate up to ¼″. If the fit is just plain poor, it's better to start over.

Attachment

With a good fit certain, now notch the rafters. Be very careful not to cut beyond the ends of your chalk lines.

Attach knee walls by nailing downward through the bottom plate and subfloor into floor joists below, and toenailing through each rafter into the cap plate. Toenail on both sides of studs and rafters, two per side. Use 12d nails. Add a block between studs to support any splice in the top plate.

Frame the opening for an access door with a header made from a pair of 2 × 4s laid flat. It isn't necessary to double jamb studs around such small openings.

With knee walls in place, you can now safely remove any collar beams. If collar beams are so low that they interfere with building and setting knee walls,

remove only enough of them at one time to build and install one section.

CEILING JOISTS

In attics where both sides of the ceiling follow the slope of the roof, you may have only a narrow area of flat ceiling. Yet this area must be supported. To establish the height of supports, measure up from the subfloor a distance equal to the ceiling height you established, plus the thickness of finish flooring material, plus the thickness of ceiling material. Mark this height on the edges of all rafters on one side of the roof, and carry the marks horizontally onto one side of each rafter. Make a similar marking on a rafter near the ends and middle of attic space on the other side.

If the distance between marks on opposite rafters is less than 4′, why not eliminate ceiling joists altogether, and let the ceiling rise to the ridge? You'll save on lumber and a lot of fitting of ceiling material; the knee walls provide adequate roof support. The only problem may be at the ridgeboard, which usually extends below the bottom edges of rafters. To circumvent this problem, carry ceiling material just short of the ridgeboard, then cover the gap with a 1 × 4 or 1 × 6 cut to width, beveled at the edges, and nailed along the ridgeboard.

If the distance is more than 8′, consider raising the ceiling height until the dimension is exactly 8′-0″. Then you can fit sheets of wallboard on the ceiling without cutting. Support the ceiling on 2 × 4 joists set with their bottom edges on new marks. Use 2 × 6s above any ceiling wider than 8′-0″.

To install ceiling joists, cut their ends to the slope of the roof; neither an exact cut nor a tight fit is necessary as long as you have ample nailing area at rafters. Set each joist on its mark and drive in one nail. Then set the joist against the opposite rafter, level it, and nail. Complete nailing at both ends with four 8d nails placed in a diamond pattern.

This procedure works as long as pairs of rafters meet the ridgeboard at the same point. Sometimes they are offset the thickness of a rafter, however, and ceiling joists won't be at right angles to the ridge. Thus you would have great difficulty installing ceiling material.

If you face this problem, cut ceiling joists so that they rest on the marks on rafters on one side, but are cut to the slope of the roof on the other side, where they butt against the undersides of rafters. At these points toenail each joist to the underside of the rafter, then cover the joint on both sides with splice plates (refer to Fig. 8-6). Use either 5″ × 8″ metal splice plates, placed with one long edge flush with the bottom edge of the rafter and an upper corner just touching sheathing; or cut triangular plates out of plywood large enough to cover at least the end 8″ of the joist.

If you plan a shed dormer on one side of attic space, see construction details later in this chapter.

VENTILATION

Attic space used solely for storage must, by today's standards, be well insulated in the floor to prevent heat loss from the rooms below, and well ventilated to carry off excess heat and to prevent condensation problems. When you convert the attic to living space, however, you now have two areas that must be insulated and ventilated: the living space itself and the remaining unused space above it.

Windows already in gables will help ventilate attic rooms, and by adding windows in dormers you improve both ventilation and light. But windows won't help ventilate the areas between rafters and above the attic ceiling. Similarly, louvers in gables won't ventilate rooms. As long as louvers lie above attic ceiling joists, they are adequate for ventilating unused space.

If you have no louvers or if their bottoms are visible below joists, the most satisfactory solution is to remove any louvers and close off the openings, then install a ridge ventilator, and add ventilation at the eaves when you don't already have it. Installation of a ridge ventilator is covered in Chapter 8 and Fig. 8-13. Methods of ventilating at eaves are shown in Fig. 8-12.

INSULATION

The insulation between floor joists of an unfinished attic is usually loose fill. Ideally, it should have been blown or poured in place over a vapor barrier. Often it is not. In either case that loose fill insulation is not reusable above finished attic space. Just leave it where it is; it will help deaden the sound of people walking on the attic floor.

Insulate attic space with blankets or batts already having a vapor barrier on one side. **Blankets** are long rolls of insulation; **batts** are blankets cut to uniform length, usually 8′, and packaged in bundles. Both types are made with nailing flanges and in several R values. An **R value** is a measure of an insulation's resistance to transfer of heat.

Blankets are more cumbersome to work with than batts, but normally you will have less waste. Order according to the spacing between rafters (16″, 20″, or 24″) and by R value. R values and thicknesses are not necessarily directly related, but as a general rule the higher the R value, the thicker the insulation. You must leave a gap of about 2″ between roof sheathing and the back side of insulation to allow air to flow between rafters. Therefore, determine the maximum thickness of insulation which meets that requirement, and buy insulation of that thickness bearing the highest R value.

You install insulation with the vapor barrier on the room side. Place the flanges against the *sides* of studs and rafters, not their edges (Fig. 10-3). There are two reasons for this. First, this method leaves a small pocket of air on the room side that increases insulating value. Second, you have a firmer surface against which to place finish materials. Install with staples driven at right angles to the edge through flanges into framing members.

Fit each blanket or batt between studs in a knee wall so that its ends just touch the two plates. Then work upward between rafters, across the ceiling, and down the other side. You'll need help to support the unattached end of a blanket. Staple every 6″ and on both sides of bends, keeping the flange as flat as possible against framing members. Cut the other end for a tight fit at the opposite plate.

When one length won't reach all the way, fit the next piece as tightly as possible against the installed piece. Whenever you leave a gap anywhere, either between lengths or between staples, you create a small hole through which heat and moisture can escape and cause problems.

Not all spacings between framing members will be a standard width. Although you should have no spaces wider than standard, you may have some narrower spaces. To narrow a blanket or batt, follow the four steps in Fig. 10-4a. Slit the backing paper at the flange (1), and trim the insulation to the narrower spacing (2). Next trim off excess flange—the difference between standard spacing and the narrower opening (3). Then fold the backing paper to the new shape (4), and staple through the folded backing paper and flange.

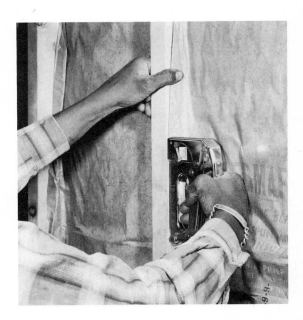

Fig. 10-3. Staple insulation to the sides, not faces, of studs and joists, with the vapor barrier on the room side. Place staples 6″ apart into joists and every 7 to 8″ into studs. (Courtesy United States Gypsum Company.)

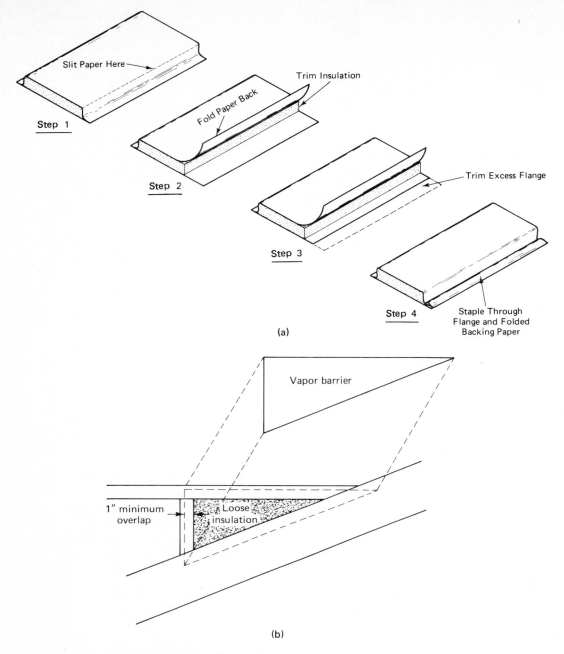

Fig. 10-4. Trimming a blanket or batt to fit narrower spaces (a), and insulating an odd-shaped space (b).

To insulate an odd-shaped space (Fig. 10-4b), remove the surface papers from a piece of scrap insulation. Save the vapor barrier, throw away the paper backing, and stuff the insulation in the cavity. Then cut the vapor barrier to overlap the cavity about 1″ on all sides. Staple the barrier to the framing, and flatten the crowns of staples flush.

PARTITIONING

After you have completed the structural frame for new attic space, provided ventilation, and installed in-sulation, it's only natural to want to partition the space to see how it will look. But hold off. It is much easier to install wall, ceiling, and floor materials first while you have large, uninterrupted areas to work in, no partitions in your way, and little cutting and fitting of materials at corners. Procedures for installing finish materials are described in Chapters 19 and 20.

Most partitions will run parallel to rafters, and you must provide some method of anchoring them at their tops. If at all possible, locate partitions where they lie directly under rafters and ceiling joists and butt against studs in knee walls. Then you can nail through the plates into existing framing members.

When partitions fall between framing members, you must build a ladder between knee wall studs, rafters, and ceiling joists. Ladder construction is shown in Fig. 8-9b. If you install finish materials before you partition, leave out the 1 × 6 and move ladder rungs forward to flush with framing members.

In space where you need a ladder, set insulating batts or blankets toward the back of the space if possible. But don't let them protrude beyond the back edges of ladders, or they will interrupt air flow.

Partitions in a prefinished attic must be built a little differently than other partitions. You can build partitions of constant height as a unit. But when they fit under rafters and therefore vary in height, it's easier to build them in sections.

Begin by marking on the floor with chalk lines the location of one edge of each partition. Then measure the lengths of all partitions, make a written note of these lengths, and cut all bottom plates. Lay these plates in position on their chalk lines. Then with 8d nails attach them to subflooring at their ends only, two nails per end.

Short Partitions

To build partitions that fit under rafters, begin by dropping a plumb bob from the point where the flat and sloping sections of ceiling meet. Mark this point on the plate that you've already installed for each such partition. Measure the distance from the mark to the knee wall, and cut another plate to this length, not from a 2 × 4 but from a 1 × 4. On this plate, called a **shoe**, mark stud locations, one at each end and no more than 16″ on centers between. Work outward from the knee wall, placing the first mark at 15¼″, then every 16″ thereafter.

To establish the length of the top plate, measure the length of the sloping ceiling. Transfer this measurement to a 2 × 4 at least 4″ longer. Use a pitch board (see Fig. 7-7 and related instructions) to mark plumb cuts at both ends. You'll use a pitch board many times as you cut parts for partitions that fit under rafters.

The upper ends of studs in short partitions get an angle cut; you cut bottom ends square. These studs are all different in length, but there is a common difference between them. That common difference is the rise of the roof (the short side of your pitch board) times the spacing between studs stated in feet. (See "Gable Wall" in Chapter 7 for more detailed discussion.)

To find the length of the first or shortest stud, measure the height of the knee wall, and subtract the following:

- The thickness of the bottom plate (1½″).
- The thickness of the shoe (¾″).
- The vertical thickness of the top plate along a

plumb cut. This thickness varies with the slope; mark a plumb cut with your pitch board and measure the length of the line.

- The thickness of a shim; allow ½″.

The resultant dimension is the length of the first stud at its shortest edge.

Cut this stud to length, add the common difference to determine the length of the next stud, and so on until you have all studs cut. Nail them on their marks on the shoe. Then attach the top plate to the end studs; make sure that they are square with the bottom plate. Then nail the intermediate studs to the top plate after squaring them. Your wall section is now assembled.

Turn the section upright and slide it slowly and carefully into position on the bottom plate. It should clear your finished ceiling enough to avoid damage. Fit shims made from roofing shingles under each stud, and carefully drive them in from alternate sides until the section is tight against the ceiling. Check the partition for plumb on both sides and at both ends. Then nail downward through the shims with 12d nails, upward into a joist or ladder, and horizontally into a stud or ladder.

Full-Height Partitions

Build partitions and sections that extend all the way to a flat ceiling in the same manner. Stud length is the distance from subfloor to ceiling less 5¾″—the thicknesses of top and bottom plates, shoe, cap plate, and clearance for shimming. A cap plate isn't required under rafters on short sections, but you need it on full-length partitions to secure other partitions that butt against it. The cap plate on one partition must overlap the top plate of the other partition (see Fig. 8-8). When short and full-height sections butt together in a straight line, nail end studs together with 8d nails in pairs spaced about every 24″ vertically.

DORMER CONSTRUCTION

A dormer is a projection through a sloping roof. It has a front wall, two side walls, and a roof. It fits into an opening in the main roof that must be reinforced like the opening for an attic stairway. Rafters on both sides must be doubled, and the ends of the opening must be closed with double headers.

Small Dormers

The narrowest practical dormer requires an opening 43½″ wide. To achieve this width you cut two adjacent rafters, assuming they are a standard 16″ o.c., and add doubling rafters on the opening side of the next two rafters. You can't use the cut rafters for doubling; all rafters must extend from rafter plate to ridge. But you can cut them into headers.

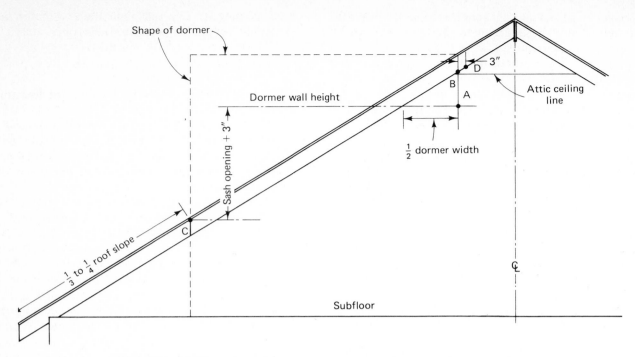

Fig. 10–5. To determine where to cut the roof for a narrow dormer, draw a section through your attic space. You must determine on paper where to cut rafters before you proceed with cutting.

If you have enough headroom, the ceiling of a dormer may be flat. More often it follows the slope of the dormer roof. To establish the area of roof to be cut open for a dormer, the only sure way is to draw a section through your attic space. Refer back to the section drawing you made earlier of your attic, and update it by drawing in the work you have completed. You need to show the locations of knee walls and any ceiling joists.

On a sheet of lightly lined graph paper draw a horizontal line representing your attic subfloor (Fig. 10-5). In the middle of the paper draw a light line that represents the centerline of attic space. Then measure the height from subfloor to the undersides of rafters where they meet the ridgeboard. If rafters are no longer exposed, measure to the ceiling or ceiling structure. Mark this height on your vertical line. Use a scale of $\frac{1}{2}$" = 1'-0" if possible; if not, use the largest scale for which you have room.

The height of dormer walls above the subfloor should be no less than 6'-7", and 7'-1" is better (the extra inch allows for thicknesses of finish floor and ceiling materials). On your drawing mark this height with a light line drawn horizontally across the rafter slope. Then measure along this line inward from the intersection a distance (at scale) equal to half the width of your planned opening for the dormer. From this point (A in Fig. 10-5) draw a vertical line to the rafters. This intersection (B) marks the location of the lower header above the opening. This point must be below the

bottom edge of the ridgeboard of the main roof, but just above the line of any attic ceiling.

The front wall of a small dormer may rise directly above the wall of the house below it, but it looks better if it rises about one-fourth to one-third of the way up the slope, measured between eave and ridge. The governing factor is the height of the dormer window. From your window supplier find out what size of rough opening (also called a **sash opening**) is required for the window you have in mind. To this height add 3"—the combined thickness of a top plate and cap plate. This total height is the minimum vertical measurement you must have between the tops of dormer side walls and the tops of rafters. From the dormer wall height on your drawing measure off this height, and draw a light horizontal line. Where this line crosses the roof line (C, Fig. 10-5) marks the location of the outer header below the dormer opening.

Framing the Opening. To get everything to work, you may have to make some adjustments—in the height of your dormer ceiling or wall or window. Get help from a carpenter if you can't solve your problem. But you must establish the locations of headers before you can proceed.

Then, working from your drawing, locate points B and C on the edges of rafters to be cut. Carry the marks vertically up from B and down from C on the sides of the rafters. Then measure *horizontally* away from mark B a distance of 3", and mark point D. Draw a line

Chapter 10 / Shaping Attic Space

through D parallel to the line through B. The lines through C and D are the lines on which you cut the rafters.

Where lines B and C meet roof sheathing, draw lines across the sheathing to rafters that won't be cut. Measure 1½" from the rafters along the lines to mark the corners of the dormer opening. Snap chalk lines along the sheathing between the corners to mark the edges of the opening. Then, at the four corners drive nails upward as vertically as possible through the sheathing and roofing. These four nails are your guide to work that must be done from the roof itself.

On the roof locate the four nails, and snap chalk lines between each pair to form a rectangle. Let all lines extend about 2' beyond their intersection so that you have a permanent guide after you remove roofing material.

Before you remove any material, have a tarpaulin handy at least 4' wider than the opening to be cut, and long enough to extend from about 1' below the opening to a point about 1' over the ridge. Also, have a dozen bricks or similar weights available to hold the tarpaulin down. You must be able to cover the opening quickly in case of sudden bad weather.

Thus prepared, check your lines for accuracy. The horizontal lines should be parallel to the tabs of roofing shingles, and all corners should be square. Recheck all measurements to be sure the opening is the size you need and in the location you need it.

Then with a roofer's knife, cut accurately along the bottom and side chalk lines through roofing shingles and the building paper below it. Remove these materials inside the rectangle until you reach the upper chalk line. If the shingles are in good condition, save them for re-use on the dormer roof. To remove a shingle, carefully lift the shingles above it, pull or cut the roofing nails, and slide the shingle out. You'll have the best luck working on a mild, sunny day if shingles are asphalt. They tend to break when they are cold and brittle, and to tear when they are hot and soft.

When you reach the upper chalk line, remove and save all shingles that lie under it. Then resnap the chalk line across the building paper and cut along the new line.

To cut sheathing, set your power saw to the thickness of the sheathing plus about ¼". Make the cuts at the side of the opening first; be careful to cut no more than necessary beyond the crossing chalk lines. Before making the end cuts, adjust the angle of the saw blade to the slope of the roof. End cuts should be plumb cuts, not made at right angles to the roof. The blade should just nick the tops of rafters you intend to remove. If you have done your work accurately, the cuts will go right along the lines you drew on the underside of the sheathing.

Pry the sheathing loose until you can draw out the nails holding it. Then set it in the attic for reuse in sheathing part of the dormer roof.

Before you forget it, reset your saw for a square cut, and change the depth setting to 1⅛". Then go inside the attic to cut the marked rafters.

To keep rafters from falling on you when you cut through them, tack lengths of 2 × 4 across both the rafters to be cut and adjacent framing rafters. Cut as far as you can with a power saw, and finish the job with either a saber saw or a crosscut hand saw. You must make the upper cuts from underneath because sheathing overhangs there.

Begin framing the opening with the doubling rafters (Fig. 10-6). They get a plumb cut where they fit against the ridgeboard, and a plumb and heel cut where they rest on the rafter plate. Use existing rafters as your guide to the length of rafter you need and the shape of the cut at the plate. Check the fit at the ends and with the cut at the sheathing before you install them.

Set each rafter in place against its mate, and nail through the doubling rafter into the main rafter about 6" from the ridgeboard just to hold it. Recheck the fit. Complete nailing with pairs of 8d nails spaced about 24" apart the length of the rafter. Toenail into the ridgeboard and rafter plate. You won't have much working room, but do the best you can.

Now measure the new width of the opening, and cut four headers from the rafters you took out. They should all be the same length, equal to the planned inside width of your dormer. Install the outer lower header first, with its outer edge flush with the tops of doubled rafters. Toenail into these rafters with three nails at each end on the front and two on the back if you can reach. Then set cut ends of cripple rafters at right angles to the header, and nail through the face of the header with three 8d nails. Set the doubling header flush with the top of the outer header, and attach it with three pairs of nails placed at about the midpoints between rafters.

The tops of lower headers are horizontal and flush with each other (Fig. 10-6). The tops of upper headers, however, must be beveled to the slope of the roof. Use your pitchboard to mark the cuts, then cut and check the fit before nailing. As before, set and nail the outer header first, with its top flush with the tops of rafters and against the overhanging sheathing. Then set the inner header also flush with the tops of rafters and the outer header. The bottom edges of these two headers will be offset slightly and won't quite extend to the bottom edges of the rafters. But don't let that worry you.

Framing a Small Dormer. Few framing members of a small dormer have square ends, and you will use your pitchboard constantly. Follow Fig. 10-7 as a guide to the shapes and relationships of members. Your

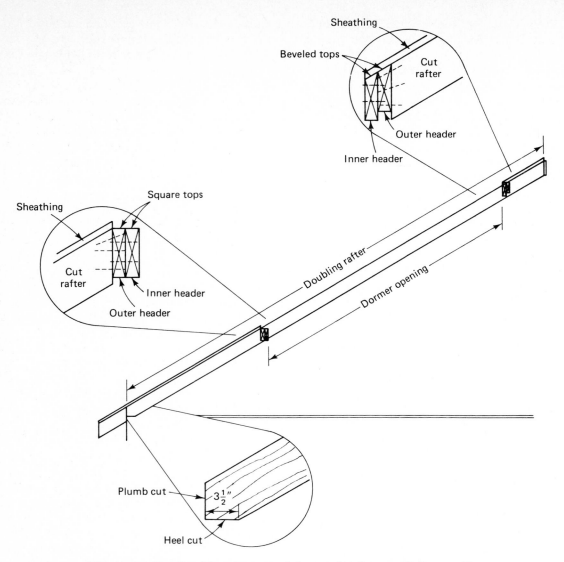

Fig. 10–6. Details of framing around the opening for a small dormer. Note that lower headers are the same size and have squared tops, but upper headers have beveled tops. They may be the same size, or the outer header may be larger to fit flush at the bottom with the inner header and cut rafters.

starting point is the size of the framed opening you worked out when you decided on window size. Cut corner posts from pairs of 2 × 4s, and bevel their lower ends. Cut the top plate to length; note in Fig. 10-7a that it extends the width of the opening plus the thickness of four studs. Assemble the posts, nail on the top plate, and install the framework by toenailing the posts into the doubled rafters. Nail just enough to hold it in place; you plumb it shortly.

Next, bevel one end of the rafter plates for side walls (Fig. 10-7c). Before cutting the other ends, however, set them in place on the rafters and front wall framework, and hold them level. The tops of these plates should be at the ceiling level you marked on your section drawing. If they aren't, you probably cut the corner posts too short or too long. Now is the time to make any adjustments or to start over; the top plates must be level and at the proper height.

When you are sure you can safely proceed, hold the front wall plumb and the top plate level, and mark its end for cutting. After you attach the top plates at both ends, finish nailing the front wall into the headers. Then add the short cap plate; it is the same length as the width of the opening.

On both top plates mark the spacing of sidewall studs and dormer rafters, spacing them 16″ o.c. from the corner. Carry the marks down onto the doubled rafters. Bevel lower ends of studs to the roof slope (Fig. 10-7d), then cut pairs to length. You can determine lengths by actual measurement, or by calculating the common difference as described for short partitions earlier in this chapter. Install studs by nailing downward through the plate and toenailing at the lower ends.

The Dormer Roof. Dormers are so light that you can use a 1 × 4 for a ridgeboard, 2 × 4s for rafters,

Chapter 10 / Shaping Attic Space

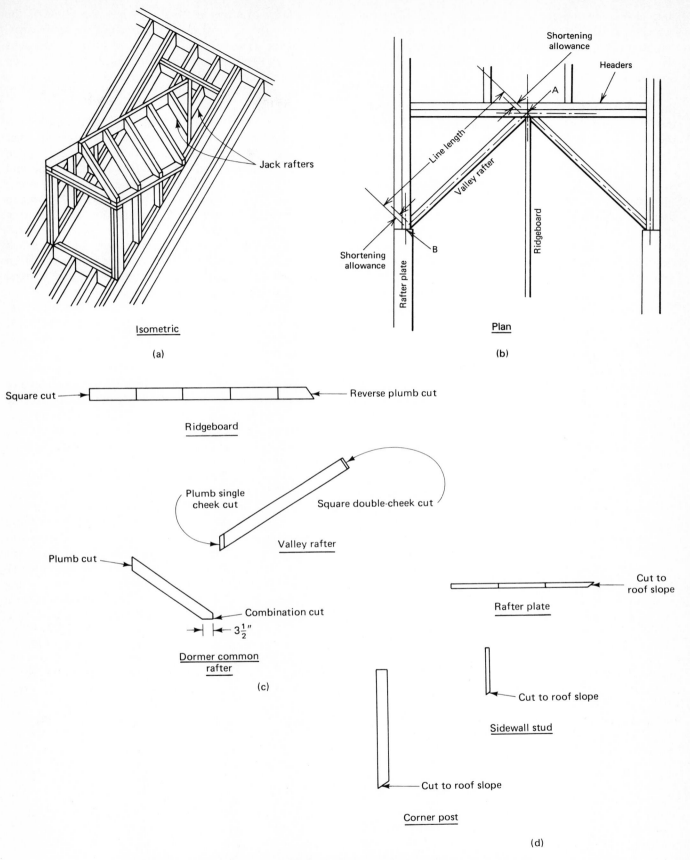

Jack rafters

Shortening allowance

Headers

A

Line length

Valley rafter

Ridgeboard

Shortening allowance

Rafter plate

B

Isometric

(a)

Plan

(b)

Square cut → ⟶ Reverse plumb cut

Ridgeboard

Plumb single cheek cut

Square double-cheek cut

Valley rafter

Plumb cut

Combination cut

$3\frac{1}{2}''$

Cut to roof slope

Rafter plate

Dormer common rafter

(c)

Cut to roof slope

Sidewall stud

Cut to roof slope

Corner post

(d)

Fig. 10–7. Framing for a small dormer in isometric (a) and plan (b). Also shown are the various framing members in the roof (c) and side walls (d), and the cuts required at their ends.

and assemble these parts in your attic. Cut the ridgeboard first; it is equal in length to the *horizontal* length of the opening, as taken from your section drawing, plus 3″ for the lower headers. The cuts are shown in Fig. 10-7c.

The best way to cut rafters is to lay out the end of the dormer on the attic subfloor at full size. You know the length of the cap plate, you know the thickness of the ridgeboard, and you know that the pitch of the roof should be the same as the pitch of the main roof. So draw on the floor a line the length of the cap plate, and draw diagonal lines at roof pitch from the ends until they meet (Fig. 10-8). Find the center of the cap plate line, and draw a line from this center to the point where the pitches meet. This line should be perpendicular to the cap plate line. Mark off half the thickness of the ridgeboard on each side of the line at its upper end, thus marking the shortening cut at the ridge. At the lower ends of rafters mark off a horizontal heel cut 3½″ long, then trim at that point with a plumb cut to form a combination cut (Fig. 10-7c).

Cut only common dormer rafters to this template. Mark their locations on the ridgeboard every 16″, beginning at the outer end, and nail them in place like any rafter (see ''Roof Assembly'' in Chapter 7). Set the partially finished roof frame on the side plates and against the upper header, and nail it securely, making sure the faces of the front pair of rafters are plumb. At each nailing point toenail from both sides into the rafter plate or header.

For valley rafters (Fig. 10-7c) use ridgeboard stock. Working out the end cuts is easy for an experienced roofing carpenter, but complex for an amateur. Go back to your drawing on the floor (Fig. 10-8). Measure the distance from the centerline of the cap plate to its end, and multiply it by 1.414. Measure off this length along the cap plate line from its midpoint. From this new point draw a diagonal line to the ridge as you did for common rafters. The length of this line is the length of a valley rafter before shortening.

Why multiply by 1.414? When the pitch of the dormer roof is the same as the pitch of the main roof, the valley rafter is the hypotenuse of a 45° triangle whose short sides are equal in length to a common dormer rafter. And the length of such a hypotenuse is the length of a short side times the square root of 2, which is 1.414.

Your layout establishes the angle of the plumb cut at the header, which is smaller than the angle of other plumb cuts. The cut itself is a double cheek cut, which you lay out as detailed in Fig. 7-18 a and c, and this end of both valley rafters is cut the same. Lay out the single cheek cut for the lower end as detailed in Fig. 7-18 a and b. One valley rafter is cut in one direction, and the other in reverse.

As a final step in framing the roof, cut jack rafters (see Fig. 10-7a) for the dormer and the main roof. Both types get a plumb cut at their upper ends, and a single cheek cut, plumb and at 45°, at their lower ends.

While you lay out and cut valley and jack rafters, check the fit frequently. An exact fit isn't mandatory, but the closer you come the better the other members of the dormer roof will fit together.

Cover the roof framing with sheathing and roofing paper before you quit work for the day. Cut and attach sheathing as described in Chapter 7. Start at the front dormer wall and work toward the main roof. At the valley cut sheathing at a 45° angle so that the two pieces butt on the centerline of the valley rafter. Then sheathe the dormer walls.

With the dormer sheathed, cut two strips of building paper 8 to 10″ wide, and long enough to extend from the front wall of the dormer to a point 8″ above the juncture of the sidewalls and valleys. Crease these strips lengthwise so that there is at least 4″ of paper on each side of the crease. Lay the strips along the joint between the existing roof and dormer wall sheathing (1 in Fig. 10-9), and tuck the upper end and lower edge under existing roof shingles but over existing building paper. Attach the strip into wall sheathing with roofing

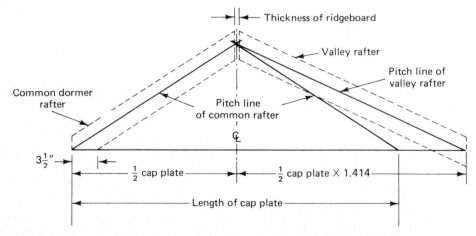

Fig. 10–8. Lay out common and valley rafters for the dormer at full size on your attic floor.

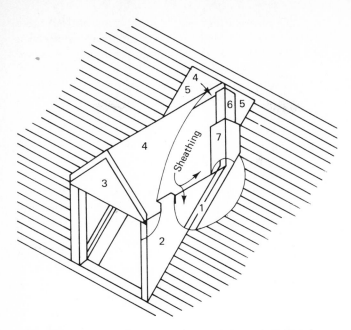

Fig. 10–9. As soon as a dormer is sheathed, protect it with building paper and flashing. The numbers indicate the order in which this protection should be applied.

nails about 8″ apart near the upper edge.

Next, cut and apply building paper to the remainder of the dormer walls (2 and 3, Fig. 10-9).

These triangular pieces should extend at the bottom to the crease at the roof line, at the top to roof sheathing, and at the side to the dormer window opening.

Then cover the roof sheathing with building paper. One width of paper isn't likely to cover from eave to eave, so use two. Let each piece (4, Fig. 10-9) overlap the ridge about 4″ and the eave about 2″. Where you have cut existing roofing paper and shingles above the dormer, tuck the ends (5, Fig. 10-9) under the old paper at least 6″. Then any water from leaks will flow downward, and not back up at joints in the paper.

To flash valleys, lay a strip of roll roofing about 12″ wide (6, Fig. 10-9) down the center of the valley. Then lay a second strip 18″ wide (7, Fig. 10-9) over the first strip, again centered. Nail both strips at the upper corners only to hold them in place; roof shingles will cover the nails. Hold the lower ends down with weights if you won't be shingling right away.

A Shed Dormer

The approach to erecting a shed dormer is similar to preparing to install a small dormer. You first establish the available ceiling height and the width of the dormer. If you have enough headroom, ceiling joists in the dormer area may rest on the outside wall of the dormer (Fig. 10-10a). If headroom is limited, they may be supported on dormer rafters (Fig. 10-10b).

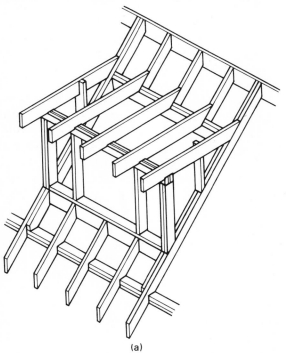

(a)

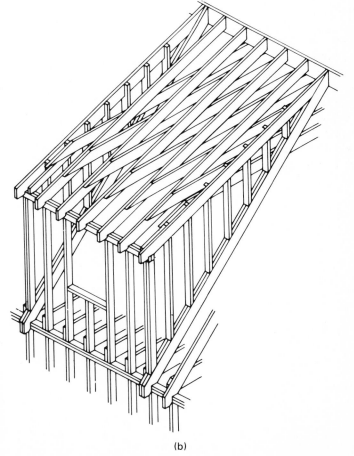

(b)

Fig. 10–10. Typical wall and roof construction for a small shed dormer with its wall inset from the house wall of the floor below (a), and for a wide dormer with its wall directly above the house wall (b). Lower ends of dormer rafters overhang the dormer wall. Upper ends may butt against headers and main roof rafters, or extend to the ridgeboard.

Begin your planning by drawing a section through the dormer. It should show half the attic space. Dormer rafters usually extend all the way to the ridge, and have the same overhang at the eave as the main roof.

The front wall may be built in two ways. It may rise directly above the wall below it, as in Fig. 10-10b, in which case studs rest on the wall's cap plate against ceiling joists. Or it may be located partway up the slope, in which case the lower end of the opening must be framed with double headers like a small dormer (Fig 10-10a). When a shed dormer is no more than 8' wide, its front wall may rest on headers like the wall of a small dormer. Front walls of wider dormers usually lie inside the headers and are attached to the attic subfloor.

Framing the Opening. Follow procedures for framing the opening for a small dormer: mark the size of the opening from the attic side, carry the corners to the roof, snap chalk lines, and have a large tarpaulin ready to cover the opening.

If you install headers at the lower end of the opening (Fig. 10-10a), remove roofing materials as previously described for a small dormer. If the dormer wall rises from the wall below (Fig. 10-10b), remove the roofing material all the way to the eave. At the ridge carefully remove and save ridge shingles. When you cover the opening at night or during bad weather, make sure that the tarpaulin extends over the ridge and covers the exposed area under ridge shingles.

Framing the Dormer. By drawing a section you established the height of the dormer wall. To determine post lengths in an inset dormer, subtract 3½" for a header in the wall, then subtract the distance from the subfloor to the top of the header in the roof. Give the tops a square cut and bevel the lower ends to the shape of the main roof. Studs in the front wall are 1½" shorter than posts, and get square cuts at both ends.

When the dormer wall lies above another wall, add to the height of that wall the thickness of subflooring and the height of an attic floor joist, then subtract either 3½" or 5½" for the wall header to determine stud length. Cut a template stud to this length with both ends cut square. Hold it against a doubled rafter, and mark the slope. Cut four corner posts to the length above the mark, and with the bottom ends beveled to the slope. Then cut the remaining full-length studs.

Now build the wall header. Use 2 × 4s as long as the widest window is not over 4' wide; otherwise, use 2 × 6s. Cut two lengths the width of the dormer opening plus 6". Then from ½" plywood cut strips 3½" or 5½" wide and as long as the header. If your dormer is so wide that you must splice the header, the splices in the lumber and plywood must fall at least 12" apart. Assemble the header with 8d nails driven in pairs at each end, on both sides of each splice, and approximately 12" between pairs.

When the dormer wall is inset, cut a bottom plate 6" shorter than the header. Mark stud locations on both the wall header and bottom plate where required (see Fig. 7-12) but not over 16" o.c. Then assemble posts, studs, header, and bottom plate flat on the attic floor. Toenail studs and posts into the header, and nail through the bottom plate into ends of studs. Leave the bottom ends of posts free. Raise the assembly into position, nail the bottom plate into the doubled roof header, and toenail posts into rafters. Use your level to keep the wall plumb during attachment.

When the dormer wall rises from the wall below, set the wall header across the floor joists to mark stud locations. If the wall is short enough so that you and a helper can raise it together, toenail the studs to the header on their marks. Then set the assembly in position and, holding the wall plumb, nail the lower ends of the studs into the joists with three 8d nails. If the wall is quite long, it is usually easier to attach the studs to the joists first, then add the header.

Dormer Rafters. Above a dormer with an inset wall you will need new rafters cut from the same-size stock as the rafters in the main roof. If the wall is at the outside of the house, and the full-length rafters you remove are in good condition, you can reuse them after making new cuts. You will need some new rafters, however, because you use two of them for doubling at the sides of the roof opening.

Before you lay out dormer rafters, cut a second pitch board for the gentler slope of the dormer roof (see Fig. 10-11). You will need it to mark plumb cuts at the ridge and eave, and for the bird's mouth at the wall. Procedures for cutting rafters are described in detail in Chapter 7. At the rafter plate all rafters should lie above evenly spaced studs, and you must mark this spacing on the exposed ridgeboard.

Cut a sample dormer rafter and test the fit. When the fit is good, mark and cut all other intermediate rafters. Use the sample also to mark the length of end rafters. In a small dormer all rafters are alike (Fig. 10-10a). Note that in a broad dormer, however, the upper ends are cut differently (Fig. 10-10b). There end rafters rest on the outer doubled rafter around the roof opening. The angle of this upper cut is the difference between the pitches of the main roof and the dormer roof. To mark the cut, mark a plumb cut at the ridge like that on intermediate rafters, using the dormer pitch board. Lay the main pitch board with its short edge along the plumb cut, and draw a line along its hypotenuse (Fig. 10-11). You cut along this line.

Side Wall Studs. Studs in the side walls of a shed dormer must be beveled at their lower ends to the slope of the main roof, just like studs in a small dormer. Upper ends, however, are notched to fit around end rafters, and trimmed to the slope of the dormer roof.

Each stud in one sidewall is a different length,

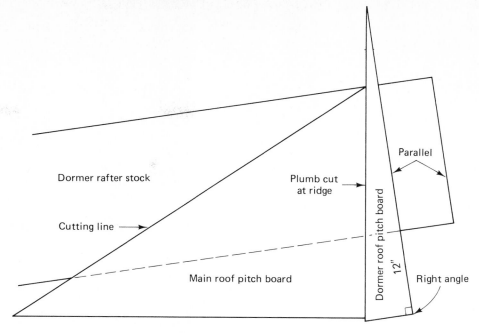

Fig. 10–11. Establishing the bevel cut for the upper ends of dormer rafters that butt against main rafters, or the plumb cut when they butt against the house's ridgeboard.

although there is one the same length in the opposite wall. But the difference between lengths is the common difference (see "The Gable Wall" in Chapter 7 for a detailed discussion). Suppose that the pitch of the main roof is 8 in 12 and of the dormer roof is 2 in 12. Then their unit rises are 8 and 2. To find the common difference between studs spaced 16″ o.c., you subtract the smaller unit rise from the larger, and multiply by 1⅓. In the example, $8 - 2 = 6$, and $6 \times 1⅓ = 8$. So the difference in lengths of adjacent sidewall studs is 8″.

You must find the length of one stud before you can apply the common difference principle, so work on the stud nearest the post. Measure off the stud spacing on both rafters, starting at the outside edge of the post. Remember to measure *horizontally*. The vertical distance between the tops of rafters at the marks is the length of the longest stud.

Attic Ceiling Joists. The ends of ceiling joists supported by shed roof rafters are cut to the pitch of the shed roof. Use your pitch board for marking the cut. Note in Fig. 10-10 that the two end joists don't touch end rafters; the notched studs are in the way. Therefore, you have to cut two cripples from a 2 × 4 as supports. One end gets a heel cut so that it rests flat on the wall header. The other end gets a bevel cut like ceiling joists. With 8d nails, attach the cripple to the header and at least one stud, and attach the end joist to both studs and the cripple.

Stub Rafters. As soon as you have the dormer framed, apply sheathing across rafters and studs, cover roof sheathing with building paper, and apply flashing where dormer walls break through the main roof, similar to Fig. 10-9.

If the front dormer wall is a vertical continuation of the wall below, you now have to complete the interrupted eave line of the main roof by adding stub rafters. Cut them to extend from the eave line to the back face of studs. Nail them not only into studs, but also toenail them to the cap plate on which they rest. Sheathing on the dormer wall should stop at the rafter tops, not continue to the floor. Cover the joint between wall and roof sheathing with flashing.

ROOFING MATERIALS

On a narrow dormer with a gable or hip roof, use the same type of shingles as are on the main roof. Attempt to match colors if you need more shingles than you could save when you cut through the roof. Intermix old and new asphalt shingles to minimize color differences. Prestain wood shingles for as close a color match as you can achieve.

On a shed dormer you can use wood shingles over open sheathing as long as the roof pitch is at least 4 in 12. You can use standard asphalt shingles over solid sheathing when the pitch is at least 3 in 12. For slopes as flat as 2 in 12, use either interlocking asphalt shingles or strip shingles with seal-down tabs. On roofs with a lesser pitch your only choice is between a built-up roof applied by a professional roofer or a metal roof, which you can put on yourself if you have the necessary metal-working tools.

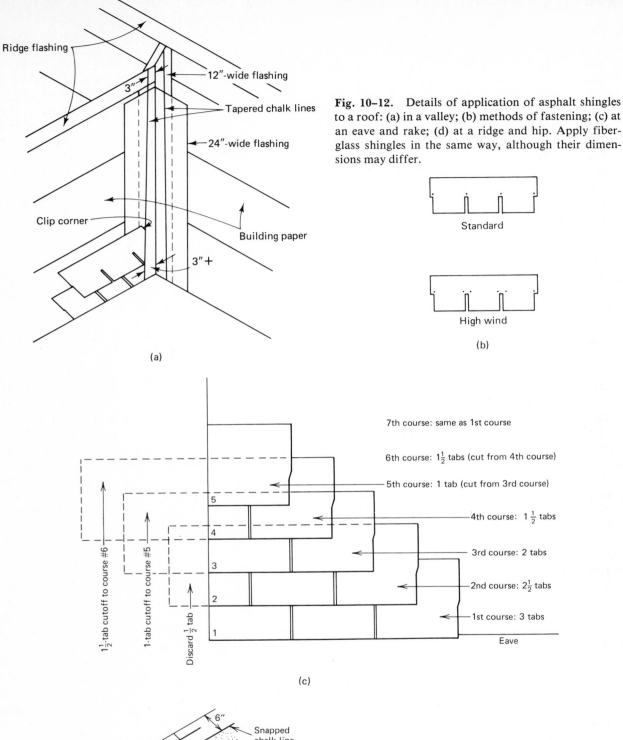

Ridge flashing

12"-wide flashing

3"

Tapered chalk lines

24"-wide flashing

Clip corner

Building paper

3" +

(a)

Fig. 10–12. Details of application of asphalt shingles to a roof: (a) in a valley; (b) methods of fastening; (c) at an eave and rake; (d) at a ridge and hip. Apply fiberglass shingles in the same way, although their dimensions may differ.

Standard

High wind

(b)

7th course: same as 1st course

6th course: $1\frac{1}{2}$ tabs (cut from 4th course)

5th course: 1 tab (cut from 3rd course)

4th course: $1\frac{1}{2}$ tabs

3rd course: 2 tabs

2nd course: $2\frac{1}{2}$ tabs

1st course: 3 tabs

Eave

$1\frac{1}{2}$-tab cutoff to course #6

1-tab cutoff to course #5

Discard $\frac{1}{2}$ tab

(c)

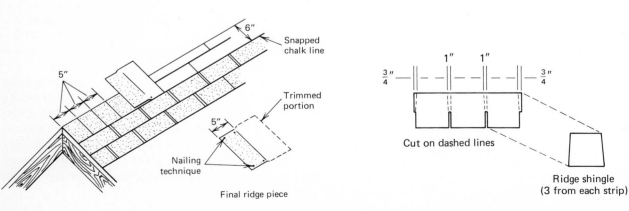

6"

Snapped chalk line

5"

Trimmed portion

5"

Nailing technique

Final ridge piece

$\frac{3}{4}''$ 1" 1" $\frac{3}{4}''$

Cut on dashed lines

Ridge shingle (3 from each strip)

(d)

Asphalt or Fiberglass Shingle Application

At the eave of a new roof you need a starter course (Fig. 10-12). Cut 3″ off a 36″-long strip of shingles for the first piece. Set this strip with its cut end flush with sheathing at the rake, its straight edge flush at the eave, and with the tabs facing *up* the roof. Fasten the starter pieces with standard roofing nails or with staples having a 1″ crown and 1¼″ legs and applied with a stapling hammer. Along the lower edge place fasteners about 3″ from the eave and 6″ apart, and fasten the upper edge at the corners of each tab. Repeat this process until you have covered the eave to the opposite rake. If you come to a hip first, cut the edge of the starter strip at 45° to match the angle of the hip.

At a valley, measure off 3″ on each side at its upper end, and mark the points with chalk (Fig. 10-12a). Then measure the length of the valley to the nearest foot, and divide the length by 8. If your measurement is 4′-9″, for example, the length to take is 5 and your answer is ⅝. Add this dimension in inches to the 3″, for a total of 3⅝″ in the example, and mark off this greater width on each side of the valley at its lower end. The valley must widen from top to bottom. Snap a pair of chalk lines between upper and lower points. Cut the starter strip and later exposed shingles to lie along the chalk lines. Seal the cut edge with a ribbon of roofing cement.

To start shingling the roof, take another strip shingle and trim square the edge that fits at the rake. Place this shingle with tabs down so that it overhangs at both rake and eave ½ to ¾″. Nail or staple as shown in Fig. 10-12b: with four fasteners in most parts of the country and with six where high winds are common. Do not sink fastener heads or crowns.

In most roofs the notches between tabs of shingles fall on the centerlines of the tabs below. To achieve this effect, lay successive courses at the rake as shown in Fig. 10-12c, with 5″ of each course exposed. At hips, trim the shingle in each course to follow the angle of the hip. At valleys, clip the upper corner of each shingle so that it won't trap water running down the valley. Set each cut edge in a ribbon of roofing cement, and make sure that the seal is watertight.

At the ridge the top course of strip shingles should end at or just below the ridge itself. Cover the ridge with a strip of roofing felt flashing 10″ wide and running up under the shingles of the main roof about 4″. Crease and bend it to the two slopes, than fasten it about 1″ from the edges and every 36″ along its length. For ridge shingles cut a strip shingle as shown in Fig. 10-12d. Bend each piece down its center, working carefully so that you don't crack the surface, and measuring to be sure the two leaves are the same width. Set one ridge shingle in position, and snap a chalk line parallel to the ridge along its edge as a guide for setting other ridge shingles.

Set the first ridge shingle in a bead of roofing cement at the rake, and nail 5½″ back from the leading edge and 1″ up both sides. Lay succeeding shingles in the same way, leaving about a 5″ exposure. Where the ridge ends at a valley, trim the last ridge shingle to end along the chalk lines. This last shingle should be a full-size ridge shingle if possible, so it's a good idea to lay out all ridge shingles before you attach the second one, and reduce exposure as required. Exposure should never be increased. Cover the two exposed nails in the last shingle with roofing cement and seal all edges.

The treatment at a hip is essentially the same as for a ridge. The shingle at the eave must be trimmed to the shape of the eave, however, and the top hip shingle should fit under the end ridge shingle.

Wood Shingle Application

Wood shingles come in lengths of 16″, 18″, and 24″, and vary in width from 3 to 14″. Use the length that matches the shingles on your existing roof. Unlike asphalt shingles, their wood counterparts absorb some rainwater, and therefore must be applied to minimize the amount of absorption and to permit natural drying by air movement.

First apply a length of beveled siding at all roof rakes with the thicker edge outward (Fig. 10-13a). This directs the flow of water down the roof away from the rake. Then lay the first wood shingle so that it overhangs the siding about 1″ and overhangs the eave 1 to 1½″. Regardless of the width of any shingle, use only two nails, one driven about 1¾″ from the rake side, and all others about ¾″ from the edge of the shingle. Use 3d nails in 16″ and 18″ shingles, and 4d nails in 24″ shingles. As far as possible, match the exposure of the main roof, and place nails so that they are covered at least 1″ by the course above (Fig. 10-13b).

Lay succeeding shingles in the first course with butt edges aligned and with a gap of ¼ to ½″ between shingles. Lay additional courses so that gaps fall at least 1½″ from gaps in the course below. Snap chalk lines at exposure points to maintain your courses in a straight line. Continue all courses to hips, but leave a ¼″ gap there, and add one more nail about an inch from the bottom corner of the hip. Stop about 24″ short of valleys.

At valleys mark the cutting line for shingles with chalk lines as described earlier for asphalt shingles. Their butt ends should clear valleys by about ½″ vertically, and must therefore be supported on 1 × 2 wood cant strips and copper cleats (Fig. 10-13c). Use the widest shingles available at valleys, and trim them to shape with a saw.

At hips cover the joint at the eave with two starter shingles about 6″ wide trimmed for a tight butt fit (Fig. 10-13d). Then nail up temporary boards to guide you to consistent width of hip shingles. Nail a shingle at least

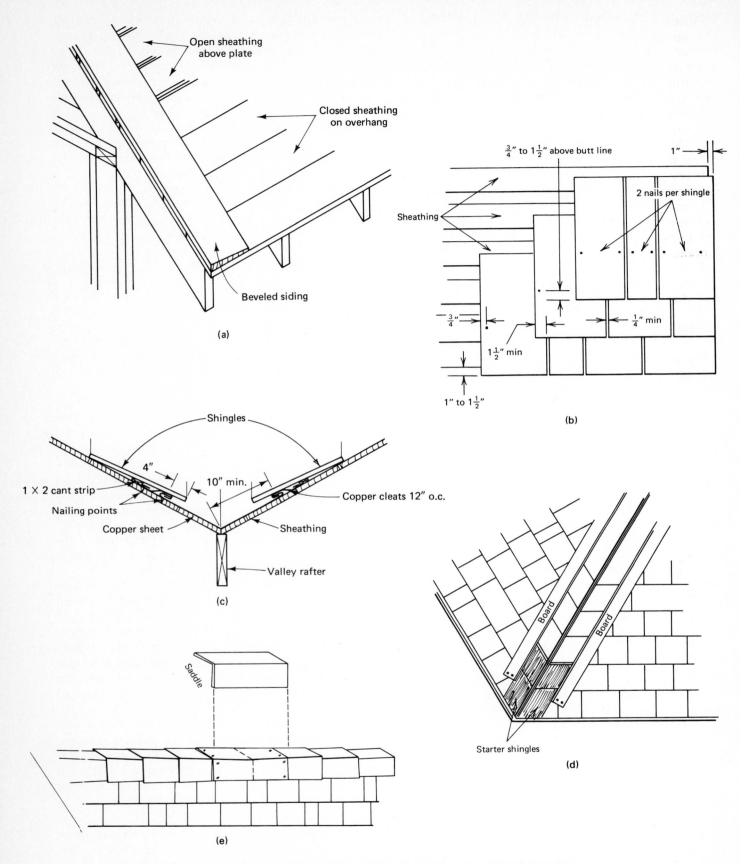

Fig. 10–13. Details of application of wood shingles to a roof: (a) preparation at a rake; (b) at an eave and rake; (c) in a valley; (d) on a hip; (e) at a ridge.

6″ wide to cover the starter shingle on one side, and let it overlap the hip. Trim off the overlap with a shingling hatchet, beveling the edge so that it lies flush with the other starter shingle. Then nail the opposite hip shingle and trim the overlap, this time to the opposite bevel. Repeat this process on up the hip, but reverse the order in each course so that the bevels are on opposite sides in alternate courses. Use 6d nails on hips and ridges.

At the ridge let the top courses gap about ½″. Cover the gap with a length of flashing 12″ wide and extending at its juncture with the main roof 4″ under existing shingles. Lay a pair of starter shingles at the rake as described for a hip. When the ridge ends in a hip, the top hip shingles act as starter shingles. Add guide strips and lay shingles as described for a hip, working from rakes inward. When a ridge extends from rake to rake, cover the center point with a **saddle**—two shingles that cover the joint with an extra course—face-nailed as shown in Fig. 10-13e.

Metal Roofing

On a shed dormer with very low pitch you can satisfactorily roof with sheets of aluminum, copper, tin-plated steel, galvanized steel, or various alloys. Each metal has its advantages and drawbacks. Local metal fabricators are your best source of a recommendation for the most practical roof for your house, and the names of metal roofing contractors if you don't want to tackle the job yourself. The work itself is not difficult, but does require considerable care and a variety of metalworking tools. Cleats and fasteners used must be made of the same metal as the roof itself to prevent destructive electrolitic action.

Roofing metal comes in strips joined together at seams. Strips running across the roof may be joined in flat-lock or loose-lock seams without solder. Strips running up the roof are usually joined in a standing seam. Figure 10-14 shows the steps in forming these seams.

At any edge that doesn't interlock with another piece, the edge must be stiffened by bending the metal back on itself twice. At the upper edge of a shed roof, where it joins an existing roof of another material, a standing seam must be flattened. These upper edges should be bent 180° and tucked at least 4″ up under existing roofing, and the joint sealed with roofing cement.

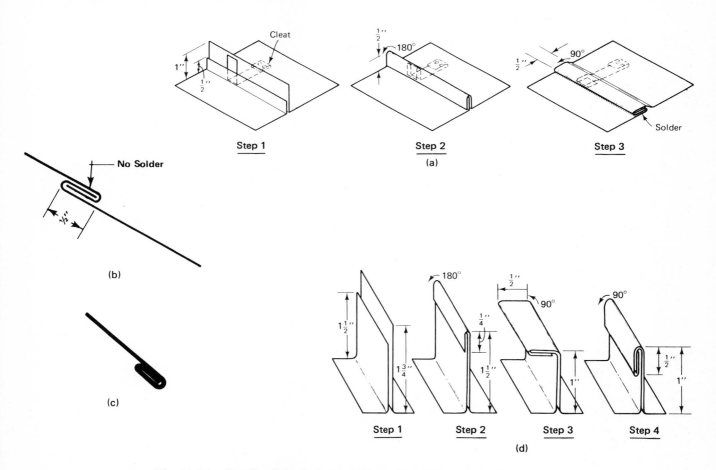

Fig. 10-14. Details of flat-lock (a) and loose-lock (b) seams for metal roofs that run across the slope, and of a standing seam (d) for connecting strips running up and down the slope. All unseamed edges must be doubled over for stiffening (c).

11

Finishing A Basement

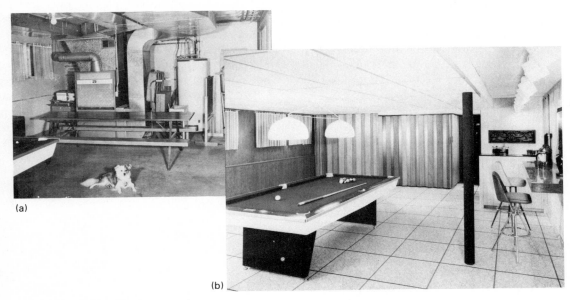

(a)

(b)

The basement space in (a) was an excellent candidate for remodeling for greater use—with a sound concrete floor, good ventilation, columns down the center of available space, and furnace and water heater at one end. The furnace is now concealed from view (b) by accordion-type doors that allow circulation of combustion air even when closed. The ceiling is furred down over the plenum duct, covered by a ceiling grid, and illuminated by lights marching down the unfurred portion. Walls are paneled and columns painted. Flooring is resilient tiles laid with feature strips. (Courtesy Azrock Floor Products.)

Many basements, especially those in houses more than 40 years old, don't lend themselves to conversion to living space. In houses built in the past 20 years they are more likely to have the features that make space usable. The idea of finishing a basement may look like an attractive solution to the need for more space because the structure is already there and the cost of fixing up the space is the most reasonable of all conversions. Nevertheless, take a long, hard look at what you have to work with before you decide to go ahead, even with planning.

For a basement to be practical for any living purpose, it must:

- *Be dry*. Water that seeps through walls can be

blocked, but to block it properly takes a lot of work.

- *Be warm*. Radiation from furnaces and boilers in older homes is usually adequate for warming one large basement area. If you partition the space, however, you must be able to tap into the existing duct or piping system to heat rooms individually. In some newer homes heat outlets are already in place.

- *Have adequate headroom*. As a rule of thumb, you should have at least 7'-8" between the basement floor and the undersides of ceiling joists if rooms will be large—say the size of a living room or family room. For smaller rooms, such as extra bedrooms, you can get away with 7'-4″.

- *Have few low-hanging pipes and ducts.* Utility lines carrying heat, water, and waste lie between joists wherever possible. But sometimes, particularly in older heating systems with round ducts, they run under joists and form an obstacle that limits room arrangement and makes an attractive finished ceiling impossible.

- *Be easily reached.* Basement stairs should be straight, with enough headroom over their entire length so that no one must duck as they descend. The ideal converted basement has an outside entrance, not only as a safety exit, but also as a way of bringing in furniture.

- *Have good ventilation.* Windows don't have to be large, but they should be located in opposite walls so that air can move freely and easily through basement space. Hopper vents—one-piece windows hinged at the bottom that open inward—are common in basements. They afford good airflow and protection against weather when you can open them at least 60°, but they can be a hazard if they open at eye level.

- *Have a level floor.* Many basement floors, like some garage floors, slope inward toward a drain. As long as the slope is slight and the drain isn't in the area you plan to remodel, you can erect partitions and lay a finished floor without major problems. But don't plan on sealing that drain. It is there for a purpose—as a way out for water that may somehow get on your floor. Your remodeling doesn't alter that purpose, or the need for that emergency exit. You may be able to hide the drain, but you can't cover it and level the floor.

Good light isn't a necessity unless you plan to use the new rooms extensively during daytime hours. A well-planned scheme of artificial light is much more important (see Chapter 5).

PLANNING THE JOB

When you are reasonably certain that your basement, or at least part of it, lends itself to finishing, draw up a floor plan to scale, as described in Chapter 3. Show the locations of all windows and any exterior doors. Draw in existing partitions; if you plan to move them, show them in dotted lines. Locate any supporting posts or columns. Accurately locate the stairs, particularly the bottom step. Show the exact location of any floor drain. Sketch in any existing equipment that can't or won't be moved: furnace or boiler, water heater, laundry tubs and equipment, water softener, and storage tanks.

Then accurately locate any overhead obstructions that will drop below a level ceiling. Show these obstructions in dotted lines. Also show dotted the locations of any grilles in the duct system that heat the basement area. Indicate the locations of any overhead lights and wall outlets.

It may help you to draw in a bright color the basement elements you can't change. Planning a basement remodeling is more a matter of what you have to work *around*, rather than what you have to work *with*.

Begin your layout of better space by lightly drawing screening partitions around mechanical and laundry equipment that you want to shield from view. Be sure to allow enough room around such equipment for repairs or future replacement; half the width of the equipment is a good minimum. While screening partitions must be attached at the floor and ceiling for stability, they don't need to be surfaced over their entire height, and often shouldn't be. Warm air furnaces, for example, need a supply of fresh air to burn fuel efficiently. By enclosing them too tightly, you may restrict that source of air. A partition finished to a height of roughly 6′ effectively screens equipment from view but permits an ample supply of air, and helps cross ventilation in the basement. It also gives you a chance to do something interesting in the way of decoration.

Partitions that will run the same direction as ceiling joists should, if at all possible, be located directly under those joists. They are much easier to attach. Also when possible, tie partitions into posts or columns, and locate them where they will close off one side of an overhead obstruction. Remember to draw partitions in full thickness, not just as a single line.

THE STAIRWAY

The typical basement stairway is utilitarian rather than a thing of beauty. It serves one purpose: to allow people to go from one floor level to the other safely. It usually ends at basement level near the longitudinal center of basement space, and therefore presents no problems of access to partitioned space. It may have a basement partition along one side, but more likely drops through a stairwell without side support. Structurally, it probably consists of a pair of sturdy stringers and a series of treads, but no risers. The treads may rest on notches in the stringers, or on cleats nailed to the insides of stringers.

To fix up a basement without improving the looks of the stairs at the same time is a mistake. The first impression anyone receives of your remodeling efforts is the stairway down, and it should be as attractive as the main entrance hall to your home or a finished stairway to upper floors. When basement layout permits, plan to close off the stairway on one side with a partition, and leave the other side open.

The procedure for building a new stairway is outlined in Chapter 9. Remodeling a stairway is much easier, because the hard part is already done—laying out the stringers. As long as you have enough headroom and the stringers are in good condition, the job moves quickly.

Build and install the flanking partition first, as described in the next section of this chapter. Stair treads may be in the way; if so, knock them loose and remove all nails. While you have the treads off and better working room, nail the stringer into the studs of the partition. Use two 8d nails at each stud. Then reset the treads on the stringers or cleat, and hold them temporarily in place with a single nail on each side, driven downward at about the midpoint of the tread from front to back.

If your stringers are notched for treads, measure the horizontal length of a notch. This dimension plus a minimum of 1″ is the depth of the new tread you need. The vertical height of a notch is the height of riser you need. Both treads and risers are actually longer than these dimensions because one end is shiplapped (see Fig. 9-10) to fit into a groove in the adjoining piece. When you replace existing treads with more finished ones and add risers, the relationship between treads and risers doesn't change. The front edge of each tread, however, will be about ¾″ farther forward, and the tread may be at the same height or ⅜″ lower. Install these stair parts as described in Chapter 9.

If treads are supported on cleats, measure back 2″ from the front edge of two consecutive treads, and mark these points on the stringer (Fig. 11-1). Remove the treads and draw horizontal lines on the stringer along the tops of the two cleats below. Remove the upper cleats and carry the 2″ marks downward to the next cleat line. Make sure that these lines are plumb, cleat

lines are level, and lines cross at 90°. Connect points where the lines cross. Measure the lengths of the two 90° lines, and from a piece of 2″ stock cut a triangle with these dimensions. Test the fit. When the fit is good, use the triangle as a template for cutting all supports, two per tread. The vertical side of the triangle is the height of riser you need (excluding the shiplapped edge), and the horizontal side is the depth of tread you need, plus 1″ overhang and again excluding the shiplapped edge.

After you have all the pieces on hand—triangles, treads, and risers—begin at the bottom of the stairway, marking, as described above, the vertical and horizontal edges of each triangle. Nail the triangles with five 8d nails into the stringer on the lines. Then install the two bottom risers with 5d or 6d finishing nails. To install the tread between them, apply glue liberally in grooves in both the tread and riser above, fit the shiplapped edge of the tread firmly into the groove in the riser, then press it just as firmly onto the lower riser. If you glue properly, you need no nails. To hold the pieces together while the glue dries, carefully drive a pair of 5d nails through the bottom of each riser into treads, working underneath the stairway.

No part of notched stringers is exposed except for the outside surface of an open stringer. Details for finishing this side are shown in Chapter 9. Much of a straight stringer is still exposed, however, and should be covered for appearance's sake.

If the inside surface of the stringers is smooth enough to take paint easily, don't resurface it. If it is scarred or gouged, however, cut triangles of ¼″ plywood or other thin, smooth material, and nail or glue them between treads and risers. Cover the opposite

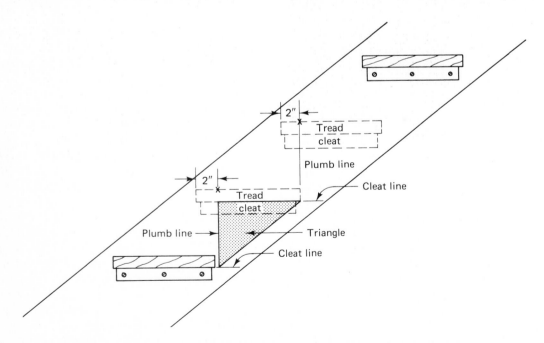

Fig. 11-1. To convert a basement stairway with open treads and no risers to a finished stairway, add a series of triangles to stringers and nail both treads and new risers into them.

side of the stringer with a finish string. Then cap the top of the stringer and the finishing material on both sides with a high-grade board or molding wide enough to overlap on both sides to cover the joint. Cut the board to length, then hold it in place and mark the notches to be cut into it for the front edges of treads.

PARTITIONING

After you have located partitions on paper to the best of your ability, transfer these locations to the floor of the basement by snapping chalk lines. Set scrap lengths of 2 × 4 between the lines or at corners where they cross to give yourself an idea of how the spaces will look when partitioned, and whether you allowed enough room around equipment. Carry with you a carpenter's level and another length of 2 × 4 somewhat shorter than ceiling height. Set this 2 × 4 upright at various points in the partition to see what problems you have at the ceiling line, if any. Now is the time to adjust locations of partitions, not after you begin assembling them.

When you are satisfied that you can proceed, cut bottom plates to length out of treated lumber. Unlike partitions between rooms above ground level, basement partitions may some day be subject to moisture. Bottom plates should therefore be cut from lumber that has been pressure-treated to resist rot.

Cut top plates of the same length out of regular 2 × 4 stock, and mark stud locations simultaneously on both plates. If the partition runs parallel to ceiling joists but not directly under one, build a ladder between joists for attachment. See Fig. 8-8 for partition construction and Fig. 8-9b for ladder construction. You can add a cap plate to the top plate for greater strength, but it is not required under existing joists, and makes attachment to ceiling structure more difficult.

To secure bottom plates into a concrete basement floor, use **concrete nails**, also called **cement nails** and **hardened nails**. Select nails not less than 2″ or more than 2½″ long. Drive in a pair of nails at each end of each bottom plate, just outside the line marking the location of the end stud or corner post. Drive in a single nail between other stud marks. But before you nail, make sure that you have the plate properly placed, and have someone hold the other end in position when you begin to nail.

With the bottom plate attached, check it for level in both directions. If it is reasonably level and ceiling joists above are also level, cut all studs the same length. To establish a length, measure up the basement wall from the plate to the wood framing above, then subtract 1½″ for the thickness of the top plate. If you have much variation from level at either end of studs, measure and cut each stud individually. Number the studs in sequence when their lengths differ, so you know the proper order of nailing.

Lay the top plate on the basement floor on edge,

and lay the studs also on edge on their marks. Nail through the top plate into studs, making sure that the edges are flush. Then raise the partition into position; you may have to bend the studs to one side to get them to fit over the bottom plate. Then hammer them into position on their marks, and adjust the partition for plumb. Nail the top plate to the ceiling framing in about the same pattern as you nailed the bottom plate.

The partition should be solid without further attachment. To be sure, however, you can always nail through the end stud into the basement wall. Use concrete nails if the wall is concrete, or masonry nails if it is built of concrete blocks, clay tiles, stone, or brick. Where another partition butts at the other end, nail through its end stud into the corner post.

When you plan to stop surface materials short of the top plate, and leave studs exposed above, install blocks between studs as a nailing surface for the top edge of material. Nail the end block through flanking studs. Nail succeeding blocks through the stud at one end, and toenail at the other. Add blocks before you raise the partition.

When only end and corner studs will be exposed, cut two lengths of 2 × 4 to fit between them. Mark the bottom of the opening on the studs, and set the top of the upper 2 × 4 just below the mark, first nailing the two lengths together. Cut studs to fit between this header and the bottom plate.

BOXING PIPES AND DUCTS

Steel columns, steel posts, and the main plumbing stack may sometimes be in the way of a partition. Almost always they will be too big to hide inside it. Therefore, you should box in vertical obstructions. You can do this so that the box juts on both sides of the partition (Fig. 11-2a) or so that one side is straight and the protrusion is all on the other side (Fig. 11-2b).

Vertical Box

To establish the *inside* measurements of a vertical box, measure the diameter of a stack or circular post, the width of a pedestal, or width of the flange and height of the web of an H column. Use the maximum dimensions of the obstruction, which may be a steel plate at the floor of a column, or a bell connection between lengths of pipe. Add ¼″ to these maximums. Then, from 2 × 4 stock, cut two top and two bottom plates of this length, and cut the other plates of this length plus 7″.

Mark the location of the box on the floor, and lay the pieces of bottom plate in position to check the fit. Nail them on their marks to the floor. Next determine stud length, allowing 4½″ for thicknesses of three plates. Cut four studs out of 2 × 2s.

Assemble a centered box in two parts as shown in

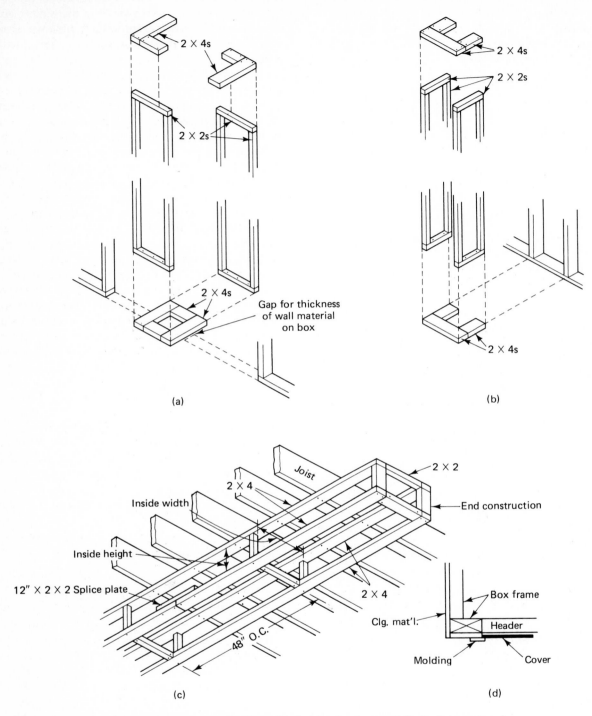

Fig. 11-2. General procedures for boxing in pipes and ducts: box centered on partition (a); box off center (b); furring framework (c). All box members are either 2 × 4s or 2 × 2s. Part (d) shows in section how to provide an access below a drain valve in a horizontal pipe line.

Fig. 11-2a. Set them in place on the bottom plates, nail them down, then toenail the top plates together. Assemble a jutting box in one piece (Fig. 11-2b). Even if you didn't need to build a ladder to attach the top plate of any partition, you will probably need one here. Usually, you can insert ladder rungs between joists after you have the box frame in position, and know exactly where you need top support.

Horizontal Box

There are three differences between boxing around a vertical pipe and a horizontal duct:

1. Wood framing must clear heat ducts by at least 1″.
2. Some long horizontal members may have to be spliced.
3. Vertical members may extend up the sides of ceiling joists.

To box in a pipe or duct that hangs below the bottoms of ceiling joists, you follow the same principles for building a light framework to which to attach ceiling material. The procedure is similar to furring a ceiling above cabinets in a kitchen (see Chapter 15). Figure 11-2c shows the typical furring framework, and the method of attachment at splices and joists.

Before you box in any piping, look for drain valves through which the pipes can be cleaned out or emptied. You must provide access to these valves. The simplest method is to leave an opening in the box large enough so you can reach and turn the valve, and frame it with headers (Fig. 11-2d). Then, after you have ceiling material in place up to the edge of the opening, add a thin molding strong enough to support a removable cover. Let the molding overlap the opening about ¼″, and cut a cover to fit closely. To remove the cover, simply raise it and slide it out of the way inside the furring, or turn it at an angle and drop it through the opening. The cover may be plywood or a piece of ceiling material. If you use plywood, paint it on both sides to equalize moisture content and prevent warping.

MOISTURE CONTROL

The primary cause of wet basement walls is sufficient moisture in the earth outside the wall under sufficient pressure to force its way through tiny openings in wall materials. There are three possible solutions to such a moisture problem: seal the wall on the inside, seal the wall on the outside, or prevent the moisture from saturating the ground.

The easiest answer is to waterproof the inside of basement walls, but this is also the least effective solution. Oh, there are several products on the market formulated for brushing or troweling onto the surface that won't let moisture through. But although these products keep moisture away from basement *space*, they won't keep it out of basement *walls*. So what happens to the moisture that gets into the walls? It stays there, and eventually will cause serious structural problems.

Between the other two solutions you rarely have an easy choice. The process of waterproofing the outside of a masonry wall, called parging, is covered in Chapter 6. Its seven steps aren't difficult to complete, and it takes about four days, allowing for drying time between steps. But to parge a wall you must completely expose it all the way to footings. Therefore, you must dig a trench around the house at least 24″ wide so that you have room to work. In so doing you would probably have to move base planting around the house, disrupt flower beds, and even dig out and replace part of a driveway, walkway, or patio. The materials for parging are not expensive, and you could do the work yourself. The cost and effort lie in getting at the wall to work on it, then putting the earth and planting back in place. If you have a usable basement except for a moisture problem, however, you would save by parging the walls and finishing the basement rather than building an addition to achieve the same amount of space.

Locate the Source of Moisture

Building an addition may solve your space problem, but it won't solve your moisture problem. So make it a family project to find the source of water. The most likely sources are:

- A spring or similar water source originating underground.
- A flat, low-lying lot, perhaps in a flood plain, that doesn't drain well.
- A driveway or other paved area that directs rainwater toward the foundation.
- An inadequate system for collecting rain off your roof and directing it away from the foundation.
- Rainwater from a neighbor's roof that flows toward your house.

Record of Rainfall

Keep a record of weather and moisture leaks in an attempt to establish a relationship between them. Get a legal-size pad of paper, and use one sheet to record conditions for each month. Divide each sheet into five columns. In the first put the date and day of the week. In the next indicate with a check mark when any precipitation fell. In the third write the amount of precipitation.

Ideally, you should have a rain gauge for measuring rainfall, and place it where it is clear of trees and protected from strong wind currents. Check the gauge every day at approximately the same time. Write down the reading in tenths of an inch, then empty the gauge and replace it in its holder. A less satisfactory alternative to a rain gauge is the statistical data sometimes given with the weather report in local daily newspapers. The problem here is that you may live 30 or 40 miles from the official measuring point, and you may have twice as much or only half as much rain as is officially reported.

In the fourth column of your chart write in the wind direction. A weathervane is a help, but you can usually tell by seeing on which side of the house windows are wet. Wind direction is particularly important if you live in an area where rains are heavy and often accompanied by wind. In the last column indicate when and where moisture appeared in the basement. Check this at the same time you check the rain gauge and wind. Be as exact as possible, giving the distance from a corner or other fixed point, and how far above the floor you can feel moisture. When you look for a leak in a roof, the relationship between the source of leak and the point where water appears is difficult to establish. In a basement, however, the source of moisture is almost always close to the point where it appears inside.

Over a period of time—and it may take six months or more—you can begin to see from your data what weather conditions cause leaks, and what the time lag is between the storm and the appearance of moisture. The shorter the time lag, the closer the cause of your problem lies to the point where the leak shows up.

If the time lag is short—perhaps within 24 hours after the end of a ½″ rain—study how water flows during and just after the next heavy rain. Your problem may be nothing more than a clogged gutter or downspout, or a hole or loose connection in a gutter that is allowing water to puddle against a wall. Or perhaps the downspout isn't directing water far enough away from the house so that it can run off instead of running back. Such problems are easily corrected with little expense. You should clean gutters annually on one of the first warm days in early spring, then every two weeks from the time leaves or needles begin to fall until most have fallen—especially if your house is surrounded by trees with large leaves, such as oaks, and conifers that shed pine straw.

Replace gutters with holes in them. When a leak occurs at a joint, buy a can of sealant at your local hardware store and follow the directions on the can. In closing a leak, however, be certain to smooth the surface of the sealant so that water flows over the joint without interruption. If the problem is at ground level, add a short length of downspout to the end of the existing line, or set concrete splash blocks to direct water away from the house. Rainwater deposited 4′

from the house isn't likely to flow toward it unless the grade is wrong.

Regrading

If the time lag is longer, the problem may be grading. When a house is built, the area around the foundation is backfilled after the wall is completed. The correct procedure is to backfill with dirt and gravel in several steps, allowing one load to settle before adding the next. But many builders don't take the time to do this. As a result, the grade at the wall settles, and is slightly lower than at a point 2 or 3′ away. Therefore, water can puddle against the wall. To correct this, simply buy a load or partial load of topsoil locally, and spread it around the foundation wall so that ground level falls at least 2″ in every 12″ away from the house for at least 48″. At the same time, however, never add soil any closer than 4″ from the bottom edge of the lowest piece of exterior trim or bottom course of shingles or siding. To do so is to invite termites and other ground-dwelling wood eaters.

In some sections of the country, such as the southeast, rains often beat down hard enough to spatter wet red soil onto the side of the house. To avoid such unsightly stains, spread a 1 to 2″ layer of gravel about 12 to 18″ wide around the foundation. The gravel prevents splattering, and lets water filter into the ground more gradually.

Drain Lines

The complete answer to basement water problems is parging plus drain lines plus good backfilling. Since parging requires digging down to footings around the entire house, laying drain tiles in the bottom of the trench is a simple process. Drain lines and backfilling are discussed briefly near the end of Chapter 6, but you will probably need professional help with the layout.

Start drain lines at the lowest corner—the corner from which the drain line leads into the disposal line to the sewer. Lay a Y or T section on the footing, and achieve the required 1″ slope in 8′ by laying lengths of tile in a base of pea gravel. The two branches must meet at their high point at the opposite corner of the house. At this high point the bottom of the line must be below basement floor level. If it isn't, lay the tiles beside the footing instead of on it.

If the end of the disposal line is below the storm sewer or natural point of drainage, you need a sump and a sump pump. A **sump** is simply a small reservoir for holding water. When water level in the sump reaches a fixed point, the sump pump goes into action to raise the water to a level high enough for disposal.

Problems caused by springs and drainage runoff can rarely be solved without professional help. Sources of help are sometimes hard to find. As a starter, call the

Chapter 11 / Finishing A Basement

nearest County Extension office, listed under "United States Government, Department of Agriculture."

LIGHT, VENTILATION, AND ACCESS

Unless your basement is woefully deficient in good ventilation and adequate light, or you need access directly outdoors, leave sound basement walls alone. To tamper with them by adding doors or enlarging windows is to invite leaks. On the other hand, don't let the risk of problems deter you from taking the steps necessary to give you maximum use of the space you're remodeling.

Let's take three common drawbacks one at a time: a poor view out windows, windows too small for living or sleeping space, and outdoor access.

A Better View

Basement windows often look out into **areaways**—small sunken courts with walls of concrete or corrugated metal. Their purpose is to hold back the soil and let a little light and air into basement windows. Properly built areaways have a drain in the bottom that leads to drain lines at the footings. Although areaways let in some light and air, the amounts are limited, and the view outward isn't worth a glance.

With a little effort and imagination, however, you can convert areaways into miniature gardens. Leave the drains in place, but remove the vertical metal or concrete walls. Then cut the slope from 90° to about 45°. In the new slope embed rocks large enough to hold the slope against washing but small enough to let you plant between them. Fill the gaps with such plantings as hens and chickens, jonquils, tulips, and other plants that thrive with little sunlight and little care. They are protected here from severe weather, and can provide a closeup view of nature that is as interesting as a fish tank or indoor planter, and a lot less trouble.

Better Light

Standard basement windows are about 2½' wide and from 15 to 23" high. Because the heads of these sashes are just below ceiling level, their sills are seldom less than 5½' above the basement floor level. The lower a window sill, the more light will reach the floor and, in so doing, will reflect farther into the room.

Generally, you can improve light conditions more effectively by lowering a sill than by widening the window opening. Widening a basement window opening also may create structural problems that you would be wise to avoid. But with proper precautions against exterior moisture, you can install standard metal windows as high as 42" simply by removing part of the wall below an existing window, and not touching the wall above or beside the opening.

Specifications for New Windows

If your drainage conditions permit lowering sills, first find out what metal windows are available that are no wider than your existing windows. Note that basement sash should be metal, if for no other reason than their imperviousness to rot in the presence of moisture. If necessary, you can always narrow an opening slightly. Widening it even slightly is much more difficult.

But a word of caution. Under most basement conditions you must install windows that open inward, such as hopper vents. The upper corners of these vents can be a serious hazard if they are close to eye level when open. So if your main purpose in enlarging windows is to increase light, consider a two-sash window with the upper sash opening in and the lower one fixed. If you need both better light and more ventilation, consider a jalousie window. A **jalousie** window consists of a series of horizontal glass plates that overlap when closed. When open to a horizontal position, they provide about 90% ventilation, but the plates do not extend beyond the window's sill.

From manufacturer's literature determine the rough-opening height and width of the new window, and compare it with the dimensions of the existing opening. The rough opening is the size of the hole needed to accept the window and its frame. Mark this size on the basement wall with chalk lines, carefully snapped to assure square corners. If at all possible, maintain a fixed position for the head of the window and one jamb.

Before you actually buy any basement windows, figure out how you are going to drape them. If draperies lie close to the wall, you must be able to open them beyond the window opening so that you can operate the hopper vents. If you are likely to want ventilation and privacy at the same time, drapery hardware must either be attached to the vent itself and move with it, or be placed far enough out from the wall to permit vent operation when draperies are closed.

Installation

Your existing basement windows may have been installed in one of three ways. If walls are concrete, the frames were probably installed in wall forms and the concrete poured around them. If walls are concrete block, the frames probably fit into jamb blocks at the sides, and the opening is sealed all the way around with concrete mortar. With other types of masonry, such as stone or brick, the frames are probably held in place with metal clips.

Unless you can remove an existing window without disturbing the wall around it, better hire a small contractor to adjust the size of the opening and install new windows. You aren't likely to have the tools or the time to do the job yourself and do it properly. Even enlarging an existing opening requires concrete cutting tools that you may not be able to rent. But you can enlarge the areaway outside the window, being careful not to disturb the drain except to shorten it, and plant the slope as previously suggested.

Outdoor Access

When you plan to use remodeled basement space for any purpose that requires moving large or long items in and out, such as a workshop, you need a stairway that is straight, fairly wide, and leads in a straight line to the outdoors. Few basement stairways meet these three requirements. Stairs that give you direct access do. Concrete steps are one answer, and manufactured basement access stairs are another.

In either case you must cut a door through an existing wall. The procedure is outlined in Chapter 6. In planning the spot for the door, keep two thoughts in mind. Outdoors it should open at a point where natural surface drainage is away from the stairwell that must be dug. Indoors it should open not only at the point of greatest convenience for moving materials to their point of use, but also where it will not break up wall space for a practical furniture arrangement or create a hallway through the living area. Block out an area of wall about 5' wide, then decide where within these limits you can install a door the most economically. Allow for a door 36" wide.

Concrete Steps

To lay out concrete steps, follow the procedures outlined in Chapter 9 for laying out an inside stairway. If you have enough yard space, work with 6" risers and 12" treads for maximum safety. Otherwise, use a maximum riser of 7" and a minimum tread of 10½". Concrete steps should never be as steep as wood steps. Allow a clear working width of 48" between the walls of the stairwell.

Establish the floor of the stairwell ¾ to 1" lower than the basement floor. Dig 4" below that level under most soil conditions; go down 6" if the soil is soft or weak. The dimension of the well floor perpendicular to the wall should be at least 18", and 24 to 30" is better if you have space. Cut the slope at the angle of pitch of your stairway, allowing the same minimum concrete thickness as for the floor (Fig. 11-3). Establish the level of the top step about 1" above grade so that water won't run off the lawn down the steps. Dig the excavation the width of your stairs plus 12", thus allowing for a 6" wall on each side. Side cuts should be as close to plumb and as straight as you can make them; then they can serve as forms for the outsides of poured concrete walls.

Before you build and erect sidewall forms, dig a hole for a drain. This drain should lead into drain lines if you have them, or else to a sump nearby. You won't have a lot of water going down the drain, but make sure that what does arrive won't go into the basement.

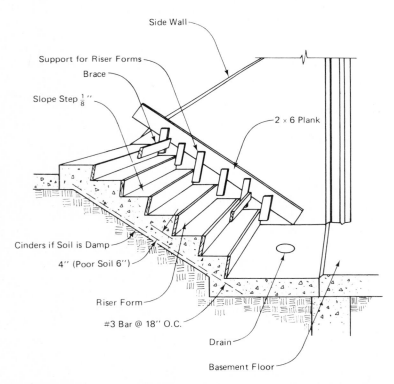

Fig. 11-3. Outdoor steps should not be as steep as inside stairs, but have wider treads sloped slightly for drainage and vertical faces undercut for maximum toe space. Note the method of forming when steps rise beside an existing masonry wall.

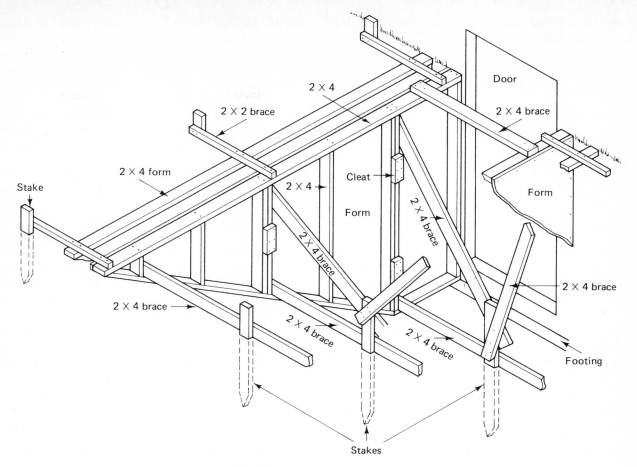

Fig. 11–4. Details of forms for walls beside a basement access stairway. The forms may be built in one piece or in smaller units clamped together with cleats.

In the figure: Stake, 2 × 4 form, 2 × 2 brace, 2 × 4, 2 × 4, Cleat, Form, Door, 2 × 4 brace, 2 × 4 brace, Form, 2 × 4 brace, 2 × 4 brace, 2 × 4 brace, 2 × 4 brace, 2 × 4 brace, 2 × 4 brace, Footing, Stakes

Form for Walls. Build wall forms out of ¾" plywood or boards, similar to those shown in Fig. 11-4. Where two forms meet, clamp them firmly together at top and bottom. Brace them diagonally to stakes in the ground and, if you form both walls simultaneously, brace between them. As you assemble the forms, line up their surfaces carefully at joints. Otherwise, that joint will show up clearly in the finished wall.

Where you use the side of your excavation for a form, you will need a low form at the top. Hold this form in place with either stakes or tie cleats, or both. Make the form out of 2 × 4s laid flat on the ground. Lay a long, straight 2 × 4 and a level between opposite forms to make sure that their tops are level and at the same height.

For best results seal the edges of your form boards or plywood with aluminum paint or shellac. Then check the flat surfaces for flaws; every defect will show up in the finished wall. Make repairs with water putty. Then oil the surfaces that will have wet concrete against them. You can use new motor oil for this purpose; used motor oil will discolor the wall. Spread the oil liberally until the surface is slippery.

Concrete Mix. For each wall you will need less than a cubic yard of concrete. For that small amount it is less expensive to rent the equipment and mix your own, rather than to buy ready-mixed. Use this formula:

- 1 part portland cement
- 2½ parts clean sand
- 3 parts crushed rock or stone 1 to 1½" in size

A sack of cement contains 1 cu ft and weighs 94 lb. From each sack with the formula above you can mix about 7 cu ft of concrete (about ¼ cu yd). To maintain proper proportions, build a plywood box with inside dimensions of 12" × 12" × 12". At points 3", 6" and 9" from the bottom draw lines inside the box on all four sides. Each 3" of depth equals ¼ cu ft of content, and a full box contains 1 cu ft.

Mix the ingredients as close as possible to their point of use. Measure dry ingredients first and dump them in the mixer. Then add water. For every sack of cement add 5 gallons of water when the sand is wet, or 6 gallons if the sand is dry. If your mix turns out too thin, add more rock. *Do not* increase the proportion of cement. If the mix is too stiff, add water. But add only a little at a time, and give the mix a chance to absorb it and reach more fluid consistency before you add any more. It's easy to add too much water.

Reinforcement. Reinforcement isn't absolutely necessary, but you will have a stronger, more durable wall with it. Use ⅜" steel rods made for this purpose. Cut two lengths a little shorter than the diagonal measurement of the bottom of the form. Tie pieces of wire around the ends, then tie or nail the upper ends of the wires to the cleats between forms. The rods should hang about an inch above the bottom of the wall and about an inch in from each form. After you fill the form about half full of concrete, work the mix with your spade, then cut the wires somewhere below the top of the wall. Add vertical reinforcement at that time, shoving one rod into the mix near each end of the wall and one between. The ends of the rods should be 4 to 6" from the bottom of the form and a few inches below the top surface.

Pouring Concrete. Set the mixer as close as possible to forms to reduce spills. If you must pour from more than 4' away, build a wood chute to bridge the distance. Pour steadily, and avoid a quick dump. Concrete is heavy, and the force with which it hits the forms could knock them loose, even when they are braced.

As you fill each form, force the concrete against the side of the form by working the spade up and down in the wet mix. This action helps to release air trapped in the mix during pouring, and pushes concrete fully into lower corners of the form. Fill forms all the way to the top, but just to the top and no farther.

Level the tops by working a short length of 2 × 4 with a straight edge back and forth in a zigzag pattern along the tops of the forms. To bring excess water to the surface, a process called **floating**, use a metal or wood float. You can use a broad trowel, but a float brings better results.

One of the secrets of good concrete work is letting the water in the concrete evaporate slowly. Cover the exposed top of the wall with wet burlap, towels, or any similar material that holds moisture for a long time. Leave this cover in place for three days in cool weather or five days in hot weather, and add moisture every day. Leave the forms in place for four days. Take them apart in the reverse order of assembly. You may use a hammer and crowbar for dismantling as long as you are careful to put no pressure on the wall itself. The wall won't fall, but the concrete won't yet be fully cured and able to withstand rough treatment for another three weeks.

Forming for Steps. Forms for concrete steps consist of a series of strips cut to length and width from 1" boards or ¾" plywood. Their width is the same as riser height, and the edges should be beveled slightly so that the risers slant inward to provide maximum toe space (see Fig. 11-3). Place these forms with the top edge of one form about ⅛" below the bottom of the form above; this gives the steps enough slope to drain. The horizontal distance between the back edges of forms is the tread width.

Form the steps before the concrete in the walls has fully cured. Nail a 2 × 6 plank into each wall just above the nosing line of the steps. Support the riser forms with short lengths of 1 × 4 nailed into the planks. Then brace across the steps between supports with another 1 × 4. Remember to seal the drain; stuffing it with rags is the easiest way.

Pouring Steps. Pour the entire flight of steps at one time, and be prepared to get pretty messy because you have to walk in the mix. Before you begin leveling, shove reinforcing rods under the steps as shown in Fig. 11-3. Aerate the mix with your spade as described for walls, and level the top step with a straightedge. Because you have no back form to guide a straightedge for leveling the other steps, use a trowel or broadknife to remove any excess concrete and to fill low spots. Then float and smooth the surface in a single operation. Obviously, you work from the top step downward, so be sure that the new door is unlocked, and that you have a place in the basement for taking off your messy clothes and cleaning up.

As with walls, cover steps with wet material to slow evaporation, and keep them damp. After four days, remove the forms. Then mix just enough concrete to patch the walls where you nailed into them, and to repair steps where edges broke loose as you removed the forms.

Manufactured Stairs

By installing a manufactured basement entrance you can avoid the messiness of concrete steps and the need for a drain in the stairwell.

Entrance units fit over an areaway of concrete or concrete blocks. They have a waterproof cover that includes two doors, a header that fits against the existing wall of the house, a sill at the outer end, and two triangular sides (Fig. 11-5). The sides and sill are bolted to the areaway, and the header fits under finished exterior wall material. The doors are hinged at the sides, open up and out, and may be locked from the inside. The stairs are a series of 2 × 10 wood treads supported on a pair of steel stringers. There are no risers.

Manufacturers' literature provides complete instructions. You need to form and pour footings (see Chapter 6) around the areaway. You build the areaway out of concrete blocks, as shown in Chapter 6, or form for a concrete pour as described earlier in this chapter. You assemble the steel frame, and position it on blocks or forms. You set the bolts that hold the frame in place, then either pour the walls or fill the holes in the top

Fig. 11–5. Manufactured basement access stairs include a pair of metal doors, the frame they rest on, stringers, and treads. You provide the concrete areaway beneath the frame. (Courtesy The Bilco Company.)

course of blocks around the bolts. Next, you caulk the perimeter of the areaway to seal it against weather. Finally, you install the stringers, and cut and fit treads. You still need a door in the basement wall to prevent heat loss and to reduce condensation.

THE BASEMENT FLOOR

One of the provisos for remodeling a basement is a level floor. But what do you do when your floor isn't level, or when you don't have a floor but need one, as in a room addition with a basement under it?

In Chapter 18 ("An Uneven Floor") you'll find a method of leveling an existing floor above ground by resurfacing it with lightweight concrete. You can follow these same general procedures for leveling an old basement floor. The floor must be in good condition, however, and free of moisture from the earth beneath it. And you must have enough headroom after you have added the extra floor thickness. At drains you must add an extender to raise the drain to the higher floor level, and slope the concrete slightly toward the drain within 12″ of it.

Over bare earth you must take six steps (Fig. 11-6) before you can pour a new concrete floor:

1. Install a basement drain line and any utility piping that lies below the floor.

2. Clean the excavation of loose dirt and debris, and have it reasonably level.

3. Add 4″ of medium-size crushed rock or gravel, and rent a power tamper to compact it. As you tamp, be careful not to knock pipes out of position.

4. Over this fill lay a polyethylene vapor barrier at least 4 mm thick, since you will be walking on it. Overlap joints at least 6″ and carry the barrier 2 to 3″ up basement walls. Let it conform to the contours of the gravel; pull it too tight and you may puncture it. Repair any punctures by cutting a patch extending at least 12″ in all directions from the hole or tear, and sealing the seams with duct tape.

5. Place temporary isolation joints. An **isolation joint** is a device for separating walls and floor so that they can move independently of each other as they settle slightly, and thus prevent cracking. On foundation walls mark the level of the finished basement floor, then set isolation joints with their tops at this level. For joint material you can use lengths of beveled siding with the butt edge up, ½″ oiled plywood, or strips of rigid in-

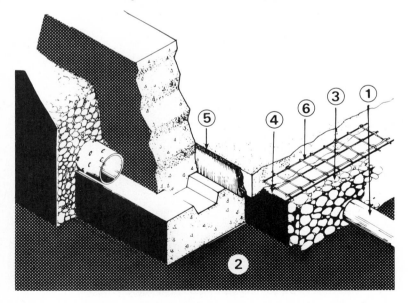

Fig. 11–6.   The six steps to take before you pour a new basement floor: (1) install drain and utility piping, (2) clean the excavation, (3) add a rock base, (4) lay down a vapor barrier, (5) install isolation joints, and (6) lay steel reinforcement.

sulation. Set isolation joints loosely in place until you pour, then adjust their position when the wet concrete can hold them in place. Later you remove the temporary material and replace it with asphalted gaskets like those atop your foundation wall.

6. Lay reinforcement. The common reinforcement is 6″ × 6″ × No. 6 wire mesh. It comes in rolls and you lay it in strips, overlapping them 1″ or so. The mesh protects the vapor barrier while you walk on it during concrete pouring and finishing.

Concrete Mix

For a basement floor use a concrete mix with these proportions:

- 1 part portland cement
- 2¼ parts of fine aggregate—¼″ or smaller in diameter
- 3 parts of coarse aggregate—½ to 1″ in diameter
- 6 gallons of water, including water in aggregate

You can mix your own, but ordering from a ready-mix plant is advisable. You'll be busy enough spreading and finishing the concrete without having to worry about mixing it, too.

The area of basement floor in most remodelings is small enough so that you can pour the entire floor at one time. If you want to mix your own concrete, form the floor in sections, and finish one area before you pour the next. The general procedure for forming and

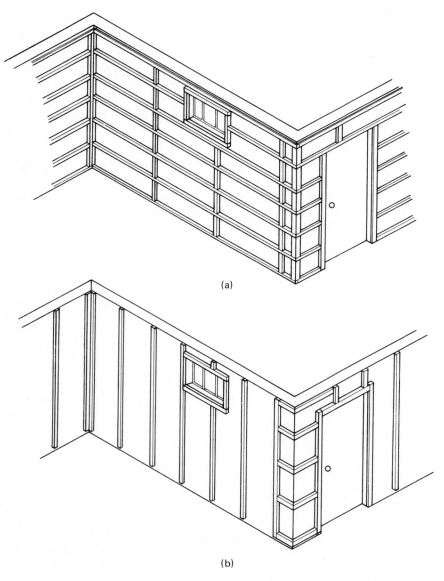

(a)

(b)

Fig. 11-7. Basement walls must be furred for application of finish panel materials. When paneling runs vertically, furring runs horizontally (a) except behind seams between panels and around wall openings. When paneling runs horizontally, furring runs vertically (b) except at outside corners and around openings.

finishing is described in Chapter 18. Use the tops of isolation joints as guides for screeding. After the concrete begins to set, replace the temporary joints with the asphalted gaskets.

When should you pour a concrete floor? Have basements walls completed, but leave access to chute the concrete into the space. Have the door cut through from your existing basement, and exit through it when you've finished the floor. Have subflooring on the floor level above to keep rain out of the basement, and the roof sheathed to keep rain off the subfloor. The more air that can circulate through the basement and the addition above, the quicker moisture from the curing floor will dissipate. So pour and finish the floor before you sheathe the walls and install windows and doors in space above the basement. By the time you finish that work, most of the moisture from the basement should be gone, and the floor dry.

PREPARING BASEMENT WALLS

Panels of finish wall materials must never be applied directly to basement walls of masonry or concrete. Instead, you must provide a network of furring strips that leaves an air space between the existing basement wall and the new surface material. Furring strips may be 1 × 2s or metal furring channels with overall dimensions of $2\frac{1}{4}'' \times \frac{7}{8}''$. A finished basement room is therefore slightly smaller than the unfinished area, reduced by the thickness of the furring and the finish material.

For Paneling

If you intend to finish walls with panels of plywood or wood fiberboard, run furring strips horizontally (Fig. 11-7a). Place the lowest strip with its bottom edge about 1″ above the floor line, and the highest strips about the same distance below ceiling joists. Add strips between no more than 16″ apart.

Cut and apply short lengths of furring vertically between horizontal strips at inside corners and wherever joints between panels will fall. At outside corners miter the ends of horizontal furring strips, and use 1 × 4s for short verticals, applied so that they are flush on the front and one side with other furring.

At doors and windows the openings must be surrounded with furring. If you can extend trim far enough to cover its exposed side, set furring flush with the opening. Otherwise, inset the furring the thickness of finish material, and carry it around the corner.

For Drywall

If you intend to apply gypsum wallboard, run main furring channels or strips vertically, ending them just above floor level and just below joist level (Fig. 11-7b). Place them in corners and every 24″ on centers around the wall. Then apply the wallboard horizontally, and cut panels if necessary so that their ends fall on strips. At outside corners run channels horizontally, spaced no more than every 24″, and miter them by cutting the wings and flanges with a hacksaw at 45°. Don't cut the web. At openings, furr with wood strips as described for plywood panels.

Application of Furring Strips

Apply wood furring strips with concrete nails driven into concrete walls or into mortar joints of masonry walls. Space nails about every 24″. Apply metal channels to concrete with $\frac{5}{8}''$ concrete nails, and to masonry with 2″ cut nails in the same manner and spacing as with wood strips. Apply panels to wood furring strips with nails; wallboard must be screwed to metal channels.

Planning Better Use Of Space

(a)

(b)

A heating plant operates most economically when near the center of a house. In that location, however, it often destroys efficient use of the space around it (a). Not so in this remodeling. The furnace is now partitioned off, but louvered doors (b) provide the necessary air for combustion. A ceiling lowered to cover a duct left space above for recessed spotlights over work counters. Note that no corner is wasted. Laundry equipment fits into a recess formed by storage closets off the room behind. (Courtesy Azrock Floor Products.)

One of the unfortunate by-products of poor residential design is wasted space. There may not be a lot of space wasted in any one room. But if you add up all the little areas in all rooms that can't be used to their maximum, you probably have enough to create another room. Making the most of available space is the approach you should study fully if you are limited by lot size, areas available for finishing or converting, or remodeling money.

For several reasons it will be difficult for you to analyze the house you live in for better use of existing space. Architects are trained in this type of analysis, and can be invaluable in guiding your thinking. Many people, even those who can read plans fairly readily, can't visualize in three dimensions from a two-dimensional layout. Moreover, they are so accustomed to the elements that cause space to go to waste that they can't spot either the main problem or its solution. That is why, early in this book, you were advised to make a list of all the annoyances, petty and otherwise, that you have adjusted to. With that list in front of you, and the steps in this chapter fully digested, perhaps you will be able to see your home through reeducated eyes, and find a way to improve it merely by adjusting existing rooms.

COMMON PROBLEMS

The three problems that afflict improperly planned rooms are too little wall space, two many doors, and too

160

much pass-through traffic. The three problems are closely related. Look at the floor plans of two living rooms in Fig. 12-1. They are identical in size: 13′ × 20′. They have about the same linear feet of wall space. They both have two doors.

Yet in Room 1 almost one-fourth of the floor space is not fully usable, while in Room 2 only a few square feet have limited utility. Room 2 is lighter and better ventilated because it has windows in two walls instead of one. The second window takes up wall space, true, but it helps improve the use of other wall space. Furthermore, the simple relocation of one door groups usable wall space at one end of the room, rather than splitting it between ends so that a practical room arrangement is impossible. In room 2 traffic passes not through the length of the room, but across a corner. And furniture can now be grouped for an intimate conversation or accommodate a party. In addition, many furniture arrangements are possible, while in room 1 there are only a few, none fully satisfactory.

Sure, you might say, that looks great, but I couldn't do something like that in my house without throwing every other room in the house out of kilter. And you would be right. That's exactly why you must analyze the relationship between *all* rooms on any floor level, not just one.

THE FLOOR LAYOUT

The starting point in your thinking, as always, must be with a floor plan of existing space. A scale of ¼″ = 1′ = 0″ is best at this point; you may need to go to a larger scale to work out details later. Begin measuring at the corner of the house from which you can most easily establish inside dimensions. If one wall is broken up with closets, lavatories, and other small spaces, leave it until last because your chances of

measuring error are greatest. Determine thicknesses of partitions by measuring the width of a casing at a door. After you have the interior length of two adjacent exterior walls established, lightly complete the rectangle, and work toward the opposite corner. Measure any wings or ells last.

You may save time and assure yourself of accuracy if you do the measuring yourself, and call out the dimensions to someone else who writes them down in columnar form. By adding up these dimensions for opposite walls, you can quickly determine the amount of error. If your error is less than an inch, ignore it; adjustment can come later. What you are after now is a working plan that shows the relationship of spaces.

On this "before" plan show the locations of windows, doors, and stairways, or any changes in floor level. For the time being, ignore the locations of heating and electrical outlets, plumbingware, counters, and appliances. In most cases they can be moved where necessary.

After you have the plan drawn lightly, strengthen the lines of walls that can't or shouldn't be moved (or draw them in a different color). They are few. They include the exterior walls, which you should now give their full thickness by drawing another set of lines around the house parallel to the inside wall lines and 6″, 8″, or 10″ away from them at scale. Their thickness depends on whether exterior material is wood, concrete block, or brick veneer, respectively. Also strengthen lines of walls flanking a stairway to a basement or second floor, and any other bearing partitions.

How do you recognize a bearing wall or partition? You can't always be positive. A one-story house with a truss roof probably has no bearing partitions. A one-story house with a roof of any shape framed with rafters has a bearing wall running parallel to the long walls of the house and about midway between them. The first floor of a multistory house will have a similar bearing

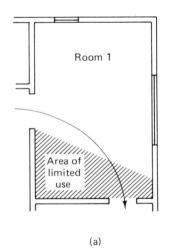

Room 1

Area of limited use

(a)

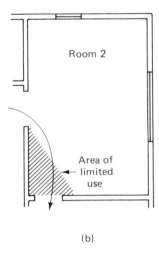

Room 2

Area of limited use

(b)

Fig. 12–1. These two rooms are the same size and have the same number of doors. Yet look at the difference in the amount of space wasted by the floor plan!

partition, and upper floors will have one at the same location unless the roof is truss construction. Few one-story houses have bearing partitions running the shorter dimension of the house. You may find them in a two-story house beneath cross partitions on the second floor.

The lines you didn't strengthen or draw in a different color should be heavy enough so that you can see them through a sheet of tracing paper. Gather half a dozen sheets of thin tracing paper, a couple of pencils with soft lead, an eraser, and a ruler. Then set your drawing on a hard, smooth surface at a table where light is good, lay a sheet of tracing paper over it, and see whether you can solve some of your plan problems.

TRAFFIC

Start with traffic patterns that may be limiting the usefulness of your rooms. On the tracing paper, rough in the walls of the rooms—that is, trace freehand those walls you drew on your "before" plan. Then draw with colored pencils lines indicating the common routes that people take to go from one room to another or to go outdoors. Look again at Fig. 4-5.

Certainly you should not have to go through a bedroom to get to any other room except a bathroom that serves only that bedroom, or perhaps doubles as a guest facility. Ideally, you should not have to cross through a living room. A door into a dining room usually doesn't carry excess traffic because most people going into the dining room are already in the living room.

A family room used primarily for quiet activities, such as reading, watching television, or working on hobbies, is most useful as a dead-end room with a single door. A family room for more vigorous activities and regularly used by children needs less wall space but more

doors—directly to outdoors, to the kitchen, and to a bathroom either directly or indirectly. An active family room may well double as a hallway, and it will likely have a floor covering that will withstand the wear and tear of activities plus the extra load of pass-through traffic.

Incidentally, floor space that allows people to move only from one room to another may seem like a waste, but a hallway often makes the difference between a good floor plan and a poor one. Long, wide halls do waste space; short, narrow ones can save it. The more doors that open off a hallway, the better the house's traffic pattern is likely to be.

Move a Doorway

Look for four ways to improve the traffic pattern. One is to move a doorway within a wall, perhaps only a few feet. In Fig. 12-2a, the locations of doors 1 and 2 are fixed by the stairways up and down. Door 3 is centered in the wall between the dining room and kitchen because at one time it was customary to center doors in walls if possible. But its location there limits the use of one corner in both rooms. By moving the door toward that corner (Fig. 12-2b) you lose any use of corner space, but you increase continuous wall space in both rooms. No longer do you have to weave your way around the dining room table, or put up with traffic through part of the kitchen. Besides, door 3, which is double-acting (it swings both ways), can now be left open against the wall in either room for better ventilation and communication.

Close a Doorway

A second way to improve traffic pattern is to close up a doorway. You can't often do this without disrupting traffic entirely, but sometimes you can seal an opening

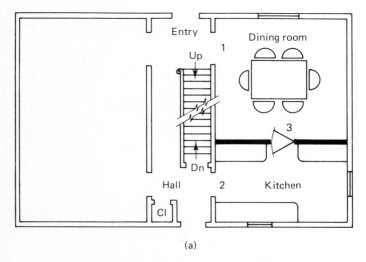

(a)

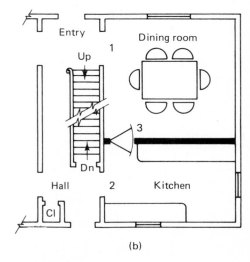

(b)

Fig. 12–2. These two plans are identical except for the location of door 3. Yet the plan in (b) has far better traffic flow and a much more workable kitchen arrangement.

Chapter 12 / Planning Better Use Of Space

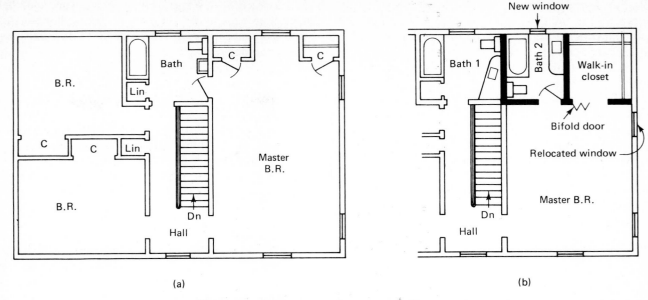

(a)

(b)

Fig. 12–3. The house in (a) has one bathroom upstairs and a large master bedroom with individual closets. Reduce the size of the bedroom (b), and you can add a master bathroom, provide better hanging space in a walk-in closet, close up the second door in bath 1, and place the lavatory in a storage counter.

as a result of another change. In Fig. 12-3a, for example, the one upstairs bathroom in a two-story house is no longer adequate for a family of four when the children become teenagers. The master bedroom is pleasant and roomy, but larger than necessary for a room used only for sleeping.

In the remodeled home (Fig. 12-3b) the two end closets are converted into one large walk-in closet, which leaves space for a second bathroom exclusively

for the owners. As a result, the second doorway to the original bathroom can be sealed, and the single lavatory is now built into a counter that makes the bathroom much more functional.

Group Doorways

A third method of solving traffic problems is to group doorways for better use of room space. In Fig. 12-4a,

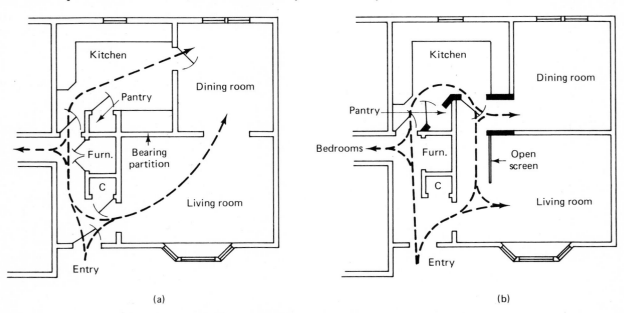

(a)

(b)

Fig. 12–4. The four doors to major rooms in the plan in (a) limit usable wall space to only half the wall available. By grouping doors (b), and in this case actually adding one, you can reduce or eliminate traffic flow through rooms, and greatly increase the wall space for furniture.

wall space in the living room is broken up by a wide doorway to the dining room. There is little wall space in the dining room for any furniture except the table and chairs. Traffic completely bisects the kitchen.

Suppose that you create a small hallway and actually add a doorway (Fig. 12-4b). Now the living room has continuous wall space on three sides. There is no longer a view from the living area of what's for dinner. Wall space in the dining room is continuous on four walls except for one corner. The kitchen, although smaller, lends itself to better arrangement because it, too, has unbroken walls for counters and appliances, and meals can be prepared out of the line of anyone walking through the room for a snack or to see what's cooking.

Relocate the Entrance

Finally, consider the possibility of relocating the main entrance. Many homes built prior to 1940 were planned —if you want to call it that—without much thought to the family car. The main entrance was traditionally on the street side of the house, and often centered in the front wall. With increased use of the car and greater informality in living, the side or service door gets 90% of the in-and-out family use, and the front door is used only by party guests, purveyors of Girl Scout cookies, strangers who are looking for an address in the neighborhood, and volunteers collecting for charities.

Relocating an entrance is more expensive than other changes, and can alter, either for good or bad, the street-side appearance of the house. But if you don't use the front door often, and its present location leads to wasted space inside, don't discard the possibility of a change.

Take two examples. The house in Fig. 12-5a was built half a century ago on a narrow suburban lot with its short wall to the street. It is a rectangle two stories tall except for an unheated entrance hall one story high on the north. The house was roomy and comfortable except for the living room. Doors in opposite corners limited practical furniture groupings. The front door was seldom used, but the closets off the entrance hall were the only place to store coats, boots, ice skates, and other sports equipment. Therefore, the living room was a hallway for the family, and carpeting suffered accordingly. In winter, arriving guests let in blasts of cold air when the door was open, and the unheated hall leaked cold air even when all doors were shut.

Moving the entry hall to the east side of the house (Fig. 12-5b) solved these problems. A new walk and exterior lights at the corner of the house direct visitors to the new front door, which is not visible from the street at a glance. Closet space is split. Hangers and shelves for guests' clothing are in the stair hall, so that people don't block the entrance while they are shedding their foul-weather protection. The closet in the entry is exclusively for family use, and is handy to both front

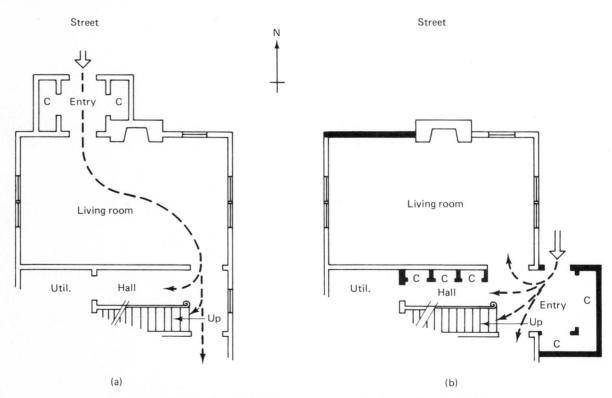

(a)　　　　　　　　　　　　　　　(b)

Fig. 12-5. Relocating the main entrance door sometimes solves cross-traffic problems, and opens the opportunity to better living space and more practical storage.

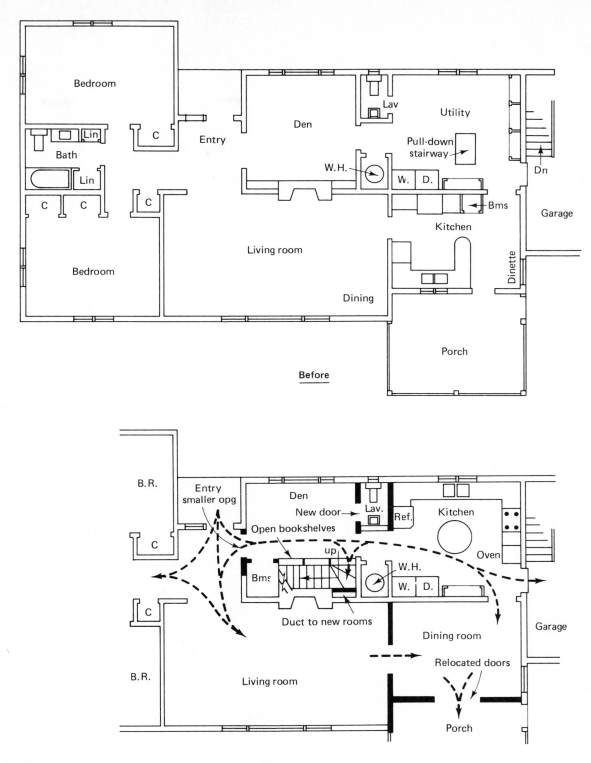

Before

Proposed stage 2

Fig. 12–6. The original house (top) did not have a good floor plan, but the building was sound and the setting superb. Proposed stage 2 relieved the problems of access to new attic bedrooms (see Fig. 12–7), a small kitchen, and limited dining space. Yet it made a hallway out of the den. In revised stage 2 (page 166) the main entrance and den are essentially interchanged to improve traffic circulation and reduce cross-traffic in the den.

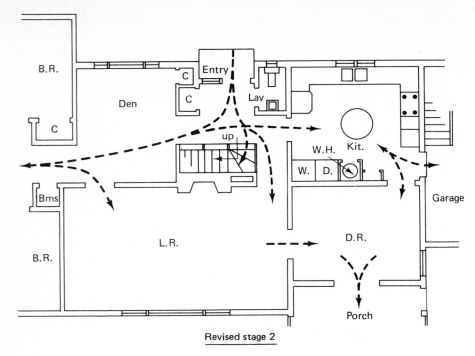

Revised stage 2

Fig. 12–6. (continued)

and rear doors. The old door to the front entry is gone, and so is the old entry hall, sharply reducing heat loss and completely eliminating the traffic problem.

But the change created a few contingent problems with the appearance of the front of the house. When the old entry was torn off, a small window in the bedroom above the hall then looked like an eye almost swollen shut. Replacing it with a window of the same size as the window in the other front bedroom, however, balances the second story nicely. Because the living room already had adequate light, the old front door opening was closed completely instead of being filled with a window. To decorate the blank wall and hide the visible effects of remodeling, holly is espaliered to the new wall, where it adds a touch of greenery all year and a splash of bright color in the drab winter months.

The other example of the advantage of changing an entrance is illustrated in Fig. 12-6. The basic problem here did not involve the entrance but several other drawbacks (Fig. 12-6a). A combination living-dining room, adequate for the original childless owners, was not practical for the family moving in with growing children. The kitchen had adequate counter space, but too many doors and too little floor space—only enough for a small dinette table. Conversely, the adjacent utility room was almost big enough for square dancing, and had a lavatory off it. A large screen porch had a superb view across a stretch of lawn to a graceful bit of river that broadened into a small lake with a park on the opposite shore. But the only entry to the porch was through the kitchen. The porch was ideal for eating and relaxation, but northern weather limited its use to four or five months of the year. A pine-paneled room on the front of the house was a bit too large for a cozy den and

too small for a family room. There was no basement, but an unfinished attic.

Plans called for a complete remodeling to be accomplished in two stages. In the first stage, attic space was finished into two bedrooms, a compartmented bathroom, and a small sewing room, all occupying a shed dormer on the south and overlooking the view (Fig. 12-7). The only possible place for a stairway was behind the chimney, with the space for it stolen from the pine-paneled room.

In the second stage plans called for the kitchen to be moved into the utility room along with laundry facilities, and the former ktichen to become a separate dining room. The door to the lavatory was to be closed to permit a better kitchen arrangement, and a new door cut through in the adjacent wall. No changes were planned to downstairs bedrooms.

Yet problems remained with proposed stage 2 in Fig. 12-6. There was no way to get from the kitchen or garage to the bedrooms, or from the kitchen to answer the front door bell, without going through the den. You couldn't go between the kitchen and living room without going through either the dining room or the den. As a result, the pine-paneled room was more of a hallway than a den.

What happens, the owners' thought, if we move the front door to the other side of the den? To do so meant also relocating the entry closet and den windows, and cutting a new door into the living room. This change—revised stage 2 in Fig. 12-6—improves access to upstairs rooms and the relationship between the kitchen and the living room and front door. It reduces traffic through the den, and provides an alternate (but no better) route through the living room. The cost isn't great if the work is done as part of the larger second stage. But is the improvement worth that cost? That's the type of question you must consider, and the answer will vary from family to family.

These examples are given solely to show you what you can do sometimes with what appears to be an impossible problem. Rough out your ideas on tracing paper as they occur to you. Sketch in freehand even if you aren't good at it. At this time your main interest is to get your ideas down on paper and study the relationship between rooms and the lines of movement between them. You may hit on something in the first couple of tries. It may take two dozen. Or you may never hit on anything you like. But however many sketches you make, *keep them all*. Many times you will reject a sketch that contains an idea worth keeping, but you won't recognize its worth until you have tried a number of different ideas and seen your problem from other angles.

When you finally have a plan roughed out that appears to work, develop it to scale with walls drawn straight and measurements checked. Where tolerances in dimension are slight, as in the relocated front hall in revised stage 2 Fig. 12-6, draw a detail at a larger scale, perhaps ½" or even ¾".

As a semifinal step, add locations of heat outlets, lights, and electrical receptacles, and where you think plumbing runs within walls. Draw these in symbols (see Fig. 3-3), with firm lines if they exist and won't be changed, and in light lines at new locations. Don't consider the prospect of relocating heating, plumbing, or electrical lines as total deterrents. You must weigh the ultimate cost of rerouting utility lines against the improvements in living that the reroutings permit.

To be certain that you have planned well, take your "before" and "after" plans to an architect, and bring along your discarded sketches in case you need them. After the architect has commended your plan or made suggestions for improving it further, you are ready to talk with a contractor and discuss price.

So much for problems relating to doors. Can you improve living by making any changes in windows?

DARK ROOMS

Many years ago the Small Homes Council at the University of Illinois developed 10 planning principles for windows. They were set forth for application to the design of new houses, but they also apply to existing houses. Here they are:

1. Glass areas should be at least 20% of floor area. Therefore, a room with 120 sq ft of floor area should have at least 24 sq ft of glass area. That's *glass* area, not window area.

2. The principal window area should face south. If this isn't possible, the descending order of preference is east, then north, and west last.

3. Windows in more than one wall of a room give more balanced light than windows in just one wall, however large they are.

4. Windows that provide ventilation should take full advantage of the prevailing summer breeze. Incoming air should reach occupants of a room at their seated level.

5. One large window is better than several small ones. You have better light, better view, and eliminate dark areas between openings.

Fig. 12–7. Some 500 sq ft of attic space, added as stage 1, now includes two large bedrooms, a compartmented bathroom, and a small sewing room, all with a view of the lake. From the street side the addition is not visible, but it improves the appearance of the rear side immeasurably.

6. Large glass areas help to extend indoor living space outward.

7. The higher a window is in a wall, the farther light penetrates into a room to brighten it.

8. A window that is basically horizontal in shape gives better light than a vertical window with the same glass area.

9. If divisions between windows or between panes interfere with a view, they are undesirable.

10. Use screens only on windows needed for ventilation. Screens shut out as much as 50% of available light.

Seasonal Sunlight

The movement of the sun during the day and from season to season plays a vital part in planning for good **fenestration**—the relationship of windows. At Christmas the sun moves along a short arc, rising in the southeast and setting in the southwest. It is low in the sky and penetrates well into room interiors. The arc is shorter in Chicago than in New Orleans, and the penetration deeper (see Fig. 12-8).

At the beginning of spring and fall the sun moves along an arc of about 180°, rising in the east and setting in the west. It no longer penetrates deeply into south-facing rooms, and the penetration is about the same in Minneapolis as it is in Atlanta.

In mid-June the sun travels its greatest arc, rising in the northeast and setting in the northwest. At midday it is almost overhead. Now its arc is greater in Seattle than in Los Angeles, and its penetration is less—just the opposite of winter sun.

Orientation. The sun enters north-facing rooms during only a few weeks in early summer. Therefore, the level of north light is fairly constant throughout the year; that's why artists and others who create on paper or canvas look for studios with north light. Summer heat is no problem on the north; cold winter winds are.

Neither cold nor sun is a major drawback on the east, except in midsummer, when outdoor temperature rises above 72° before the sun is off east windows.

Windows on the south are protected from winter cold by the house itself. The sun penetrates deeply in winter when you want its heat, and doesn't enter in summer when you don't want its heat. Only at mid-morning and midafternoon in summer, when the sun is below the peak of its arc, does the sun need to be carefully controlled on the south.

West is the problem orientation. Windows on the west bear the full brunt of winter winds, yet also face the typical summer breeze out of the southwest. Heat is at its maximum on the west side of a house throughout the year, and west walls give off radiant heat long after the sun has dropped below the summer horizon. As it sets, its rays penetrate almost to the ceiling on walls opposite west windows.

What good is all this information? It can be useful not only in helping you improve light and ventilation, but also in helping you avoid new problems when you make changes.

Add a Window

Look again at Fig. 12-4a. The original house has no windows in the right-hand wall. By remodeling you have the opportunity to add a window in both the living room and dining room. Should you?

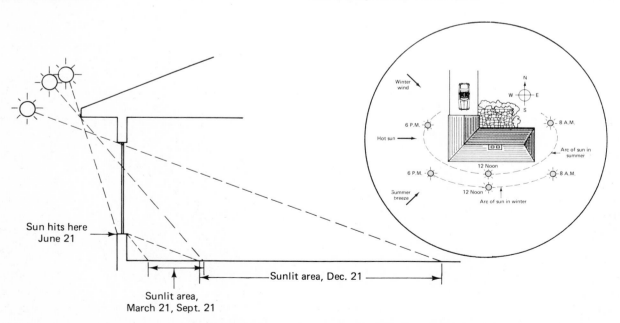

Fig. 12–8. The position of the sun at sunrise, midday, and sunset varies greatly with the seasons.

Chapter 12 / Planning Better Use Of Space

Take the dining room first, and apply the 10 principles listed earlier in this section. If the glass area of existing windows meets the 20% requirement, you already have enough light. Besides, unless the dining room is used frequently during the day, lots of light isn't important. And an added window reduces the wall space you gain by relocating the door.

Even if glass area doesn't meet the 20% requirement, think twice before you add a window if the blank wall faces west. The window will let in extra heat and glare during the summer right at dinner time. When the blank wall is on the north, east, or south, an extra window could make the room more pleasant, and low-angle sunlight isn't a deterrent. You might center the window in the dining room wall of a traditional house. But consider the possibility of placing it opposite the kitchen door, just far enough from the corner so that you can drape it satisfactorily. The exact placement will vary with the location of existing studs. With the window off center, light can then bounce off the interior partition for better balance; and the dining table, while cradled between solid walls, is well lighted at both ends. You also provide maximum cross-ventilation.

What size window should you add? Match one of the existing windows when orientation is on the east or south, and thus heat loss or gain through the window will have little effect on heating or air conditioning needs. Otherwise, consider a narrow fixed window with insulating glass that adds light but little heat or cold. Now exterior appearance comes into play. And what you do in the living room affects your choice in the dining room.

In the living room in Fig. 12-4b, principle 3 relating to balanced light is the main consideration, even if the large bay window meets the 20% requirement. On overcast days there won't be enough light in the corners of the room for reading without lamps on. A window in the blank wall won't help balance light throughout the room, but it will brighten the seating area, which is what you are after. It is worth adding even if the blank wall faces west.

Before you decide where to place a new window, work out several furniture arrangements so that it serves you well even when you rearrange the furniture. Here, if you decide to match windows, match the new window in the dining room in shape and size. The shape doesn't have as much effect on the living room interior as it does outside. The new window will afford the best daylight if centered in a north or south wall, and if closer to the dining room partition in an east or west wall.

When it comes to a choice of locations, interior appearance should take precedence over exterior appearance. Your purpose in remodeling is to correct interior problems, not create them. You can usually hide an awkward exterior problem with planting.

You won't often be faced with major changes in windows that require decisions on your part. In fig. 12-6, for instance, a relocation of the den windows does not affect the interior and has little effect on exterior appearance. Only in the kitchen remodeling does a window change make a major difference, and solutions are discussed in Chapter 15.

ADDING PARTITIONS

For three specific reasons there are advantages to adding partitions. One, obviously, is to reduce a wastefully oversized room to more manageable proportions and thereby create a new small area that fulfills a single need. The new partitions in Fig. 12-3b are a good example. These are full-height and full-length dividers.

Another reason is to define the shape of an area of a room used for a secondary purpose. The bedroom in Fig. 12-9 is large enough not only for sleeping and dressing, but also for sewing. Addition of a stub partition only 30″ long not only defines the space, but also permits you to organize it with cabinets, drawers, a large work surface, and excellent working light.

The third reason is to make an honest hallway out of space in a room that carries a lot of traffic. Look first and again at Fig. 12-4b. One side of the room is a corridor, and can't be used for much else. When the living area is small to begin with, it would become even smaller if you partitioned off the corridor; it could make the room appear too cramped for comfort. With a large enough room, however, you could add a partition to help shape the living area. As a test, hold up a bedsheet along the proposed partition line to see what effect it has on the proportions of existing space.

Then design the partition to work for you. A floor-to-ceiling partition a standard 4½″ thick serves the basic purpose, but shuts out light in the corridor. Instead, consider a storage partition perhaps 16″ deep. Make it closed to a height of about 30″, and add doors for storage. Above that point add a decorative screen or bookshelves open on both sides, as was done in the den in Fig. 12-6. Now light can filter through into the corridor, and you have an attractive and useful feature in an otherwise sterile living room.

REMOVING PARTITIONS

It's physically possible to remove any partition, but it is seldom practical or economical to remove a bearing partition. Structurally, the partition can be replaced with posts and a beam to bear the weight of the building above. But because they do carry weights and are centrally located, bearing partitions usually contain heat ducts, pipes, and wiring, and even furnace flues and soil stacks. These accoutrements can be moved, but at considerable expense and sometimes to the detriment of the mechanical system.

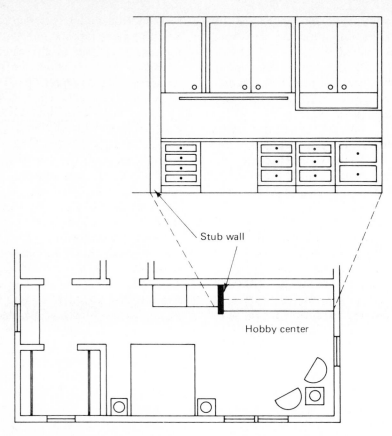

Fig. 12-9. Sometimes the addition of a short partition will define an area of a large room used for more than one purpose. This complete hobby center with a well-lighted work counter is a good example.

So before you even think about removing a partition, determine whether it is bearing and what systems it contains. You may be able to cut a doorway through it, or widen an existing opening, or even remove part of the wall. But be sure that by so doing you won't have to reroute anything more than electrical conduit or water piping.

Nonbearing partitions create far fewer headaches.

Take the partition in Fig. 12-10a between two cramped bedrooms. By removing it (Fig. 12-10b) you have one large bedroom with good ventilation, good storage, and ample space. The location of the bedroom door is less than perfect, but you have little alternative. You can turn the location into an advantage, however, by using one end of the room for sleeping and the other, brighter end as a play area if the occupants are children, or a

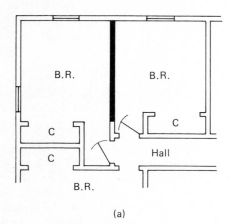

(a)

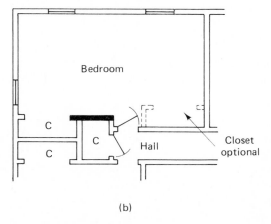

(b)

Fig. 12-10. Tearing out a partition between two small bedrooms (a) creates one large room (b) big enough for secondary use, and brings the bonus of an extra closet at the end of the hall.

work or hobby area if the occupants are adults. In addition, you gain a closet off the hallway for linens, luggage, or out-of-season clothing.

Tearing out a partition is not difficult, but it leaves you with some work to do before the combined space looks finished. There will be a gap between finished materials on two walls, the ceiling, and the floor that must be covered. You'll be prudent, then, to allow in your remodeling budget for redecorating to conceal the patches and combine the decors of the two spaces into one.

PREPARATION

Planning an interior remodeling is both frustrating and rewarding. Don't be concerned that your final design develops through trial and error. A professional designer goes through much the same process, although his or her experience makes the task move more quickly and surely. Eventually, however, you will have a rough

sketch that satisfies you, and a more accurately drawn and dimensioned plan to work from. Now the question is: Who is going to do what?

How much you and your family do depends on your ability, your toolroom, your time, your finances, and your family's patience. Any remodeling is messy. Tearing out is fun, and in your eagerness at seeing changes take place you tend to overlook the dust and grit and discomfiture. Building back up is not as messy, but it is slower, and family life can't begin to return to normal until you finish.

So decide first of all what you won't or can't do. Then make up an honest schedule for the work you think you can do. The following chapter tells you how to go about the early stages, and Chapters 18 to 22 tell how to finish the job. Make up your schedule on a week-by-week basis, leaving the starting time open. Set a starting date only if you intend to do all the work yourself. Otherwise, select a contractor and work out your schedule with him. Then stick to it.

13

Structural Changes

In a remodeling involving extensive interior changes, it's usually best to strip to bare structure. At right a broad new opening cuts through a bearing partition, and a warped joist above it was replaced. The partition at left is new, and ends against a post (far left) that supports a girder above adjoining space. Doors shipped in their frames are ready for installation. (Courtesy American Plywood Association.)

The order of work you establish for completing a remodeling of existing living space is influenced by a number of factors. You can build an addition, convert a garage, porch, or carport, or finish an attic or basement without seriously disturbing family routine. But when you are working in rooms that you need now for living, you face more complex problems.

Consider these factors:

- The physical extent of the work to be done. In other words, how many living spaces will be temporarily disrupted?
- Your estimate of the time required to complete the work.
- Your ability and experience in construction.

- The availability of any contractor.
- Your family's tolerance of inconvenience.
- Availability of funds, especially if the work is extensive and may need to be completed in stages.
- Weather conditions when you must open up exterior walls.

EXTENT OF THE WORK

Under ideal conditions you do all the tearing out first, then complete new structural work, then resurface, and finally decorate. In this way, as you master a technique, you use your newly developed knowledge and skills continuously, rather than at several times during remodeling while you try to remember how you did the same job the last time.

The primary limitation on the ideal, however, is space. You must clear the floor area in the room where you work, and move furniture and accessories out of the way. In a small house you may have to continue to use the room because there is no other place to go, or perhaps keep an area cleared for movement of people and materials. Usually, the most practical approach is to complete all work in one area, or carry it as far as possible. Then move on to the next area. This method also works best when your time is limited, your pace will be slow, you must limit the amount of inconvenience, and you intend to remodel on a pay-as-you-go basis.

The main drawback to completing one area at a time is the purchase and storage of building materials. Unless you have adequate storage space, protected against weather and theft, you must buy in smaller quantities and possibly at a higher price than when you have materials delivered in bulk. You must weigh the advantages against the drawback.

LOWERING A CEILING

Heat rises. In an uninsulated house built around the turn of the century with gracefully high ceilings, there may be as much as a 20° difference between air temperature at the ceiling and at seated level. In a warm-air heating system, some of this heat is recirculated throughout the house. In a hot-water or steam system, the heat is wasted. Insulating the walls will save the most fuel (see Chapter 10). But you can also save heating costs and increase comfort by lowering the ceiling.

There are two ways. One is to install new ceiling framing at a lower level. If you want a smooth ceiling surface, such as in a living room or bedroom, this is the only practical method. The other way is to install a metal grid, then lay pieces of wallboard or acoustical tiles in the grid. This is the easier method and is particularly practical in rooms, such as kitchens and family rooms, where soft overhead lighting is advantageous.

As the first step in planning, decide what new ceiling level you would like and what, if anything, you intend to do with the concealed space. The exact height isn't important. More important is the effect the lowered ceiling will have on the room itself and existing windows and doors. The tall, narrow windows common in houses built before the turn of the century may look peculiar and awkwardly out of scale in a room with a lower ceiling. One way to help you visualize the new room is to draw a one-point perspective (Fig. 13-1).

Draw a Perspective

First draw a floor plan of the room to scale, and add dimensions (Fig. 13-1a). Then decide how much of the room you want to show in a perspective, and draw a dashed line (A) on the plan at this point. This line is called the **picture plane**. In Fig. 13-1a you see about two-thirds of the room. Find the midpoint of this dashed line between walls, and through it draw a light line to the bottom of the drawing (B). From the points where the picture plane line meets sidewalls, draw 30° lines (C) to the centerline. The three lines should meet at one point (S_1). In your perspective you are standing at this point.

Now you can start drawing a perspective (Fig. 13-1b). At any convenient scale (the larger the better), draw a rectangle equal in width to the length of the picture plane (line A) and equal in height to existing ceiling height. This rectangle represents a section through the room at the picture plane. At one side of the rectangle measure up 5′ from the floor and mark that eye-level height (D). Then measure the actual heights of window sills and door and window headers, and transfer these heights at scale to one side of the drawing.

At eye-level height draw a light horizontal line across the rectangle, and extend it to both sides (E). Find the midpoint of this line within the rectangle. Then, on the plan drawing, measure the distance at scale between the picture plane and point S_1. On line E in the perspective, mark off this measurement on each side of the midpoint, at the scale of the perspective if different. These points, V_L and V_R, are the left and right vanishing points of the perspective. A **vanishing point** is that point where parallel lines seem to meet in the distance. The midpoint is S_1.

Now draw light lines from the four corners of the rectangle to point S_1. These are the floor and ceiling lines of the side walls. To find where they touch the end wall, draw lines W-X and Y-Z on the floor plan, beginning at the corners of the room and drawing at a 45° angle until they cross the picture plane line. Now measure the distance on the plan between the end wall and the picture plane. Along the floor line of your rectangular section measure off this distance from each corner, and mark the points X and Z.

Next draw light lines from X to V_L and from Z to V_R. Where these lines cross the floor line of the side walls, draw vertical lines to the ceiling line of the side walls. Finally, between similar ends of these vertical lines, draw horizontal lines. Now strengthen the vertical and horizontal lines; they indicate the shape of the end wall. Strengthen the floor lines for the side walls; do not strengthen ceiling lines yet.

To mark the heights of window and door openings, begin with the height marks you made at the right edge of your perspective. Draw light lines between these points and point S_1 until they meet the right vertical corner line of the end wall. If there are openings in the end wall, carry lines for them horizontally to the opposite corner of the room. From there draw outward from point S_1 back to your picture plane.

To locate the sides of openings in the *end wall*,

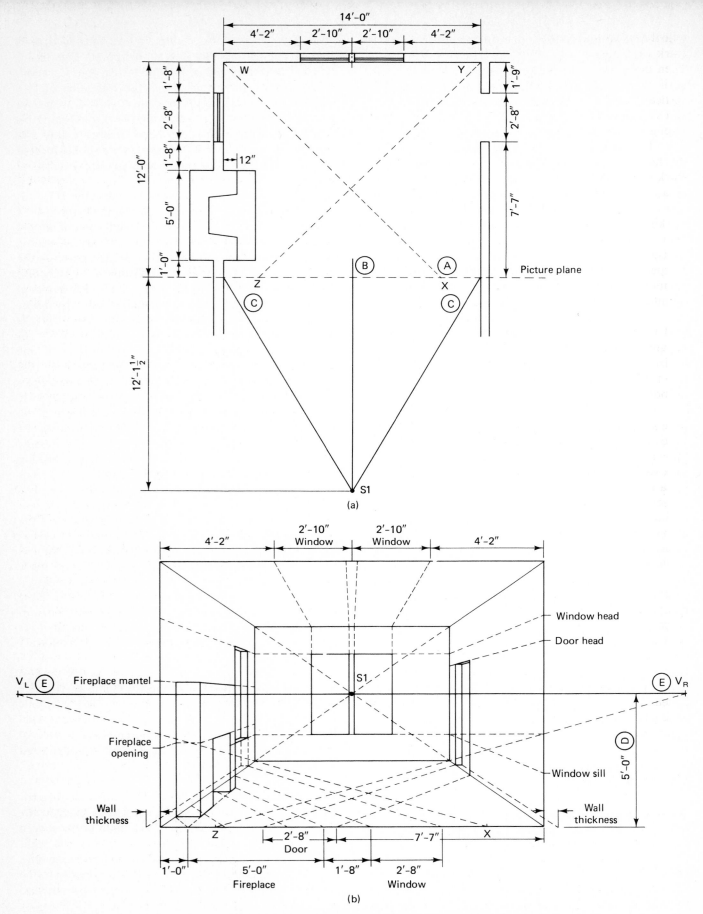

Fig. 13.1 A one-point perspective (b), drawn from a floor plan (a). A perspective like this helps you to visualize the effects of changes that you are planning to make in the proportions of a room.

take the horizontal measurements off the floor plan and mark them on the *top* of the picture plane rectangle. Then draw light lines from all these points toward S₁ until they touch the ceiling line. From there draw vertical lines to the horizontal lines marking the heads and sills of windows, or to the floor if there are doors. Strengthen the lines around each opening.

To locate the sides of openings in *side walls*, take the horizontal measurements off the floor plan and mark them on the *bottom* of the picture plane rectangle. Measure from the left side for openings in the left wall, and from the right side for openings in the right wall, working from the picture plane, not the corners. Draw light lines from these marks toward their respective vanishing points until they touch the floor line in the perspective. Then carry the lines vertically until the openings are all shaped. Strengthen the four lines around each opening.

To add thickness at side openings, measure off wall thickness on the floor line of the picture plane rectangle, then carry lines toward S₁ until they meet horizontal lines below window and door openings. This step isn't necessary, however. Your purpose is to study proportion, not detail.

If you strengthened the ceiling lines, you would have a perspective of the room as it now exists. Instead, following the procedure for establishing the ceiling line, draw another ceiling line lightly where you think it will look well. If you aren't sure where you want the ceiling, lay a sheet of tracing paper over your perspective and try several heights. When you like the results, draw the ceiling line on the end wall, and carry it in perspective along side walls. Where it touches the picture plane, measure the height to scale. That is the height at which to place the new ceiling.

After laying out a perspective, you'll probably find that actual construction seems a lot easier by comparison. You can make the drawing a lot simpler by keeping all lines light until you are sure they are right. And keep that pencil sharp. Incidentally, if you have any jogs in the room, such as a projecting fireplace, you follow the same basic procedures. When a wall jogs into the room, measure inward along the picture plane line. When it jogs out, measure out. And remember that the ceiling and floor lines of all walls parallel to the picture plane are drawn horizontally, not toward vanishing points.

Use of Above-Ceiling Space

A suspended ceiling isn't strong enough to support any weight but its own. The space above, however, is useful for heat and air conditioning ducts, light fixtures, and any new plumbing lines. All such equipment must be installed before you begin work on a new ceiling.

A new ceiling gives you an excellent opportunity to improve overhead lighting. Determine where you need more light in the room, and whether that light should be general or specific (see Chapter 5). To light a specific area, such as a dining room table, you can install recessed fixtures in a joist-supported ceiling. Just add a pair of 2 × 2s between joists and flush with their undersides at the point you need the light. The 2 × 2s support the flanges of the fixture. For general light you can hang light fixtures a few inches above a suspended ceiling, and insert a translucent panel in the grid instead of a solid panel. No other change in the ceiling system is necessary.

If you have high ceilings in all rooms and are short on storage space, think about lowering the ceiling in one room and making between-ceilings storage space accessible from an adjoining room. Or perhaps leaving ceilings high in rooms off a hallway, dropping the hall ceiling as low as 7'-6", and making the space above usable for storage and accessible from both sides. Simply frame the access openings like a window, install casings, and add cabinet doors. You'll find details on cabinets in Chapter 15.

The only reason for deciding whether to use the concealed space is to get that work out of the way before you start on the ceiling. Unless a large area can be devoted to storage, and the items stored are heavy, your use of the space shouldn't affect the size of wood joists required.

Framing with New Ceiling Joists

The joists you install to support a lowered ceiling can run in either direction. They are easier to handle if they run the short dimension of the room, but either way is all right if you can span the long dimension without splicing. The only advantage to running joists the long way is that application of wallboard is easier. Wallboard should be applied across joists, and if you can span the short dimension of the room with one piece, you save a lot of work concealing butt joints.

On all walls mark the height of the undersides of joists, which is the ceiling height you established less the thickness of ceiling material. Locate studs in walls and partitions, and mark the centerlines on the wall about 6" above your ceiling lines. Cut ledgers from 2 × 4s and, with a pair of 12d nails at each stud, nail them with their bottom edges on the ceiling line. Ledgers don't need to be cut for an exact fit in corners, but joints between them should fall between future joists.

Start at one wall and mark joist locations on the ledger. The first mark should be 15¼" from the corner, with an × on the far side of it. Make all other spacings 16", all with ×s on the far side. Let the last spacing be whatever is left, provided that it isn't more than 16". Then mark the opposite ledger in the same way.

Because walls in old houses aren't always exactly parallel, measure the length of each joist separately. For spans of 12' or less, use 2 × 4s and measure the span

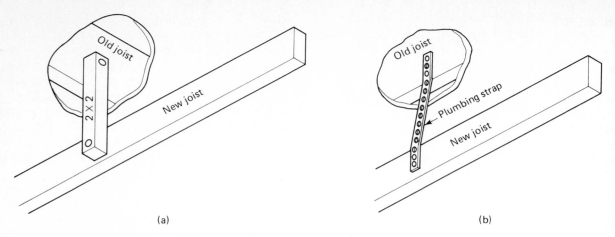

Fig. 13-2. When new joists run perpendicular to old joists, support them with 2 x 2s through holes in the old ceiling (a). When they run parallel but not in vertical alignment, use metal strapping (b).

between ledgers. For greater spans use 2 × 6s, measure from wall to wall, and notch the ends to fit over the ledgers. If you can't span with available lengths of lumber, use 2 × 6s and splice with 5 × 8 metal splice plates, one on each side.

Toenail each joist through its side into the ledger so that it covers the ×. Use four 12d nails per end. You'll need someone to hold the other end in position while you nail. Check the open end for square with the wall before you nail.

To assure that joists won't sag from the weight of ceiling materials, add 2 × 2 vertical supports near the center of each joist. Cut the supports a little longer than the distance between the old and new ceilings. Chop holes in the old ceiling large enough so that you can nail the upper end of each support to the side of an existing joist. When old and new joists don't cross or lie within vertical reach, use metal strapping instead of 2 × 2s (see Fig. 13-2).

Framing with a Metal Grid

A suspended ceiling consists of four main parts (Fig. 13-3). Around the wall at finished height are metal angles. The angles support the ends of main tees which usually run the long dimension of the room. Between main tees are cross tees installed at right angles. Main tees and cross tees interlock in various ways, depending on the manufacturer of the suspended ceiling system. At each intersection the tees are supported by thin wires attached to the existing ceiling or its structure. There must be at least 2″ of vertical clearance between the existing ceiling and the tops of tees. Otherwise, you can't fit ceiling panels into the grid.

Plan the Layout. Even before you mark the ceiling height on walls, plan the layout of your ceiling. First measure all four walls at the ceiling line. Then establish the size of individual ceiling panels. Standard

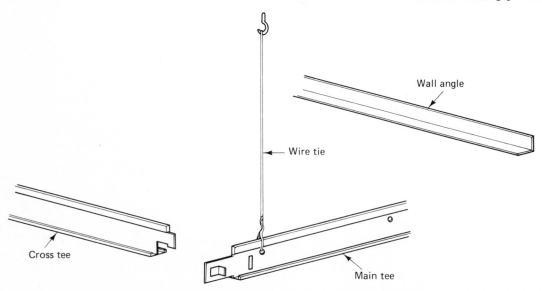

Fig. 13-3. The main parts of a suspended ceiling supported in a grid system: wall angles, main tees, cross tees, and wire ties to existing structure.

panels of acoustical tile come in squares 12", 16", and 24", and in rectangles 12" × 24", 16" × 32", and 24" × 48". In most rooms the two larger rectangular sizes are the most practical and economical.

Edge panels closest to opposite walls should be the same width and at least half a panel wide. Suppose that your room is 13' × 18' and you want to use 16" × 32" panels with their long dimensions running the same direction as the long dimension of the room. For the 13' dimension (156") you need eight panels of full width (128") and two edge panels of 14" (28"). A grid of nine full panels and 6" edge panels violates the half-panel rule. For the 18' dimension (216") you need five panels 32" long (160") and two edge panels of 28" (56").

Locate Tees.   To mark the ceiling height on the walls, measure up the desired height and add the width of the leg of a wall angle, which is usually ¾". Place two marks at this height on each wall near the corners— eight marks in all. Snap a chalk line between pairs of marks on each wall, and check the lines for level. Adjust marks as necessary; they may be off if your floor isn't level. You set the upper edge of the angles on the lines, and they must be level for your ceiling to be level. And it should be, even if your floor isn't.

Set wall angles in position and nail them into studs. At inside corners let the angles overlap. At outside corners cut them so they extend beyond the corner a distance equal to the width of the angle's bottom leg, then miter matching corners at a 45° angle. Check the level of each piece before you nail.

Run main tees the long dimension of the room. If you have an even number of full panels across the room, you will have a main tee down the center of the ceiling. Mark the centerlines of end walls at ceiling level, and lay out tees from the center tee toward side walls. Then, even if side walls aren't exactly parallel, the ceiling grid will still be symmetrical.

If you have an odd number of full panels across the room, mark the centerlines of end walls, then measure half the width of a full panel in both directions and make new marks. Here you work from the new marks toward side walls, rather than from the centerline.

Repeat the marking process for side walls. In the example, you have an odd number of full-length panels, so you would measure off 16" on each side of the centerline to establish a new starting point for laying out cross tees.

Once you have established your longitudinal and latitudinal starting points, stretch taut strings from the bottoms of angles between starting marks on opposite walls. The two strings should cross exactly at right angles. If they don't, repeat the marking process until they do. They *must*.

Install Eyes.   When all is square, snap a chalk line across the old ceiling directly above the longer

string. It is along this line that you install eyes for supporting wires, and the eyes must be screwed into something solid. You may be lucky enough to have a joist directly above your chalk line and running the same direction. If not, snap a chalk line on the ceiling above the other string. Centered on this chalk line nail a 1 × 2 furring strip into joists. Then, every 4' in each direction nail parallel furring strips, with the final strip no farther than 4' from end walls.

If joists run at right angles to your first chalk line, nail a furring strip centered on that line and every 16" (or whatever your cross spacing is) in each direction. The last strip can be no farther than this spacing from side walls.

Locate the first eye directly above the crossed strings. Install additional eyes every 4' along the first chalk line to support the first main tee.

Install Tees.   Cut the main tee to length. A standard length is 12', and if your main tee is longer than that, you can fit two lengths together. They have a locking device of some sort at each end.

To accept cross tees, main tees are also slotted or punched, and these points of connection must be located according to your ceiling layout. In the example, the first cross tee is 28" out from an end wall. Therefore, you cut the main tee 28" from the *point of attachment*, not from its end. If you have a long main tee, cut one end, assemble additional lengths, and then cut the other end.

Lay the first main tee on the wall angle at one end directly over the string, and fasten it with a wire to the first eye you installed where the strings cross. Run the wire through the hole in the tee (Fig. 13-4) directly below the eye, and attach it temporarily so that the tee is at string level. Next tie the main tee at all other eyes above it, and recheck both the level and the alignment of the tee. Then wire it permanently.

For all other tees repeat the process of installing

Fig. 13-4.   How to wire-tie a main tee to an eye. (Courtesy Armstrong Cork Company.)

the first main tee. Relocate the string as the first step. Complete installation of all main tees before you begin to place cross tees.

Cross tees may be one of two types. Some are made the same length as main tees and snap into slots in them. You simply cut this type to length, measuring from the point of intersection with the nearest main tee. Other cross tees are made in shorter lengths to fit between main tees. Only the tees running between the wall angle and the first main tee require cutting. With this type install cross tees between main tees first, and the cut lengths last.

Install the first cross tee under the second string, and recheck it for level and square with the main tees. All cross tees and main tees must meet at right angles if ceiling panels are to fit easily. Repeat the installation process for other cross tees until the grid system is complete.

Insert Panels. To complete the ceiling, measure the opening for each edge panel on all four sides, and cut a panel to fit. The panels should be about ⅛" shorter in each dimension than the opening itself.

When panels are translucent plastic for placement below light fixtures, cut them with a circular saw fitted with a combination blade. Cut acoustical tiles face up with a coping saw or sharp utility knife. If you install panels of gypsum wallboard, use ⅜" material. Measure all grid openings along one wall, and lay them out on the face of a sheet of wallboard. Allow ⅛" for cuts. Score the surface along the longest line on the wallboard, then snap and trim as described in chapter 19 and shown in fig. 19-5. Make shorter cuts in the same way.

Install edge panels first, then center panels. Slide each piece upward at a diagonal through its opening, then gently set it on the flanges of the main tees and cross tees or angles. If a grid opening is not rectangular, and the cut panel has an irregular shape, put an × in one corner of the panel, such as lower left, so that you always know how to get the correct fit on the first try.

TEARING OUT A WALL

When your remodeling plans require work on a partition between rooms, clear the floor area within at least 4' of the partition on one side. Unless you intend to remove the entire surface, mark the width and height of any new opening. Then remove trim that is in the way.

Remove Trim

Begin with the base shoe. If it is in two pieces, start at the joint; if it is a single piece, start in the middle. Work a wood chisel between the base and the shoe, with the flat side against the baseboard. In this way you limit any damage to the shoe alone, where it is easier to repair and

less conspicuous than damage to the base. Also, if you snap the shoe, it costs less to replace than a new base.

Shoe may have been nailed into the base or into wood flooring. If nailed to the base, it will pop off fairly easily. If it tends to twist and remain attached at the bottom, pry alternately against the base and the floor. The nails will probably pull through the shoe. Let them; you can fill the holes when you renail.

As you come to a corner there will be a nail a few inches from the end of the shoe. The end itself will be wedged in a miter joint against the piece of shoe on the adjoining wall. Pry from underneath at the nail until the shoe springs loose in the corner. Then gradually raise the trim until it is free.

Store each piece of trim that you remove, and mark on the back in pencil where it came from, such as "east wall, l.r." Over the years the mill dimensions of trim have shrunk, so you may not be able to match what you retain. That's why you should use extreme care to avoid breakage.

Using the same care and following the same procedure, next remove the base and any ceiling trim. Mark and store each piece. Trim is cut from hardwood, and is strong and flexible. But because its dimensions are slender, it also breaks easily. Store trim where it won't get wet or stepped on. Lay it flat and straight; it will take on a bow if you don't.

Leave door trim in place unless it is in the way. Even then, remove only the casing around the door, jamb pieces first, then the head. Because trim will be crossnailed at corners, try to remove all three pieces at once. Then either store it that way, or separate the pieces where you have more working room. Leave the door on until you have torn off surface materials, and take it off just before you remove the door frame. The door will give some protection against dirt and dust filtering into the next room.

Remove Surface Materials

With the surface material now fully exposed, knock a hole with a hammer at about the center of the area to be removed. Your purpose is to learn what, if anything, lies inside the wall that may alter your plans, and exactly where studs are. After you uncover one stud, measure to the next one on each side to establish the spacing on centers. If you are not removing the entire partition, but only cutting a new opening through it or reducing its length, mark the stud spacing on the wall's surface. Then see how that spacing agrees with the location of the cut you marked previously. Sometimes by adjusting the location an inch or two you can save lumber.

Keep in mind that two studs are required on each side of a door or window opening. To determine the space to allow between inside studs, you need to know the rough opening for the door or window. If you are relocating a door, measure the existing opening. Figure

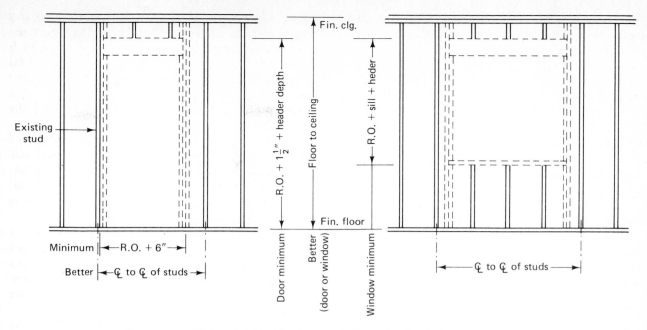

Fig. 13-5. When a new opening in an existing wall already has a stud at the jamb, clear away surface materials as shown at the left. Resurfacing is much easier if you clear from centerline to centerline of untouched studs. When the new opening lies between existing studs (right), again clear from centerline to centerline of the adjacent unaltered studs.

13-5 shows the width of wall surface to remove when you build against an existing stud (left), and when all four studs are new (right).

Above an existing door remove enough surface so that you can cut the cripples that rest on the header, and have room enough to toenail the remaining cripples into the header. Measuring from the bottom of the partition's bottom plate, allow rough-opening height plus the depth of the header plus about 1″ clearance. Since you have to install a new piece of wall material above the door anyway, it may be easier to cut all the way to the ceiling. Then you have only two vertical joints to conceal and no horizontal joint. Follow the same general procedure for cutting and marking below a window sill.

How you cut away excess material depends on the material. Cut wood paneling with a power saw, with the blade set to the thickness of the material when there are studs behind it. To cut gypsum wallboard, use a power saw with a carbide-tipped blade; don't use a new blade because you will dull it. Or else drill a small hole to get started, then cut with a utility saw along cut lines.

Begin removing plaster by knocking a hole through it large enough so that you can see the plaster's thickness and what sort of lath is behind it. Unlike plywood and wallboard, plaster won't break along a straight line. Use a power saw with a carbide-tipped blade set to the thickness of the plaster to cut along your marks. Cut a little deeper than the plaster when lath is gypsum or wood. Cut a little shallower if lath is wire mesh. Remove enough plaster at the cut edge so that

you can get at the lath. Cut gypsum lath as you would wallboard. Cut wire mesh with a metal cutting blade or metal shears. Use a saw with a crosscut blade for wood lath. The cut edge doesn't have to be smooth, but it must be straight enough so that you can cover it with new trim around the opening.

Assuming that the opening is free of obstructions, mark its edges on the back side of the opposite wall material. Then drill small holes at a couple of points to guide you in marking the exposed surface. Remove materials in the manner just described until the opening is clear of surface materials.

The easiest way to remove studs is by cutting them into two pieces, then working each piece back and forth until you loosen the nails into plates. Then pry studs loose at the plates and remove bent nails. Your cutting points for studs are at the top of the future header and the bottom of a future window sill. Leave the bottom plate intact.

Fill the New Opening

Build a new door or window frame as a unit, complete with header, any sill, and jamb studs, measuring frequently to make sure that the assembly will fit the opening (see Fig. 7-11). Then insert the assembly in the opening and nail with pairs of 8d nails every 12″ into existing studs. If you don't have a stud already in place on one side, mark its location on the top and bottom plates and install it before you begin the assembly. At the header toenail upward into cripples on both sides of the header, and at any sill nail downward into cripples, two nails per stud. Now cut through the bottom plate flush with framing studs, and remove the cut piece.

If you are simply moving an existing door to a new location, determine before you remove it which way the door will swing in the new opening. When the swing is the same, pry the casings at jambs and heads from behind until you work them loose and the casing nails pull through. The lengths may be crossnailed where they meet, and won't separate easily. In this case try to remove the casing as a unit and pull the nails after you get it out where you have room to work on it. Otherwise, you split the wood.

When you change the door swing, plan to buy a new door already prehung in its frame. It is possible to reuse the old head of the frame without change, but jamb casings must be reversed, with the painted sides toward studs. Then you must cut new grooves for the head member, and cut new mortises for hinges and the strike plate. Furthermore, you must relocate hinges on the existing door, and fill the old mortises. All this takes precise work, and even then your patchwork will show.

Regardless of casing changes, you can reuse the door stop, although you may have to relocate it on casings to adapt to a new door swing.

Fill the Old Opening

To fill the old opening, first nail down the length of bottom plate you cut out for the new opening. It will be a little short, but that won't matter. Then determine the locations of any studs needed for attachment of wall materials at panel edges. Usually, this won't be necessary. Finally, cut studs to length, space them no more than 16" apart in the opening, and toenail them to plates at top and bottom.

REMOVING A BEARING PARTITION

You can't completely remove a bearing partition, and you can't remove any of it without replacing it with some sort of support for the weight it carries. That replacement is a header or beam.

Suppose that you have a bearing partition 12' long with a door 3' wide in it, and you want to replace the door with a cased opening 6' wide. The rough opening, then, is 6'-1½", allowing for a ¾" casing on each side. The header is supported by a pair of studs on each side. Therefore, the overall width of the frame assembly is 6'-7½". If existing studs are spaced 16" on centers, the space between every fourth stud is 6'-6½". To take advantage of existing construction, then, you may want to narrow your finished opening by 1".

Determine the locations of studs as previously described in this chapter, and mark on the wall the area of surface material you must remove. Then mark to the centerline of the next stud on both sides of the opening.

You must remove material to these centers so that you can insert temporary supports until you have the new opening framed.

Temporary Support

The temporary supports are jacks, which you can rent from large building supply dealers or rental stores. When the load on the partition is relatively light, you can place a jack on the bottom plate next to the stud on each side of the new opening. When the load is relatively heavy, use a pair of jacks with a length of I-beam between, and set the jacks just outside the plate on each side of the partition. To determine what is "light" and what is "heavy", talk to your building materials dealer, telling him what lies above the partition. To be absolutely safe, consult with an architect or structural engineer.

Raise the jacks until the top plate of the partition bears fully and horizontally on the I-beam or the jacks themselves. Then remove the studs in the opening.

Frame the Opening

Measure the distance between flanking studs, and build a solid header of this length out of 2 × 12s with a piece of ½" plywood between (Fig. 13-6). Since the top of the header fits against the underside of the top plate, its bottom will be approximately 13¾" below ceiling level. That places the top of the cased opening about 6'-10½" above the floor. If your other doors are 6'-8" high, add a 2 × 4 flat against the bottom of the header. If your ceiling is higher than a nominal 8' (it's about 8'-1½" with modern construction) work dimensions from the bottom up. Set the bottom of the header 1" above the height of other doors, then fill between the header and top plate with cripples. Mark the header's location on the sides of existing studs.

Cut jamb studs to length, which is the rough opening dimension less the thickness of the bottom plate. Cut for a tight fit. Lay the studs in the opening at a slight angle, with their bottom ends toward the center of the opening. Then, while one or two people hold the header in position, knock the cut jamb studs upright. If you cut all pieces accurately, the assembly should stay in position without nails. Check the header and jamb studs for plumb in the opening, then nail with 10d nails. Nail through existing studs into the header, using three nails into each 2 × 12 at each end. Nail through jamb studs in pairs at top and bottom and every 16" between. Next add the second pair of jamb studs; nail as before, but adjust nailing locations so that you don't hit other nails. Finally, toenail upward through all four jamb studs with 8d nails into the header on both sides. Attach any cripples.

Now you can remove the jacks. Lower them slowly so that the header can adjust to its new load. Then cut the bottom plate between new jamb studs.

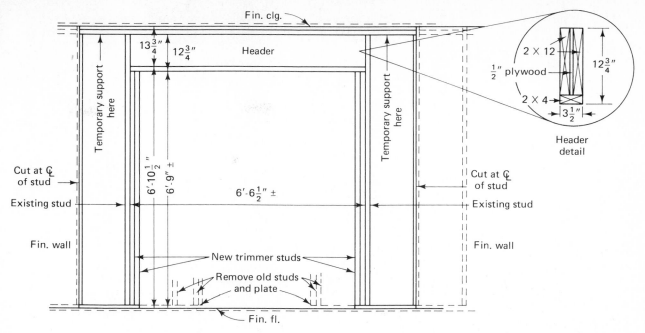

Fin. clg.

$13\frac{3}{4}''$ $12\frac{3}{4}''$ Header

Temporary support here

Temporary support here

2×12
$\frac{1}{2}''$ plywood
2×4
$12\frac{3}{4}''$
$3\frac{1}{2}''$

Header detail

Cut at ℄ of stud

Existing stud

Fin. wall

$6'\text{-}10\frac{1}{2}''$ $6'\text{-}9''\pm$

$6'\text{-}6\frac{1}{2}'' \pm$

Cut at ℄ of stud

Existing stud

Fin. wall

New trimmer studs

Remove old studs and plate

Fin. fl.

Fig. 13-6. A broad opening cut through a bearing partition must be framed with a header supported on each side by a pair of studs that are nailed to existing studs. A minimum header consists of two 2 x 12s separated by a piece of ½" plywood.

The procedure for removing most of a wall is more complex. You need a beam to support the load, and posts on each side to support the beam. In today's construction most long headers are built to dimension in a sawmill. They consist of lengths of lumber laid side by side and laminated with glue under heat and pressure (Fig. 13-7). Laminated beams may be constructed of dimension lumber for finishing at the site, or of thinner pieces selected for appearance and their ability to take paints and stains.

Posts are built of as many 2 × 4s as are necessary to carry the weight of the beam and the load on the partition. The design of both beams and posts is beyond the scope of nonprofessionals, and should be worked out with an architect, structural engineer, or competent builder. There's no reason why you can't remove surface materials yourself to save time and money, but hire experienced people to design the support system and install it.

Floor Repair

When you remove the unneeded section of bottom plate in an opening and thus expose the subflooring, you face one of four basic conditions:

1. The finished flooring is the same resilient tile or carpeting on both sides of the partition.

2. The finished material is wood flooring of the same thickness on both sides.

3. The finished flooring does not match, but floor levels are the same.

Fig. 13-7. Many long headers today are laminated beams built to order. This beam across a garage door opening is made of eight 2 x 4s glued together side by side under heat and pressure. (Photo: Drew: Leviton-Atlanta.)

4. Finished floor levels are not the same.

Tile or Carpet. With the first condition, you will probably need to cover the subfloor with a piece of underlayment to bring the level in the opening up to the level of the underside of the finish flooring. Clean the subfloor, scraping away any adhesive that may be there. Cut the piece of underlayment for a close fit against other underlayment and for a loose fit at jambs. Apply

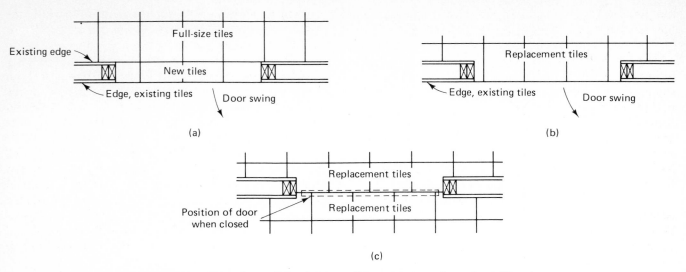

Fig. 13-8. Plan views of the three conditions you may face when tiling the floor at a new opening, and where to lay new or replacement tiles.

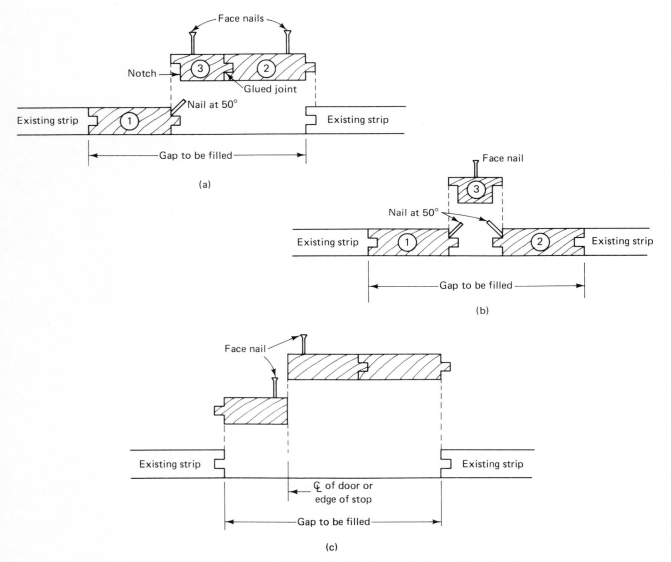

Fig. 13-9. Sectional views of the three conditions you may face when filling a gap with wood strip flooring at a new opening.

the piece with either nails or adhesive, depending on how much total thickness you need for leveling.

If you are lucky enough to have a matching piece of carpet stored somewhere, cut it for an exact fit. Then loosen the edges of existing carpet at the opening, and slip under each edge a piece of tack strip, placed so that half the strip's width is exposed in the opening. Stretch the old carpeting as far into the opening as you can, and press it onto the tack strip. Repeat this step on the other side. Then fit the loose piece of carpeting on the exposed half of both strips, and secure it with glue appropriate for the purpose. Add weights until the glue dries.

If you have a tile floor, first measure the widths of edge tiles in the room *away from which* the door swings. When edge tiles are full size, lay filler tiles from the existing edge (Fig. 13-8a). When they are less than full size, see whether you can cover to the edge tiles in the next room with a new full tile. If so, remove the partial tiles to the first seam beyond the jambs of the opening, and replace them with new tiles cut to fit (Fig. 13-8b). If you can't quite cover the gap, check the size of edge tiles in the adjoining room. If you can't cover the gap by replacing edge tiles in that room, work from the existing edge in the first room.

The point is that you should avoid laying any tile that is not at least half its original size.

If you have partial tiles along both edges, remove them on both sides of the partition, and replace them with larger tiles that meet under any door when it is closed (Fig. 13-8c).

For procedures on laying underlayment and floor tiles, see Chapter 20.

Strip Flooring. With wood strip flooring, the strips may run parallel to the wall (condition 2) or perpendicular to the wall (condition 3).

When strips run parallel to the wall, you may again have three conditions: tongues exposed on both sides, grooves exposed on both sides, or a tongue on one side and a groove on the other. When a groove and tongue face each other, fit piece 1 in Fig. 13-9a, drive it tight, then nail just above the tongue at about a 50° angle. Use spiral screw nails or cut steel floor nails; for most strips a 7d nail is the best length, but ask the dealer from whom you buy the flooring. Then cut and notch piece 3 so that the combined width of 2 and 3 equals the gap to be filled. Fill the groove in piece 2 with glue, force in the tongue of piece 3, wipe off the excess, and let the glue dry thoroughly. Then insert the assembly in the gap, and face-nail where shown.

When tongues face each other, nail pieces 1 and 2 in place as just described, and cut piece 3 to bridge the gap (Fig. 13-9b). Face-nail as shown.

When grooves face each other, make up two glued assemblies that will meet under any door (Fig. 13-9c). Fit the two assemblies into the grooves simultaneously, force them in cautiously so that you don't damage the tongues, then face nail at the meeting edges.

You'll find complete details on laying strip flooring in Chapter 20.

Nonmatching Flooring. When you face condition 3—flooring at the same level but not matching—your only choice is to fill the gap up to finish floor level with whatever materials are available of the required

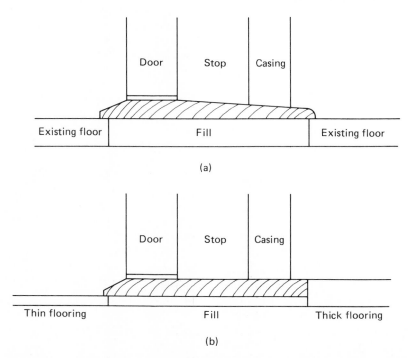

(a)

(b)

Fig. 13-10. When flooring materials beside a newly cut opening don't match (a) or are different thicknesses (b), use a threshold to cover the gap. These views are sections through the opening.

thickness. Then cover the gap with a threshold (Fig. 13-10a).

Standard wood thresholds are 3½" wide and come in various lengths. Standard metal thresholds also come in various lengths, but in widths of 3½", 3¾", and 4". The odds are high that the gap between edges of finish flooring is more than 3½", and may be more than 4". If you can't buy a threshold wide enough to cover the exposed edges of both flooring materials, your only real choice is to have one made to your specifications out of oak or maple. It should be as thin as possible, but thick enough to be durable. One-half inch at the center and tapered at the edges is about right. Predrill holes for four nails about ¾" from the corners, and attach the threshold with 3d casing nails. Countersink them slightly and fill the holes.

Nonmatching Levels. When floors are at different levels, clean the gap and fill it to the lower level with whatever material will do the job. Again, the only cover for the gap is a threshold. Now, however, one end of the threshold should be equal in thickness to the difference in finish floor levels, be flat to its midpoint under the door, then taper to the opposite edge (Fig. 13-10b). Butt the threshold against the thicker material, and let it overlap the thinner material about ¼". Face-nail into predrilled holes.

Door Frames

Thresholds and carpeting should be installed after door casings but before door stops and trim. Other flooring materials are applied before casings. Therefore, if you intend to reuse an existing door, frame, and trim, you should achieve a good fit without cutting.

Doors that are manufactured and shipped already in a frame you install as a unit, then add trim. With a relocated door you can also reassemble the frame on the floor, add the stop, and hang the door. By prehanging the door you are assured of a good fit and smooth operation. At the same time, however, you will handle more weight during installation. If you do preassemble, tack braces across the frame on both sides to keep it square, not only during assembly but during installation. Be sure that the braces don't extend beyond the edges of the frame.

Set the assembled frame, with or without the door, in its rough opening. Behind the hinge jamb insert five pairs of wedges—one wedge from each side of the frame in each pair (Fig. 13-11). Pieces of wood shingle make excellent wedges. Locate one pair at the head of the frame, one at the bottom, and the others behind hinge locations. Behind the latch jamb set four more pairs of wedges, one at the bottom, one at the top, one behind the latch, and the fourth midway between the latch pair and the top pair.

Hold your carpenter's level against the frame, and

gently tap on the wedges until the frame is plumb at all points. Then nail through each pair of wedges with two 8d finishing nails placed about ½" from the edges of the frame. Recheck the plumb after driving each pair of nails. The door frame should not touch structural framing around the opening at any point.

Now install any threshold, and measure the height of the reduced door opening. The door should clear the frame by ⅛" at the top. It should clear finish flooring and carpeting about ½", or a threshold by ⅛". Since your door is already trimmed at the top to fit existing hinge locations, any shortening must be done at the bottom. Mark the location of the cut on one side of the door, and tack a piece of scrap plywood or 1 × 2 to the bottom of the door on the opposite side. Then set your power saw to cut a little deeper than the thickness of the door. The scrap lumber will keep the face on the back side from splintering. Sand or plane the cut smooth on both sides before rehanging the door. Finish the job by replacing the casings.

Fill the Old Opening

People may still need to move from room to room while you are trimming out a new door opening. For that reason leave the old opening until you have the new one in operation.

Measure the opening to be filled, and cut the bottom plate to length first. Cut it for a tight fit, and wedge it between existing studs. It will be somewhat higher than the bottom plate in the existing wall, and should be toenailed to studs rather than nailed downward through existing flooring.

At the sides of the opening add lengths of 1 × 4 to serve as a nailing surface for finish wall material. Do not cut these pieces for a tight fit; gap about ⅛" at top and bottom. Cut studs to exact length to fill the remaining space at no more than 16" on centers. Toenail them to the bottom plate and old door header.

Procedures for installing surface materials are described in Chapter 19.

CHANGING AN EXTERIOR OPENING

Procedures for cutting a new opening in an exterior wall and filling the old one do not differ radically from those for an interior partition except that time and weather become important factors. You must have on hand the materials to protect the opening against weather and burglary, and the materials for closing the opening as fast as possible, including insulation.

Enlarge an Existing Opening

Enlarging an existing opening creates special problems, and therefore is the subject of the following discussion. Suppose, for example, that you have a small window

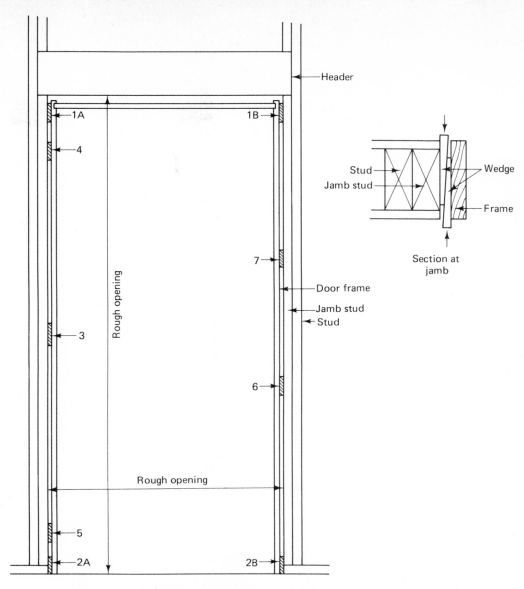

Fig. 13-11. Use nine pairs of wedges to plumb and square a door frame in its opening. Install pairs near the top and bottom (1A, 1B, 2A, 2B), one behind each hinge (3, 4, 5), one behind the latch (6), and one midway between 1B and 6 (7).

centered high in a dining room wall and want to replace it with a larger window, lower in the wall but still centered. Order the window and find out from the dealer what size rough opening you need.

Clear the floor area within 4′ of the wall, and mark on the wall the rough opening. Remove ceiling cover, baseboard, and base shoe as previously described in this chapter, and store them for reuse. Remove and dispose of window trim—casings at the jambs and head, and the apron and stool at the sill. This material is not reusable.

Once you remove surface materials and the old window, you have no marks to go by. So measure from the corners of the room to the sides of the rough opening, and write down the dimensions. At the same time establish the height of the head and sill. The head

should usually be at the same height as the heads of other windows in the room. Write down these two heights also.

Before you tear out, transfer the location of the rough opening from inside the house to the outside. One good way is to work from a vertical centerline through a window muntin and a horizontal centerline through another muntin. If your windows have no muntins, measure from the edge of a pane of glass or some other point that is the same both inside and outside the window. Snap chalk lines on the marks, and let them extend at least 2′ beyond the sides of the rough opening.

In a Frame Wall. Although the windows or doors themselves are identical, manufacturers set them in two different types of frames: one for walls with

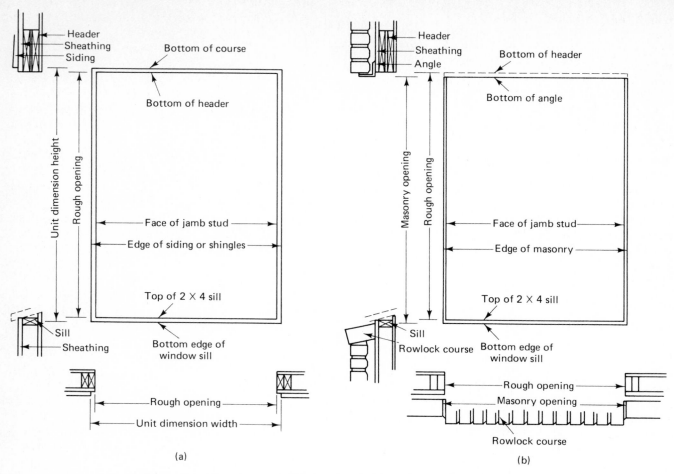

(a)

(b)

Fig. 13-12. Elevations and sections showing the relationships between window manufacturers' rough opening dimensions and structural framing for windows designed for installation in a frame wall (a) and a masonry veneer wall (b).

exterior materials of shingles, siding, or sheets, and the other for masonry walls. The frame will project beyond the surface of the wall of a frame house, and extend beyond the rough opening about an inch on all sides. The overall dimensions of these frames are shown in manufacturers' literature as **unit dimension height** and **unit dimension width** (Fig. 13-12a). Find these dimensions and determine their relationship to rough-opening dimensions. If unit dimension width is 2″ greater than rough-opening width, for example, the frame extends 1″ beyond the rough opening on each side and also at the head. To determine the amount of extension at the sill, find the difference between the unit dimension height and rough opening height, and subtract half the difference in widths—1″ in the example.

Mark on the exterior wall the locations of the unit dimension height and width, and snap a second set of chalk lines vertically and horizontally around the new window opening or doorway.

If the exterior wall material is in courses, such as shingles or siding, notice where these new chalk lines fall. Ideally, they should fall at the edge of a course, but this will happen only by chance. If your chalk lines are

close to a course line, consider raising or lowering the window slightly so that they fall on course lines, particularly at the head. You will save yourself some cutting, and reduce the chance of window leaks. A wall looks better, too, when course lines are continuous across the wall at the head and sill.

In a Masonry Wall. The frame for a new door or window in a masonry wall, whether solid masonry or brick or stone veneer, is inset about 4″ from the exterior surface. Manufacturers of windows and doors here provide dimensions for the **masonry opening**. The two dimensions, one horizontal and one vertical, are the overall dimensions of the frame, which are slightly longer than rough-opening dimensions. The masonry opening width is the actual distance between masonry faces at the jambs (Fig. 13-12b). Masonry opening height is measured from the underside of the steel angle supporting masonry above the opening down to the top of the rowlock course of bricks at the sill.

Find the masonry-opening dimensions and determine their relationship to rough-opening dimensions. If the difference in widths is about ¾″, say, then ⅜ʺ of that dimension lies on each side of the marks for the rough-opening width. Snap vertical chalk lines at these new points. The difference between chalk lines at the head should be the same as at the jambs, so snap a new chalk line at the masonry-opening height. Forget the sill for the moment.

The chalk line marking the masonry opening at the head must fall at the top of a brick, block, or stone course. If it doesn't, raise or lower the window in its opening until it does, and make a note of the amount of change.

Then see where the vertical lines fall. Ideally, they will fall at vertical joints in alternate courses. If they don't, move the window opening slightly until this happens on one side, and make a note of the change.

Finally, mark these changes on the interior wall surface by relocating the lines marking the rough opening. Only then are you ready to start tearing out inside.

Tearing Out

First, tear out all interior surface material to the centerline of the stud one stud space beyond the rough opening. Remove insulation. If the wall isn't insulated, consider tearing off all surface material and insulating all stud spaces before resurfacing. You'll never have a better opportunity to reduce fuel costs and heat loss.

On the top and bottom plates mark the edges of the rough window opening, and add another set of marks 1½ʺ beyond these marks. Cut studs to length, and toenail one on each of the second marks. On these two studs mark the head and sill heights for the rough opening.

Next measure the length of and cut all structural framing parts—the header, sill, jamb studs, cripple studs below the sill, and cripple studs above the header, if any. You can take all dimensions off the wall as you have framed it and marked it so far. What you do next depends on the exterior materials.

Removing Shingles, Siding, or Sheet Materials. The lines marking the unit dimensions on the outside wall are of only temporary value, because you must remove all exterior material to a point at least 6ʺ beyond your marks on all sides. With either shingles or siding begin at the top and work downward. Determine the top course to be removed; it is the course that will touch the top of the window or door frame.

Wood shingles are attached near their tops, and the fasteners are hidden by the course of shingles above. Gently raise the bottom edge of the shingle course above the course to be removed, until you can see the fasteners. Then pry beneath the nails until you loosen them enough either to pull them out or cut off their heads. The top course is the hard one to remove; after that nail heads are exposed and you have enough room to work.

Most types of wood siding are attached near their bottoms, and the nails usually do not penetrate the course below. Gently pry loose the bottom edge of the top course to be removed along its entire length. You should remove the whole piece, even though it extends many feet past the opening. It should slide right out. If not, lift the bottom edge of the course above to see if the nails holding it are also holding the length to be removed.

The top edges of metal and vinyl siding interlock with the bottom edge of the course above, and lengths in each course overlap at their ends. To avoid damaging the siding itself or its finish, you will probably have to start at the top of the wall. Remove any top trim, exposing nails holding the top course, then pull the nails until the course is free to unlock from the course below.

Asbestos-cement siding and shingles are either top-nailed like wood shingles or are supported unfastened in channels that are nailed into sheathing. You remove them like wood shingles or metal siding. But be extremely careful. Asbestos-cement is very brittle. To minimize breakage, loosen fasteners by driving small wedges on either sides of the nails until the heads are loose. Then remove the nails with pliers so that you don't have to press against the shingles.

Sheet materials such as plywood are usually fastened with exposed nails in the middle of the sheet— called the **field**. Edges are commonly covered with battens cross-nailed into the joints between sheets. Remove any battens first, then insert a crowbar or similar pry into the gap between sheets. If edges are shiplapped or tongue-and-groove, work outward from the old window, and be careful not to damage the edges. With square-edged material work from any convenient edge toward the opposite side.

As you remove each piece of material, mark it on the back so that you know where it goes after the new window or door is installed, even though you have to trim it. You replace coursed materials from the bottom up, so consider the bottom as course 1. You also work from undisturbed materials toward the new opening, so consider the outside piece on the left side of the opening as L1, and the outside piece on the right as R1, or some similar system. You'll save time if you have someone stack the pieces as you remove them. Usually, you install them in the exact reverse order in which you take them off.

Removing Masonry. A window or door frame is fitted into a masonry wall first, then masonry units are laid in mortar around the opening on all four sides. To set the frame you must remove one course above the chalk line marking the masonry opening at the head (Fig. 13-13). At a jamb where the masonry opening lines up with ends of masonry units, remove a brick from the alternate courses. At the other jamb go at least a half-brick beyond the chalk line but no more than a full

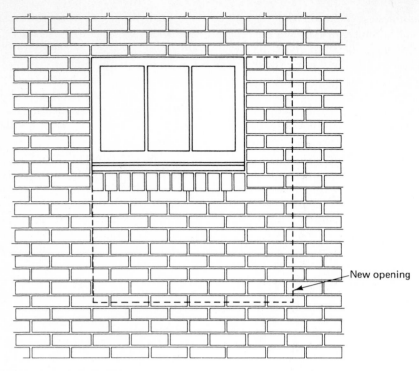

Fig. 13-13. Wall elevation showing the old window and the shape of the opening for the new window (dashed lines). If any part of a brick appears inside those lines, it must be removed to allow installation of the frame.

brick. Above the masonry opening remove at least one full brick on each side of jamb lines.

As you approach the sill, measure down from the upper masonry opening chalk line, and snap another horizontal chalk line to mark the masonry opening at the sill. Often the measuring points for the rough opening and masonry opening at the sill are the same. You need to remove two full courses of bricks below this chalk line.

If you have masonry units larger than standard bricks to remove, clear an area one course above the opening, at least 6″ on each side, and at least 5″ at the sill.

Before you remove any masonry, check with local suppliers to see whether you can match existing materials in color, size, and texture. As long as you are enlarging an opening, you take out more bricks than you reuse. But if you are relocating a door, for example, you will probably need all the bricks you remove. You're bound to break some bricks even if you are painstakingly careful. So know what your limitations are before you begin to tear out.

Removing masonry units is slow, hard work. You need only two tools: a masonry chisel and a chipping hammer. A power saw with a masonry cutting blade is helpful for cutting at the head and sill where you have long mortar joints, but it won't help you at jambs. For safety's sake, wear safety glasses to protect your eyes and work gloves to protect your hands. This equipment should be worn when you are tearing out anywhere.

Because you will be working above ground level outside, you need a sturdy working platform. A ladder won't do. Sometimes you can rent tubular scaffolding that you assemble yourself and can erect to the working height and width you need. You provide the planking or plywood for a platform. A less acceptable alternative is a pair of jacks that you raise to desired height, and with a platform laid on the projecting arms.

To save bricks, chisel near the center of mortar joints, chipping until the mortar cracks and continuing to chip until you can remove the bricks. Start at an upper corner and work toward the opposite corner. The first brick is the hardest. Unless mortar is old and crumbly, you don't need to worry about bricks falling out that you don't intend to remove.

After you clear the opening area, clean out all mortar so that the edges of all bricks—those exposed and those to be reused—are as clean as you can get them. It pays to rent two sets of tools so that someone is cleaning mortar off the bricks you've removed while you are cleaning the opening. All bricks that will touch fresh mortar must be free of mortar dust and loose mortar for a good bond. Stack reusable bricks on a pallet where they are off the ground and near a source of water. More about that later.

Install a Window in a Frame Wall

Before you go any further, study manufacturer's drawings of frame installation to see whether the frame

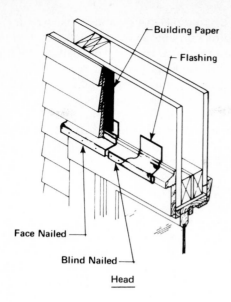

Building Paper

Flashing

Face Nailed

Blind Nailed

Head

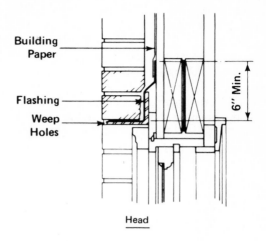

Building Paper

Flashing

Weep Holes

6" Min.

Head

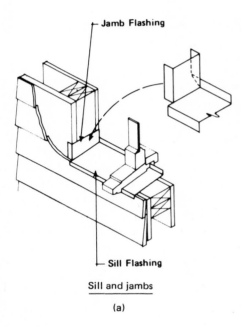

Jamb Flashing

Sill Flashing

Sill and jambs

(a)

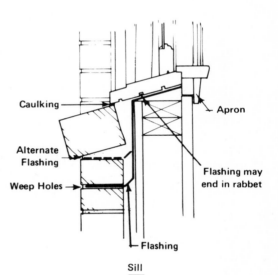

Caulking

Alternate Flashing

Weep Holes

Apron

Flashing may end in rabbet

Flashing

Sill

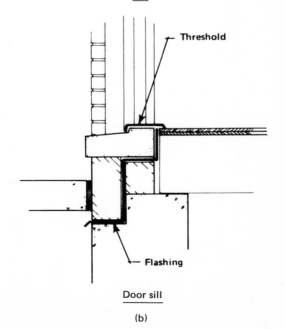

Threshold

Flashing

Door sill

(b)

Fig. 13-14. Details of flashing at the head, sill, and jambs of openings in walls with wood exterior materials (a) and with brick veneer (b).

fits over wall sheathing or against wood framing members. Most windows and doors for installation in frame walls fit over sheathing. You simply cut it flush with the structural frame around the rough opening, as in Fig. 13-12. Under such conditions cut strips of building paper 10 to 12″ wide to serve as flashing around the opening. Cut the sill piece 6″ longer than the rough-opening width, and slit at the corners so that it turns up the sides of the opening (Fig. 13-14a, Sill & Jamb). Cut jamb flashing to the same width and to the height of the opening. Nail or staple the sill flashing to sheathing first, then the jamb flashing. If you're installing a door, flash at the sill as shown in Fig. 13-14b, Door Sill.

Place a pair of shims on the sill flashing, and set the window frame on them, centering the frame in the opening. Sometimes jamb members of frames have horns that extend above the header and below the sill; trim them to fit the opening. Then, working from inside the house, insert wedges beside the jambs near the top, bottom, and midpoint of the frame. Have someone outside to hold the frame in the opening while you do this. Gently tap on the wedges until the frame is plumb at both the side and edge of the jamb.

Next, drive an 8d galvanized casing nail or finishing nail through the casing and sheathing into the framing member at an upper corner. Then drive a nail part way into the opposite upper corner. Recheck plumb before driving this nail home.

Now drive nails part way in at the lower corners. Again check level and plumb. When you are satisfied that the frame is properly set, drive these two nails home. Finish nailing window casings with 8d galvanized casing nails every 8 to 12″ around the frame. Finish nailing an exterior door casing with 16d nails spaced 12 to 16″ apart and about ¾″ from the outer edge of the casing. With the frame secure, trim off the excess length of wedges.

As a final step before replacing exterior and in-terior wall materials, flash above the window. Some manufacturers provide a piece of metal or vinyl flashing that fits over top trim, and you nail through it into sheathing. If none is provided, cut a piece of thin galvanized metal about 6″ wide and the length of the top trim piece. As the simplest method of attachment, face-nail it as shown in Fig. 13-14a, Head. For a more finished appearance nail one edge to the trim, then bend the metal 180° and shape it to the surface of the trim before nailing it again at its upper edge.

Install a Window in a Masonry Wall

The procedure for installing a window or door frame in a masonry wall is identical except that you install flashing afterward. Across the top of the opening, however, you need a lintel. For a wall of brick or stone veneer a nominal 4″ thick, order a steel angle of the size shown in Table 13-1 according to the width of the masonry opening, and of a length equal to the masonry opening width plus 8 to 12″. In a brick cavity wall you need two angles, usually identical in size, and in a solid brick wall with a 2″ stone veneer you need two angles of different sizes.

With the frame in place, cut a strip of building paper about 10″ wide and as long as the lintel. Nail or staple the strip as far up as you can reach. Then set the lintel in position; if the legs are unequal in width, make sure that the longer leg is vertical. Shape the flashing over the angle and trim along its leading edge.

At the sill of either a door or window attach flashing to the top edge of sheathing (Fig. 13-14b, Sill and Door Sill) and shape it to fit down the wall and across the top course of untouched bricks.

Preparing to Replace Bricks

For small jobs that require little mortar, mix it on a mortar board. For larger quantities mixed by hand, use

Table 13-1. Sizes of steel angles needed as lintels above door and window openings.

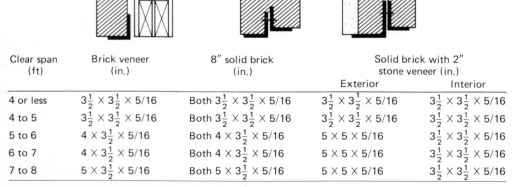

Clear span (ft)	Brick veneer (in.)	8″ solid brick (in.)	Solid brick with 2″ stone veneer (in.)	
			Exterior	Interior
4 or less	$3\frac{1}{2} \times 3\frac{1}{2} \times 5/16$	Both $3\frac{1}{2} \times 3\frac{1}{2} \times 5/16$	$3\frac{1}{2} \times 3\frac{1}{2} \times 5/16$	$3\frac{1}{2} \times 3\frac{1}{2} \times 5/16$
4 to 5	$3\frac{1}{2} \times 3\frac{1}{2} \times 5/16$	Both $3\frac{1}{2} \times 3\frac{1}{2} \times 5/16$	$3\frac{1}{2} \times 3\frac{1}{2} \times 5/16$	$3\frac{1}{2} \times 3\frac{1}{2} \times 5/16$
5 to 6	$4 \times 3\frac{1}{2} \times 5/16$	Both $4 \times 3\frac{1}{2} \times 5/16$	$5 \times 5 \times 5/16$	$3\frac{1}{2} \times 3\frac{1}{2} \times 5/16$
6 to 7	$4 \times 3\frac{1}{2} \times 5/16$	Both $4 \times 3\frac{1}{2} \times 5/16$	$5 \times 5 \times 5/16$	$3\frac{1}{2} \times 3\frac{1}{2} \times 5/16$
7 to 8	$5 \times 3\frac{1}{2} \times 5/16$	Both $5 \times 3\frac{1}{2} \times 5/16$	$5 \times 5 \times 5/16$	$3\frac{1}{2} \times 3\frac{1}{2} \times 5/16$

Note: The first dimension is the length of the vertical leg, the second dimension the length of the horizontal leg, and the third dimension the angle's thickness.

a mortar box. If you are finishing an entire wall, use a power mixer.

A good formula for a small amount of mortar is:

- 1 part type II masonry cement
- 3 parts well-graded sand from coarse to fine, with 5 to 15% fine

Or you can buy ready-mixed cement in bags with the sand already included, to which you add only water.

Whatever mortar you use, mix up a very small test batch to check color. If you have to buy bricks of a slightly different color to supplement those you saved, the variation won't be noticeable as long as the new and old mortars match. Let the batch dry thoroughly before you check the color match. You can buy mortar dyes in small quantities for adding to the mix. It may take you awhile to hit the right combination, but it's worth the time and effort provided that the window or door is installed and you can protect the unfinished opening from weather.

The day before you are ready to lay bricks, soak them *thoroughly*. Sprinkling won't do. Play a stream of water on them from a hose until water runs off all around, or let the hose run into an old pail, in the bottom of which you've punched holes. Let the bricks drain overnight. If you try to work with dry bricks, they will suck up so much moisture from the mortar that you won't get a good bond.

To test whether bricks are ready, draw a circle around a quarter with a grease pencil on a brick's surface. Then place 20 drops of water in the circle, and time how long it takes the brick to absorb the water. If it takes more than 90 seconds, the bricks are ready; if less than 90 seconds, they are still too dry to use.

For tools you need as a minimum a narrow-heel brick trowel, a pointing trowel, a bricklayer's hammer, a jointer, a steel dusting brush, and a mason's level. (You can use a carpenter's level, but unless you clean off mortar constantly, it will never be the same again.) If you have any long courses to lay, you also need a mason's line, line pins, and a sled runner.

LAYING BRICKS

The moment you finish mixing your mortar it is ready to use. From that moment on its consistency changes as water begins to evaporate. So try to work on a cloudy, cool day when the humidity is fairly high. Avoid hot, windy days that increase evaporation. You can add water to mortar that has not set up—that is, begun to harden—and remix to regain original consistency. This is called **retempering**. But the less retempering you have to do, the more time you can devote to bricklaying.

Pick up mortar on the blade of your trowel, working from the edge of the mortar board to the center of the pile. Ideally, the mortar will be shaped like a

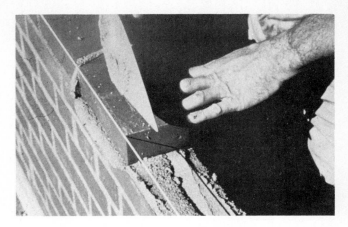

Fig. 13-15. Riffle the mortar bed to spread mortar to the edges of bricks for tightest bond. (Courtesy Brick Institute of America.)

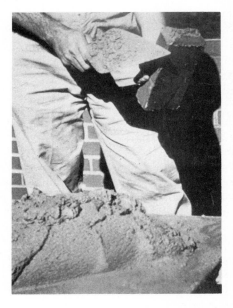

Fig. 13-16. Butter one end of a clean brick with plenty of mortar. (Courtesy Brick Institute of America.)

torpedo when you pick it up professionally. To test for proper consistency, hold your trowel at a 45° angle. If the mortar stays on the trowel, it is stiff enough.

If you are bricking in an opening, complete the course above the lintel first so that the course you left temporarily suspended doesn't begin to crack. Lay bricks in the opening without mortar to establish the spacing. Use the second course above the lintel as a guide.

Sling a bed of mortar onto the steel angle near each end—enough for about three bricks on each side. **Slinging** is the term for getting the mortar to flow off the trowel and form a bed of relatively uniform thickness. To make the bed as uniform as possible, **riffle** the mortar with the point of your trowel—that is, plow a furrow down the center of the mortar bed (Fig. 13-15). This step pushes mortar toward the edges of bricks.

Now pick up the first clean brick and butter one end of it with mortar (Fig. 13-16). Use plenty; you can always scrape off any excess. Most brick jobs that fail do so because too little mortar was used in the bed and at **head joints**—the vertical joints between bricks in a course. If the brick you are about to lay will have a new course above it, the brick is ready for positioning. If the brick will fit into a cavity between an angle and an existing course, butter the top and bottom of the brick as well as its end.

Set the brick in position from above the mortar bed when you have enough working room, and gently tap it on the unbuttered end and on its top until you squeeze a little mortar out of both joints. When you are setting the brick in an opening only one course high, slide it into the heavily mortared opening close to final position, then tap it sideways for a tight head joint. If a lot of mortar oozes out, you have a well-filled joint.

To clean away excess mortar, called **cutting**, hold your trowel as shown in Fig. 13-17 and use a slow sideways stroke. Do not cut with an upward or downward stroke; you'll pull the mortar away from surrounding bricks and leave a crack that can cause a leak.

Continue to lay bricks following these steps, slinging a bed of mortar for three bricks on one side of the opening, laying the three bricks, then repeating the operation on the other side. When you come to the last brick in the course—the **closure**—you should have a space wide enough for a brick and two head joints. If not, shape the brick to size with the chisel end of the bricklayer's hammer. Then fill the opening about half full of mortar, butter the brick on all edges, and shove it into the opening, being careful not to dislodge the bricks already laid on either side.

When you have several horizontal courses to lay, stretch a mason's line from corner to corner of the house at the level of the top of each course as a guide.

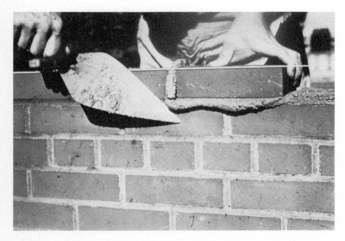

Fig. 13-17. Cutting a mortar joint to remove excess mortar. The angle of the trowel blade and a slow sideways stroke are critical to a leakless joint. (Courtesy Brick Institute of America.)

Make sure that the line is taut and level. Use line pins or wood blocks to hold the line in place at the corners.

As you lay each brick, check its relationship with the guide line and its plumb in the wall. Make adjustments before you move on to the next brick. Constantly use a level, plumb bob, framing square, and your lines. If later you find a brick out of alignment or discover you made a mistake, don't try to correct it. You'll break the bond and have a leak. You can't repair the mistake; you must start over by relaying the errant brick and all those that are newly laid above it in an inverted triangle. And that takes a lot longer than checking your work after each brick is laid.

To complete the wall at window or door jambs, start at the bottom and work upward. Now you are working toward a vertical line. One way to establish this line is to drive a nail into a mortar joint somewhere above the jamb, and hang a plumb bob from it. Just remember to fill the nail hole with mortar when you remove the bob.

If you planned properly in advance, you should be able to complete one jamb with nothing but half bricks laid in alternate courses. When this neatness isn't possible at both jambs, measure the lengths of bricks you need. Sometimes you can buy **kings**, which are three-fourths of the length of a full brick, and **queens**, which are one-fourth of full length. Whatever the dimension, the jamb brick in each course should never be less than one-half brick. In any course with a jamb brick less than half, lay that brick against an existing brick in the course, then finish the course with a full brick at the jamb.

At the sill lay a **rowlock course** (Fig. 13-12) in which bricks are laid with enough slope for drainage, fit under the wood window sill, and have their ends and part of one side exposed. The course should slope about 2″ from back to front, and overhang regular courses about 1″. Calculate how many bricks you need, and cut or shape them to length. Allow the same width of mortar joint as in other courses—about ½″, but no more than ⅝″ or less than ⅜″. Remember that you will have one more joint than you have bricks.

Before you begin, check the flashing you placed earlier. The upper end should be tucked into a rabbet in the underside of the sill. Near the center of the flashing it should have a 90° bend so that it fits against wall sheathing and across the top brick in the regular course below the sill. It should extend just beyond the lower course, and be bent to fit down over it about ¼″ (see Fig. 13-14b).

Fill the cavity beneath the wood sill with mortar so that each rowlock brick rests in a full bed and also a full back. Butter the side of the first brick by wiping mortar off the trowel on both edges so that mortar is thickest at the center. Lay the brick in approximate position; it should fit with little gap at the sill and extend at least 1″ under it. Tap the brick sideways against jamb bricks until you have the proper thickness of joint. Repeat this process with the first brick at the opposite jamb. Then check both bricks for fit at the sill, plumb in the wall, and level from brick to brick.

Continue laying bricks toward the center of the opening until only the closure is missing. Butter that brick on both sides, and gently fit it into the gap from above. Then cut away excess mortar.

Tooling Joints

The purpose of tooling joints is to force mortar tight against bricks. Jointers come in several shapes that give you a concave joint (a half circle), a V joint, or a flush joint. Match the joints in existing masonry.

Mortar is ready for tooling when it is **thumbprint hard**—that is, it is stiffening but still soft enough so you can see your thumbprint in it. Tool vertical joints first, applying just enough pressure to force the mortar against bricks on both sides of the joint. The jointer should be slightly wider than the joint itself. When you tool horizontal joints last, they are cleaner and emphasize the horizontal effect of a masonry wall.

Precautions

You should be able to complete the job of enclosing a new opening in a matter of hours. To assure the best possible job, observe these precautions:

- Work on a day when air temperature is at least 50°F, the air is comparatively still, and humidity is above average.
- Even though the bricks you lay are damp, the surfaces in the existing wall on which you spread mortar must be clean and dry.
- Keep all materials, both masonry units and mortar ingredients, off the ground and under cover until you are ready for them.
- Protect completed brickwork against rain for 48 to 72 hours. A sheet of polyethylene works well, and lets light into the house.
- If your work is interrupted for more than 30 minutes, remove all excess mortar around laid bricks and tool all completed joints. Then, before you resume work, clean the surfaces around your completed work with a wire brush to remove all dried mortar.
- Scrape excess mortar off tools and wash and dry them before storing them.

REPLACING SIDING

The work of resurfacing an old wall around a new opening with siding goes quickly. Retain existing course lines, and begin with the lowest course and work upward.

Cut reusable siding to its new length, and fill old nail holes from both front and back with wood putty. Apply the pieces with new nails driven near the old nail holes, but slightly above and to one side of them. Be sure that the nails miss the top of the course beneath. To assure good attachment through siding exposed to the weather for many years but still in good condition, use threaded nails of the same length as those you removed. At window and door frames seal all joints tight with caulking.

If you must notch siding at a window sill, hold the piece to be cut against the bottom of the sill, with its end in alignment with the end of the adjoining piece. Mark the width of the sill on the siding. Then measure the amount of offset between the loose piece and the course in which it will fit. Make vertical cuts of this length on the two marks, then make a horizontal cut between them. Press the piece into caulking around the sill, and nail.

If you must notch above an opening, mark and cut the siding as just described. Before installing it, however, cut a piece of metal flashing to the width of the window frame. Tuck the upper end at least 2″ up sheathing, letting the building paper overlap it. Then bend the lower edge to conform to the shape of the drip cap above the window. As you nail the notched siding in position, be careful not to puncture the flashing. Caulk where the siding fits at jambs.

REPLACING SHINGLES

To make sure that your courses of replacement shingles are level, get a 2 × 4 long enough to extend from the window or door frame across the area to be shingled and under about 36″ of existing shingles. Hold this guide under the butts of existing shingles, and set replacement shingles on it for position. Apply each shingle with two nails if it is no wider than 8″. Otherwise, use three. Nail approximately ¼″ from outside edges and about 1″ above the butt line of the course above, varying these dimensions as necessary to avoid reusing existing holes. You don't need to fill old nail holes in shingles, but should use new nails of the same type as you removed.

APPLYING NEW SIDING

When you apply new siding on an entire wall, whether that wall is existing or is the side of an addition, the first and most important step is establishing the exposure. **Exposure** is the visible vertical height between parallel butt edges.

Beveled wood siding comes in three nominal sizes: ½″ × 6″ with a recommended exposure of 4½″, ⅝″ × 8″ with a 6″ exposure, and ¾″ × 10″ with an 8″ exposure. You can reduce recommended exposures, but any reduction of more than about ¼″ isn't economical. You should not increase recommended

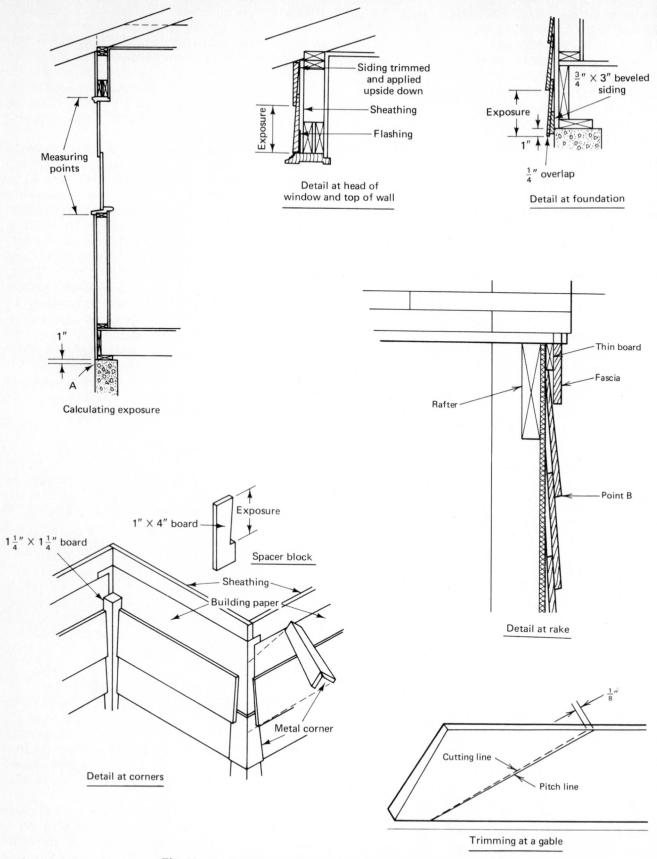

Measuring points

Siding trimmed and applied upside down
Sheathing
Flashing

Exposure

Detail at head of window and top of wall

$\frac{3}{4}'' \times 3''$ **beveled siding**

Exposure

1"

$\frac{1}{4}''$ **overlap**

Detail at foundation

1"

A

Calculating exposure

Thin board

Fascia

Rafter

Point B

Detail at rake

Exposure

$1'' \times 4''$ **board**

Spacer block

$1\frac{1}{4}'' \times 1\frac{1}{4}''$ **board**

Sheathing

Building paper

Metal corner

Detail at corners

$\frac{1}{8}''$

Cutting line

Pitch line

Trimming at a gable

Fig. 13-18. Details showing method of application of wood siding.

exposure by more than ¼". Plywood and hardboard siding are designed for an 8" exposure that is adjustable. Metal, vinyl, and asbestos-cement siding are designed for an 8" exposure that can't be varied.

What type of siding and what exposure should you use? Match the type and exposure on the main house when it has siding. Otherwise, work out the best exposure, then make your decision.

Figuring Exposure

To determine exposure, make a chalk mark on your foundation wall 1" below its top. This is point A in Fig. 13-18. Then measure from point A to the undersides of window sills, from undersides of sills to heads of windows and doors, and from heads to the top of the wall. The top of the wall may be a sloped soffit on the undersides of rafters, a horizontal soffit level with the ends of rafters, or the tip of a gable.

Now divide each dimension by 8" and see what you get. Suppose that your stack of dimensions is 32¼", 55½", and 16½"—for a total height of 104¼". Eight doesn't go into any of the numbers exactly, but comes very close—close enough so that you can use any siding with an 8" exposure, and have butt lines fall within caulking distance of sills and heads of openings. You adjust at the top of the wall by varying the width of trim.

But suppose instead that your dimensions are 33¾", 52½", and 14¾", for a total of 101". Here an 8" exposure doesn't fit at all. You could notch at heads and sills and adjust at the top with trim, but the wall wouldn't look well. If at all possible, butt lines should fall at heads and sills of openings. So your most logical solution is to use a siding with an exposure that you can adjust to your given dimensions.

To find the best exposure, divide the combined height from point A to window heads by increasing numbers of courses to establish an average exposure. Then see how close the average fits your three individual dimensions. In the second example, for instance, 12 courses over 86¼" gives an exposure of just over 7⅛", but that exposure doesn't work at all into the three dimensions. Thirteen courses, however, gives you an average exposure of about 6⅝". With five courses below windows, exposure is 6¾". Eight courses beside windows would have exposures of 6¹¹⁄₁₆". Above windows two courses of 6⅝" and trim 1½" wide is exact. Similarly, you can come close with 15 courses: 6 below windows at 5⅝" and 9 beside windows at 5¹⁵⁄₁₆". Above the windows use a 6" exposure and wider trim.

Actually, you can vary exposure on a wall as much as ½" to adjust to conditions without the difference being noticeable, but the more consistent you are the better the wall's appearance. If you decide on a 6⅝" exposure, you must order 10" siding. With the 5⅝" exposure you can work with 8" siding.

Preparation

Behind siding you must have a moisture barrier. Both gypsum sheathing and insulating sheathing have an asphalted surface that prevents penetration of moisture. Plywood sheathing does not. Therefore, cover plywood sheathing with 24"-wide strips of building paper applied horizontally with staples or roofing nails. Wrap the strips around corners. Apply the first strip flush with the top of the foundation wall, and overlap succeeding strips about 2".

Next decide how to handle corners. At inside corners, such as where an addition meets an existing wall, the best solution is to nail into the corner a board trimmed to 1¼" × 1¼" (see Fig. 13-18). Then, as you renail old siding or shingles that you removed temporarily to allow for new construction, you butt them against the corner board. If the existing wall is masonry, replace units you removed until they touch the sheathing of the addition, then add the corner board. The board should extend from the top of the foundation to the top of the wall. Before you install it, paint it with a primer-sealer on all four sides and both ends to prevent deterioration from moisture. Use 16d nails spaced about 12" apart and driven through sheathing into a stud in the addition.

At outside corners the simplest, quickest, and cleanest closure is metal corner caps. Cut siding to stop about ½" short of the corner on both sides (see Fig. 13-18). Bend a metal cap, available at most lumberyards, to fit the angle at the corner of the wall. Slip its bottom flange under the butt edges of the siding in each course, and push the cap upward. To assure a tight fit, tap gently on a wood block held against the cap. Then secure it with a pair of 2d or 3d nails driven through predrilled holes into the siding.

With corner boards in place and metal corner caps on hand, measure down ¾" from the top of the foundation wall at two widely separated points on each surface. Then snap chalk lines between pairs of marks, and check the level all the way around the foundation. On each chalk line set the thicker edge of a beveled board, and nail it every 16" through sheathing into the sill plate (see fig. 13-18). The board should be at least 2" wide and no more than ½" thick at its bottom edge. For this backerboard you can either rip a length of beveled siding or bevel a 1 × 3 or 1 × 4. The purpose of the backerboard is to direct rain running down the wall away from the top of the foundation wall.

The First Course

Cut each piece of siding about ¹⁄₁₆" too long, and prime the ends before you install it. Whenever possible use a single length for a course. When a wall is too long to do this, cut ends to meet at the centerlines of studs, which you will have to mark on new building paper. No length of siding should be less than 32".

Apply the bottom course so that it overlaps the backerboard by ¼", thus giving you the location of point A you used in determining exposure. Begin at inside corners and work toward outside corners. Set each piece with a slight bow, nail into predrilled holes near its ends, then spring it into place for a tight fit. In between ends use one nail per stud, again driven into predrilled holes. Place nails so that they just clear the top of the backerboard.

Nails should be either aluminum or hot-dipped galvanized steel so that they don't rust and stain the siding. If you plan to paint, use casing nails, countersink them, and fill the holes with putty. If you intend to stain, use siding nails driven flush with the siding's surface. For attachment to plywood sheathing use 6d threaded nails with 6" siding, and 8d threaded nails with 8" and 10" siding. Use 8d nails for applying 6" siding to any other type of sheathing, and 9d nails with 8" and 10" siding.

Additional Courses

To assure uniform exposure according to your plan, make a spacer out of 1 × 4 (see Fig. 13-18). The depth of the notch is slightly less than the butt thickness of siding, and its length is equal to your exposure. Fit the spacer against the course you have already installed, and set the next course on the top of the block. Check level frequently. Drive nails so that they just clear the course below. Install corner caps as the last step in each course. Then caulk all joints—at corners, at butt joints, around openings—before you coat the surface.

At window sills, notch if necessary as described under "Replacing Siding" earlier in this chapter. At the top of the wall measure from the soffit to the butt edge of the top course, and subtract your exposure dimension. Then rip a length of siding or a board to this dimension, and install it upside down as a trim piece (see Fig. 13-18).

At the rakes of roofs in gables, use your pitch board to mark the slope on the ends of each length of siding. Then measure off ⅛" outward (toward the rake) on the top edge. From this point draw a new line to the end of the pitch line at the butt edge (see Fig. 13-18). Cut on this new line and test the fit. Use a block plane as necesssary for a tighter joint.

These instructions are for application of beveled siding. Application of other types of wood siding is essentially the same. With any type of manufactured siding—metal, vinyl, or asbestos-cement—follow the manufacturer's instructions. They will also be similar, but are likely to vary somewhat.

APPLYING NEW SHINGLES

Wood shingles come in lengths of 16", 18", and 24", and vary in width from 3" to 14". The two shorter lengths are usually applied by **single-coursing**—the entire wall is covered with two thicknesses of shingle and three at butts, and all nails are hidden (Fig. 13-19a). The 24" shingles permit **double-coursing**—the entire wall is covered with two thicknesses, but there are four thicknesses at butt ends, and half the nails are exposed (Fig. 13-19b).

Exposure

As with application of siding, the first step is to plan exposure. Maximum exposures are 7½" for single-coursed 16" shingles, 8½" for single-coursed 18" shingles, and 16" for double-coursed 24" shingles. Measuring points for exposure (see Fig. 13-18) are the same as with siding, and the procedure is the same. Similarly, plywood sheathing must be covered with building paper; other types do not require it.

As with siding you need a backerboard behind the bottom course of shingles to direct rain away from the top of the foundation wall. With shingling, however, the most common backerboard is a doubled course of shingles (Fig. 13-19d). Thus the bottom course is thicker (as at the rake of a roof), and the exposed layer overlaps the undercourse ¼" at butts.

Preparation

At inside corners use a corner board as shown in Fig. 13-18, but use a nominal 2 × 2 to allow for the extra thickness of exterior material. At outside corners you can buy a one-piece molding called a **corner bead** or **corner post**; it is 1¼" wide on each side and comes in 10' lengths (see Fig. 13-19c). Prime and install moldings at both inside and outside corners before you begin shingling.

Snap a level chalk line ¼ to ½" below the top of the foundation wall on all sides, and lay an undercourse of shingles with their butts on the chalk lines. Attach the shingles 1 to 2" above their butts, two fasteners per shingle. Use rust-resistant siding nails if the sheathing is plywood; use self-clinching or patented threaded fasteners with other types of sheathing.

The First and Other Courses

Install the bottom course of shingles so that the exposed butts are 1" below the top of the foundation. On this course mark at several points the exposure you selected, and tack a long, straight 2 × 4 on the marks as a leveling guide for the next course. Continue up the wall in this manner, and trim at the top with a beveled board or manufactured trim.

For a wall with some texture and strong horizontal joint lines, lay shingles without gapping (called **closed jointing**). For maximum texture but less horizontal

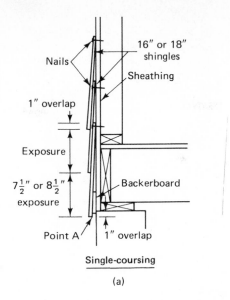

Single-coursing

(a)

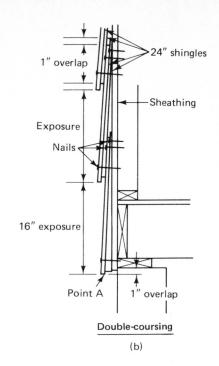

Double-coursing

(b)

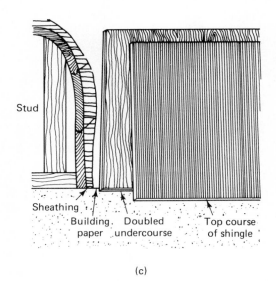

(c)

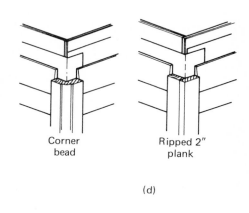

(d)

Fig. 13-19. Sections (a) and (b) show the amount of overlap and exposure in single-coursing and double-coursing methods of application. Treatments at the foundation wall in these sections are alternatives to those described in the text. Details (c) and (d) show application of wood shingles at the foundation and outside corners respectively. You can buy a corner bead, or make your own by cutting a 2 x 4 or 2 x 6 into two pieces, one exactly 1½" wider than the other.

effect, gap about ⅛" **(open jointing)**. Vertical joints in lapping courses must be staggered at least 1½". If the edges of shingles aren't plumb, shave them with a shingling hatchet or power plane.

You may leave shingles to weather naturally, or you may paint or stain them. For best results and longest life, dip shingles in a bucket of stain or thin primer, and let them dry before you apply them. Add finish coats after all shingles are in place and you have caulked at corners and around openings.

14

Designing A Better Kitchen

(a)

(b)

Typical kitchens around the turn of the century (a) had too few windows, too many doors, high ceilings, and little work or storage space. Yet they are salvageable. In (b), a lowered ceiling gives the room more pleasing proportions, and broader windows provide more balanced light. Replacing one door with a window eliminated cross-traffic. The table with a drop-leaf extension not only seats six, but also acts as an extension of counter and as a barrier that keeps the work triangle free of traffic. (Courtesy Azrock Floor Products.)

Planning a kitchen remodeling is among the most frustrating of design tasks. Yet a well-planned kitchen brings the most gratifying results. Few people who spend much time in their kitchens say they love to work there.

Extremely rare is the kitchen that can't be remodeled and wouldn't benefit from remodeling. Yours is undoubtedly among them. It may be so large that it is inefficient, or it may be too small to be efficient. It rarely has enough counter space or cabinet space. Much of the storage space it has is inconvenient—at the wrong level, in the wrong place, of the wrong size.

Why are there so many poor kitchens? One main reason is their changing use over the decades. For many generations the kitchen was the "family room" of older houses. It was a kitchen as we know it part of the time, a dining room part of the time, a study hall, game room, and even bathroom at other times. At all times it was the center of family activities. It was seldom a store room, however; a pantry and cellar served that purpose. So old kitchens were frequently large, close to square, with ample room around a table. The sink was wide, had its own drainboard, and often provided the only counter space. The only appliance in sight was a stove; the icebox was relegated to a porch or other location near a back door where water from melting ice could easily be disposed of.

As often happens, when the pendulum of lifestyles began to swing, it swung to the other extreme.

One by one the uses of the kitchen shifted to other rooms. The "Saturday Night Live" bath was taken or administered in the privacy of a new room with indoor plumbing. Development of gas and electric ranges did away with the need for space to store wood or coal. The advent of the refrigerator and the automobile changed food buying and storage patterns. Smaller families meant smaller tables for informal dining. Basement recreation rooms became the center of the family's group activities. By the mid-1950s the kitchen was little more than a center for preparing and serving food, and cleaning up after meals.

It wasn't until kitchen space shrank so drastically that home economists began to time-study kitchen-related processes. Over a period of time they developed recommendations for kitchen planning that, modified by further changes in living patterns, improvements in appliances, and increases in building costs, are still valid today.

Most important of these recommendations is the **work triangle**. The three basic functions of a modern kitchen are:

1. Storage and mixing.
2. Food preparation and cleanup.
3. Cooking.

The areas of the kitchen where these functions occur should be separate, but related to each other in the shape of a triangle, with the sink, range, and refrigerator at the corners. The combined length of the three sides of the triangle should be no less than 12' or more than 22'. Convert these figures to steps, and in the most efficient kitchen the range and refrigerator should be on opposite sides of the sink and no more than three steps from them.

Kitchen experts further recommend counter space on both sides of the sink, both sides of the range, and on the handle side of the refrigerator. They recommend storage space near the refrigerator for the utensils used in mixing, baking dishes and similar containers, and the ingredients most commonly mixed. They recommend storage space near the sink for soaps and detergents, brushes, towels, and other cleaning supplies. They call for storage space near the range for the vessels and tools used in conjunction with cooking and serving. China, glassware, and tableware used daily should be stored between the sink and range. Best china, crystal, and silver should be stored close to the formal dining area.

APPLIANCES

A disposal unit must obviously fit under the sink, but in that location it cuts in half the storage space available in the sink cabinet. A dishwasher should fit next to the sink; on which side depends on your method of rinsing dishes. If you hold dirty items in your left hand and scrape with your right, then the dishwasher should be to the left of the sink so you don't have to shift hands to put the dish, glass, or utensil in its proper rack. If you work in reverse, the dishwasher should be to the right of the sink. A dishwasher doesn't reduce storage space, because it is a storage cabinet much of the time itself.

The most logical place for a built-in oven is in a corner at the end of a counter. If much of what you bake or broil goes directly to the dining table, a corner nearest the dining table is the best location. But if you are long on baking cakes that require frosting, or cooking foods that need further preparation after they cool, then next to the mixing area is a better spot. Use the space above and below the oven for platters, cake plates, serving tools, and utensils used in or at the oven. There is no rule that says all your tools for food preparation must be kept in the same drawer or area.

A separate freezer can go anywhere you have room for it. Because of its size, an upright unit may block light from a window unless it is in a corner. It should have at least 15″ of counter space on the handle side if possible.

The proliferation of small appliances has created some storage problems. If you're one of those people who must keep everything out of sight, plan cabinets large enough to store utensils near their point of use. If you prefer the convenience of leaving frequently used appliances, such as a can opener and toaster, where you can get at them quickly, allow in your planning for the extra counter space they occupy.

LAYING OUT YOUR KITCHEN

With all the rules and variables involved in kitchen arrangement, where do you start to plan your remodeling? You simply establish the physical limitations of the space you have available, and go from there. For a kitchen that serves only the three main purposes, you need between 100 and 125 sq ft of floor space. A kitchen with eating space for four to six people should have 160 to 200 sq ft. These are practical minimums, depending on the shape of the space.

Assume first that you won't go to the expense of relocating any bearing partition or exterior wall. Then look at the other side limitations. Can you move or remove any other walls and, if so, will the effect on adjoining rooms be beneficial or harmful? If you reduce existing kitchen space, what is the best use of the space you gain? If you must enlarge existing space, where is the best place to borrow it?

To find answers to space questions, measure your existing kitchen, and draw an accurate plan of its boundaries. For preliminary planning use a scale of ¼″ = 1'-0″; better still, work on graph paper with lines ⅛″ or ¼″ apart. Later, after you have worked out a rough arrangement, you can redraw the plan of the proposed remodeled kitchen at ½" scale. On your preliminary plan show the locations of doors and windows, and measure and draw the plans of adjoining rooms. Ignore all else.

Now study the six basic kitchen shapes shown in Fig. 14-1 with your plan drawing in hand.

Basic Plans

A **one-wall kitchen** (Fig. 14-1a) takes up the least floor space but is also the least efficient. Consider it a possibility only when your available space is narrow (between 6 and 8') and long (15 to 18'). The work triangle flattens to a straight line. A one-wall kitchen is adequate for vacation houses and apartments; it is rarely practical for full-time houses unless it occupies one wall of a larger area such as a family room.

A **corridor kitchen** (Fig. 14-1b) takes a little wider space (8 to 9') than a one-wall kitchen, but a little less length (12 to 14'). Of all shapes it is the most efficient with the shortest work triangle, *provided* that the kitchen is not also an aisle. The term "corridor" refers to shape only, not usage. The sink and range are against opposite walls, and the refrigerator and any oven can go against either wall. Since counters are straight, the kitchen has no inside corners with deep storage space that is difficult to reach.

A **U-shaped kitchen** (Fig. 14-1c) takes up about the same floor area as a corridor kitchen, and fits nicely into spaces where the shape varies from half again as long as wide (such as 12' × 8') to square. The work triangle is quite efficient, and the work area is completely out of the line of any traffic through the room. The U-shaped kitchen has two disadvantages, however. It has two corners that offer only limited and hard-to-reach storage space. And it doesn't lend itself to use by more than one person at a time, whether the other people are helping with the dishes or simply after a snack in the refrigerator or cookie jar.

An **L-shaped kitchen** (Fig. 14-1d) has all appliances, counters, and cabinets on adjoining walls. Its work triangle is flatter than in a corridor or U kitchen, but is still efficient. Minimum dimensions are about 8' × 12' without eating space. An L-shaped kitchen of slightly larger dimensions can include a dinette table that is easy to serve and equally easy to clear. Traffic is not a problem, there is room for help when you need it, and only one corner is lost for storage.

A **peninsula kitchen** (Fig. 14-1e) has a plan shaped like the letter F. It is a basic U with one counter extended, or a basic L with a stub. Two storage corners are partially wasted, but traffic is no problem. The stub may contain the range, sink, or refrigerator, or simply provide added counter space. A peninsula kitchen occupies quite a little floor area, and for that reason is most often placed at one end of a family room or in-formal dining area. It is ideal for use by more than one person, because any one of the three basic kitchen functions can be separated by the stub from the other two. The smaller work area can also be a wet or dry bar.

An **island kitchen** (Fig. 14-1f) has continuous counters along one, two, or three walls, and an isolated work area adjacent. The island serves as a buffer against traffic, and may be used as a cooking center, dishwashing area, serving counter, buffet, or snack bar. The island and its storage space are accessible from all sides. Minimum floor space is about 12' × 12' and approximately square.

The **family kitchen** (Fig. 14-1g) that virtually disappeared during the mid-decades of the twentieth century has made a comeback in slightly altered form. Its abundant but wasted space has been organized. The kitchen area itself may take any one of the six common shapes, and is open to the rest of the room. At the center of remaining space is a table surrounded by specialized storage. You may adapt the space to your family's individual needs: as a supervised play area for toddlers where they are close but not under foot; as an after-dinner study area for older children; as a meeting room for teen activities; as a hobby area for all members of the family; and as a focal point for family gatherings at and after meals.

Draw a Floor Plan

Not all common kitchen shapes will suit your needs and the space available, but at least one will. So go back to your floor plan and lightly draw in lines 2' away from all walls. Let them run all the way around—under windows, across doorways, everywhere. The light lines represent the approximate depth of counters and major appliances.

Next measure the distance between parallel counter lines. If that measurement isn't at least 4' at scale, you have a choice. Either you can't have counters on opposite walls or you must move one wall until space between counters is at least 4'. If you can't move the wall for structural or economic reasons, you are stuck with a one-wall kitchen. If moving the wall is the only way to widen the room enough for a corridor kitchen, lay a sheet of tracing paper over the existing plan, and draw the new shape of the kitchen with the wall moved. Don't erase on your original drawing; you need it as you drew it.

Next look at doorways, and determine which ones can't be moved under any circumstances. There may be some. Examples are doors leading to basement stairs or opening into a narrow hallway. Measure from room corners to these openings and subtract 3". Transfer these dimensions to your drawing at scale, and draw lines between the wall and countertop line at right angles to both. Then erase the counter line in front of the door between the two lines.

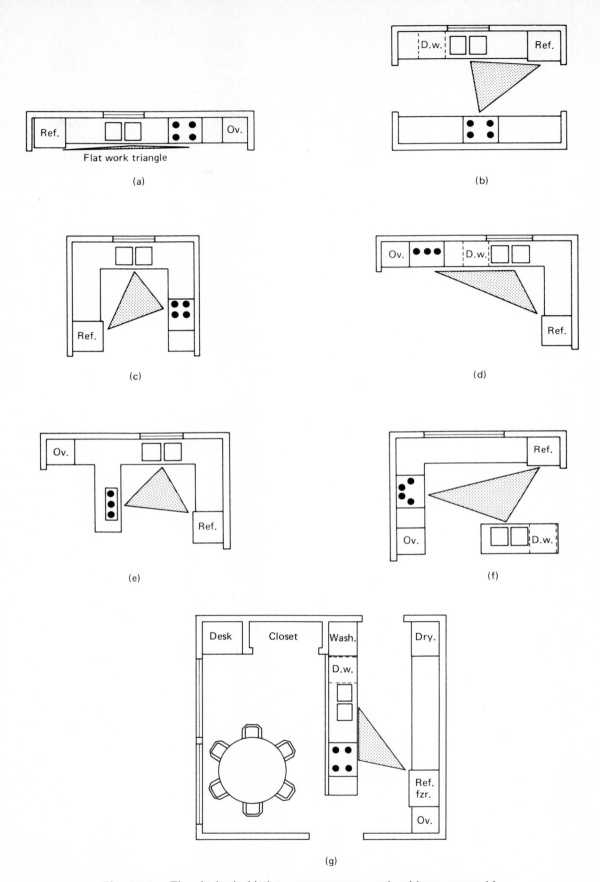

Fig. 14–1. The six basic kitchen arrangements, each with an acceptable work triangle between the refrigerator, sink, and range: (a) one-wall; (b) corridor; (c) U-shaped; (d) L-shaped; (e) peninsula; (f) island. A family kitchen (g) combines one of the six plans with additional space for other shared uses.

Then cut three rectangles out of a sheet of sturdy colored paper. Make one 24″ × 32″ (½″ × ¹¹⁄₁₆″ at ¼″ scale), one 24″ × 30″ (½″ × ⅝″), and one 32″ × 28″ (¹¹⁄₁₆″ × ⁹⁄₁₆″). Let these represent your sink cabinet, range, and refrigerator, respectively. If you plan to reuse existing appliances, take their actual measurements. In a newly remodeled kitchen, however, your old appliances will look out of place and you'll probably end up buying new ones anyway. Mark the rectangles with an S, Rg, and Rf so that you don't get them mixed up.

First find the best location for the sink. Most people prefer it under a window so that during the day they can look out and have good light on the sink area. Ignore your present sink location, and don't be deluded into thinking that the best sink location is where the present sink is. The cost of moving water and drain lines is minor compared to the mental and physical cost of working at a sink in an inconvenient spot. The sink should be near the center of a wall or of a confined work area.

Mark a centerline on your drawing for the sink as you have tentatively located it. Set the sink cutout in

place, but don't paste it down. Then look for a place for the refrigerator.

The heaviest traffic to the refrigerator is from the service entrance of the house and to the sink. Therefore, the best corner is one nearest the service door where it can be reached by people with an armful of groceries and children with a stomachful of hunger to satisfy. Keep in mind which way the refrigerator door swings so that you have counter next to the handle. The doors of most new refrigerators don't require extra space for swinging. You should allow 1 to 1½″ clearance on one side, however, for sliding the unit in and out for repairs and cleaning. Set the refrigerator cutout in place.

Finally, find the most logical place for the range. Of all corners of the work triangle, the range should be farthest away from traffic for safety's sake. It should be close to dining areas to save serving steps. It may be against an inside partition, on a stub, or in an island. If you cook with gas, it should not be under a window where draperies create a fire hazard. If you plan to install a hood over the range to vent outdoors the heat and odors of cooking, try to place the range against or close to an exterior wall. Then you can exhaust directly

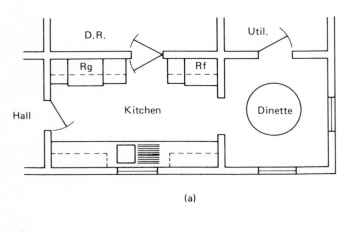

(a)

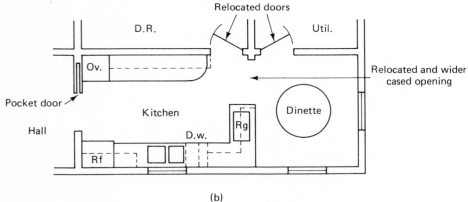

(b)

Fig. 14–2. In the "before" plan (a), doors break up work areas and permit traffic problems. During remodeling the doors are grouped (b), and one troublesome door swing avoided with a seldom-closed door that slides into a pocket. The refrigerator is now near the service entrance, the range handy to both dining room and dinette, and the dinette table out of the pathway between the kitchen and utility space.

through the wall, rather than through a duct above the ceiling.

Set the range cutout in place, and study the arrangement of counter space. The more continuous your counter space is, the better it is. The minimum practical width for any section is 12″, and 15″ is a far better minimum. Do you have counter beside the refrigerator, on both sides of the range, and on both sides of the sink? Good. Then cut 24″ squares of colored paper (½″ × ½″) for any separate oven or dishwasher, and fit them onto your plan. The dishwasher won't reduce counter space; the oven will. A built-in oven doesn't need counter next to it, and should go in a corner or other out-of-the-way spot where it won't block light. A microwave oven, whether built-in or resting on a counter, must have work space adjacent to it.

Now figure out where to put the remaining doors you need to reach other rooms. Draw light lines 3″ at scale from existing door jambs at right angles to the counter and wall. With doors in these positions, does your counter space still meet minimum requirements? If not, look for another place to cut through a door. Sometimes you can achieve a better kitchen layout and simultaneously reduce cross traffic by grouping door openings. Figure 14-2 shows a good example of a change in door location that improves both counter space and traffic problems. Be sure, however, that the doors in these openings don't swing against each other.

Draw Elevations

When you are reasonably satisfied with your efforts, redraw your plan at ½″ scale, delineating walls and fixed windows and doors in firm lines and everything else in light lines. Then draw elevations of all four walls to see how the kitchen will look, and where to place cabinets. Again use ½″ scale.

Counter Heights. First establish counter height. Standard height for a kitchen counter is 36″. But since you are remodeling this kitchen for your family's use, ignore standards. Ask whoever will use the kitchen the most to stand with an arm extended as if to shake hands. Then measure from floor to elbow, subtract 3″, and place the counter at that height.

This is the best height for a counter at which you work standing up. For work sitting down, plan a counter level of 26 to 28″. Allow at least 20″ of width below it for knees; 24″ is better.

Clearances. Between any cabinet that rests on the floor, called **base cabinet**, and any cabinet above a counter, called a **wall cabinet** or **overhead cabinet**, allow a minimum clearance of 15″; 18″ is better. Above a sink allow 24″ clearance. Usually, there is a window there, and over-the-sink cabinets are neither possible nor

practicable. If you place the sink elsewhere, be sure to provide artificial light. Fluorescent tubes attached to the underside of the cabinet and shielded by its bottom rail work well.

The clearance between a range top at counter level and cabinets above it is established by building code. Check with your local Building Department to verify the minimums in your community. As a rule of thumb you must provide 24 to 26″ clearance when you install a hood that catches grease and absorbs or carries away the heat of cooling, and about 33″ clearance without a hood.

Set the underside of a cabinet above a refrigerator 69″ above the floor. Over a washer or dryer the minimum is 15″. If your laundry equipment is top-loading, the cabinet should clear an open door by at least 1″.

Cabinet Tops. Most people can reach items on a shelf 18″ above their heads without standing on anything but tiptoe. Reduce that height by 3″, however, if you have to reach over something, such as a refrigerator or range hood. As a rule the top rail of a frequently used cabinet should not be more than 84″ above the floor. Unless you need the storage space above that height for little-used kitchen items, fill the gap between the top of the cabinet and the ceiling with furring. **Furring** is a light framework that you finish like an ordinary wall or ceiling, and to which you attach wall cabinets. More about furring in the following chapter.

By following the heights and clearances above, you can draw on your elevations the horizontal lines representing counter levels and the tops and bottoms of wall cabinets. Draw these lines lightly.

Then draw in the shapes of all appliances, using actual dimensions when you know them, or the dimensions given on page 202 if you don't know them yet. Allow for side clearances where required. If you plan to replace any appliance, now is the time to select it so that you know exactly how much space it will occupy, and can adjust either your choice or your plan when what you would like and what you have room for don't agree. Manufacturers' literature tells you what clearances are required, if any, at the sides and back of their products.

The cabinet above a refrigerator should be the same width as the space below it. Similarly, the cabinet above a range should be as wide as the range, or the cabinet containing it when it is built in. To denote the edges of these cabinets, draw vertical lines downward from the counter and upward at the same point from the undersides of base cabinets (Fig. 14-3). A kitchen always looks best when upper and lower cabinets line up.

At this point in your planning you know the approximate heights and widths of the spaces available for cabinets. Before you can begin remodeling, you need to work out the design of each cabinet. Even

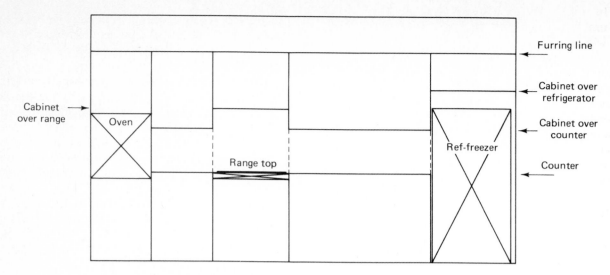

Fig. 14-3. Whenever possible, wall cabinets should be the same width as the appliances or base cabinets directly below them. Your elevation drawing of a kitchen wall should look like this at this stage in planning.

before that, however, make sure what other changes you must make or want to make in the kitchen and adjoining spaces.

IMPROVING LIGHT

For those short trips into the kitchen for a snack or to store groceries or to help you see your way through the room, you need only a low level of general light. A small window or a skylight in a one-story house

Fig. 14-4. Windows in the wall between counter and overhead cabinets provide good daylight on the work counter. This kitchen, now 30 years old, proves that good design never goes out of style, even though individual elements here—windows, lighting, countertops, and hardware—have been improved in the intervening years. (Courtesy Andersen Corporation.)

provides ample light during the day. A single center light or a light panel in a ceiling grid (see Chapter 13) is adequate at night. For cooking, mixing, food preparation, and cleanup, however, general light is useless. You need specific light without shadows on all work surfaces—the sink, the range, and counters. (See Chapter 5.)

Daylight

The closer the sill of a window is to counter height, the better working light the window provides. Well-designed counters have a **backsplash** or **splashboard**, an extension of countertop material up the wall behind. Standard height for a backsplash is 4″, making the typical sill level 40″ above the floor. You can carry fixed glass or awning windows all the way to counter level, but you will be cleaning glass frequently that isn't easy to reach.

Heads of windows can be at one of three heights. One is just below the ceiling. More common is the same height as other windows in the wall of the house. Then the heads of all windows line up outside for better appearance. A standard height is 6′-8″ above floor level. Thus you can extend furring above cabinets in a continuous line across windows, and recess lights into the furring for specific illumination on the sink or counter below.

The third height for the heads of windows is just below the bottoms of wall cabinets. A series of awning windows tucked between counter and cabinets provides excellent working daylight and good ventilation (Fig. 14-4). This approach has two problems, however. Strip windows may look fine in the kitchen but could look peculiar on the exterior of a staid old house. Second, controlling glare off the counter from low-angle west or east sun is difficult.

In small kitchens where wall space is at a premium, it is always difficult to decide whether to have wide windows for good daylight but limited storage space, or narrow windows and more cabinets. The best solution is to arrange doors so that you have the maximum unbroken space for cabinets on the wall opposite windows. Let light from the windows illuminate the cabinets' contents, then light the counter artificially. In this way you don't need as much outside wall for cabinets, and can widen the window area. Cabinets flanking windows block some daylight anyway, and a window less than 36″ wide won't let in much light.

Artificial Light

A light recessed into furring above the sink and operated by a switch within reach of that sink provides the best light for cleanup. The light should be centered about 6″ from the wall, so that the head of anyone washing dishes doesn't cast a shadow on the sink.

Range hoods are equipped with a light that affords ample light on the cooking area. Clean the lens at least once a month, however; it will get dirty from grease and smoke. The light is operated by a button on the hood.

Fluorescent tubes attached to the undersides of overhead cabinets provide the best specific light on counters. The bottom rail of the cabinet keeps the light out of your eyes, and light reflected off the wall and counter itself all but eliminates shadows. Tubes should be continuous from one end of the cabinet to the other. They can be wired so all come on at the flip of a wall switch, or you can buy individual tube lights that you plug into a nearby outlet and activate with a button.

VENTILATION

Because cooking generates both heat and odors, and all appliances give off heat, a kitchen needs better ventilation than other rooms. Cross-ventilation out the kitchen window will remove much of the heat and odors, but when the wind blows in, it simply distributes the odors and heat throughout other rooms. Since you can't control the wind, a vent fan is a better answer.

There are three types. One type fits in an existing wall and is operated by a switch. When the fan is running, the force of outgoing air raises a protective cover that prevents rain, snow, or dust from entering at other times. To serve its purpose a wall fan must be within 3′ of the cooking area. A wall fan is a satisfactory solution to ventilation only when the range is on an outside wall, or on a side wall or in a stub counter within 3′ of that wall.

The other two types of fans are integral parts of range hoods. One type (Fig. 14-5) has a filter that catches particles of grease as the fan sucks air out of the kitchen, through a duct, and exhausts it outdoors. For

Fig. 14-5. A range hood that exhausts outdoors through a duct is the most effective way to remove heat and cooking odors from a kitchen. To keep duct runs as short as possible, the range should be against or close to an exterior wall. (Courtesy Vent-A-Hood.)

maintenance you merely wash the filter in detergent periodically. The range hood fan does the best job of ventilating, provided that you have space for the duct. It rises through the cabinet above the hood, then runs horizontally to the outside wall. When the range is against an outside wall, the only disadvantage compared to a wall fan is loss of overhead storage space. When the range is against a wall perpendicular to the outside wall, you can run the duct in furring, and you aren't limited in location. When the range is against the wall opposite the outside wall, you can run the duct above the ceiling between floor joists that run at right angles to the outside wall. Then you have to cut the outside joist to let the duct through, and reinforce the cut.

In the other type of range hood the fan sucks air through a charcoal-activated filter that absorbs grease and odors, then blows the cleansed air back into the room. This type of hood works wherever you place the range, even in an island. There is no ductwork and therefore no loss of storage space in the cabinet above. There are two drawbacks, however. The filter must be washed frequently to be effective, and the hood does a poorer job of removing heat than other types.

WIRING

Electrical codes are quite specific about the requirements for electrical outlets for appliances, both fixed and portable. The National Electrical Code is updated every three years, and in most communities you must comply with the current code when you remodel, regardless of the age of your house. Unless an old house has been rewired since it was built, considerable new wiring may be required to meet code. If you plan to hire an electrician, go over your plans with him before you start work, so that you both know where you want outlets for convenience and where he must install them to pass inspection. If you plan to do the work yourself, make a wiring diagram and have it approved by the electrical inspector before you begin any tearing out.

You should observe the same procedure for providing power to any appliance that operates on more than 120 volts. You must establish the location of the power outlet on your drawing. The conduit from this outlet to the point of connection to the appliance gives you at least 18″ of leeway in final positioning.

FUEL LINES

In most communities a homeowner is not permitted to cut off existing gas lines or install new ones. When you have worked out a tentative floor plan, then, call your local gas company and arrange to go over your plans with their engineer. Gas is piped to a fixed point near each appliance, then continues to its connection at the appliance through flexible tubing. All you have to agree on is the fixed point. The tubing gives you a leeway of at least 18″ in exact location of the appliance.

PLUMBING LINES

Unlike electrical circuits and gas lines, which end in the kitchen, plumbing lines continue beyond it. Not only must incoming hot and cold water lines be connected to existing lines, but drain lines must be fitted into existing drain piping and vented into an existing stack or a new one. As long as plumbing is accessible beneath the kitchen floor, the job of rerouting incoming piping presents no major problems. Connecting to outgoing piping is not as easy if you relocate the sink more than a foot or two from its present location.

Don't let potential problems and expense deter you from making a change in sink location as long as it improves kitchen arrangement and efficiency. Do talk to a plumber in the early planning stages, however, and have him look over the conditions he faces. If he sees no major obstacles, relocate the sink where you tentatively placed it. If he can reduce his costs by having you move the sink and other plumbed appliances a few inches, and the changes don't cause you problems, his suggestion is probably worth following. But if he suggests a major change, such as putting the sink against a different wall, evaluate the saving in cost against the loss in kitchen efficiency. Then make a decision either to pay the extra cost, to follow his suggestion, or to find another plumber.

After you check out any problems with power, fuel, and plumbing lines, are satisfied with your solutions to light and ventilation, and still like your kitchen arrangement, you can get back to cabinet design.

MANUFACTURED CABINETS

Kitchen cabinets of wood or metal are made by a number of manufacturers. Quality of appearance ranges from adequately attractive to beautiful. Quality of construction ranges from mediocre to excellent. Differences lie in the grade and species of wood, method of jointing and attachment, durability of finish, and quality of hardware. Price range from top to bottom is close to 100%, and generally varies with quality but not necessarily with finished appearance.

The better manufacturers make as standard stock items anywhere from 30 to 50 different sizes, with all dimensions on a 3″ module except for the height of base cabinets. Common heights of wall cabinets are 12″, 15″, 18″, 24″, 30″, and 33″, although no one manufacturer makes all of them. Base cabinets are designed for a 36″ finished height with countertop, which you order separately from a local supplier or make yourself. Widths of wall and base cabinets range from 9″ up to 48″ in 3″ increments, although not all manufacturers make all widths.

Suppose that you have a space 60″ wide for a wall cabinet. You can fill it with two 30s, two 21s and an 18, a 24 and a 36, or any number of other widths totaling 60″. The closer that door widths are to equal, the better the cabinets will look. And the wider the doors, the more useful the storage space. If your space is 62″ wide, you buy the same cabinets plus a 3″-wide filler strip that you trim to fill the gap wherever it will look best. Cutting the strip into two equal widths is the common answer for ultimate appearance.

Special units are available for corners, sinks, ovens, and drop-in ranges. Except for oven units these special cabinets have no drawers.

Most manufacturers of kitchen cabinets provide design service. You give them an accurately dimensioned plan of the room, showing its relationship to other rooms, window locations, and door swings, and they will send you a kitchen layout showing you which of their cabinets to order. There is usually no charge for this service; manufacturers are after your order.

If you can't work out a good kitchen plan yourself or are unsure how good your own plan is, you can rely on manufacturers to send you a sound and serviceable, although perhaps pedestrian, arrangement. Always send along your plan with the request for design service. Unless you have violated some cardinal rule of kitchen planning, the layout staff will adapt your layout to their products, and provide you with a workable plan.

BUILDING YOUR OWN CABINETS

To design and make your own cabinets is not difficult if you have the proper tools for cabinetry. As a minimum you need a circular saw, with attachments for cutting dadoes, and a router. Useful but not absolutely necessary are a saber saw, power drill, power sander, and power plane. You can sand, drill, and plane by hand, but you'll get a much more professional result with equivalent power tools.

Cabinet Design

Before you put a line on paper you must make several decisions:

- What are the maximum outside dimensions of each cabinet?
- What materials will you use for the framework?
- What kind of joints do you want to make?
- What type of doors will look best?
- What size should drawers and doors be?
- What type of hardware is needed?

Cabinet sizes. In many cases the width of cabinet you build is limited by width of available space. As a rule for general storage, however, consider a 14″ width as a practical minimum. From that dimension outward the dimensions of the cabinet itself, its stiles, doors, and shelves are governed by economy of material usage. A wide cabinet is usually much easier to build and install if you design it as a series of smaller cabinets built individually and installed one at a time instead of as one large unwieldy unit. If, for example, you need a complete storage wall and have 8′ of width, plan two 48″ units, three 32″units, four 24″ units, or some combination rather than a single 96″-wide cabinet.

Materials. You can build the frame of a small cabinet with 1 × 2s and add a skin of ¼″ plywood or hardboard (Fig. 14-6a). Cut the frame for large cabinets out of ¾″ plywood (Fig. 14-6b), which provides structural strength and skin in a single material. The back of a plywood cabinet can be cut from ¼″ plywood or hardboard. Stiles and rails for the front may be cut from 1″ lumber or ¾″ plywood. Therefore, the inside dimensions of a framed cabinet are 2″ less in width and 1¾″ less in depth than its outside dimensions. Inside dimensions of an all-plywood cabinet are 1½″ less in width and 1″ less in depth than outside dimensions.

Cabinets that stand on the floor usually rest on a base that keeps the bottom shelf above floor level. The typical base is made of 1 × 4s or ¾″ plywood. It may be flush with the front of the cabinet, as in a unit with storage space behind doors at the bottom and bookshelves above. But if the cabinet serves as a base for a counter, its base should be recessed 2″ to provide toe space for anyone working there.

Joints. For connecting cabinet framing members the simplest joint is a butt joint, held together with glue and corrugated fasteners (Fig. 14-7a). Far stronger if you have the tools to shape them are mortise-and-tenon and dadoed joints (Fig. 14-7b and c). You cut them with a power router and its attachments, then glue the pieces together.

For connecting plywood either end to end or at a corner, the simplest joint is a plain dado or shiplap (Fig. 14-7d). Glue at a dado joint and, at a shiplap joint, use glue together with either screws or nails driven into predrilled holes and countersunk.

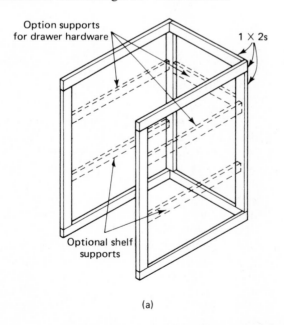

(a)

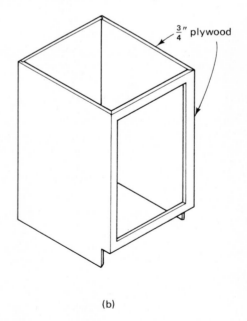

(b)

Fig. 14–6. You can build simple base cabinets using 1 × 2s for the frame and a skin of ¼″ sheet material (a), or cut the front and sides out of ¾″ plywood (b). Construction of wall cabinets is similar.

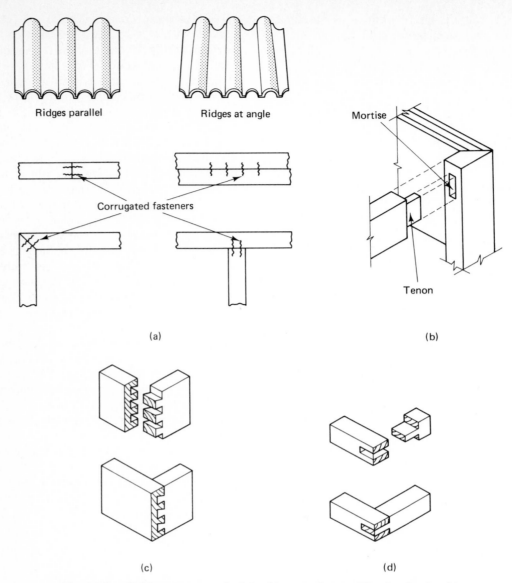

Ridges parallel

Ridges at angle

Corrugated fasteners

Mortise

Tenon

(a)

(b)

(c)

(d)

Fig. 14–7. Cabinet parts may be joined in several ways. The simplest is with corrugated fasteners (a). Far stronger but requiring power tools are mortise-and-tenon (b), dadoed (c), and shiplapped (d) joints.

Doors and Drawer Fronts. Hinged cabinet doors and the fronts of cabinet drawers may be overlaid, flush, or lipped. **Overlaid doors** (Fig. 14-8a) are the simplest to build, but also require the most material. They overlap an opening all around—about ½" at the top and sides, and about ⅛" below the shelf at the bottom. The frame prevents doors from closing too far.

Edges may be left square, but you can improve appearance and cut down on bruises from bumping into sharp edges in two ways. One is to round off vertical edges. Known as a **waterfall edge**, it eliminates sharp corners. The other method is to bevel edges inward. Doors must be cut slightly larger so that you have at least ⅜" overlap on the narrower side. But you eliminate the cost of knobs or pulls, which are needed on doors of other shapes. The beveled edges serve as finger grips for opening.

Flush fronts (Fig. 14-8b) lie in the same plane as the frame, and are inset into openings. Pulls are required. The doors must be cut about ⅛" smaller than the opening to allow for clearance and expansion. Cut them too large and they will bind; cut them too small and you leave ugly and uneven gaps around the edges. Both doors and drawers must be fitted with some kind of stop to prevent them from closing too far.

The **lipped front**, sometimes called an **inset front** (Fig. 14-8c), is the most difficult to make, but overcomes the disadvantages of the other two types. Fronts project ⅜" beyond the frame, and edges are rounded. Pulls are required. Edges of doors are dadoed ⅜" on all four sides, leaving ¼" lap and ⅛" clearance. Drawers supported by sliding hardware at their sides are cut the same way. Drawers that slide on bottom glides are dadoed ⅜" at the top and sides, but only ¼" at the bottom for zero clearance.

Chapter 14 / Designing A Better Kitchen

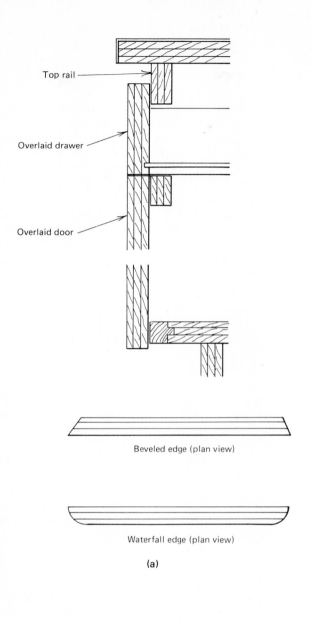

Top rail

Overlaid drawer

Overlaid door

Beveled edge (plan view)

Waterfall edge (plan view)

(a)

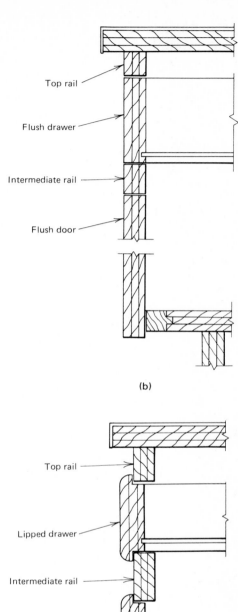

Top rail

Flush drawer

Intermediate rail

Flush door

(b)

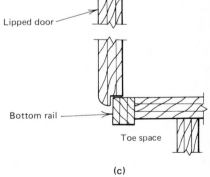

Top rail

Lipped drawer

Intermediate rail

Lipped door

Bottom rail

Toe space

(c)

Fig. 14-8. Drawer fronts and hinged cabinet doors may overlap the frame (a), lie flush with it (b), or be partly inset (c). These are sections through the front of a base cabinet.

Sliding doors are an alternative answer for some broad cabinets, especially those holding items that you don't use often but are small enough to move in and out of a restricted opening. **Sliding doors** operate in pairs, and expose slightly less than half the width of the cabinet when open (Fig. 14-9). They slide in parallel tracks at top and bottom. You can buy tracks of metal, plastic, or nylon, and simply cut them to length. Or you can make your own tracks by cutting grooves in hardwood boards. Doors should be cut from $\frac{1}{4}''$ thick material. Hardboard, either plain or perforated, is less subject to warp than plywood, but it wears more quickly. You operate the doors either with a recessed pull or a hole $1''$ in diameter drilled through each door.

Door Sizes. When you cut doors, drawer fronts, sides, and perhaps stiles and rails from sheet material such as plywood, it pays to work out sizes that can be cut with a minimum of waste. A standard sheet is $48'' \times 96''$, but you can sometimes buy sheets $48''$ wide and either $72''$ or $108''$ long. Allow about $\frac{3}{16}''$ for each saw kerf—the width of the cut.

Base cabinets have two standard depths: $24''$ in kitchens and utility areas, and $21''$ in bathrooms. Therefore, you can cut two sides each $23\frac{7}{8}''$ wide out of a standard width of plywood panel with no waste, or two $20\frac{7}{8}''$ sides with $6''$ of material left over for stiles. The grain of the plywood on its visible face should run vertically in *all* cabinet parts.

Wall cabinets are not standard in depth, but if you cut sides $11\frac{7}{8}''$ wide, you can get four pieces out of a width of plywood without waste. Economical dimensions for a combination cabinet-bookshelves are $15\frac{7}{8}''$ at the base and $11\frac{7}{8}''$ for the shelves.

Because doors use up a lot of plywood, establishing economical dimensions is worth your time. The maximum practical width of a door is a nominal $24''$, and minimum practical width for normal storage is $12''$. For openings 24 to $36''$ wide use a pair of doors. Wide openings make storage of large items easier than an opening bisected by a stile, but a clean appearance is more difficult to achieve. Where two doors meet, regardless of the type, they should gap no more than $\frac{1}{16}''$. Do not give meeting edges a beveled or waterfall cut. Either cut them square so that each door may be opened separately, or shiplap the edges. Shiplapping blocks any view into a cabinet, but sometimes you have to open one door to open the other.

Let's take one example to illustrate how to adjust door sizes. Suppose that you have a space $54''$ wide above a washer and dryer, and you plan to build a pair of cabinets each $27''$ wide. If you use $1\frac{1}{2}''$ stiles—the minimum width—you have an opening $24''$ wide for a single door. A flush door $23\frac{7}{8}''$ wide fits perfectly without any cutting waste. But a lipped door would have to be $24\frac{1}{2}''$ wide. An overlaid door with square or waterfall edges would have to be $25''$ wide, and an overlaid door with beveled edges would have to be about $25\frac{1}{2}''$ wide. All are uneconomical widths. What do you do? You cut the door $23\frac{7}{8}''$ wide, regardless of its type. Then you widen both stiles equally to narrow the opening: to $1\frac{3}{4}''$ with a lipped door, to $2''$ with one type of overlaid door, and to $2\frac{1}{4}''$ with an overlaid door

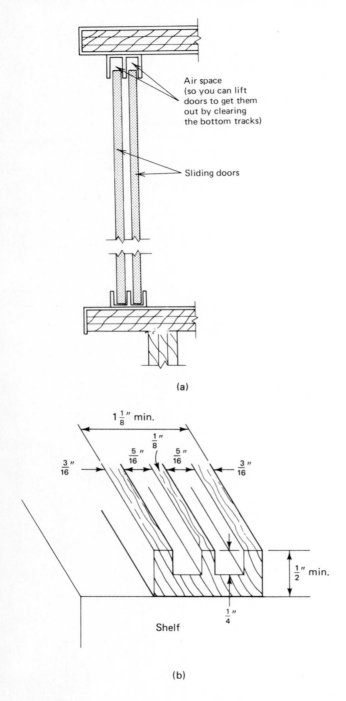

(a)

(b)

Fig. 14-9. Sliding doors are practical on some cabinets. The doors themselves are pieces of $\frac{1}{4}''$ sheet material that move either in manufactured tracks of metal or plastic (a) or in boards that you groove yourself (b).

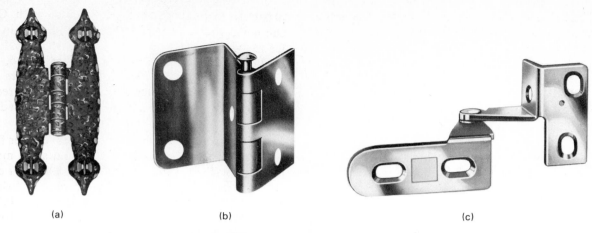

(a)   (b)   (c)

Fig. 14–10. Typical cabinet hinges: flush-mounted H hinge of hammered brass with a black enamel finish (a), pin-type offset hinge of polished bronze (b), and a semiconcealed hinge (c). (Courtesy Amerock Corporation.)

with beveled edges. Always cut out doors and drawer fronts first. You are bound to have some long strips left over from which to cut stiles.

Apply the same type of thinking to door heights, especially if you have a lot of doors of equal height. Keep in mind, however, that you can't adjust the widths of rails in a row of cabinets. All top and bottom rails should be the same height, usually 1½″ but no less.

Hardware. Door and drawer pulls are available in a wide variety of shapes and sizes, and in materials from wood to metal to ceramic. Select what you think will work best, look best, and blend well with door hinges.

The type of hinge depends on the type of door. On flush doors you must use flush hinges, mounted on either the front or back surface of the door. (Screws don't hold well in edges of plywood.) Several types are available. You mount one type (Fig. 14-10a) on the front of the door; the hinges are described by their shape—H, L, or strap. They are made of hammered brass, often have a black enamel finish baked on, are decorative as well as practical, and easy to install. Another common type, pin hinges (Fig. 14-10b), are like

ordinary door hinges but smaller. You mount them on the inside of the door and cabinet stile, and only the pins show outside. They come in bronze, brass, or chrome finishes, all either dull or polished. You mount the third type, invisible hinges (Fig. 14-10a), on the back of the door and stile. They do not show when the doors are closed.

Lipped and overlaid doors require offset hinges to overcome the difference between planes of the doors and their stiles. Offset hinges may be the pin type or semiconcealed. Semiconcealed hinges pivot in a slot cut in the door. The horizontal leaf is attached to the door and the vertical leaf to the stile.

To keep doors shut use either spring-loaded hinges that automatically swing the door closed when it is ajar, or else magnetic catches made for use with either a single door or pair of doors. One piece of the catch is a small metal box with magnetic leaves in it. You attach it to the underside of a center shelf or to the edge of a stile near its vertical midpoint. The other piece is a flat metal plate attached to the inside of the door; it closes against the box.

Think you can build your own cabinets? Then look in the next chapter for procedures.

15

Remodeling The Kitchen

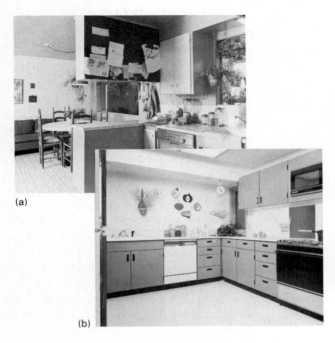

(a)

(b)

(c)

In many middle-aged homes kitchens are small and open to the only eating space available (a). As children age, however, neither space remains adequate. In this major remodeling an enlarged kitchen with continuous counters on three walls (b) occupies both the original kitchen and dining area. A new and more formal dining space (c) adds depth to one end of the living area, and is connected to the kitchen by a pass-through and snack bar. (Courtesy American Plywood Association.)

Planning a kitchen remodeling takes much time and thought, but organizing the job and scheduling the work are just as important. In all of the remodeling projects discussed so far a certain amount of disruption occurs, and you and your family can put up with it for a while. But when you interrupt kitchen operation, you close down the shop. You must plan every moment of the job to keep interruptions as short as possible and to as few as possible.

At the time you remove the first nail in the tearing out process, you must have

- A floor plan showing the kitchen layout, either your own or one you had drawn for you.

- Elevations showing cabinet arrangements on all walls. If you drew the plan and elevations, have a couple of prints made of each, and put the originals in a safe place.

- Posted the plan on a door or wall that won't change; you will refer to the plan frequently.

- Selected any new appliances and have a record of their dimensions and instructions for installation.

- Ordered, received, and safely stored any new windows and doors.

- Selected, ordered, and stored any new flooring material.

- Chosen any cabinets you plan to purchase rather

than build, and estimated the date you want them delivered.

- Estimated quantities of materials you need for ceilings, walls, and cabinets.
- Found a source for any countertop you intend to have made for you.
- Selected and consulted with any plumbing and/or electrical contractor whose services you intend to hire.
- Alerted the local gas company if you plan to make any change in gas lines or gas-burning appliances.
- Made arrangements for disposal of building materials you throw out, existing appliances you replace, and for temporary storage of any salvageable cabinets and countertops.
- Decided where to store temporarily the contents of existing cabinets.
- Assembled all tools needed, and put them in top physical and mechanical order.
- Applied for and posted a building permit.
- Worked out a sequence of operation and a schedule for each step.

SCHEDULING

For the purpose of working out a practical schedule, let's assume that you plan to gut the existing kitchen and remodel it completely. The work includes installing new windows, relocating an interior door, lowering the ceiling and adding new lighting, resurfacing cracked walls, replacing worn linoleum with vinyl tiles, installing new wall cabinets, increasing base cabinet storage and work surfaces, and buying all new appliances—sink, dishwasher, range, separate oven, disposal unit, and combination refrigerator-freezer. You will do all the work yourself except for wiring, plumbing, and gas piping.

A kitchen doesn't function very well with half its contents stored in another room, but it will function and you can survive. You can slide the old refrigerator into another area and plug it into another outlet until you have a spot for the new one. You can cook with small ovens or hotplates while the range is disconnected. You can operate without a dishwasher or disposal unit. But a kitchen is virtually out of business without a usable sink. So schedule your work so that you can pin down the day you have the new one installed, and make sure that your plumbing contractor will be available on that day.

This doesn't mean that you replace the sink first. That day comes late in the remodeling. Until you learn what problems you face unexpectedly when you start tearing out, and how fast the various phases of work move, you can't set a date. But set that date as soon as

possible so that you are without a usable sink for no more than a couple of hours.

Assemble cabinets first, ready to install as soon as the kitchen's surfaces are ready to accept them. Then tear out only as much wall area and as many cabinets as are in the way of installing the new windows and relocated door. Next, if you are resurfacing walls rather than installing new wall materials, cover exposed studs with pieces of wallboard of the same thickness as the existing wall material.

Then work from the ceiling downward. Cover counters and appliances with polyethylene to protect them while you remove all wall cabinets and other obstructions to a point at least 54″ below the ceiling. Work primarily on one wall at a time, although you may have to clear part of adjacent walls for working room. Build and install furring first. Surface the **soffit** (the underside) of furring, then apply the upper sheet of wall material horizontally. Finally, install the overhead cabinets on that wall.

With rare exceptions you can have the upper half of the kitchen operational before you touch the bottom half. Patch the existing ceiling or install a ceiling grid at this time. If the level of the grid is above the level of furring, add wall material to the **fascia** (the vertical face) of the furring. At this time, while space above the ceiling and behind walls is still accessible, you are ready for the electrician to wire to ceiling fixtures, lights in the soffits of furring and under wall cabinets, and the range hood. He can also install wall outlets and extend wiring to new locations for appliances.

Organization of work on the lower half of the room is more complicated. Finished flooring should extend from wall to wall, even under base cabinets. To find out the condition of existing flooring and where it stops, remove base trim at the floor and pry off the front of the cabinet's base. You will probably ruin it, but that can't be helped. If existing flooring is in good condition, leave the part under cabinets alone and resurface only the exposed floor area. If you must refloor from wall to wall, find the midpoint of the room. You must clear out all cabinets and appliances in half the room, lay new flooring, and surface the lower portion of walls before you can install new base cabinets. At this point you decide whether the sink will be in the first half you complete or the second half, and give your plumber a timetable.

By the time you have the upper half of the kitchen in order, you should have an idea of how long it takes you to complete the various tasks involved. To lay a new floor will take about as long as to install a ceiling grid. You lay underlayment from one corner of the room toward the opposite corner, but you lay floor tiles from the center of the room toward the walls. So hope that flooring under existing cabinets is in good condition. Then you can work on one wall at a time instead of one entire half of the room.

With your order of work established and a timetable tentatively worked out, you are ready to begin beautifying your kitchen. But before you begin to assemble cabinets, recheck every horizontal dimension to make sure that cabinets will fit the space available. One way to be sure is to mark locations on the existing wall. Remember to allow for the thickness of wall materials that may be different from existing thicknesses. If, for example, your present walls are ¾" lath and plaster and you plan to install ½" wallboard, you will gain ¼" in each corner. If, on the other hand, you plan to add a surface layer of ¼" wallboard over the existing wall, you will lose ¼" at each corner. Allow also for the width of trim around doors and windows, and for clearances beside appliances, if any.

ASSEMBLING CABINETS

After you have established and verified cabinet dimensions, cut base members first (Fig. 15-1b). Cut the front piece from the best finish material and let it extend the full width of the cabinet or, when you have a series of cabinets in a line, across the entire group. In cutting other base pieces remember to allow for joints and skins. Rabbet the ends of members where necessary.

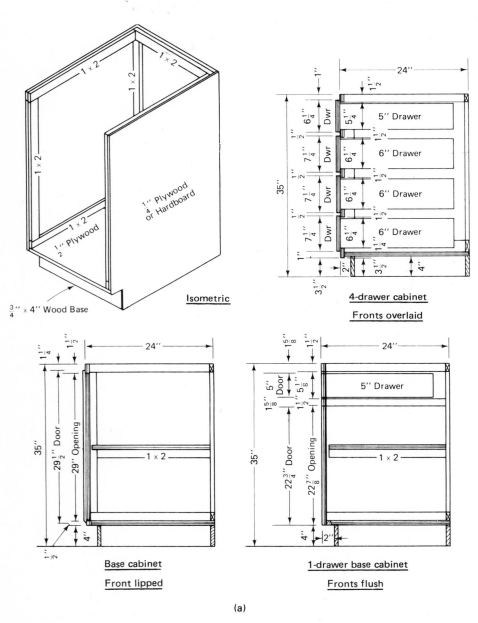

(a)

Fig. 15-1. Details of a base cabinet, with typical dimensions for the three common types (a). Note that the base (b on page 215) is narrower and shallower than the cabinet itself. Note also (a, isometric) how framing members relate in length to the materials they support, and how they meet at corners.

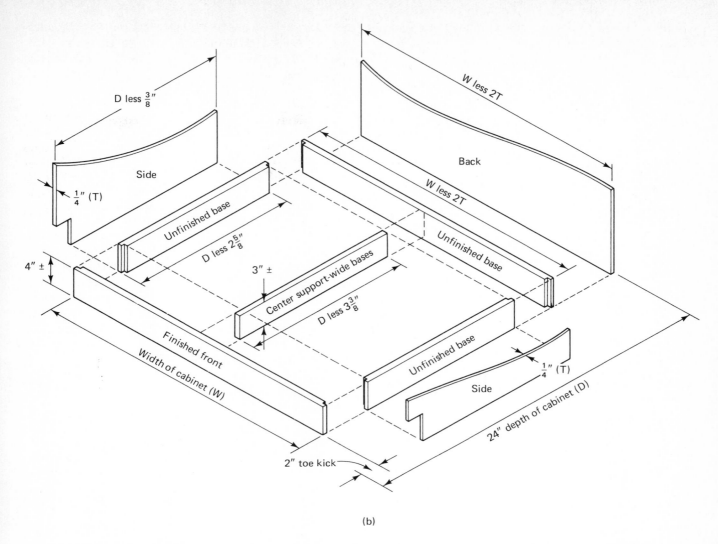

D less $\frac{3}{8}$"

Side

$\frac{1}{4}$" (T)

4" ±

Unfinished base

D less 2$\frac{5}{8}$"

3" ±

Center support-wide bases

D less 3$\frac{3}{8}$"

Finished front

Width of cabinet (W)

2" toe kick

W less 2T

Back

W less 2T

Unfinished base

Unfinished base

Side

$\frac{1}{4}$" (T)

24" depth of cabinet (D)

(b)

Assemble the base with glue and screws, making sure it is absolutely square at all corners. Include any cabinet-wide front piece; leave off an assembly-wide piece for the moment.

Base Cabinets

Cut the bottom shelf. It should fit the base flush at both rear corners, and overlap 1¼" at the front. If the cabinet has a bottom rail (see Fig. 14-8c), you can leave the front edge of the shelf unfinished; the rail will cover it. If the edge will be exposed when the door is open, add a ¾ × ¾" strip of finish material to cover it. Nail the shelf to the base, countersink the nails, and fill holes with wood putty.

From this point on the procedures are the same for cabinets with or without a base. Cut 1 × 2 framing members to length, allowing for butt joints (Fig. 15-1a, isometric). Then cut side panels, notching for the toekick. Next cut the back panel; side panels usually overlap the back panel.

With glue and corrugated fasteners assemble the three framing members that lie flat against side panels. Use clamps to keep corners square. After the glue dries,

attach the frame to the sides by fastening through the panels with screws 1" long. The frame will fit flush at the top and front edge, and be ¼" short at the back. It will be flush at the bottom if there is no base, and fall short the thickness of the bottom shelf if there is a base.

Again with glue and fasteners assemble the four framing members that lie flat against the back. Note in Fig. 15-1a, isometric, that the ends of horizontal members are inset ¾" from the sides of vertical members. Again check square, and clamp the assembly until the glue dries. Then attach the frame to the back as you did the sides. The frame will be flush with the back at the top and both sides, flush at the bottom without a base, or otherwise be short the height of the base and bottom shelf.

Before you put the sides and back together, cut and attach any 1 × 2s for special purposes. You need them to support shelves, for attachment of drawer hardware, and for stiffening the backs of wide cabinets.

Finally, fit the back and sides together and glue them wherever framing members meet. To assure square corners and add strength, cut small triangles of plywood or 1" boards and glue them in the top corners. If necessary to hold the cabinet frame square and plumb until the glue dries, tack cleats of scrap material across the top.

Wall Cabinets

You assemble wall cabinets like base cabinets except that framing members at the bottom should be good finish material (see Fig. 15-6). They will be exposed to view. Before you attach the back to the sides, cut the bottom shelf. Its dimensions are the same as the overall dimensions of the frame, but you have to notch at all four corners to fit around vertical framing members.

Other shelves in wall cabinets are usually fixed, resting on 1 × 2 framing members. If you prefer adjustable shelves, either attach metal standards to sidewalls, or drill holes for supporting clips. **Standards** are slotted metal strips installed in sets of four. Clips in the slots support the corners of shelves. With adjustable shelves, however, the sides of cabinets should be at least ½"-thick plywood. Thinner sides won't hold the screws for attaching standards or provide the depth of hole for clips.

Fixed shelves in manufactured wall cabinets are fixed at the midpoint of vertical height. In your kitchen this may or may not be the best location. To customize your cabinets, establish what will be stored in each cabinet, and allow 1" clearance between the underside of the shelf above and the tops of glasses, a stack of dishes, cereal boxes, or bottles.

Cabinet Fronts

When you designed each cabinet you worked out the widths of stiles and rails. From materials of these widths cut stiles and rails to length, and shape the ends of both for the joints you use. Assemble the stiles and rails and clamp them together until the glue dries.

Then measure the openings for doors and drawers to verify that their dimensions are what you planned. Cut doors and drawer fronts to size, and shape their edges as necessary. When the glue in the front has dried, remove the clamps, lay the front face up on the floor, and try the doors and drawer fronts for size. When the fit is good, attach the cabinet front to its frame with glue and finishing nails. Countersink the nails and fill holes with wood putty.

Cabinet Doors

It is easier to hang cabinet doors before you install the cabinet, but it is easier to install the cabinet without the doors on. The logical compromise is to mark the locations of hinges and knobs before you install the cabinet, attach the hardware to the doors at your convenience, then hang the doors after you put up the cabinet.

An exact location for hinges and knobs isn't critical in a single cabinet. But if you have a row of them, be consistent. The most common location for hinges is 3" from the top and bottom of cabinet doors, whatever their type. Therefore in a row of wall cabinets all top hinges are at the same level, and bottom hinges go up or down as the heights of cabinets vary. In a row of base cabinets all bottom hinges are at the same level and upper hinge locations vary, depending on whether the cabinet has a drawer.

To locate door knobs draw a line at a 45° angle from the upper corner of doors in base cabinets, and from the lower corner of doors in wall cabinets (Fig. 15-2). Measure 2" along the line and drill a hole at that point for a knob. If you decide on pulls instead of knobs, use this hole for the bottom screw on wall cabinets and for the top screw on base cabinets. Install pulls vertically on doors and horizontally on drawers. Center pulls from top to bottom on all drawers up to 8" deep. On deep drawers locate them 3 to 4" from the top of the drawer front. On drawers up to 16" wide a single centered pull or knob is adequate. On wider drawers install a pair, each placed about 3" from the sides of the front.

To mark the locations of screw holes for hinges,

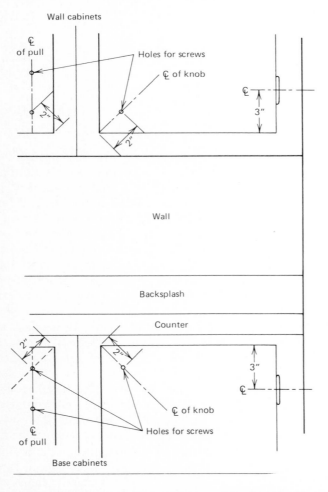

Fig. 15-2. Where to locate hinges and knobs of wall cabinets (top) and base cabinets (bottom).

use the template provided by the hardware manufacturer. Make starter holes with an awl or screw starter. When you finally hang the doors, attach the hinges to the stile with a single screw and test the fit. When the fit is good, make the remaining starter holes and drive all screws home. Use the manufacturer's template to locate magnetic catches.

Drawers

A drawer is difficult to build with ordinary hand tools, but easy if you have a router and a variety of bits. Drawer parts are stock items at most lumberyards. You determine the dimensions of each drawer, how you will join the parts, and how the drawer will slide.

Method of Operation. The simplest but least durable guide is a runner of smooth wood or plywood attached at the front to a rail, at the back to a horizontal framing member, and centered in the drawer opening (Fig. 15-3a). To keep the drawer in line during operation, notch its back to ride on the guide, or attach a grooved block on the drawer bottom to ride on the guide, or do both. The block fits toward the back of the drawer and hits against the rail to prevent the drawer from coming all the way out.

For smoother operation you can buy hardware consisting of metal tracks, nylon rollers, and stops (Fig. 15-3b). Diagrams with the hardware show how and where to install the parts. The track may be below, above, or beside the drawer, and you must select the hardware in advance so that you provide the necessary clearance and points of attachment for the tracks.

Dimensions. Excluding its front, a good drawer has exterior dimensions $\frac{1}{8}$″ less than the width of its opening and $\frac{3}{4}$″ less than its height. A close fit at the sides prevents the drawer from wiggling on its track, and the extra clearance permits you to remove the drawer for cleaning. Except for storage of special items of odd dimensions, exterior width should be no more than $20\frac{3}{4}$″ and no less than $11\frac{1}{4}$″. Minimum practical depth is 4″ and maximum depth 8″. In a stack of four drawers the top drawer is the shallowest, the next two the same size or slightly deeper than the top drawer, and the bottom drawer the deepest. The sizes in Fig. 15-1a are typical.

When you determine the length of a drawer, leave at least 2″ clearance between its back and the inside of the cabinet frame to allow for hardware. The ultimate length depends then on the type of front—lipped, flush, or overlaid—and the method of assembly.

Materials. Stock drawer sides and backs are $\frac{1}{2}$″ boards of various widths and planed smooth. If you cut your own, use 1″ boards or $\frac{3}{8}$″ or $\frac{1}{2}$″ plywood. For bottoms use either $\frac{1}{4}$″ plywood or hardboard.

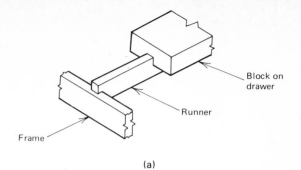

(a)

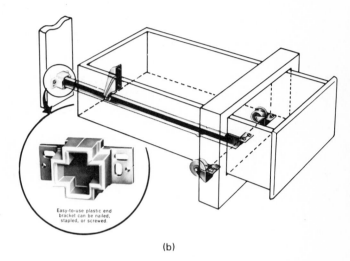

Easy-to-use plastic end bracket can be nailed, stapled, or screwed.

(b)

Fig. 15-3. You can make your own drawer runners out of wood, but drawers will operate more smoothly and for a longer time with manufactured hardware. (Photo courtesy Amerock Corporation.)

Joints. Drawer sides may be attached to backs in several ways. The simplest is a lapped joint (Fig. 15-4a). Stronger but more difficult to cut are a tongued lapped joint (Fig. 15-4b), mortise-and-tenon, and dovetail dado (Fig. 15-4c). The strongest joint is a continuous dovetail (Fig. 15-4d) cut with a dovetail attachment on a power router.

Fronts may also be attached in several ways. A continuous dovetail works well only with flush fronts. Lapped and tongued lapped joints work well with lipped fronts. All types shown in fig. 15-4 may be used with overlaid fronts. Another alternative usable with any type of front is a double front. You cut an inner front just like a drawer back, add the bottom and sides to form a box, then attach the inner front to the exposed front with screws.

Assembly. Cut the back first to the width of the drawer opening less clearance. Then cut the sides to length, allowing for the depth of joint of your selection at both ends. From the bottom of the back and both sides measure up $\frac{3}{8}$″ to $\frac{1}{2}$″, and mark the location and thickness of the groove for the drawer bottom. Rout the groove for a tight fit to a depth of about $\frac{1}{4}$″.

If you have not already done so, cut the drawer

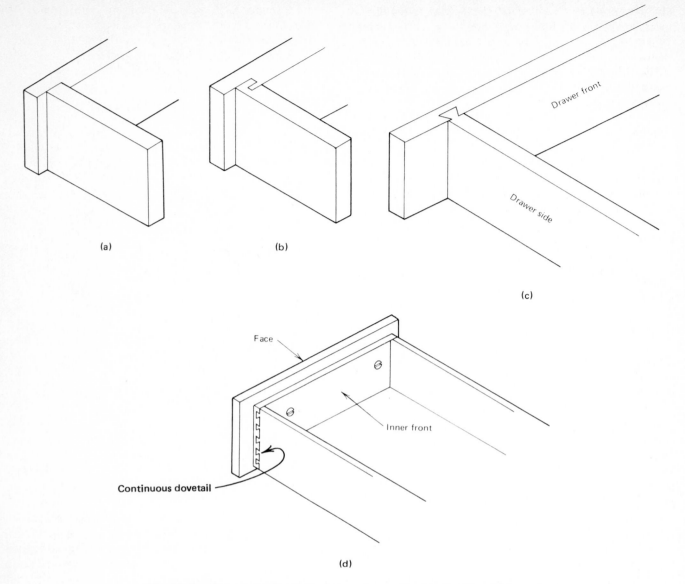

(a)

(b)

(c)

Drawer front

Drawer side

Face

Inner front

Continuous dovetail

(d)

Fig. 15-4. Four methods of attaching a drawer front to its sides: (a) lapped, (b) tongued lapped joint, (c) dovetail dado, and (d) continuous dovetail. Backs and sides may be attached in lapped joints or in a continuous dovetail, as used (d) to attach the inner front to drawer sides.

front to size and shape. Then mark the location of the groove for the bottom. It will seldom be at the same height as in drawer sides and back, but some ½ to ¾" higher. The exact location depends on the type of drawer guide, its location, and the type of drawer front.

Next cut dovetails (or whatever joint you choose) in the backs and sides of drawers where they meet. Assemble the pieces but do not glue. Make sure that all corners are square, then use the assembly to mark the locations of cuts in the front to accept the sides. Fit the front on the sides and check your overall dimensions to make sure that the drawer will fit its opening with planned clearances.

Next measure the size of the drawer bottom from

inside of groove to inside of groove, and cut it for a tight fit. Then spread glue in the joints where sides meet the front, and in the grooves in the front and both sides. Don't spare the glue. Glue the front to the sides, and slide the bottom into place in the three grooves. Spread glue in the open joints in the sides and back and in the groove in the back, and fit the back in position. Check joints for a tight fit and verify the square of all corners. Finally, use clamps to hold the parts tight until the glue dries. No other fastening is necessary.

Following the hardware manufacturer's directions, install drawer slides and guides in the cabinet. Make sure that all screws are tight so that hardware won't work its way loose over years of use. Install matching hardware on the drawer itself according to instructions, and again test for tightness. Fit the drawer in place and test its operation. It should move easily, not bind at the opening, and open in a straight line with little sideways movement at any open position. Make sure that the drawer closes tight, and won't come all the way out when you open it.

Then try the same tests with a couple of bricks or similar weight in the drawer. Make any adjustments; usually, it is the location of the hardware that needs to be altered slightly. If the drawer seems to drag on the rail below or is loose in its opening, install a nylon glide in the lower corners of the opening. When the drawer works smoothly, add the knob or pull, remove the drawer, and set it aside until you install the base cabinet. If you have a number of drawers of the same size, mark them on the bottom so that you reinsert each draw in the opening to which you fitted it.

INSTALLING FURRING

When you need to furr down over a wall cabinet, build a simple framework of 2 × 4s (Fig. 15-5a), then cover all surfaces with a finish wall material. Build the furring so that it projects 1½ to 2″ beyond the face of the cabinet. In Fig. 15-5 all long horizontal pieces are the same

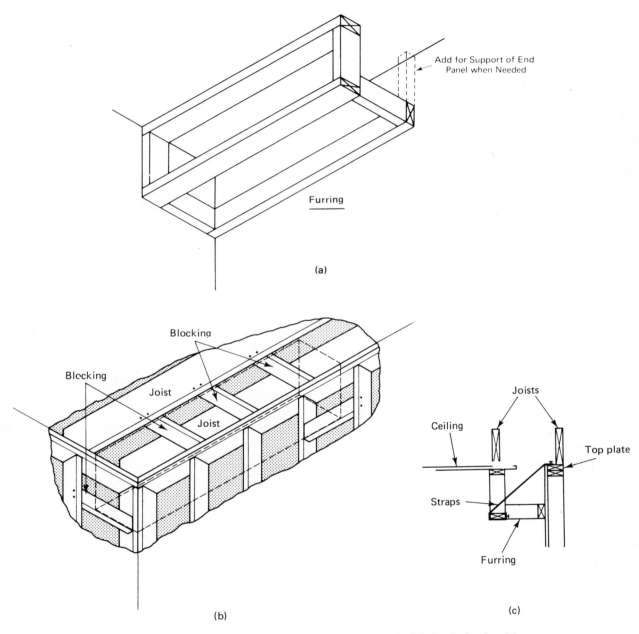

Fig. 15-5. To lower the ceiling above wall cabinets, build simple furring (a). Attach furring to blocking between joists (b) or to the joists themselves when you have access to them. Otherwise, tie furring to existing structure with metal strapping (c).

length, and all short horizontal pieces are the same length. Vertical members are the same length, too, except for a support that you may need at an exposed end for finish material.

Assemble the vertical framework and horizontal framework separately, then crossnail the frames together. Raise the assembly into position, and mark the height of the bottom of the frame in a corner of the room. Next, snap level chalklines on the two walls at the height of the bottom of the furring.

Furring must be nailed into structural members. So locate the studs in the wall behind the furring, and determine which way ceiling joists run. If they run at right angles to the cabinet, mark their locations. Then attach the furring with 12d nails driven upward into joists and horizontally into studs.

When Joists and Furring Run Parallel

If joists run the same direction as the cabinet, hold the framework along the chalklines on the walls and against the ceiling. Then draw along the inner edge of the long top member from the wall to the point where it meets the outside vertical (Fig. 15-5b). Remove the framework and, with a square, draw a line from the end of this line to the wall at right angles to both.

Nailing into studs alone won't support the furring, so you must also support it from above. If you can get at ceiling joists from above, locate the two joists that flank the furring. Cut 2 × 4 blocking to fit between them, space the blocks 16" on centers, and nail them through joists flush with their undersides. If ceiling joists aren't accessible, cut holes in the ceiling large enough so that you can nail perforated metal strapping to a top plate or joist. Cut the holes about 4 to 6" from each end of the furring, and at the midpoint of any furring more than 48" long. Bend the straps around the bottom chord of the furring (Fig. 15-5c), and nail them on the back side.

If you are resurfacing walls and can get at existing studs, also add blocking there. You need a block to support the end of the furring framework. You need blocking just below furring for attaching the tops of wall cabinets. You need blocks between studs to support the bottoms of wall cabinets (see Fig. 15-6). And you need blocking to attach the tops of base cabinets (see Fig. 15-8).

DUCT FOR VENTILATING

Install any duct that runs from a range hood to an outside wall between ceiling joists or in furring now, while you can still get at the space. Follow the manufacturer's instructions as to size of duct and where it attaches to the hood. If the duct goes through the wall below ceiling level, install only the section that goes through the wall. Cut holes in the back and bottom of the cabinet for the next section, and install this section after the cabinet is in place.

Wait to install the hood itself, whether connected to a duct or ductless, until after the range is in place. Installation may be a bit awkward, but at least you won't hit your head on the edges of the hood while you are working below it. Similarly, wait to install a vent fan in an outside wall until you have removed any old base cabinets but before you install new ones. Then you have full and easy access to the wall in which you place the fan.

SURFACING THE UPPER WALL

Wall materials in a kitchen should be fire resistant, and the best material for the amateur to apply is gypsum wallboard. For covering old wall surfaces order ¼" wallboard. It is manufactured in a single width of 48" and in lengths of 8' and 10'. It should be applied *only* over a solid surface, and never directly to studs or joists, or to an existing wall surface in poor condition.

Over exposed studs and joists use ½" gypsum wallboard. It also comes in a single width of 4', but in lengths of 6', 8', 9', 10', 12', 14', and sometimes 16'.

Both types of wallboard should be applied horizontally in a kitchen. Order the longest length that will cover with a minimum of vertical joints. Suppose that your kitchen is 13' × 15'. If you are applying ¼" wallboard, order four pieces 8' long and eight pieces 10' long. On the short walls use an 8' length and half a 10' length on the upper half of the wall, and an 8' length and the other half of the 10' length on the lower half, offsetting the joints. Use 1½ 10' lengths on each half of the longer walls, again offsetting the joints.

If you are applying ½" wallboard, order 14' lengths for the shorter walls, and either 8' or 10' lengths for the longer walls, depending on where studs fall. End joints must be centered on studs. Stud location is not critical with ¼" wallboard.

Detailed procedures for cutting and applying wallboard and finishing joints are covered in Chapter 19. Apply wallboard to horizontal surfaces first—ceilings and soffits of furring. Then cover vertical surfaces. Do not finish joints that will be concealed by cabinets.

INSTALLING WALL CABINETS

Whether you build or buy wall cabinets, the procedure for installing them is the same. Begin by measuring the heights of all cabinets. If there is any slight difference, work with the greatest height. Then measure down this height from the soffit of the furring (or from the ceiling if you don't furr), and snap a level chalk line at that point along the wall. If you have cabinets of more than one basic height, snap chalk lines to mark the bottom edges of other heights, too. Use your carpenter's level to make sure that all lines are level, even if the ceiling and floor are not.

Next mark the widths of all cabinets along the chalk lines as a setting guide. Allow a slight gap—about ⅛″—at corners unless the cabinets completely fill the wall or unless you have a corner cabinet that extends along an adjacent wall. Gap base cabinets the same way so that your cabinets line up vertically.

Attach wall cabinets at three points: upward into furring just inside the top rail, horizontally through the frame at the top into blocking, and horizontally through the bottom shelf support into blocking (Fig. 15-6). If you don't have blocking and aren't sure of hitting a stud, attach cabinets with screws into wall anchors inserted in the wall's surface material.

Predrill holes in cabinets for all screws, and use the holes to mark the locations of any anchors. Center the holes in cabinet framing members about 3″ from the ends of the cabinet and no more than 16″ between. Drill holes into walls at a slight angle to give you room to operate a ratchet screwdriver.

Setting wall cabinets takes two people, one to hold the cabinets in position and the other to drive screws home. You can hang cabinets one at a time, but it is easier to assemble a group on the floor and install an entire assembly. Clamp cabinets together so that they line up at stiles and the bottom rail. Then attach them to each other with screws driven into predrilled holes at the four corners. By preassembling you assure that cabinets will line up properly at the bottom.

Begin installation in a corner. If you have a corner cabinet, install it first and by itself, setting it on the horizontal chalk lines and vertical marks. This cabinet is your guide to locating abutting cabinets and must be set straight. If you have no corner cabinet, but two cabinets meet at a corner, start there. If you have a straight run of cabinets, start at either corner. Most right-handed people find it easier to work from left to right, and left-handed people the opposite way.

If you need a filler strip to fit your kitchen's dimensions, as with manufactured cabinets, gap for it in a corner. With a complete wall of cabinets, leave gaps of identical width at both ends, and insert fillers of equal width for symmetrical appearance. Because the gaps may not be constant in width, cut filler strips only after the cabinets are in place. Cut for a friction-tight fit.

With your helper holding the cabinet on its marks and firmly against the wall and furred soffit, drive home the top screws at the back of the cabinet. Use flat-head wood screws (FHWS) long enough to go at least 1″ into blocking or anchors. These screws will hold the cabinet in place while you check it for level and plumb. Then drive screws upward into the soffit. If you have a gap over any cabinet, as you may have with an uneven ceiling or cabinets of slightly different heights, fit a shim in the opening and drive the screw through it. Cut shims

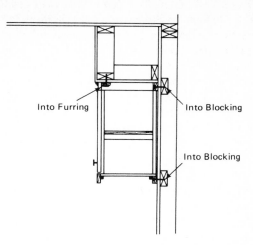

Fig. 15-6. Where and how to attach wall cabinets to furring and blocking in walls.

flush with a sharp knife. Then drive the last set of screws into the wall, and test the installation by tugging on it.

When all wall cabinets are in place, cut and fit filler strips. Hold them in place with long, thin screws driven through cabinet stiles. Then fill all screw holes with matching putty stick or wood putty. It is easier to do this now while you can still reach wall cabinets without stretching over base cabinets. But if there is any doubt about the work you have done so far, such as alignment of base cabinets, hold off until you have every cabinet in place.

Complete Wall Cabinets

You still have three steps to complete. First, cut shelves to size, notching where necessary to fit around frames. Shelves should gap ⅟₁₆ to ⅛″ at the sides, ⅛″ at the front, and none at the back. In cutting shelves, remember to allow for any finishing strip on the front edge.

With shelves in place, hang the doors. Insert one screw in each hinge and drive it in. Then test the swing before attaching the remaining screws. Add any magnetic closers according to their manufacturer's instructions.

As a final step install trim at the ceiling line. Use a small cove molding, and attach it with brads driven upward into the furring through the cove's concave surface. Thus the trim will remain tight against the furring, even if cabinets drop slightly under the weight of their contents. Miter at inside and outside corners. If you have to splice a long piece, set both pieces in a miter box, overlap them slightly, and cut them simultaneously for an exact fit. Wall cabinets are now ready for use.

The Lower Wall

Compared to installation of wall cabinets, setting base cabinets goes slowly. Whether you apply new wall materials or resurface, you have a horizontal joint and corners to finish. You have appliances and plumbing fixtures to disconnect and reconnect. You may have flooring and underlayment to install. So be prepared to have your kitchen disrupted for a week at the least.

Where you start depends on your kitchen layout. It's usually preferable to start on a wall with no corner cabinets, so that you can get the feel of the job and its problems before you tackle cabinets and a countertop that touch two walls. If possible, leave the wall with the sink until last.

Before you tear out anything, mark on the floor the corners of all base cabinets, as you did with wall cabinets. From these marks determine the exact size of the countertop. More on dimensions in a moment.

BUILDING COUNTERTOPS

You can order countertops built for an exact fit. Most dealers in manufactured cabinets have a source for countertops, and their package price includes them. If you build your own cabinets, you can have the countertops built at a local cabinet shop, ready to install. Just give your supplier the overall dimensions, the type of edge you want, and the amount of backsplash.

Building your own countertops is not difficult, although you won't be able to duplicate the rounded edges of professionally built tops. Cut the base out of ¾″ plywood or particleboard, and apply plastic laminate to it. The backsplash may be built as part of the countertop, which is the better way when walls are straight and corners of the room are square. Otherwise, build the backsplash as a separate unit for best appearance against uneven walls.

You can finish edges in three ways. The simplest is with a metal molding attached with small nails or screws provided with the molding (Fig. 15-7a). No special tools are required. Another way is with a plastic tee molding that fits into a slot which you cut in the edge of the countertop (Fig. 15-7b); you fasten it with brads driven upward. For this edge you need a tool for cutting the slot. The third way, a self-edge, is the most professional and most attractive (Fig. 15-7c). To the edge of the countertop you add a 1 × 2 or strip of base material, and cover it with the same plastic laminate used on the countertop itself. For this type of edge you need a router (inset) for finishing the joint in the laminate.

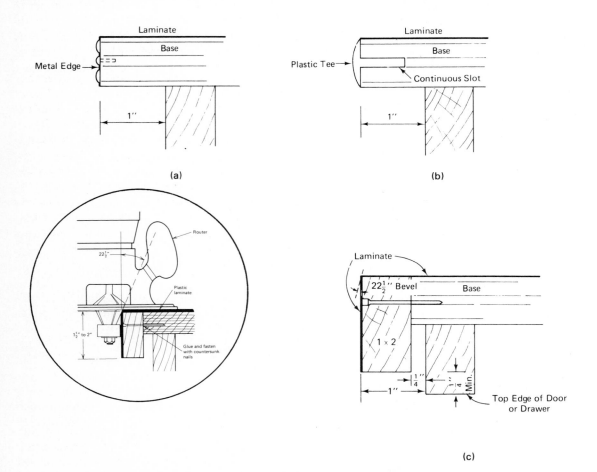

Fig. 15-7. The edge of a countertop may be finished with a metal molding (a), plastic drive-on strip (b), or plastic laminate (c) that matches the countertop itself. The inset shows how to bevel a laminated edge with a router.

The Base

The standard overall dimension from a wall to the front edge of a countertop is 25″. With a separate backsplash and drive-on edge, the width of the base is a full 25″. With a separate backsplash and self-edge, the base is 24¼″. With an attached backsplash and drive-on molding, the base is also 24¼″. With an attached backsplash and a self-edge, the base is 23½″. Only with this latter combination can you cut two widths of countertop out of a single width of base material. This may therefore be the most economical use of materials. On the other hand, if you also cut backsplashes and the bases for edging out of base material (you can use a ripped 1 × 6 or a 1 × 2 as alternatives), you will use about 32″ of a 48″ width of base, and have enough left over for shelving up to 16″ wide. The point is, lay out your countertops on paper before you cut any pieces to assure the most economical use of your base material.

Overhangs. A countertop should overhang the front and any exposed side of a base cabinet by 1″. Beside a refrigerator or freezer cut the overhang to ¾″ if self-edged, or to ½″ with a drive-on edge. This dimension should not be included in the clearance required for moving the appliance in and out. Beside any appliance that is the same height as a counter, such as a freestanding range, allow no more than ⅛″ and leave the edge unfinished.

Layout. The ideal countertop has no joints, and the best planned kitchen is designed so that appliances form natural end points no more than 8′ apart. Even L-shaped sections should be cut in one piece. When a seam in the base is necessary, locate the butt joint between side frames of a small base cabinet for maximum support.

Lay out your countertops on the base material carefully and accurately. Check the square of the room's corners, and allow for any deviations. The base should fit as tightly as possible against all walls along its entire length. After you cut, test the fit. This may be difficult with existing cabinets and counters in the way, but a good corner fit is vital.

Cutting. The surface to which you apply plastic laminate must be smooth, dry, and free of any foreign material such as grease. Fill all holes and gouges with crack filler, let it harden, then sand the surface lightly until smooth. Wipe away wood dust and let the surface dry thoroughly. If you plan a drive-on edge, sand the edges, too.

Next cut the backsplash and edge pieces. Backsplashes extend from 4 to 5½″ above the counter. Governing factors are the height of any window sill and ceiling height. The shorter dimension is almost standard in today's homes, but in a kitchen with a high ceiling a

higher backsplash usually looks better. Measure the height of a separate backsplash from the top of the countertop's base; measure the height of an attached backsplash from the bottom of the base.

The base for a self-edge is 1½ to 2″ high, but must clear the tops of doors and drawers in base cabinets by at least ¼″. As a general guide, cut edges 1½″ high with a 4″ backsplash and 2″ high with a higher backsplash.

With glue and finishing nails spaced every 6 to 8″, attach any edge strips to the base. Make sure that the top edge and the surface of the base are flush at all points. Countersink the nails, fill the holes, and sand smooth. Repeat this process for any attached backsplash.

Laminate

Plastic laminate comes in sheets no more than ₁⁄₁₆″ thick, in lengths of 5′, 6′, 7′, 8′, 10′, and 12′, and in nominal widths of 24″, 30″, 36″, and 48″. Most manufacturers make the sheets wider than nominal, however, so that you can cut two 25″ widths out of a single 48″-wide sheet. Laminate comes in a wide range of colors and patterns to suit your new color scheme.

Unsupported, laminate is very brittle and chips easily. Once you bond it properly to the countertop base, however, it can withstand boiling water, temperatures up to 275°F, and considerable impact without damage. A good bond is the key.

Cut laminate to dimensions ⅛ and ¼″ greater than the dimensions of the base so that it overlaps at all edges except against an attached backsplash. Avoid joints if at all possible. Cut so that one piece of laminate covers the entire base without a seam. If you must seam, seam only at the edge of a countertop range or at a 45° angle in a corner. Do not seam at a sink; the seam won't be visible, but moisture will seep into a poor joint and cause delamination. Equally, important, do not place a seam in laminate within 12″ of any joint in the countertop base.

Cutting. You can cut plastic laminate in two ways. With either method you must provide support during cutting as close as possible to the cut edge. The best cutting tool is a router, and you cut with the decorative side of the laminate *face down*. Less effective alternates are a fine-toothed handsaw or metal shears; with them you cut with the decorative side *face up*. No other tool will do the job without danger of ruining the tool or the laminate or both.

Adhesive

Two adhesives will bond laminate to its base satisfactorily. Slow-setting glues give you time to correct a mistake; but you must clamp the laminate to the base until the glue dries, and a uniform bond is rather difficult to achieve. Contact cement provides an excellent bond, but requires great care. Correcting a mistake is almost impossible. The best advice? Use contact cement, but follow instructions exactly.

Laminate the Edge

Apply laminate to any self-edge first. With a brush apply two coats of contact cement to the base for the edge, and a single coat to the back of the strip of laminate. Let the coats dry until they are slightly tacky to the touch; information on the can's label tells you how much time to allow. Then carefully position the strip of laminate flush with the bottom edge of its base, with only the two edges making contact. Now press the laminate in place. Once the two coats of cement touch, you won't be able to budge the laminate. So accuracy in placement is critical. To assure a tight bond, place a wood block flat across the laminate and tap it with a hammer. Repeat this step as you move the block over the entire surface. Finally, use a router to trim excess laminate flush with the top of the countertop's base, and a file to smooth the edge. Always file toward the laminate, never toward you, to avoid breaking the bond.

When an edge turns an inside corner, set the first strip of laminate flush in the corner, and let the second strip overlap it. Treat an outside corner in the same way as the top edge of the self-edge.

Laminate the Top

Because you are working with wide sheets of laminate, you take an extra step in finishing the countertop itself. As with edge laminate, apply two coats of contact cement to the countertop base and one coat to the laminate. This time, however, use a roller or notched spreader instead of a brush. Let both coats dry until tacky.

Next cover all the cement on the base with strips of brown wrapping paper 18 to 24″ wide. Let the pieces overlap where they meet. Then position the laminate on the paper so that it overlaps at edges but butts against the rear edge or backsplash. The paper lets you slide the laminate until you have it positioned correctly.

Then, starting at one end, gently pull out the first piece of paper a few inches at a time, while simultaneously pressing the laminate into the uncovered cement. This is the critical time, because you must not knock the laminate out of position when you move the paper. Continue this process down the entire length of counter. Then assure good bond by pressing on the laminate with a hand roller, working from the center of the countertop toward both edges. Press hard so that you bond every square inch of laminate to its base. Then wipe off any excess adhesive.

Under most humidity conditions you have about two hours to complete the job from first application of cement to final bond. The label on the contact cement can tells you how much open time you have.

Trimming. If you apply a drive-on edge, trim the laminate flush with the edge of the countertop base. With a self-edge trim the meeting edges of laminate with a router and a bevel trimming bit set at $22\frac{1}{2}°$ (see inset, Fig. 15-7). As an alternative, use a block plane and hand file, but file only on the downward stroke.

Do not apply laminate yet to the backsplash. Whether it is part of the countertop or a separate piece, it must be nailed to the wall first.

Before cutting a hole for a sink or countertop range, let contact cement set for at least four hours. Then with a grease pencil or chalk line, mark the centerlines of the hole. Manufacturers of sinks and ranges provide a template to guide you. If you are reusing existing equipment, take off existing measurements. The usual clearance is $\frac{1}{16}″$ on all sides. Drill a hole large enough to accept a saber saw, then cut to and around the edge of the outline. Do not install the sink or range until you have the countertop in place.

SURFACING THE LOWER WALL

With base cabinets and countertops ready to install quickly, clear the area of existing cabinets, countertops, and appliances. Remove any wall material that you plan to replace, and any flooring or underlayment that must be replaced in that half of the room. Clean the area thoroughly.

Install wall materials first, carrying them to about $\frac{3}{4}″$ above the finished floor line, not the subfloor. Then apply the first of three coats of joint cement at seams (see Chapter 19 for details). While this coat is drying, find the centerlines of the room and snap chalklines at these points on the floor. Carry the lines up the walls a short distance for future guidance.

FINISHING THE FLOOR

If underlayment is required, lay the first piece in a corner, trimming it to fit against the walls. How much you lay at this time depends on the kitchen layout and dimensions. Since you lay new flooring from the crossed centerlines, you must apply underlayment at least to this point. Underlayment should be laid at right angles to rectangular subflooring. Over diagonal subflooring you may lay it whichever direction is the most practical for conditions. Joints in underlayment must never fall at the same point as joints in subflooring; they will telegraph through your finished flooring. Also, joints in rows of underlayment should be staggered for the same reason.

Lay underlayment past the midpoint of the room, even if edges remain temporarily staggered. Instructions are covered in Chapter 20. Then resnap new chalklines on the underlayment to mark the midpoints of the room. Now, before you go on to the next step, is a good time to apply the second coat of joint cement on walls.

The procedures for finding the starting point for laying floor tiles, applying adhesive, and setting the tiles are also covered in Chapter 20. In spreading mastic, be careful not to go beyond the starting point of the first line of tiles. As soon as you lay the first row, scrape off any excess mastic. If you don't, you will have a high spot when you lay tiles in the remainder of the room.

SETTING BASE CABINETS

Let mastic set overnight before you walk on or work above freshly laid tiles. The next morning apply the final coat of joint cement to the seams in new wallboard. Then mark on the floor the locations of base cabinets, aiming for tight fits. After marking, recheck the overall dimension on the floor with the length of your countertop to make sure that you have the planned overhang at ends and appliances.

Next, snap a chalk line on the floor marking the edge of the toekick. Then, starting at a corner, carry each base cabinet to its location and set it gently on its marks. Check first for fit at corners and at openings for appliances. Then check the level not only from side to side but from front to back. If the top edges of cabinets don't quite line up, mark on the wall the height of the tallest cabinet, and snap a level chalk line through that point. Then remove each cabinet one by one, add shims at out-of-line corners, and reposition and relevel the cabinets. Only when all fronts line up and tops are level can you install the first cabinet.

Like wall cabinets, base cabinets are attached at three points (Fig. 15-8). But you attach them at only two points until all are positioned. Through holes predrilled through cabinet frames drive screws upward at about a 30° angle into blocking or anchors behind the upper frame at the back, then downward at a 30° angle just above the bottom shelf.

Align, level, and install each succeeding cabinet.

Then clamp pairs of cabinets together and connect them with wood screws driven into predrilled holes in the stiles. Wall cabinets may be connected before installation. Base cabinets should not.

Finally, drive the last set of screws at a 45° to 60° angle through the base into the floor. If you have shimmed along the base line, screw through the shims, then trim them flush with the base. Later, cover the seam with base shoe or a manufactured cove base.

INSTALLING COUNTERTOPS

In the four corners of each base cabinet, predrill a hole for a screw upward through each triangular brace. The countertop rests on the level base cabinets, and is attached at four points to each cabinet. If there is no cabinet under any part of your countertop, such as above a revolving corner storage unit or a kneehole of a desk, nail 1 × 2s to the wall with their tops level with the tops of base cabinets. When a pair of 1 × 2s forms a corner support, add a triangular block as in base cabinets, and predrill it for a screw to hold down the corner of the countertop.

Now hold your breath and try the countertop for a final fit. Set it—don't drag it—about 4″ from the back wall. Then gently but steadily push it into place against the wall and see what problems you face. There is still time to correct them.

The surest way to avoid problems is to measure and cut your countertops after you install base cabinets. Then you know exactly the size you need. You save a day to a day and a half of kitchen downtime by building countertops in advance, but you risk an error in calculations. That's why you are better off building backsplashes separately. They can compensate for errors of as much as ⅜″.

The important point of fit is at the front edge of the counter. Establish the 1″ overhang along the length

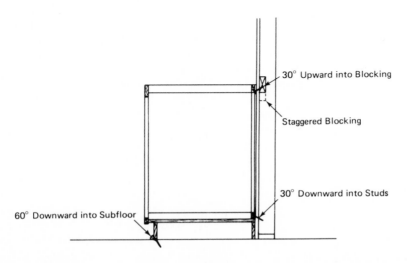

Fig. 15-8. Where and how to attach base cabinets to blocking or studs in walls and into flooring.

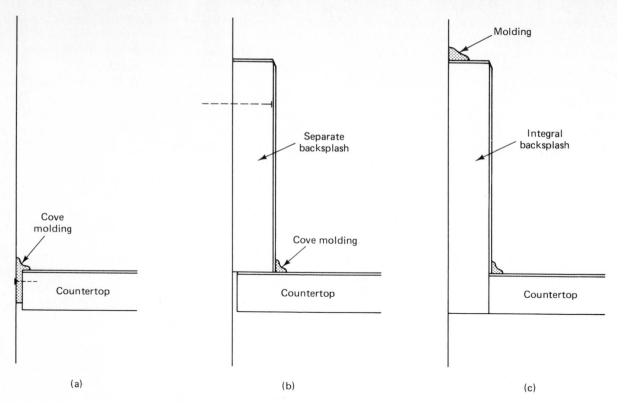

Fig. 15-9. Use small plastic moldings to close the gap between a countertop and a wall (a), a countertop and backsplash (b), or a backsplash and an uneven wall (c).

of counter and see what happens at the back wall. If the gap is small—not over ⅛" maximum—you can close it by fitting a rubber or plastic cove on the back of the counter (Fig. 15-9a). The cove compresses, hides unevenness, and actually eliminates the need for a backsplash.

With a larger gap at any point, cut the base for a backsplash, mitering at corners, and attach it to the wall with 4d finishing nails. Laminate the front and top of the backsplash as described earlier in this chapter for a self-edge, and close the joint at the countertop with a cove molding set in mastic (Fig. 15-9b). If the fit at the wall is still uneven, add the cove shown in Fig. 15-9c.

When you are satisfied with the appearance of your countertop, have someone hold it firmly in position while you drive screws upward through base cabinets into its under side. Use screws that go no more than halfway into the base, and draw the base down tight. Only a cove at the back of a countertop without a backsplash should be installed before the countertop itself. All other work should be done afterward.

Hang base cabinet doors, and insert drawers. Then paint or paper the wall before you connect appliances.

THE SINK CABINET

Before you start work on the wall with the sink cabinet against it, plan carefully what you must do to accommodate plumbing. Assuming that you have a dishwasher next to the sink, you will undoubtedly have plumbing and electrical connections through the back, bottom, and side of the sink cabinet. You or your plumber must disconnect any lines coming through the back and side of the present sink cabinet, then disconnect and pull through the floor any piping leading downward. Otherwise, you won't be able to remove the present sink and its cabinet or to slide the new one in place.

As on other walls, mark on the floor the widths of new base cabinets to establish the exact location of the sink cabinet. If you can reuse existing connections, find the centerlines of existing piping. When you measure, remember to allow for the thickness of any new wall or flooring materials. If you are relocating your sink, contact your plumber. He can tell you exactly where he plans to run his piping, and at what point in the remodeling process he wants to do his work. He may have to come through the wall with water connections, but more likely he will bring all water and drain lines upward through the floor.

On the back and bottom shelf of your sink cabinet mark the necessary centerlines. Then drill holes for the pipes about ¼" greater in diameter than the pipe. Drill from the inside of the cabinet for the neatest results.

Once the sink is disconnected and drain piping dropped below the floor line, follow the process already described in this chapter for finishing the wall, applying underlayment, laying flooring, and fitting cabinets. The only possible difference is which cabinet to set first after you have positioned all of them and determined what shimming you need. Unless cabinets fit tightly in corners and you have little tolerance for error, set the sink cabinet first. It is easier to place while you can still work on all sides of it.

Set the sink cabinet gently on its marks on the floor about 4″ from the wall, and slide it slowly until the stubs of any pipes coming through the wall protrude through the holes you drilled for them. Then adjust the position until the holes for piping coming through the floor line up directly with the holes you drilled in the bottom shelf of the cabinet. Attach the sink cabinet at the two rear wall points (Fig. 15-8).

Set the Sink

Before you fit the sink into its cabinet, place rings of plumber's putty around the holes for faucets, and set the faucets in position. Then tighten nuts on the underside. It is much easier to reach the nuts before you set the sink than afterward. Clean off excess putty, then fit the sink into its cutout.

clamps over the curved end of the rim, and tighten the screws until the putty seal is squeezed closed. Remove excess putty with a putty knife.

TYPES OF PIPES

The existing piping in your house may be made of lead or brass if the house is very old, of steel, cast iron, or copper if it is newer, or of plastic if it is less than 15 years old. Regardless of what you now have, any new piping that you install yourself should be plastic where permitted by code. Plastic is easy to cut with a saw and just as easily spliced with cement-solvent.

Some codes limit the use of plastic. It is now generally accepted for drain lines, often for cold water lines, but only occasionally for hot water lines. (Hot-water piping has a different plastic formulation than cold-water piping.) Some plastic pipe is rigid and you assemble lines with cement. Other pipe is flexible and connected with an insert fitting and clamps.

To connect rigid plastic pipe, clean pieces with a dry rag and fit one halfway into the other. It should fit easily but not loosely. Position the two pieces the way

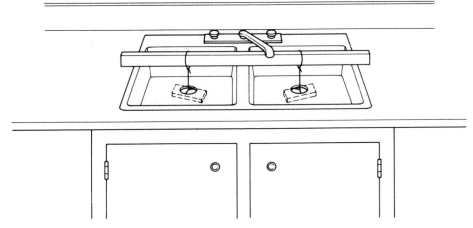

Fig. 15-10. While you clamp a sink into its cutout in a counter, support its weight on short lengths of 2 × 4 under drain holes; they are wire-tied to a longer 2 × 4 laid across the counter.

If the sink is **self-rimming**—that is, the rim is part of the sink—apply a bead of plumber's putty all the way around the under edge of the rim. Then carefully set the sink in position, check it for square, and press down firmly all the way around the edge to form a watertight seal. Next, secure it to the countertop with clamps provided by the manufacturer. Use two clamps at each corner, and one at the midpoint of the front and back.

If the sink has a separate T-shaped rim, coat the underside of the rim on both sides of its stem with plumber's putty. Fit the rim on the sink and set the sink in its cutout. Support it temporarily by running a wire through the drain and wrapping the wire around two short lengths of 2 × 4, one beneath the drain and the other across the sink and counter (Fig. 15-10). Then fit

you want them, mark the position, then pull them apart. Brush a light coat of solvent on the two mating surfaces. Then, no more than 30 seconds later, apply a thin coat of cement on the inner surface of the female fitting and a thick coat on the outer surface of the male, but not so much that you block the opening. Immediately push the pipe into the fitting, twist it about a quarter-turn to spread the cement, then line up your marks. An even bead of glue should appear around the joint; if it doesn't pull the pipe out at once and add cement. Hold the connection firm for a moment, and wait five minutes before you add any other fitting. Wait at least two hours before using the pipe.

Connect flexible plastic pipe by slipping clamps about ½″ from ends, and inserting a rigid fitting into

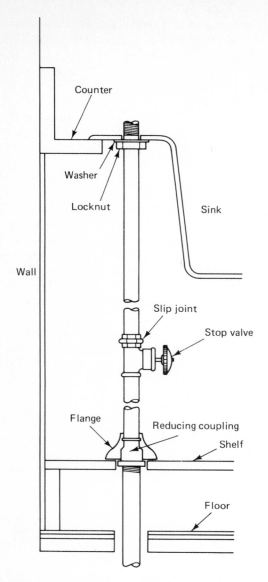

Counter

Washer

Locknut

Sink

Wall

Slip joint

Stop valve

Flange

Reducing coupling

Shelf

Floor

Fig. 15-11. This side view shows the plumbing needed to bring water from its source under the kitchen floor to sink faucets. The reducing coupling, which is not always required, may be either above the cabinet shelf or below the kitchen floor.

both pieces until the ridges are no longer visible. Tighten clamps with a screwdriver.

Copper pipe and tubing are the next easiest materials to work with, but are more expensive and require some special tools. You can cut them with a hacksaw, but a tube cutter does a better, surer job. You may need a tube bender for shaping flexible copper tubing to the required configuration. You need a soldering iron to make sweat joints, or a flaring die for shaping ends for connection with flare nuts. Making either a good sweat joint or flared joint takes practice.

Steel pipe and fittings fit together in threaded joints. Fittings come already threaded; pipe does not. To thread pipe yourself you need either a hand- or power-operated threading machine. To cut steel pipe

you need a pipe cutter, and should have a pipe vise and reaming tool. At most plumbing supply houses you can buy pipe of the size you need, and have it cut and threaded to your specifications. You assemble pipe and fittings by coating the male (exposed) threads with pipe compound.

If you hire a plumbing contractor to install new piping, he will decide what type to use to meet code requirements and the quality of job required. If you intend to do all plumbing yourself, you must have full knowledge of local codes, plumbing materials, and fitting methods.

The plumbing instructions in this book are limited to the remaining condition—where you hire a plumber to run new lines to new plumbingware and water-using appliances, but you finish the connection to the lines he stubs through the wall or floor. Therefore, work out with your contractor which materials he wants to use, and have him advise you on what materials local codes permit and any restrictions on the way lines are assembled. Obviously, you can connect your steel piping to his, your copper piping to his, and your plastic piping to his. With special transition fittings you can connect your plastic, copper, or steel lines to whatever he stubs in. But you must know in advance.

CONNECTING WATER LINES

In most areas of the country plumbers avoid running water lines in exterior walls to eliminate the danger of freezing. If your water lines are stubbed through the wall, pack insulation behind them. Then make connections as described for lavatories in the next chapter.

When water lines come through the floor and the base of your sink cabinet, you need from the floor upward a reducing coupling, a length of pipe, a stop valve, slip joint, another length of pipe, and a washer and locknut (Fig. 15-11). Work out in advance with your plumber whether you need to install the reducing coupling above the shelf, or whether he will install one below the floor. This coupling is required only when the supply pipe from the main water line is larger than the water line to sink faucets specified by the sink manufacturer.

Remove the capped stub provided by the plumber, and install a **nipple**—a short length of pipe. If you install the reducing coupling, the nipple must be long enough to extend ½" above the bottom shelf of the sink cabinet. Coat the male threads of the nipple with pipe compound, and insert it in the supply pipe. Then fit on the reducing coupling and a length of pipe that reaches about 16" above the cabinet shelf. Assemble only; do not install.

If the reducing coupling is below the floor, insert in it a nipple that carries the water lines to that point 16" above the shelf. Again fit but not install.

To the end of the pipe fit a slip joint and a shutoff valve or stop valve. Then measure the distance from the underside of the faucet pipe to the end of the valve. Cut pipe to this length. Use flexible tubing if possible so that you can adjust for any vertical misalignment. Fit the length in place. When all pipes are of acceptable length and the fit is good, take the line apart and reassemble the pieces in the same order as before. Use pipe compound at every threaded joint, but applied only to the male threads.

CONNECTING WASTE LINES

Usually, a kitchen sink lies beneath a window. Therefore, the drain pipe downward and the vent pipe upward are not directly behind the sink, but offset. To run from the sink drain to the main drain line, then, your sink piping must run from side to side as well as front to back.

Both compartments of a two-compartment sink may discharge into a **continuous waste** and a single trap *except* when you have a garbage disposal unit. Then they must have separate drain connections and you can't use a continuous waste (Fig. 15-12c). A continuous waste may discharge in the center if you have no offset to contend with (Fig. 15-12a), or at one end to achieve the offset (Fig. 15-12b).

First install the strainer unit in the bottom of the sink, and connect the tailpiece underneath with a washer and slip nuts. Then assemble the continuous waste as a separate unit. Continuous wastes are standard in length to fit common sink dimensions. Fit the parts of a two-piece waste into a tee, or fit a one-piece waste into an elbow at one end and a tee at the other. Attach the assembly to the sink.

You can plumb from the tee to the outlet pipe in several ways (Fig. 15-13). You save under-sink storage space if you run from the required P-trap to the drain pipe close to the wall (Fig. 15-13a). So fit the P-trap temporarily in place, then take measurements. First measure the vertical distance between the open end of the trap and the centerline of the drain pipe coming through the wall (A in Fig. 15-13e). Then measure the distance between the end and centerline of an elbow; this measurement (B) will be about 2½″, depending on the size and type of pipe you use.

If the end of the trap lies above the drain pipe, add A and B to get the length of nipple needed between the tee and trap. If the end is below the drain pipe, and B is greater than A, the difference is the length of the nipple.

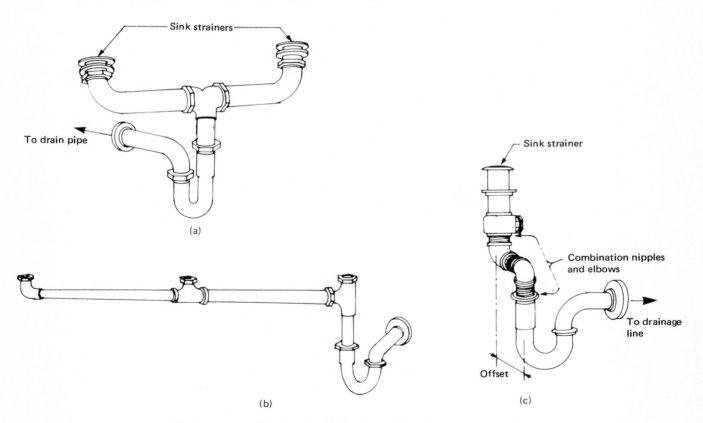

Fig. 15-12. Waste from a two-compartment sink flows into an outlet pipe through a series of fittings called a continuous waste, which may discharge directly below the center of the sink (a) or to one side of it (b). A garbage disposal unit cannot be connected to a continuous waste, but must discharge through its own trap to the drain line (c).

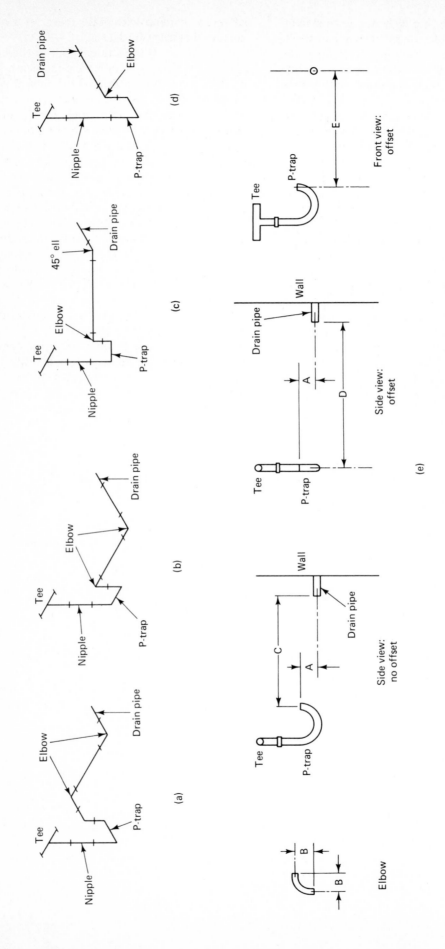

Fig. 15-13. Four ways to plumb from the tee under the sink to the outlet pipe in the wall: back toward the wall then sideways (a), sideways then back toward the wall (b), back at a 45° angle (c), and straight back (d). Lower drawings (e) show where to measure to find the lengths of various nipples.

If the end is below the drain pipe, and A is greater than B, the difference is the length of nipple needed between the trap and elbow. This is not a common condition.

Next measure horizontally from the end of the drain pipe through the wall to the centerline of the open end of the trap. If you don't have an offset (Fig. 15-13d), measurement C will be between 10 and 11"; the length of connecting nipple is C minus B (for the elbow). If you have an offset (Fig. 15-13b), measurement D will be about 14"; the length of nipple connecting to the drain pipe is D minus B.

With an offset only, measure parallel to the wall between the centerline of the trap and centerline of the drain pipe (E). From this dimension subtract measurement B twice, once for each elbow. The remainder is the length of slightly sloping pipe that runs parallel to the wall.

Assemble all pieces of pipe and the necessary fittings to test the fit. Then take them apart and re-assemble them permanently. Work outward from the wall to the trap, and from the tee down to the trap. The trap is the final fitting to install. When your plumbing is complete, open the main shutoff valve in the house, keep the stop valve off, and check water lines as far as the valve for leaks. Then open the valve and check the next section for leaks. Finally, turn on the faucets and check drain piping for leaks.

CONNECTING A GARBAGE DISPOSER

Manufacturers of garbage disposal units provide complete installation instructions with their products. Check those instructions carefully before you lay out your plumbing. Most units drain out the side (see Fig. 15-12c) and require a separate trap. The trap may be under the sink; but if space there is limited, as it is when you also have to plumb for a dishwasher, you can run the drain pipe down through the bottom of the sink cabinet, through the floor, and install a P-trap there.

CONNECTING A DISHWASHER

Dishwasher manufacturers also provide complete installation diagrams. Water lines to the appliance usually branch off hot and cold water piping to the sink. Waste piping must be separate; it can't be directly connected to any part of the waste piping from the sink or disposal unit.

Remodeling The Bathroom

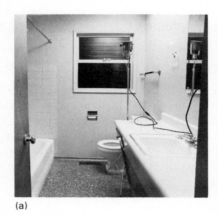

(a)

(b)

Bathrooms tend to be functional and cramped (a). Yet thoughtful remodeling can add both space and beauty while retaining functionalism. As part of an overall remodeling (b) a 3½' × 6' shed-roofed addition transformed the once sterile bathroom. A new beam replaces the original exterior wall above a sunken tub. A fixed window provides better light and a view out, while a high wall blocks the view in. The area where the tub used to be is now free for laundry equipment, linen storage, more counter, or whatever you need the space for. (Courtesy American Plywood Association.)

In all too many remodelings the bathroom, if not ignored entirely, is left alone except for freshening with new paint or wallpaper and perhaps a new shower curtain. Yet bathrooms become out of date as quickly as kitchens. That's part of the problem; they become outmoded but their fixtures seldom wear out. As long as the plumbing works, why remodel?

Historically, bathrooms and kitchens have moved in tandem in shape and convenience. The first indoor facilities were installed in large houses of the well-to-do, and the bathroom was huge. Frequently, the bathtub occupied one wall, the toilet another, and a freestanding washbowl a third. The window was the same size as bedroom windows. There was ample space for drying off

and dressing, but no storage space of any kind. Bathrooms were large enough to accommodate whole families at once, but the mores of the day virtually dictated one at a time, please.

Gradually, with the advent of smaller plumbingware, bathrooms shrank. A generation ago the 5' × 7' bathroom, considered a practical minimum, became virtually a standard. Fixtures were grouped together, often along one wall to save space and plumbing costs. The bathroom was economical allright, but it was practical for only one person at a time, and inconvenient for a family of four or five living in a one-bath house.

The next and still current phase has moved in two directions. One movement has been toward larger bathrooms compartmented for simultaneous use by more than one person in privacy. The other has been to stay with small rooms but provide more of them. The most common bathroom remodeling today, as it has been for some years, is the bathroom addition.

PLANNING PRINCIPLES

The amount of space needed in a bathroom is affected by the size of the fixtures, by clearances required by building codes, by the purposes for which you intend to use the room, and by good architectural planning principles.

Obviously, you need a door. Standard width is 30″, although a 28″ door is acceptable when you can find that width in stock. But size isn't the most important factor; swing is. The door should open into the bathroom. It should swing so that it screens rather than exposes anyone in the tub or on the toilet, particularly in a bathroom that serves guests. It should never swing toward the front of a toilet or against a lavatory where someone could be hit by it. Instead, it should swing against a short section of wall, or against the side of the tub toward its rear, not its drain end.

Should there be more than one door? Experts disagree here. A bathroom tucked between two bedrooms is a space saver, privacy protector, and convenience. But if the occupant of one room locks the door to the other room and forgets to unlock it, all the advantages disappear in a hurry.

A window in a bathroom is not required, but ventilation is. To conserve exterior wall space for rooms that need windows, many designers now place bathrooms in windowless areas, then specify a vent fan in the ceiling to carry off odors and excess moisture. Some types of vent fans include a light fixture with a bulb for general lighting and an infrared heat lamp to warm someone stepping out of a shower or bath until they are dry.

A bathroom window may be double-hung, sliding, casement, or awning type, but not a hopper vent that opens in. The obvious place for a window is above the tub to conserve other wall space. But it is also the poorest location for three reasons. First, you can't easily open or shut the window without stepping into the tub. Second, it permits cold air in winter to spill down onto a bather and create an unpleasant draft. Third, the window is constantly exposed to maximum moisture from steam and shower water. Wood windows tend to rot out quickly, and metal windows tend to discolor unless wiped off regularly.

One solution in a bathroom under a roof is a skylight. You can buy circular, square, or rectangular skylights, complete with frames, in sizes ranging in area from 1½ sq ft up to 73 sq ft. They provide good glareless daylight during the day, and preclude the need to turn on the light every time you use the room. On the other hand, they don't provide enough light during early morning and late evening hours when most bathrooms receive maximum use. Some types are hinged, and can be opened for ventilation.

The Bathtub

The standard rectangular bathtub is 5′-0″ long, although lengths of 4½′, 5½′ and 6′ are available. Widths vary from 28 to 32″ for all lengths. Square tubs, approximately 4′ on a side, are made with the bathing area running diagonally. All sizes are made in two configurations, one to fit in an alcove with only a side exposed, and one to fit against walls on one side and the drain end. And they are made for either right-hand or left-hand installation; a left-hand tub is drilled for plumbing at the left end as you prepare to step into it.

On rare occasions tub plumbing must be repaired or unclogged. To make repairs the plumber needs an access door in the plumbing wall at the front of the tub, accessible from the adjoining room. A framed opening 12″ wide and centered on the shower pipe and 15″ high from floor to header is adequate. You can make the door from ¼″ plywood and hold it over the opening with clips. The access door is usually hidden in a cabinet or closet.

Tub Clearances. Between the open side of a tub and any adjacent fixture allow at least 3″, and as much clearance as space permits if the faucets are at the same end of the tub as the nearby fixture (Fig. 16-1a). Between the side of the tub and any fixtures against the opposite wall, or any opposite wall without fixtures, allow 20″ minimum and at least 28″ when space permits.

Faucets and the drain mechanism may be at either end of the tub. If you have a choice, plan for a left-hand tub if the majority in your family are right-handed, and a right-hand tub if most are left-handed.

The Shower Stall

A showerhead above a tub requires no special planning as far as floor layout is concerned. You must carry water-shedding wall materials 6′ above the floor, however, and cover the sill and jambs of any window below this level. You also must provide blocking for a shower curtain rod or a sliding shower door.

Separate shower stalls are manufactured in three shapes. Square stalls (Fig. 16-2) are 32″, 36″, or 40″ on each side; a rectangular shower is 32″ × 48″ with the long dimension against a wall. Corner showers are either 36″ or 40″ on two sides, about 20″ on two others, and the doorway or curtained opening is on a diagonal between the short sides. Drain locations vary. Stalls are made of metal or plastic, and are easily attached to exposed studs or furring. Wall material is not required behind them.

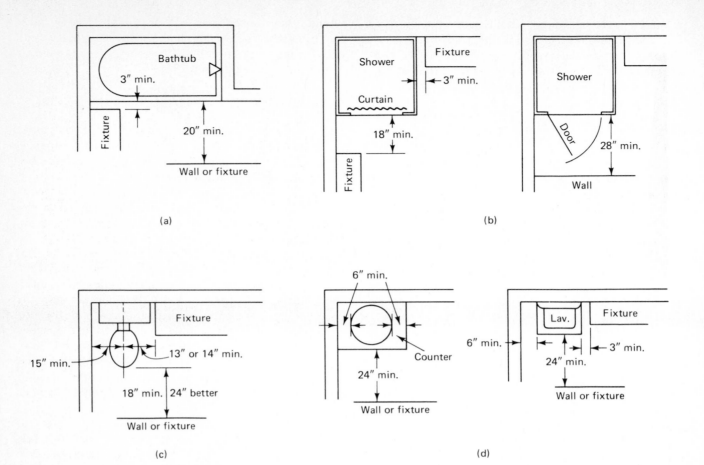

(a)

(b)

(c)

(d)

Fig. 16-1. Plumbing codes require minimum clearances between fixtures and either walls or other fixtures: (a) bathtub, (b) shower stall, (c) water closet, and (d) lavatory.

Fig. 16-2. Typical shower stalls are square like the one shown, or rectangular, or have five sides and fit in a corner. (Courtesy Eljer Plumbingware.)

Shower Stall Clearances. Between the outside of a stall and any adjacent fixture allow at least 3″ for cleaning. Allow at least 18″ between a stall with a shower curtain and any fixture on the opposite wall. When the stall has a door, allow at least 28″ (see Fig. 16-1b).

The Toilet

Known in plumbing circles as a **water closet** or **w.c.**, a toilet may be a one-piece or two-piece fixture and have any of five methods of flushing. Two-piece units (Fig. 16-3a and b) are the most common. One-piece water closets are more complex and therefore more expensive, but are easier to keep clean (Fig. 16-3c). Most common flushing actions for residential water closets are the siphon-vortex type and siphon-jet type. Both are quiet and efficient.

In the best planned bathroom the water closet is screened from view when the door is open. Why? Custom and tradition primarily. There is no code reason for doing so, and no cosmetic reason except when the w.c. is in use, in which case the door should be closed.

More important is its relationship to the soil stack. Ideally, the stack should be in the wall behind the fix-

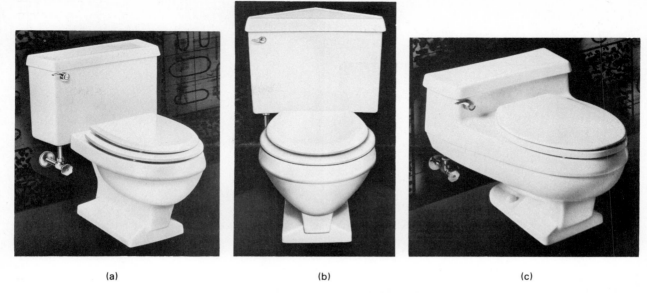

Fig. 16-3. Two-piece water closets (a) and (b) have a separate bowl and tank. In one-piece units (c) the bowl and tank are formed as a unit. A relatively new design has a triangular tank for use in a corner of a room with limited floor space. (Courtesy Eljer Plumbingware.)

ture and on the same centerline as the drain. Codes do permit a maximum distance of 6' between the stack and drain, but the plumbing is more complex. The stack must fit between studs, and the **closet bend**—the curved pipe running from the bowl to the soil stack, must fit between floor joists. So plumbing is much simpler when the drain and stack line up a minimum distance apart.

Clearances.   The space occupied by a water closet is no more than 31″ high, 22″ wide, and 30″ front to wall. Allow a minimum of 15″ from the centerline of the fixture to any side wall (see Fig. 16-1c). Allow no less than 14″ between the centerline and a lavatory or cabinet, and 13″ between the centerline and the edge of a bathtub. If you have the space, allow at least 30″ for the water closet between any flanking walls or fixtures. Furthermore, between the front edge of the seat and any wall or fixture opposite, allow at least 18″. You will be a lot more comfortable with 24″.

The Lavatory

You have more choices in lavatories than any other item of plumbingware (Fig. 16-4). They vary in depth from 12 to 20″ and in width from 12 to 36″. Some types are designed to hang from the wall, others to stand on slender legs, and others to fit in a counter. If space is critical, you can even buy a corner lavatory. Lavatories may be round, oval, or rectangular. They may be made of vitreous china, like water closets, enameled metal, or shaped plastic. But they all have one common feature: the water inlet, faucets, and drain are all located within the dimensions of the fixture.

Counters for lavatories have different dimensions than sink countertops. Depth is usually 21″. Height varies from 30″ to 33″ in bathrooms used primarily by adults, and from 28 to 30″ in children's bathrooms. Widths vary with the space available. Minimum should be the width of the lavatory plus 6″ on each side. The maximum is whatever room you have; it is almost impossible to have too much counter space in a bathroom.

Clearances.   Allow 3″ between the lavatory itself and any adjacent fixture. Allow 6″ between a lavatory and a side wall. Between the front edge and any fixture opposite it allow 24″ (see Fig. 16-1d).

Other Fixtures

Plumbingware manufacturers produce a few other specialty items in small quantities for a limited and generally affluent market. There isn't room in a small bathroom for them, but in a spacious room they add a note of elegance and self-indulgent luxury.

One is the special tub, and its design varies with a constantly changing market. The Roman tub, for example, is of standard depth, but is circular and big enough for two or more. The hot tub is also circular, but has a smaller diameter and is deep enough to stand in. It also accommodates a friendly group, and has shown some popularity in less inhibited regions of the country.

Not yet popular in the United States but common in Europe and parts of Asia is the **bidet.** It is shaped somewhat like a small water closet, without a seat. You

(a)

(b)

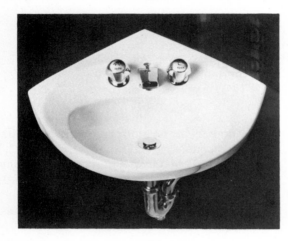

(c)

Fig. 16-4. Most lavatories are either recessed into a counter (a) or hang from a wall (b). They come in a wide range of shapes and sizes. A rectangular lavatory similar to the wall-hung type is supported at the front by a pair of metal legs. Taking up the least space is a corner lavatory (c). (Courtesy Eljer Plumbingware.)

sit in it, not on it. It has hot and cold water faucets and a drain like a lavatory, and is designed for cleansing the genital area.

LAYING OUT THE SPACE

In new construction it is economical to place all fixtures against one wall to save plumbing costs. This is also a commendable goal in remodeling, but should be lower in order of importance. More important are the contents of the room and the relationship of remodeled bathroom facilities to existing rooms.

First, how many rooms and how many people must your bathrooms serve? A bathroom off the master bedroom for two adults getting up and going to bed at the same time should be different from a bathroom used by two or three children of varying ages, or from a bathroom used by both children and overnight guests.

Master Bath

In a rectangle of 35 sq ft you can design a master bath used most often by one person at a time with a toilet, bathtub with showerhead, and a lavatory in a counter-

top (Fig. 16-5a). With a shower stall instead of a tub the area should be about the same, but the shape closer to square (Fig. 16-5b). But be sure that both of you are willing to forgo a bathtub before you leave it out or include it in another bathroom.

In 50 sq ft you can design a bathroom large enough for two people to use simultaneously. Although there are times when you wish you had installed two toilets, separate lavatories in a countertop are a great convenience that takes up little space (Fig. 16-5c).

When space is limited, consider the possibility of placing a second lavatory in the bedroom against one wall of the bathroom to conserve plumbing. With careful planning (Fig. 16-6) you can create a complete washing–dressing area that minimizes the time you have to waste waiting for someone to get out of the bathroom.

A Second Bathroom

A bathroom that serves the bedrooms of two or more children should have a water closet, a combination tub–shower, and two lavatories (Fig. 16-7). Allow 50 sq ft, and add another 10 sq ft for each simultaneous user more than two. Somewhere in the room provide a

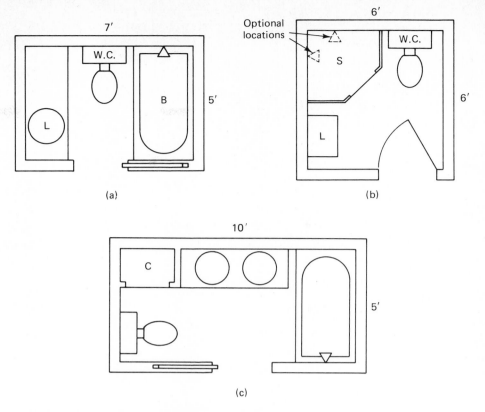

(a)

(b)

(c)

Fig. 16-5. Minimum bathroom sizes with a bathtub (a), corner shower stall (b), and twin lavatories (c). Minimums should never be remodeling goals, however, unless better space is not available.

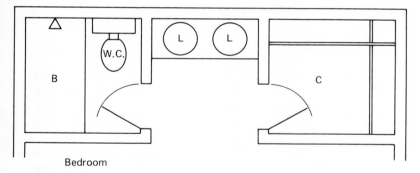

Bedroom

Fig. 16-6. Off a master bedroom you may be able to combine a master bath with a dressing area. Sliding instead of swinging doors would be more convenient here, but they are not as quiet to operate—a drawback if the bedroom's occupants have different bedtime and rising hours.

Fig. 16-7. Second bathrooms should serve as many purposes and people as possible. In a space 7½′ × 10½′ you can include laundry equipment and storage for clean linen and clothes to be washed.

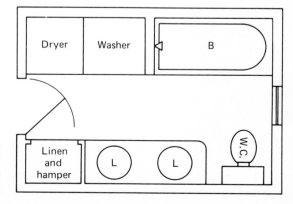

237

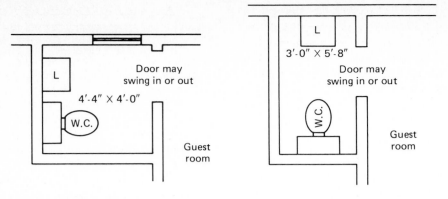

Fig. 16-8. In 20 sq ft you can fit a bathroom off a guest bedroom—a special convenience for older visitors. These are the two most practical plans.

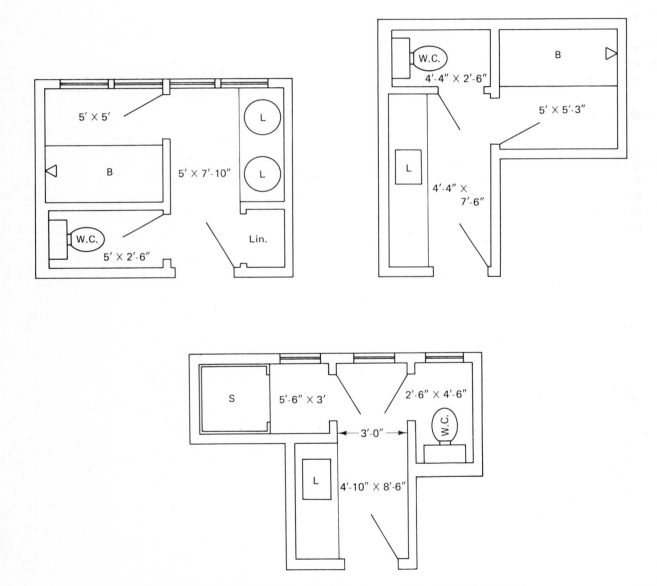

Fig. 16-9. One compartmented bath can do the work of several separate rooms in less space. As these three plans show, you can often work a compartmented bath into odd spaces available in an existing house.

hamper for dirty clothes. By getting children in the habit of disposing of soiled clothes at a single point, you save yourself time in assembling clothes for washing. Since most items to be washed come from the bedrooms anyway, consider the possibility of placing your washer, dryer, and linen storage area either in the second bathroom or adjacent to it.

Guest Facilities

No greater luxury exists for overnight guests than a half-bath directly off the guest room. In less than 20 sq ft you can tuck a lavatory and water closet (Fig. 16-8). A private bath is of particular value if many of your guests are older people who may need to get up in the night. Going down the hall for a bath or shower is a minor inconvenience compared to trying to find your way to a toilet in the dark.

When guests share a bathroom with children, there must be a door directly off the hall. When guests share your bath facilities, they should be able to reach them without going through your bedroom.

The Compartmented Bath

Convenience of location is extremely important in planning bathrooms when you have the space and funds for more than one. But when the plan of your existing house defies an arrangement with separate bathrooms, look for a single spot large enough to accept a compartmented room.

A compartmented bath takes up a lot of space—as much as 60 to 80 sq ft. But it has two big advantages. First, its shape can almost always be adapted to the space you have available (Fig. 16-9). Second, plumbing costs can be held to the lowest possible for the number of people served.

The purpose of a compartmented bath is to permit use of the space by several people at one time, but with privacy preserved when privacy is important. In effect you put together one or two cubicles for water closets, one or two cubicles for bathtubs or shower stalls, each with a door opening off a central area containing lavatories and storage space. Cubicle sizes, excluding the thickness of walls, can be as small as $2\frac{1}{2}' \times 4'$ for a toilet, $3' \times 5\frac{1}{2}'$ for a shower, and $5' \times 5\frac{1}{2}'$ for a bathtub. With a lot of cubicles together, door swings can be a problem, but you can solve many of them by installing sliding doors instead of hinged doors. Sliding doors are not advisable for the main entrance to bathrooms because they are noisier than swinging doors.

A BATHROOM ADDITION

The problem that most people want to correct by bathroom remodeling is the single occupied bathroom. Even though a single bathroom is unoccupied 95% of a 24-hour day, it's like rush hour on the freeway the other 5%. And since you are footing the bill, why not concentrate on adding a second bathroom serving only the master bedroom? This is usually the simplest and least costly solution.

Generally, you face one of three conditions. In

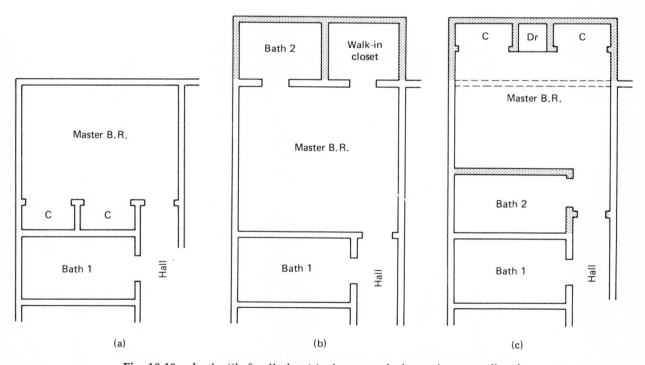

(a)   (b)   (c)

Fig. 16-10. In the "before" plan (a), the master bedroom is too small and another bathroom is needed. Two possible solutions are shown in (b) and (c).

one, the master bedroom is on the back or side of the house where you can expand within setback restrictions (Fig. 16-10a). See chapter 4 for a discussion of property limitations. Here you build an addition the width of the bedroom and 5 to 6' in the other dimension over a crawl space. Then you have a choice. Either place the new bathroom, together with new closets and a dressing area, in the addition (Fig. 16-10b); or else put the new bathroom next to an existing bathroom where it can share plumbing, and extend the bedroom into the addition (Fig. 16-10c).

From a planning standpoint the second solution is better. The bedroom has better light, better ventilation, plumbing costs are less, and the second bathroom can be used in an emergency by others without interrupting your bedroom privacy. From a structural standpoint, however, the first solution is likely to be simpler and less costly overall, and less disruptive of family life during the remodeling. The chances are that ceiling joists bear on the rear wall you would need to remove; you must provide support in some form, such as a beam exposed below ceiling level right down the middle of the room. If joists happen to run the other direction, the second solution is much the better.

In the second condition, the master bedroom is located on the front or a side where expansion is out of the question (Fig. 16-11a). Here the simplest solution is to switch bedrooms. The other bedroom that you expand may be smaller, and probably is. But you can regain the lost floor area by removing existing closets, and placing in the addition a complete bathroom–closet–dressing room complex (Fig. 16-11b). You tear out little rear wall, and frame joists into the existing

wall. A window in the dressing area provides good light and ventilation, and plumbing in the new bathroom is adjacent to existing plumbing. You do lose the window in the existing bathroom, but a fan can take care of ventilation, and children seldom look out the bathroom window anyway.

In the third condition, the master bedroom is on the second floor of a two-story house. Here your choice is more limited, because you also want to make maximum use of the first-floor space you add. The wall between the bedroom and the addition is a bearing wall. So work out the size and basic layout of the upstairs space first, then see what you can do with the added first floor space. If you need 6' × 12' upstairs, for example, and can't make practical use of less than 9' × 12' downstairs, the size of needs downstairs should dictate the size of the addition at both levels. Then you plan how to make maximum use of the bonus space upstairs. Possibilities might be a dressing area, a built-in sewing alcove, a small home office, or a cozy reading alcove with bookshelves.

A RELOCATED BATHROOM

In many small houses with two bedrooms and one bath, the only logical place for a third bedroom and larger new bathroom can be reached only by converting the existing bathroom into a hallway (Fig. 16-12). If you have an acceptable alternative, you can probably remodel more economically. But don't let fear of tearing out an existing bathroom stop you from doing so if that step offers the best solution.

As in Fig. 16-12, you will seldom be able to reuse

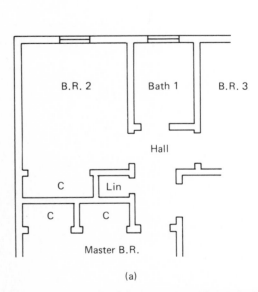

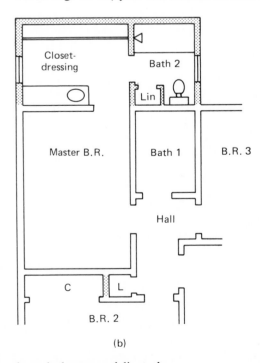

Fig. 16-11. To interchange bedrooms is sometimes the best remodeling solution.

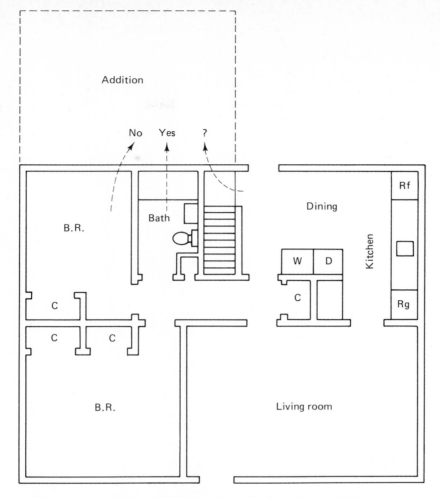

Fig. 16-12. In many small homes the only place for an addition is at the rear, and the only practical access to that addition is through an existing bathroom.

existing stacks, plumbingware, or piping. To keep the existing bathroom operable during remodeling, you must plan carefully. Build the foundation for the addition, frame it, and enclose it as far as possible without cutting through any connection to the existing house.

Then install the new bathtub, and have your plumbing contractor run his rough plumbing to new connections with existing water and drain lines. Next, finish the new bathroom and install the remaining fixtures. While your plumber is completing finish plumbing and making the new bathroom usable, he will also stub off connections to existing fixtures. While he is doing this, you tear out enough wall of the old bathroom to provide access to the new. Only then can you complete the job of enclosing the addition, and begin to remove existing plumbingware and wall materials in the old bathroom.

A NEW BATHROOM IN EXISTING SPACE

To a renovation of an existing bathroom apply the same step-by-step planning principles. Establish the location

of the water closet first. Avoid moving it if possible, and move it no more than 6' from your existing soil stack. Then establish the location of the tub and/or shower, then the lavatory, and finally storage space for medicines, towels, and bathroom supplies.

Before proceeding, review your plans in your house with a plumbing contractor. He can tell you where he will run his piping, and where he will come through the wall with water lines and the floor with drain lines. Mark these locations with chalk.

PLUMBING SYSTEM

It isn't difficult to tie new hot and cold water lines into existing lines in a basement or crawl space, or even in a common wall between the old and new bathrooms. They can run vertically or horizontally wherever necessary between structural members and, within code limits, through framing members (Fig. 16-13).

To remain within code limits when cutting a top plate (Fig. 16-13a), you must reinforce on both sides with steel strapping at least three times as long as your

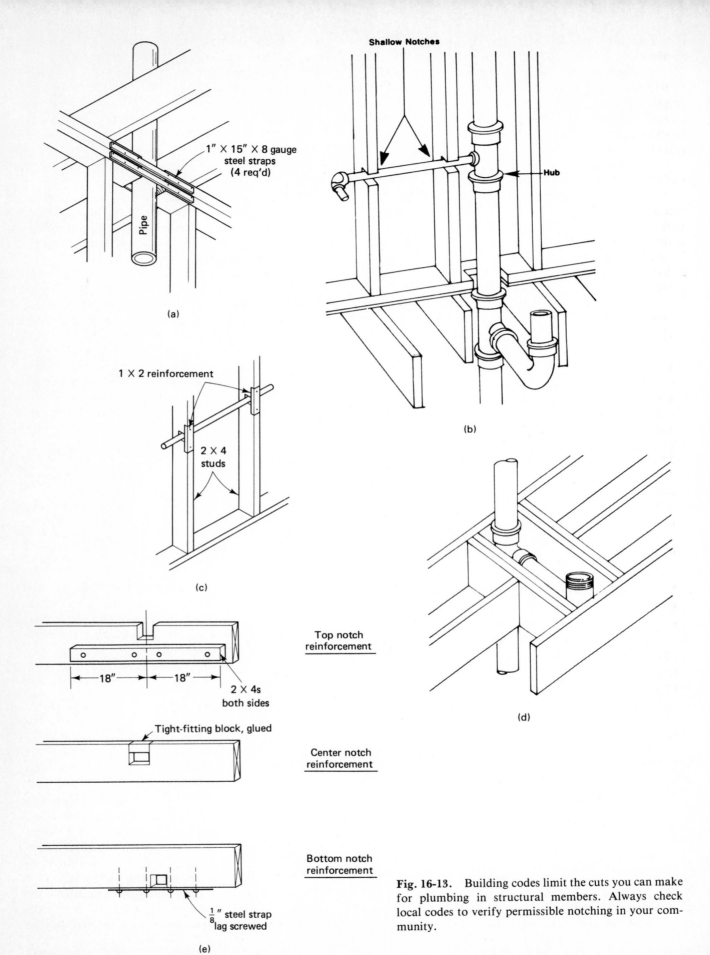

Shallow Notches

1" × 15" × 8 gauge steel straps (4 req'd)

Pipe

Hub

(a)

(b)

1 × 2 reinforcement

2 × 4 studs

(c)

(d)

Top notch reinforcement

18" 18"

2 × 4s both sides

Tight-fitting block, glued

Center notch reinforcement

Bottom notch reinforcement

$\frac{1}{8}$" steel strap lag screwed

(e)

Fig. 16-13. Building codes limit the cuts you can make for plumbing in structural members. Always check local codes to verify permissible notching in your community.

cut. You can cut a bottom plate (Fig. 16-13b) without reinforcing it.

You can notch studs up to one-third of their depth provided that the notch is not in the middle third of the length of the stud (Fig. 16-13b). If you notch more than two adjacent studs, you must reinforce all cut studs with blocks of clear stock of stud thickness, cut for a tight fit and glued in place (Fig. 16-13c).

You can never notch a girder or cut a joist except within 24″ of its point of support. Any such notch can be no deeper than one-sixth of the depth of the joist, and must be reinforced in one of three ways (Fig. 16-13e): with 2 × 4s on both sides extending at least 12″ beyond the cut, with a clear wood block cut for a tight fit and glued, or with a piece of $\frac{1}{8}$″ × $1\frac{1}{2}$″ steel plate as long as the cut plus 36″ and attached with $\frac{1}{8}$″ × 2″ lag screws.

When necessary, joists may be cut and supported on both sides of piping by doubled headers (Fig. 16-13d).

Water Lines

The size of your water supply line from the city main or a well to the house is determined by the total water demand of all fixtures, water pressure in the main, the length of the service pipe from main to house, and the difference in elevation between the water meter and the highest fixture, usually a showerhead. Without increasing incoming pipe size you can add a second bathroom to a house with one bathroom, kitchen with disposal unit, and a washer provided that:

- Pressure is approximately 100 psi (pounds per square inch).
- The service pipe is less than 100′ long.
- Your water supply line is $\frac{3}{4}$″ in outside diameter.
- Your house is no more than two stories high.

To determine water pressure call your water company or read the decal on your water pump if you have a well. If your house doesn't fit the four conditions, call your water company or a plumber.

Drain Lines

With drain lines and **waste piping**—pipes that carry waste from fixtures other than the water closet—you have far less flexibility. At some point in your house all waste must enter the **house drain,** which is the waste connection from the house to a city sewer, a septic tank, or similar waste disposal facility. The size of the house drain is seldom critical. Any drain with an outside diameter of $3\frac{1}{2}$″ or more is adequate to take care of a second bathroom, provided that it slopes the minimum of $\frac{1}{4}$″ per foot as required by code. If you're adding a third bathroom, however, you need either a pipe with a $4\frac{1}{2}$″

outside diameter (o.d.) or a slope of $\frac{1}{2}$″ per foot. You can't determine existing slope because the drain is buried. You can probably measure the diameter of the pipe at the cleanout where it rises through the floor of the basement or crawl space.

The soil stack rises vertically from the point where the house drain becomes visible through the basement floor or ground. The stack's location is critical to your plans. You can tie an extra water closet into an existing soil stack provided that the centerline of its drain is no more than 6′ from the centerline of the stack. If the distance is more than 6′, you need a separate stack, called a **secondary stack.** To connect it to the house drain, you or your plumber will have to dig under the floor or crawl space to make the connection.

Only the water closet is affected by the 6′ rule. Other fixtures may be farther away. But then the slope rule comes into effect. Suppose that the distance from the trap under a bathtub to the soil stack is 20′. In that horizontal distance the waste pipe must drop uniformly at a rate of $\frac{1}{4}$″ per foot, or a total of 5″ vertically. By the time you allow for the tee at the soil pipe and the extra diameter of fittings at joints, you won't be able to stay between the depth of 2 × 8 joists without interfering with headroom below. In such a case you must install a separate soil stack.

Because a sound knowledge of plumbing methods and codes is vital to a successful bathroom reorganization or addition, talk to a plumbing contractor as soon as you have developed a floor plan you like. He may approve your plans as drawn and tell you where he will run his lines. Or he may suggest a change that could reduce his costs and yours without seriously affecting your basic plans.

REPLACING EXISTING FIXTURES

To remove existing plumbingware either for relocation or replacement, follow these general procedures.

The Water Closet

When you have a firm floor plan for your bathroom remodeling on paper, visit plumbingware dealers and select the water closet. The manufacturer provides an installation diagram that shows two important dimensions: the location of the fixture drain and the position of the water inlet through the wall.

The centerline of the drain is the centerline of the fixture, and 12 to 13″ from the *finished* wall line. If you are installing a new fixture at the same place as the old one, find the centerline of its drain by measuring from the wall to the centerline of the two bolts holding the water closet to the floor; they are on the same line as the drain. If your old water closet has four bolts, measure to the bolts nearest the wall. As long as the wall-to-drain dimension of the new fixture is no greater than that dimension for the old fixture, the new water closet will fit.

The water inlet hole is off center and from 5 to 9" above the floor. If the locations of the old and new inlet are different, you can bridge the difference with a piece of flexible copper tubing.

To remove an existing water closet, first shut off the water. There should be a valve in the water line just below the toilet tank. If not, there is a valve somewhere in the supply line in your basement or crawl space. Flush the toilet, and with a sponge soak up all water remaining in the tank and bowl. Then loosen the slip nut on the inlet pipe to the tank.

If the tank is mounted on the bowl, remove the two nuts from the bolts underneath the tank, and lift the tank off the bowl. If the tank is mounted on the wall, loosen the slip nuts at both ends of the pipe between tank and bowl, and remove the pipe. Then, while someone temporarily supports the tank, remove the nuts from the hanger bolts and pull the tank off the wall.

The bowl is held to the floor by bolts threaded on a closet flange. Pry off or unscrew the porcelain caps, then remove the nuts and washers. You may need pene-trating oil to loosen them. To break the seal between floor and bowl, rock or twist the bowl until it comes loose. Then lift it straight up; be careful not to damage the closet flange if you plan to reuse it. Into the open drain line stuff a rag to keep out dust and debris and to prevent sewer gas from escaping into the room. Scrape the flange clean with a putty knife. Either wax or putty may have been used as a seal.

Finish flooring usually extends to the edge of the drain hole, and the water closet rests on that flooring. When you intend to lay a new floor, then, you must do so after you remove the old water closet but before you set the new one. It is possible to cut resilient flooring, such as linoleum and vinyl tiles, to fit the shape of the bowl at the floor line, but you won't have as clean-look-ing a result. With ceramic tiles the work must be com-pleted before you install the water closet. Details of lay-ing flooring are discussed in Chapter 20.

Water Closet Installation. To install the new bowl, turn it upside down and fit a new wax gasket around the protruding drain outlet, called the **horn**. If a

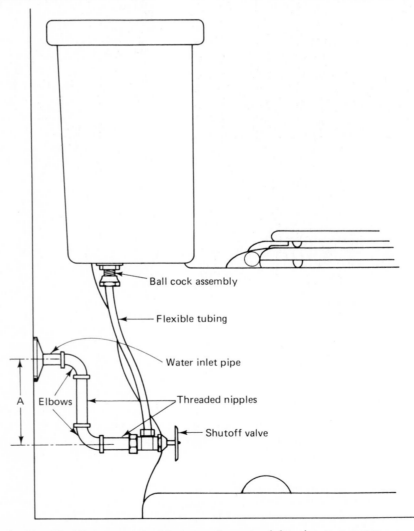

Fig. 16-14. The fittings required between the water inlet pipe to a water closet when the tank of the new fixture sets lower than the old one.

Chapter 16 / Remodeling The Bathroom

new floor covering has increased the dimension between the top of the flange and the floor's surface, use a gasket with a plastic sleeve; the sleeve faces away from the horn. Then remove the rag you stuffed in the drain, turn the bowl upright, and gently set it over the bolts of the floor flange.

With a carpenter's level, check the bowl's level from side to side and front to back. Usually, you can level it with pressure; if not, use shims. For shims use small pieces of sheet metal; do not use wood. When the bowl is level, press it down firmly and with a slight twisting motion to tighten the seal between bowl and drain pipe. Then recheck level. Fit the washers and nuts on the bolts until they make contact with the bowl, but don't tighten them.

If your water closet has a separate tank, set the tank cushion in place, lining up its holes with the holes in the bowl. Thread the rubber washer provided by the manufacturer around the flush-valve opening on the bottom of the tank. Then set the tank in place so that bolt holes line up. Insert the bolts, add washers and nuts, and tighten. Then recheck bowl level, and alignment of the tank with the wall. They should be parallel. When all is level and aligned, tighten the nuts at the floor and replace the ceramic caps. Install the seat and its cover.

The bottoms of present-day water closet tanks are closer to the floor than older models, and the water inlet pipe may be too high for a direct connection. To adjust its level, either turn an existing elbow so that it points down, or add an elbow that does. Then add a threaded nipple, another elbow, and another threaded nipple (Fig. 16-14) until the open end of the water line is approximately below the inlet hole in the bottom of the tank.

Most water piping to fixtures has an inside diameter (i.d.) of ½″, and an outside diameter (o.d.) of about ⁵⁄₁₆″. To determine the length of nipple you need, measure the distance between centerlines of parallel pipes (A in Fig. 16-14) and subtract 1¼″. Threaded ends fit ½″ into the elbows and tees. You can buy nipples cut to length and threaded at many good hardware stores.

To assemble the water line, apply joint compound to the threads of the nipple *only* (the male end of the connection), working toward the end of the pipe. Wipe off excess compound; it is important not to get any compound inside piping where it impedes the flow of water. Turn the nipple into the elbow by hand as far as you can. Then finish the connection with two wrenches, one holding the elbow in place and one turning the nipple. When the joint is tight, only two or three threads of the nipple should be exposed.

At the open end of the water inlet line fit the shut-off valve. If your old line didn't have a valve, add one. Slip the flexible supply pipe in place, and connect the bottom end to the valve and the upper end to the ball cock shaft. Tighten the connections, then turn on the water and check for leaks.

As a finishing touch, after you are sure that the water closet is functioning smoothly and all connections are watertight, apply a seal of bowl setting compound or plaster of Paris at the floor line around the bowl.

The Bathtub

Unlike other bathroom fixtures, the bathtub is installed before any finish wall and flooring materials. It has flanges on the sides that fit against walls, and the flanges are slotted or drilled for nails that hold the flange against studs or blocking in the wall. Finish wall material covers the flange, and finish flooring butts against the tub.

To remove an existing tub, remove the waste control lever and drain plug. Then tear out enough wall material so that you can get at the flanges to remove the nails. Usually, the tub's weight holds it to the floor, and there is no seal to be broken. With a crowbar or similar pry, lift at the front outside edge of the tub until the waste fitting in the bottom of the tub rises out of its seat in the drain pipe. Then raise the rear until you can get a grip under the side of the tub. Pull until the tub is free on all sides. This isn't easy. Removing a bathtub without damaging surrounding surfaces is next to impossible. So don't plan on reusing an old tub in a new location, and do plan on resurfacing walls where the tub used to be.

Installation. First select the fixture and study the installation diagram provided by the manufacturer. It will show the height above flooring of the slots in flanges. Install blocking at this height. Use either a length of 1 × 4 notched into studs (Fig. 16-15), or a series of 2 × 4s set between studs and staggered for easier nailing. At the front of the tub remember to provide a framed opening for an excess door and a cut in subflooring for the drain line. You must also provide blocking at both ends of the tub for either a shower curtain rod or a sliding shower door. Blocking should line up with the inside edge of the rim of the tub.

The bathtub must be in place before water and drain lines are fitted to it. As you move the tub into position, treat it with care. Vitreous china chips easily if you accidentally drop a hammer on it, and molded plastic will sometimes shatter under a sudden impact. With the tub in its final location, check its level at all rims. Some types have supports that rest on the floor, and you may need to shim. Other types require blocks under the inner rim, and you must establish level so that you know the length of blocks to cut. Attach the tub flange to blocking with 8d nails. Flanges aren't finished, so there is no danger of damage.

The Showerhead. The generally accepted standard for the above-floor height of the water inlet pipe for a showerhead is 6′-6″. Thus the shower nozzle is

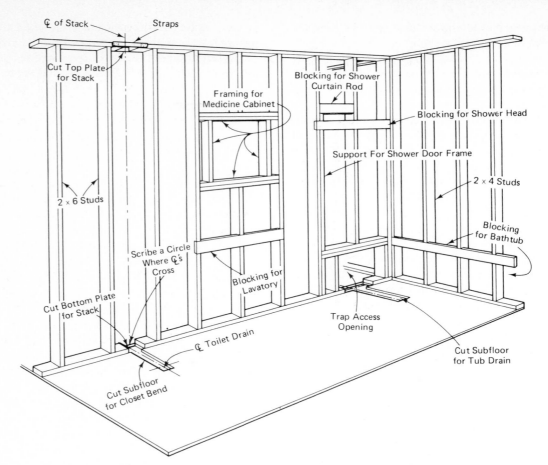

Fig. 16-15. Where blocking is required behind surface materials in a typical bathroom.

about 6′ above the floor of the tub or shower stall. Some tall people find this height too low, and short people often find it too high. So before you place blocking for the shower pipe, determine the most practical height for your family. Then place blocking in the front wall with its top 3″ above this level (Fig. 16-15). The plumber attaches the supply pipe to the blocking just below the elbow that turns the water line horizontal.

Protect the Tub. While you finish the bathroom you will sometimes be working above and in the tub. To protect its surface you can buy a special covering made for the purpose. Or you can make your own out of newspapers and a powdered adhesive mixed with water. Don't use any sections with slick paper or color, and read the label to make sure that the adhesive won't harm the tub's finish. Mix the adhesive and coat the tub with it, then add layers of newspaper to form a cushion. To remove the protection, soak the papers thoroughly and they will peel right off.

Connect Piping. At the time you finish the walls around the tub, the plumber will have installed the trap and drain lines, and carried beyond studs the pipe stubs

for the showerhead, tub spout, and controls for the drain plug and hot and cold water lines. To protect the ends of these stubs, he probably installed plugs. Remove the plug at the spout, and thread on the spout fitting until it is tight and aims downward. Remove the plug at the showerhead, screw on the length of chrome-plated gooseneck pipe, fit an **escutcheon** (a decorative ring) over the pipe, then screw on the showerhead.

Manufacturers of controls provide installation instructions, which vary with the type of control. In general, however, remove the plugs from the pipes, coat the valve stems with pipe compound, fit them into the pipes with the handles still on, and hand-tighten them. Then unscrew the handles and tighten the stem with a wrench and packing nut. Make sure that the wrench fits tightly on the nut so that you don't damage it by rounding its edges. To prevent damage to fittings, too, wrap the jaws of wrenches and pliers with tape. Finally, slip escutcheons over the stems and add the handles. The H handle (for hot) should be on the left, and the C on the right.

The Lavatory

At the time you install a lavatory, the wall behind it must be finished, and finish flooring laid. Rough plumbing for water and drain lines must be stubbed through the wall.

You install a lavatory in a counter, whether self-rimming or with a separate rim, in the same way as a sink (Chapter 15). A lavatory fully or partly supported on a wall, however, is hung by a longer procedure.

With the lavatory comes a hanging bracket (Fig. 16-16). Set the fixture upside down on the floor, and place the bracket on its back against the clips. Then measure from the top of the bracket to the top of the lavatory (dimension A), and from the top of the rim to the top of the lavatory (dimension B).

Now mark on the wall the vertical centerline of your lavatory (step 1 in Fig. 16-16). It should pass right through the center of the nipple for the waste line. Next, determine the height of the rim of the lavatory (dimension C); standard is 30 to 33". To dimension C add dimension B and subtract dimension A. Draw a horizontal line at this point across the vertical centerline, using your level (step 2).

On the bracket mark its vertical centerline. Line up the bracket on the wall with its top on the horizontal wall line and the two vertical centerlines aligned (step 3),

and mark the locations of holes for screws. Drill holes into blocking or studs, and attach the bracket with No. 12 FHWS (flat-head wood screws) long enough to go 1" into the wood.

Before you hang the lavatory, place a ring of plumber's putty around the faucet fitting or individual faucets and set it or them in position. Then tighten the nuts on the underside. Clean off excess putty, making sure that none gets into the water lines.

Installation. With a crayon or grease pencil mark the centerline of the lavatory on its top near the back. Line up this mark with the centerline on the wall, and fit the lavatory onto the bracket, holding it firmly on both sides. Then very slowly let go, ready to catch the fixture if you missed alignment or the bracket isn't tight. When the bracket accepts the weight without flinching, prop up the front of the lavatory with a board until you can fit any legs.

Attach the legs loosely to the lavatory, and adjust them so that they are plumb in all directions. On the floor mark the points where legs touch; they have a small tip at the end. Recheck plumb, then remove the

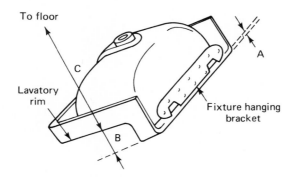

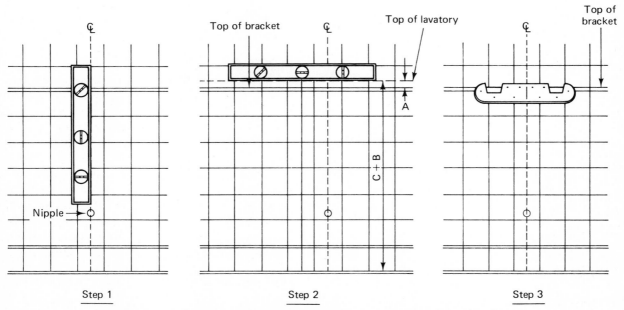

Fig. 16-16. Lavatories that hang on a wall or are partially supported on legs have a two-piece bracket that must be carefully fitted to the wall.

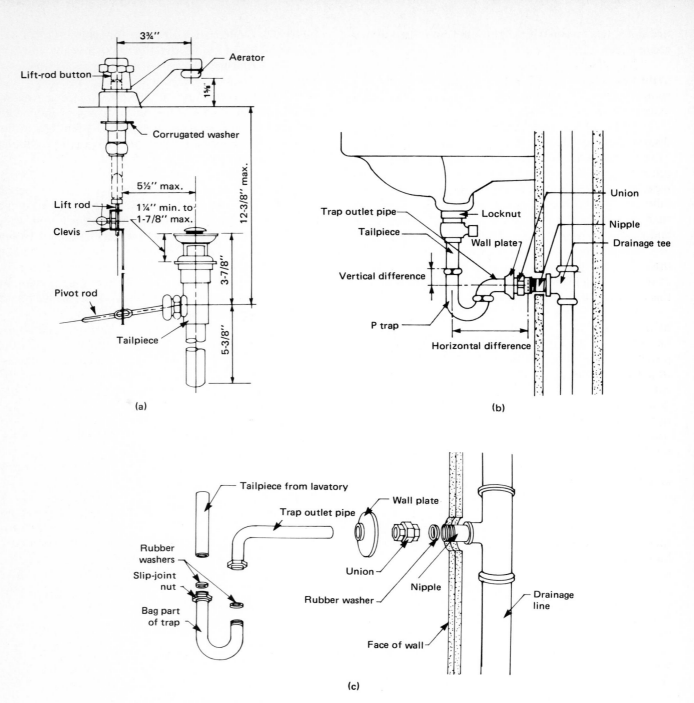

(a)

(b)

(c)

Fig. 16-17. Details of the assembly of the waste line at a lavatory: popup fitting (a); finished waste piping (b); points of measurement (c).

legs and drill a small hole in the flooring to hold the legs in position. Replace them and tighten until they carry the weight of the lavatory, and the fixture is level.

Connect the Waste Line. The fitting that goes into the drain outlet in a lavatory is called a **tailpiece** (Fig. 16-17a). The tailpiece leads into a P-trap with a cleanout (Fig. 16-17b), which in turn leads into a tube drain that connects with a nipple through the wall. Most tailpieces have a pop-up drain operated by a button or lever on the water control fitting.

Begin the waste line, by putting a ring of plumber's putty around the drain outlet in the lavatory. Set the tailpiece in the drain; make sure that the tailpiece is plumb and that the washer on the underside of the lavatory is accurately positioned. With a wrench, tighten the locknut on the tailpiece. Then clean away any excess putty.

Use an adjustable P-trap. It has a swivel neck that lets you adjust for any slight variation in points of connection. Slip the P-trap on the end of the tailpiece. Until you have worked out dimensions and assembled the entire waste line to check the fit, do not final-tighten any connection.

The waste pipe your plumber stubbed through the bathroom wall probably projects several inches into the room. Remove the stub and replace it with a nipple that extends about ½" beyond the wall's surface.

Now take two measurements. Measure the vertical distance between the centerline of the nipple and the end of the P-trap (X in Fig. 16-17c). Then measure the distance between the end and centerline of the trap outlet pipe (Y). If X is greater than Y, you must shorten the tailpiece by the difference in dimensions. If Y is greater than X, you must extend the tailpiece with a coupling and short nipple.

Then measure the horizontal distance (Z) between the end of the nipple through the wall and the centerline of the open end of the P-trap. Cut the trap outlet pipe to this length.

Remove the trap, and assemble the various parts of the drain line from the wall outward. Fit a washer and union on the nipple, slide an escutcheon onto the trap outlet pipe, then fit the pipe onto the union. Set trap washers in place, and hold the trap in position against the end of the tailpiece and the end of the trap outlet pipe to recheck the fit. When the fit is right, tighten the union or slip nut at the nipple. Then push the trap upward onto both the tailpiece and outlet pipe, and tighten the nuts at the slip joint.

To connect the pop-up mechanism (Fig. 16-17a), attach the pivot rod to the tailpiece, and fit the lift rod in place. Fit the clevis onto the lift rod, then fit the pivot rod through its spring clip into the clevis. Push both the pop-up and lift rod lever as far down as they will go, then tighten the clevis screw. Make any adjustments by loosening and retightening the screw in a different position.

Connect the Water Lines. The plumber may have a short stub or a capped nipple extending through the wall. Make sure that the water is shut off at the main valve, then either remove the cap or replace the stub with a nipple extending ½" through the wall. Then check the lavatory manufacturer's diagram for the size of pipe the fixture requires. If the inlet pipe and fixture supply are the same size, proceed with measurements. But if the inlet pipe is larger, say ½" when you need a ⅜" fixture supply line, add a reducing coupling. Remember always to use pipe compound at threaded fittings, always applied to the male threads only.

Between the lower and threaded ends of faucet fittings you need a slip joint or union, a length of vertical pipe, a stop valve to shut off the water supply, a length of horizontal pipe, and either a union or a reducing coupling. The length of the vertical pipe is the distance from the end of the faucet pipe to the centerline of the water inlet less the dimension from the horizontal centerline to the outlet of the valve (Fig. 16-18). The length of the horizontal pipe is the distance from the

centerline of the faucet pipe to the nipple or coupling, less the distance from the vertical center of the valve to the outlet. If you have any trouble making accurate measurements, use flexible tubing for the vertical run.

Preassemble the horizontal and vertical pipes into the stop valve, but again don't tighten the connections. Fit a slip nut over the vertical pipe, and an escutcheon and slip nut over the horizontal pipe. Then fit the assembly in place and tighten all nuts. If you have to thread the horizontal pipe into a reducing coupling, complete this connection first.

Now turn the water on at the main valve, but leave the stop valve closed. Check for leaks in the horizontal line. If none appear, open the valve and check for leaks as far as the faucets. When all is still dry, turn on the faucets and check the drain line for leaks. If you have done your plumbing well, your installation is complete. If you find a leak, seal it with pipe compound and let it harden before retesting.

REMOVING EXISTING FITTINGS

When you relocate fixtures and don't intend to reuse existing supply and waste lines, you must remove fittings and close off the lines behind the wall's or below the floor's surface. With most fixtures you simply disassemble the water and drain lines in the reverse order in which they were assembled, as just described. Be sure that the water is turned off.

To remove the tub spout, stick a piece of wood or the handle of a hammer into the spout and turn counter-clockwise. Remove a shower head with a wrench. All other fittings can remain attached to the plumbingware and be removed with it.

Where water lines come through the wall, remove all piping, including the last nipple that fits into the

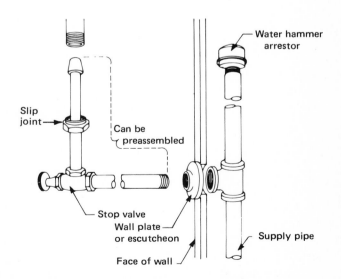

Fig. 16-18. Detail of the assembly of the water line at a lavatory.

main supply pipe. This is the only connection you need to be concerned with, so leave a piece long enough to grip with two wrenches. Once you have the pipe loose, coat the threads of a plug with plumber's putty and insert it in the opening. You may have to enlarge the hole in the wall to accomplish this. Do not patch the hole (see Chapter 19 for patching instructions) until you let water flow through the supply pipe again and are sure that your plug is watertight.

Drain lines must be sealed not only to keep out odors but to prevent any possibility of sewage backing up. Close drain lines that go through a wall in the same way as water lines. Close drains that go through the floor, such as from a bathtub or water closet, with a gasket and cover. Sealing existing plumbing lines may well be a job to turn over to your plumber. He has the special tools and knowledge to do the job quickly and correctly.

Better Storage Space

When you plan open storage space, keep in mind the dimensions of items to be stored or displayed. Here vertical supports are spaced at random. All shelves, whether plywood or glass, rest on standards, and can therefore be adjusted in height. Desk top fits 16" into its niche, projects 8" from it, and is 36" wide. Rack of overhead lights provides both decorative and practical working light. (Courtesy American Plywood Association.)

Few houses have enough storage space. Many of them built in the 1800s had no closets. People stored their clothing in furniture—wardrobes with hanging space and massive chiffoniers for flat clothing. They rarely traveled, so had little or no luggage. Early automobiles included luggage and a rack on which to strap it. Books and magazines were also stored in furniture—bookcases and magazine racks. About the only major storage area was the pantry—a separate room that housed virtually everything now stored in the kitchen.

Yet rooms in very old houses are usually large enough so that you can add storage space where or close to where you need it. Houses built half a century ago are much smaller, bedrooms have some closet space, kitchens have a sprinkling of overhead cabinets and storage space below short counters, and perhaps a bookshelf or two.

Houses built during the era when built-ins were the rage—the 1950s and early 1960s—probably have the most storage space of any ever built. But as building costs have risen, the storage space provided in most houses is limited to the bare essentials—bedroom closets with good access, kitchen cabinet space ranging from minimal to adequate, a shelf or two in the laundry area, and sometimes in more expensive houses bookshelves flanking a fireplace.

Houses with good storage space are so rare that when they come on the market they sell quickly and for top dollar, even though they may have other flaws. You can sharply upgrade the value of your house with well-thought-out storage, so why not add it now while your family can benefit from it?

CLOSETS

A well-planned and fully usable closet has dimensions within specific limitations:

- A minimum width for single closets of 36″; 48″ is better and 60″ is ample.
- A minimum depth of 24″ and a maximum of 30″. Any greater depth wastes space.
- Minimum dimensions for walk-in closets with rods and shelves on both sides of 48″ front to back and 72″ side to side. With a rod on one side only and flat storage on the other, increase depth to 60″ and width to 84″. Other workable layouts with dimensions are shown in Fig. 17-1.
- A minimum door opening width of 30″. Far superior and worth the cost of remodeling are doors that open up the entire width of the closet.
- Clothes rods centered 12 to 14″ from the wall behind them. Standard height above floor level for a rod is 66″ for men; add or subtract ½″ for each 1″ of a man's height above or below 6′-0″. For women standard height is 62″; add or subtract ½″ for each 1″ of her height over or less than 5′-6″. Rods for children's clothes should be adjustable in height, and no lower than 42″.

- A 3″ clearance between the top of a rod and the bottom of the shelf above it. Depth of the shelf should be no less than 12″ (a 1 x 12 will do) or more than 14″.
- A 9″ clearance between the bottom shelf and the underside of any upper shelf. Maximum convenient height above floor level for a shelf is 84″. Depth of the upper shelf should be the same as the lower shelf unless the closet is a walk-in type or has full-width floor-to-ceiling doors. Then its depth can be as much as 18″.

Work within these specifications if you are adding new closets. It will probably not be worth the money to change the shape of existing closets to conform to the ideal, but you can achieve tremendous improvement in many cases simply by widening the door opening, adjusting rod locations, and adding shelves.

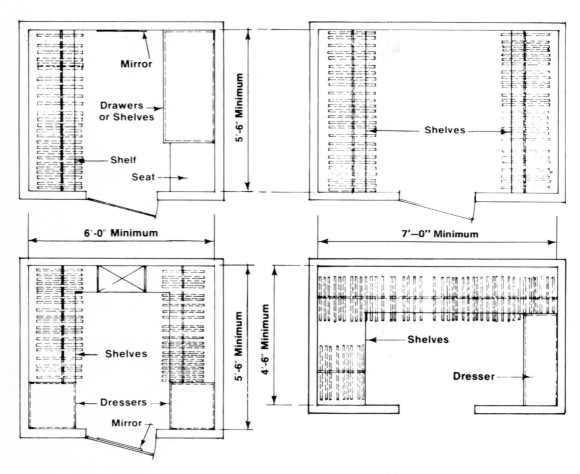

Fig. 17-1. Four good arrangements for walk-in closets, with their minimum practical dimensions.

A NEW CLOSET DOOR

Among life's greatest frustrations is a closet 5' wide with a 2' door. Hanging and shelf space are adequate but access is miserable. You can resolve the problem simply by installing bifold doors.

A **bifold door** is made in two sections hinged together in the middle to open outward. A standard unit consists of a pair of two-section doors. Standard heights are 6'-8", 7'-6", and 8'-0", and standard widths are an even 3', 4', 5', and 6'. Doors are made of prefinished metal or plastic, or unfinished wood that may be painted or stained. Many bifold doors are louvered to allow circulation of air into the closet.

You can also use a pair of hinged doors or a pair of bypass doors on a wide closet. Hinged doors take more floor space to open than bifold doors, although they do provide full access. **Bypass doors**, which slide past each other on parallel tracks, take up no floor space, even when open, but you can never reach more than half the storage space at any one time. Bifold doors open up the entire space and, because they fold against themselves, take up little floor space when open.

Decide on the most appropriate and practical size of doors to install, then proceed as if you were installing a new opening in a wall as described in Chapter 13. Remove the old door, and empty the closet to keep its contents clean. Then remove surface material on both sides to the side walls of the closet on the inside, and to the centerline of a stud beyond the opening you marked on the outside. Before marking the size of the opening, look at the door manufacturer's literature. The opening dimensions given are likely to be for the finished opening, not the rough opening, and you must allow for thicknesses of casings and the recommended clearances.

Case the New Opening

Order casing material of a width equal to the finished thickness of the closet wall. Check one end of jamb casings for square, and trim if necessary. Then measure up the height of the finished door opening, and mark a notch for the head casing. Cut the notch for a tight fit, using a radial arm saw with a dado head, a circular saw with a dado head, or a portable router. It's possible to cut a groove competently with hand tools, such as a backsaw in a miter box, but you'll get a better fit with power tools.

Cut the head casing to length, which is finished opening width plus twice the depth of a notch (usually ⅜"). Insert the head casing into the notches, and nail through the jamb casings with three 12d casing nails into each end of the head casing (Fig. 17-2a). Hold the pieces against a framing square to assure right angle joints. Fit the assembly into the rough opening, plumb and level it with wedges, and nail it into studs (see Fig. 13-11). Recheck the frame for square; bifold doors

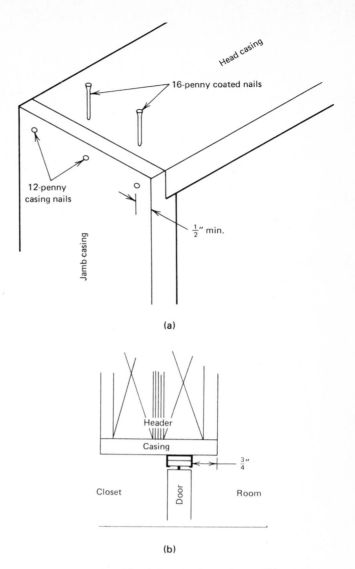

(a)

(b)

Fig. 17-2. Details of installation of a casing at the head of a bifold door, showing method of notching and nailing (a) and where to position the door in its frame (b).

won't work properly unless their frame is absolutely square, even if the surrounding wall is not.

Door Installation

Metal and plastic doors come complete with all hardware, and usually with hinges and knobs already attached. Wood bifold doors may or may not be already hinged, and hardware may not include knobs. If the doors weren't hinged at the factory, connect pairs according to manufacturer's drawings.

Doors pivot at jambs on pins in sockets set in an overhead track, and are supported by a nylon guide where they meet. On the head casing mark the location of the track. There is no set location, but the standard place is ¾" back from the front edge of the door casing (Fig. 17-2b). Hold the track on its mark, and circle the locations of holes for screws. Predrill the holes and in-

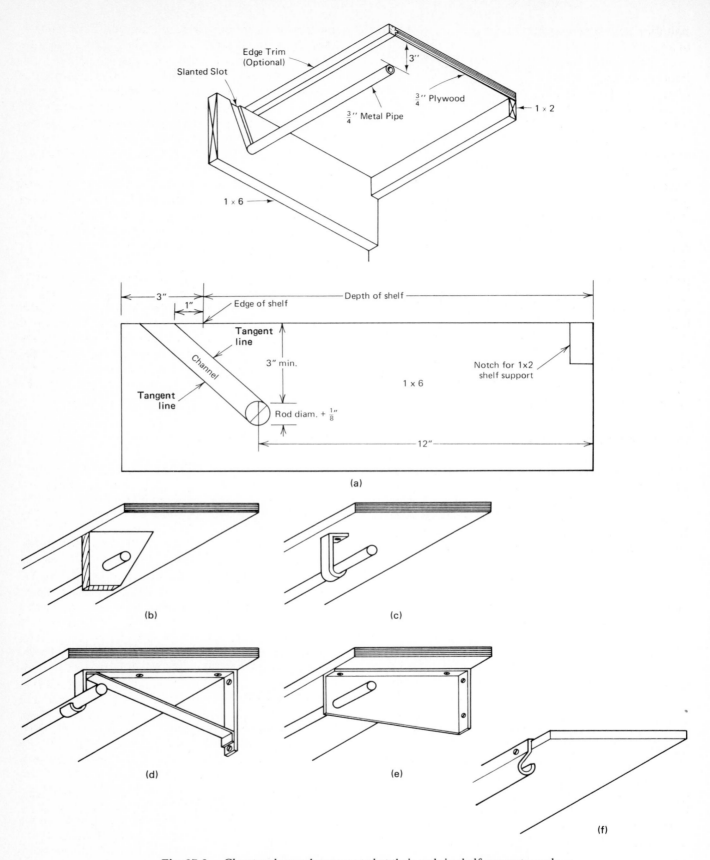

Fig. 17-3. Closet rods may be supported at their ends in shelf supports made from 1 × 6s (a). When shelves are short, rods may hang from the shelves themselves (b, c), and when they are long on brackets that also support the shelves (d, e). One type of manufactured rod support also stiffens a shelf (f).

stall the track. It should fit without cutting, with a gap of about ⅛" at each end.

Before you hang the doors you must finish the floor in the new opening in one of the ways described in Chapter 13. The exception is carpeting; it is better to screw the bottom sockets into the floor first, then cut the carpet to fit around them.

From the hole for the pivot in each top socket drop a plumb bob, and mark the location of the bottom sockets. The pairs of pivot holes must line up exactly. Then fold one pair of doors together, and set the bottom pivot in the bottom socket. Depress the spring-loaded top pivot and snap it into the pivot hole in the top socket. Repeat the operation for the other pair of doors. Then test their ease of movement in the track, their fit against each other, and their horizontal alignment. Doors should clear finish flooring or carpeting by ½ to ¾". You can adjust the level of the doors with a wrench by loosening or tightening the nut on the bottom of the doors.

As the final step, close the doors and, on the inside at the bottom where they meet, mark the locations of closers. When the doors are shut, the closers should fit directly over each other. Attach them with screws, add any door knobs, and the job is done.

RODS AND SHELVES

You can make very useful and attractive shelves out of ½" plywood with screen molding tacked along the cut edge. The molding is ⅝" wide. You can install it flush with the top edge of the shelf for a clean look that hides any raggedness in the cut. Or you can fit it flush with the bottom edge if you prefer a shelf with a stop that prevents stored items from sliding off.

Each shelf must be supported at its ends and on the back wall. A continuous 1 × 2 is adequate for shelves up to 6' long. Longer shelves should be supported also on a center bracket (see Fig. 17-3d, e, and f). End and center supports can also support the closet rod. You can use as rods wood dowels with diameters of 1¼" or 1⅜". Under heavy weights and over a period of years, however, wood fibers stretch and the rod will tend to sag. Less attractive but rigid under heavy loads is a ¾" steel pipe. Its smaller diameter makes hanging easier, too. Center brackets are made to fit these various diameters.

Cut end supports from a 1 × 6 longer by 3" than the depth of the bottom shelf. Notch the back corner (Fig. 17-3a) for any 1 × 2 support. Next, mark the height of the rod, following the rules given earlier in this chapter. Draw a circle with a diameter ⅛" greater than the diameter of the rod. Then measure out 1" from the front edge of the shelf along the top of the 1 × 6, and make a mark.

From the mark draw a line tangent to the circle on the back side. Then draw another line parallel to this line tangent to the other side of the circle. Following the lines, dig a slot ⅜" deep with a router. Then round off, cover, or sand smooth the leading edge of the 1 × 6.

On the three walls mark the height above floor level of the underside of the shelf, according to the rules for good closet design stated earlier. Draw a continuous line through the marks, making sure that it is level at all points. Set the end supports with their top edge on the line, and attach them with 1½" flat-head wood screws, one near each corner. Screw into studs if possible; otherwise, set wall anchors into the surface material and drive the screws into the anchors. Predrill screw holes and countersink the heads. If you expect the installation to be permanent, cover the screw holes with wood putty. In a child's closet drive the screws flush with the wood's surface, and leave them exposed for later removal.

Next install the 1 × 2 cleat and any center bracket level with the shelf line. The 1 × 6s support the ends of the 1 × 2, so a screw every 16" into a stud provides ample intermediate attachment. Cut the shelf to size and set it in place, but don't nail it down. Finally, cut the rod to length with no more than 1/16" clearance at the ends. Drop it in place, paint or stain the shelf and supports, and your new storage space is ready for use for years to come.

LINEN STORAGE

Closet shelves, even the deepest upper ones, are not a good place to store linens, blankets, and spare pillows. You can't protect them easily from dust and mildew, the shelves aren't deep enough, and the items are not easily or safely taken down or stored.

If you plan to add a new linen closet somewhere, build it with inside dimensions of 18 to 20" in depth and 24 to 27" in width with a door 24" wide. An 18" × 24" shelf accommodates two stacks of folded bath or beach towels, a stack of sheets for any size bed, folded blankets, and extra pillows. Cut shelves to fit flush with the inside of the front wall up to a height no greater than 72". Shelves above that height are hard to stock. To use the upper space, case the opening above the closet door on three sides (Fig. 17-4). At the bottom cut a shelf that extends all the way to the outside of the front wall, and support it on fixed 1 × 2s at the back and sides. Then cut a single cabinet door or pair of smaller doors to fit the upper opening, and trim around both doors. You'll find details on cabinet construction and doors in Chapter 15.

A closet that is too deep for practical clothes storage makes an adequate if not ideal linen closet. Remove the rod, shelf, and supports, then patch the holes in the wall with spackling compound. Next add standards, a pair on each side wall.

Locate studs and mark their centerlines with vertical lines drawn on the wall. Then establish the maximum practical height for the top shelf, and the mini-

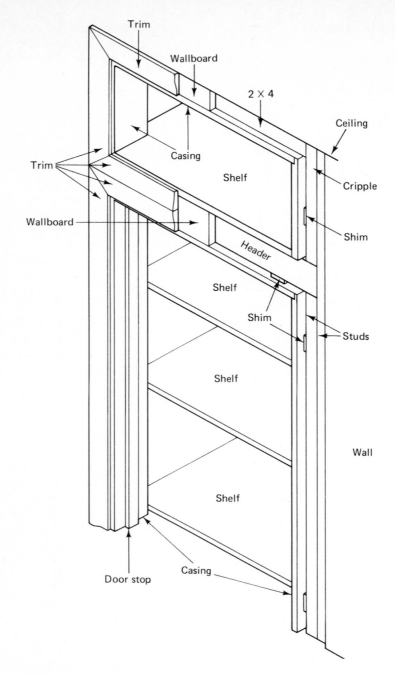

Fig. 17-4. Detail of construction of high storage space above a linen closet, which you enclose behind a pair of cabinet doors.

mum practical height for the bottom shelf. Mark these heights on the centerlines. Standards must extend at least 5″ below the level of the bottom shelf in order to hold snap-in brackets. They do not need to extend above the top of the top shelf.

Cut one standard to length, hold it on the centerline, and mark the locations of top and bottom screw holes. Then, with a level, carry these heights across all other centerlines. Predrill holes for screws 1½″ long. Cut the remaining standards so that the distances from the end of each standard to the nearest screw hole are identical. Attach standards with screws at the top and insert brackets. Then check the level across all pairs of

brackets. If necessary to achieve level, drill new top holes. When all brackets are level, insert the bottom screws. Then drill screw holes through all other holes in the standards, and add screws.

Snap-in brackets have a little nodule at the end that prevents narrow shelves from sliding off. These nodules are in the way of larger shelves. Cut linen shelves to size; don't measure from wall to wall, but allow about ⅛″ clearance at standards. Set the shelves in place, and mark on the underside where you need to provide any recess for the nodules. At each mark drill a hole ¼″ in diameter and ⅛ to ³⁄₁₆″ deep. The nodules fit into the holes and hold the shelves secure.

Standards and brackets are ideal whenever you need adjustable shelves anywhere. You can hang shelves on walls or in kitchen or utility cabinets. Just make sure that you attach them into wood framing or wall anchors; the screws may pull out of wallboard or plaster. And be sure to set the brackets firmly in the slots in standards. Otherwise, they could pop out and the shelves collapse.

STORAGE IN WASTED SPACE

If you're short of storage space—and nearly everyone is—walk around each room of your house looking for space that you don't often use, that you don't fully use, or that would be more useful for storage than its present purpose. Don't overlook any area and, most important, do not dismiss any area as impractical until you have let your mind run free. Let's take a couple of examples.

Suppose you have a closet that is too deep for clothes and in the wrong location for linens. Could you reduce the depth of the closet to 24″ by building a thin partition, and reach the partitioned space from some other direction (Fig. 17-5a)? Perhaps you would end up with a space 3′ deep and only 8″ wide. That is an excellent shape for card tables, serving trays, boxed games, tennis racquets, and gift wrapping paper.

Suppose that you have rooms with high ceilings. Rather than lower the ceiling in the entire room, could you build a long cabinet just below the existing ceiling on one or two sides of the room (Fig. 17-5b)? Perhaps the space is only 18″ deep and 12″ high inside. It would not be convenient to reach without a short stepladder, but it could hold items that you use only two or three times a year, such as a turkey roaster, portable heater, picnic basket, boxed out-of-season clothing, or jars for canning. Or perhaps you would prefer a long open shelf in place of a cabinet for displaying china and glassware,

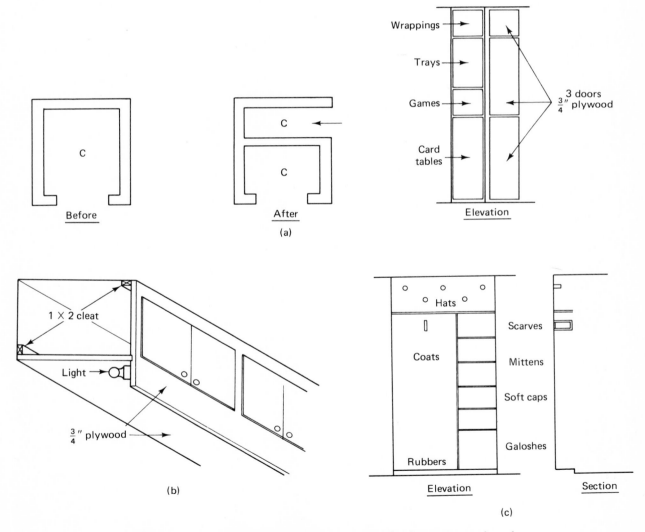

Fig. 17-5. Here are ideas for making better use of a deep, narrow closet by dividing it (a); of a high ceiling by hanging cabinets around the perimeter of the room (b); and of a wide hallway by building in a shallow closet for outdoor clothing (c).

or a special collection of some kind. You can make either cabinets or shelves serve a dual purpose by adding a fascia and installing lighting behind it.

Suppose that you have no guest closet. Can you spare enough hall space for a floor-to-ceiling cabinet only 9″ deep outside and only 48″ wide (Fig. 17-5c)? In space this shallow you can hang four winter coats, store five hats on pegs, set six pairs of galoshes or rubbers, and still have shelf space for mittens and scarves.

The design of such storage cabinets depends on the space available, the size and shape of items to be stored, and convenience to their point of use. All you have to do is come up with the locations and the dimensions.

18

Repairing The Interior

Some decorative wall treatments are complex. This one isn't. Old wall surfaces are covered with horizontal furring strips of ¼" plywood—at the floor, ceiling, and two intermediate points where maximum bumping is likely to occur. Vertical strips are spaced to take half-width (23 7/8") strips of decorative plywood, with a gap of 1½" between. Exposed areas of the strips are painted first, then plywood applied with glue and a few finishing nails. Finished gap at floor and ceiling will also be 1½". (Courtesy American Plywood Association.)

So far the information in this book has concentrated predominantly on structural improvements and better space arrangements. The next four chapters cover the final stages toward completion of a remodeling: repairing existing surfaces in this chapter, applying new surfaces in the next two, and trimming in Chapter 21.

Being a fibrous material, wood tends to deflect under loads over a period of time. Codes and building practices allow for some deflection; materials strong enough not to deflect would add unnecessarily to the already high cost of construction. Only when wood framing gets so far out of shape that you must prevent further deterioration, or when parts (such as doors) don't function properly, or when you can't apply sur-

face materials by standard procedures, should you spend the extra money for structural repair.

A SAGGING FLOOR

Floors that slope downward from exterior walls are the most common problem. There are a number of possible causes, but all can be attributed either to age or poor building practices. When a floor slopes in the same direction that joists run, the usual cause is stretched fibers in the joists or a drop in the supporting beam near the center of the house. When a floor slopes across joists, especially in platform construction, the builder

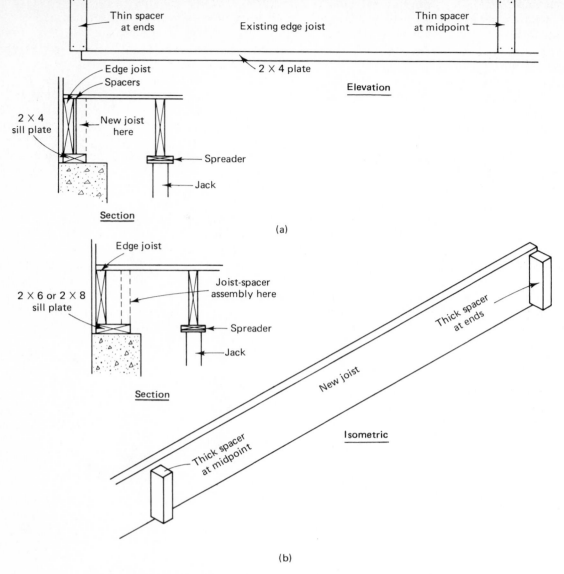

Fig. 18-1. To prevent further sag at sidewalls, add spacers to edge joists, then add a new joist when sill plates are 2 × 4s (a). If sill plates are wider (b), add spacers to a new joist, then toenail the assembly in place.

may have omitted the joist just inside the edge joist, and the weight of inadequately supported sidewalls on the subfloor causes the sag.

When lumber has been overstressed for a period of time, it's almost impossible and generally not advisable to remove all sag. By correcting the support problem you create new problems in surface materials. Each situation is unique, but as a rule of thumb the most practical solution is to stop further sag and to reduce existing sag no more than two-thirds. How much headroom you have to work with bears strongly on what you can do.

Add a Missing Joist

When a joist is missing under a side wall, rent a pair of jacks and set them at the third points of the next joist in-

ward. If the span is less than 12', use a single jack under midspan. Use pieces of ¾" scrap plywood about a foot square to spread the weight at the base, and about a foot long and as wide as the jack support at the top. Raise the jacks each day about ¼" and not more than ½" until the dimension from the sill plate to the subfloor at the top of the foundation wall is equal to the depth of a joist.

Then measure the distance from the side of the edge joist to the edge of the sill plate. It should be 4", but may be 2" or 6". From this dimension subtract 1½" for the thickness of the new joist. If the remainder is about ½", cut spacer strips of plywood of that thickness 3" wide and as long as the depth of a joist. Nail a spacer at the ends of the edge joist and at its midpoint (Fig. 18-1a). Then cut a new joist to length, fit it against the spacers, and nail to them with 8d nails.

If the remainder is 1½" or more, rip spacers out of scrap 2 × 4s with their width equal to the remainder and their length about an inch shorter than the depth of the edge joist. Attach these spacers to a new joist cut to length (Fig. 18-1b). Fit the joist in place, then toenail it into the plate and into joists or beams at each end.

Finally, at the same slow rate, lower the jacks. This process relieves the pressure of the wall on the sub-floor and joists close to the wall, and helps furniture on the floor above near the wall to stand straighter. It won't help to straighten joists distorted from the weight. To correct that problem fully you have to run a steel I-beam beneath the midpoints of joists, and support its ends on columns. Even if you have enough headroom for a beam, the cost in money and appearance is likely to be too great for the results you achieve.

Raise a Center Beam

A more common cause of sag, particularly in old houses, is a main wood girder that has settled, letting the joists it supports settle with it. The solution is simpler. The girder is almost always beneath the center of the house, and in that position divides basement space. Adding columnar support under the beam doesn't further divide the space nor affect headroom.

For beam supports you can use either steel columns or permanent jacks. The jacks are more expensive, but they do permit you to adjust for any further settling that results from weak soil under the house rather than weak structure. Both columns and permanent jacks must be supported on a concrete cap (Fig. 18-2) formed either on an existing basement floor or on a footing in a crawl space. At the top you bolt a steel plate to the under side of the beam. You can use 4 × 4 or 6 × 6 wood posts for support if you prefer, but they will compress slightly under the weight of the floor.

Spacing of Supports. The maximum dimension between supports should be 8'-0". Stress on the beam is greatest at its midpoint, which would indicate a need for a column there. With a single column, however, all weight is transmitted downward at a single point, and it may be more than an old concrete floor can stand without cracking. A safer solution is a pair of columns 4 to 6' apart and placed equidistant from the midpoint of the beam.

From the ends of the beam at the centerline of its

Fig. 18-2. Details of support for a steel column (a) and a wood post (b) where they rest on a basement floor and how they support a girder.

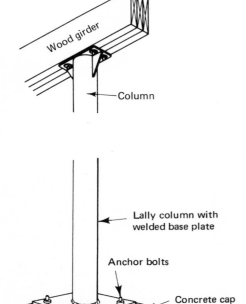

(a)

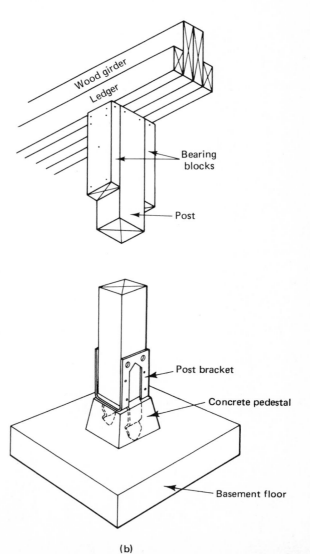

(b)

thickness drop a plumb bob, and mark the points where the end of the bob touches the floor or ground. Then with a chalk line or straight line, connect the two points. Next mark on the underside of the beam the points of support you established, and drop a plumb bob from these points. Mark the new points on the floor or dirt to establish the cross centerlines of the concrete cap or pedestal.

Now place temporary jacks under the beam along the chalk line where they won't interfere with forming and pouring the base, or with installing and attaching the columns—at least 24″ from crossed centerlines. Place the jacks and raise the beam as described earlier in this chapter until its low point is about ¼″ higher than its ultimate height.

Form the Base. While you are raising the beam, prepare concrete forms. From a piece of scrap plywood cut a template 12″ square—the shape of a cap. Use four 18 to 20″ lengths of 2 × 4 if you're working on a concrete floor; use 2 × 6s if you're working on dirt. Lay the lengths around the template so that they butt at one end and lap at the other (Fig. 18-3a). Nail them together, then remove the template.

Set the forms in place. If you are working over dirt, set each form so that its corners are all on crossed centerlines. In a basement you probably won't want the

corners of the base sticking so far into usable space. Therefore, mark the midpoints on the sides of the form, and tack on strings that run from midpoint to opposite midpoint. Turn the form over, and line up the strings with the crossed centerlines.

With each form positioned, check its level in both directions. Cut away dirt at high corners; do not fill at low corners. When the top of the form is absolutely level, drive stakes just outside the corners, and nail the form extensions to them.

The process of pouring concrete can easily move a form unless it is firmly held in place. On a concrete floor set each form in place and level it by shimming at low corners. Then place bricks or stones around the form. This blocking must not extend above the tops of the forms.

To form a pedestal for a post, use ¾″ plywood or 1″ boards. The shape is a truncated pyramid (Fig. 18-3b). Inside dimensions at the top should be equal to the exact size (not the nominal size) of the post. Inside dimensions at the bottom should be 3″ greater, and the height of the form 6″. Cut opposite sides alike, with two sides overlapping the other two. Nail the four pieces of form with duplex (double-headed) nails, one set near the top and the other 3″ down from the top.

To hold the bottom of the form together, build a collar out of 1 × 4s (Fig. 18-3c). Its inside dimensions

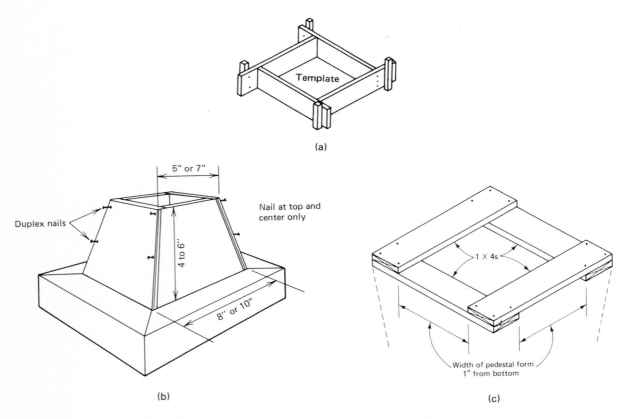

Fig. 18-3. The forms to build for a concrete cap (a) under a steel column and for a concrete pedestal (b) under a wood post. The collar (c) fits over the form in (b) to prevent it from spreading.

are equal to the outside dimensions of the form 1″ above its base. Slip the collar over the form, and set the form on its marks. Level it as described for a cap form. Set bricks or stones on the collar to hold the form in place during pouring.

Pour the Base. For the little concrete you need, order a sack of premixed high-strength concrete to which you add only water. Slowly pour the concrete into the form; be very careful not to knock it out of position. While the mix is still wet, insert reinforcement. In a cap use ½″ steel rods 9″ long and placed to form a square about 1″ above the bottom of the form. In a pedestal form a similar square with rods about 3″ shorter than the bottom dimension of the form. Then add two 5″-long rods vertically near the corner.

Level the top of the cap or pedestal with a trowel, using the edges of the form as your leveling guide. In a cap you then insert anchor bolts—leaving off the washers and nuts—about 2″ in from each corner so that they rise just inside the reinforcement. In a pedestal insert the metal bracket into which the post fits. Make sure that both bolts and brackets are plumb. Then with your trowel, repair any humps or hollows in the top of the concrete until it is again level and smooth.

Keep the concrete moist for at least 48 hours. Then remove the form by pulling the duplex nails. Let the concrete cure for another 72 hours. In the meantime measure the distance from the top of the concrete to the underside of the beam to be supported. If you are using a steel column, subtract ¼″ for the overjacking you did. This dimension is the length of the column including the plates at top and bottom. If you are using a wood post, subtract the same ¼″ at the top, plus the thickness of the bracket on the pedestal, plus another ¼″ for bottom clearance. To prevent rot, the end of the post should not touch the concrete. This dimension is the length of post required.

Install a Column. When you order a column, the steel fabrication shop will weld to it a top plate braced and drilled, and a drilled bottom plate. You need to tell the fabricator the overall length of the column *with* plates, the width of beam being supported, the size of the concrete cap, whether the axes of the bottom plate are parallel or at 45° to the long axis of the top plate, and the locations of bolt holes in the bottom plate. For accuracy make a template out of cardboard, set it on the cap, punch out the holes for bolts, mark the axis of the beam above, and give it to your fabricator. Otherwise, the plate may fit at the base but be 90° off at the beam. The holes in the bottom plate must be large enough so that you can fix the bottom plate over the anchor bolts and still slide the top plate under the beam.

Fit the plate on the cap, plumb the column, add washers, and turn the nuts finger-tight. Then lower the jacks until the beam just touches the top plate but does not rest on it. Recheck plumb, then mark the locations of bolt holes. Drill holes in the bottom of the beam for bolts, add washers, and finger-tighten the nuts. Once again check plumb. When plumb is perfect, tighten all nuts with a wrench.

Install a Post. Recheck the posts for length. Then at the top add bearing blocks (see Fig. 18-2b) so that the width of the post and blocks is approximately equal to the width of the beam. In the bracket at the bottom set a pair of shims to support the post until you attach it. Pencils work well as shims. Set the post in place and plumb it; it should clear the beam by about ¼″. While someone holds the post plumb, start nails into the bottom holes in the bracket. Recheck plumb. Then drive the nails home and remove the shims. Through the top holes in the bracket insert lag screws, and tighten them with a wrench.

Finally, drop the jacks until the beam just touches the post. Recheck plumb one more time. Then toenail upward through the post and bearing blocks into the beam in one direction, and downward through the beam into blocks in the other direction.

Now lower the jacks until they are clear, and remove them.

AN UNEVEN FLOOR

With jacks and additional supports you can correct many floor problems where the amount of deflection is not more than 1% of the span. If you face one or two other conditions, try a different approach. Perhaps your floor surface is uneven—has some low spots and some high spots. The most likely causes are joists that weren't level to begin with or have dropped at different rates, or a warped subfloor. Perhaps a foundation wall has sunk, and the floor of a room slopes downward toward that wall.

If you have enough headroom and working space, you can level an unevenly supported floor by setting an I-beam on jacks and slowly raising the beam until all joists rest on it. Then bolt the beam to each joist, and support it on steel columns. Under most conditions this is a job for a building contractor.

If the problem is warped subflooring, you must remove existing finish flooring, cover the uneven subflooring with a rigid underlayment, and lay a new floor. It may be possible to apply underlayment directly over an existing floor of wood or resilient material, but you are likely to have problems with floor levels at doorways.

Resurfacing

Often, the most practical solution, not only to an uneven floor but also a floor that slopes downward in one direction only, is a new floor base of lightweight con-

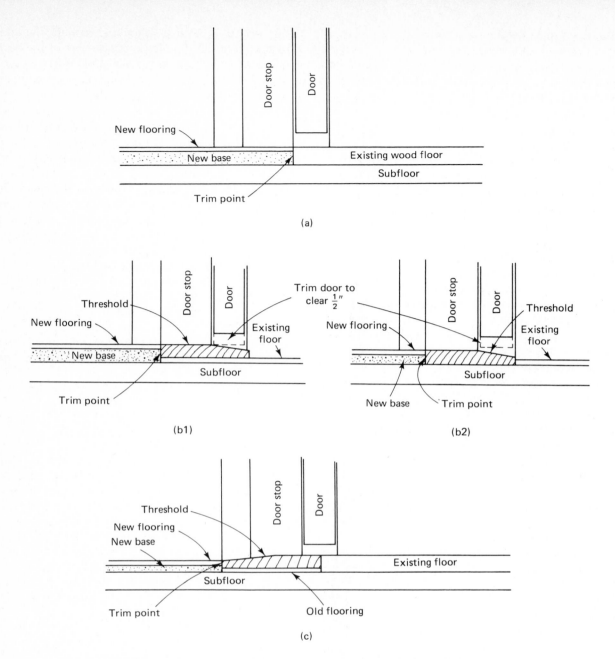

Fig. 18-4. Three ways to establish the level of new finish flooring laid over a lightweight concrete base. Note how the point for trimming existing flooring varies with conditions.

crete. As long as you own or can rent the tools for mixing the cement and smoothing its surface, you can do the job yourself. You can pour the cement base over an existing subfloor or underlayment that is firm and clean. You must remove existing finish flooring.

The concrete base is sufficiently light so that no extra structural support is necessary. To prevent further settling, however, you should support the structure under it with columns or permanent jacks as described earlier in this chapter. You can taper the thickness of a concrete base to no more than a skim layer, but should do so only as a last resort. The base is less likely to crack and spall off if you aim for a minimum thickness of ¼".

Establish Floor Level. The first and most difficult step is establishing the final floor level. Often the high point of a floor is at a doorway, so start there. You have three options (Fig. 18-4). If the flooring in both rooms is wood (Fig. 18-4a), let the floor height at the doorway be the finish floor height in the unremodeled room, and subtract the thickness of new finish flooring to establish the height of the base. For new finish flooring apply either resilient tiles or thin wood blocks. Allow $\frac{1}{16}$" for the thickness of mastic into which to lay the tiles or blocks.

If the flooring in both rooms is thin tiles or linoleum (Fig. 18-4b1), you need a threshold at the doorway and must trim the bottom of the door to clear it. The threshold may be installed on the existing floor, and flooring removed up to the back side of it. Or, to save a little height, you can remove flooring to the front edge of the threshold (Fig. 18-4b2), and set it on the subfloor. In either case the height of the concrete base is the height of the threshold when installed less the thickness of new finish flooring.

If flooring in the two rooms is different (Fig. 18-4c), proceed as if it was the same in both rooms, with the level of the floor in the adjoining room at the starting point for planning.

Mark Base Level. To prepare for pouring a concrete base, clear the room completely. Then carefully remove trim at the floor; you should be able to reuse all of it with little or no adjustment. At some point around the edge of the room, measure the thickness of the finish flooring you must remove.

If you are going to need a threshold, confirm the base level you worked out before you tear up the floor. Buy a thin wood threshold and set it loosely in place on the finish floor. Mark its height on both door jambs. If you follow Fig. 18-4b1 or b2, subtract the thickness of new finish flooring, including mastic, and make another set of marks. If you follow Fig. 18-4c, subtract the heights of both existing flooring and new flooring, and make another set of marks. Mark the new level with chalk lines snapped on all walls.

Then, while two people stretch a taut string from chalk line to chalk line across the room at various points, you measure from string to floor wherever they seem closest together. As long as the measurement is at least ¼″, the base level you marked is acceptable. Otherwise, snap new chalk lines to assure this minimum thickness at any point.

If you don't need a threshold (Fig. 18-4a) you must tear out the floor before marking the level of the base, because it will be below the level of existing flooring.

At each doorway mark the point to which you will remove existing flooring, depending on which option you chose—the back edge of door stops, the back edge of the threshold, or the front edge of the threshold. Center the threshold on jamb casings.

Remove Old Flooring. To remove flooring, work from an outside wall toward a doorway. Use a crowbar under the long sides of wood strip flooring. Pry against a 2 × 4 laid across at least two studs to protect the wall while you loosen the first few strips. When you reach the trim point, set a power saw to the thickness of the flooring, and rip along the trim line.

To remove linoleum or resilient tiles, loosen the first edges with a putty knife, then work with a broadknife. You must remove not only the flooring but the adhesive in which it was laid and any building paper. At the trim line cut with a roofer's or linoleum knife. This stage of your work is done when the subfloor or underlayment is exposed from wall to wall and the edge shaped at doorways. Clean the area thoroughly with a broom. Then, if you have an attachment to your vacuum cleaner for cleaning chair cushions, use it to pick up fine dirt and grit that sweeping missed.

One step remains before pouring the base. If you chose the option of Fig. 18-4a, snap chalk lines around the wall at a level equal to the height of flooring at the doorway less the height of new finish flooring. If you chose the option of Fig. 18-4 b or c, install the threshold. Cut it to width, set it in place, and mark on the door stops the amount they must be trimmed to fit to the top of the threshold. Remove and trim the stops, set the threshold in mastic, and replace the stops.

Form at Edges. Finally, nail 1 × 1 strips along the wall with their top edges on the chalk lines. When the distance between the subfloor and chalk lines is less than ¾″, cut strips to length, lay them against the wall, rest them on the floor, and level them. Then with a scriber measure the distance between the top of the strip and the chalk line.

With the scriber set to this dimension and one leg on the subfloor, draw a line along the side of the strips. Remove each one, rip it along the line, and reset it. Its top should lie on the chalk line, and its bottom on the uneven floor. Nail strips to the wall, or to the floor if they are too thin to attach horizontally. The strips not only establish the height of the concrete base, but serve as a runner for a screed to level it. They also act as a carpet strip when needed.

Mix and Pour the Base. Mix enough base so that you can complete the job in a single pouring if possible. If you can't, establish a logical stopping point, such as the midpoint of the long dimension of the room. At this point measure the width of the room from screed strip to screed strip, and cut a 2 × 2 to that length. Fit the 2 × 2 in position, level it, and scribe its bottom so that its top fits level with the strips. Set this temporary form back in place, and hold it there with small blocks nailed to the subfloor with duplex nails.

To finish the concrete base you need a shovel or spade, a screed, a darby, a float, and a mason's trowel. A **screed** is nothing more than a straight length of 2 × 4. It must be long enough to rest on opposite form strips, yet short enough so that you can wiggle it back and forth as you draw it toward you to level the base. The width of the room less ¾″ is about the correct length. At most tool rental shops you can rent a **darby**, used for compacting the surface, and the float and trowel.

Once you start work there is no turning back and no place to stop until you reach a temporary form or the other wall of the room. It is important therefore to know what to do, how to do it, what is likely to happen, and how to correct mistakes *before* you begin.

You need at least four people: one to mix the concrete base and bring it to the room, one to work the wet mix as soon as it is poured, and two to operate the screed. Work in moderate weather so that you can open windows, and work toward the door through which you exit. Because you will be working in a confined area, plan to work only as much floor area as you can darby from outside that poured area. Small darbies come in 3′ and 6′ lengths.

As soon as the mix is poured in an area, use the spade to force it against the strips and to spread it evenly to a level slightly higher than the strips. Begin screeding immediately, starting at one wall and working toward the unfinished area. Move the screed back and forth across the surface in a slight zigzag pattern. Have the helper with the spade keep an eye out for low spots, and fill them before the screed gets there.

As soon as an area is leveled with the screed, it must be darbied to further smooth and compact the surface. Darbies have a slightly curved blade that slides smoothly on the surface. While using one, be careful not to step or lean on the screeded surface.

As quickly as one area is darbied, repeat the process in the next area, and continue until the entire surface has been darbied. All the ingredients in the mix are heavier than water and, as they settle, they force water to the surface. You must screed and darby before this action, called **bleeding**, can occur. Even after you darby, some water will appear on the surface. Do not touch the darbied surface, however, until this water evaporates.

The next step is **floating**, the process by which you level any little uneven areas, compact the surface material, and erase any marks left by the darby. The proper time for floating is difficult to judge. The base should still be plastic enough so that floating brings fine particles to the surface, but firm enough to bear your weight. Many experts work with the float in one hand and their weight supported on the darby in their other hand.

Do not walk on a surface before or during floating. Kneel on a **kneeboard**; you can make one out of plywood and 1 × 2s (Fig. 18-5). You need two, one to kneel on and one to step onto when you start work on another floor area.

The base is ready for the final step, troweling, when it is hard enough to produce a ringing sound as you scrape the edge of a trowel across it. If water still comes to the surface when you start to trowel, stop; the base isn't ready for troweling.

As you use a darby, float, or trowel, keep the tool as flat on the surface as you can, especially a trowel. An old tool with slightly rounded edges does a better job than a new one, and will leave fewer marks. If you plan to cover the base with carpeting or wood flooring, a single troweling is adequate. But if you intend to apply resilient flooring, trowel once with a large trowel, then go over the surface an hour or so later with a smaller trowel. The more you trowel, the smoother surface you obtain.

CRACKED CEILINGS

Because of the angle from which you view it, a droopy ceiling isn't as noticeable as a sagging floor. That's good, because it isn't easy to correct. As with a sagging floor, the cause lies in joists that have deflected either

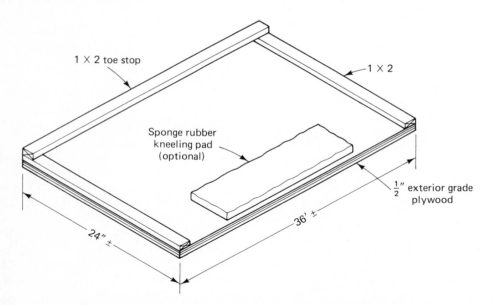

Fig. 18-5.   While you float flat concrete, a kneeboard not only spreads your weight and prevents damage to the fresh surface, but also makes it easier on your knees. You can make a kneeboard from plywood and 1 × 2s.

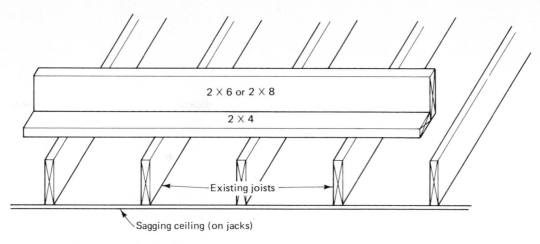

Fig. 18-6. To build a strongback attach a full-length piece of joist material to a 2 × 4 to form an L. Then nail through the 2 × 4 and toenail through the vertical member into each ceiling joist to strengthen the structure against sag.

because of age or because they are undersized for the weight they carry. Two structural corrections and several cosmetic solutions are possible.

Structural Repairs

If you can work in the space above ceiling joists and don't plan to finish it, find the midpoint of the sag. If the entire ceiling droops, carefully and very slowly raise it with jacks. Place pieces of plywood about 24″ square on the jacks to spread the upward thrust over as broad a ceiling area as possible. Then cut a length of joist material to stretch across sagging joists from one end of the ceiling to the other. Use no less than a 2 × 6, and a 2 × 8 is better if you have the height available. Attach this stiffener, called a **strongback**, to a 2 × 4 and nail both members at each joist (Fig. 18-6). The strongback will help support the weight of the ceiling structure and finish ceiling materials.

If the area above the ceiling is unfinished but you intend to finish it, raise the joists with jacks as just described. Then lay a plywood subfloor as shown in Chapter 10. Use no thickness less than ¾″; 1″ or ⅞″ plywood is much stiffer. And use only tongue-and-groove plywood, which will act like a beam to prevent deflection.

When ceiling droop is not uniform but in only one area, chances are that a joist has split or was installed with its crown down. To raise a single joist, place a jack directly below the point of greatest sag, and raise the ceiling to just above final level. Then cut two blocks of joist-sized material, the pieces equal in length to spaces between joists. Install a block between the bad joist and each adjacent joist at the midpoint of their span, offset them slightly, and nail through the sides of the joists into the ends of the blocks. The blocks help spread the weight carried by a weak joist.

To strengthen a split joist, jack up the ceiling and

apply metal splice plates (see Chapter 8) on both sides of the joist at the point of weakness. Then block as just described with four blocks, a pair at each end of the splice plates.

If you can't work above the ceiling, the only way to make structural corrections is to remove ceiling materials and work from below. Unless your ceiling is in very bad shape, however, this approach is messy, slow, and expensive. Resurfacing may do the job just as effectively.

Resurfacing

You can resurface a ceiling with four materials. If the surface is uneven but otherwise in good condition, roll or brush on a textured paint. Light reflecting off a smooth surface accentuates its flaws. Textured paint has a slightly rough surface that hides those flaws. It is available at most paint stores.

Paint may also hide small cracks for awhile, but if structural stress continues, those cracks will eventually begin to show through. With another material this is much less likely. Called the Pleko Wall Coating System, it is a combination of polymer and aggregate that has exceptional resistance to cracking. It stretches with the movement of the structure, and may be applied on both exterior and interior surfaces over most types of existing materials—even some metals. The surfaces must first be coated with a special sealant. You apply the Pleko coating with a trowel to a thickness of $\frac{1}{16}$ to $\frac{1}{8}$″, then immediately add texture with a trowel or a perforated foam roller. Manufactured by Kern-Tac, Inc.,* the product is available through a growing network of dealers around the country. It comes in a number of earth tints and requires no painting.

*For the name of the nearest dealer, write Kern-Tac, Inc., P.O. Box 98287, Tacoma, WA 98498.

If your ceiling is cracked, but the material is still firmly attached, you can also cover it with ¼" gypsum wallboard. Ceiling structure must be sound, however, because the new ceiling will add weight. Use the longest pieces available, and work out the ceiling pattern in advance, as described in Chapter 19, so that you have a minimum of butt joint to finish.

Thin wallboard is somewhat heavy, quite flexible, and breaks easily. To do the job right you need three people, one at each end of a sheet to lift and hold it in position while the third begins attachment at the center of the sheet and works outward. Details of application are shown in Chapter 19. To raise yourself to working level, build a temporary scaffolding of sawhorses and sheets of plywood or planks. As an alternative you may be able to rent **stilts**—adjustable metal extenders that you clamp on your legs. With them you can walk anywhere in the room at the proper level. Just don't drop your tools.

With the fourth choice of ceiling material, acoustical tiles, you can camouflage a sag, cover unevenness, and add sound control all at one time. When headroom permits, you can install a ceiling grid as shown in Chapter 13. When headroom is limited, install individual tiles.

As long as your existing ceiling surface is firm, apply the tiles with mastic. By using the minimum thickness of mastic at low points in the ceiling and greater thicknesses at high points, you can achieve a level ceiling—or close enough to it so that you can't tell the difference from eye level. If you have a cracked or

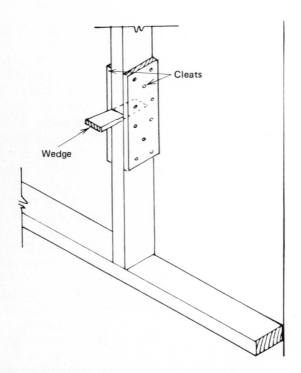

Fig. 18–7. Correct a crooked stud by cutting part way through it, straighten it, fill the cut with a thin wedge, then add strengthening cleats on both sides.

loose ceiling surface, install a series of 1 × 2 furring strips as a base for attaching tiles with staples. As you install the strips, shim them at high points so they are level on the bottom. Procedures are described in Chapter 19.

WAVY WALLS

Luckily, unevenness in wall surfaces is not common—luckily because it is difficult to correct. You can check for waviness by placing the edge of a long, straight 2 × 4 against the surface, first vertically, then horizontally. If the wall bows from top to bottom along its entire length, particularly a bearing wall, it is carrying more weight than it was built for. Call a contractor into consultation to see whether you should live with the problem or if it is likely to get worse and the wall should be rebuilt. There is no simple way to straighten a deflecting wall.

If the wall bows from top to bottom at just one point, and bows at the same point when you hold the 2 × 4 horizontal, the most likely cause is a crooked or cocked stud. If walls are plaster, the problem may be variable thickness of plaster that can be corrected with a power sander.

Crooked Studs

A crooked stud is not a sign of structural weakness, and you're better off to live with the uneven wall than to try to correct it. But if you plan to resurface the wall anyway and want to correct the flaw, mark on the wall the point of greatest bow. Then clear enough wall material around that point so you can get a saw blade into the offending stud and can swing a hammer on both sides of it.

At the point of greatest bow cut about two-thirds of the way through the stud. The cut will relieve the bow. With your level plumb the stud. Then drive a thin wedge into the cut (Fig. 18-7) with its end sticking out. To replace the strength lost by cutting, nail a 12" length of 1 × 4 on each side of the stud. Make sure that the stud is plumb before you nail, and that the 1 × 4s are flush with the stud's edge. Then toenail the wedge and trim the excess.

PATCHING PLASTER

What you find between a plaster surface and the structural members behind it depends largely on the age of your house. The oldest houses have a plaster base of wood lath, followed by three coats of plaster—a scratch coat, brown coat, and finish coat. Wood lath was the standard base as late as the 1920s. With the development of expanded metal early in this century, metal lath replaced wood lath in more expensive homes because it provided a better bond and was less susceptible to changes in air temperature and moisture content. Beginning in the 1930s gypsum lath became the standard as a base for three-coat plaster work. Gradually, the brown coat was eliminated, and two-coat plaster prevails today.

You may have to patch a small hole, such as around a new pipe or electrical outlet. Or you may have a large area to resurface, such as the old location of a door you moved. The procedures vary with the type of lath originally used and the size of the hole.

Small Patch, Wood Lath

Wood laths are 4' long and nailed to all studs. When you break through a lath, however carefully, you are likely to break the plaster bond. A cut wood lath provides little support. The only way to patch, then, is to carefully cut away the plaster and lath flanking the hole, and replace them.

Mark on the wall the area to be cut away. Its height should be no less than the total width of broken lath. If the hole is around new pipes stubbed through the wall, cut the hole at least 1" above and below the pipe. Reach into the hole and feel how many laths are broken. The width of patch should be from inside to inside of adjoining studs, not to their centerlines. Make horizontal cuts first, using either a power saw with a carbide-tipped blade or an old utility saw. Plaster dulls blades quickly, so don't use good tools.

With the opening cut, nail short strips of 1 × 4 to the sides of end studs as a base for gypsum lath. The strips don't need to be any longer than the height of the opening. If you are patching around pipes, drill or cut a

hole in the precut patch of gypsum lath at the proper point, and fit the patch over the pipe before nailing. Use lath nails made for the purpose. Then brush away all loose plaster around the opening.

To the lath apply a coat of patching plaster to a depth of about ¼". Then immediately add a second coat to a depth no more than ⅛" below the finished wall surface. Use the largest tool that will fit the opening—a broadknife, trowel, or putty knife. Level the surface of the second coat as much as possible. Then, while it is setting, roughen the surface slightly with a nail, the tines of a serving fork, or something similar. This process, called **scratching**, assures a good bond with the finish coat.

You may apply the finish coat after the basecoat has set and is still damp, or wait until it dries. If you wait, wet the patch's surface with a spray or brush before applying the final coat. Fill the remaining depth full, and level it flush with the surrounding surface with a trowel. Continue to trowel the surface rapidly until the plaster has set. Any fine cracks must be troweled before final set occurs.

Small Patch, Metal Lath

To cut a hole in plaster attached to metal lath, or when you aren't sure what kind of lath you have, mark the size of the area to be removed, and carefully chip away the plaster until the lath is exposed. Cut metal lath with wire snips or metal shears as close to the edge of the plaster as possible.

If the hole to be patched is around pipes, follow the procedure described for wood lath. When you can

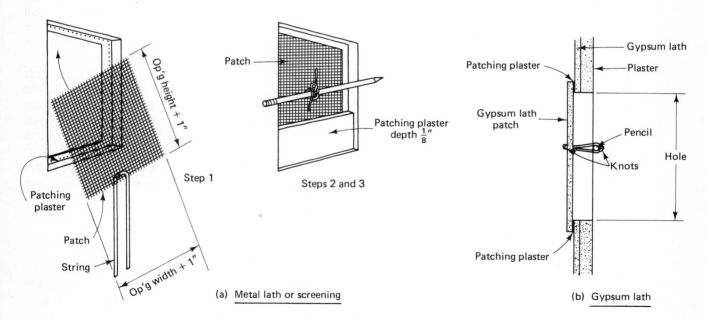

(a) Metal lath or screening

(b) Gypsum lath

Fig. 18-8.   You can patch a small hole in plaster by plastering over a base of metal screening (a) or gypsum lath (b). The string and pencil hold the base in place until it has bonded to the back of existing base material. The method shown in b is also used to patch a small hole in gypsum wallboard.

fit your hand into the hole, cut a patch of metal base about an inch larger in both dimensions than the hole. For this patch use metal lath if available; if not, a piece of stiff metal screening will do. Plastic screening will not.

Mix up a small amount of patching plaster, then brush water onto the edges of exposed plaster around the hole. On the back side of the lath around the hole spread a coat of patching plaster with a putty knife. You may have to distribute it by hand if the hole is quite small. Then apply enough patching plaster to the wet edges to narrow the hole about ½".

Through the metal patch thread a string 6 to 8" long. Then, while you hang onto the string, fit the patch through the hole, turn it upright, and pull it against the patching plaster on the back of existing lath (Fig. 18-8a, step 1). Lay a pencil across the hole, and tie the loose ends of the string to it to hold the patch in place while the plaster sets.

Later, remove the pencil, wet the surface of the patch, and fill the hole to within ⅛" of the finished surface with another coat of patching plaster (Fig. 18a, step 2). Hold onto the string while you do this so that you don't push the patch through the wall. Level this coat, then cut the string flush. After this coat sets, fill the remaining depth with a thin coat of patching plaster, again dampening the surface first. Level with a trowel as described for patching over wood lath.

Small Patch, Gypsum Lath

Follow the procedures for patching over metal lath with two exceptions. Cut the patch out of gypsum lath. Then drill a small hole near the center, tie a knot in a piece of string, and thread both ends through the hole (Fig. 18-8b). The knot prevents the string from pulling through.

Large Patches

The procedure for making a large patch is identical to patching a small hole in plaster on wood lath through the application of gypsum lath. From that point on everything is different. You need additional tools, you use a different type of plaster, and you may need to add grounds.

To illustrate, suppose that you are filling a former door opening. After you apply the new lath across

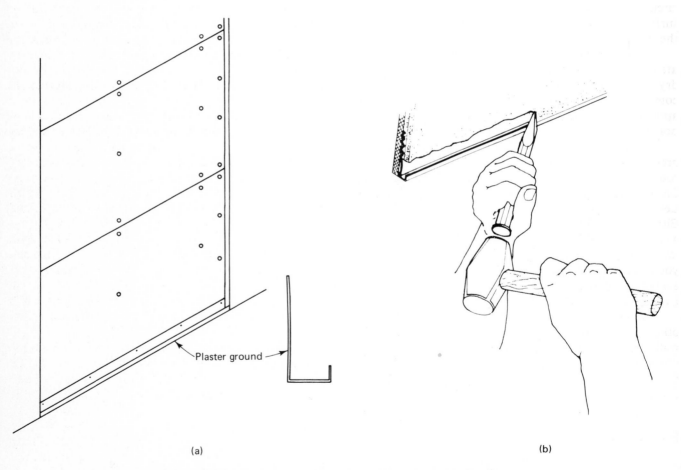

(a)

(b)

Fig. 18-9. A ground (a) is a simple device for establishing the thickness of plaster in a large patch when you have no other guide. After you apply base-coat plaster, chip away that coat at the ground (b) to establish a good bond with the finish coat.

studs, you need to install a ground at floor level. A **ground** is nothing more than a guide to finish thickness. Install a metal ground (Fig. 18-9a) if the thickness of existing plaster is the same as the dimensions of standard grounds available. Otherwise, rip a 1 × 1 to the required thickness.

You will need a container in which to mix plaster and a **hawk** (mortarboard) from which to spread it. You'll need a regular trowel for spreading the plaster, a straightedge for leveling it, and a float for finishing it.

Use ready-mix basecoat plaster for the first coat and ready-mix gypsum plaster for the finish coat. Both types come with aggregate already in them, and all you add is water according to the instructions on the bag. Mix only as much as you can apply in an hour. You should be able to apply each coat easily within that time limit.

Mix the basecoat plaster, transfer some of it to the hawk, and spread it with the trowel. Apply a coat to a depth of about ¼″, then immediately add a second coat to within ⅛″ of the finished surface and bottom ground. Level the surface with the straightedge, then compact it with the darby, as with concrete described earlier in this chapter. Get the surface as level as you can under the circumstances; exact level isn't required. Roughen the surface with a scratcher. Then trim back the basecoat at the ground (Fig. 18-9b).

Basecoat plasters set between two and four hours after mixing. After the basecoat has set and is partially dry, mix and apply the finish coat. If the basecoat is completely dry, wet it with a spray or brush before applying finish plaster. Otherwise, the two coats won't bond properly.

Apply a skin coat less than ⅛″ thick with enough pressure on the trowel to assure a good bond with the roughened basecoat. Then immediately apply a thin finish coat to bring the patch up to final thickness. Level it with a straightedge; a featheredge is better. Either tool should be long enough to rest on the finished wall on both sides of the patched area to assure the levelest possible surface. Then float the surface, just as you float concrete (page 266). After water in the plaster evaporates and the surface looks dull, it is ready to trowel.

With the trowel in one hand and a wet brush in the other, brush the surface slightly with water. A wallpapering brush is excellent for this purpose. Follow the brush immediately with the trowel, and continue this process until the plaster sets and all signs of fine cracks disappear.

PATCHING WALLBOARD

If your house has walls and ceilings of gypsum wallboard, you may find a single thickness of ⅜″, ½″, or ⅝″, or two layers totaling ¾″. The basic patching procedure is the same; only the patching material varies.

Around Pipes

The time to patch is before finish plumbing is completed. Once you carry piping beyond the stub through the wall, patching is difficult.

When a hole around pipes or other obstacles is no wider than 1″, you can usually fill it adequately with ready-mixed joint cement (see details in Chapter 19). With a putty knife, fill the hole liberally with the cement so that at the pipe it extends about ¼″ beyond the surface of the wall. This may take two applications. Then slowly draw the putty knife around the pipe, at the same time pressing slightly until the cement at the pipe is about ⅛″ below the surface of the wall at the pipe and is flush at the outer edge of the hole.

Let the cement set overnight. The next day fill the depression with another coat of joint cement level with the wall's surface. Let it set for a few hours, then sand lightly if necessary. Since you will probably cover the patch with an escutcheon anyway, sanding is seldom necessary. The main reason for patching is to prevent entry by insects and vermin.

When a hole is too large to patch solely with joint cement, backblock and finish as described below. Cut two pieces of backblocking, one to fit on each side of the pipe.

Backblocking

To patch any kind of hole when the patch is too small to nail to studs or joists at both ends, the best answer is backblocking. **Backblocking** is a procedure for installing wallboard that minimizes the chance of a ridge showing where two pieces meet. As a support for a surface patch, cut a backblock out of gypsum wallboard at least 1″ larger in each dimension than the hole to be filled, but small enough so you can fit it through the hole. Drill a hole near the center of the backblock, and insert a knotted string into it as shown in Fig. 18-8.

On the finished surface of the backblock around all edges apply a bead of joint cement about ½″ high and ⅜″ wide. Fit the backblock into the hole, turn it so that all edges are in full contact with the back of existing wallboard, and pull on the string to press the patch tight. Tie the string around a broom handle laid across the opening, and leave it for 24 hours.

The next day cut a piece of wallboard of the required thickness and no more than ⅛″ smaller than the opening to be filled. Make the cuts with a utility knife along a metal straightedge on the surface of the wallboard, cutting from one edge of the board to the other (refer to Fig. 19-5). Cut deeply enough to go through the surface and score the gypsum core. Then snap the board over your knee, with the scored side up. The board will break cleanly along the cutting line. Then cut through the paper backing to complete the patch.

With a spreader having a serrated edge, coat the

back of the patch with beads of joint cement ⅜" wide and 1½" apart. The height of the beads depends on the depth of the hole you are filling. Usually a ⅜" bead is about right; as you push the patch into position the beads will flatten to a depth of ⅟₁₆ to ⅟₃₂".

Remove the broom, but leave the string in case you push too hard and displace the backblock. Then set the bottom edge of the patch at the bottom of the hole and gently push inward. If the patch goes in too far at the bottom, remove it and increase the thickness of joint cement. If it won't go in far enough, skim a little cement off the tops of the beads. The patch should fit level with only enough pressure to spread the cement and should gap evenly on all sides. Fill the gaps with joint cement, let it dry, and sand smooth.

Fill a Large Area

When you cover a large opening with wallboard, first add 1 × 4 nailing strips to studs at both sides. Then cut lengths of wallboard to fit horizontally. Apply the first piece at the bottom of the opening; the baseboard will cover the tapered edge. Trim the width of the next piece to fit the remainder of the opening, and set it with its tapered edge against the tapered edge of the piece below. *Do not* set a tapered edge against a butt edge. Fill the gaps around the edge with joint cement, let it dry, and sand smooth. Finish the tapered joint in the center with joint treatment as described in the next chapter.

Surface Finishing—Ceilings And Walls

Nothing can change the appearance of a house more than resurfacing the exterior. Here asbestos-cement shingles are covered first with a layer of building paper, then vertically grooved plywood panels are nailed over them. Later, extra trim is applied around openings and at corners to compensate for the extra thickness of exterior walls. (Courtesy Georgia-Pacific Corporation.)

Only two materials are practical for homeowners to apply on ceilings—wallboard and acoustical tiles. Only two are practical for walls—wallboard and wood paneling. And to apply these materials in any room, whether an addition with exposed framing or an existing room being resurfaced, you start at the top and work down.

CEILING TILES

There are two basic types of ceiling tiles—fiber and mineral. Fiber tiles are made of vegetable or wood fibers pressed to a thickness of ½" or ¾". Their exposed surface is dotted with small holes or fissures to absorb sound. The factory finish may be flame retardant,

although the tiles themselves will burn.

Mineral tiles won't burn. Usually ¾" thick, they are manufactured with a variety of surface patterns ranging from random fissures to decorative designs. Methods of application are identical.

Both types of ceiling tiles may be applied with mastic directly to an existing ceiling surface of plaster or gypsum wallboard in good condition. Or they may be stapled to furring strips nailed to ceiling joists over existing ceiling material. Because they won't burn, mineral tiles may also be applied to furring strips nailed directly to exposed ceiling joists.

Tiles are manufactured in squares 12", 16", and 24" on a side, and in rectangles 12" × 24", 16" × 32", and 24" × 48". The larger sizes are most commonly used in a ceiling grid (see Chapter 13). For remodeling done by the homeowner the 12″ squares or 12″ × 24″ rectangles are the most popular. Their sides may be square-cut, slightly beveled, tongue-and-groove, or slotted. Which type you select depends on your method of installation.

Make a Layout

Regardless of the type of tiles or method of application, first make a ceiling layout. For the best appearance, your layout must follow three rules:

1. Any cut tiles—that is, tiles less than full size—should go at the edges of the ceiling. Trim covers the cut edges.

2. Cut tiles on opposite edges of the ceiling should be equal in width.

3. No cut tile should be less than half a tile in either dimension. Small tiles not only don't look well, but are difficult to apply.

Applying the Rules. Suppose that you want to apply 12″ square tiles to the ceiling of a room that measures 14′-2″ by 9′-6″. Across the longer dimension you can't use 14 full-size tiles and a 2″ tile; that violates rule 2. Nor can you use 14 full-size tiles and two 1″ tiles; that violates rule 3. Therefore, you plan for 13 full-size tiles and a 7″ tile at each edge; that meets all the rules.

Across the shorter dimension, a layout with nine full-size tiles and one half-tile meets rule 3 but violates rule 2. So you plan for eight full-size tiles and a 9″ tile at each edge. For the entire job, then, you need 150 tiles— 104 at full size, 26 at 12″ × 9″, 16 at 12″ × 7″, and 4 at 9″ × 7″ in the corners.

To cut a tile you need a sharp utility knife and clean hands. Tiles damage and soil easily. Lay the tile face up, measure along two edges, and mark the cut by scoring the surface along a straightedge with your utility knife. Then complete the cut either with the knife or a coping saw.

TILES APPLIED WITH MASTIC

For application with **mastic**, also called **ceiling cement**, select tiles with either square or beveled edges. Some types of bevel-edge tiles have slots in opposite edges for plastic splines. The splines help to hold tiles in alignment and at the same level. If you are careful and take your time, however, you can install a level ceiling without taking the extra step of inserting splines after every row.

Ceiling Preparation

Begin by washing the ceiling clean of dust and dirt and especially any grease. Then measure all four edges to establish the number of full tiles and the width of edge tiles along each wall. Near corners of the room measure out the width of edge tiles, and mark those widths on the ceiling's surface. Then measure the distance between pairs of marks near opposite walls. The measurements must be identical and the dimension divisible by the width of a full tile. Let the widths of edge tiles vary to compensate for any differences in width of ceiling. Snap chalk lines through the marks to form a rectangle outlining the area to be covered with full tiles, formed in Fig. 19-1 by chalk line A and the other three perimeter chalk lines. Dimension B is the difference in length between chalk lines at right angles to each other. The two marks identify the corners of a square formed with the other three starting chalk lines. Lines C are diagonals that serve as a guide to accurate application of tiles.

Now check the corners for square. Use the 3–4–5 triangle method (see Fig. 3-5). From the point where each pair of chalk lines cross, measure out 3′ along one line and 4′ along the other. Then measure between these two points; the measurement should be exactly 5′. If it is, you're ready to install the first tile.

If your corners aren't square, first recheck all measurements. If they are accurate, the room itself may be off square. When this happens, find the midpoint of the ceiling along each wall, then snap chalk lines from midpoint to midpoint. These lines will cross in the exact center of the room. Then from these lines measure at several points to the edge of the area to be covered with full tiles. Keep in mind that the measurement will be in even feet if the number of full tiles is even, and will be even feet plus 6″ if the number of tiles is odd. Wash off the previous edge chalk lines, and snap new ones through the new marks.

Where to Start

Next, decide in which corner of the room you'd like to start. From the point in that corner where chalk lines cross, measure along the longer chalk line the distance to the corner mark on the shorter chalk line, and make a mark. If, for example, your full-tile area is 13 tiles by 8 tiles, measure off 8′ along the 13′ chalk line (dimension B in Fig. 19-1). Repeat this step along the other longer chalk line. Then snap diagonal chalk lines (C) between the marks and your starting corners. These diagonal chalk lines act as a directional guide. The corners of tiles should fall exactly on the diagonals.

Application

Cut the corner tile (1 in Fig. 19-2), and two edge tiles of each size (2, 3, 4, and 6). Provided that your corner is square, tiles 2 and 4 will be the same size and 3 and 6 will be the same size. If the room is not square, you must measure from the chalk line to the wall for each tile, and cut each individually. You can safely gap as

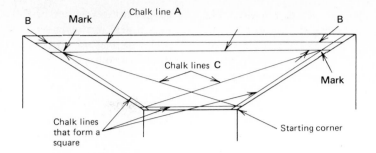

Fig. 19-1. The first step in laying out a ceiling for tiles is snapping chalk lines to mark the rectangle of full-size tiles.

much as ⅛″ at the wall to allow for dimensional variation.

Install tiles in the numerical order shown in Fig. 19-2. Place a dab of mastic on the back of each edge tile about an inch from each corner. Use a putty knife, and make each dab slightly smaller than a golf ball. As long as your existing ceiling is level or close to it, dabs should be equal in size. When the ceiling slopes, you can compensate somewhat by using larger dabs on tiles at high points—usually at the walls—and smaller dabs on tiles at low points.

Hold tile 1 close to its final location with the mastic just touching the ceiling. Then with a little sideways motion slide it into position, at the same time pushing upward to spread the mastic against the ceiling. The normal distance between the old ceiling and the back of a tile should be ⅜ to ½″.

Along the chalk lines install tiles 2 and 3 in the same way. Then lay your carpenter's level across tiles 1 and 3, 1 and 2, and 2 and 3. If a tile or edge is too low, push straight up to spread the mastic a bit more. If the tile is too high, remove it, increase the thickness of mastic, and reset it.

From tile 3 on you lay tiles in a diagonal pattern. Tiles 4, 5, and 6 form the next diagonal. Set tile 4 against tile 2 and the chalk line. Set full tile 5 against 2 and 3, and make sure that its outer corner is exactly on the diagonal chalk line. When you prepare any full-size tile, add a fifth dab of mastic on the back at the center; the pattern should look like the fives on a pair of dice.

Set tile 6 against tile 3 and the other chalk line to complete the first diagonal. Continue in this pattern, carefully checking each tile for level in both directions before you apply mastic to the next one.

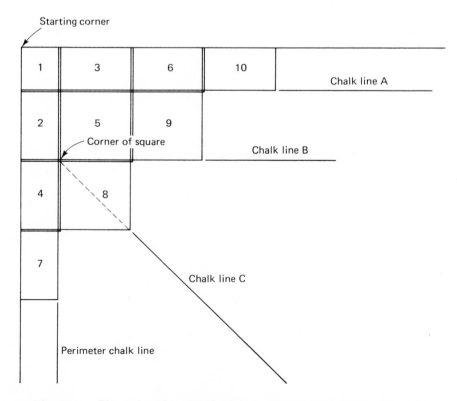

Fig. 19-2. The order of installation of the first six ceiling tiles. From this point they are usually laid diagonally across the ceiling.

If you use splines, apply tiles until you are ready for the edge tiles against the wall opposite row 1-3-6. Then insert the spline before fitting the corner tile in place. The flexible spline should slide in easily if you have leveled the tiles properly. Fit the spline into the slot of the corner tile as you swing it into place. Incidentally, you must set the first row of edge tiles and insert a spline before you continue in a row-on-row, not diagonal, pattern.

In the last unfinished corner, cut each tile to fit by measuring the space available for it. If you use splines, preassemble the last four tiles with a short spline and insert them as a unit.

You can simplify the job of applying tiles with mastic in two ways. One, have someone at floor level apply the mastic while you work from a ladder to set the tiles. This saves a lot of climbing. Two, keep all hands clean and out of the mastic. It can be messy to work with and hard to remove from tiles.

Mastic hardens slowly, so don't rush the job. If, when you set a tile, you find that a tile in the previous row is not level, you still have time to adjust it. Once mastic sets, however—and it takes a couple of hours—make no further adjustments. You'll have to live with your workmanship.

TILES STAPLED TO FURRING STRIPS

Standard furring strips are 1 × 3s that must be both flat and straight; otherwise, you won't have an adequate stapling surface. They must be placed at right angles to joists and nailed into them. Therefore, the first step is to determine which way joists run, and their spacing. Use a stud finder if you can't check space from above the ceiling.

Over an Existing Ceiling

Manufacturers of fastening tools do not recommend applying ceiling tiles with staples directly to an existing ceiling. Gypsum doesn't have the holding power of

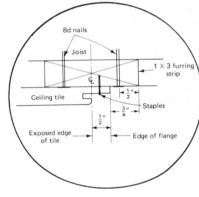

Fig. 19-3. Laying out furring strips for ceiling tile application. Use 1 × 3s except against walls, where 1 × 2s are adequate. If you apply tongue-and-groove tiles with staples, you must allow in your layout for the ½″ difference between the edges of exposed faces and stapling flanges (inset). Note the placement of nails and staples so they do not hit.

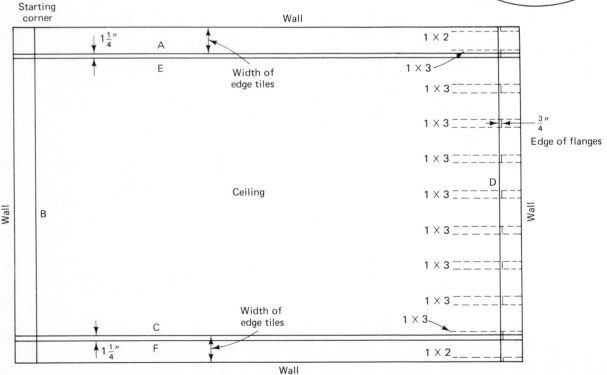

wood, and that is the reason for furring strips. They provide a firm base for stapling.

As with the mastic application just described, determine the exposed sizes of edge and corner tiles, wash the ceiling clean, and lay out chalk lines marking the rectangle to be covered with full-size tiles.

Decide in which corner you want to start. Then, from the chalk line running across joists (A in Fig. 19-3), measure *out* 1¼″ and snap a new chalk line (E) parallel to line A. (The 1¼″ dimension is half the width of a 1 × 3.) Along chalk lines B and D measure with a steel tape from line E every 12″ (or whatever the width of your tiles), and make chalk marks on the ceiling. Snap chalk lines between pairs of marks. The last chalk line (F) should be 1¼″ *closer* to the opposite wall than line C and parallel to it.

To make sure your layout is still square, measure the lengths of lines B and D between chalk lines E and F, and the lengths of E and F between B and D. The pairs of lengths must be the same. Then measure the diagonals. If your layout is square, the two diagonal measurements will be equal.

As a final step before applying furring strips, mark on the ceiling as accurately as possible the centerlines of joists. Mark near opposite walls, then snap chalk lines between pairs of marks as a guide to nailing the strips.

Across Exposed Joists

The main difference between laying out furring strips on exposed joists instead of an existing ceiling is that you snap the chalk lines on the joists themselves. Determine the exposed width of edge tiles, add 1¼″ to that dimension, and snap a chalk line across the joists (E in Fig. 19-3) on the side of the room where you plan to begin work. Snap additional chalk lines across the room parallel to line E the width of a full tile apart. The final chalk line (F) should be 2½″ closer to the wall than line E.

Install Furring Strips

Across the joists against opposite walls nail a 1 × 2 furring strip; you can rip a 1 × 3 as an alternative. Then nail a 1 × 3 against each of the chalk lines, making sure that you are consistent in which edge of the strip you set on the lines. If your ceiling is not level, the low point is likely to be at the center of the room. So nail there first. Use two 8d nails at each joist, and drive the nails straight upward about ½″ in from the edges of the strips. If you nail any closer to the edge, you may split the wood; if you nail any closer to the center, the nails could interfere with staples.

Work outward from the center as you nail, and check the level of the furring strips constantly. If necessary, shim with pieces of wood shingle and nail through the shims.

Mark the Tile Layout

For application to furring strips, select tongue-and-groove tiles with a stapling flange. Overall dimensions of flanged tiles are ½″ greater than exposed surface dimensions. You line up the *flanges*, not the exposed edges, on chalk lines. Therefore, you must allow for that ½″ as you snap chalk lines for edge tiles along the remaining two walls.

In your starting corner measure out from the wall parallel to joists a distance equal to the width of a tile plus ½″. Snap a chalk line across furring strips at this point. If you are working beneath an existing ceiling, this line should be parallel to the edge chalk line (B in Fig. 19-3) and ½″ closer to the center of the room. From this chalk line measure off the size of full tiles along the two edge furring strips, and mark until you reach the opposite wall. Snap chalk lines between pairs of marks. The last chalk line should be parallel to the wall and the width of an edge tile less ½″ from it.

Finally, measure ¾″ in from the edge of each furring strip along the chalk lines (Fig. 19-3), and snap parallel chalk lines. You now have a grid on the furring strips marking the edges of the flanges of all tiles.

Apply Tiles with Staples

Cut the first corner tile by trimming the tongued edges and leaving an *exposed* surface equal in dimension to the corner tile you planned in your layout. Set it in place on the chalk lines, and staple through the flanges. Use staples with a ½″ crown and a ⅞″ or 1″ leg. Set staples at a slight angle to the edge of the flange for greatest strength. Drive three staples into the longer flange, and one into the shorter flange near the outer corner.

Apply the next five tiles—four edge tiles and a full tile—in the order shown in Fig. 19-2. Slide the tongue or tongues of each tile into the grooves of adjacent tiles for a snug fit. Be firm but gentle; you can easily damage edges with too much pressure.

Work across the room diagonally. After you staple every third tile, sight down the chalk lines and also diagonally across the room to make sure your pattern is true. When you reach the opposite walls, trim the flanged edge of edge tiles so that the exposed surface of each tile is the same size you planned in your layout. Check the fit, then nail at cut corners with 1½″ nails driven flush with the face of the tile. Trim will cover the nailheads.

WALLBOARD OVER EXISTING CEILINGS

For resurfacing an existing ceiling when you don't want to use ceiling tiles, the best material is gypsum wallboard ¼″ thick. This thin material must be applied over an existing surface; it should never be applied directly to structural members. It comes 4' wide and 8' and 10' long, packaged two panels to a bundle. Ends are cut square; edges are tapered and must be finished with joint treatment before you paint or wallpaper.

Ceiling Layout

In making the most practical layout of gypsum ceiling panels, your primary objective is to have the fewest possible feet of butt joint, which is harder to finish smooth than edge joint.

Several rules apply to layout:

- Always install wallboard on a ceiling before walls.
- When ends of panels butt, place the joints as far from the center of the room as practicable.
- Stagger butt joints at least 16″ in adjacent panels.
- Never place a butt edge against a tapered edge. Place tapered edges against each other.
- If you must rip a panel to width, place the cut edge against the wall.

You can apply panels on a ceiling with their long dimension running either direction, but it pays to make a layout both ways. Take the room used as an example to explain ceiling tile layout, which has dimensions of 14'-2″ by 9'-6″. Each ceiling requires 160 sq ft of wallboard, including scrap—either 5 panels 4' × 8' or 4 panels 4' × 10'. With panels running the long dimension of the room (Fig. 19-4a), you have 9½' of butt end and 28'-4″ of edge to finish, whether you use 8' or 10' lengths. With 8' panels running across the room (Fig. 19-4b) you have more than 14' of butt end and 28'-

6″ of edge. If you use 10' lengths (Fig. 19-4c), you still have 28'-6″ of edge but no butt ends. Obviously, the last alternative is the best layout.

But suppose that the room is 15' by 11'. With a lengthwise layout you have 11' of butt end and 30' of tapered edge, but with a crosswise layout you have 15' of butt end and 33' of tapered edge. Therefore, the lengthwise layout is preferable.

Preparation

Gypsum wallboard may be attached with 1¾″ annular ring nails driven with a wallboard hammer, or with 1⅝″ type W wallboard screws driven with a power screwdriver. For the amateur, nail application is easier; screw application is better, but proper operation of a power screwdriver takes considerable practice and a fine touch. Even a wallboard hammer must be used with care. It has a slightly rounded head with a surface scored for accuracy in driving nails. Nails must be driven straight at right angles to the surface to a point just below that surface without breaking the paper. This process is called **dimpling**. The head of an ordinary hammer, with its sharper edges, is likely to break the surface.

To prepare for installation, carefully remove any ceiling trim. Mark each piece on the back so that you know where it goes after you resurface, and store the trim somewhere out of the room. Check the square of all corners of the room at ceiling level. If you have a choice of where to start, begin in a square corner. Alignment of succeeding pieces is much easier and, when you need to trim a later piece to fit, it will be narrower and easier to handle.

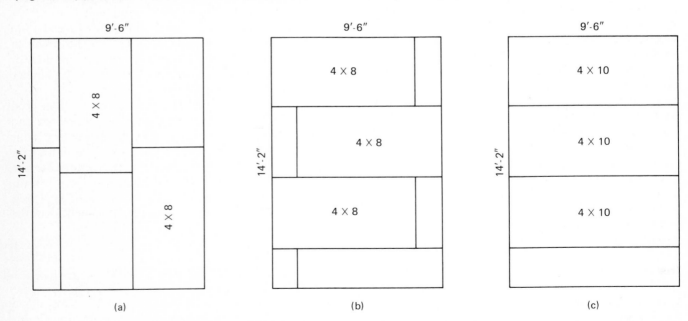

(a)   (b)   (c)

Fig. 19-4. The best layout for wallboard on a ceiling is the one with the fewest feet of butt joint to finish.

(a)   (b)   (c)

Fig. 19-5. The three steps in cutting gypsum wallboard to size are: (a) scoring the surface paper and core along the cutting line; (b) snapping the board either as shown or over your knee from behind; and (c) cutting the paper on the back to separate the two pieces. (Courtesy United States Gypsum Company.)

Then locate joists with a stud finder or by trial and error. Snap chalk lines across the ceiling on the centerlines of these joists to guide your cutting and nailing. All panels must end on centerlines, so mark their locations accurately. Carry the lines about 2″ down the walls.

Mark the first gypsum panel to gap ⅛″ in the corner and to end on a centerline. Use a metal T-square for measuring and marking, and as a cutting guide. Make straight cuts with a wallboard knife, following the steps shown in Fig. 19-5. Smooth cut edges with a rasp.

Thin wallboard must be supported when you measure, mark, and score. The firm, flat working surface can be a wall or floor, but the best cutting base is a platform of ½″ or ¾″ plywood set across three sawhorses. Use this base for cutting each panel, then as a scaffolding that places your head just below ceiling level.

Installation

Raise the first panel with one helper at each end and you under the center. If only one person is available, make a T-brace (Fig. 19-6) to act as a third person on the unfastened end. Position the panel on a centerline and

gapping slightly at both walls. Don't force the fit; if it's not right, either trim that panel or cut a new one.

Begin nailing at the center of the panel and work outward toward the ends and edges. Space nails about 7″ apart in the **field** (the middle of the panel) and place them ⅜″ in from ends and edges. Omit the last row of nails at walls unless you have no ceiling trim. The trim supports the edges, and the wallboard will deflect slightly to provide a good fit.

Complete the first row of panels end to end before you start the second row. Then repeat the process in each adjacent row, remembering to offset butt joints in adjoining panels.

You won't have many obstacles to work around in a ceiling installation, but there may be two—a light fixture and a jog in the room. Remove the light fixture and bulb or tube. Then measure from the wall (if the cut is in the first panel) or the end or edge of adjoining panels to the edge of the fixture. Transfer these measurements to the panel to be cut; be sure to measure from the correct end and edge when you transfer. Inside the marks drill a hole at some point large enough to accept the blade of a keyhole saw. Cut from the hole over to the nearest mark, then cut along the marks. As you near the end of a circular cut, support the cutout to

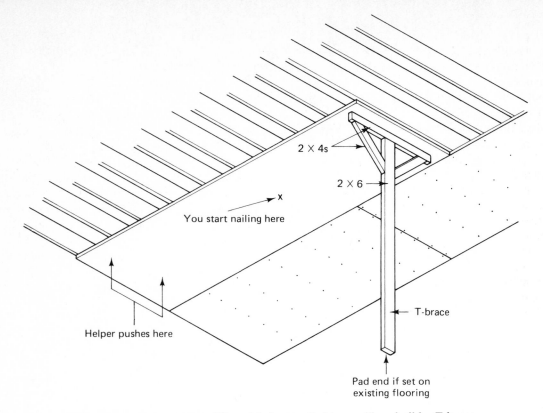

2 × 4s

2 × 6

You start nailing here

T-brace

Helper pushes here

Pad end if set on
existing flooring

Fig. 19-6. To support wallboard being applied to a ceiling, build a T-brace
out of 2 × 4s. The cross member should be about 4 ′ long and the stem of the
T about 1 ″ shorter than the room's height from floor to finished ceiling.

assure a clean edge. If the cutout is rectangular, make a turn before you reach the corners. Then, after you remove the cutout, go back to each corner and cut it square with the saw.

To fit around a jog, mark the two cutting lines on the panel with your T-square. Cut along the shorter line with a drywall saw or keyhole saw to the intersection of the two lines. Then score and snap along the longer line as shown in Fig. 19-5.

WALLBOARD ON EXPOSED JOISTS

The procedure for nailing ½ ″ wallboard across exposed joists is the same as for ¼ ″ wallboard. Now, however, you always omit nails at the walls. Panel edges rest on the wallboard you apply across studs. But you should take a couple of extra preparatory steps to make sure that the resultant ceiling is level.

First, check corners for square. Then check the alignment of joists by laying the edge of a long, straight 2 × 4 against their bottom edges. All bottom edges should be in the same plane. If they are not, and you have room to work above joists, align them with a strongback (see Fig. 18-6). If necessary, push upward on low joists with a 2 × 4 to assure a solid fit between all joists and the 2 × 4 in the strongback.

If joists support a second floor and there is no

place for a strongback, cut six pieces of solid bridging. Push the poorly set joist into alignment, and support it temporarily in the position. Then nail the bridging between it and its neighbors.

Also look for cocked joists—joists whose sides aren't plumb. Their bottom edges therefore won't be horizontal, and you will have a ridge in your ceiling, especially if ceiling panels happen to butt on that joist. Straighten the offending joist with solid bridging (see Fig. 7-4).

Finally, look for anything that protrudes below the edges of joists, such as blocking, bridging, and nailheads. All such obstructions must be trimmed or removed. Only when the under sides of joists are flat, level, and smooth should you proceed with installation.

WALLBOARD ON WALLS

The procedure for applying gypsum wallboard over an existing wall surface is only slightly different from ceiling application. Mark the centerlines of studs on the upper 5′ of wall as a guide to nailing top panels, then use the row of nails in top panels as a guide to nailing lower panels. Check corners of the room for plumb. Remove and store existing trim at the ceiling, floor, and around openings. Check the straightness of walls as described in Chapter 18 in the section "Wavy Walls," and correct the problem if practical.

If you are applying wallboard directly to studs, check them for plumb, and look for any protrusions beyond their nailing surfaces. Replace any studs with crook in them.

Lay out walls for a minimum of joint, and place butt joints toward the corners of rooms, not the centers of walls. Most professionals start on the shorter walls first and apply wallboard horizontally from top to bottom. At inside corners the panels overlap. At outside corners they must be cut to overlap flush; then you trim the edge with **corner bead**, a manufactured strip attached with nails or staples. The metal nose protects the exposed corner from damage by bumping.

Precut all panels so that they butt on centerlines of studs. Also mark and precut panels to fit loosely at window and door openings. They must be nailed to structural framing at their edges.

Mark carefully the locations of holes you need to drill or cut for pipes and electrical outlets and switches. The diameters of holes should be no more than $\frac{1}{8}''$ greater than the diameters of pipes they fit around. Holes for electrical connections should be the same size as the electrical boxes around them, or not more than $\frac{1}{4}''$ larger in either dimension.

At the time of installation, capped stubs for water and waste piping must be in place. So must boxes for electrical outlets, switches, and wall lights. In new construction you fit panels around pipe stubs and against electrical boxes. When you resurface an old wall, remove the electrical plates and the screws into the boxes that hold the ears of the switch or outlet against the wall. As a safety precaution, turn off the power. Then pull the switch or receptacle out of its box and let it project straight out into the room. Feed it through the hole you precut for it. After you nail the panel in place, push the wires back into the box and fit the switch or receptacle back into position. You will probably need longer screws than you removed to fasten it back in the box. Make sure that the ears fit firmly against the new wall surface.

JOINTS IN WALLBOARD

To give wallboard a smooth, unbroken surface you need two materials and three or four tools.

Joint compound is a ready-mixed material with a consistency similar to caulking compound. It comes in a can ready to use. **Joint tape** is a strong, fibered paper product with tapered edges and hundreds of pinholes in it. The tape comes in rolls 2″ wide and from 60 to 500′ long, and has a slight crease down the center for fitting into corners.

You apply joint compound in three stages, and embed the tape where necessary in the first stage. For this first stage you need a flat-bladed finishing knife 4″ wide. Use a 6″-wide knife for stage two, and a 10″ knife for stage three. A corner tool with an L-shaped blade is

useful, but you can fit tape into corners with a 4″ knife almost as well.

Preparation

Before you apply any joint compound, press on each panel of wallboard along the rows of fasteners to make sure that you drove all nails firmly. Then run your finishing knife across the heads of nails. If you hear metal hit metal, sink that nail a little deeper. But don't break the surface of the paper. Make sure that panels are level across joints, and gap no more than $\frac{1}{4}''$ at tapered edges. If they do, fill the joint with compound spread with the 4″ knife, and let it dry for 24 hours. Fill any gap between butt ends in the same way. Then remove any dust and grit from the entire wall surface with a damp sponge.

First Stage

Apply a first coat of joint compound in nail dimples with the 4″ knife, and fill them level with the surrounding surface. Then butter tapered joints with compound. Fill the channel full and evenly but don't overfill it. Next, center joint tape over the seam and force it into the fresh compound with the knife held at about a 45° angle to the wall. Exert enough pressure so the compound oozes through the perforations in the tape. Compound should be thick enough at the center of the joint to hold the tape firmly, but no more than $\frac{1}{32}''$ thick at the edges. Then immediately apply a thin skim coat of compound to a width of about 3″ to prevent the edges of the tape from wrinkling. Follow this same process at butt joints. The steps in this first stage are shown in Fig. 19-7.

You can embed tape as it comes off the roll if you like. Most people find it easier, however, to cut the tape to length first, the length being $\frac{1}{2}$ to 1″ shorter than the length of the joint itself.

Let the compound applied in stage 1 dry thoroughly. Drying time varies with the room's temperature and humidity. Assuming that room temperature will be no less than 60°F (16°C) or more than 80°F (27°C), let the compound dry for 24 hours when humidity is 50% or less. Allow 48 hours when humidity is between 50 and 80%. At high humidities the drying time increases exponentially; at 70°F and 95% humidity, for example, allow six days.

Second Stage

To dimples apply a thin second coat of compound with any of your knives. To tapered joints apply a second coat of compound with a 6″ knife, and feather the edges about 2″ beyond the first coat on each side. To butt joints apply the second coat with a 10″ knife, and feather the edges to a total width of about 10″.

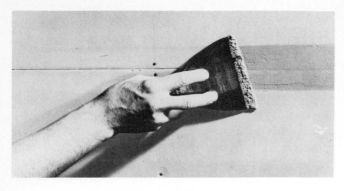

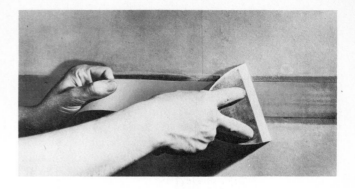

(a)   (b)

Fig. 19-7. To treat joints in wallboard, first butter tapered joints with compound (a). Then embed the joint tape in the compound with enough pressure so that a film of compound oozes through the tape (b). (Courtesy United States Gypsum Company.)

Let the second coat dry thoroughly. Then sand the joint lightly to smooth the surface.

Third Stage

To dimples apply a thin finish coat of compound that extends at least 1″ beyond them all the way around. To tapered joints apply a thin finish coat with a 10″ knife, and feather the edges about 2″ on each side of the joint beyond the second coat. Total width of joint compound should now be between 11 and 12″. To butt joints apply a thin finish coat of compound with a trowel, and feather the edges to a total width of about 18″.

After this finish coat has dried thoroughly, sand it lightly, and wipe the wall clean with a damp sponge. The surface is now ready for decorating.

Inside Corners

You finish inside corners like tapered joints, with a few minor exceptions. Butter the joint so that compound is almost ⅛″ thick in the corner. Then crease the tape down its center, place it in the corner, and press it into the compound with the 4″ knife, working from top to bottom. Embed about 2′ of tape on one side of the crease, then on the other, and continue alternating sides on down the corner. Be careful not to split the tape with the sharp edge of the knife blade. With a corner tool you can embed the tape in a single operation. A ridge of compound will build up at the tape's edges, however; remove the excess with a flat-bladed knife. Use long vertical strokes to spread the compound evenly.

Application of second and third coats of compound is the same as for tapered joints.

Outside Corners

During preparation for taping, cut a strip of corner bead for each outside corner so that it gaps about ⅛″ at ceiling and floor. Check the rounded nose for plumb, then nail or staple the bead into studs, even if you are resurfacing.

With a 4″ knife apply the first coat of compound on both sides of the corner, letting the knife ride on the nosing. No tape is needed at outside corners. After the first coat is dry, apply a second coat with a 6″ knife, and feather the edges about 6″ on both sides of the corner. Let this coat dry, then sand it lightly. Apply the final coat with a 10″ knife, and feather it 8 to 10″ on both sides. After this coat dries, sand it lightly, The rounded nose of the bead will still be exposed, but paint or wallpaper covers it easily.

INSULATING WALLBOARD

Insulating wallboard is regular wallboard with a backing of aluminum foil instead of heavy paper. Its use is limited to ceilings below unfinished attics and to exterior walls, where it acts as a vapor barrier and reflective insulation. The foil side of the wallboard goes against studs or joists, and there must be an air space of at least ¾″ behind the foil between framing members. You apply and finish insulating wallboard just like regular wallboard.

PREDECORATED WALLBOARD

Instead of the easily decorated paper surface of regular wallboard, **predecorated wallboard** has an exposed surface of vinyl on a fabric backing that is laminated to the gypsum core. The vinyl comes in a wide range of solid colors, and in patterns from woodgrains to textiles to marblized. Panels are 4′ wide, 8′ and 10′ long, and ⅜″, ½″, and ⅝″ thick.

Predecorated wallboard is manufactured with three types of edges. Square and beveled edges are wrapped with the surface vinyl, and are left exposed. Eased edges have a 2″ flap of vinyl along one edge that overlaps the adjoining panel, eliminates joints, and covers fasteners to form an uninterrupted wall surface.

Predecorated wallboard is recommended only for walls and not for ceilings. Panels must be applied vertically. They may be nailed over an existing surface or directly to studs. The nails, provided by the manufacturer, have heads painted to match the vinyl. Panels may also be applied directly to studs with adhesive. Manufacturers also make special moldings for trimming at joints and corners.

Preparation

Decide first in which corner to start. The best place is the most conspicuous inside corner. In new construction plan your layout with full panels in this corner and the diagonally opposite corner, then butt cut panels in the other two less prominent corners. If you are resurfacing a wall, you will probably have to trim the first panel so that the untrimmed edge falls on a stud's centerline.

For the most attractive appearance of wood-grained and textured patterns, consider applying every other panel upside down. To do this, number each panel on the back in the order in which you want to install it, with an arrow pointing to the top.

Check the starting corner for square and plumb. The first panel must be plumb or all panels will be slightly askew. Then, if you are applying panels over an existing wall, mark centerlines of studs as a guide to positioning.

Before you put up the first panel, read the manufacturer's instructions for installation. Usually, they say to place nails $\frac{3}{8}$" from the edges of panels and to space all nails 8" apart along vertical edges and in the field. They may or may not call for nails along ends. Nails should penetrate at least $\frac{3}{4}$" into studs.

When you cut a panel, always cut the vinyl face with a sharp utility knife, regardless of how you complete the cut. After scoring the face, cut holes for switches and receptacles from the back side so that the vinyl won't delaminate.

Installation

Place the first panel in your starting corner with any cut edge in the corner and the finished edge on a centerline. Begin nailing at about eye level in the field. Check the fit and plumb after you have started a couple of nails. Complete nailing in the corner. If you use divider moldings between panels, slip the molding over the untrimmed edge of the panel, and nail through the exposed flange into the stud. Insert the next panel into the divider.

Complete the wall to the opposite corner. Then, starting again at the first corner, complete the second wall. If you use inside corner moldings, fit the molding against the first panel in the first wall, nail through its flange, and slip the first panel of the second wall into it.

After you finish two walls, start in the untouched corner of the room and repeat the process for the other two walls. Cut the last two panels to fit, slip the inside corner molding over the cut edge, and swing each panel against the wall. If necessary, nail the panel at top and bottom just outside the molding where the nails will be hidden by ceiling and floor trim.

At outside corners to be finished with molding, cut the first panel for a flush fit and install it. Then fit the outside corner molding over the end of that panel and against the wall, and nail through the exposed flange. Fit the next panel into the trim. When you don't turn the corner with predecorated wallboard, or it butts against another material, slip an end cap molding over the edge of the panel, and push it tight before applying the panel.

You apply manufactured snap-on moldings after all panels are in place except at outside corners where panels overlap. If you prefer wood or plastic moldings, you apply all of them after panels are in place throughout the room.

WATER-RESISTANT WALLBOARD

The paper surface of regular wallboard will absorb water, and water will eventually destroy the gypsum core. Therefore, regular wallboard is not a good material for finishing the walls of new bathrooms behind a tub or shower. But water-resistant wallboard is. It has a water-repellent paper on the surface that can be painted, covered with water-repellent wallpaper, or finished with tiles.

Preparation

The bathtub or shower base must be attached to framing before you can apply water-resistant wallboard, and all plumbing lines must be stubbed through the wall. Framing members around the tub must be aligned, and all blocking for accessories such as towel racks and soap dishes must be in place. These requirements are covered in Chapter 16.

Application

Water-resistant wallboard must be applied horizontally. Measure the wall above the long edge of the tub, and cut the first piece to length. Then brush sealant liberally on both ends; the wallboard manufacturer provides sealant in 1-pint cans. To keep the core dry, you must coat all cut edges and any nicks or gouges with sealant.

On the edge of the tub or shower base set a pair of spacers about $\frac{1}{4}$" thick to support temporarily the lower edge of the first piece of wallboard. Pencil stubs make good spacers. Set one long edge of the wallboard on the spacers, then nail the panel in place. Space nails 8" apart unless you intend to finish the walls with ceramic tiles. In that case nail every 4" to carry the extra weight.

Cut end panels to length. If your tub is standard size, you can cut one side panel and two end panels out of a single 10' length of water-resistant wallboard. Mark the locations of holes for stubbed plumbing, drill or cut the holes, and seal the edges of holes and the ends of panels with sealant. Install the end panels, again on spacers.

Repeat this process without spacers for the upper panels, installing them with the cut edge toward the ceiling. Water-resistant wallboard should extend no less than 6' above the floor of your tub or shower. Then remove your spacers, and fill the joint around the tub or shower base with joint caulking.

If you are going to paint or paper over the wallboard, finish joints with joint treatment as described earlier in this chapter. But if you are going to tile, simply brush sealant over all nailheads. *Do not finish the joints.*

For an alternative method, finishing a tub enclosure with tileboard, see the section "Tileboard" later in this chapter.

CERAMIC WALL TILES

There is nothing difficult or mysterious about tiling walls—or floors either, for that matter. It takes a little knowledge, a couple of special tools, and quite a little time, care, and patience. But the results can be worth the effort.

Two types of tiles are commonly installed in homes today. Individual glazed tiles have been around for more than 5000 years. The typical standard size is 4¼" × 4¼", and the shapes in that size (Fig. 19-8) fit all wall conditions. Standard trim pieces are 2" × 6" for straight runs and 2" × 2" in corners. Tile thickness is ¾". Tile manufacturers also make toilet paper holders, towel racks, and soap dishes to fit regular tile patterns.

You can also buy smaller, thinner tiles mounted face down on sheets of paper usually 12" × 24". The tiles may be all the same color, or in a variety of analogous colors either scattered at random or forming a pattern. They may be all the same size or several sizes. Thickness is ¼ to ⅜"; unglazed tiles are thinner than glazed tiles. Edges may be cut square or slightly rounded.

Ceramic tiles may be applied to walls in several ways, but the easiest method for homeowners is with organic adhesive or epoxy mortar. Both types of adhesive hold tiles to either unfinished wallboard or plaster. Some types can be applied over painted surfaces; others cannot. So read the instructions carefully before you buy. After you narrow the possibilities, see what the label says about **open time**—the length of time before the adhesive begins to set. Open times vary from 30 minutes to 3 hours. If you are new at tiling, select an adhesive with a longer open time so that you have more opportunity to correct any mistakes.

Preparation

Any finished tiling job is only as good as its base. The surface must be flat or nearly so; you can bridge low

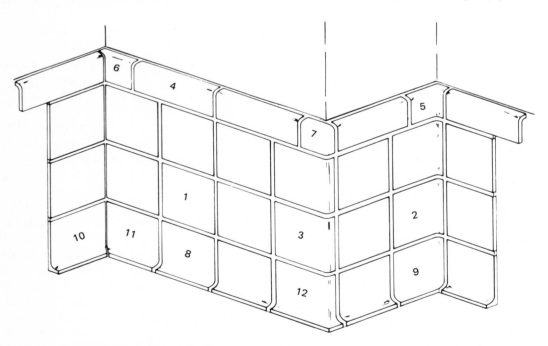

Fig. 19-8. Standard shapes of ceramic wall tiles are: 1, field tile; 2, inside corner; 3, outside corner; 4, field trim tile; 5 and 6, inside trim corners; 7, outside trim corner; 8, field base tile; 9, 10, and 11, inside base corners; and 12, outside base corner. Pieces 7, 9, and 12 are also made for the opposite corner condition.

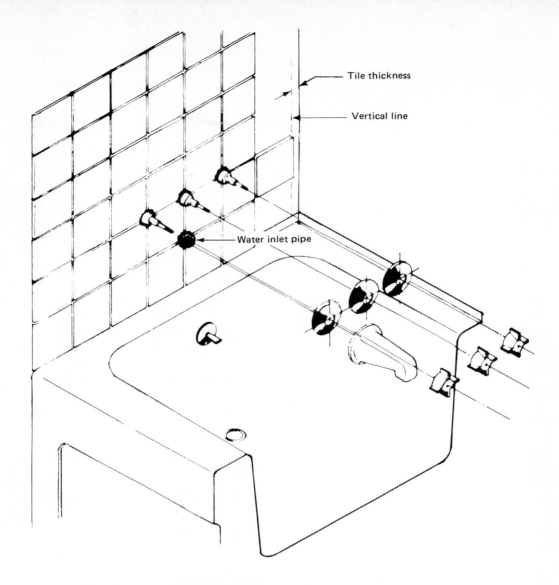

Fig. 19-9. On the wall above the drain end of the bathtub, measure off the thickness of a tile and draw a vertical line. In a good layout the water inlet pipe and water control valves should come through the wall at tile joints.

spots with either adhesive or tiles. The surface must be clean; dust, grease, oil, or loose particles form a film that prevents adhesive from sticking. If walls are already painted, follow instructions on the can of adhesive for preparing the surface. The surface must not be glass smooth. To give it a little roughness brush on a coat of **size**—a thin glue-like liquid that helps adhesive stick better.

Where a pipe comes through a wall, seal the opening with caulking or adhesive so that moisture can't work its way into the wall. Make sure that the seal is smooth and without bumps that would throw tiles out of line. Let the sealant set overnight.

Lay Out the Job

The most difficult aspect of tile-setting is cutting tiles to fit. Plan your layout, then, so you have the fewest

possible tiles to cut. Space tiles so that pipes fall at joints, not in the middle of a tile. If it comes to a choice, straight cuts are easier to make than rounded cuts.

Vertical Starting Line. Begin your layout on the wall where pipes protrude. If he knows you are going to use $4\frac{1}{4}$" tiles, a good plumber will space piping with faucet controls exactly $4\frac{1}{4}$" apart, and the spout $4\frac{1}{4}$" below the center faucet. Check the corner for plumb, then snap a vertical chalk line on the end wall the thickness of a tile from the corner (Fig. 19-9). Next, measure from the line to the centerline of the water inlet pipe. The dimension should be about 13"—the width of three tiles plus three joints. Tiles are manufactured with spacer lugs that leave a joint from $\frac{1}{32}$ to $\frac{1}{16}$" wide. You can increase the width of joint slightly if necessary to get spacing correct, but no more than $\frac{3}{32}$".

In inside corners the tiles will butt against tiles on

the long wall above the tub. But where do you stop at the other end of a short wall? You have several choices. One is at the edge of the tub's rim; usually, the edge of a full tile will line up with that edge. Rather than cut tiles in the last vertical row and set edge tiles flush with the rim, use full tiles in the last row and carry trim tiles all the way to the floor. You can usually do this without cutting as long as the wall continues straight. If the wall turns at the rim, you must either set trim tiles flush with the corner, or else carry tiles around the corner until you can trim. Tile walls must be edged with trim tiles.

Horizontal Starting Line. Next, lay your carpenter's level on the rim of the tub. If the rim is level along its entire length, find something $\frac{1}{16}$" thick to use as a spacer. A piece of cardboard will do. Set a base tile on the spacer in one corner, and draw a line across the wall at the top of the tile. Carry this line horizontally across all three walls around the tub. If you're lucky, the line will pass right through the centerline of the water inlet pipe and be about $4\frac{5}{16}$" below the horizontal centerline through faucet controls. If you aren't lucky, you'll just have to work with available conditions.

When the rim of the tub is not level, find the lowest point as determined with your carpenter's level. Set the spacer and a tile at that point, mark the top of the tile, and carry the line around all walls. You'll have to trim some of the tiles in the bottom row to fit.

To all three walls just below your chalk line tack a straight wood strip, such as a 1 × 2 or screen molding, as a guide for laying the first course. You can work without the strip, but with it you are certain of getting off to a straight start.

Finally, lay out a row of full tiles along the wood strip on the long wall, beginning with a full tile in your starting corner. Measure the space between the last tile and the other corner, and take one of three steps:

1. If the space is more than $1\frac{1}{4}$", lay all tiles lug to lug.

2. If the space is less than $1\frac{1}{4}$" but at least $\frac{3}{4}$", increase the spacing equally between tiles so that the edge of the last full tile is $\frac{3}{4}$" from the corner. Then place the edge of the first row on the back wall against the long wall, instead of butting it against side wall tiles as shown in Fig. 19-9.

3. If the dimension is less than $\frac{3}{4}$", count the number of full tiles you laid out. With an odd number, find the centerline of the long wall and snap a vertical chalk line at that point. With an even number again find the centerline, but then measure half a tile to one side of that centerline and snap a chalk line through that point. In both cases your starting point is the vertical line, and your cut tiles in both corners will be equal in width.

With your layout complete, count the number of tiles of each type you need, including edge tiles, and order them. Order accessories at the same time. When they come, mark their locations on the wall with an × inside the rectangle of wall space they will occupy. Do not spread adhesive inside these rectangles.

Spread Adhesive

Before spreading adhesive or epoxy mortar, read the instructions on the container. Then follow them exactly. They do vary, but they will work if you respect the manufacturer's knowledge and use it.

To apply adhesive you need two tools—a notched spreader and either a pointed trowel or a 4" broadknife. Lift the adhesive from the can to the back of the spreader with the knife or trowel. Then hold the spreader at a 30 to 45° angle to the wall to spread the adhesive. Coat only as much wall area as you can tile in 30 minutes. Unless the adhesive manufacturer tells you otherwise, it doesn't matter whether the ridges run horizontally, vertically, diagonally, or in swirls. What does matter is that you completely cover the area and leave very little adhesive against the wall between ridges. Your chalk lines should show through easily.

Set Tiles

Set the first tile on the wood strip and against your vertical starting line—either the corner or the wall's midpoint. Rest the tile on the strip and tip it forward into the adhesive. Press it into place with a little squirming motion—just enough to flatten the ridges and assure bond, but not so hard that you force adhesive to build up on the outside of lugs.

Complete the first course of full tiles as far as you spread adhesive. Then go back and pry loose the first tile. If you are setting tiles properly, at least half the back of the tile will be covered with adhesive. You can safely replace this tile without spreading more adhesive.

As you work, constantly check horizontal and vertical alignment. To do this, hold your level along the edges of the tiles, but keep it out of the adhesive. Continue to spread adhesive and set full tiles until you come to a corner or a spot where tiles must be cut. With your broadknife or a putty knife, scrape away any adhesive spread beyond your stopping point, including any against lugs.

How to Cut Tiles

To make a straight cut in a tile, mark the cut line on the unglazed edges with a pencil. Score the glazed surface between marks with a glass cutter available at any hardware store. Then set the tile over a wire coathanger, line up the marks on the wire, and break the tile by pressing down hard on the parallel edges (Fig. 19-10a). Clean off rough spots with a small triangular file or carborundum block.

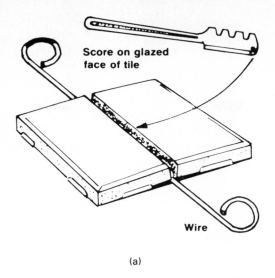

Score on glazed
face of tile

Wire

(a)

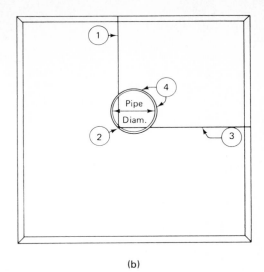

(b)

Fig. 19-10. To make a straight cut in a ceramic tile, score the surface with a glass cutter, then break it over a coathanger (a). To shape a hole you make a straight cut to the area, then complete the hole with a coping saw, glass cutter, and nippers (b).

To cut an arc in the edge of a tile, mark the cut lines on the edge and back. Then, for best results, make a starting notch with a triangular file and cut with a coping saw. If you don't have a coping saw, you'll need a pair of **tile nippers**. You operate nippers like pliers, but they have carbide-tipped edges that chew through the tile. Holding the marked tile with the finished side up, bite off pieces no more than ⅛″ in size. Start at a corner, then nip off pieces side by side as you enlarge the chipped area until you reach your mark. Take too big a bite and you may crack the tile. To prevent chips from flying into your eyes, always wear safety glasses when cutting or chipping tiles.

If you have to cut a hole in the middle of a tile, the simplest way is to rent a hole cutter or power hole saw, cut the hole, then knock out the plug with a well-directed hammer blow. Cut on the glazed side. The next best way is to drill a pilot hole inside the area to be cut out, using a power drill with a carbide-tipped bit. Then score the cut along the mark, and make the actual cut with a coping saw. Make the hole slightly larger than marked if it will be covered with an escutcheon or collar.

If you have only hand tools and the hole will be visible, make a short straight cut with a coping saw tangent to the hole (1 in Fig. 19-10b). With a glass cutter, score the face of the tile along a 90° arc (2), then score to the edge of the tile at right angles to the straight cut (3). Cut on the arc with the coping saw, then snap along the remaining scoring line. Nibble the tile to the remaining circular mark (4), and set the two pieces on the wall separately.

If the hole will be hidden, mark the centerline of the pipe on the tile, score along that centerline, and snap the tile into two pieces. Then nibble the hole in both

pieces. Use a coarse file or carborundum block to smooth edges.

Complete Corners

You probably won't be able to fit a spreader into a corner to set cut tiles. Instead, use a putty knife to butter the backs of cut tiles, and push them firmly into place. Always complete the first wall, including trim tiles, before you start adjoining walls.

Let the adhesive dry for a day. Then set bathroom accessories. Spread a thin coat of adhesive not only on the wall in the rectangles you left, but also on the back of the accessory. Let both coats dry for about 30 minutes. Then fit the accessory in place, and hold it either by bracing it with a stick or fastening it to the wall temporarily with masking tape. If you don't, it will fall, break, and damage the tub or shower base. Remove support after 24 hours.

Clean and Grout

As soon as you finish tiling an area you coated with adhesive, clean the tiles with the cleaner recommended by the manufacturer of the adhesive. Use it carefully. The cleaner is a solvent that not only dissolves the adhesive you smear on tiles and your hands so that it can be wiped off, but also softens the adhesive holding tiles on the wall.

Wait for at least 24 hours after you set the final tile or accessory before grouting the joints. **Grout** is a dampproofing compound similar to mortar but thinner in consistency and finer in texture. It comes in powdered form and you sift it into clean, cold water to form a smooth paste. Most grout is white, but it is available in some colors.

Grout has an open time of about 30 minutes, so you must work quickly. Apply the compound with a small trowel, working it into joints with the edge of the tool. Fill joints full, then draw a squeegee diagonally across tiles to remove the excess. This step leaves a thin film of grout on the face of tiles. Wet a sponge in clean, cold water, hold the flat side against the wall, and gently wipe off the film. Do not press the sponge into joints.

Grout reaches final set in about 10 minutes. At that time compact the joints; the handle of an old toothbrush is an ideal compacting tool. The handle forces the grout into joints, compacts it, and leaves a slight depression below the surface of the tiles. Again clean the excess with a damp sponge, and polish with a dry cloth.

Grout won't completely harden for 10 to 14 days, and needs to be moistened occasionally during this period to prevent too rapid drying and formation of hairline cracks. You can shower in 24 hours after grouting, but don't soak the grout or leave excess water on the wall's surface.

Small tiles in sheets are installed like individual tiles, although you must allow for the reduced thickness when you make your layout. Leave a small gap between sheets for grout. Because tiles are smaller, you can probably work from corner to corner without cutting any tiles. As you press mounted tiles onto a wall, adhesive will ooze through the backing or around tiles face-mounted on paper. Leave any face paper in place until the adhesive has set fully. Dampen the paper with a sponge to remove it. Then recheck the alignment of tiles before you grout.

OTHER TYPES OF TILES

Metal and plastic tiles are a lighter weight but acceptable substitute for the more expensive ceramic tiles. Installation procedures are identical except for layout and cutting. These tiles are only $\frac{1}{8}$" thick, and you must allow for this thinness in planning tile layout in corners. The tiles may also be slightly smaller or slightly larger than $4\frac{1}{4}$" square.

To cut metal tiles use ordinary metalworking tools, primarily a hacksaw, metal shears, and a file and pliers to smooth and straighten rough edges. Plastic tiles break as easily as ceramic tiles. You make straight cuts with a coping saw and curves with nippers. Or you can use a soldering iron to melt the plastic to a cut line, or burn a hole in the middle of a tile.

TILEBOARD

Tileboard is a form of hardboard tempered to resist moisture and coated with a baked enamel finish. Its surface may be grooved into squares to resemble tiles, or smooth with a marbleized appearance. Standard thickness is $\frac{1}{4}$", and sheets 5' × 7' and 4' × 8' are the most common sizes. You can cover walls around a tub for less cost and in less time with tileboard than any other way. But you must work carefully to prevent leaks.

Above a recessed tub 5'-wide tileboard is ideal. One sheet covers the long wall, and half a sheet covers short walls. You must not have horizontal joints in any wet area. Manufacturers of tileboard make moldings of chrome-plated aluminum or of plastic to finish edges and corners. Although shapes for specific purposes are similar, they vary somewhat from manufacturer to manufacturer. Instructions tell you whether a molding goes in place before or after you set a panel.

Preparation

Tileboard must be applied over a solid backing at least $\frac{3}{8}$" thick. That backing—whether plaster, wallboard, or plywood—must be clean, dry, flat, and fully fastened. Its surface may be already painted, but be sure to remove any flaking paint or plaster. Also, repair any holes and fill any depressions with spackling compound or wood putty.

Unless pipes are capped, turn off the water at the main shutoff valve. Then remove faucets, the tub spout, soap dishes and other accessories, and the showerhead if it is in the way. Caulk all joints, holes, and cracks around pipes. Unwrap panels 24 hours before you apply them so that they can adjust to humidity in the house. Stand them face out against a wall, and check for surface damage. Do not install damaged panels.

Installation

Cut a length of tub molding to fit against the tub on its long side. Use a hacksaw on metal trim and a sharp utility knife on plastic or vinyl trim. Lay a heavy bead of waterproof caulking along the edge of the tub. Embed the molding in it, and nail through the flange into studs.

Establish the upper edge of tileboard panels, and snap level chalk lines (AB, AC, and BD in Fig. 19-11) at that height on all three walls. In the corners measure from the chalk line to the bottom of the recess in the tub molding. These measurements will be identical if the rim of the tub is level. Next, locate the center of the long wall along line AB, drop a plumb bob from that point (E), and mark the centerline (F) on the wall just above the molding. Now measure from E to A, E to B, F to G, and F to H. Subtract $\frac{1}{8}$" from each of these measurements, and write them down.

Check both upper corners to see whether line AB is at 90° to either AC or BD. If either corner is therefore square, begin at the same corner of the tileboard panel and lay out the dimensions you took in the paragraph above. If neither corner is square, mark the centerline of the panel and work from there.

Trim the panel to size and shape face up with a fine-toothed hand saw or plane saw. Cut on the

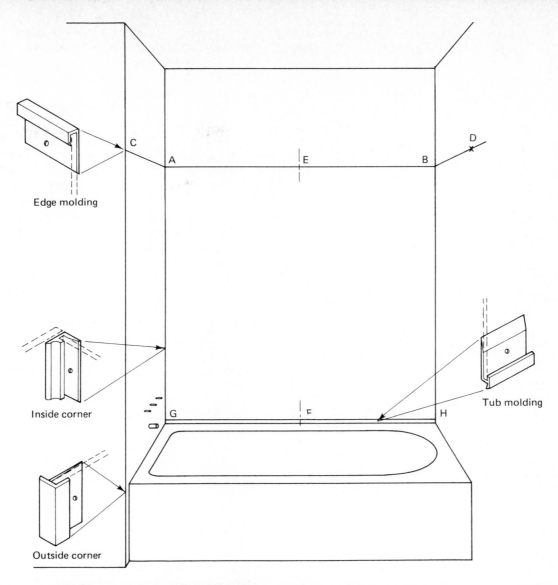

Fig. 19-11. Typical moldings for use with tileboard, and how to measure the sizes of panels.

downstroke only—that is, with the blade moving toward the finished surface. Otherwise, you may chip the enamel. Set the panel in the molding to test the fit. It should gap ⅛" at the corners and just touch your chalk line. Mark and cut any openings for a soap dish or towel bar.

Fill the tub molding at least half full of caulking. Then spread adhesive on the wall according to the manufacturer's instructions. Set the panel back into the tub molding and press down until the chalk line at the top is just visible. Press the panel into the adhesive on the wall, pushing on the entire surface to assure a complete and uniform bond. Press from the molding upward. Then, before you reach the top, cut a piece of edge molding to length, and force it onto the upper edge of the panel. Press the rest of the panel and the molding into the adhesive.

Follow the same general procedure to panel end walls. If you plan to stop tileboard at the edge of the tub, measure from the finished corner to the beginning of the downward curve of the tub, and subtract ⁵⁄₁₆" for an edge molding. Cut tub moldings to length and install them.

Then cut inside corner molding so that its exposed length fits between the top of the tub molding and the bottom of the edge molding. You'll have to trim part of the back flange of the corner molding to keep it from overlapping the flanges of the other two moldings. Apply a bead of caulking on the face of the installed panel along its edge, embed the corner moldings in the caulking, and nail 16" on centers through the flange.

Insert the end panel opposite plumbing fittings for fit. Its outside edge should extend ⅛" beyond the tub molding. Draw a plumb chalk line at this point, then remove the cut panel. Caulk the inside corner and tub moldings half full, then apply adhesive to the wall. Insert the panel into the two moldings simultaneously until the top and side chalk lines are just visible. Next, cut the top and side edge moldings to length, and miter the corner where they meet. Caulk these two moldings and force them onto the panel. Then press the entire panel to the wall.

Repeat this same process for the opposite panel. To locate the holes for piping, make a template out of cardboard. Set the cardboard all the way into the tub molding after you install it but before you caulk it. Mark the circles for the pipes and cut them out. Then trim ⅛″ off the bottom of the cardboard, lay the template on the panel, and mark the holes for cutting. Drill starter holes and complete the cuts with a keyhole saw. Be sure to caulk around the pipes and let the caulking dry before you spread adhesive on the wall.

After all panels are in place, press again on the entire surface to assure a complete bond. Remove excess caulking with water and a soft cloth, and wipe off adhesive with mineral spirits and another soft cloth. Don't use the tub or shower for 24 hours.

HARDBOARD PANELING

Other types of hardboard may be used to finish walls in rooms not subject to moisture. Standard panel size is 4′ × 8′ by ¼″ thick, but you can buy longer panels for rooms with high ceilings. Hardboard is manufactured unfinished with a hard, smooth surface suitable for painting, or with a surface perforated with small holes. It is also made prefinished, with the surface either striated or embossed, and with patterns that simulate wood, masonry, stone, leather, and fabrics. Some finishes are printed; better quality finishes are vinyl.

Hardboard less than ¼″ thick must be applied over a solid backing, and can be used to resurface any smooth wall except masonry. In new construction or on uneven walls, the best application is on furring strips. These strips must be used behind perforated hardboard and any hardboard applied over masonry.

Furring Strips

To install solid hardboard over existing walls or across bare studs, cut furring strips 2″ wide from ¼″ plywood, either finished or unfinished and preferably scrap material. To install perforated hardboard you need 1 × 2 furring strips so that you have room to insert hanging fixtures. Over masonry walls use 2 × 2s.

Furring strips are required behind the top and bottom of each panel and no less than every 16″ between (Fig. 19-12a). Joints between these long strips must fall on studs. You also need shorter strips on studs that support joints between panels, around door and window framing, and at other openings for such things as heating grilles. Apply the strips with common nails long enough to go at least ¾″ into studs.

Masonry walls must be coated with a waterproofing compound to seal against moisture before you apply the strips. Set the bottom horizontal strip about ¼″ above the finished floor level. Attach the top strip to ceiling joists when they run perpendicular to the wall (Fig. 19-12b), and to 6″ nailing blocks when joists are parallel to the wall (Fig. 19-12c).

Apply Hardboard

Hardboard may be applied in three ways: with nails to furring strips, with adhesive to furring strips, or with adhesive to an existing wall surface that is clean and level.

You can nail either with 3d finishing nails or colored nails that match the paneling. Space fasteners every 4″ along all four edges, and 8″ apart in the field. Drive colored nails with a plastic-headed hammer that won't chip the paint, leaving the heads flush with the hardboard surface. Predrill holes for finishing nails, countersink the heads slightly, and fill the holes with putty stick of a matching color.

To attach panels to furring strips with adhesive, you must pretrim panels to size and cut holes in them where necessary. Then apply adhesive with a gun. Check the manufacturer's instructions and information on open time before you start. On furring strips behind joints between panels, lay a bead of adhesive about ⅛″ wide and ½″ from each edge. Lay the bead down the center of all other strips.

If you have a long enough open time, press each precut panel into the adhesive to spread it. Then remove the panel and immediately reset it permanently. This extra step helps the adhesive set more quickly and gives a better bond. Nail only along the top and bottom to hold the panel until the adhesive dries.

To attach hardboard to an existing surface with adhesive, follow the basic procedures earlier in this chapter for the application of tileboard.

PLYWOOD PANELING

Like hardboard, plywood paneling may be applied to furring strips as just described, or with adhesive to an existing wall. Unlike hardboard, however, it is enough stronger and more flexible that you may also apply it directly to studs.

Prefinished panels are 4′ wide, come in lengths of 7 to 10′, and in thicknesses from 4 mm (about $\frac{5}{32}$″) to $\frac{5}{16}$″. The most popular panels have vertical V-grooves cut apparently at random, but there is always a groove 16″, 24″, and 32″ from each edge. Thus full panels can easily be split into one-third, one-half, and two-thirds panels down a groove.

The tones of face veneers range from dark browns to pale tans, with some tones toward a cool gray and others toward a warm yellow. The grain may be prominent or subdued. Before you select plywood, set three or four panels side by side to see the effect. You

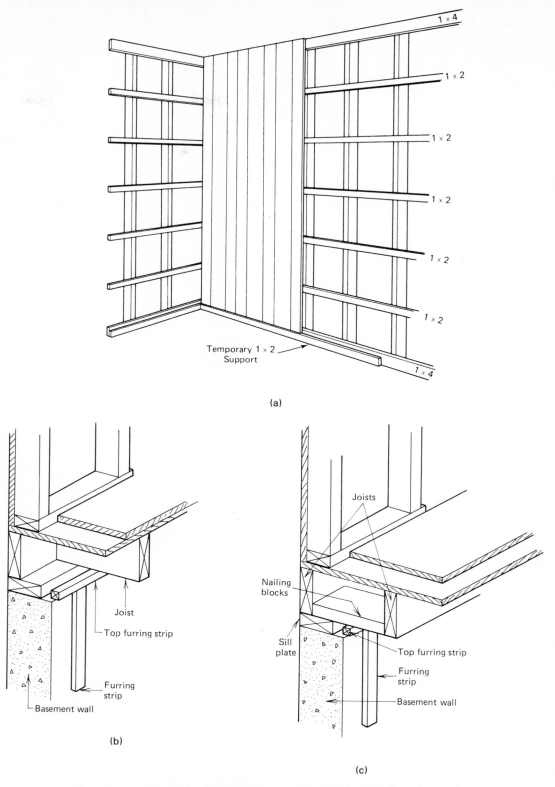

Fig. 19-12. Where furring strips are required behind hardboard paneling applied over studs (a). When you apply paneling to a foundation wall, attach the top furring strip to joists that run perpendicular to the wall (b), or to nailing blocks between the edge joist and first joist when they run parallel to the wall (c).

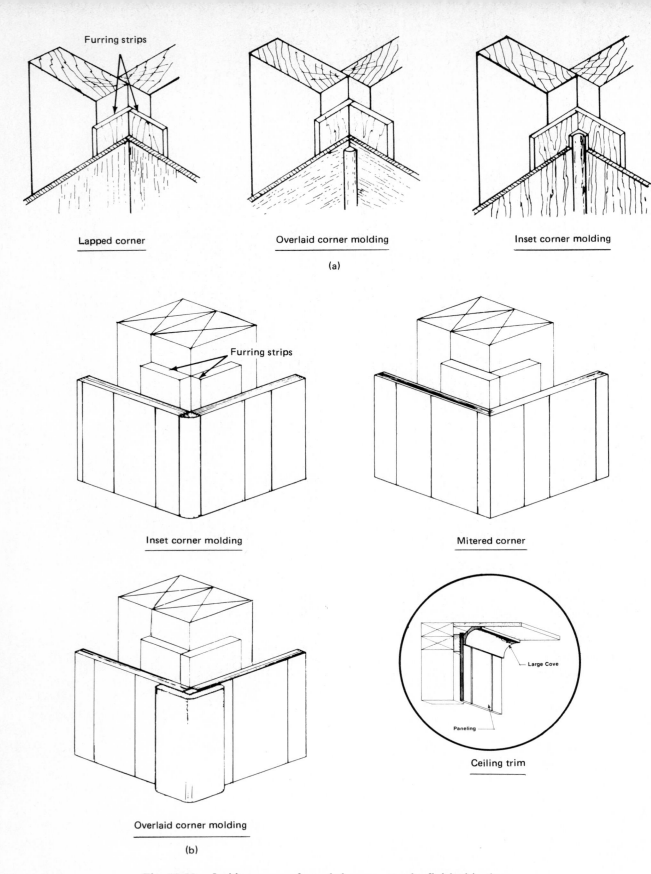

Furring strips

Lapped corner   Overlaid corner molding   Inset corner molding

(a)

Furring strips

Inset corner molding   Mitered corner

Large Cove

Paneling

Overlaid corner molding   Ceiling trim

(b)

Fig. 19-13. Inside corners of paneled rooms may be finished in three ways (a) and outside corners also in three ways (b). At the ceiling (inset) select a cove molding large enough so that you can nail it firmly through paneling into furring and avoid having to nail into the ceiling.

can't tell how an entire wall will look by seeing a single panel.

Layout

Use full panels wherever possible, because factory-finished edges are made to fit well together. At openings it is quicker and, in the long run, more economical to apply full panels, than trim away the excess with a router or fine-toothed saw.

Lay out your panels by standing them against the wall to study the overall effect. You may want to install alternate panels upside down to relieve monotony of appearance. Where you must cut a panel to width, figure out in advance where you can use the remainder. Then number each panel on the back in order of application, and mark the top with an arrow.

Preparation

Order plywood to arrive at least 24 hours before you plan to apply it. Plywood expands and contracts less than hardboard, but will nevertheless change dimensions slightly. So remove the panels from their carton to let them adapt to moisture content in the room. Remove at one time as many panels as are packed between protective sheets. Then lift them one by one; avoid sliding them, which mars the surface. After you number the panels lay them flat again. Otherwise, they will take on a bow and be more difficult to install. To prevent damage from bumps in a room that will be actively used after remodeling, add 2 × 4 blocking between studs about 36″ up from the floor and 36″ down from the ceiling.

Installation

To apply plywood to furring strips or over an existing surface, you follow the procedures just outlined for hardboard. Space nails 12″ apart along edges, and 16″ apart in the field, however.

Begin application to studs at the most prominent corner of the room. Set the corner panel in place, and mark the centerline of the stud on which the outside edge falls. Then check the fit in the corner, and scribe the edge if necessary. The first panel must be applied plumb and on the centerline. Precut any holes for switches or electrical receptacles.

Obviously, a standard 8′ high panel won't cover a wall that measures about 8′-1″ from subfloor to finished ceiling. So set the panel with gaps at both ends—no more than ½″ at the floor and the remainder at the ceiling. You cover the gap later with trim.

Install the pretrimmed corner panel first. If you use nails, nail into grooves wherever possible. To avoid splitting the wood, nail at an angle into the side of the groove. When you nail directly to framing, space nails every 6″ along edges and every 12″ in the field.

If you use contact adhesive, precut each panel and mark the centerlines of studs on their backs. Then brush two coats of adhesive on the faces of all studs behind the panel, and three coats about 2½″ wide along centerlines on the back of the panel. After the coats have dried thoroughly, fit the edge of the first panel into the corner, holding it at an angle to the studs. Then slowly swing the panel into position. You must be accurate. Once the coats of adhesive touch, you can't move the panel without destroying it. With the panel in place, pound with a rubber mallet or press with a roller along the entire length of each stud to assure a permanent bond.

Continue along the first wall to the corner, then work from the first panel to the opposite corner. In a rectangular room start work on the last two walls in the corner diagonally across the room from the first panel, and repeat the process.

At Corners. You can finish inside corners in three ways (Fig. 19-13a). You can overlap panels as long as the edge of the lapping panel fits without trimming or scribing. You can gap the panels slightly and fit a quarter-round or small cove molding over the gap. Or you can nail a ¾″ corner molding into the corner and butt panels against it. In many rooms this method works well, because it puts the edges of corner panels on the centerlines of studs.

Outside corners are more likely to be bumped, and therefore need greater protection. Again you have a choice. The more attractive but more difficult solution is to cut panels flush with studs and inset a corner molding (Fig. 19-13b). A simpler answer is an overlaid corner molding, which may also be the better solution depending on stud spacing.

TRIM AT OPENINGS

When you resurface any wall, keep in mind that the extra thickness is going to affect the fit around door and window openings. The backs of trim are **plowed** (slightly hollowed) so that they can adapt to some difference between the planes of a finished wall and the edges of casings. Even then, joints at corners where two pieces of casing meet may have to be remitered to fit well. The point to remember is that you should be aware of the problems that added thickness causes *before* you apply a new surface material, and not be surprised by them when the bulk of your work is behind you.

Surface Finishing—Floors

Floors eventually wear down in very old houses, and often the only practical solution to maintaining appearance of rooms is new flooring. Matching the Colonial style of this room and its furnishings is a wood plank floor, laid in alternate widths of 2¼ and 3¼ inches. Edges and ends come beveled to emphasize the joints. (Courtesy Fine Hardwoods/American Walnut Association.)

Flooring materials are installed in one of two ways—with nails or with adhesive, including mortar. Those that you are most likely to work with require underlayment and are set in adhesive.

Thin flooring materials such as linoleum and tiles of asphalt, vinyl, rubber, or vinyl-asbestos **telegraph**—that is, transmit to the surface—the cracks or joints in the support material beneath them. It is possible to lay a plywood subfloor so smooth that joints don't show, but even a slight unevenness in the tops of joists makes this difficult. Although it takes a little more time and a little more material, you should always cover subflooring, whatever it is, with a thin layer of smooth sheet material before you lay thin flooring. The most common of these underlayments are ¼″ hardboard and underlayment grade of ¼″ plywood.

PREPARING FOR UNDERLAYMENT

The surface over which you install underlayment may be a new subfloor in an addition, a badly and unevenly worn finish floor, or an old but reasonably smooth finish floor. In new construction begin by sweeping the subfloor clean. Fasten down with screws or additional nails any cupped edges of plywood or particleboard that may have warped while you were building. If necessary, rent a power sander to remove ridges and other high spots. Sand lightly; it doesn't take much pressure with a sander to remove more than you intended.

To be thorough in an existing house, you should tear out old flooring down to the bare subfloor. Often, however, this is a slow job that takes a lot of effort. If the added thickness of underlayment and new flooring won't cause problems at doors, leave the old flooring in place. Otherwise, accept your fate and get to work removing the old floor.

Remove Old Flooring

First remove the base and base shoe, and pull all nails left either in the trim or the wall. With sheet flooring start in a corner, forcing a putty knife under the edge of the sheet. If there isn't room to do this, score through the flooring near a corner and pry along the cut until you loosen a piece. Then work toward the center of the room with a broadknife. Remove not only the sheet flooring but the adhesive beneath it. If the flooring was laid over building paper, it should go, too, and makes removal of adhesive a lot easier.

With thin tiles begin either in a corner or at any loose corner of a tile, and follow the same procedure.

To remove a wood strip floor, begin at one side of the room and work across it. Usually, strip flooring is laid parallel to the long wall. Use a crowbar to loosen nails holding the flooring down, working over joists so that you pry against the most resistance.

After you have the old flooring off, check the condition of the subflooring. Refasten any cupped edges or corners of sheet subflooring, and sand ridges as smooth as you can get them. Then sweep and vacuum the surface.

If your subflooring is wood, nail down any loose boards and replace any broken or badly cupped ones. Clean the surface thoroughly. Then cut strips of 15-lb roofing felt and lay them out on the subfloor—across diagonal boards or at right angles to long boards laid straight. Felt comes in rolls 30″ wide. Butt the strips; don't overlap them. Then set the strips aside and cover the subfloor with mastic spread with a finely notched trowel. Spread only enough adhesive at one time for one strip. Set each strip in the adhesive and roll it with a heavy roller immediately to assure a tight, even bond. The roofing felt serves two purposes. It prevents dust and dirt from falling through cracks between subflooring boards, and it reduces the chances of squeaks in the floor. Felt isn't required over sheet subflooring.

Installation of Underlayment

When you lay out underlayment over board subflooring, begin in a corner with a full sheet trimmed to fit in that corner and with one outer edge on the centerline of a joist. Complete the first row of sheets end to end, then start the next row with a half sheet, the third

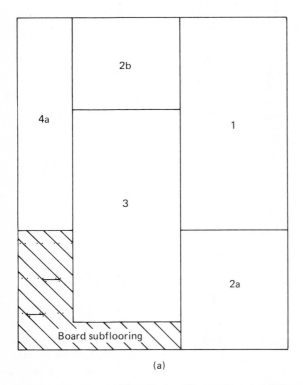

(a)

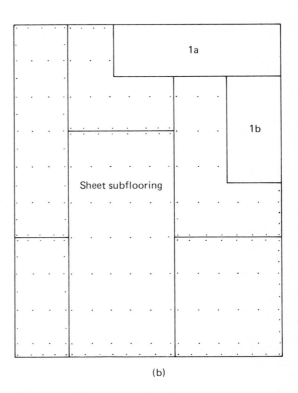

(b)

Fig. 20-1. Over a board subfloor (a), begin laying underlayment with full sheets, and stagger joints between rows. Sheet 2b is the offall of full sheet 2. Over sheet subflooring (b) begin underlayment with partial sheets so that joints in the subfloor and in the underlayment are as far apart as possible.

row with a full sheet, and so on (Fig. 20-1a). Staggered joints give you the smoothest base.

Over a plywood subfloor, cover a full sheet of plywood with a partial sheet of underlayment half the width and two-thirds the length of a full sheet (Fig. 20-1b). Complete the first row with half-width sheets, then use full-width sheets until you near the opposite wall. Stagger end joints either 32″ or 48″, whichever is more economical. In this way you bridge joints in the subfloor, which you must do.

Apply underlayment with special underlayment nails spaced 3″ apart along edges and 6″ apart in the field. Drive the first nail in the center of each sheet, and work outward to avoid any waviness.

RESILIENT TILES

In the simplest tile floor the tiles are all the same color and they are laid with their joints parallel to walls. As easy to lay but more complicated to lay out is a floor with several colors of tile in a pattern—even a diagonal (Fig. 20-2). More difficult to lay is a floor with tiles actually running diagonally. Most difficult, but also the most interesting, is a floor of tiles or linoleum with feature strips—1″-wide strips of sharply contrasting color value.

points of the short walls, and lay a cord between them. The cord should pass through the midpoint; if it doesn't, recheck your measurements. Snap a chalk line between wall midpoints. Then, using the 3–4–5 triangle method (see Fig. 3-5), locate a second chalk line through the room's midpoint at 90° to the first chalk line. It should reach long walls at their midpoints.

When a room isn't rectangular but walls are parallel, find the maximum dimensions of the room. Divide these dimensions in half, and measure off these distances from the corner where the two longest adjoining walls meet. Then measure the same distances from the opposite walls (Fig. 20-3). Snap chalk lines between opposite points. Then lay a cord on the diagonal; it should pass through the midpoint where chalk lines cross.

In a room with a wall or two curving or off angle, decide which wall you want tiles to parallel. Then establish a starting point by a method similar to that in Fig. 20-3.

Tiles Running Parallel. Divide room dimensions by the width of a tile; most tiles are either 9″ × 9″ or 12″ × 12″. Suppose, for example, that room dimensions are 104″ × 164″, and you selected 9″ tiles. You need 11 + tiles in one direction and 17 + in the other. But 11 full tiles would leave border tiles only 2½″ wide, and they should be at least half a tile wide. Therefore,

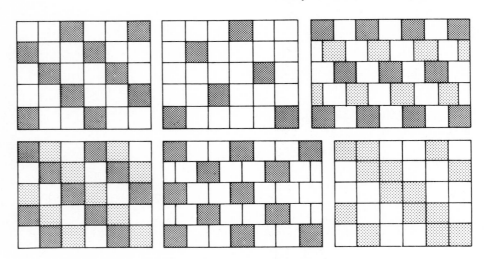

Fig. 20-2. The only limit to patterns in which you can lay floor tiles is your own imagination. Here are just a few diagonal patterns that can be achieved by laying tiles parallel to walls.

Lay Out Tiles

Laying out a tile floor is very similar to laying out an acoustical tile ceiling. Begin by checking all corners for square. Then measure the room accurately, and write down its dimensions in inches. Use the longest dimensions, regardless of the shape of the room, as the basis for your tile layout.

In a room that is rectangular or close to it, snap diagonal chalk lines across the subfloor. Where they cross is the midpoint of the room. Next find the mid-

plan on 10 full tiles and 7″ border tiles. In the long direction 17 full tiles cover 153″, and you need border tiles 5½″ wide.

Now look at Fig. 20-4. The solid lines represent your crossing chalk lines. If you have an odd number of full tiles, you must move the centerline half a tile in either direction by snapping a new chalk line. Therefore, you have four possible starting points. If the number of full tiles in *both* directions is *even*, lay the first tile as shown in Fig. 20-4a, using your existing chalk lines. If the number of tiles in *both* directions is

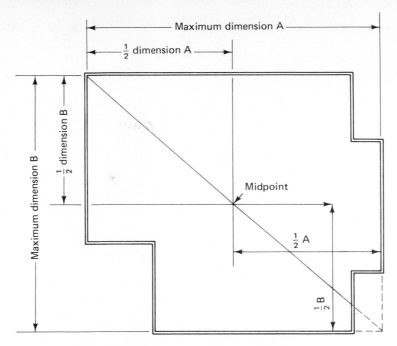

Fig. 20-3. To find the starting point for laying floor tiles in a room of irregular shape, work from the midpoints of its maximum dimensions.

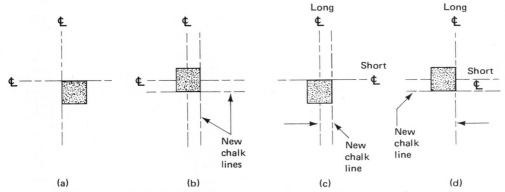

Fig. 20-4. The starting point for laying the first tile may be one of four places, depending on the number of full tiles running each direction.

odd, snap new chalk lines (shown dashed) and lay the first tile as shown in Fig. 20-4b. Follow Fig. 20-4c if the *long* dimension is *odd* and the *short* one *even*, as in the example. Follow Fig. 2-4d if the *long* dimension is *even* and the *short* dimension *odd*.

Tiles Running Diagonally. From the centerline of the longest wall measure to the midpoint of the room, then swing your tape 90° and mark this same dimension on the floor. Between this point and the midpoint snap a chalk line; it will be at 45° to the wall and other chalk lines. Set tiles along this line to see what happens in the corner. Ideally, a 45° line outward from each corner should lie under the center of a row of tiles. Sometimes you can adjust the diagonal line by half a tile width to make this happen. Otherwise, carry your diagonal chalk line across the rest of the room and work from it.

Special patterns. To work out your own design for flooring, draw a floor plan of the room at the largest possible scale. Use graph paper if all flooring units will be the same size. Use plain paper if you plan to use feature strips or an **insert**—any special design such as an initial or coat of arms. The 1″ feature strips come in a variety of plain colors and you can develop interesting designs with them. Inserts are most easily cut out of sheets of resilient flooring and hand-fitted into the space provided for them.

Tile Adhesive

To avoid any problems with incompatible materials, always use the adhesive recommended by the tile manufacturer. Most manufacturers make their own brand. There are three types. One type you spread with a trowel like adhesive behind wall tiles, but use a trowel with finer notches so that ridges aren't as high or wide. Another type is like contact cement, and you apply it with a brush. It must be applied with one-directional strokes, and allowed to dry for about 1 hour. A third type is applied to the backs of tiles at the factory, and protected by a sheet of paper. All you do is peel off the paper and set the tiles in place. You must brush wood sealer on underlayment and let it dry, however, to permit the adhesive to dry slowly and bond well. Not all types, colors, and patterns of tiles are available with an adhesive backing.

Lay the First Tile

Some professionals prefer to lay floor tiles like ceiling tiles, working from a corner outward. They establish with chalk lines the area to be covered with full files, then lay the first tile just inside the chalk lines at one corner. They cover half the room, then lay border tiles before going on to the other half. This may be the most practical method for you when you are completely remodeling a kitchen, and need to keep the room in as full operation as possible.

For most do-it-yourselfers it is safer to start in the middle of the room at one of the four points shown in Fig. 20-4, and work toward walls.

For at least 24 hours before you apply tiles, store the boxes where air temperature is at least 65 °F. Tiles must be flexible when you lay them; stiff tiles are brittle and may break.

Spread adhesive on no more than half the underlayment; in a large room cover only one-fourth of the floor area. Work in a well-ventilated room; most

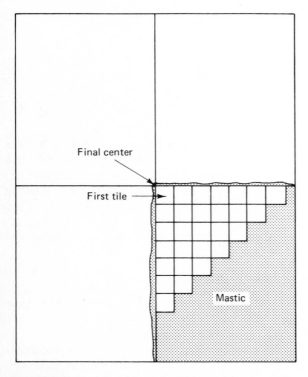

Final center

First tile

Mastic

Fig. 20-5. Lay tiles in a pyramid, working from the center starting point toward walls. Cover a fourth of the floor of a large room with mastic; in a small room you can cover half the floor at one time.

adhesives will burn and have a strong odor that dissipates quickly. Apply the adhesive in a thin coat. When applied with a trowel, only the adhesive that squeezes through the notches should remain on the underlayment.

It's all right to cover up your chalk lines, but leave the ends of lines and the midpoint where they cross exposed. After the adhesive becomes tacky—that is, no longer plastic but slightly sticky to the touch—resnap chalk lines over the coating. To tell when adhesive is tacky, touch it with your finger. If your finger doesn't stick, the adhesive is ready. But there is no rush; floor tile adhesive has a much longer open time than wall tile adhesive. Check the label on the can to determine how much.

Hold the first tile above the point where your finally established centerlines cross, and make sure it lies exactly on both lines. Then lower it into position. Never slide or twist a tile into place; by doing so you build up a ridge of adhesive on the edge of the tile and won't get a tight joint. In a good tiling job you can scarcely see the joints.

Lay succeeding tiles in the shape of a pyramid (Fig. 20-5). The patterns of many tiles have grain to them, and a floor looks best when the grain is at right angles in consecutive tiles. Place the edge of each tile against the edge of its neighbor at a slight angle to the floor, and swing it into position. Work slowly, especially as you kneel or walk on freshly laid floors. It's easy to push a tile out of line and hard to get it back into line. Wipe off any mastic that gets on the face of a tile with a wet cloth dipped in the solvent recommended by the adhesive manufacturer.

Border Tiles

When the edge of the last row of full tiles is parallel to a wall, place a loose tile atop the last full tile in a row (A in Fig. 20-6a), with the grain at right angles to that tile. Slide the loose tile against the wall. Use the edges of tile A as a guide to scoring the loose tile with a linoleum knife. Then cut along the scoring line. The cut piece will fill the gap.

If the last row of full tiles is not exactly parallel to the wall, lay a narrow strip of tile on the underlayment against the wall. Then lay a full-sized tile upside down on the strip and the finished row, with the grain running the proper direction (Fig. 20-6b). Push the tile flush against the wall, with its shorter edge directly above the joint in the finished row. Mark the edges of the loose tile where it crosses the finished tile line. Turn the tile over, set a straightedge between the edge marks, and score the face with a linoleum knife. Then cut along the scoring line. When the angle off parallel is slight, the cut piece (A in Fig. 20-6b) will fit almost exactly. With a greater angle the tile will gap slightly at the wall, but that gap will be covered by base trim. Piece B may fit at the end of some other row.

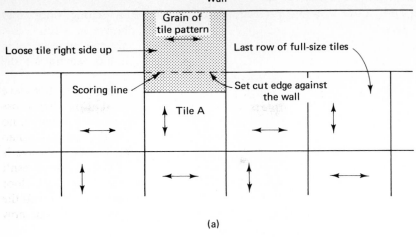

(a)

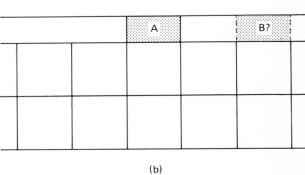

Fig. 20-6. Cutting border tiles when the wall is parallel to the edges of full tiles (a), when the wall is off parallel (b), and when tiles run diagonally (c).

(b)

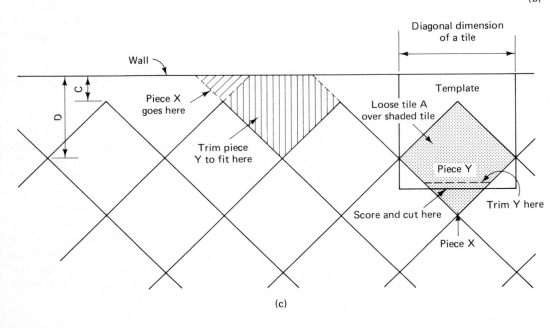

(c)

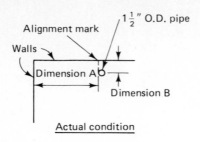

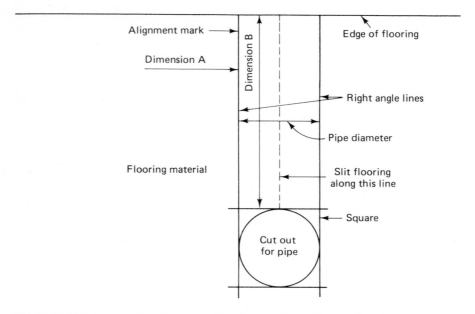

Fig. 20-7. How to mark and cut sheet flooring or tiles to fit around a pipe.

Border tiles in a diagonal pattern must be cut differently. First make a template out of cardboard, with its sides equal in length to the *diagonal* dimension of a full tile. With 9″ tiles the template should be 12¾″ on a side; with 12″ tiles 17″ per side. Next, place a loose tile (A) face up over the last full tile in a row (shaded in Fig. 20-6c). Then lay the template over tile A with one edge against the wall and its long sides just touching the corners of the loose tile. Score tile A along the edge of the template, then complete the cut. One piece (X) will fit the border. Trim the remainder of tile A (Y) to fit at some other point in the border. Measure from the wall to the 45° corners (dimension F or G) to determine how to cut piece Y with minimum waste.

At corners, follow border procedures in two steps. In the first step mark the cut to fit against one wall, and in the second mark the cut against the second wall. Around irregular shapes, such as a door jamb, set a loose tile on the closest full tile to the obstacle. Then use another loose tile, moving it around the obstacle, to mark the first tile for cutting. As an alternative to a loose tile, use a scriber. Set the legs of the scriber to the width of your tile, then move it along the irregular shape. Be sure to keep the scriber always at right angles to the edge of the tile to be cut.

SHEET FLOORING

Sheet flooring, also called **roll goods**, comes in long rolls and you buy it by the square yard. For years the only sheet flooring available was linoleum. Now vinyl flooring is more popular because it doesn't absorb grease or stains, is thinner, and is easier to handle. Sheet flooring comes in 6′ and 12′ widths, and in a wide variety of smooth and embossed patterns, either matched or unmatched at edges. You lay sheet flooring, like resilient tiles, over underlayment in adhesive, but the procedure is quite different.

Layout

Where you start depends on the flooring you select and the size and shape of the room. In a room less than 12′ wide, run sheet flooring the long dimension of the room. In a room more than 12′ in both dimensions, run the flooring whichever direction requires the least cutting and seaming.

When the material has no matching pattern for you to worry about, plan to place the first strip along a long, unbroken expanse of wall, and work across the room. When the material does have a matching pattern, work from a chalk line down the centerline of the room and toward walls.

Flooring must extend into doorways. For that reason work toward doorways if possible, so that you are laying the narrower strips there. Keep this extension in mind as you lay out your work. If a room 12' wide has a doorway on one side, your material won't be wide enough, and you'll have to run it the other direction.

Fitting

Set the roll of flooring so that it laps up the end wall about 3", and unroll it along the long wall. Cut the opposite end to lap about 3" also. Push the strip against the long side wall to check the fit. It should not gap at any point more than about ⅛". If it does, mark the edge with a scriber and cut along the scribing line.

After the fit is good at the side wall, force one end of the strip tightly into the corner between wall and floor. Score the flooring at the corner, pull it away from the wall, and cut on the scoring line. Repeat this process at the other end. To make sure that the strip doesn't slip between cuts, mark both its surface and the long wall at some point, and use the two marks as coordinates for realignment.

If there is an obstacle between the two end walls (Fig. 20-7, top left), mark an alignment point on the wall and flooring, then carry the line onto the underlayment at right angles to the wall. Reset the strip against the pipe, with its edges parallel to the wall and the marks aligned. Draw lines on the flooring at right angles to the wall a distance apart equal to the diameter of the pipe. Then measure from the wall to both sides of the pipe or obstacle, and transfer these dimensions to the flooring, measured from its edge and allowing for any gap. Inside this square (Fig. 20-7) draw a circle with a compass. Cut out the circle with a linoleum knife, then slit the flooring between the circle and the edge. Cut the slit at an angle to the surface, and the seam will be almost invisible.

Cut Seams

You can cut all strips before laying any, or you can lay each strip before you cut the next. With either method, prepare and cut the seam between sheets before the adhesive dries.

With the first strip either laid or in position for laying, set the next strip so that it laps up the walls 3" and lies flush with the first strip. Place an alignment mark at least 2" long across the seam at some point near the midpoint. Next, move the strip so that it overlaps the previous strip ¾" or to a pattern matching point (Fig. 20-8). Then trim the ends to fit snug at the walls.

For cutting a seam use a metal straightedge or the longest straight piece of metal you can find or borrow. Mark points ⅜" from the edge of the top strip close enough together so you can connect them with the straightedge. First, score along this cutting line with a sharp knife. Next, cut entirely through the top strip and

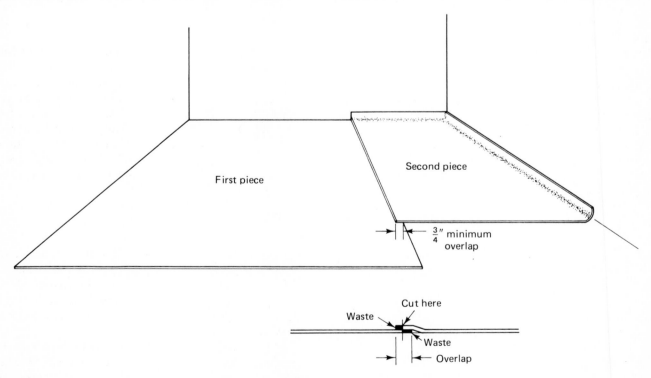

Fig. 20-8. Where two lengths of resilient flooring meet, lay them so they overlap. Then cut through both thicknesses for an exact match at the seam.

far enough into the bottom strip to score it. Temporarily move the top strip out of the way, and discard the narrow strip you cut off. Then cut the bottom strip along the scoring line. Cut only through the strip; avoid dulling your knife by scarring the underlayment. Finally, slide the second strip against the first to check the fit. It should be exact.

When you cut, hold your knife at a slight angle to the vertical. Cut both strips with the handle of the knife tilted toward the edge of the strip to be cut off. By undercutting the seam this way, you leave the thinnest flooring at the top, and the edges squeeze together in a tight seam.

At Corners

To fit the final piece in a room, measure the width of the uncovered area at several points. Then trim the strip to a width about 2″ or 3″ greater if the wall has no doorway, a full 3″ wider into a doorway where the door opens into the room, and 4″ wider when the door opens out. Like all others, this strip should lap end walls 3″. Set this strip against the adjoining strip, mark an alignment point, then reset it with a ¾″ overlap as in Fig. 20-8.

For the best fit at an inside corner, make a U-shaped cut at the corner of the strip. Lay the strip flush with the side wall and lapping up the end wall. Measure the amount of overlap in the corner. Then measure the width of floor to be covered and add ¾″. Transfer these measurements to your strip. With the strip flat, make a U-shaped cut through the points you marked. Then realign the strip on your alignment marks, and trim the end to fit. Repeat this operation in the opposite corner. The ends should now fit, but the strip will still lap up the

side wall. Now follow the process just outlined for cutting seams.

At an outside corner, slit the strip where it turns up the wall (Fig. 20-9). Cut straight down so that part of the strip still laps the wall but the remainder drops around the corner. At a doorway repeat this step at the opposite jamb. Then trim the excess flush with the wall. In the doorway carry the flooring to the edge of the door stop, and trim it there. Cut at the near side of the stop when the door swings in, and the far edge when the door swings out. Cut at the centerline of a swinging door that has no stop.

Around Obstacles

To fit around an irregular shape, such as a toilet bowl, mark on the flooring the centerline of the bowl. Cut along this line to a point that allows the flooring to lap about 2″ up the front of the bowl. Then cut slits at the front corners, and scribe the flooring for a flush fit at the front. Cut out some of the excess material that will be in your way, allowing a 2″ overlap at the sides, until you can locate the back corners. Then slit and fit, first on one side, then the other. Trim along the back of the bowl to your first cut to complete the job.

Application

Clean underlayment thoroughly with broom and vacuum cleaner before you begin to lay your strips. Set the first precut strip in position to recheck the fit, especially if you precut one day and lay the next. Mark with a chalk line on the underlayment the outer edge of

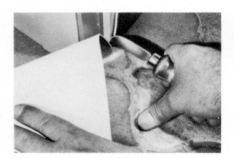 

Fig. 20-9. Trimming resilient flooring around a door jamb. (Courtesy Armstrong Cork Company.)

the strip. Then fold the strip back on itself, but don't crease it.

Following instructions on the can, spread adhesive with a notched trowel from an end wall to the folding point, and from the side wall to within 2″ of the chalk line. Set the flooring in the adhesive, aligning it on the chalk line and at the end and letting it fall gently into place. Then roll the surface with a 100-lb roller to within 4″ of the chalk line. Next, fold the uncemented flooring onto the cemented half and repeat the process. Be careful not to spread new adhesive into the old; it will leave a ridge that will telegraph through the flooring.

Follow the same process for all remaining strips. With the second strip folded onto itself, first spread adhesive with a putty knife or broadknife under the edge of the previous strip. Then spread adhesive for half the new strip. If you don't precut remaining strips until after you lay the first strip, cut the seam after you roll the second strip. Then wet the seam with a damp cloth and reroll it.

CERAMIC FLOOR TILES

The ¾″-thick ceramic tiles often used in bathrooms for flooring require an underlayment of ¾″ exterior-grade plywood covered by felt, and are set in a bed of mortar at least ¾″ thick. Because of the problems created by the differences in floor levels between rooms, these tiles are not practical for reflooring.

But the thinner tiles mounted on paper or fabric will work nicely. You lay them directly on a smooth subfloor in waterproof mastic. They come in squares 24″ on a side, and individual tiles are either 1″ square or 1″ × 2″. Because of their small scale, you can begin laying the floor at any convenient point.

In a new bathroom lay a tile floor after you install the bathtub or shower stall but before any other fixtures are in place. In an existing room remove any base trim and, when you come to them, the legs of lavatories. With careful nipping you can achieve a good fit against a toilet bowl or base cabinet without removing them.

All the tiles in a sheet may be the same color, or several colors in either a random or geometric pattern. Yet even tiles of one color vary slightly in shade. For best appearance lay out full sheets on the bare subflooring, then fit in partial sheets at walls and other obstacles. Let a row or two of tiles run up the walls for now, and cut small pieces with tile nippers later.

Lay Out the Sheets

When you are satisfied with your floor's appearance, number each sheet in the order in which you plan to lay it, then stack the sheets in numerical order. If possible, plan your work so that you don't ever have to kneel or step on laid tiles, and end up at a door to another room. In a kitchen this is usually not difficult, but in a small bathroom it takes quite a little planning. Always begin with a full sheet, preferably in a square corner, but with at least one side flush with a straight wall or cabinet.

Lay Tiles

Using the mastic recommended by the tile manufacturer, spread just enough to cover the area you can reach from bare subflooring. At walls, obstacles, and between sheets, leave a gap equal to the space between tiles to allow for grouting. Where the edges of a cut sheet fall on a grout line, cut the backing or surface paper along the line before you set the partial sheets. Where you must fit around an irregular shape that doesn't follow grout lines, start cutting tiles at one edge and fit as you work toward the next edge.

Press sheets firmly into the adhesive until it surrounds each tile. It should ooze no more than about one-third of the way up the side of a tile. If paper covers the exposed tile surface, rub it with a damp sponge until it comes loose. Recheck tile alignment as soon as you lay a sheet or partial sheet. If you must kneel on laid tiles, wrap padding (an old towel will do) around a short length of 1 × 8 to spread your weight and save wear and tear on your knees. Recheck alignment once more when you stand up.

Ceramic wall tiles have rounded edges, and you fill the gaps between tiles with grout only to the beginning of the curve. Ceramic floor tiles, on the other hand, have square edges, and joints should be filled with grout flush with the tile surface. Thus water from washing won't collect in joints, and the floor is easier to clean and keep clean.

To withstand wear, use a thicker grout than with wall tiles. Your tile supplier can recommend the best type. After the adhesive has dried for 24 hours, apply the grout with a trowel. Fill joints flush, then carefully wipe off excess grout with a squeegee and damp sponge. Avoid digging into joints.

You can polish the floor in 24 hours with a coarse cloth, such as burlap. Don't wash it for at least three weeks, however; it takes that long for the grout to set completely, although you can walk on the floor immediately. Avoid strong cleaning compounds for at least six months. You shouldn't need them anyway.

Save the tiles you don't use, either as partial sheets or as individual tiles if they are easier to store that way. Then you have spares if some day you must repair the floor.

THIN WOOD BLOCKS

Wood flooring comes in three forms: prefinished blocks, prefinished strips, and unfinished strips. Blocks are by far the easiest to install. Their standard size is 9″ × 9″, and thicknesses range from ⁵⁄₁₆″ up to ¹³⁄₁₆″. You set thin blocks in adhesive over a plywood subfloor or smooth concrete. You nail thicker blocks to a sub-floor of plywood or boards.

Thin wood blocks (less than ½″ thick) are the less expensive of the two types and are made like plywood. The grain of the top and bottom plies runs the same direction, and the two plies are aligned. The grain of the core runs at right angles to the other two, and that ply is offset slightly to form a groove on two sides and a tongue on the other two. Blocks are usually laid in a **parquet** pattern—that is, with the grain in each block running perpendicular to the grain in the four adjoining blocks.

Some types of thin wood blocks are made with a self-sticking adhesive already on the back and protected by a sheet of paper. Just peel off the paper and away you go. The adhesive has almost no open time, however, and you must lay each block accurately the first time. When you spread mastic yourself, you have time to correct any misalignment. Use the mastic recommended by the block manufacturer.

To lay blocks, you establish a starting point in the center of the room as shown in Figs. 20-3 and 20-4, then follow procedures for laying resilient tiles. Fit the tongue of each block fully into the groove of adjoining blocks, being careful not to knock other blocks out of line as you do so. Recheck alignment frequently so that joints are straight in both directions. A wood block

Fig. 20-10. A nailing machine in use. The plunger is activated by the hammer. Note that strip flooring is laid loosely in place so that you can see how the various lengths and grains will look together. (Courtesy National Oak Flooring Manufacturers Association.)

floor looks beautiful when you're finished, but misalignment shows up all too clearly.

At walls cut blocks to gap about ½″. About ⅜″ from their corners drill holes for finishing nails, and face-nail the blocks to the subfloor. Omit nailing if the base is concrete. Trim will cover both the gap and nailheads.

Use a power saw with a fine-toothed plywood blade for making straight cuts. For irregular cuts use a coping saw.

THICK BLOCKS

Thick blocks are the same thickness as wood strip flooring, and are actually made of edge-laminated strips. In some types the strips all run the same direction; in others the strips are shorter and form a swirl pattern. Both types have grooves on two opposite sides and tongues on the other two.

Cover the subflooring with felt as described on page 295, with one exception. Instead of butting edges of strips, overlap them 4″. The felt serves as a moisture barrier that prevents the blocks from warping.

As with thin blocks, find the center starting point and lay the first block there. Position it so that the tongues face in the direction you are going to work. After you nail each block, fit the grooves of the next block over the tongues.

To nail blocks a standard ²⁵⁄₃₂″ thick you can use 7d or 8d cut nails, 7d or 8d spiral nails, 6d barbed fasteners, or 8d coated nails. Professionals use a nailing machine and, if you can rent one locally, your work will go more quickly and surely. You load the nailing machine with fasteners, adjust it to the thickness of flooring you are installing, hold the machine against the tongue, and strike the plunger with a rubber mallet (Fig. 20-10). The machine automatically drives nails at the proper angle. You stand on the first block to hold it in place while you nail. For later blocks stand on the completed floor wherever you are comfortable.

To nail with a hammer, hold the nail just above the shoulder of the tongue, and drive it into the subfloor at about a 50° angle (Fig. 20-11). Nail about ¾″ from the end of each tongue.

Each block should fit against its neighbor without a gap. To permit this, tongues are shorter than grooves are deep. To avoid damaging tongues, however, rip a block in half, set a half with the groove over the tongue of the piece to be fitted, and hammer along the edge of the scrap piece to assure a tight fit. Never pound on the tongue itself; you will damage it and prevent a tight fit.

After you have driven nails as far in as possible with a hammer, lay a nailset flat on the recess over the nailhead, and hammer on the side of the nailset to drive the nails home. The heads don't need to be countersunk, but should be as flush as possible.

Make straight cuts with a power saw with a fine-

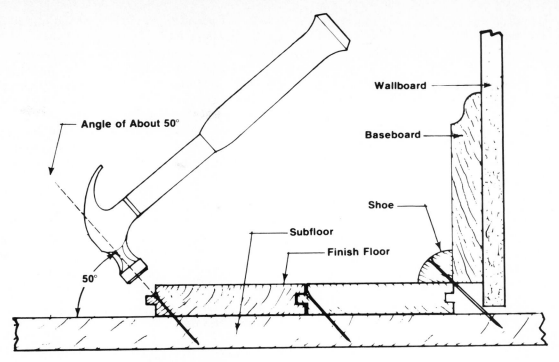

Fig. 20-11. Thick wood blocks and strip flooring may also be nailed with an ordinary hammer. Note that nails should be driven at about a 50° angle just above the tongue of each piece, and well into subflooring.

toothed blade, and irregular cuts with a coping saw. Leave a gap of about ¼″ at walls and obstructions, and blind-nail. If nailheads won't be covered by trim, countersink the heads, and fill the holes with matching wood putty or putty stick.

When you face-nail, it is worthwhile to predrill nail holes to keep from splitting the wood. If you don't have a small enough bit, you can make one by snipping the head off a No. 6 finishing nail and using the shank as a bit. Bore holes ½″ from the grooved edge.

WOOD STRIP FLOORING

There are two types of prefinished wood strip flooring. The most common strips are ²⁵⁄₃₂″ thick and 2¼″ wide. Edges and ends are tongue-and-groove, and corners are cut square to meet in tight joints. Prefinished planks are similar in thickness, but range up to 6″ in width. Both strips and planks may be nailed directly to and across floor joists, but you have a stronger, quieter floor when they are fastened with nails over felt to a wood subfloor. Wood strips may also be nailed to sleepers laid over a concrete floor. Sleepers are nothing more than horizontal furring strips.

Where to Start

The floor plan of your house, relationship of rooms, and the direction of joists all have a bearing on where you start. If you are flooring a single room, run strips parallel to the longest wall. If you are flooring several rooms open to each other, run all the strips the same direction in all rooms. You'll have the sturdiest floor if strips run across joists, but as long as you have a subfloor, the other two considerations are more important.

Begin work in the most prominent room. Measure out from the ends of the long wall a distance equal to about three widths of flooring. At that point either stretch a string at finished floor height or snap a chalk line. Position the first row of strips by measuring from the string, which is straight even if your wall isn't.

Over Subflooring

Start with a long strip, placed with its grooved edge ½ to ¾″ from the long wall and its grooved end ½ to ¾″ from the side wall. Make sure that the strip is parallel to the string or chalk line, then face-nail through predrilled holes at the end. You can use any of the nails recommended for thick blocks earlier in this chapter. Recheck alignment, then nail every 10″ at about the midpoint of the strip or plank. Do not nail within 5″ of the open end, so that you can fit the next strip more easily. You almost always have to face-nail the first strip nearest the long wall, because there isn't room to operate a nailing machine or swing a hammer. See Figs. 20-10 and 20-11 for nailing procedures.

Complete the first strip of flooring, trimming the tongued end to fit at the wall with a ½″ gap. To trim, turn the strip end for end and mark the cutting line. Then saw off the tongued end.

Now lay out 10 or 12 rows of strips. Strips vary in length, grain pattern, and uniformity of color, and it is important to maintain a variation throughout the floor. If you start with all light-toned strips, you will end up with darker strips at the other wall. Similarly, if you use up all the long strips first, you'll end up with all the short strips at the other wall. Intersperse short strips among the long ones throughout the floor. Place the prettiest strips where they will show, and save less attractive strips for less conspicuous areas such as closets and corners. Stagger butt ends at least 12" between rows.

When you are satisfied with appearance, position and nail strips at tongues. You can complete each strip before starting the next, but most professionals work from one side wall outward, laying increasingly shorter strips, then work on a diagonal toward the corner of the room opposite the corner where they started.

When you reach the point at the opposite wall where you have no room to toenail, fit the last two rows in position and force them tight with a crowbar. Place a scrap block behind the crowbar to protect the wall. Face-nail the final rows.

Sometimes you need to double back, such as into a closet. To do so, insert a plastic spline into the groove of the last strip you can lay in the normal way. Then cut the adjoining piece to length, and fit it over the spline so that the two strips are groove to groove. Toenail this strip, then complete the floor area as just outlined, working in the opposite direction.

Over Sleepers

Sleepers laid in mastic are the common base for strip flooring in a remodeled room with an existing concrete floor. Details are covered in Chapter 8 and shown in Fig. 8-3. They must run at right angles to flooring strips.

Time is a factor when flooring over sleepers, because you must not only set the sleepers but lay the floor before the adhesive hardens. So buy a mastic with a long open time, and precut sleepers.

The method of applying flooring to sleepers is the same as to a wood subfloor except for spacing of nails, which must hit the sleepers. No felt is required; the mastic itself forms a vapor barrier.

WOOD PLANKS

Planks are manufactured with edges cut at right angles or slightly beveled. The bevels reflect light and add to the beauty of the finished floor. The basic method of attachment is similar to nailing strip flooring, but does vary somewhat from manufacturer to manufacturer. Planks with tongue-and-groove edges are blind-nailed like strip flooring. Square-edged planks must be face-nailed. Space nails 24 to 32" in planks up to 4" wide, and every 16" in wider planks. Use spiral screw nails or finishing nails.

To achieve the effect of an old pegged floor, some plank manufacturers predrill holes near the ends of the planks. You blind-nail at tongues, face-nail at grooves, then fasten the ends with flat-head wood screws in the holes. Manufacturers provide plugs of contrasting wood (flooring is usually oak and the plugs walnut). Screw down the planks as you go, but leave the screwheads exposed until you floor the entire room and sweep it clean. Then blow debris out of the screw holes, and cover screwheads with glue. Fit the wood plugs with their tops flush with the planks, and wipe off any excess glue. At the same time cover the heads of countersunk nails with wood putty.

To protect your new wood floor, keep a container of some sort in the last corner of the room you plan to finish, and throw into it all bent nails and scrap flooring that might damage the prefinished surface. When you finish the floor, sweep it clean.

CARPETING

Carpeting is manufactured in rolls or squares and you buy it by the square yard. The one-foot squares, made with an adhesive backing protected by paper, are easy to lay although more expensive to buy. Roll carpeting must be secured at all edges.

To apply carpet tiles find the center starting point as if you were laying resilient tiles (see Figs. 20-3 and 20-4). Then work from the center of the room toward walls. In formal living areas make sure all squares come from the same dye lot so that you achieve the effect of uniform color throughout the room. In active rooms you may select squares of various colors and lay them in a pattern of your choice. Follow the manufacturer's recommendations for preparing the subfloor and installing the squares.

To lay roll carpeting over either a new or old subfloor, begin by nailing carpet strips around the perimeter of the room about ⅛" from all walls. A **carpet strip** is a thin, narrow length of wood, metal, or heavy fabric with barbs sticking upward at various angles. The barbs hold the carpet in place while you stretch it.

And stretch it you must. To do this properly you need either a carpet stretcher or a knee-kicker. A **carpet stretcher** is a mechanical device of adjustable length that holds carpet stretched until you can tack it down. A **kneekicker** serves the same purpose, but you strap it to one knee and do the stretching with leg power.

Layout

Carpeting comes in 12' widths (sometimes 15') and can run either direction in a room. When you fit two pieces together, they should lie edge to edge, rather than at right angles to each other. To keep costs down, develop a layout that requires the minimum length of carpet, since the width is fixed.

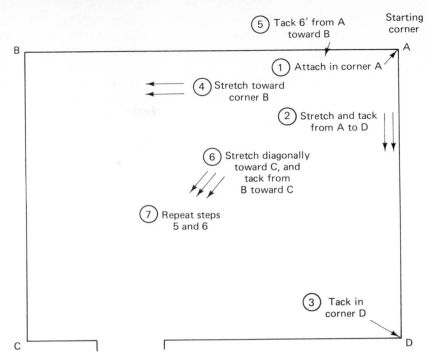

Fig. 20-12. The seven steps in carpeting a room after you cut a piece to the size of the room plus overlap.

Suppose that you have a room 15′ × 18′. If you run 12′ carpet the long way of the room, you need 36′ of length, or a total of 48 sq yd:

$$\frac{36' \times 12'}{9}$$

But if you run the carpet the short way, you need only 30′ of length or 40 sq yd. And you have less seam to match.

Be careful in a room just 12′ wide with a side doorway. By stretching you can usually gain 1 to 1½″, enough to reach a door stop. But get the assurance of the supplier before you buy. A heavily traveled doorway is no place for a seam.

Lay the Carpet

First check the cut of the open end of the roll. If the cut isn't square, use a sharp utility knife, carpenter's square, and a straightedge to trim it. Then set the roll flush against your starting wall, with the open end tight in a corner (A in Fig. 20-12). Unroll just enough so that you can press the corner onto the carpet strip against the starting wall to hold it. Then, being careful to keep the roll flush with the wall, unroll it toward the opposite corner of the room (B in Fig. 20-12).

At that wall unroll enough carpet so that you can fold it back and get the main roll away from the corner. Press the carpet into the corner, letting it lap up the wall several inches. At the corner (B in Fig. 20-12) make a cut about 2″ long. Repeat this process in the third corner

(D). Then mark a cutting line across the back of the roll between the two short cuts. If your room is square, the cutting line should be at right angles to both edges. Cut along this line. When you have a doorway in this wall, be sure to leave enough carpeting to fit into the opening. Carry the remainder of the roll out of the room.

Lay the cut piece of carpet flush with both walls in your starting corner (A in Fig. 20-12), and fasten it to the carpet strip. Then stretch the carpeting toward the opposite wall with a carpet stretcher or kneekicker. Tack the carpet to hold it in corner D. Then tack along the side wall between corners A and D. Let any excess carpeting lap up the wall.

Next, working first in your starting corner (A), stretch the carpet the other direction, and tack down about 6′ of it along the adjacent wall. Then stretch at a slight diagonal across the room so that you stretch the carpeting not only the short dimension of the room but also keep it taut the long dimension. Continue to the final corner (C) in this way, tacking edges to strips as you go. Then trim off the excess at walls with your utility knife, cutting as close to the wall as possible.

At Seams. As you approach any center seam, lay a strip of adhesive carpet tape on the floor so that the edge of the first piece of carpeting falls on the centerline of the tape. Press the carpet firmly onto the tape. Finish tacking the first piece along three walls. Then set the next piece on the tape, squeezing the two edges together for as tight a fit as you can make. Attach the second piece as you did the first. The fibers in each piece will bush beyond the cut edges and hide the seam.

At Doorways. At a doorway where carpeting stops and other flooring begins, use a carpet bar to conceal the edge when the carpeting is thicker than adjoining flooring, or a threshold when it is thinner. Cut the metal carpet bar to length—the dimension from door stop to door stop—and nail it in place. Thin flooring in the adjacent room may stop at the bar or run under it to conceal its edge. Stretch the carpeting as far into the open bar as you can, then bend the top of the bar over the raw edge to hold the carpeting firmly.

If the carpeting ends against wood flooring, tack the raw edge to the subfloor after cutting it to fit. Then buy a wood threshold of a thickness that will leave its top flush with the wood flooring when in place. Cut the threshold to length, set it flush, and nail it down over the gap. Countersink the nails and fill the holes. You may have to trim the bottoms of door stops to fit atop the threshold.

Trimming Out

One purpose of trim is to beautify, but outdoors its main purpose is to cover joints to prevent penetration of moisture. Here some soffit boards are in place to finish the underside of the roof rake of an addition. A fascia board is being added to the fly rafter to overlap the outer edge of the soffit. The final trim piece (standing upright) will be installed just under the overlapping edges of asphalt shingles. (Photographer: Jay, Leviton•Atlanta.)

Once you have finished ceiling, wall, and floor surfaces, the bulk of your work is done. The installation that remains—trimming—is the easiest in some respects and the hardest in others. You work with lightweight pieces of material and you have no time constraints. Yet trim is sometimes awkward to handle, is easy to damage, and requires extreme accuracy in cutting and fitting.

As was pointed out earlier in this book, trim has changed steadily over the years. Hardwood is still the dominant material, although trim is now also made of hardboard, vinyl, and plastic reinforced with glass fibers. But trim dimensions, both thicknesses and widths, have changed so much that you may not be able to come close to matching the trim you remove. That's why you should remove each piece carefully and store it

safely for reuse. If you must have a small amount of new trim that matches the old, you can have it made to order. But you pay for the privilege. Or with adequate power-shaping tools, you can make your own. Or you can substitute. In a room addition your best bet is to select something you like and not worry about matching the existing trim in the rest of the house.

REUSING OLD TRIM

If you marked the location of pieces of trim you saved at the beginning of your project, those that don't have to be shortened should fit neatly. Working on a solid supporting surface, lightly sand edges and ends with medium sandpaper to remove excess paint, then sand surfaces to take off any loose paint. Smooth the back sides where you have pulled nails through, and fill holes from the back with wood putty.

While the putty dries, drill starter holes for new nails. Do not attempt to reuse existing nail holes. Drill just deeply enough to avoid splitting old, dry trim; ⅛″ is enough. Now fill visible nail holes and any gouges with wood putty, and seal any cracks or splits with an aliphatic resin glue. Use clamps or weights to hold split pieces together until the glue dries, which is usually less than 5 minutes. Then sand again lightly where you filled and glued.

Set in place each piece of trim you've prepared, plus abutting pieces, to check the fit. If the fit is still good, apply a coat of primer-sealer to the visible surface and any unpainted surfaces on the back. After the primer dries, apply one finish coat of semigloss enamel to the surfaces that will be visible when the trim is installed. When that coat dries, nail the trim in place, countersink the nails, and seal the holes. Later, sand the holes and touch up the sanded areas with enamel.

To cut existing trim, you'll get the best results with a backsaw and miterbox. As an alternative, use a fine-toothed crosscut saw and clamp the trim to your workbench. Always cut with the exposed surface up. Hand tools work better here than power tools. Old trim is likely to be dry and brittle, and you can cut more accurately with hand tools.

NEW CEILING TRIM

Of all trim, ceiling trim is the most difficult to fit, so get it out of the way first. The reason is that typical cove moldings bridge across, not fit against, corners formed by a ceiling and wall. At inside corners you must cope

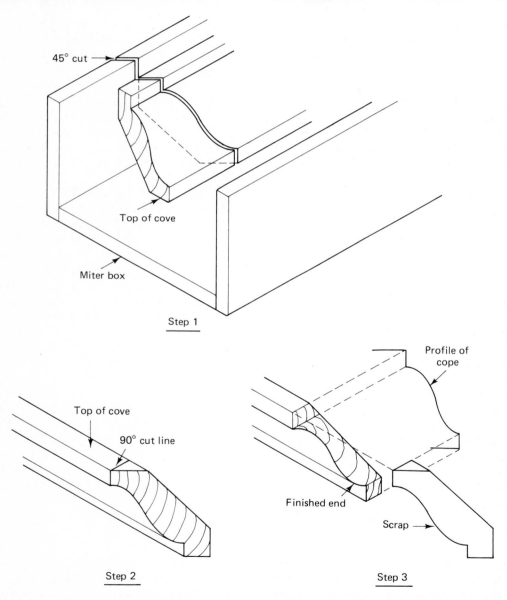

Fig. 21-1. The three steps in coping a ceiling cove to fit at an inside corner.

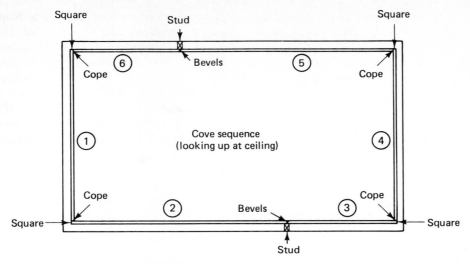

Fig. 21-2. A typical sequence of installation of ceiling cove. This view is looking upward at the ceiling. Note that long pieces must meet at a stud.

the joint for a good fit; a mitered joint seldom looks well. You do miter outside corners, however.

Coping

In a **coped joint** the cut follows the shape of the molding. You make it in three steps. In step 1, place the cove upside down in your miter box, and cut the end at a 45° angle (Fig. 21-1). In step 2, mark on the top of the cove a 90° line drawn from the front edge of the 45° cut. In step 3, cut with a coping saw, beginning at the 90° line and following the contours of the cove. For the best fit undercut slightly—that is, follow the contour line exactly but cut away a little more material than you would with a square 90° cut. The coped end should fit exactly against another piece of cove held at right angles to it.

Plan the Cove Layout

To install a ceiling cove, start on a short wall and work around the room—to the left if you are left-handed and to the right if you are right-handed. Standard lengths of cove are 10′, 12′, 14′, and 16′, although your dealer may also have other lengths. If possible, buy lengths that stretch from wall to wall. When a wall is longer than you can trim with a single length, the joint between pieces must fall at a stud.

Figure 21-2 shows a typical sequence of application, looking up at the ceiling. In a long rectangular room you make 12 cuts: four square cuts, four copes, and four bevels.

Installation

With your steel tape, measure the length of the starting wall at ceiling level. Cut piece 1 to that dimension, with both ends square. Fit the piece in place, making sure that it is flush against both wall and ceiling. With finishing nails long enough to penetrate at least ¾″ into framing members, tack the first piece temporarily in place. Nail 4″ from each end first, then every 8 to 10″ between.

Just where on the surface you nail depends on the shape of the cove. Nail a convex molding (Fig. 21-3a) at the outermost point of the curve. Nail a concave molding (Fig. 21-3b) both sideways and up and near the outer edges. If trim is hardwood (and most wood trim is), predrill the holes to prevent splitting and to make installation easier.

For piece 2 in Fig. 21-2, select a length of cove that will end on a stud with minimum waste, and cope the left-hand end. Bevel the opposite end, with the short side of the cove against the wall. Fit and tack piece 2, but don't nail yet within 12″ of the beveled end.

Measure the unmolded length of wall from the inside edge of the bevel cut to the next corner, and select a piece (3) long enough to fit. Bevel the left end so that it fits against piece 2, and cut the right end square. Cut piece 3 slightly long, and spring it into place. Adjust the bevel if necessary for a tight fit. Then tack the piece in position, nailing at ends first.

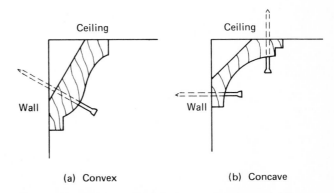

Fig. 21-3. Where to nail ceiling coves. If you nail a concave molding (b) solidly into studs, the nails upward may not be necessary except at beveled joints.

Cut piece 4, coping the left end and squaring the right end. Tack it in place. Then cut piece 5 in the same way that you cut and fitted piece 2.

Measure from the inside edge of the bevel cut on 5 to the wall at the final corner to determine the length of piece 6. Give one end a bevel cut and cope the other. As with piece 3, cut it $\frac{1}{16}$ to $\frac{1}{8}$″ long to assure a tight fit, and spring it into place. Then tack it.

Now check the appearance of the cove around the room. This is your last chance to refine inexact fits. The advantage to cutting pieces slightly long is that you have enough material to trim a bit if necessary. When you cut short, you have no choice but to cut a new piece.

All trim should be primed on all surfaces, including cut ends. If you are confident in your ability to make accurate cuts, prime each piece before you tack it in place. For most do-it-yourself remodelers, it is easier to remove the tacked moldings, number them in the order of attachment, then prime and first-coat all pieces in two operations, and finally reinstall them with permanent nailing.

Whichever way you work, when you are satisfied with the fit, drive the nails home, countersink their heads, and fill the holes. It isn't wise to fill joints, because the joints will eventually open up. Cut them right the first time and you won't have any joints to fill.

DOOR CASINGS

Typical casings for doors and windows are about $\frac{3}{4}$″ thick and 2 to 4″ wide. Their backs are plowed to allow a good fit when the edge of a jamb and a wall are not exactly in the same plane. Door trim consists of two jamb casings and a head casing that meet at mitered corners. Their inner edges are not flush with the door frame, but are set back $\frac{1}{8}$ to $\frac{1}{4}$″. Use a $\frac{1}{4}$″ setback for best appearance when space permits.

Casings come in random lengths from 7′ on up.

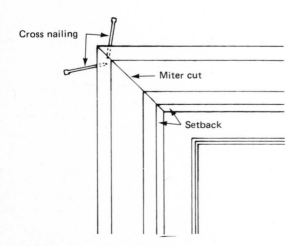

Fig. 21-4. Detail of casings where they meet above a window or door. Pieces should touch at a miter joint. Crossnailing prevents them from separating.

Around interior hinged doors you'll need on each side two 7′ pieces and one 3′ piece, neatly cut without waste from one 10′ and one 7′ length. Before you order casings determine the individual lengths you need. Remember that the length of a jamb casing equals door height plus one setback plus the width of a casing. The length of a head casing equals door width plus two setbacks plus two widths of casing. Sometimes you can buy casings by the package, already cut, primed, and ready to install.

Installation

Measure off the setback and mark it at eight points: at the bottom and midpoint of both jambs, and at the side and top of each corner. Square the lower ends of the two jamb casings and set them on the finished floor. Line up each piece on the setback marks, and mark on the inside edge the start of the miter cuts at upper ends (see Fig. 21-4). Lightly mark the miter cut on the casings's surfaces so that you know which way to go; the cuts are opposite on opposite jambs. Make the cuts with a backsaw in your miter box.

Tack the two casings temporarily in place at their ends. Use 4d or 5d casing nails at thin edges, and 7d or 8d nails at thicker edges, driven into predrilled holes.

Miter one end of the head casing and test the fit. Make any adjustments with a block plane. Then measure the distance between the outer edges of side jambs, mark this length on the thicker edge of the head casing, and miter the uncut end in the opposite direction from the first miter. Cut slightly long so that you can adjust the fit when necessary. Test the fit at both ends. If the miters aren't parallel at a joint, plane one end until they are. If the miters are parallel, but the head casing is too long or too short, adjust the side setbacks to compensate.

When the fits are good, remove, prime, and first-coat the casings, then nail them permanently. Space nails about 16″ apart. At corners crossnail with 6d nails (Fig. 21-4) to prevent corners from opening up.

WINDOW CASINGS

At the sides and top, you trim windows just like doors. At the sill, however, trim may be a fourth piece of casing or, more commonly, a stool and apron. The **stool** forms an inner sill and the **apron** supports it.

If you case on all four sides, fit the casings flush without setback. Measure the opening along all sides and check corners for square. If opposite lengths are equal and corners square, cut two identical jamb casings and two identical horizontal casings, giving each a miter cut at both ends. When measurements aren't the same, you have two options. Either adjust the miter cuts to something less or more than 45° and have the frame out of square; or cut the corners at 45°, have a setback, and

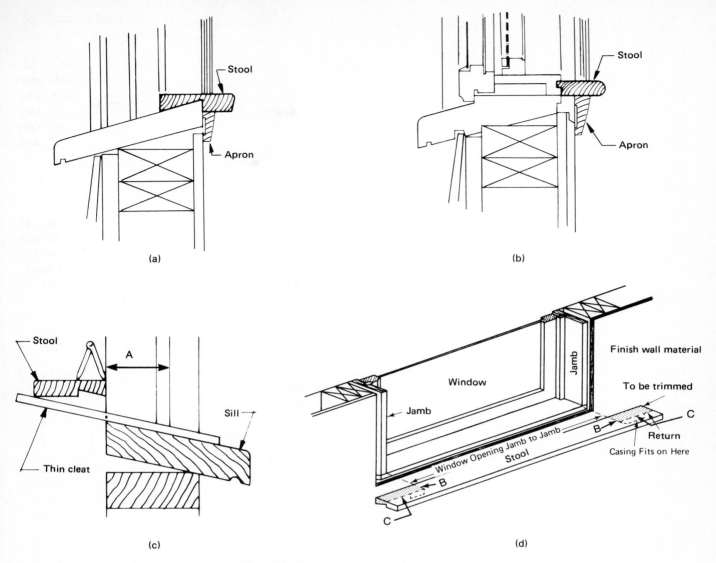

Fig. 21-5. Stools beneath windows with a sloping sill are rabbeted to fit over the slope (a). Those that fit over a flat sill are flat on the bottom and routed at the outer edge (b). The section (c) and isometric (d) illustrate the two basic steps in cutting and fitting a stool.

let the width of the setback vary to compensate for the lack of square at the window opening.

When you have a stool and apron, you start with the stool. There are two basic shapes (Fig. 21-5). One type (a) has a rabbeted underside that fits over the sloping sills of double-hung and some awning windows. The other type (b) is flat on the bottom to fit against frames around casement and sliding windows.

Install a Stool

From thin plywood cut a couple of cleats about 2″ × 8″ and tack them to the window sill (Fig. 21-5c). Center the stool on the window opening, with its back edge against the wall, its front edge on the cleat, and held level. On the top of the stool mark the width of the opening into which it must eventually fit. If window stops are in the

way, remove them temporarily. The stool fits under stops.

With a scriber measure the distance between the inner edge of the stool and the roomside face of the window sash (A in Fig. 21-5c). Mark off this distance on lines (B) drawn through your two width marks perpendicular to the edge (Fig. 21-5d). Then check to see how flat the edge of the stool is against the wall on both sides.

If the stool is flush, draw lines (C) at 90° to lines B to the ends of the stool. If the stool doesn't fit flush, use your scriber to mark the wall's contours from lines B to the ends. Cut along lines B with a saber saw, and along lines C with a saber saw (for straight cuts) or coping saw (for scribed cuts).

Now cut the stool to length. Its length equals the width of the window opening plus the width of two jamb casings plus two returns. **Returns** are the extensions at the sides of the window beyond the casings; a typical return is 1". Round the cut ends to match the contour of the front edge.

Test the fit, again holding the stool absolutely level. It should be flush at the walls and at jambs in the opening, and clear the sash about ⅟₃₂" to allow for coats of paint.

Prime the stool thoroughly on all sides, and predrill nail holes. With 8d casing or finishing nails, attach the stool to the sill. Blind-nail at jambs where casings will cover the holes, and about every 6" between. Don't countersink the nails until you install the apron.

Install an Apron

With the stool in place, cut and install window casings in the same way as door casings. Then measure from outside of casing to outside of casing. This is the length to cut the apron.

Aprons and casings look alike, except that aprons aren't plowed on the back. If they were, you would see a gap at their ends. You can cut those ends square, but they look more professional if you cope them to the apron's contours. Center the apron under the stool, and mark the location of either end lightly on the wall. Prime it, then predrill holes for nails spaced to hit studs. Nail the apron twice to each stud with 8d casing nails. Then with 3d nails fasten the stool downward to the apron at about the same places. Be careful to drive these small nails straight so that they don't break the apron's surface.

Now countersink all nails and fill the holes.

NEW FLOOR TRIM

In most rooms floor trim consists of a **baseboard** or **base** and a **base shoe**. With shag carpeting a shoe isn't necessary. With other types of carpeting it is optional, but does protect the base from a vacuum cleaner.

Plan the Layout

You cut baseboard square against door casings. You cope joints in inside corners and miter at outside corners. Where two lengths meet on a long wall, bevel the ends as with ceiling cove.

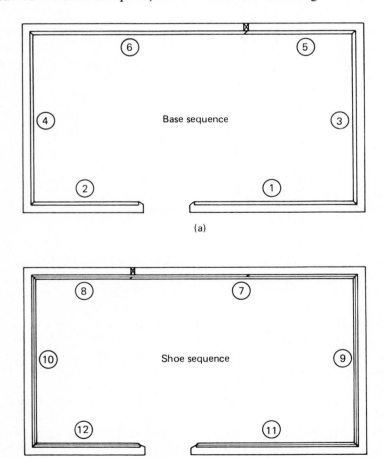

Fig. 21-6. Typical sequences of installation of a base (a) and base shoe (b). These views look down at the floor.

Begin your layout at door jambs and work toward a room's corners. Figure 21-6 shows a typical sequence. Try to end on the longest wall, because long pieces are easiest to spring into place. You can buy base in lengths from 10 to 16′, and base shoe in a range of lengths from 6 to 16′. Determine the individual lengths you need, convert the total into the lengths of raw material to buy, and follow your plan to minimize the number of joints you must cut.

Install the Base

Measure from door jambs to room corners with a steel tape held at floor level. Cut both ends of pieces 1 and 2 square (Fig. 21-6a), and tack them in place. Then cut and fit pieces 3 and 4, which should be the same length, coping the end abutting either piece 1 or 2 and cutting the other end square.

On the last long wall cut the shorter piece (5) first. Cope one end and at the other, which must fall on a stud, cut an inward bevel. Tack this piece in place. Then measure from the inside edge of the bevel on piece 5 to the wall, add $\frac{1}{16}$″, and cut piece 6 to that length. Give one end an outward bevel and cope the other. Spring this piece into place and tack it, working from both ends toward its center.

When the fit at all joints is good, prime and paint the base, drive the nails home, countersink them and fill the holes, and touch up the holes. Attach base pieces with 8d nails placed about $\frac{1}{2}$″ down from their tops. Nail near their ends and into studs every 16″ between. If you don't need a base shoe, drive a second set of nails slightly downward into the bottom plate, and space them every 8 to 10″. At outside corners miter the pieces and crossnail one piece of base to the other.

Install the Shoe

To cover the joint between base and floor you can use either a $\frac{3}{4}$″ quarter-round or a shoe molding, which is about $\frac{3}{4}$″ high, $\frac{1}{2}$″ thick, and rounded on the exposed surface. Both types of trim are flexible and easy to work with, but also break and split easily.

Begin on the long wall by cutting pieces 7 and 8 (Fig. 21-6b) so they have square ends and meet over a stud at a beveled joint. Cut the longer piece first so that the joint falls as far as possible from the joint between base pieces 5 and 6. Cut pieces 9 and 10 to fit at a coped joint against 7 and 8 and square at the other end. These pieces, remember, will be shorter than base pieces 3 and 4 by twice the thickness of the base.

With the first four pieces tacked in place, cope one end of pieces 11 and 12, and fit them in the corner. Then mark the cut at the door casing. For a perfect fit you'll probably need to make two cuts—a short square cut where the shoe fits against door trim, and a beveled cut from the edge of the casing outward.

You can nail the shoe in two ways—either at a 30° angle through the base into the bottom plate, or at a 60° angle into the subfloor. Usually, the first method is easier and better, because the shoe then moves with the base if there is any structural settling. Any crack is less noticeable at the floor than it is at the base. Be sure to use nails long enough to go through the base into framing members, and predrill holes to prevent splitting and to make nailing easier.

CORNER TRIM

Unless you have paneled walls, you probably won't have any corner trim to install. With wood walls, however, you need vertical strips to cover cut edges. Inside corner moldings are small, thin coves. Outside corner moldings are wider and thicker to withstand bumps. Trim may be wood, hardboard, vinyl, or plastic.

Always install ceiling and floor trim first. Rooms look best when horizontal trim is continuous, and you cut corner moldings to fit between. Measure the distance between ceiling cove and base in each corner, and check all corners for square at their top, midpoint, and bottom. If corners are not square, use vinyl or plastic corner trim rather than wood because it is flexible enough to fit odd angles. If you insist on wood, you can plane the backs of moldings where necessary.

After you cut corner trim pieces to length, check at top and bottom for face lap. Where trim is thicker than base or cove, gently taper edges over the last inch for a flush fit. Any overlap at the center won't be noticeable. Use sandpaper wrapped around a wood block to taper inside corner trim, and a block plane on outside corner trim.

MISMATCHED MOLDINGS

When you don't have enough original trim to reinstall, and you can't find or afford matching trim, don't try to match. Mismatched trim looks better than a trim similar to the original that just misses matching.

At the floor you have a choice. If the base along most of one wall is hidden by furniture or cabinets, cut the original trim to fit along the other three walls. Then, for the fourth wall, buy a clear board long enough to cover and at least as wide as your existing base. Cut the board to length and trim it to width. Then with sandpaper or a plane, ease the exposed top edge. Install this trim piece first, and cut old base pieces square to fit flush against it (Fig. 21-7c). Add shoe, which you should be able to match.

As an alternative, install the flat-faced base against opposite walls. Cut the ends of all pieces square. Miter only if you are good at it.

A ceiling cornice presents a more difficult

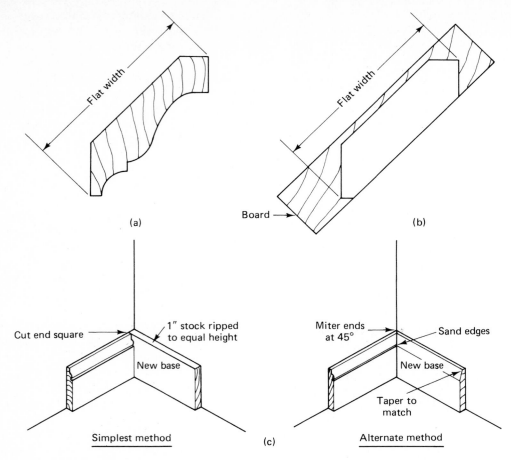

Fig. 21-7. When you cannot match existing broad trim, make your own. The new cove (b) matches the old cove (a) in size, but doesn't have the shape, which you can either omit or cut with a router. New base (c) should have the same dimensions as the old base it replaces, but can be plain, with only the top edge eased.

problem, since trim on one wall is usually as visible as trim on the other walls. Here opposite trim looks best when matched, so reuse the old cove along the longest walls and new trim on the shorter walls.

For new trim buy clear boards of adequate length and as wide as the flat width (not the installed width) of original cove. Make a template of the shape of the old cove (Fig. 21-7a), and mark the top and bottom cuts on the ends and edges of the new pieces (Fig. 21-7b). With a plane or router, reshape the board along the lines. The new trim will be flat on the sloping side, but all other surfaces will match. Install these pieces as 3 and 4 in Fig. 21-2, and cope adjoining pieces to fit.

LOOKING BACK

Nearly everyone starts a remodeling with enthusiasm. If you don't have enthusiasm at the beginning, you might as well not start because you need that initial momentum to carry you through. Enthusiasm begins to wane part way through any phase, then rebuilds as you near the end of that phase and look forward to the next one.

The critical time is as you approach the end, particularly the end of a remodeling that has stretched over many months. You're tired and want to get the job over with. As your pace slows and the job becomes physically easier and with more break points, it is easy to put things off, or to cut corners to hasten the end, or to hurry your work to get it behind you.

If you ever resisted temptation, resist it then. The structural work you did was properly done because it had to be. But nobody sees that quality now. *You* know it's there, and that's what counts.

Yet everyone sees your finish work, and its quality is just as important to the final result as structural quality. So take that extra step, even if you dread it now. Add a little more putty where nailholes still show. Brush on another finish coat where the first one isn't as good as you would accept if you were paying to have the work done. Throw out that strip of wallpaper that you didn't cut quite right and doesn't fit inconspicuously.

Perhaps no one will ever spot your mistake. But you know it's there, and you'll have a lot more lasting satisfaction when you know it *was* there, but you corrected it.

Index